What makes *SOC* special?

SOC offers instructors scholarly content and unmatched currency in a succinct magazine format that engages students. SOC consistently encourages students to foster their sociological imagination, get involved, and make a difference in the world around them.

What's Inside

Engaging pedagogy designed to be eye-catching and visually appealing can be found throughout the text. SOC shows students how they can apply sociological concepts to their everyday lives.

PopSOC teaches sociological concepts through popular culture familiar to students.

Personal Sociology

Personal Sociology gives down-to-earth explanations of sociological concepts using the author's experiences as examples.

SOCVIEWS on . . .

SOCTHINK

SOCThink questions throughout each chapter prompt students to think more deeply about a topic discussed in the text.

get involved!

Get Involved advises students on how to actively participate in sociological issues that are relevant to them.

Functionalist View
Conflict View
Interactionist View

MAKE THE CONNECTION

SOCViews offers students a summary diagram of how the three major perspectives provide insight into key topics in sociology. **MAKE THE CONNECTION** presents questions to prompt students to look at their own lives through the lens of the three sociological perspectives.

As You
READ

As You Read begins the chapter with important questions discussed in the chapter.

For
REVIEW

For Review summarizes the key points of each chapter in an easy-to-read format.

fresh
POP CORN
DELICIOUS NUTRITIOUS

At the Movies lists movies that relate to the sociological topics in each chapter.

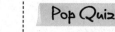
Pop Quiz

Pop Quiz allows students to review chapter material.

SOC 2011

VICE PRESIDENT, EDITORIAL **Michael Ryan**

AUTHOR **Jon Witt**

EDITOR AT LARGE **Gina Boedeker**

FIELD CORRESPONDENT **Richard T. Schaefer**

MANAGING EDITOR **Rhona Robbin**

DEVELOPMENT **Briana Porco**

STYLE DIRECTOR **Brittany Pogue-Mohammed**

FILM ADVISORS **Polina Novozhenets**

MARKETING MANAGER **Patrick Brown**

PRODUCTION EDITOR **Anne Fuzellier**

BUYER II **Tandra Jorgensen**

COMPOSITOR **Laserwords Private Limited**

PRINTER **Quad/Graphics**

ART MANAGER **Robin Mouat**

DESIGN MANAGER **Cassandra Chu**

INTERIOR DESIGNER **Maureen McCutcheon**

COVER DESIGNER **Linda Beaupré**

PHOTO WRANGLERS **Brian J. Pecko, Nora Agbayani, Sonia Brown**

ILLUSTRATION **Ayelet Arbel, Lineworks, John and Judy Waller, and Laserwords**

AUTHOR PORTRAIT **Arthur Mount**

To our esteemed author, Dr. Richard Schaefer: We thank you for your invaluable contributions to *SOC*.

To Lori: If I had only one friend left . . .

SOC 2011

Published by McGraw-Hill, an imprint of The McGraw-Hill Companies, Inc., 1221 Avenue of the Americas, New York, NY 10020. Copyright © 2011, 2010. All rights reserved. No part of this publication may be reproduced or distributed in any form or by any means, or stored in a database or retrieval system, without the prior written consent of The McGraw-Hill Companies, Inc., including, but not limited to, in any network or other electronic storage or transmission, or broadcast for distance learning.

This book is printed on acid-free paper.
Printed in the United States of America.

3 4 5 6 7 8 9 0 QDB/QDB 1

ISBN 978-0-07-352829-8

MHID 0-07-352829-3

Front cover: © Josef Lindau/Corbis
Back cover: © Purestock/Getty Images
Foldout: © ballyscanlon/Getty Images, © Ryan McVay/Getty Images, © RubberBall Productions, © Amos Morgan/Getty Images, © Amos Morgan/Getty Images, © Ryan McVay/Getty Images, © RubberBall Productions, © Corbis/PunchStock, © Ryan McVay/Getty Images, © Josef Lindau/Corbis

---

Library of Congress Cataloging-in-Publication Data

Witt, Jon.
   Soc / Jon Witt. — 2nd ed., 2011 ed.
      p. cm.
   Includes bibliographical references and index.
   ISBN-13: 978-0-07-352829-8 (alk. paper)
   ISBN-10: 0-07-352829-3 (alk. paper)
   1. Sociology.   I. Title.
   HM586.W58 2010b
   301—dc22

                                        2010026622

www.mhhe.com

Name: Jon Witt (though my mom calls me Jonathan)

Education: I got my BA from Trinity College in Deerfield, IL, and earned my PhD from Loyola University in Chicago.

Occupations: Sociologist, father, and dog-walker

Hobbies: I like reading, writing, and riding a bike—and I'm addicted to my iPhone and iPad.

Childhood ambition: To be a printer like my dad until I decided to be a teacher like my mom.

Family: Lori and I have been married for 26 years, and we have two daughters, Emily, 16, and Eleanor, 14.

Last book read: Haruki Murakami's Norwegian Wood

Favorite film: Right now it's Toy Story 3—though I love all of Pixar's animated films.

Favorite soundtrack: Singing songs from Glee with Em & El on road trips.

Latest accomplishment: This book!

Quote: There may be fields of sociological science quite beyond the average mind, and rightly left to the learned specialist; but that is no reason why we should not learn enough of the nature and habits of society to insure a more profitable and pleasant life.
—Charlotte Perkins Gilman, Human Work, 1904

My Blog: www.soc101.com or follow SOC on Twitter @soc101

WHAT'S NEW IN SOC

> New SOCViews feature in each chapter on the three major perspectives encourage students to look through these lenses.

> New Gender and Sexuality chapter with coverage on the spectrum of sexual orientation, the social construction of gender, heteronormativity, sexual practices in the United States and around the world, and third-wave feminism.

> Revised discussions on defining the self, mate selection, alternative families, economic systems, and racial and ethnic identity. New topics include the 2010 Gulf oil spill, health care reform, and public trust in government with numerous new pop culture examples throughout.

> New section on practicing sociology in personal and professional lives.

> Updated statistics and examples, including 2010 data, throughout.

SOC 2011 Edition

BRIEF CONTENTS

"I have taught this class for almost 10 years without a standard textbook, as I did not find one that worked for me. Too many were "highschooly," while others were dense with too many terms and not enough contemporary examples to keep the students' interest. . . . Quite frankly, I like SOC so much, that I organized my course format/chronology around it."

–ANDREA M. BRENNER, *American University*

Thanks for your feedback. **SOC** *was designed with students in mind. And one thing students appreciate is engaging content that can travel with them wherever they go.*
—*The Editors*

"The tone and energy of the text are wonderful. I really like the graphics and the range of different ways the students have to interact with the material—At the Movies, SocThink, PopSoc, etc. The text has a lot of breadth and almost none of the boring textbook tone and heavy framing."

–LAUREN SMITH, *University of Wisconsin, Whitewater*

That's great news! Jon Witt developed the narrative and features to reach students where they are, so that instructors can take them where they need them to be. **SOC** *asks students to think critically about issues close to their lives. We're glad you think this will work well for your students.*
—*The Editors*

"The design of *SOC* is most appealing. What is good is that substance is not sacrificed for style. The students get good information in an engaging design that still adheres to the traditional framework of sociology classes."

–JOHN TENUTO, *College of Lake County*

"I like how the Witt text looks like a magazine. It also has lots of graphs, interesting facts, and cool pictures to hold my attention."

–SKYE PETERS, *student at Parkland College*

From the cover to the interior design, images, graphs, charts, and pedagogy, **SOC** *was designed to make sociology accessible and thought-provoking for students. The visuals reinforce the solid scholarship throughout.*
—*The Editors*

Table of Contents

5 > Social Structure & Interaction 100

9 > Government and Economy 208

10 > Social Class 234

11 > Global Inequality   260

12 > Gender & Sexuality   286

1

THE SOCIOLOG

THE INDIVIDUAL AND SOCIETY

George Bailey feels trapped. He dreamed about going to college and traveling the world, hoping one day to become an engineer and design skyscrapers. Instead, he is stuck in the small town in which he grew up, and pressured into taking over the family business that is on the verge of collapse. George is so disillusioned with what his life has become that he finds himself on a snowy bridge ready to commit suicide. Hardly the makings of a happy story, but so begins the holiday film classic *It's a Wonderful Life*.

George's desire to leave home and go out on his own is likely familiar to many of us. What happens next is not. George gets to see what the world would have looked like had he never existed. An angel named Clarence arrives just in time to show him and it's not a pretty sight. People die whom George helped save, homes are lost that his family building-and-loan business helped finance, and life in the local community takes a serious turn for the worst. George learns that he has had a huge impact on family, friends, and the community. In the words of Clarence, "One [person's] life touches so many others, when he [or she's] not there, it leaves an awfully big hole." George changes his mind and rushes home to waiting family and friends who have united to save his business from financial ruin.

The film's focus on the relationship between the individual and society is fundamentally sociological. On the one hand, it shows that we as individuals can make a difference. Our actions influence others. On the other hand, the film shows the power society has over our lives through family, community, and social context. Our options are limited by our social position and the groups to which we belong.

Perhaps there is a bit of George Bailey in all of us. We create society by the choices we make and the things we do. At the same time, we are products of society, shaped by the people around us. For each of us, many endings are possible—that is the nature of individual choice—but not all endings are equally probable—that is the nature of social position and the unequal distribution of resources. Sociology seeks to describe and explain this interrelationship between the individual and society.

As You
READ

>>

- What is sociology?
- How do sociologists look at the world?
- How might someone practice sociology?

>> What Is Sociology?

We need each other. We may like to think that we can make it on our own, but our individualism is made possible by our interdependence. We praise the Olympic gold medalist for her impressive skill, dedicated training, and single-minded determination. Yet, if it weren't for her mom driving her to the pool every day, for the building manager waking up at 4:00 A.M. to make sure the pool is open, for the women working overnight to make sure the locker room is clean and safe, and so many others who fade into the background in such moments of glory, she would never have had that chance to shine.

> **sociology** The systematic study of the relationship between the individual and society and of the consequences of difference.
>
> **sociological imagination** An awareness of the relationship between who we are as individuals and the social forces that shape our lives.

Sociologists seek to investigate and understand the full scope of our interdependence. **Sociology** is the systematic study of the relationship between the individual and society and of the consequences of difference. We will examine the components of that definition in detail later, but in general, sociology focuses on social relationships, looking at how others influence our behavior; how major social institutions like the government, religion, and the economy affect us; and how we ourselves affect other individuals, groups, and even organizations. In doing this analysis, sociologists focus less on what one individual does or does not do than on what people do as members of a group or in interaction with one another, and on what that means for individuals and for society as a whole.

Through sociology we can ask and answer questions about our interdependence. With whom do we connect? How do we organize those connections? What gets in the way? Who benefits? Whether sitting in a classroom, working in an office or a factory, or exercising in a health club, we rely on others who shape how we think and act. As individuals, we do choose, but we cannot divorce our individual preferences from the influence of parents, teachers, friends, enemies, the media, and more, or from our access to resources such as money, social networks, and knowledge. We influence and are influenced by the world around us. Sociology studies those influences.

THE SOCIOLOGICAL IMAGINATION

Sociology helps us to see our place in the world in new ways. In an effort to describe how we might do that, American sociologist C. Wright Mills (1959) created a concept called the **sociological imagination,** an awareness of the relationship between who we are as individuals and the social forces that shape our lives. Mills described the sociological imagination as our ability to see the interaction between history and biography. By "history" he meant not just the times in which we live but also our positions in society and the resources to which we have access. "Biography" encompasses our personal experience, our actions and thoughts, and the choices we make. As Mills put it, "neither the life of an individual nor the history of society can be understood without understanding both" (p. 3). As we saw with George Bailey, we act, but we do so within the confines of society.

The sociological imagination involves our recognition of the significance of our social location. In other words, it enables us to see how factors such as age, gender, race, ethnicity, class, and level of education shape our preferences, perceptions, and opportunities. One way to gain insight about ourselves and our social worlds is to imagine how our practices might look to an outsider. Consider sporting events, for example. In the United States, thousands of fans pack stadiums to cheer for well-trained football players. In Bali, Indonesia, dozens of spectators gather around a ring to cheer on well-trained roosters engaged in cockfights. In both instances, the spectators root for their favorites and might bet on the outcome. Yet what is considered a normal sporting event in one part of the world is considered unusual in another.

In applying the sociological imagination, Mills (1959) suggested that we distinguish between **private troubles,** obstacles that individuals face as individuals, and **public issues,** obstacles that individuals in similar positions face. Unemployment, for example, is unquestionably a personal hardship (private trouble) for a man or woman without a job. But when millions of people lose their jobs,

Discovering the larger patterns related to unemployment—in other words, treating it as a public issue—helps us to predict its impact on individuals and communities and to respond appropriately.

The sociological imagination is an empowering tool. It enables us to see the world and its people through a broader lens. This might be as simple as understanding why a roommate prefers country music to hip-hop, or it may open up a whole new way of understanding other people around the world. For example, in the aftermath of the terrorist attacks of September 11, 2001, many Americans used the sociological imagination to better understand how Muslims throughout the world perceived the United States.

5 Movies on THE SOCIOLOGICAL IMAGINATION

Castaway
A man is isolated from society on a remote, deserted island.

Children of Men
A dystopian vision of society where humans can no longer reproduce.

Harry Potter and the Sorcerer's Stone
An 11-year-old orphan is introduced to a new society of wizards.

Fish Tank
A volatile teenage girl tries to escape her chaotic life in a British housing project.

One Flew over the Cuckoo's Nest
A scheming convict sent to a mental institution takes on Nurse Ratched.

THE HAMBURGER AS MIRACLE

We can use the sociological imagination to better understand our interdependence. Many people take for granted that it would be easy to provide for their needs if they had to, and they are eager to strike out on their own and prove themselves. Suppose you had to do something as seemingly simple as making a hamburger but had to do so without relying on any knowledge, skills, tools, or resources obtained from someone else. Without an interdependent network of people performing myriad small tasks that we take for granted, we would be hard-pressed to provide for our basic needs. As we will see, like all things we might produce, a hamburger is a miracle because it is a symbol of our society's shared knowledge and skills.

private troubles Obstacles that individuals face as individuals rather than as a consequence of their social position.

public issues Obstacles that individuals in similar positions face; also referred to by sociologists as "social problems."

How hard can it be to make a hamburger from scratch? Considering the ingredients,

unemployment becomes a public issue. Social factors, such as shifts in the economy, rather than individual failings contribute to large-scale unemployment. For example, from February 2008 to February 2010, the unemployment rate in the United States rose from 4.8 to 9.7 percent. This increase was tied to factors such as the banking crisis, the stock market plunge, and the decline in new home construction. At such times, blaming unemployment only on individuals is like treating symptoms without addressing the disease that caused them.

SOC THINK

Imagine spending the afternoon people watching at the mall. What differences might you observe in how people present themselves? What social factors might shape how they dress and talk, whether they are alone or in a group, and how much they buy? How might C. Wright Mills have explained such differences?

which seem fairly simple, there are any number of ways to proceed. Let's begin with the burger itself. First, you need to find a cow.

How hard can that be? Well, you can't buy one from a farmer, as doing so means relying on resources from others. For the same reason, you can't go out to the country (getting there itself might present something of a challenge) and steal one from a farm (which implies a farmer, which means dependence on another person). So you need to find a wild cow.

Assuming you do find a wild cow, you then have to kill it. Perhaps you might bash it with a large rock or stampede it off a cliff. Next, you need to butcher it, but cow hide is tough. Imagine what it takes to produce a metal knife (finding ore, smelting, forging, tempering, and so on). Perhaps a sharp rock will do. Assuming you came up with a cutting tool, you now have a chunk of raw cow meat. Given that it's hamburger we're after (though you might be ready to settle for steak at this point), next you need to grind the meat. You might use a couple of those rocks to pulverize the meat into something of a meat mash, although a meat grinder would work better if only it weren't so hard to make one. In any event, at last you have a raw hamburger patty.

Now you need to cook it. How will you do that? Where will you get the fire? Perhaps you could strike two rocks together in hopes of creating a spark, or maybe rub two sticks together. If you were allowed to get help from an outside source, you might check how Tom Hanks' character did it in the film *Cast Away*—but you aren't. Perhaps it would be easiest to wait around for lightning to strike a nearby tree. However you might accomplish it, after you get fire, you still have to cook the meat. No frying pans are available, so either you make one or perhaps cook it on that handy rock you used to kill the cow. Or you could just put the meat on a stick that you cut down and whittled with the knife you made (or was that a "sharp" stone?) and roast it over the fire.

Assuming you are successful, you now have a cooked hamburger patty. But, of course, you aren't done yet. There are still many other steps that need to be completed. You need to bake a bun, which involves figuring out how to come up with flour, water, salt, oil, sugar, yeast, and an oven. What about condiments such as ketchup, mustard, pickles, and onions? What if at the end of all that you decide to make it a cheeseburger? Hopefully you milked the cow first.

Making something that seems so simple, that we take for granted, that we can get for a dollar at McDonald's, turns out to be quite complicated. The knowledge and skill to acquire and prepare all the ingredients in a hamburger are beyond the capacity of most individuals. Yet if we eat a burger, we think nothing of it. When you think about it—when you apply the sociological imagination—a hamburger is a miracle. It's miraculous, not in a supernatural sense but as a symbol pointing to the astonishing complexity and taken-for-grantedness of our human interdependence and to the knowledge we share collectively without even realizing it. Of course, this is true not just for hamburgers but for virtually any product we use.

It could be a veggie-burger, a book, a desk, a shirt, a car, a house, or a computer. Look around you and try to imagine making, by yourself, all the things that we as humans have produced. The knowledge and skill that such products represent is astounding. Thankfully, our interdependence means that we do not have to rely on our own knowledge and skill alone for our survival.

> The function of sociology, as of every science, is to reveal that which is hidden.
>
> Pierre Bourdieu

KEY COMPONENTS OF SOCIOLOGY

A more detailed breakdown of the four key components of the definition of sociology will help us to better understand the foundation upon which the sociological imagination is built.

Systematic Study Sociologists are engaged with the world, collecting empirical data through systematic research. Relying on such data means that sociologists draw their conclusions about society based on experiences or observations rather than beliefs or the authority of others. If they want to understand the impact of television on community or the phenomenon of binge drinking on college campuses, they must gather data from those involved in these activities and base their conclusions upon that information.

Sociological research historically has involved both quantitative and qualitative approaches to data collection. Quantitative approaches emphasize counting things and analyzing them mathematically or statistically. The most common way to collect this type of data is through surveys. In contrast, qualitative approaches focus on listening to and observing people and allowing them to interpret what is happening in their own lives. The most common way to collect this type of data is through participant observation, in which the researcher interacts with those she or he studies. In practice, sociologists often draw on both techniques in conducting their research. We will investigate these research techniques, along with others, in more detail in Chapter 2.

The Individual Although sociology is most commonly associated with the study of groups, there is no such thing as a group apart from the individuals who compose it. As individuals we are constantly choosing what do to next. Most of the time, we follow guidelines for behavior we have learned from others, but we have the ability to reject those guidelines at any time. A term sociologists sometimes use to describe this capacity is **agency,** meaning the freedom individuals have to choose and to act. In professional sports, for example, we use the term "free agent" to describe a player who has the power to negotiate with whatever team he or she wishes. We, too, have such freedom. We could choose not to go to class, not to go to work, not to get out of bed in the morning, not to obey traffic signals, not to respond when spoken to, not to read the next sentence in this book, and on and on.

Because our self exists in an interactive relationship with its environment, we act within the context of our relationships. The same is true for that sports free agent. While he or she can choose any team, in order to get a big payday, he or she is limited to choosing within the confines of the league. Our choices, too, are constrained by our positions. Having access to varieties of resources, we choose among an array of options with knowledge of various possible outcomes. We usually follow "paths of least resistance"—the accepted and expected actions and beliefs—but the choice of whether to continue to follow them is ours each and every second of our lives (Johnson 1997).

"*Actually, Lou, I think it was more than just my being in the right place at the right time. I think it was my being the right race, the right religion, the right sex, the right socioeconomic group, having the right accent, the right clothes, going to the right schools . . .*"

Society The study of society is at the core of sociology. Although we will spend most of this book describing various aspects of society, we can begin by thinking of it as our social environment. Society consists of persistent patterns of relationships and social networks within which we operate. The social structure it provides is analogous to a building: The structure of a building both encourages and discourages different activities in different rooms (such as kitchens, bedrooms, and bathrooms), and many of the most essential operations of a building (such as heating and air conditioning) are mostly invisible to us. In the same way, the structure of our *institutions*—a term sociologists use to describe some of the major components of social structure, including economy, family, education, government, and religion—shapes what is expected of us. For example, the choices that are available to us in the context of the modern family, such as to go off and pursue our own education and career, are much different from the obligations we would face in more

> **agency** The freedom individuals have to choose and to act.

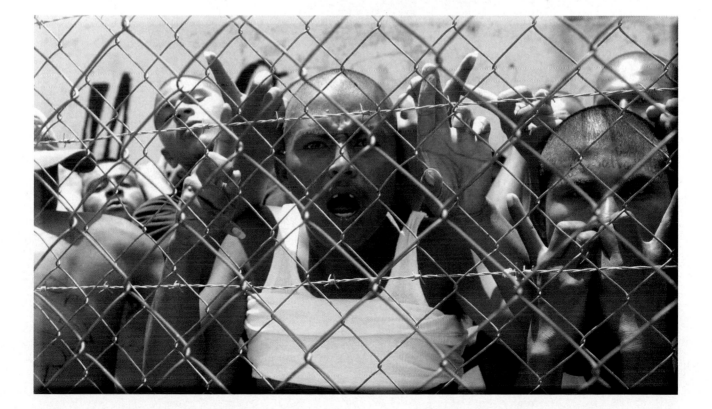

traditional family contexts. Nested within institutions are the groups, subgroups, and statuses that we occupy. We will look at the details of these institutions in coming chapters, but it is helpful to remember that we construct culture and engage in social interaction within the context of society.

The Consequences of Difference The final part of the definition of sociology involves the consequences of difference. Sociology does more than just describe our structure, culture, and interaction; it also looks at how economic, social, and cultural resources are distributed and at the implications of these patterns in terms of the opportunities and obstacles they create for individuals and groups. Since the founding of sociology, sociologists have been concerned with the impact our social location has on our opportunities or lack thereof.

> **social inequality** A condition in which members of society have differing amounts of wealth, prestige, or power.

Sociologists have noted, for example, that the 2004 Indian Ocean tsunami affected Indonesian men and women differently. When the waves hit, following traditional cultural patterns, mothers and grandmothers were at home with the children; men were outside working, where they were more likely to become aware of the impending disaster. Moreover, most of the men knew how to swim, a survival skill that women in these traditional societies usually do not learn. As a result, many more men than women survived the catastrophe—about 10 men for every 1 woman. In one typical Indonesian village, 97 of 1300 people survived; only 4 were women. The impact of this gender imbalance will be felt for some time, given women's primary role as caregivers for children and the elderly (BBC 2005).

The analysis of social power deserves particular attention because it shapes how and why we think and act as we do. The simple fact is that those who have access to and control over valued material, social, and cultural resources have different options available to them than do those without such access. One of the main tasks of sociology is to reveal and report the degree of **social inequality**—a condition in which members of society have differing amounts of wealth, prestige, or power. That is why the definition of sociology draws particular attention to the consequences of difference.

In combination, these four aspects of sociology help us to understand the things that influence our beliefs and actions. Coming to terms with the reality that our choices are constrained by the positions we occupy can seem depressing, but sociology actually empowers us by providing

U.S. Employment Trends

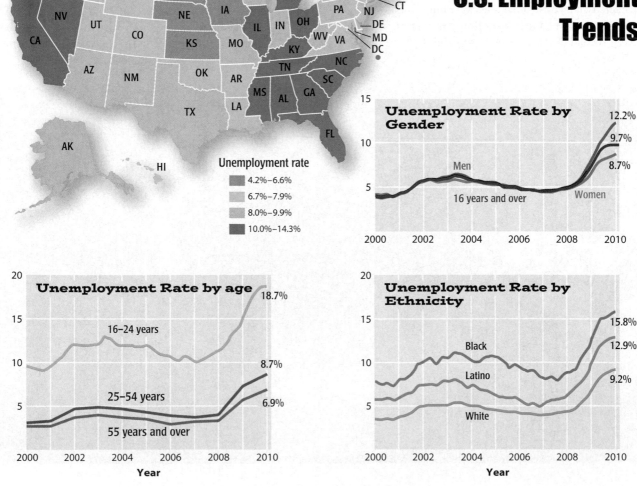

a more complete picture of the worlds within which we live. French sociologist Pierre Bourdieu (1998a) put it this way: "Sociology teaches how groups function and how to make use of the laws governing the way they function so as to try to circumvent them" (p. 57). Only by appreciating the degree to which our thoughts and actions are determined by our social location are we free to make more realistic choices to change ourselves and our worlds.

SOCIOLOGY AND THE SOCIAL SCIENCES

Is sociology a science? The term **science** refers to the body of knowledge obtained by methods based on systematic observation. Just like other scientific disciplines, sociology involves the organized, systematic study of phenomena (in this case, human behavior) in order to enhance understanding. All scientists, whether studying mushrooms or murderers, attempt to collect precise information through methods of study that are as objective as possible. They rely on the careful recording of observations and the accumulation of data.

Of course, there is a great difference between sociology and physics, and between psychology and astronomy. For this reason, the sciences are commonly divided into natural and social sciences. **Natural science** is the study of the physical features of nature and the ways in which they interact and change. Astronomy, biology, chemistry, geology, and physics are all natural sciences. **Social science** is the study of the social features of humans and the ways in which they interact and change. The social sciences include sociology, anthropology, economics, history, psychology, and political science.

These social science disciplines have a common focus on the social behavior of people, yet each has a particular orientation. Anthropologists usually study past cultures and preindustrial societies that continue today, as well as the origins of humans. Economists explore the ways in which people produce and exchange goods and services, along with money and other resources. Historians are concerned with the peoples and events of the past and their significance for us today. Psychologists investigate personality and individual behavior. Political scientists study international relations, the workings of government, and the exercise of power and authority. Sociologists, as we have already seen, study the influence that society has on people's attitudes and behavior and the ways in which people interact and shape society.

Let's consider how different social sciences might study the impact of the global economic crisis that began in late 2008. Historians would compare recent events to those that occurred in previous crises such as the Great Depression of the 1930s. Economists would conduct research on the financial impact of the current crisis for individuals, nations, and the world as a whole. Psychologists would study the behavior and reactions of individuals to assess the emotional trauma such crises cause. And political scientists would study the stances taken by political leaders and their governments' responses to the crisis.

What approach would sociologists take? Following Mills' lead, they would view the economic downturn as a public issue, seeking to understand how the positions we occupy influence our experience of the crisis. This would include gathering data about the impact of this crisis on different social locations of people based on factors such as social class, race and ethnicity, gender, age, and region of the country. We can get a glimpse of the impact social position has on a person's likelihood of unemployment by viewing the graphs on page 00. Understanding how different groups are affected helps policy makers decide which actions to take to solve the crisis. A singular or universal solution is unlikely to be effective in addressing the different needs of the various groups. On a more local scale, sociologists would seek to understand the impact such changes have on communities, neighborhoods, families, and individuals.

Sociologists would take a similar approach in studying episodes of extreme violence. In April 2007, just as students at Virginia Tech were beginning to focus on the impending end of the semester, tragedy struck. In a two-hour shooting spree, a mentally disturbed senior armed with semi-automatic weapons killed a total of 32 students and faculty at Virginia's largest university. Observers struggled to describe the events and place them in some social context. For sociologists in particular, the event raised numerous issues and topics for study, including the role of the media in reporting breaking news events, the presence of violence in schools, the politics of gun control, concerns about gender, the inadequacy of the nation's mental health care system, and the stereotyping and stigmatizing of people who suffer from mental illness (Glassner 2010; Newman and Fox 2009).

science The body of knowledge obtained by methods based on systematic observation.

natural science The study of the physical features of nature and the ways in which they interact and change.

social science The study of the social features of humans and the ways in which they interact and change.

SOCIOLOGY AND COMMON SENSE

At times all of us practice some form of the sociological imagination, weighing the balance between individual and society. So what's the difference between sociology and common sense—the knowledge we get from our experiences and conversations, from what we read, from what we see on television, and so forth? Commonsense

Sociological research shows that the choice of a marriage partner is heavily influenced by societal expectations.

knowledge, although sometimes accurate, is not always reliable, because it rests on commonly held beliefs rather than on systematic analysis of facts.

Contrary to the common notion that women tend to be chatty compared to men, for instance, researchers have found little difference between the sexes in terms of their talkativeness. Over a five-year period, they placed unobtrusive microphones on 396 college students in various settings, on campuses in Mexico as well as the United States. They found that both men and women spoke about 16,000 words per day (Mehl et al. 2007).

theory In sociology a set of statements that seeks to explain problems, actions, or behavior.

Similarly, "common sense" tells us that in the United States today, military marriages are more likely to end in separation or divorce than in the past due to the strain of long deployments in Iraq and Afghanistan. Yet a study released in 2007 shows no significant increase in the divorce rate among U.S. soldiers over the past decade. In fact, the rate of marital dissolution among members of the military is comparable to that of nonmilitary families. Interestingly, this is not the first study to disprove the widely held notion that military service strains the marital bond. Two generations earlier, during the Vietnam War era, researchers came to the same conclusion (Call and Teachman 1991; Karney and Crown 2007).

Like other social scientists, sociologists do not accept something as fact just because "everyone knows it." At times, the findings of sociologists may seem like common sense because they deal with familiar facets of everyday life. The difference is that such findings have been tested by researchers, analyzed in relation to other data, and evaluated in light of what is known by sociologists in the form of sociological theory.

>> What Is Sociological Theory?

Sociology, like all sciences, involves a conversation between theory and research. We gather data through systematic research, and we seek to describe and explain what we find using theories. Theories represent our attempts to tell the stories of our lives, but they do so in a particular way. Initially, theories might be general and vague. However, over time, as they become more fully informed by research, they are modified and refined into fuller, more accurate accounts of why we think and act as we do. We look first at theories and in Chapter 2 at methods.

FORMULATING SOCIOLOGICAL THEORIES

Why do people commit suicide? Émile Durkheim's answer to this question over a hundred years ago helped to establish sociology as a discipline. Among the traditional commonsense answers that Durkheim rejected were the notions that people inherit the desire to kill themselves or that sunspots drive people to take their own lives. He even suspected that psychological or biological explanations that pointed toward depression or chemical imbalance as causal factors were insufficient. He believed that social forces existed that influenced an individual's likelihood of committing suicide and set out to prove his theory.

Durkheim developed a theory that offered a general explanation of suicidal behavior. We can think of theories as attempts to explain events, forces, materials, ideas, or behavior in a comprehensive manner. In sociology a **theory** is a set of statements that seeks to explain problems, actions, or behavior. An effective theory may have both explanatory and predictive power. That is, it can help us to see the relationships among seemingly isolated phenomena, as well as to understand how one type of change in an environment leads to other changes.

Durkheim theorized that people commit suicide because they lack the social connections and obligations to prevent them from taking this most final and individualistic of all acts. His hypothesis was this: "Suicide varies inversely with the degree of integration of the social groups of which the individual forms a part" ([1897] 1951:209). He initially chose religious affiliation as an indicator of social integration, arguing that Protestants are less socially integrated than are Roman Catholics. He claimed that Catholicism is a traditional faith with a hierarchical system of authority in which variation in belief (on such topics as birth control, abortion, married priests, and women priests) is not up to the individual. Protestantism, in contrast, puts the Bible into the believers' hands to interpret. The many schisms found among Protestants occurred as a consequence of individuals choosing to interpret matters of faith based on their own understanding of God's word. Whereas there is only one Roman Catholic Church, Protestantism includes Baptist, Methodist, Reformed, Episcopalian, Presbyterian, and many other denominational and nondenominational churches. These contrasting contexts shaped the degree to which individuals were integrated into the religious community, leading Durkheim to predict that Protestants would be more likely to commit suicide than Catholics.

TESTING SOCIOLOGICAL THEORIES

In order to test his theory, Durkhiem gathered data from different countries to see if suicide rates varied. Looking at France, England, and Denmark, he found that England had 67 reported suicides per million inhabitants, France had 135 per million, and Denmark had 277 per million. Durkheim concluded that Denmark's comparatively high suicide rate was due to the fact that Denmark was a more Protestant nation than either France or England. In other words, it was the social makeup of these nations that shaped their suicide rates. More recent research focusing on individual rather than national rates continues to find this same relationship.

In extending his analysis to look at other indicators of social integration, Durkheim continued to obtain results that confirmed his underlying theory: The unmarried had much higher rates of suicide than married people; and people without children were more likely to take their lives than people with children. In addition, there were higher rates in times of economic instability and recession rather than in times of prosperity. Durkheim concluded that his theory was correct: The suicide rate of a society reflects

SOC THINK

If Durkheim is correct and level of social integration influences the likelihood of suicide, why do rates vary for the groups listed in the Suicide Rates figure? Why is the rate for men four times higher than that for women? Why is the rate for non-Hispanic Whites higher than that for any other racial/ethnic groups? Why do White, non-Hispanic males have the highest suicide rate of all? Why is the rate for the elderly so high? Why is there a midlife suicide peak? What might the top-five or bottom-five states have in common? What might these patterns suggest about the social integration of people in these categories?

the extent to which people are or are not integrated into the group life of the society. Durkheim presented his results in his landmark work *Suicide,* published in 1897.

APPLYING SOCIOLOGICAL THEORIES

Built into Durkheim's theory is the presupposition that we find meaning in life through our interconnections with others. The more interconnected and interdependent we

Suicide Rates

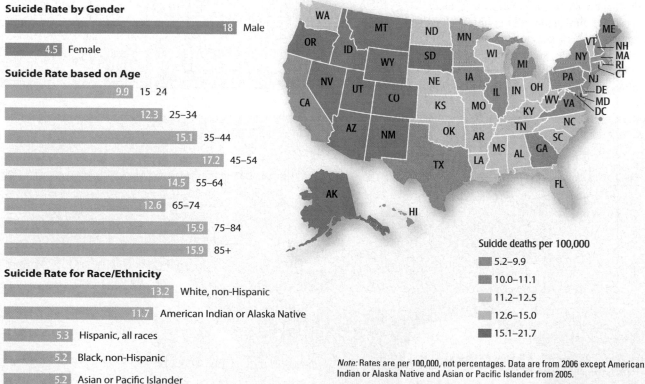

Suicide Rate by Gender

- 18 Male
- 4.5 Female

Suicide Rate based on Age

- 9.9 — 15 24
- 12.3 — 25–34
- 15.1 — 35–44
- 17.2 — 45–54
- 14.5 — 55–64
- 12.6 — 65–74
- 15.9 — 75–84
- 15.9 — 85+

Suicide Rate for Race/Ethnicity

- 13.2 White, non-Hispanic
- 11.7 American Indian or Alaska Native
- 5.3 Hispanic, all races
- 5.2 Black, non-Hispanic
- 5.2 Asian or Pacific Islander

Suicide deaths per 100,000
- 5.2–9.9
- 10.0–11.1
- 11.2–12.5
- 12.6–15.0
- 15.1–21.7

Note: Rates are per 100,000, not percentages. Data are from 2006 except American Indian or Alaska Native and Asian or Pacific Islander from 2005.

Source: Heron et al. 2009; National Center for Health Statistics 2007.

work. He theorized that social forces shape individual actions. He tested this theory by investigating suicide as one such individual choice—perhaps the most individual of all choices—and demonstrated that the likelihood of committing suicide varied based on group membership. Analysis of more recent data (see figure on page 11) shows that suicide rates continue to vary based on social position. Durkheim concluded that if social forces are at work in this most extreme example of individual choice, they similarly shape all other individual choices. He argued that if social forces have such power in our lives, there should be a discipline dedicated to their study. As a result, Durkheim established Europe's first department of sociology at the University of Bordeaux in 1895.

>> The Development of Sociology

Given the complexity of human life, sociologists have developed a wide range of theories in which they describe and explain the diversity of social behavior. Sometimes their theories can be grand in scope, seeking to encompass the "big picture"; other times they can be more personal,

feel, the less likely we are to kill ourselves. Attempting to summarize the significance of our attachment to society, Durkheim put it this way: "The individual alone is not a sufficient end for his activity. He is too little. . . . When, therefore, we have no other object than ourselves we cannot avoid the thought that our efforts will finally end in nothingness. . . . Under these conditions one would lose the courage to live, that is, to act and struggle" ([1897] 1951:210). Human beings are, at their very foundation, social beings. According to Durkheim, we cannot consider what it means to be an individual apart from our position in society. This social dimension of individual behavior is what Durkheim wants sociology to explore, elaborate, and explain.

Durkheim's work on suicide provides a classic case of sociological theory at

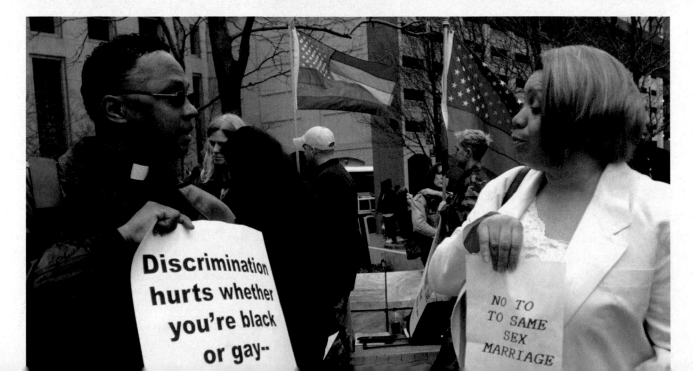

intimate, and immediate. Although we will spend most of the rest of this book investigating the insights sociological theories provide, here we will briefly address just five questions sociologists have frequently asked. These questions represent significant doors sociologists have opened to provide additional tools for the sociological imagination. The questions are these: How is social order maintained? How do power and inequality shape outcomes? How do we construct our worlds and ourselves through everyday interaction? How does group membership (especially class, race, and gender) shape opportunity? How should sociologists respond?

HOW IS SOCIAL ORDER MAINTAINED?

The discipline of sociology grew up in the midst of significant social upheaval. The advent of the Industrial Revolution and urbanization in the early 19th century led to changes in patterns of government, thought, work, and everyday life. Aristocracy was on the decline while democracy was spreading; people were moving from a primary reliance on religious explanations to more scientific ones; and the world of the village and farm was rapidly giving way to life in the city and factory. It was in this context that French sociologist and philosopher Auguste Comte (1798–1857), in hopes of emulating what natural scientists did for nature, sought to establish a science of society that

Harriet Martineau ([1838] 1989) argued that we could learn a lot about a culture by analyzing the ideas, images, and themes reflected in their popular songs. She wrote, "The Songs of every nation must always be the most familiar and truly popular part of its poetry. . . . They present also the most prevalent feelings on subjects of the highest popular interest. If it were not so, they would not have been popular songs." What might we learn about American culture based on analysis of the lyrics of the current top-10 songs? (Lists are available at "The Billboard Hot 100" or www.top10songs.com.)

would reveal the basic "laws of society." Comte believed that knowing these laws would help us to understand two key principles which he referred to as "social statics"—the principles by which societies hold together and order is maintained—and "social dynamics"—the factors that bring about change and that shape the nature and direction of that change. Sociologists would then use their knowledge of these laws to help lead us toward the good society, balancing the needs for social order with positive social change. To give this new discipline a name, Comte coined the term *sociology*—which literally means "the study of the processes of companionship" (Abercrombie, Hill, and Turner 2006:367).

English-speaking scholars learned of Comte's works largely through translations by the English sociologist Harriet Martineau (1802–1876). Seeking to systematize the research essential to conducting a science of society, Martineau ([1838] 1989) wrote the first book on sociological methods. She was also a pathbreaking theorist in her own right, introducing the significance of inequality and power into the discipline. Martineau's book *Society in America* ([1837] 1962) examined religion, politics, child rearing, and immigration in the young nation. It gave special attention to social class distinctions and to such factors as gender and race. In Martineau's ([1837] 1962) view, intellectuals and scholars should not simply offer observations of social conditions; they should act on their convictions in a manner that will benefit society. Martineau spoke out in favor of the rights of women, the emancipation of slaves, and religious tolerance.

These two themes—analysis of social order and analysis of social inequality—have shaped the theoretical paths sociologists have pursued since this beginning. In early sociological theory, they find their fullest development in the works of Émile Durkheim and Karl Marx, respectively. As we will see throughout this book, they continue to be primary concerns for sociologists.

Émile Durkheim (1858–1917) emphasized the significance of social order. As we saw in his analysis of suicide, he saw society as a real, external force existing above the level of the individual and exerting its influence on individual behavior. Durkheim was particularly concerned about what happens when the influence of society declines, resulting in weakened social integration. He theorized that an increase in the division of labor, a defining characteristic of modern societies, meant that individuals shared fewer common experiences, ideas, and values. As workers became much more specialized in their tasks, they were at greater risk of what Durkheim called **anomie**—the loss of direction felt in a society when social control of individual behavior has become ineffective. Anomie increases the likelihood of alienation, loneliness, and isolation. Inspired by Comte's vision, Durkheim sought to establish sociology as a science to study these processes.

> **anomie** The loss of direction felt in a society when social control of individual behavior has become ineffective.

HOW DO POWER AND INEQUALITY SHAPE OUTCOMES?

Karl Marx (1818–1883) was also concerned about social order and integration, but his work particularly emphasized the significance of power and control over resources. Marx viewed our creative capacity to transform raw materials into products—for example, to take clay and make a pot, or cut down a tree and make a desk—as the key factor distinguishing humans from other animals (whose behavior is ruled by their instincts). For Marx, human history is the progressive unfolding of human creativity in the form of new technology through which we establish our relationship to the natural world and with each other. Unfortunately, for most of human history, we lacked sufficient technology to provide enough material goods (such as food, clothes, and shelter) to meet everyone's needs, so not all people had enough.

Emile Durkheim

Social inequality for Marx, then, is determined by ownership, or lack thereof, of key material resources. Those who own and control the means of production—the tools and resources necessary for that transformation to happen—rule the world. Members of the working class, in contrast, own only their capacity to transform raw materials into products, which requires access to the means of production controlled by the ruling class. Whereas Durkheim was concerned with anomie, Marx was concerned with alienation, by which he meant loss of control over our creative human capacity to produce, separation from the products we make, and isolation from our fellow workers. We will consider Marx's work as it relates to capitalism in more detail in a later chapter. His influence on sociological theory, however, extends beyond social

Karl Marx

class to an analysis of group identification and association, such as how class, gender, race, ethnicity, nationality, and age influence individual opportunity.

Seeking to expand sociological theory further, Max Weber (1864–1920; pronounced "VAY-ber") offered a more general theory of power that was less wedded to capitalism and ownership of the means of production. Weber argued that, although social class and its associated control over material resources may determine who has power in most instances, these are not the only possible foundations for power. Others he identified include social status, in which people defer to others out of respect for their social position or prestige, and organizational resources, in which members of a group gain power through their ability to organize to accomplish some specific goal by maximizing their available resources. Weber argued that these social resources draw their power from people's willingness to obey the authority of another person, which in turn is based on their perception of the legitimacy of that person's right to rule.

HOW DOES INTERACTION SHAPE OUR WORLDS?

Much of the work of Durkheim, Marx, and Weber involves **macrosociology,** which concentrates on large-scale phenomena or entire civilizations. This top-down approach focuses on society as a whole and how broad social forces shape our lives. A later school of sociologists turned away from this approach in favor of **micro-sociology,** which stresses the study of small groups and the analysis of our everyday experiences and interactions. This bottom-up approach emphasizes the significance of perception, of how we see others and how they see us. Sociologist Erving Goffman

Max Weber

(1922–1982) popularized a method known as the *dramaturgical approach* (see Chapter 4), which compares everyday life to the setting of the theater and stage and sees people as theatrical performers. Just as actors project certain images to an audience, all of us seek to present particular features of our personalities to others even as we hide certain qualities. Thus, in a class, we may feel the need to project a serious image; at a party, we want to look relaxed and friendly. In this approach, sociologists must analyze our lived experience at the everyday level where our actions create, sustain, and modify our understanding of reality itself.

... According to the Thomas theorem, established by sociologists W. I. Thomas and Dorothy Swaine Thomas, "If men define situations as real, they are real in their consequences" (Thomas and Thomas 1928:571–572). In other words, our perceptions of what is real determine how we act more so than does reality itself.

Did You Know?

came up short. Part of the task for the sociologist, then, is to bring to light such inconsistencies that may otherwise go largely unnoticed. This is something Wells-Barnett sought to do in her groundbreaking publications in the 1890s on the practice of lynching African Americans, as well as with her advocacy of women's rights, especially the struggle to win the vote for women. Like feminist theorists who succeeded her, Wells-Barnett used her analysis of society as a means of resisting oppression. In her case, she researched what it meant to be African American, a woman in the United States, and a Black woman in the United States (Wells-Barnett [1928] 1970).

HOW DOES GROUP MEMBERSHIP INFLUENCE OPPORTUNITY?

Over time, sociologists came to more fully understand and appreciate the consequences that group membership, especially class, race, and gender, has for opportunity. Black sociologist W.E.B. Du Bois (1868–1963; pronounced "dew BOYS") combined an emphasis on the analysis of the everyday lived experience with a commitment to investigating power and inequality based on race. He was critical of those who relied on common sense or on all-too-brief investigations, arguing that a researcher has to be more than just a "car-window sociologist" because true understanding demands more than "the few leisure hours of a holiday trip to unravel the snarl of centuries" (Du Bois [1903] 1994:94). Through engaged and sustained research on the lives of African Americans, he documented their relatively low status in Philadelphia and Atlanta. His research revealed the social processes that contributed to the maintenance of racial separation, which extended beyond material differences to include social separation, which he referred to as the "color line."

Similarly, feminist scholarship has broadened our understanding of social behavior by extending the analysis beyond the male point of view that dominated classic sociology. An early example of this perspective can be seen in the life and writings of Ida Wells-Barnett (1862–1931). Carrying on a tradition begun with Martineau, Wells-Barnett argued that societies can be judged based on whether the principles they claim to believe in match their actions. Wells-Barnett found that when it came to the principles of equality and opportunity for women and African Americans, America

HOW SHOULD SOCIOLOGISTS RESPOND?

Throughout sociology's history, a recurring theme has been the idea that sociological theory and research should contribute to positive social change. In the early 1900s, many leading sociologists in the United States saw themselves as social reformers dedicated to systematically studying and then improving a corrupt society. They were genuinely concerned about the lives of immigrants in the nation's growing cities, whether those immigrants came from Europe or from the rural American South. Early female sociologists, in particular, often took active roles in poor urban areas as leaders of community centers known as settlement houses. For example, Jane Addams (1860–1935), an early member of the American Sociological Society, cofounded the famous Chicago settlement, Hull House, which provided social, education,

macrosociology Sociological investigation that concentrates on large-scale phenomena or entire civilizations.

microsociology Sociological investigation that stresses the study of small groups and the analysis of our everyday experiences and interactions.

Did You Know?
... Michelle Obama received a bachelor of arts degree in sociology from Princeton University in 1985. She used that degree as a stepping-stone to law school at Harvard.

Personal Sociology

Hooked on Sociology

When I took "Soc101" in college, it took me a long time to understand the sociological imagination. I still remember feeling overwhelmed by all the concepts, facts, and figures. Eventually, as we studied the impact of the media and the power of inheritance, things began to fall into place; I took another course and was hooked. As you begin your study of sociology, my advice is to stay focused on how our individual choices are shaped by our social positions and access to resources. How do our circumstances influence how we understand ourselves and others? I hope that after encountering sociology, you will come away with a new way of seeing, equipped to act in new and more informed ways.

and cultural programs for recent immigrants. Addams and other pioneering female sociologists commonly combined intellectual inquiry, social service work, and political activism—all with the goal of assisting the underprivileged and creating a more egalitarian society. Working with Ida Wells-Barnett, Addams successfully prevented racial segregation in the Chicago public schools, and her efforts to establish a juvenile court system and a women's trade union reflect the practical focus of her work (Addams 1910, 1930; Lengermann and Niebrugge-Brantley 1998).

This commitment to positive social change was not unique to Addams and her colleagues. From the very beginning and on down to the present, sociologists have recognized an obligation to go beyond explaining how the world works and become actively engaged in making the world a better place. In the words of French sociologist Pierre Bourdieu, "I have come to believe that those who have the good fortune to be able to devote their lives to the study of the social world cannot stand aside, neutral and indifferent, from the struggles in which the future of that world is at stake" (1998a:11). For some this has meant releasing the results of their research to the public so that we might make more informed decisions; for others it has meant active engagement in establishing social policy or assisting in the lives of others. For example, Durkheim, who considered an educated citizenry essential to democratic success, used his appointment to the Department of Science of Education and Sociology at the Sorbonne in Paris, along with his political connections and appointments, to shape French educational policy and practice. Du Bois cofounded the National Association for the Advancement of Colored People, better known as the NAACP. In fact, one of the dominant reasons students choose to major in sociology is because they want to make a difference, and sociology provides a pathway to do just that.

functionalist perspective
A sociological approach that emphasizes the way in which the parts of a society are structured to maintain its stability.

>> Three Sociological Perspectives

The answers to the five questions that sociologists ask provide us with just a glimpse of the mosaic of sociological theories that have developed over time as sociologists consider the complexity of human behavior. Some theorists focus on society as a whole; others concentrate on individual interactions. Some are particularly concerned with inequality; others focus on maintaining social cohesion. Some approaches seem to overlap; others seem at odds with each other. But, regardless of their stance, all theorists share a common commitment to provide us with greater understanding of why we think and act the way we do. Each theory, whether broad or narrow, offers a way of seeing that allows us to perceive things we might have otherwise missed.

To simplify the rich array of sociological theories (especially for someone new to sociology) sociologists have classified various theories into three major theoreticial perspectives or approaches: functionalist, conflict, and interactionist. Each perspective offers a different set of lenses, focusing our attention in slightly different ways. Or, to put it another way, it is like three different people standing on the edge of a circle looking in at the same thing but each seeing it from a different point of view, able to recognize things that others might not even see.

According to the **functionalist perspective,** society is like a living organism with its various parts working together (or functioning) for the good of the whole. Functionalists posit that society and its parts are structured to provide social order and maintain stability. Aspects of society that appear dysfunctional, seemingly contributing to a decrease in social order or integration, will either wither away over time or actually contribute some hidden benefits that researchers seek to reveal. Durkheim's research into

Three Sociological Perspectives

	Functionalist	Conflict	Interactionist
View of society	Stable, well integrated	Characterized by tension and struggle between groups	Active in influencing and affecting everyday social interaction
Level of analysis emphasized	Macro	Macro	Micro, as a way of understanding the larger macro phenomena
Key concepts	Social integration Institutions Anomie	Inequality Capitalism Stratification	Symbols Nonverbal communication Face-to-face interaction
View of the individual	People are socialized to perform societal functions	People are shaped by power, coercion, and authority	People manipulate symbols and create their social worlds through interaction
View of the social order	Maintained through cooperation and consensus	Maintained through force and coercion	Maintained by shared understanding of everyday behavior
View of social change	Predictable, reinforcing	Change takes place all the time and may have positive consequences	Reflected in people's social positions and their communications with others
Example	Public punishments reinforce the social order	Laws enforce the positions of those in power	People respect laws or disobey them based on their own past experience
Proponents	Emile Durkheim Talcott Parsons Robert Merton	Karl Marx W. E. B. Du Bois Ida Wells-Barnett	George Herbert Mead Charles Horton Cooley Erving Goffman

social order and its challenges, especially within modern societies, is a classic example of the functionalist perspective. Durkheim assumed that, over time, society would progress toward greater order as it came to terms with apparent threats or challenges.

Whereas the functionalist perspective emphasizes consensus and cooperation, the **conflict perspective** focuses on power and the allocation of valued resources in society. According to conflict theorists, social order cannot be fully understood apart from an analysis of how the status quo is established and maintained by those who control key resources. Such resources include material resources (such as money, land, and property), social resources (such as family connections, social networks, and prestige), and cultural resources (such as education, beliefs, knowledge, and taste). The existing social structure helps maintain the privileges of some groups and keep

Jane Addams

others in inferior positions. Marx's work on inequality, social class, and alienation provides a classic example of the conflict perspective.

Finally, whereas functionalist and conflict theorists both analyze large-scale, society-wide patterns of behavior, theorists who take the **interactionist perspective** generalize about everyday forms of social interaction in order to explain society as a whole. For interactionists, society is the product of our everyday interactions (with parents, friends, teachers, or strangers) through which we establish shared meanings and thus construct order. Because society is dependent upon this ongoing construction, society is fluid and subject to change. Goffman's dramaturgical approach is an example of the interactionist perspective.

The three-perspectives model has the advantage of providing us with conceptual hooks that allow us to recall some of the key concerns and issues sociologists have raised. A disadvantage, however, is that it gives the illusion that these three are discrete categories with fundamentally different and incompatible ways of looking at the world. In practice, research rooted in one perspective almost inevitably draws on or address insights from the other two.

conflict perspective
A sociological approach that assumes social behavior is best understood in terms of tension between groups over power or the allocation of resources, including housing, money, access to services, and political representation.

interactionist perspective
A sociological approach that generalizes about everyday forms of social interaction in order to explain society as a whole.

>> Practicing Sociology

One of the questions that students frequently ask about sociology is "What can I do with it?" This query often comes from students who really like sociology, and might want to pursue it further, but are uncertain about where it leads. The good news is that there are many ways people can practice sociology.

PERSONAL SOCIOLOGY

We don't have to become professional sociologists to practice what we have learned. The sociological imagination can help all of us to better understand our beliefs and actions and to make more informed choices. We can all practice **personal sociology** by recognizing the impact our individual position has on who we are, and how we think and act. Doing so also calls us to take responsibility for the impact our actions have on others. For example, by drawing on insights gained from sociological theory and research, we might watch the news and ask whose interests are being represented. When we walk through the mall, we might observe how people display their social status and how they are treated accordingly. When we go in for a job interview, we might abide by the largely unspoken norms of conduct that shape interaction and influence our likelihood for success. Personal sociology empowers us by allowing us to see things that were previously invisible and to act on those insights.

personal sociology The process of recognizing the impact our individual position has on who we are and how we think and act, and of taking responsibility for the impacts our actions have on others.

applied sociology The use of the discipline of sociology with the specific intent of yielding practical applications for human behavior and organizations.

ACADEMIC SOCIOLOGY

Many students opt to take their sociology education further, and the number of U.S. college students who have graduated with a degree in sociology has risen steadily (see figure below). The American Sociological Association (ASA) conducted research on recent sociology graduates and discovered that the top reasons for choosing sociology as a major are that students found the sociological concepts interesting, they particularly enjoyed the first course, sociology helped them to understand the relationship between social forces and individual relationships, they wanted to make a difference in the world, and it helped them to understand themselves better (American Sociological Association 2006a, 2006b). As part of their

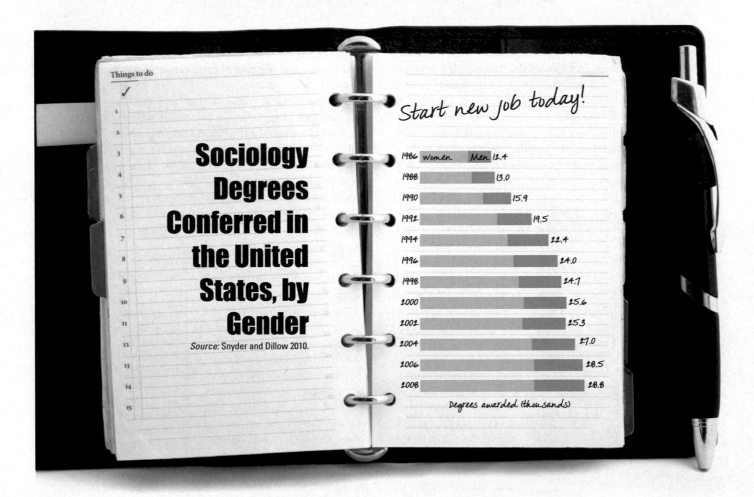

Sociology Degrees Conferred in the United States, by Gender

Source: Snyder and Dillow 2010.

Start new job today!

	Women	Men	
1986			12.4
1988			13.0
1990			15.9
1992			19.5
1994			22.4
1996			24.0
1998			24.7
2000			25.6
2002			25.3
2004			27.0
2006			28.5
2008			28.8

Degrees awarded (thousands)

sociology education, students cultivate a variety of skills, such as developing evidence-based arguments, evaluating research methods, writing a research report understandable to nonsociologists, using computer resources including statistical software to organize and analyze data, and identifying ethical issues in research. Sociology majors who later use these skills in their jobs express the highest levels of job satisfaction (Spalter-Roth and Van Vooren 2008a, 2008b).

The jobs that sociology majors find shortly after graduation, according to the ASA study, are in a range of fields. The most common occupational category is social services. Examples of jobs include caseworker for abused and neglected children, funds coordinator for Hurricane Katrina victims, manager for a not-for-profit organization, case manager for HIV-positive individuals, and child advocate. Researchers also found that graduates were employed in a variety of other positions, including teacher, librarian, paralegal, immigration specialist, office manager, quality assurance manager, crime scene investigator, police officer, probation officer, marketing consultant, research assistant, program evaluator, statistician, and editor (Spalter-Roth and Van Vooren 2008a).

According to the ASA study, of sociology majors who pursued graduate school degrees, only about one-quarter did so in sociology. Instead, most used their sociology major as a stepping-stone into graduate study in social work, education, law, psychology, engineering, and business management (Spalter-Roth and Van Vooren 2009:9). Those who do opt to pursue a master's or doctorate in sociology are most likely to do so in hopes of teaching

SOCTHINK

How much responsibility do individuals have to make things better for society?

or conducting sociological research. In fact, one of the rewards of a career in sociology is to be able to continue the search for answers through ongoing study of other sociologists' work and one's own research.

APPLIED SOCIOLOGY

Applied sociology is the use of the discipline of sociology with the specific intent of yielding practical applications for human behavior and organizations. Often, the goal of such work is to assist in resolving a social problem. For example, in the past 40 years, eight presidents of the United States have established commissions to delve into major societal concerns facing our nation. Sociologists are often asked to apply their expertise to studying such issues as violence, pornography, crime, immigration, and population.

One example of applied sociology involves the growing interest in the ways in which nationally recognized social problems manifest themselves locally. Sociologist Greg Scott and his colleagues sought to better understand the connection between illicit drug use and the spread of HIV/AIDS. The study employed 14 researchers from colleges and public health agencies, assisted by 15 graduate and 16 undergraduate students. By combining a variety

Where Are They Now?

Occupational categories of recent sociology majors

- Social services 26.5%
- Administrative, clerical support 15.8%
- Management 14.4%
- Other (includes PR and IT) 10.2%
- Sales, marketing 10.1%
- Services 8.3%
- Education 8.1%
- Research 5.7%

Graduate school programs of recent sociology majors

- 22.4% Sociology
- 16.9% Social work
- 11.4% Education
- 10.5% Law
- 9.4% Other social sciences
- 8.6% Psychology/counseling
- 7.3% Engineering
- 5.1% Other
- 4.5% Business/management
- 3.8% Public policy/affairs

Note: Percentage based on sociology majors attending graduate school 18 months after graduation.

Source: Spalter-Roth and Van Vooren 2009.

(1931) wrote about clinical sociology more than 75 years ago, but the term itself has become popular only in recent years. The Association for Applied Clinical Sociology was founded in 1978 to promote the application of sociological knowledge in interventions for individual and social change. This professional group has developed a procedure for certifying clinical sociologists—much as physical therapists or psychologists are certified.

Applied sociologists generally leave it to others to act on their evaluations, but clinical sociologists take direct responsibility for implementation and view those with whom they work as their clients. This specialty has become increasingly attractive to graduate students in sociology because it offers an opportunity to apply intellectual learning in practical ways. A competitive job market in the academic world has made such alternative career routes appealing.

Regardless of at which level it is done, practicing sociology is about so much more than a career; it is a way of looking at the world around us and understanding its complexity and interconnections in a new way. It is about understanding others from their perspective and even understanding ourselves through their eyes. It is a way of assessing the accuracy of claims and refining our knowledge about why we think the way we think and act the way we act. Sociology is something you do; it's a way of life.

>> Developing a Sociological Imagination

Learning to apply the sociological imagination may be more important now than ever. Through **globalization**—the worldwide integration of government policies, cultures, social movements, and financial markets through trade and the exchange of ideas—our lives are more connected with and dependent upon diverse groups of people around the world whose beliefs and practices may be quite different from our own. University campuses often provide a microcosm of this trend, drawing together people from around the world with radically different values, political views, customs, and more into a relatively confined social space and providing opportunities for them to interact. If such interactions are to be meaningful, positive, and respectful, we must learn to use the sociological imagination to better understand ourselves and our culture.

of methods, including interviews and observation, with photo and video documentation, these researchers found that across all drug users, HIV/AIDS transmission is highest among users of crystal methamphetamine. Meth users are also most likely to engage in risky sexual behavior and to have partners who do so. Fortunately, of all drug users, meth users are the ones most closely connected to treatment programs, which allows them to receive substance abuse education and treatment from their health care providers. Their cases, brought to the forefront by Scott and his team, highlight the need for public health officials to identify other individuals who engage in high-risk sexual behavior and to get them into appropriate treatment programs (G. Scott 2005).

clinical sociology The use of the discipline of sociology with the specific intent of altering organizations or restructuring social institutions.

globalization The worldwide integration of government policies, cultures, social movements, and financial markets through trade and the exchange of ideas.

CLINICAL SOCIOLOGY

The growing popularity of applied sociology has led to the rise of the specialty of clinical sociology. Whereas applied sociology may involve simply evaluating social issues, **clinical sociology** is dedicated to facilitating change by altering organizations (as in family therapy) or restructuring social institutions (as in the reorganization of a medical center). Louis Wirth

Sociologists expect the next quarter century to be perhaps the most exciting and critical period in the history of the discipline. That is because of a growing awareness—both in the United States and around the world—that current social problems can only be addressed by recognizing the full scope of our economic, political, and social interdependence. Through theory and research, sociologists offer us the tools we need.

SOC THINK

Consider the obstacles to cross-cultural interaction on college campuses. Why might people be unwilling to interact with others who have different cultural practices? How might it perpetuate inequality?

Investigate! Descriptions of the major sociological theorists in this chapter only begin to scratch the surface of these fascinating and creative people. Learn more at Sociology Professor (www.sociologyprofessor.com), a website where you can find biographical information on a variety of historical figures in the discipline.

get involved!

For REVIEW

I. **What is sociology?**
    - Sociology is a way of seeing that joins theory and research to investigate the relationship between the individual and society and the impact unequal distribution of resources has on opportunity.

II. **How do sociologists look at the world?**
    - Sociologists develop theories that provide windows into our lives, allowing us to better understand social order, inequality, and interaction.

III. **How might someone practice sociology?**
    - Sociology can provide a pathway to a career in a related applied, clinical, or academic context. But more than that, we can practice sociology in our everyday lives by utilizing the sociological imagination to better understand ourselves and others.

Functionalist view

Society is like a **living organism** with its various parts **working together** for the good of the whole.

The parts of society are structured to maintain **stability and social order.**

Society influences individual behavior and thus helps maintain **social integration through shared experiences.**

INTEGRATION
KEY CONCEPT

Conflict View

Society represents a **struggle over resources.** Those who control valued resources have **greater power** to get their way.

Valued resources include **material** (money, land, property), **social** (status, prestige, authority), and **cultural resources** (knowledge, beliefs, taste).

The existing social structure helps maintain the **privileges** of some groups while keeping others in subservient positions.

KEY CONCEPT
POWER

MAKE THE CONNECTION

After reviewing the chapter, answer the following questions:

Interactionist view

Society is the product of our everyday interactions by which we establish **shared meanings** and construct **social order.**

By generalizing from our everyday forms of social interaction (on the **micro level**), we can explain society as a whole.

The self exists in **relationship** with others and we come to **perceive** who we are and what our reality is through our interactions.

KEY CONCEPT
CONSTRUCTING SOCIAL REALITY

1

Why might having multiple theoretical perspectives help us when we practice the sociological imagination (p. 17)?

2

How might each perspective differ in how it looks at what it takes to produce something (such as a hamburger, a house, a book (p. 17)?

3

How might each perspective approach the study of unemployment? Of suicide? (p. 17)

4

How does each perspective enable you to see the way you participate in sports, either as a fan or as an athlete, in a different light?

Pop Quiz

1. Sociology is
   a. the analysis of individual motivations and internal struggles.
   b. concerned with predicting what particular individuals do or do not do.
   c. the systematic study of the relationship between the individual and society and of the consequences of difference.
   d. the integration of government policies, cultures, social movements, and financial markets through trade and the exchange of ideas.

2. According to C. Wright Mills, the sociological imagination focuses on the intersection between
   a. natural science and social science.
   b. power and access to resources.
   c. theory and research.
   d. history and biography.

3. What is the primary sociological lesson we learn from the hamburger as a miracle example?
   a. We take our interdependence and the knowledge we collectively share for granted.
   b. An individual could easily survive on his or her own without assistance from others.
   c. Modern technology makes it difficult for us to provide for our individual needs.
   d. Interdependence is no longer necessary because we can provide for our needs through modern technology.

4. In their attempts to describe the relationship between sociology and common sense, sociologists argue that
   a. common sense provides time-tested answers that are reliable most of the time whereas sociological facts change all the time.
   b. sociology depends on systematic analysis through research whereas common sense does not.
   c. sociology cannot assess or test the truthfulness of commonsense claims.
   d. there is no significant difference between the two.

5. Émile Durkheim's research on suicide found that
   a. Catholics had much higher suicide rates than Protestants.
   b. the more socially integrated someone is the less likely he or she is to commit suicide.
   c. married people are more likely to take their lives than single people.
   d. suicide is a solitary act, unrelated to group life.

6. Karl Marx argued that in order to understand social order we must include analysis of
   a. anomie.
   b. ownership of the means of production.
   c. the sociological imagination.
   d. microsociology.

7. Which sociologist made a major contribution to society through his in-depth studies of urban life, including both Blacks and Whites?
   a. W.E.B. Du Bois
   b. Émile Durkheim
   c. Auguste Comte
   d. Erving Goffman

8. What is the sociological term for the loss of direction felt in a society when social control of individual behavior has become ineffective?
   a. suicide
   b. alienation
   c. anomie
   d. agency

9. Thinking of society as a living organism in which each part of the organism contributes to its survival is a reflection of which theoretical perspective?
   a. the functionalist perspective
   b. the conflict perspective
   c. the Marxist perspective
   d. the interactionist perspective

10. The career path with the specific intent of altering social relationships or restructuring organizations is known as
    a. dramaturgical sociology.
    b. applied sociology.
    c. academic sociology.
    d. clinical sociology.

1. (c); 2 (d); 3 (a); 4 (b); 5 (b); 6 (b); 7 (a); 8 (c); 9 (a); 10 (d)

2 United States® Census 2010

...IN OUR HANDS
...NSUS.GOV

SOCIOLOG

ASKING QUESTIONS AND FINDING ANSWERS

Part of the fun of sociology is asking questions and finding answers, and sociologists Patricia and Peter Adler seem to have had more fun than most. Their search to understand our social lives has led them to spend extended periods of time with college athletes, drug dealers, school kids, Hawaiian resort workers, graduate students, self-injurers, and others. In each such study their underlying sociological commitment has remained the same: to answer the questions "Why do we think the way we think?" and "Why do we act the way we act?"

To better understand the tourism industry, for example, the Adlers spent eight years gathering information at five Hawaiian hotels, studying the staff and operations in minute detail (Adler and Adler 2004). This allowed them to better understand how tourist experiences are scripted (including the ceremonial lei provided upon arrival) and the significance of race, ethnicity, and social class when it comes to access to resources (including the kinds of jobs available to new immigrants such as Filipinos, Samoans, and Vietnamese).

Similarly, in their effort to better understand self-injury—including self-cutting, burning, branding, biting, and bone-breaking—the Adlers conducted lengthy, emotionally intense interviews with self-injurers over a six-year period, becoming friends with many. "Rather than remaining strictly detached from our subjects," they write, "we became involved in their lives, helping them and giving voice to their experiences and beliefs" (2007:542).

In other studies they found that college athletes go to big-time college sports schools with the best of intentions to be good students but get worn down by the obligations of being an athlete, and resign themselves to inferior academic performance (Adler and Adler 1985).

As is the case with all good sociological research, such studies seek to tell our stories and help us to understand ourselves in light of our interdependence. Sociologists such as the Adlers systematically gather our stories together through research and make sense of them with theory.

ICAL RESEARCH

- What steps do sociologists take when seeking to answer why people think and act the way they do?
- What techniques do sociologists use to collect data?
- What ethical concerns must sociologists consider while conducting research?

>> Steps in the Research Process

Sociology at its core represents a conversation between theory and research. Sociologists seek to describe and explain the patterns and practices of our lives through systematic investigation of what we do and why we do it. If we want to know why people think and act the way they do, we need to know more about what they actually think and do. We need to observe them, ask them questions, participate in their lives, or in other ways come to understand their experiences from their perspective. We cannot sit back and guess.

Sociology inherits this commitment in part from early attempts by some sociologists to emulate the scientific method. The **scientific method** is a systematic, organized series of steps that ensures maximum objectivity and consistency in researching a problem. Although not all sociologists today would tie the task of sociology as strongly to the natural science model, the commitment to making sense of the world through engagement with the world remains.

scientific method A systematic, organized series of steps that ensures maximum objectivity and consistency in researching a problem.

Conducting sociological research in the spirit of the scientific method requires adherence to a series of steps designed to ensure the accuracy of the results. Sociologists and other researchers follow five basic steps in the scientific method: (1) defining the problem, (2) reviewing the literature, (3) formulating the hypothesis, (4) selecting the research design and then collecting and analyzing data, and (5) developing the conclusion (see the figure at right). To better understand the process, we will follow an example about the relationship between education and income from start to finish.

The Scientific Method

Define the problem
Investigate existing theories

Review the literature

Ideas for further research

Formulate a testable **hypothesis**

Develop the **conclusion**

Select a **research design**
Collect and analyze data
Survey • Observation • Experiment • Existing sources

DEFINING THE PROBLEM

Does it "pay" to go to college? Many people make great sacrifices and work hard to get a college degree. Parents borrow money for their children's tuition. Students take part-time jobs or even work full-time while attending evening or weekend classes. Does it pay off? Are there sufficient monetary returns for getting that degree?

The first step in any research project is to state as clearly as possible what you hope to investigate—that is, to define the problem. Typically, this means explicitly identifying both the concepts we are interested in learning more about and the nature of the relationship we suspect might exist between those concepts. In our example, we are interested in knowing if increased education influences economic position.

In defining the problem, we draw on existing theories about why people think and act the way they do. These theories might be fairly simple and tentative guesses about the relationships, or they might be more elaborate and fully formed, such as we saw in the works of Karl Marx, Max Weber, and Émile Durkheim. For example, Durkheim developed a prediction regarding suicide based on his theory that social integration influences individual action, and he set about to test this theory using social research. Through research we seek to assess and refine our theories so that the explanations and descriptions of the world we get through sociology are fuller and more complete, more accurately reflecting both the simplicity and the complexity of human behavior.

Several competing theories exist concerning the relationship between education and income. One approach states that society needs people to develop their skills in order for society to realize its full potential, so it rewards those who make the sacrifices necessary to develop those skills through education (Davis and Moore 1945). Another theory states that education does not so much provide opportunity as reinforce the existing system of inequality by providing the illusion of opportunity. In this theory, people more or less end up in the same economic position in which they began their educational journey (Bowles and Gintis 1976). Which theory we start with will shape the kind of data we collect. We will look into both of these theories about education in a later chapter, but for the purpose of our example, we will focus on the first.

Often the concepts in our theories are too general or abstract to study in a systematic fashion. In order to investigate those concepts, we need to move from the abstract to the concrete. To do so, social science researchers develop an operational definition of each concept being studied. An **operational definition** transforms an abstract concept into indicators that are observable and measurable, allowing researchers to assess the concept. For example, a sociologist interested in status might use membership in exclusive social clubs as an operational definition of status. Someone studying religiosity might consider the frequency of a person's participation in religious services or the amount of time spent in prayer or meditation as an operational definition of how religious the

> Without theory we are blind—we cannot see the world.
>
> **Michael Burawoy**

person is. In our example, we need operational definitions for both education and earnings. Although we could argue that education involves more than just years of schooling completed, it is conventional to operationalize it that way. Similarly, income is conventionally operationalized as the total income an individual reports having received in the last year.

operational definition Transformation of an abstract concept into indicators that are observable and measurable.

hypothesis A testable statement about the relationship between two or more variables.

variable A measurable trait or characteristic that is subject to change under different conditions.

REVIEWING THE LITERATURE

The next phase of research involves a review of the literature: investigating previous research conducted by sociologists and others regarding the concepts we wish to study. Analyzing how others have studied these concepts allows researchers to refine the problem under study, clarify possible techniques for collecting data, and eliminate or reduce avoidable mistakes. An excellent place to start such research is the many sociological journals that regularly publish articles in which sociologists carefully document their findings. (See the "Finding Information" table on page 28 for more useful tips.)

In our example, we would need to seek out existing research about the relationship between education and income. In that literature we would find significant evidence that the two are linked. We would also learn that other factors besides years of schooling influence earning potential. For example, a person's occupational category (such as plumber, tool-and-die worker, secretary, or professor) might shape her or his income in a way different from just educational level alone. We also find that additional background factors such as class, gender, and race affect income. For example, the children of rich parents are more likely to go to college than those from modest backgrounds, so we might consider the possibility that the same parents may later help their children secure better-paying jobs (Walpole 2007). This might lead us to consider adding additional concepts to our definition of the problem.

FORMULATING THE HYPOTHESIS

After reviewing earlier studies and drawing on the contributions of sociological theorists, we would next formulate our hypothesis. A **hypothesis** is more than just an educated guess; it is a testable statement about the relationship between two or more factors known as variables. Income, religion, occupation, and gender can all serve as variables in a study. We can define a **variable** as a measurable trait or characteristic that is subject to change under different conditions.

Finding Information

Begin with material you already have, including this text and others.

Beware of using online sources such as Wikipedia; they can be a helpful place to start, but always double-check claims with a reputable source or organization.

Use newspapers.

Search using computerized periodical indexes to find related academic journal articles.

Use the library catalog.

Examine government documents (including the U.S. Census).

Contact people, organizations, and agencies related to your topic.

Consult with your instructor, teaching assistant, or reference librarian.

---

causal logic The relationship between a condition or variable and a particular consequence with one event leading to the other.

independent variable The variable in a causal relationship that causes or influences a change in a second variable.

dependent variable The variable in a causal relationship that is subject to the influence of another variable.

By formulating a hypothesis, we are trying to explain why something happens. In doing so, we must clearly define the potential variables that influence the event we want to explain. This assumes that **causal logic,** the relationship between a variable and a particular event in which one leads to the other, is at work. Durkheim, for example, wanted to explain why people commit suicide, and he hypothesized that social integration is a powerful factor. In our example we are suggesting that increased education leads to higher income.

In hypotheses, the causal variable that brings about change is called the **independent variable.** The variable that is affected is known as the **dependent variable** because change in it depends on the influence of the independent variable. In other words, the researcher believes that the independent variable predicts or causes change in the dependent variable. For example, a researcher in sociology might anticipate that the availability of affordable housing (the independent variable; often referred to in equations as x) affects the level of homelessness in a community (the dependent variable; typically represented in equations as y).

We can put these pieces together to generate a generic hypothesis statement: knowledge of the independent variable (x) allows us to better explain or predict the value or position of the dependent variable (y). We could then place variables we are interested in studying, such as those

Did You Know?

... U.S. government agencies regularly release reports with information on income, education, poverty, and health care. According to the Census Bureau, median household income in 2008 was $50,303. According to the U.S. Department of Education, of people aged 25–29, 87.8 percent had received their high school diploma or equivalent, and 30.8 percent had earned a bachelor's degree or a higher degree.

Source: DeNavas-Walt, Proctor, and Smith 2009a; Snyder and Dillow 2010.

in the figure to the right, into this statement to clearly present the nature of the relationships we expect to find between variables we wish to study.

In our example, our hypothesis suggests that knowing how many years of schooling a person has completed will allow us to better predict how much money he or she will earn. Our independent variable is the level of education, and income is the dependent variable. Further, we expect that this relationship will be positive, meaning the higher a person's educational attainment, the more money she or he will make.

When interpreting results, however, we need to distinguish between correlation and causation. A **correlation** is a relationship between two variables in which a change in one coincides with a change in the other. Just because variables change in a way that appears related does not mean that the relationship is necessarily causal. For example, research shows that the source individuals use to get their news influences how knowledgeable they are. Those who watch television news are less knowledgeable than those who read newspapers and newsmagazines. The correlation between the two variables is actually caused by a third variable, people's training in processing large amounts of information. People with poor reading skills are much more likely than others to get their news from television, whereas those who are more educated or skilled turn more often to the print media. Thus, although television viewing is correlated with lower news comprehension, it does not *cause* it. In the

Causal Logic

Independent variable		Dependent variable
x	→	y
Level of educational degree	→	Level of income
Degree of integration into society	→	Likelihood of suicide
Availability of affordable housing	→	Level of homelessness
Parents' church attendance	→	Children's church attendance
Time spent preparing for quiz	→	Performance on quiz
Parents' income	→	Likelihood of children's enrolling in college

words of sociologist Pierre Bourdieu, "One has explained nothing by establishing the existence of a correlation between an 'independent' variable and a 'dependent' variable" (1984:18). Correlation does not equal causation. Sociologists seek to identify the *causal* link between variables; the suspected causal link is generally described in the hypothesis (Neuman 2006).

> **correlation** A relationship between two variables in which a change in one coincides with a change in the other.

Correlation

Source: http://xkcd.com/552/.

COLLECTING AND ANALYZING DATA

To assess their hypotheses, sociologists, like all scientists, collect data. There are a variety of ways, known as research designs, that sociologists go about doing this, including surveys, observation, experiments, and use of existing data. Because the design selected is so critical to the research process, we will go into greater depth about each of those research designs later in this chapter. For now we will focus on some key issues that researchers must address regardless of which research design they select.

Selecting the Sample

Sociologists cannot study everybody, so they seek ways to select individuals and groups that are representative of the population that is the subject of the research. In most large-scale studies, social scientists carefully choose what is known as a **sample**—a selection from a larger population that is statistically representative of that population. There are many kinds of samples, but the one social scientists use most frequently is the random sample. In a **random sample,** every member of the entire population being studied has the same chance of being selected. Thus, if researchers want to examine the opinions of people listed in a city directory (a book that, unlike the telephone directory, lists all households), they might use a computer to randomly select names from the directory. The results would constitute a random sample. The advantage of using specialized sampling techniques is that sociologists can be confident that the results they obtain will be representative of the larger population, freeing them from having to question everyone in the population (Igo 2007).

sample A selection from a larger population that is statistically representative of that population.

random sample A sample for which every member of an entire population has the same chance of being selected.

It is all too easy to confuse the careful scientific techniques used in representative sampling with the many nonscientific polls that receive so much more media attention. For example, television viewers are often encouraged to "visit our website and express your views" in an online poll about headline news or political contests. Such polls reflect nothing more than the views of those who happened to see the television program and took the time to register their opinions. These data do not necessarily reflect (and indeed may distort) the views of the broader population. Not everyone has access to a television or radio, time to watch or listen to a program, or the means and/or inclination to vote in this way. Even when these techniques include answers from tens of thousands of people, they will be far less accurate than a carefully selected representative sample of 1500 respondents.

For the purposes of our research example of education and income, we could use information collected in the General Social Survey (GSS) or information from the U.S. Census. Since 1972, the National Opinion Research Center (NORC) has conducted this national survey 26 times, most recently in 2010. In the GSS, administered in both English and Spanish, a representative sample of the adult population is interviewed in depth on a variety of topics. The U.S. Census also offers a wealth of data. In addition to the national census conducted every 10 years (including in 2010), it regularly collects data using samples of the U.S. population, including annual reports regarding income (DeNavas-Walt, Proctor, and Smith 2009a).

Ensuring Validity and Reliability To have confidence in their findings, and in keeping with the scientific

Did You Know?

. . . A classic case of sampling error occurred when pollsters for *Literary Digest* declared that Alf Landon would defeat President Franklin Roosevelt in 1936. They predicted Landon would win 55 percent of the vote; he received only 37 percent. Although the *Digest* polled 2 million people, they selected names from telephone books and auto registration records. With the country in the midst of the Great Depression, phones and cars were luxuries many people could not afford. As a result, the poll underrepresented poorer people, who were more likely to support Roosevelt (Squire 1988).

method, sociologists pursue research results that are both valid and reliable. **Validity** refers to the degree to which a measure or scale truly reflects the phenomenon under study. In our example, a valid measure of income would accurately represent how much money a person earned in a given year. Although income can be a touchy subject, various studies show that people are reasonably accurate in reporting how much money they earned in the most recent year. If a question is written unclearly, however, the resulting data might not be accurate. For example, respondents to an unclear question about income might report partial-year earnings or total household income (perhaps including their parents' or spouse's income as well as their own).

Reliability refers to the extent to which a measure produces consistent results. Using the same instrument to collect data from the same people in similar circumstances should provide the same results. For example, if you give people the same questionnaire about income and education at two different times, unless something significant has changed between times, the responses should be the same.

DEVELOPING THE CONCLUSION

After conducting research, sociologists assess their results. This can involve data entry, statistical testing, transcribing and coding interviews, and more, depending on the research method used. The key is to ensure that your conclusions are fully supported by your data.

Supporting Hypotheses In our example, we find that the data the graph below support our hypothesis: People with more formal schooling do earn more money than those with less schooling. Data consistently show that those with a high school diploma earn more than those who failed to complete high school, that those with some college earn more than do those with just a high school diploma, that those with a college degree earn still more, and on up the line so that those with graduate degrees earn the most. Those with a high school diploma or less have a very small portion of the high-income slice of the pie compared to those who have more education.

> **validity** The degree to which a measure or scale truly reflects the phenomenon under study.
>
> **reliability** The extent to which a measure produces consistent results.
>
> **control variable** A factor that is held constant to test the relative impact of an independent variable.

Of course, this is not true for all individuals. There are people who have a high school degree or less who end up with high incomes, and there are those with advanced degrees who earn modest incomes. A successful entrepreneur, for example, might not have much formal schooling, and a holder of a doctorate may choose to work for a low-paying, not-for-profit institution. Sociologically speaking, both these findings—that education shapes income and that the relationship is not perfect—are interesting and would likely lead to more questions about how and why such variation occurs.

Sociological studies do not always generate data that support the original hypothesis. In many instances, the results refute the hypothesis, and researchers must reformulate their conclusions. This often leads to additional research in which sociologists reexamine their theory and methods, making appropriate changes in their research design.

Controlling for Other Factors Given the complexity of human behavior, it is seldom sufficient to study only one independent and dependent variable. While such analyses can provide us with insight, we also need to consider other causal factors that might influence the dependent variable. One way to do this is to introduce a **control variable,** which is a factor that the researcher holds constant to test the relative impact of an independent variable. For example, if researchers wanted

Impact of a College Degree on Income

High school diploma or less

7%	$80,000 and over
10%	$60,000–79,999
23%	
45%	$40,000–59,999
	$20,000–39,999
16%	under $20,000

Associate's degree or more

| 28% |
| 18% |
| 27% |
| 22% |
| 5% |

Note: High School category includes those with some college but not degree.
Source: U.S. Census Bureau 2009d:Table PINC-03, part 28.

Sixty-one percent of people with a high school diploma or less (left) earn under $40,000 a year, while only 17 percent earn $60,000 or more. In contrast, 46 percent of those with an associate's degree or higher (right) earn $60,000 or more, while only 27 percent earn less than $40,000.

to explain neighborhood crime rates as a dependent variable, they might look at the neighborhood's poverty rate as an independent variable. It is likely, however, that additional factors influence crime rates, so they might introduce familiarity—the degree to which neighbors know and regularly interact with each other—as a control variable. They would find that neighborhoods with a high level of familiarity do have lower crime rates than those with low familiarity rates. The introduction of the control variable allows us to see that some of the variation in neighborhood crime rates that was initially assumed to be due to poverty is actually due to the influence of the control variable.

research design A detailed plan or method for obtaining data scientifically.

survey A study, generally in the form of an interview or questionnaire, that provides researchers with information about how people think and act.

In our example, as we have already implied, we might want to control for the effect of additional variables that shape income. Not everyone enjoys equal educational opportunities, a disparity linked to income inequality. We might ask: What impact does a person's race or gender have? Is a woman with a college degree likely to earn as much as a man with similar schooling? In later chapters, we will consider such additional factors and variables. That is, we will examine the impact that education has on income while controlling for variables such as gender and race.

IN SUMMARY:
THE RESEARCH PROCESS

We began with a general question about the relationship between education and income. By following the steps in the research process—defining the problem, reviewing the literature, formulating a hypothesis, collecting and analyzing data, and developing a conclusion—we were able to show that education does pay. One of the ways we can check the validity of our findings is to share them with sociologists, policy makers, and others in a public forum in the form of a paper at a professional conference or an article in a refereed academic journal. By exposing what we did, how we did it, and what we found, others can serve as a useful check to make sure we did not miss anything and that we proceeded in an appropriate manner.

Research is cyclical in nature. At the end of the process, researchers almost always find that they have more questions they would like to pursue, and most research papers include a specific section addressing how they might define the problem and carry out the research next time.

Along the way, researchers may have discovered new concepts they should consider, better ways to ask questions to get the information they need, individuals or groups they should include in the study, or a whole host of other possibilities. In the end, the studies researchers produce become part of the literature review for the next project, whether theirs or someone else's.

>> Major Research Designs

As we have seen, sociologists go about gathering and making sense of the stories of our lives in a variety of ways. Sometimes sociologists want to tell our larger collective story; other times they want to tell the stories of individuals and groups who are often left out of such large-scale accounts. Different research designs are available to tell these different types of stories. For example, large national surveys allow us to get a sense of the national mood about issues such as politics or religion, and statistics can give insight into where we stand in relation to each other on such issues. To explore the stories of individuals, researchers may employ methods, such as observation, that emphasize more direct and personal interaction with their subjects.

Sociologists draw on a variety of research designs when considering how to collect their data. A **research design** is a detailed plan or method for obtaining data scientifically. Often a research design is based on the theories and hypotheses the researcher starts with (Merton 1948). The choice requires creativity and ingenuity because it directly influences both the cost of the project and the time needed to collect the data. As noted previously, research designs that sociologists regularly use to generate data include surveys, observation, experiments, and existing sources.

SURVEYS

Almost all of us have responded to surveys of one kind or another. We may have been asked what kind of detergent we use, which presidential candidate we intend to vote for, or what our favorite television program is. A **survey** is a study, generally in the form of an interview or questionnaire, that provides researchers with information about how people think and act. Among the United States' best-known opinion surveys are the Gallup poll and the Harris poll. As anyone who watches the news during presidential campaigns knows, these polls have become a staple of political life.

Issues in Designing Surveys As indicated earlier, a survey must be based on precise, representative sampling if it is to genuinely reflect a broad range of the population.

Presidential Approval Ratings

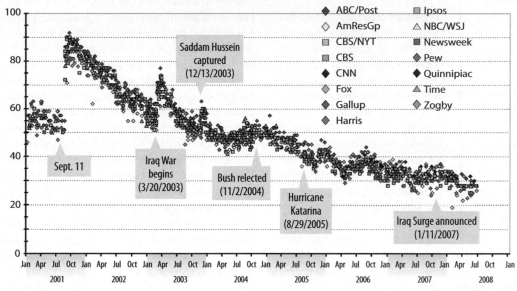

Source: www.pollkatz.homestead.com.

We might be skeptical that feedback from just a few hundred people can provide an accurate picture of how more than 300 million people think, but properly run surveys can do just that. When it comes to presidential polling, for example, we can compare the results of such polls against actual election results. In a study of the historical accuracy of presidential polls, political scientist Michael W. Traugott (2005) reports that, based on one common measure of assessing results, the polls from 1956 to 2004 were, on average, within 2 percent of accurately predicting the final result. We can also get a sense of the accuracy of polls by looking at "polls of polls" that combine various results into a single report or graph to better see the pattern that the polls collectively demonstrate (see the figure above). Examples of such polls for presidential and congressional approval ratings are available at sites such as www.pollster.com. While the pollsters sometimes fail to "get it right" (for example, predicting that Dewey would defeat Truman in the 1948 presidential election), most often they do, and with amazing precision.

In addition to developing representative samples, sociologists must exercise great care in the wording of questions. An effective survey question must be simple and clear enough for people

Going GLOBAL

Research Abroad

Researchers can gather information even under difficult circumstances. Even as the Obama administration was escalating the war in Afghanistan against the Taliban in 2009, researchers conducted surveys about people's attitudes in the region. In late 2009, they found that 79 percent of Afghans felt the Taliban had a negative influence, though residents in the south, a Taliban stronghold, were somewhat less negative. At the same time, 45 percent approved of U.S. leadership in Afghanistan, down from 50 percent earlier in the year (Ray and Srinivasan 2010a, 2010b).

to understand. It must also be specific enough that researchers have no problems interpreting the results. Open-ended questions ("What do you think of the programming on educational television?") must be carefully phrased to solicit the type of information desired. Surveys can be indispensable sources of information, but only if the sampling is done properly and the questions are worded accurately and without bias.

Studies have also shown that the characteristics of the interviewer have an impact on survey data. For example, female interviewers tend to receive more feminist responses from female subjects than do male researchers, and African American interviewers tend to receive more detailed responses about race-related issues from Black subjects than do White interviewers. The possible impact of gender and race indicates again how much

interview A face-to-face or telephone questioning of a respondent to obtain desired information.

questionnaire A printed, written, or computerized form used to obtain information from a respondent.

quantitative research Research that collects and reports data primarily in numerical form.

mean A number calculated by adding a series of values and then dividing by the number of values.

median The midpoint, or number that divides a series of values into two groups of equal numbers of values.

care social research requires (D.W. Davis and Silver 2003).

Types of Surveys There are two main forms of the survey: the **interview,** in which a researcher obtains information through face-to-face or telephone questioning, and the **questionnaire,** in which a researcher uses a printed, written, or computerized form to obtain information from a respondent. Each of these has its advantages. An interviewer can obtain a higher response rate because people find it more difficult to turn down a personal request for an interview than to throw away a written questionnaire. In addition, a skillful interviewer can go beyond written questions and probe for a subject's underlying feelings and reasons. For their part, questionnaires have the advantage of being cheaper, especially in large samples. Either way, what we can learn from surveys can be amazing.

Why, for example, do people have sex? A straightforward question, but until recently one that rarely was investigated scientifically, despite its significance to public health, marital counseling, and criminology. In an exploratory study published in 2007, researchers surveyed nearly 2000 undergraduates at the University of Texas

at Austin. They began phase 1 of the research by asking approximately 400 students in a variety of psychology courses to answer this question: "Please list all the reasons you can think of why you, or someone you have known, has engaged in sexual intercourse in the past." The explanations were highly diverse, ranging from "I was drunk" to "I wanted to feel closer to God."

In phase 2 of the research, the team asked another sample of 1500 students to rate the importance of each of the 287 reasons given by the first group. Nearly every one of the reasons was rated most important by at least some respondents. Although there were some gender differences in the replies, there was significant consensus between men and women on the top 12 reasons (see the table below). Based on their overall results, the researchers identified four major categories of reasons why people have sex: Physical (pleasure, stress reduction), Goal Attainment (social status, revenge), Emotional (love, commitment), and Insecurity (self-esteem boost, duty/pressure) (Meston and Buss 2007, 2009). After reviewing the study results, critics argued that the researchers' sample was not sufficiently representative to permit generalizing their findings to the population as a whole. The researchers acknowledged as much from the beginning, having undertaken the project as exploratory research. They have since conducted research using a more representative sample, and their findings were largely the same (Melby 2007).

Quantitative and Qualitative Research Surveys most often represent an example of **quantitative research,** which collects and reports data primarily in numerical form. Analysis of these data depends upon statistics, from the simple to the complex, which provide basic summaries describing what variables look like and how they are related. Basic descriptive statistics, such as percentages, are likely familiar. The **mean,** or average, is a number calculated by adding a series of values and then dividing by the number of values. The **median,** or midpoint, is the number that divides a series of values into two groups of equal numbers of values. The median is most often used when there are extreme scores that would distort the mean. The **mode** is the single most common value in a series of scores and is seldom used in sociological research. The mean, median, and mode all seek to provide a single score that is representative of or provides a summary for the whole distribution of scores. When it comes to analyzing relationships between variables, researchers usually rely on computer programs to deal with more complex analysis of quantitative data.

While quantitative research can make use of large samples, it can't offer great depth on a topic. That is why researchers also make use of **qualitative research,** which relies on what they see in field and naturalistic settings, often focusing on small groups and communities rather than on large groups or whole nations. Here, too, sociologists rely on computers to assist their analysis. Numerous software programs allow researchers not only to record

Top 12 Reasons Why Men and Women Had Sex

Men	Reason	Women
1	I was attracted to the person	1
2	It feels good	3
3	I wanted to experience the physical pleasure	2
4	It's fun	8
5	I wanted to show my affection to the person	4
6	I was sexually aroused and wanted the release	6
7	I was "horny"	7
8	I wanted to express my love for the person	5
9	I wanted to achieve an orgasm	14
10	I wanted to please my partner	11
17	I realized I was in love	9
13	I was "in the heat of the moment"	10

Source: Meston and Buss 2007:506.

Research is formalized curiosity. It
is poking and prying with a purpose.

Zora Neale Hurston

observations but to identify common themes, concepts, or concerns expressed in interviews. The most common form of qualitative research is observation.

OBSERVATION

Investigators who collect information by participating directly and/or by closely watching a group or community are engaged in **observation.** This method allows sociologists to examine behaviors and communities in greater depth than is possible using other methods. Though observation may seem a relatively informal method compared to surveys, researchers are careful to take detailed notes while observing their subjects.

An increasingly popular form of qualitative research in sociology today is **ethnography**—the study of an entire social setting through extended systematic observation. Typically, the emphasis is on how the subjects themselves view their social life in some setting. In some cases, the sociologist actually joins the group for a period to get an accurate sense of how it operates. This approach is called *participant observation.*

During the late 1930s, in a classic example of participant observation research, sociologist William F. Whyte moved into a low-income Italian neighborhood in Boston. For nearly four years, he was a member of the social circle of "corner boys" whom he described in his classic book *Street Corner Society.* Whyte revealed his identity to these men and joined in their conversations, bowling, and other leisure-time activities. His goal was to gain greater insight into the community that these men had established. As Whyte ([1943] 1981:303) listened to Doc, the leader of the group, he "learned the answers to questions that I would not even have had the sense to ask if I had been getting my information solely on an interviewing basis." Whyte's work was especially valuable since, at the time, the academic world had little direct knowledge of the poor and tended to rely for information on the records of social service agencies, hospitals, and courts (P. Adler, Adler, and Johnson 1992).

The initial challenge that Whyte faced—and that every participant observer encounters—was to gain acceptance into an unfamiliar group. It is no simple matter for a college-trained sociologist to win the trust of a religious cult, a youth gang, a poor Appalachian community, or a circle of skid row residents. It requires a great deal of

mode The single most common value in a series of scores.

qualitative research Research that relies on what is seen in field or naturalistic settings more than on statistical data.

observation A research technique in which an investigator collects information through direct participation and/or by closely watching a group or community.

ethnography The study of an entire social setting through extended systematic observation.

patience and an accepting, nonthreatening type of personality on the part of the observer.

Observation research poses other complex challenges for investigators. Sociologists must be able to fully understand what they are observing. In a sense, then, researchers must learn to see the world as the group sees it in order to fully comprehend the events taking place around them.

This raises a delicate issue. If the research is to be successful, the observer cannot allow the close associations or even friendships that inevitably develop to influence the subjects' behavior or the conclusions of the study. Anson Shupe and David Bromley (1980), two sociologists who have used participant observation, have likened this challenge to that of walking a tightrope. Even while working hard to gain acceptance from the group being studied, the participant observer *must* maintain some degree of detachment.

In 2006, the issue of detachment became a controversial one for social scientists embedded with the U.S. military in Afghanistan and Iraq. Among other studies, researchers participated in the creation of the Army's Human Terrain System, a $4-million effort to identify the customs, kinship structures, and internal social conflicts in the two countries. The intention was to provide military leaders with information that would help them make better decisions. Although the idea of scholars cooperating in any way with soldiers struck many social science researchers as inappropriate, others countered that the information they developed would help the military to avoid needless violence and might even facilitate the withdrawal of troops from the region (Glenn 2007).

EXPERIMENTS

When scientists want to study a possible cause-and-effect relationship, they conduct an **experiment**—an artificially created situation that allows a researcher to manipulate variables. Researchers carefully control the experimental context in order to measure the degree to which the independent variable causes change in the dependent variable under study. Although experiments can prove insightful, sociologists tend not to use them as frequently as the other

experiment An artificially created situation that allows a researcher to manipulate variables.

experimental group The subjects in an experiment who are exposed to an independent variable introduced by a researcher.

control group The subjects in an experiment who are not introduced to the independent variable by the researcher.

Hawthorne effect The unintended influence that observers of experiments can have on their subjects.

secondary analysis A variety of research techniques that make use of previously collected and publicly accessible information and data.

Personal Sociology

Newfound Respect

research designs, because they are typically more interested in understanding people's natural responses.

In a classic experiment, researchers begin by dividing subjects with similar characteristics into two groups in order to see the impact of one independent variable. The **experimental group** is then exposed to an independent variable; the **control group** is not. Thus, if scientists were testing a new type of antibiotic, they would administer the drug to an experimental group but not to a control group.

One of the disadvantages of experiments, just as in observation research, is that the presence of a social scientist or other observer may affect the behavior of the people being studied. The recognition of this phenomenon grew out of an experiment conducted during the 1920s and 1930s at the Hawthorne plant of the Western Electric Company near Chicago. A group of researchers set out to determine how to improve the productivity of workers at the plant. The investigators manipulated such variables as lighting and working hours to see what impact the changes would have on how much workers produce. To their surprise, they found that every step they took seemed to increase output. Even measures that seemed likely to have the opposite effect, such as reducing the amount of lighting in the plant down to moonlight levels, led to higher productivity (Mayo 1933).

Why did the plant's employees work harder even under less favorable conditions? The researchers initially concluded that the workers modified their behavior because they knew they were being studied. They responded positively to the novelty of being subjects in an experiment and to the fact that researchers were interested in them. Since that time, sociologists have used the term **Hawthorne effect** to describe the unintended influence that observers of experiments can have on their subjects even though later studies show the situation there was more complex (Brannigan and Zwerman 2001). It highlights the difficulties experiments present in seeking to understand how people behave in their real-world environments.

Sociologists do sometimes try to approximate experimental conditions in the field. Sociologist Devah Pager (2003) devised an experiment to assess the impact of a criminal background on individuals' employment opportunities. She sent four polite, well-dressed young men out to look for an entry-level job in Milwaukee, Wisconsin. All four were 23-year-old college students, but they presented themselves as high school graduates with similar job histories. Two of the men were Black and two were White. One Black applicant and one White applicant claimed to have served 18 months in jail for a felony conviction—possession of cocaine with intent to distribute.

The experiences of the four men with 350 potential employers were vastly different. The White applicant with a purported prison record received only half as many call-backs as the other White applicant—17 percent compared to 34 percent (see the graphic above). But as dramatic as the effect of his criminal record was, the effect of his race was more significant. Despite his prison record, he received slightly more callbacks than the Black applicant

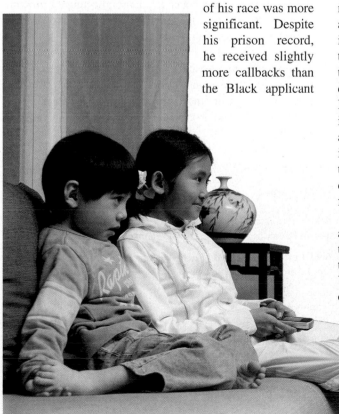

White Privilege in Job Seeking

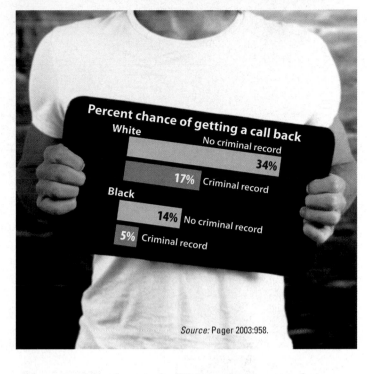

Percent chance of getting a call back

White
No criminal record **34%**
17% Criminal record

Black
14% No criminal record
5% Criminal record

Source: Pager 2003:958.

with no criminal record (17 percent compared to 14 percent). Race, it seems, was more of a concern to potential employers than a criminal background.

USE OF EXISTING SOURCES

Sociologists do not necessarily need to collect new data in order to conduct research and test hypotheses. The term **secondary analysis** refers to a variety of research techniques that make use of previously collected and publicly accessible information and data. Generally, in conducting secondary analysis, researchers use data in ways that were unintended by the initial collectors of the information. For example, the federal government (primarily through the U.S. Census Bureau) compiles a treasure trove of data that it relies on to make policy decisions. These data are then made available for public use. Marketing specialists, for instance, may use the data to advise clients about where to build commercial properties, anything from bicycle stores to fast-food restaurants (Weiss 2000).

Sociologists can learn a great deal using available information. For example, every year the Social Security Administration receives thousands of registrations for newborn babies. Using these data, we can recognize shifts in cultural trends in the population. As the figure "What's in a Name?" on page 38 shows, for example, John has been an extremely popular boy's name for more than a century. In 2008, more

What's in a Name?

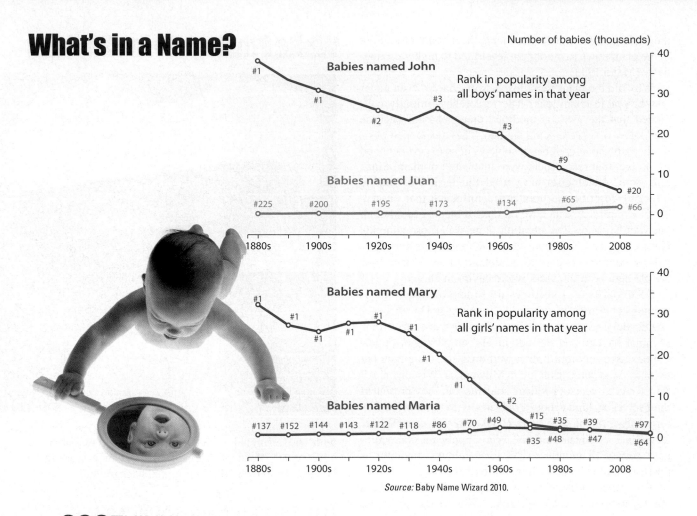

Number of babies (thousands)

Babies named John

Rank in popularity among all boys' names in that year

#1 #1 #2 #3 #3 #9 #20

Babies named Juan

#225 #200 #195 #173 #134 #65 #66

1880s 1900s 1920s 1940s 1960s 1980s 2008

Babies named Mary

Rank in popularity among all girls' names in that year

#1 #1 #1 #1 #1 #1 #1 #1 #2

#15 #35 #39 #97

Babies named Maria

#137 #152 #144 #143 #122 #118 #86 #70 #49 #35 #48 #47 #64

1880s 1900s 1920s 1940s 1960s 1980s 2008

Source: Baby Name Wizard 2010.

SOC THINK

"NameVoyager" at www.babynamewizard.com is a very cool application that allows you to type in any name to trace its popularity over time. Go there and enter several names to see how they have changed over time. Considering some of the specific names you tried, what factors might have contributed to their rise and fall? How popular is your first name? How and why has its popularity changed over time?

than 3000 babies were named John, making it the 20th most popular name that year. Though only about half as many babies were named Juan in 2008, that name has been gaining in popularity in recent generations, reflecting the growing impact of the Latino population in the United States. We see a similar patten for the names Mary and Maria.

Existing data from another source confirms this shift. Analysis of data released by the U.S. Census Bureau tracking people's family names in 2007 revealed that although Smith remained the most common surname in the United States, Garcia and Rodriguez had risen into the top 10.

Major Research Designs

Method	Examples	Advantages	Limitations
Survey	Questionnaires Interviews	Yields information about specific issues	Can be expensive and time-consuming
Observation	Ethnography	Yields detailed information about specific groups or organizations	Involves months if not years of labor-intensive data collection
Experiment	Deliberate manipulation of people's social behavior	Yields direct measures of people's behavior	Has ethical limitations on the degree to which subjects' behavior can be manipulated
Existing sources/ Secondary analysis	Analysis of census or health data Analysis of films or TV commercials	Cost-efficiency; nonreactive	Limited to data collected for some other purpose

The announcement marked the first time in the nation's history that a non-Anglo name had been counted among the most common names. Such name changes reflect an overall shift in the U.S. population from a nation composed primarily of European descendants to one that is more globally diverse, a trend sociologists expect will continue (Baby Name Wizard 2010; Levitt and Dubner 2005; Word et al. 2007).

Part of the appeal of secondary analysis to sociologists is that it is nonreactive—that is, doing this type of study does not influence what you find. For example, Émile Durkheim's statistical analysis of existing suicide data neither increased nor decreased human self-destruction. Researchers, then, can avoid the Hawthorne effect by using secondary analysis. However, there is one inherent problem: The researcher who relies on data collected by someone else may not find exactly what he or she needs. Social scientists who are studying family violence can use statistics from police and social service agencies on reported cases of spouse abuse and child abuse, but how many cases are not reported? Government bodies have no precise data on all cases of abuse.

Secondary analysis also allows us to study social contexts, both present and past, through careful analysis of cultural, economic, and political documents, including newspapers, periodicals, radio and television tapes, the Internet, scripts, diaries, songs, folklore, and legal papers. In examining these sources, researchers employ a technique known as **content analysis**—the systematic coding and objective recording of data, guided by a given rationale.

Using content analysis, Erving Goffman (1979) conducted a pioneering exploration of how advertisements portray women. The ads he studied typically showed women as subordinate to or dependent on others, or as taking instruction from men. Women engaged in caressing and touching gestures more than men. Even when presented in leadership roles, women were likely to be shown striking seductive poses or gazing out into space. Jeanne Kilbourne's content analysis of ads demonstrates that women continue to be portrayed as objects. She found that advertisers' primary message is that women should spend their time, energy, and money trying to attain the idealized, airbrushed image of female beauty only achievable with the assistance of Photoshop. She quotes supermodel Cindy Crawford as saying, "I wish I looked like Cindy Crawford" (Kilbourne 2010).

Researchers have also used content analysis to investigate media portrayals of other public health issues. For example, Sargent and Heatherton (2009) analyzed the top 25 films for each year from 1990 to 2007 and found that the average number of smoking occurrences fell from 3.5 to 0.23 per film. They compare this with the declining smoking levels of U.S. eighth-graders, an average of 1.3 percent per year after 1996. Given the complexity of possible factors, they cannot assert a direct causal link between the two, although they point to other research which demonstrates that exposure to smoking in films does affect youth smoking rates (National Cancer Institute 2008).

Concerns about childhood obesity have recently led researchers to analyze commercials aired during Saturday children's television programming on broadcast and cable channels. For example, in an analysis of more than 1200 ads, Stitt and Kunkel (2008) found that food ads made up almost half of the commercial time, an average of 11 food ads per hour. Of these ads, 9 out of 10 were for high-calorie, low-nutrient food products such as sugared snacks, sugared cereals, and fast food. The researchers also found that the most common strategy used to persuade viewers to try the products was to associate the product with having fun or happiness.

Other researchers have found a growing difference in the way men and women use sexually explicit language. For example, an analysis of the lyrics of *Billboard* magazine's top 100 hits indicates that, since 1958, male artists have increased their use of such language while female artists have decreased theirs (Dukes et al. 2003). In all such cases, content analysis allows us a better understanding of our cultural practices.

content analysis The systematic coding and objective recording of data, guided by some rationale.

Primary Themes in Children's Television Food Commercials

- 47% Fun/happiness
- 18% Taste/flavor/smell
- 12% Product's uniqueness
- 10% Other
- 8% Physical strength
- 5% Popularity of product
- 0% Healthy product

Source: Stitt and Kunkel 2008.

POPSOC

Sociologists Stephen J. Scanlan and Seth L. Feinberg suggest that we can better understand key sociological concepts by analyzing the *The Simpsons*. One example they provide, among many, is the episode "Lisa vs. Malibu Stacy," in which eight-year-old Lisa is outraged because her talking doll says things like "Let's buy makeup so the boys will like us." They say this raises sociological issues related to gender socialization, inequality, consumerism, and more. Additional issues raised in other episodes include social class, deviance, education, marriage and family, and religion. What might we learn about society by analyzing popular culture through the lens of sociology?

>> Research Ethics

A biochemist cannot inject a drug into a human being unless the drug has been thoroughly tested and the subject agrees to the shot. To do otherwise would be both unethical and illegal. Sociologists, too, must abide by certain specific standards in conducting research, called a **code of ethics.** The professional society of the discipline, the American Sociological Association (ASA), first published its *Code of Ethics* in 1971 and revised it most recently in 1997. It puts forth the following basic principles:

- Maintain objectivity and integrity in research.
- Respect the subject's right to privacy and dignity.
- Protect subjects from personal harm.
- Preserve confidentiality.
- Seek informed consent when data are collected from research participants or when behavior occurs in a private context.
- Acknowledge research collaboration and assistance.
- Disclose all sources of financial support.

Because most sociological research uses people as sources of information—as respondents to survey questions, subjects of observation, or participants in experiments—these principles are important.

CONFIDENTIALITY

In all cases, sociologists need to be certain they are not invading their subjects' privacy. Generally, they do so by assuring subjects of anonymity or by guaranteeing the confidentiality of personal information. In addition, research proposals that involve human subjects are now subject

Content analysis of popular song lyrics shows that over the last 50 years, top female artists such as Beyoncé Knowles have used fewer sexually explicit words, while male artists like Jay-Z have used more.

to oversight by a review board, whose members seek to ensure that the research does not place subjects at an unreasonable level of risk. If necessary, the board may ask researchers to revise their research designs to conform to the *Code of Ethics.*

These basic principles and procedures may seem clear-cut in the abstract but can be difficult to adhere to in practice. For example, should a sociologist who is engaged in participant observation research always protect the confidentiality of subjects? What if the subjects are members of a group involved in unethical or illegal activities? What if the sociologist is interviewing political activists and is questioned by government authorities about the research?

Like journalists, sociologists occasionally find themselves facing the ethical dilemma of whether to reveal their sources to law enforcement authorities. In May 1993, sociologist Rik Scarce was jailed for contempt of court because he declined to tell a federal grand jury what he knew—or even whether he knew anything—about a 1991 raid on a university research laboratory by animal rights activists. At the time, Scarce was doing research for a book about environmental protestors and knew at least one suspect in the break-in. Although he was chastised by a federal judge, Scarce won respect from fellow prison inmates, who regarded him as a man who "wouldn't snitch" (Monaghan 1993:A8).

The ASA, in defense of the principle of confidentiality, supported Scarce's position when he appealed his sentence. Scarce maintained his silence. Ultimately, the judge ruled that nothing would be gained by further incarceration, and Scarce was released after spending 159 days in jail. The U.S. Supreme Court ultimately declined to hear Scarce's case on appeal. The Court's failure to consider his case led Scarce (1994, 1995, 2005) to argue that federal legislation is needed to clarify the right of scholars and members of the press to preserve the confidentiality of those they interview.

SOCTHINK

Should researchers sometimes deceive subjects, even if it might result in their emotional harm, in order to get more-genuine responses?

RESEARCH FUNDING

An additional concern of the ASA's *Code of Ethics* is the possibility that funding sources could influence research findings. Accepting funds from a private organization or even a government agency that stands to benefit from a study's results can clash with the ASA's first principle of maintaining objectivity and integrity in research. As such, all sources of funding should be disclosed. The previously mentioned controversy surrounding the involvement of social scientists in the U.S. Army's Human Terrain System is one example of this conflict of interest.

Another example is the Exxon Corporation's support for research on jury verdicts. On March 24, 1989, the Exxon oil tanker *Valdez* hit a reef off the coast of Alaska, spilling over 11 million gallons of oil into Prince William Sound. Until the Deepwater Horizon spill in the Gulf of Mexico in 2010, the *Valdez* disaster was regarded as the world's worst oil spill in terms of its environmental impact. In 1994, a federal court ordered Exxon to pay $5.3 billion in damages for the accident. Exxon appealed the

> **code of ethics** The standards of acceptable behavior developed by and for members of a profession.

verdict and began approaching legal scholars, sociologists, and psychologists who might be willing to study jury deliberations. The corporation's objective was to develop academic support for its lawyers' contention that the punitive judgments in such cases result from faulty deliberations and do not deter future incidents.

Some scholars have questioned the propriety of accepting funds under these circumstances, even if the source is disclosed. The scholars who accepted Exxon's support deny that it influenced their work or changed their conclusions. To date, Exxon has spent more than $1 million on the research, and at least one compilation of studies congenial to the corporation's point of view has been published. As ethical considerations require, the academics who conducted the studies disclosed Exxon's role in funding the research. In 2006, drawing on these studies, Exxon's lawyers succeeded in persuading an appeals court to reduce the corporation's legal damages from $5.3 to $2.5 billion (Freudenburg 2005; Liptak 2008a, 2008b). In 2008, the amount was further reduced to $508 million, though in 2009 the Ninth U.S. Circuit Court of Appeals ordered Exxon to pay on additional $500 million in punitive damages, court costs, and interest payments.

VALUE NEUTRALITY

The ethical considerations of sociologists lie not only in the methods they use and the funding they accept but in the way they interpret their results. Max Weber ([1904] 1949) recognized that personal values would influence the topics that sociologists select for research. In his view, that was perfectly acceptable, but he argued that researchers should not allow their personal feelings to influence the

More recently, feminist sociologist Shulamit Reinharz (1992) has argued that sociological research should not only include the research of sociologists who are outside

> If we knew what it was we
> were doing, it would not be
> called research, would it?

Albert Einstein

interpretation of data. In Weber's phrase, sociologists must practice **value neutrality** in their research.

As part of this neutrality, investigators have an ethical obligation to accept research findings even when the data run counter to their own personal views, to theoretically based explanations, or to widely accepted beliefs. For example, Émile Durkheim challenged popular conceptions when

SOCTHINK

To what extent is it possible to maintain value neutrality when studying a social group with which you might disagree (such as White supremacists or convicted child molesters)? Why might sociologists choose to study such groups?

he reported that social (rather than supernatural) forces were an important factor in suicide.

Some sociologists believe that such neutrality is impossible. They worry that Weber's insistence on value-free sociology may lead the public to accept sociological conclusions without exploring researchers' biases. Others have suggested that sociologists may use objectivity as a justification for remaining uncritical of existing institutions and centers of power (Gouldner 1970). Despite the early work of W.E.B. Du Bois and Jane Addams, for example, sociologists still need to be reminded that the discipline often fails to adequately consider all people's social behavior.

Sociologists should not focus only on those in the majority but must also seek out the stories of those who are often invisible due to their relative lack of power and resources. In fact, sociologists have learned much about society by listening to the voices of those who are excluded from mainstream sources of power and denied access to valuable resources. In her book *The Death of White Sociology* (1973), Joyce Ladner called attention to the tendency of mainstream sociologists to investigate the lives of African Americans only in the context of social problems.

value neutrality Max Weber's term for objectivity of sociologists in the interpretation of data.

the mainstream but should also be open to drawing on relevant research by nonsociologists who might provide additional depth and understanding of social life. The issue of value neutrality does not mean that sociologists can't have opinions, but it does mean that they must work to overcome any biases, however unintentional, that they may bring to their analysis of research.

FEMINIST METHODOLOGY

Although researchers must be objective, their theoretical orientation necessarily influences the questions they ask—or, just as important, the questions they fail to ask. Because their contributions have opened up so many new lines of inquiry, sociologists using the feminist perspective have had perhaps the greatest impact on the

5 Movies on SOCIOLOGICAL RESEARCH

Kinsey
The father of modern sexual research employs individual case studies.

Thank You for Smoking
A satire about the tobacco industry, showing how statistics can lie.

Supersize Me
A reporter investigates the American fast-food industry by eating at McDonald's for one month.

49 Up
Documentary following 14 children as their lives progress from age 7 to 49.

Black Gold
A film exposing the inequalities in the global coffee trade.

current generation of social researchers. Until the 1960s, for example, researchers frequently studied work and family separately, as if they were two discrete institutions. Feminist theorists, however, reject the notion that these are separate spheres. They were the first sociologists to look at housework as real work and to investigate the struggles people face in balancing the demands of work and family (Hochschild 1989; Lopata 1971).

Feminist theorists have also drawn attention to researchers' tendency to overlook women in sociological studies. For most of the history of sociology, researchers conducted studies of male subjects or male-led groups and organizations, then generalized their findings to all people. For many decades, for example, ethnographic studies of urban life focused on street corners, neighborhood taverns, and bowling alleys—places where men typically congregated. Although researchers gained valuable insights in this way, they did not form a true impression of city life, because they overlooked the areas where women were likely to gather, such as playgrounds, grocery stores, and front stoops. These are the arenas that the feminist perspective focuses on.

Feminist scholars have also contributed to a greater global awareness within sociology. To feminist theorists, the traditional distinction between industrial nations and developing countries overlooks the close relationship between these two supposedly separate worlds. Feminist theorists have called for more research on the special role that immigrant women play in maintaining their households, on the use of domestic workers from less developed nations by households in industrial countries, and on the global trafficking of sex workers (Cheng 2003; K. Cooper et al. 2007).

Finally, feminist researchers tend to involve and consult their subjects more than other researchers, contributing to a significant increase in more qualitative and participatory research. They are also more oriented toward seeking change, raising the public consciousness, and influencing policy, which represents a return to sociology's roots (Harding 2003; Naples 2003; Sprague 2005).

Sociologists must be engaged with the world. While there are numerous ways in which they accomplish this, first and foremost this involvement comes through research. As we have seen throughout this chapter, it is not enough for sociologists to stand back and theorize or even hypothesize about why we think and act the way we do. We must go out, collect data, and use it to inform our interpretations and explanations of human behavior. Having done so, we bear a responsibility for that knowledge, whether that means simply sharing it with other sociologists through conference presentations and journal articles or actively working for positive social change.

Investigate! Learn more about what sociologists are discovering. *Contexts* magazine provides a "thought-provoking take on modern life in our communities," including accessible summaries of the latest findings from social science research, op/ed pieces from sociologists, and more. It is produced by the American Sociological Association. Visit www.contexts.org; see also the ASA's website at www.asanet.org.

get involved!

For
REVIEW

I. **What steps do sociologists take when seeking to answer why people think and act the way they do?**
   - They need to define the problem, review existing literature, formulate a hypothesis, collect and analyze data, and develop a conclusion.

II. **What techniques do they use to collect data?**
   - Research designs used to collect data include surveys, observation, experiments, and use of existing sources.

III. **What ethical concerns must they consider while conducting research?**
   - They have a responsibility to follow the ASA *Code of Ethics*, particularly respecting confidentiality, revealing research funding, maintaining value neutrality, and overall, treating their subjects with respect.

Functionalist view

Sociological research seeks to better understand how the various parts of society **fit together** to create social order and stability.

Researchers focus on **consensus and cooperation** and on the large-scale (or **macro**) level, looking at society from the top down.

Research can also help determine whether the facets of our society are **functioning** as intended. For example, does more education "pay off" in higher income?

STABILITY, CONSENSUS, COOPERATION
KEY CONCEPTS

Conflict view

Sociological research seeks to better understand how **power** operates and how **resources** are distributed and controlled.

Focus of research tends to be on the large-scale (or **macro**) level, looking at society from the top down.

Key questions behind research include: Who benefits? How does the status quo maintain **privileges** for some and denial of opportunity for others? How does **access** to resources shape outcomes?

INEQUALITY, STRATIFICATION, INTERESTS
KEY CONCEPTS

Interactionist view

Sociological research seeks to better understand how we construct meaning and establish order through **everyday interactions** with others.

Focus of research is on the small-scale (or **micro**) level, looking at the construction of society from the bottom up.

Researchers are most likely to use **participant observation** because it provides a window into people's everyday lived experiences.

ROLES, SYMBOLS, LABELING
KEY CONCEPTS

MAKE THE CONNECTION

After reviewing the chapter, answer the following questions:

1

Which perspective do Patricia Adler and Peter Adler (p. 25) seem to favor in their research? Why?

2

How might a researcher's perspective influence the research design he or she picks? Give an example for each perspective.

3

How might each perspective interpret Devah Pager's findings in her experiment about race and job seeking (p. 37)?

4

How might each perspective study the relationship between education and income in a slightly different way?

Pop Quiz

1. The first step in any sociological research project is to
   a. collect data.
   b. define the problem.
   c. review previous research.
   d. formulate a hypothesis.

2. An explanation of an abstract concept that is specific enough to allow a researcher to measure the concept is a(n)
   a. hypothesis.
   b. correlation.
   c. operational definition.
   d. variable.

3. In sociological and scientific research, a hypothesis
   a. is an educated guess.
   b. is a testable statement about the relationship between two or more variables.
   c. insists that science can deal only with observable entities known directly to experience.
   d. ensures that the people being studied are representative of the population as a whole.

4. The variable hypothesized to cause or influence another is called the
   a. dependent variable.
   b. hypothetical variable.
   c. correlation variable.
   d. independent variable.

5. The degree to which a measure or scale truly reflects the phenomenon under study is known as
   a. reliability.
   b. sampling.
   c. validity.
   d. control.

6. Which research technique do sociologists use to ensure that data are statistically representative of the population being studied?
   a. sampling
   b. experiments
   c. correlation
   d. control variables

7. Ethnography is an example of which type of research design?
   a. surveys
   b. observation
   c. experiments
   d. use of existing resources

8. In the 1930s, William F. Whyte moved into a low-income Italian neighborhood in Boston. For nearly four years, he was a member of the social circle of "corner boys" whom he describes in *Street Corner Society*. His goal was to gain greater insight into the community established by these men. What type of research technique did Whyte use?
   a. experiment
   b. survey
   c. secondary analysis
   d. participant observation

9. The unintended influence that observers of experiments can have on their subjects is known as
   a. the correlation effect.
   b. confidentiality.
   c. validity.
   d. the Hawthorne effect.

10. According to Max Weber, researchers should not allow their personal feelings to influence the interpretation of data. He referred to this as
    a. the code of ethics.
    b. content analysis.
    c. value neutrality.
    d. secondary analysis.

1 (b); 2 (c); 3 (b); 4 (d); 5 (c); 6 (a); 7 (b); 8 (d); 9 (d); 10 (c)

3

FREE HUGS

CULTURE

BREAKING RULES AND LOWERING BARRIERS

Juan Mann was depressed. His fiancée had left him. His parents had just divorced. He had dropped out of college, and his friends had scattered. He felt all alone in the world. So on Wednesday, June 30, 2004, he decided to do something different. He took a homemade sign to the Pitt Street Mall in Sydney, Australia, that said "Free Hugs." Someone at a party had given him his first hug in a long time, and it had brightened his day. He figured that if he needed a hug like that more than he even knew, there were probably many other people out there feeling similarly isolated who might want one too. Every Thursday he would head back to the mall to offer more. Before long, with the help of a viral video on the Internet, Juan's "Free Hugs Campaign" went global with more than 57 million views on YouTube alone. People were not just watching the video; in many countries and in many languages, they were making their own signs and heading out to a public place to offer hugs. (A YouTube or Google image search on "free hugs" will turn up the original video along with many other videos and images of people from around the world who were inspired by it.)

One of the interesting things about this movement is that it calls for us to go outside our comfort zones and act in ways that are not "normal." As children we are told not to talk to strangers, much less hug them. If we see a stranger offering a hug, we wonder if something suspicious is up. We have rules about such things—laws even. When people do things differently, we get nervous. It disrupts our sense of order. We want and need the actions of others to be predictable, so we create both formal and informal rules to guide our behaviors. Such rules are part of culture.

But culture is not set in stone. We create it, and we therefore have the power to change it. People doing new things, stepping outside the lines of expected behavior, is precisely how change happens. So, when confronted with the offer "Free Hugs," we face a choice: Act like the majority of people who pass free huggers by, thus reaffirming expected behaviors, or seize the opportunity to do the unexpected, thereby creating new pathways for us to follow. It is in such moments that new culture is born.

As You READ >>

- Why do humans create culture?
- What does culture consist of?
- How does culture both enable and constrain?

>> Culture and Society

We need culture. As humans, we lack the complex instincts other species are born with that enable them to survive. Unlike birds, for example, our genes do not provide us with the knowledge of how to build nests (or homes) for ourselves, and we lack the good sense to fly to warmer climates for the winter. In place of such instincts, we construct culture through which we establish relationships both to the natural world and with each other. **Culture** consists of the totality of our shared language, knowledge, material objects, and behavior.

Even though we create it, culture shapes our perception, knowledge, and understanding of the external world. While our senses experience the external world in a physical way, we must interpret the meaning and significance of those sensations. We do not perceive nature directly; we perceive the world around us through the lens of culture. Our retinas may send visual images to our brains, but recognition comes only through culture. We see this at work with optical illusions: We can look at the same thing over and over, but it is not until someone says to us, "No, look at it this way" that we recognize it.

Culture thus provides us with a kind of tool kit of habits, skills, and styles (Swidler 1986). It allows us to take for granted that others will understand what we mean, and it

culture The totality of our shared language, knowledge, material objects, and behavior.

helps make it possible for us to get what we want. Shared culture simplifies day-to-day interactions. For example, when we say hello, we expect a similar response in return. If we buy a flat screen TV or an airline ticket, we expect that the clerk will accept a credit card rather than demand huge sums of cash. When we show up for the first day of class, we assume that the students will sit at their desks

Do you see the old woman or the young one?

SOC THINK

Sometimes we can see something over and over and still not recognize patterns until someone points them out (such as the arrow in the FedEx logo). What might this tell us about the importance of authorities for recognition?

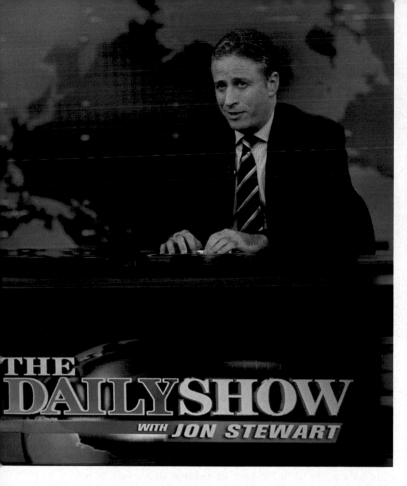

interaction. How we structure society constrains the kind of culture we construct. Some ways of thinking, acting, and making are more acceptable, whereas other ways may not even be recognized as possible. People often confront this reality when they travel abroad and find their taken-for-granted ideas and actions to be out of place and inappropriate.

> **society** The structure of relationships within which culture is created and shared through regularized patterns of social interaction.

Cultural preferences vary across societies. Educational methods, marriage ceremonies, religious doctrines, and other aspects of culture are learned and transmitted through human interaction within specific societies. Parents in India are accustomed to arranging marriages for their children; in the United States, parents typically leave marital decisions up to their children. Lifelong residents of Cairo consider it natural to speak Arabic; lifelong residents of Buenos Aires feel the same way about Spanish.

>> The Development of Culture Around the World

Through our creation of culture, we have come a long way from our prehistoric heritage. The human species has managed to produce amazing works of art such as novels by Toni Morrison, paintings by Picasso, poems by Langston Hughes, and films such as *Schindler's List*. We now take for granted what once seemed impossible, from air travel, to the cloning of cells, to organ transplants, to always-on wireless Internet access. We can peer into the outermost reaches of the universe or analyze our innermost feelings. In all these ways, our cultural creativity sets us apart as remarkably different from other species of the animal kingdom.

and the professor will take his or her place up front. Our interactions are cultural exchanges in which we trust that our assumptions are shared by others.

Because our culture represents the core of who we are, including our knowledge, values, beliefs, rules for behavior, and more, we seek both to preserve it and to pass it along to others. We preserve it through books, art, video recordings, and other means of expression. We pass it along in families, through mass media, among peers, and, more formally, at school, investing substantial amounts of resources to do so. Were it not for the social transmission of culture, each generation would have to start from scratch, reinventing not just the wheel but all other forms of culture as well.

Although it is through culture that we establish a relationship to the external world, society provides the context within which those relationships develop. **Society** consists of the structure of relationships within which culture is created and shared through regularized patterns of social

—**SOC**THINK—

How does social context influence how we relate to others? If you were talking about how school is going, how might you respond differently at home with your parents as compared to in a dorm with friends or at work with colleagues?

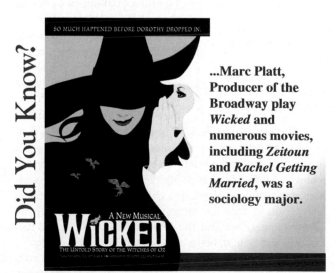

Did You Know?

...Marc Platt, Producer of the Broadway play *Wicked* and numerous movies, including *Zeitoun* and *Rachel Getting Married*, was a sociology major.

Source: http://www.baltimoresun.com/entertainment/movies/bal-ae.platt28feb28,0,487820.story.

CULTURAL UNIVERSALS

Given that we have a certain amount of freedom to construct culture in a multitude of ways, one of the early sociological questions was whether there are any aspects of culture shared by all people. Some sociologists sought to discover whether there are fundamental laws of society, equivalent to long-known laws of nature. Such patterns were referred to as **cultural universals**—common practices and beliefs shared by all societies. What this search revealed was that components of culture can be called universal only if they are expressed in the most general terms. Many cultural universals are, in fact, adaptations to meet essential human needs, such as the need for food, shelter, and clothing. Anthropologist George Murdock's (1945:124) list of cultural universals included sports, cooking, funeral ceremonies, medicine, marriage, and sexual restrictions.

The debate about the existence of general cultural universals raises an important question: Are our actions shaped by biology, or are we free to construct culture as we might choose? To put this nature vs. nurture debate in black or white terms, "nature" means that the genes we inherit determine our outcomes, as if our fates were programmed by computer code over which we have limited control. On the other side, "nurture" means that our destiny is shaped primarily by the social and psychological influences of others around us (especially parents); human nature is malleable, depending on how we choose to organize our social relationships. Over time most researchers have realized that this either-or argument is inadequate or misleading, because the relationship between the two forces is more fluid, better represented by shades of gray.

While researchers are increasingly coming to the conclusion that this nature-nurture dichotomy is too simplistic, significant differences remain. **Sociobiology** is a discipline

cultural universal A common practice or belief shared by all societies.

sociobiology The systematic study of how biology affects human social behavior.

The foods people eat, and the customs around eating and preparation of food, reflect their culture as well as their economic circumstances.

that places primary emphasis on studying how biology affects human social behavior. For example, sociobiologists look at the development of cultural universals as a product of our biological evolution. They argue that explanations of our thoughts and actions as a species must ultimately take into account our genetic makeup. On the other hand, while most sociologists would agree that our biology influences our social behavior, the degree of variation within and between societies suggests that sociobiological theories are limited as a means to explain complex human behavior. For example, one society may not allow marriage between first cousins while another encourages it.

Not only does the expression of cultural universals vary from one society to another, but it can change dramatically over time. For example, it was once thought that women were not capable of success in college because their brains were too small and their reproductive organs made them too emotional. Over time we learned that such presuppositions are false—women now make up almost 60 percent of college graduates—but at one time these assertions were accepted as "natural" and therefore resistant to change. Claims such as this have been used in the past to justify inequality (claims that were later revealed to be scientifically untrue), leading many sociologists to question biological explanations for human behavior (Lucal 2010). One of the lessons we learn about culture throughout human history is that variety and change are the norm.

More recently, researchers in both the natural sciences and sociology have sought a nuanced understanding of the relationship between biology and culture. In the scientific community there has been growing support for gene-culture coevolution, in which each shapes the other through the course of human development. From this perspective, how

Going GLOBAL

Communication, Corporations, and Consumerism

Communication, corporations, and consumerism combine to spread particular cultural preferences around the globe. What are the consequences of such diffusion for local cultures around the world?

individuals turn out isn't simply a matter of whether or not they inherited a set of "bad genes" or "good genes." Instead, researchers argue that an interdependent relationship exists between genes and environment. How genes are expressed (whether or not they are triggered, in other words) can depend upon our natural, social, and cultural contexts. From this perspective, genes are responsive to environmental factors and do not inevitably trigger predetermined responses at predetermined times (Rutter 2010; Rutter, Moffitt, and Caspi 2006; Shenk 2010). Some sociologists have also pursued research on the role that our biological foundation plays in shaping social behavior, and in 2005, the American Sociological Association established a new section called "Evolution, Biology, and Society," dedicated to the study of evolutionary sociology (Machalek and Martin 2010).

> **innovation** The process of introducing a new idea or object to a culture through discovery or invention.

INNOVATION

Humans have the freedom and ability to create new things. While a robin's nest in the year 2011 looks very much like one in 2001 or 1001 because robins act on a nest-building instinct, human abodes, however, vary widely. We can live in a cave, a castle, a sod house, a pueblo, a high-rise apartment, a McMansion, or a dorm room. Such variation is possible because we are free to innovate. **Innovation**—the process of introducing a new idea or object to a culture—interests sociologists because it can have ripple effects across a society.

SOCTHINK

How has the invention of the automobile changed our lives and our communities? How has the cell phone changed the way we interact?

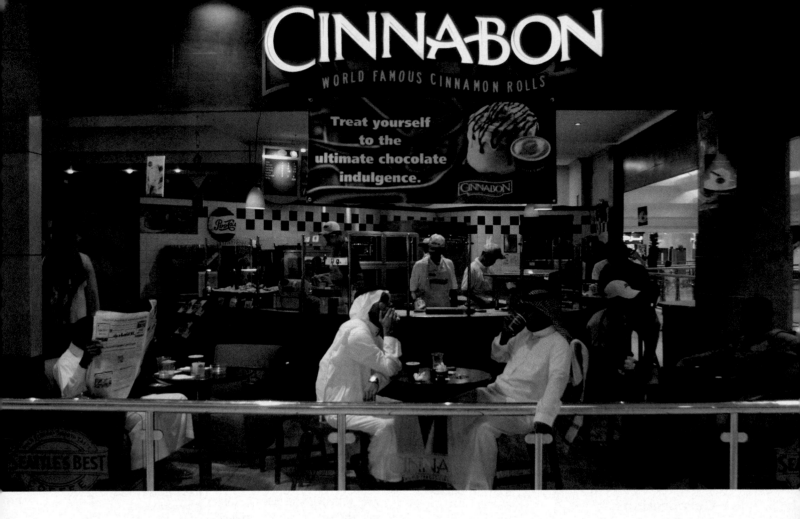

There are two main forms of innovation: discovery and invention. **Discovery** involves making known or sharing the existence of an aspect of reality. The identification of the DNA molecule and the sighting of a new moon of Saturn are both acts of discovery. A significant factor in the process of discovery is the sharing of newfound knowledge with others. By contrast, an **invention** results when existing cultural items are combined into a form that did not exist before. The bow and arrow, the automobile, and the television are all examples of inventions, as are abstract concepts such as Protestantism and democracy.

discovery The process of making known or sharing the existence of an aspect of reality.

invention The combination of existing cultural items into a form that did not exist before.

diffusion The process by which a cultural item spreads from group to group or society to society.

GLOBALIZATION AND DIFFUSION

Cultural innovation has global consequences in today's world. Imagine walking into Starbucks with its familiar green logo and ordering a decaf latte and a cinnamon ring—only this Starbucks happens to be located in the heart of Beijing's Forbidden City, just outside the Palace of Heavenly Purity, former residence of Chinese emperors. The first Starbucks in mainland China opened in 1999, and by 2009 there were more than 350, with 69 stores in Beijing alone. The success of Starbucks in a country in which coffee drinking is still a novelty (most Chinese are tea drinkers) has been striking. In fact, for many, drinking coffee has now become a status symbol of middle-class success (Christian 2009; Lu Haoting 2009).

The emergence of Starbucks in China demonstrates the cultural impact of globalization. Starbucks' expansion affects not only coffee consumption patterns but also the international trade in coffee beans, which are harvested mainly in developing countries. Our consumption-oriented culture supports a retail price of two to three dollars for a single cup of premium coffee. At the same time, the price of coffee beans on the world market has fallen so low that millions of farmers around the world can barely eke out a living. Worldwide, the growing demand for coffee, tea, chocolate, fruit, and other natural resources is straining the environment, as poor farmers in developing countries clear more and more forestland to enlarge their fields.

Even as people in Asia have begun to drink coffee, people in North America have discovered the Japanese cuisine known as sushi. More and more cultural expressions and practices are crossing national borders and influencing the traditions and customs of the societies exposed to them. Sociologists use the term **diffusion** to refer to the process by which some aspect of culture spreads from group to group or society to society. Historically, diffusion typically occurred through a variety of means, including exploration,

2009   285.6 million subscribers

2005   207.9

2000   109.5

1995   33.8

1990   5.3   = 7 million subscribers

1985   0.3

Technology makes it possible for us to keep in touch with almost anyone anywhere, as these numbers showing the explosion in the number of wireless phone subscribers since 1985 demonstrates.
Source: CTIA 2010.

war, military conquest, and missionary work. Today, societal boundaries that were once relatively closed due to the constraints of transportation and communication have become more permeable, with cross-cultural exchange occurring more quickly. Through the mass media, the Internet, immigration, and tourism, we regularly confront the people, beliefs, practices, and artifacts of other cultures.

Diffusion often comes at a cost. In practice, globalization has led to the cultural domination of developing nations by more affluent nations. In these encounters, people in developed nations often pick and choose the cultural practices they find intriguing or exotic, whereas people in developing nations often lose their traditional values and begin to identify with the culture of the dominant nations. They may discard or neglect their native language and dress, attempting to imitate the icons of mass-market entertainment and fashion. In this way, Western popular culture represents a threat to native cultures. Similarly, Walt Disney's critics have called his work "perhaps the primary example of America's cultural imperialism, supplanting the myths of native cultures with his own" (Gabler 2006). So something is gained and something is lost through diffusion, and often it is the poorer societies that sacrifice more of their culture.

>> Elements of Culture

To better understand how culture operates, it is helpful to distinguish among its different forms. A classic twofold model of culture was proposed by sociologist William F. Ogburn

Wireless Phone Usage

(1922). He drew a line between material and nonmaterial culture. **Material culture** refers to the physical or technological aspects of our daily lives, including food, houses, factories, and raw materials. **Nonmaterial culture** refers to ways of using material objects and to customs, ideas, expressions, beliefs, knowledge, philosophies, governments, and patterns of communication. While this simple division is helpful, the concept of nonmaterial culture is so inclusive that we will break it down into four key components: language, values, norms, and sanctions.

> **material culture** The physical or technological aspects of our daily lives.
>
> **nonmaterial culture** Ways of using material objects, as well as customs, ideas, expressions, beliefs, knowledge, philosophies, governments, and patterns of communication.

MATERIAL CULTURE AND TECHNOLOGY

It is easy to underestimate the degree to which we live in a humanly constructed world. Even for those of us who live close to nature, material culture is everywhere. It includes the clothes we wear, the books we read, the chairs we sit in, the carpets we walk on, the lights we use, the buildings we live in, the cars we drive, the roads we drive on, and so much more. Even those things that seem natural, like yards or parks, are human constructs.

SOC THINK

By the end of 2009, people were sending an average of 5 billion text messages per day in the United States—the equivalent of 17 messages per day per person. How might frequent "texting" and less talking affect the nature of our relationships, both positively and negatively?

Culture, Technology, and Superheroes

Some superheroes (Superman and the X-Men) are born that way, but others gain their powers the old-fashioned way: they invent them. Characters such as Ironman and Batman appeal to us in part because they rely on human innovation for their strength and stamina. Technology makes them faster than a speeding bullet or more powerful than a locomotive. To what extent does technology provide us with superhuman powers?

Technology is a form of material culture. We tend to think of it only as the physical object itself, but sociologist Gerhard Lenski suggests that it represents a way of knowing. He defined **technology** as "cultural information about how to use the material resources of the environment to satisfy human needs and desires" (Nolan and Lenski 2006:37). In other words, technology is a means of interacting with the world around us.

Technology enhances our human abilities, giving us power, speed, and even flight. The steam engine, for example, represented a critical turning point during the Industrial Revolution. It provided us with historically unprecedented strength and stamina—the ability to lift and move extremely heavy objects and to do so over sustained periods of time. It made modern coal mining practical, provided manufacturing machinery with the power needed for early factories, and powered early tractors and locomotives, setting the stage for modern global mobility.

What is sociologically important about material culture is the role it plays, like all forms of culture, in connecting individuals with one another and to the external environment. Advances in technology, especially when it comes to the revolutions in communication and transportation, have linked more individuals in a global network than was ever possible in the past. Cell phones, for example, enable us to stay in touch with friends and family from almost anywhere, and laptop computers allow us to bring the workplace with us wherever we go.

Sometimes technological change outstrips our capacity to interpret and understand the impact of such changes. Because it goes to the core of our perception of reality, nonmaterial culture is often more resistant to change than is the material culture. Ogburn introduced the term **culture lag** to refer to the period of adjustment when the nonmaterial culture is struggling to adapt to new conditions of the material culture. For example, the ethics of the Internet—particularly issues concerning privacy and censorship—have not yet caught up with the explosion in Internet use and technology.

LANGUAGE

Turning to nonmaterial culture, we begin with language, its most basic building block. **Language** is a system of shared symbols; it includes speech, written characters, numerals, symbols, and nonverbal gestures and expressions. It provides the foundation of a common culture because it facilitates day-to-day exchanges with others, making collective action possible. There are approximately 7000 languages spoken in the world today. Of these, 500 are considered nearly extinct, with fewer than 100 living speakers, and 3000 are considered endangered, with fewer than 10,000 speakers.

Language is fundamentally social in nature. There are no inherent meanings in the sounds we make when talking or in the written alphabet we use. Instead, words get their meaning from us. We come together to agree that certain sounds or shapes mean certain things, and then we act based on those shared meanings. What matters most is our shared perception rather than the actual sound or image we use. We could, for example, teach a dog the wrong meanings of commands (*fetch* means stay, *roll over* means shake, and so on). The dog would never know the difference, but we would laugh because its responses would clash with our expectations. In fact, when we start to learn a new language, we are at the mercy of those who teach us. We rely on their authority, and the only way to test our fluency is through interactions with other speakers. Because language is socially constructed, it

Inventing New Words

I was reminded of our ability to create new words while on a family hiking trip in Oregon. Eleanor, who was four at the time, was riding on my shoulders along the trail while her sister, Emily, and my wife, Lori, were falling behind. Eleanor turned and yelled as loud as she could, "Stop chickenjagging!" We knew immediately what she meant and have used this word ever since. Anyone can create words, but they become meaningful only when they are shared with others. For Eleanor's new word to become part of the common language, the chickenjagging network must extend beyond our immediate family into the wider world. Have you ever done something similar with friends or family?

allows change. We create new words and modify existing ones—especially in our modern global culture where innovation is never-ending. Dictionaries are regularly modified in an effort to try to keep up. In 2009, Merriam-Webster added more than 100 new words to its collegiate dictionary, including *staycation, frenemy, locavore, flash mob, carbon footprint,* and *waterboarding.*

Some linguists, including amateurs, have seized upon the socially constructed nature of language in hopes of creating whole new languages from scratch, with varying motivations (Okrent 2009). Some, inspired by the scientific revolution, were appalled by the inefficiencies and irregularities of existing languages. They invented new languages in the 17th and 18th centuries (such as Francis Lodwick's *Common Writing* or John Wilkins' *Philosophical Language*) in hopes of providing us with a logical system of communication in which the relationships between concepts were rational and everything fit together into a coherent whole. They didn't want words to be arbitrary sounds we attach to things, hoping instead to map the essence of things through language. Even though they succeeded in creating coherent systems, the languages they created were difficult to use and failed to attract widespread acceptance.

During the 20th century, other language inventors, driven in part by a desire to come to terms with globalization and increased contact across cultures, combined various aspects of existing languages. Their goal was to create a universally accepted language that would transcend national and ethnic differences. Rather than focus on purity of representation, such inventors emphasized practicality of communication. The most successful language of this type was Esperanto, which continues to be used today. It was originally created by Ludwik Zamenhof

in 1887 and literally means "one who hopes." It was Zamenhof's hope that his hybrid language would not only facilitate international commerce and communication but would also contribute to world peace by reducing the cultural differences that separate us.

In spite of the relative success of Esperanto, none of these invented languages has achieved widespread adoption. Part of what they seem to miss is that language is a community endeavor built up over generations of shared experiences that lead to common understandings of how the world works. Though it is technically possible to create a language from scratch, it undercuts the importance that such experiences have in shaping who we are. As linguist Arika Okrent put it in her history of invented languages, "[Languages] are the repositories of our very identities. . . . [Esperanto, along with other invented languages,] asks us to turn away from what makes our languages personal and unique and choose one that is generic and universal. It asks us to give up what distinguishes us from the rest of the world for something that makes everyone in the world the same" (Okrent 2009:112). To the extent that Esperanto has succeeded, it has done so by creating a community of shared participants who are committed to keeping the language alive.

Because different groups share different languages, the ability to speak other languages is crucial to intercultural relations. Throughout the Cold War era, beginning in the 1950s and continuing well into the 1970s, the U.S. government encouraged the study of Russian by developing special language schools for diplomats, intelligence agents, and military advisors. And following the terrorist attacks of September 11, 2001, the nation recognized how few skilled translators it had for Arabic and other languages spoken in Muslim countries. Language quickly became a key not only to tracking potential terrorists but also to building diplomatic bridges with Muslim countries willing to help in the war against terrorism (Furman, Goldberg, and Lusin 2007; Taha 2007).

technology "Cultural information about how to use the material resources of the environment to satisfy human needs and desires."

culture lag A period of adjustment when the nonmaterial culture is still struggling to adapt to new material conditions.

language A system of shared symbols; it includes speech, written characters, numerals, symbols, and nonverbal gestures and expressions.

Sapir-Whorf hypothesis The idea that the language a person uses shapes his or her perception of reality and therefore his or her thoughts and actions.

Sapir-Whorf Hypothesis Language does more than simply describe reality; it also shapes what we see. For example, the Slave Indians of northern Canada, who live in a frigid climate, have 14 terms to describe ice, including eight kinds of "solid ice" and other terms for "seamed ice," "cracked ice," and "floating ice" (Basso 1972). Most people in the United States lack such verbal distinctions and thus are less likely to notice different types of ice.

Linguists Edward Sapir and Benjamin Whorf studied the relationship between language and perception. In what has come to be known as the **Sapir-Whorf hypothesis**,

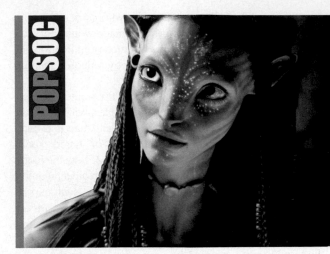

...The Na'vi language used in the film *Avatar* was created by linguist Paul Frommer, a communications professor at the University of Southern California. He built a complete language system (including grammar, syntax, and vocabulary), making it possible for people to use the principles he established to fill in gaps for words and concepts not yet created. An introduction to the language, along with a Na'vi-English dictionary, is available at www.LearnNavi.org. Tsa-ri nga-ru Irrtok!

Source: Okrent 2010.

they concluded that the language a person uses shapes his or her perception of reality and therefore his or her thoughts and actions. Based on their research, they argued that, since people can conceptualize the world only through language, language *precedes* thought. Thus, the word symbols and grammar of our language organize the world for us. The Sapir-Whorf hypothesis also holds that language is not a given. Rather, it is culturally determined and encourages a distinctive interpretation of reality by focusing our attention on certain phenomena.

In a literal sense, language may color how we see the world. Berlin and Kay (1991) noted that humans possess the physical ability to make millions of color distinctions, yet languages differ in the number of colors they recognize. For example, the English language distinguishes between yellow and orange, but some other languages do not. In the Dugum Dani language of New Guinea's West Highlands, there are only two basic color terms—*modla*

for "white" and *mili* for "black." By contrast, there are 11 basic terms in English. Russian and Hungarian, though, have 12 color terms. Russians have terms for light blue and dark blue, while Hungarians have terms for two different shades of red (Roberson, Davies, and Davidoff 2000; Wierzbicka 2008).

Feminists have noted that gender-related language can reflect—although in itself it does not determine— the traditional acceptance of men and women in certain occupations. Each time we use a term such as *mailman, policeman,* or *fireman,* we are implying (especially to young children) that these occupations can be filled only by males. Yet many women work as *letter carriers, police officers,* and *firefighters*—a fact that is being increasingly recognized and legitimized through the use of such non-sexist language.

Linguist Suzette Haden Elgin went so far as to invent a new language that gives voice to women's experience

(Elgin 1984). She argued that "existing human languages are inadequate to express the perceptions of women," which leads to inadequate perception of critical issues in the lives of women (Elgin 1988). Drawing on her expertise in the Navajo language (*Diné bizaad*), she created Láadan as a test of the Sapir-Whorf hypothesis. She argued that using Láadan would open up new dimensions of reality that are not easily accessible using languages such as English. Láadan lessons for beginners are available at www.LáadanLanguage.org.

Language can also transmit stereotypes related to race. Look up the meanings of the adjective *black* in dictionaries published in the United States, and you will find "dismal, gloomy or forbidding, destitute of moral light or goodness, atrocious, evil, threatening, clouded with anger." By contrast, dictionaries list "pure" and "innocent" among the meanings of the adjective *white*. Through such patterns of language, our culture reinforces positive associations with the term (and skin color) *white* and negative associations with *black*. Is it surprising, then, that a list meant to prevent people from working in a profession is called a "blacklist," while a fib that we think of as somewhat acceptable is called a "white lie"? Such examples demonstrate that language can shape how we see, taste, smell, feel, and hear.

—SOC THINK—

What are some slang terms we use to refer to men and to women? What images do such terms convey for what it means to be male or female?

Nonverbal Communication Of course, we communicate using more than just words. If you do not like the way a meeting is going, you might suddenly sit back, fold your arms, and turn down the corners of your mouth. When you see a friend in tears, you may give her a quick hug. After winning a big game, you may high-five your teammates. These are all examples of **nonverbal communication**—the use of gestures, facial expressions, and other visual images to communicate. We are not born with these expressions. We learn them, just as we learn other forms of language, from people who share our culture. We learn how to show—and to recognize—happiness, sadness, pleasure, shame, distress, and other emotional states (Burgoon, Guerrero, and Floyd 2010).

Like other forms of language, nonverbal communication is not the same in all cultures. For example, people from various cultures differ in the degree to which they touch others during the course of normal social interactions. Even experienced travelers are sometimes caught off guard by these differences. In Saudi Arabia a middle-aged man may want to hold hands with a male partner after closing a business deal. The gesture, which would surprise most Americans, is considered a compliment in that culture. The meaning of hand signals is another form of nonverbal communication that can differ from one culture to the next. For instance, in both Australia and Iraq the thumbs-up sign is considered rude (Koerner 2003; Passero 2002).

VALUES

Although each of us has our own personal set of standards—which may include caring or fitness or entrepreneurship—we also share a general set of objectives as members of a society. **Values** are these collective conceptions of what is considered good, desirable, and proper—or bad, undesirable, and improper—in a culture. Values may be specific, such as honoring one's parents and owning a home, or they may be more general, such as health, love, and democracy. Even individualism represents a collective value. As American essayist Richard Rodriguez points out, "American individualism is a communally derived value, not truly an expression of individuality. The teenager persists in rebelling against her parents, against tradition or custom, because she is shielded . . . by American culture from the knowledge that she inherited her rebellion from dead ancestors and living parents" (2002:130). Of course, all members of a society do not uniformly share its values. Angry political debates and billboards promoting conflicting causes tell us that much.

> **nonverbal communication** The use of gestures, facial expressions, and other visual images to communicate.
>
> **value** A collective conception of what is considered good, desirable, and proper—or bad, undesirable, and improper—in a culture.

The values of a culture may change, but most remain relatively stable during any one person's lifetime. Socially shared, intensely felt values are a fundamental part of our lives in the United States. Sociologist Robin Williams (1970) has offered a list of U.S. basic values. These include achievement, efficiency, material comfort, nationalism, equality, and the supremacy of science and reason over faith. Obviously, not all 310 million people in the United States agree on all these values, but such a list serves as a starting point in defining America's national character.

In recent decades, scholars have made extensive efforts to compare values in different nations, even while

—SOC THINK—

Consider Williams' list of basic values. Do you think most people value these things? How might some values, such as achievement and equality, conflict? How do we resolve such conflicts?

In Arab cultures, men may hold hands as a sign of affection and friendship.

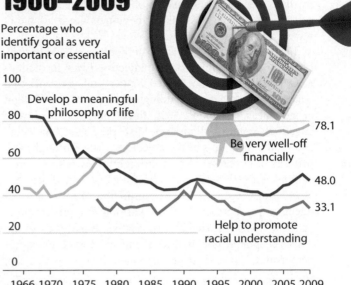

Life Goals of First-Year College Students in the United States, 1966–2009

Percentage who identify goal as very important or essential

Develop a meaningful philosophy of life

Be very well-off financially — 78.1

— 48.0

— 33.1

Help to promote racial understanding

1966 1970 1975 1980 1985 1990 1995 2000 2005 2009

Source: Pryor et al. 2007, 2009.

recognizing the challenges in interpreting value concepts in a similar manner across cultures. Social psychologist Shalom Schwartz has measured values in more than 60 countries. Around the world, certain values are widely shared, including benevolence, which is defined as "forgiveness and loyalty." In contrast, power, defined as "control or dominance over people and resources," is a value that is endorsed much less often (Davidov, Schmidt, and Schwartz 2008; Hitlin and Piliavin 2004).

Each year more than 200,000 first-year college students at approximately 300 of the nation's four-year colleges fill out a questionnaire asking them which values are most important to them. Because of its coverage, content, and scope, this survey provides a kind of barometer of the nation's values. The top value of the freshman class of 1966, the year the survey was first conducted, was "developing a meaningful philosophy of life," with 80 percent of the new students identifying it as either essential or very important. By contrast, only 44 percent choose "being well off financially." Since that time, the relative position of these two values has flipped (see graph above). Among the freshman class of 2009, 78 percent selected being well-off as a significant value, its highest level since the Higher Education Research Institute started conducting the survey. By contrast, while "developing a meaningful philosophy" has rebounded in the past five years, the 48 percent who identified this as a top value in 2009 represents a 3.4 percent decline since 2008 (Pryor et al. 2009).

Researchers also studied other family and community values among first-year students. For example, the second-highest value identified by the 2009 class was "Raising a family," which has increased to 75 percent. Students were also committed to "Helping others who were in difficulty" (69 percent), though only 42 percent selected "Influencing social values" as either essential or very important. The proportion that identified "Helping to promote racial understanding" fell to 33 percent, a decline of 4.2 percent from the previous year. As these numbers demonstrate, a nation's values are not necessarily fixed.

Because it challenges honesty as a shared value, cheating is a significant concern on college campuses. Professors who take advantage of computerized services that can identify plagiarism, such as the search engine Google or TurnItIn.com, have found that many of the papers their students hand in are plagiarized, in whole or in part. When high school students were asked how many times they had copied an Internet document for a classroom assignment in the past year, 36 percent said that they had done so at least once. When asked how many times they had cheated during a test at school in the past year, 64 percent said that they had done so at least once (Josephson Institute of Ethics 2008). Perhaps cheating has become a normal part of student culture even if it is at odds with the dominant school values.

Sometimes values shift in response to historic events. Americans have always valued their right to privacy and resented government intrusions into their personal lives. In the aftermath of the terrorist attacks of September 11, 2001, however, many citizens called for greater protection against the threat of terrorism. In response, the federal government broadened its surveillance powers and increased its ability to monitor people's behavior without court approval. In 2001, shortly after the attacks, Congress passed the USA PATRIOT Act, which empowers the FBI to access individuals' medical, library, student, and phone records without informing them or obtaining a search warrant.

NORMS

While values express our core beliefs, norms provide guidance for how to act: "Wash your hands before dinner." "Thou shalt not kill." "Respect your elders." All societies have ways of encouraging and enforcing what they view as appropriate behavior while discouraging and sanctioning what they consider to be improper behavior. **Norms** are the established standards of behavior maintained by a society. However, they are more than just the rules we think about and know—we come to embody them as part of our everyday actions.

For a norm to become significant, it must be widely shared and understood. For example, in movie theaters in the United States, we typically expect that people will be quiet while the film is shown. Of course, context matters, and the application of this norm can vary, depending on the particular film and type of audience. People who are viewing a serious artistic film will be more likely to insist on the norm of silence than those who are watching a slapstick comedy or a horror movie.

Types of Norms Sociologists distinguish between norms in two ways. First, norms are classified by their relative importance to society. When presented this way, they are known as *folkways* and *mores*. **Folkways** are norms governing everyday behavior. They play an important role in providing general guidelines for how to act within a culture. Such norms are less rigid in their application and their violation raises comparatively little concern. **Mores** (pronounced "MOR-ays") are norms deemed highly necessary to the welfare of a society, often because they embody the most cherished principles. Each society demands obedience to its mores; violation can lead to severe penalties. Thus, the United States has strong mores against murder, treason, and child abuse, which have been institutionalized into formal norms.

> **norm** An established standard of behavior maintained by a society.
>
> **folkways** Norms governing everyday behavior, whose violation raise comparatively little concern.
>
> **mores** Norms deemed highly necessary to the welfare of a society.
>
> **formal norm** A norm that generally has been written down and that specifies strict punishments for violators.
>
> **laws** Formal norms enforced by the state.
>
> **informal norm** A norm that is generally understood but not precisely recorded.

Clothing provides an example of the difference between the two. For example, fashion is a folkway, and there is wide latitude in what we might wear. But what about not wearing any clothes in public? For most of us, most of the time, that would be crossing the line into the territory of mores, and we might expect a strong and swift response if we did so. However, even this may be undergoing a change: In recent years, the nude vacation business has been booming (Higgins 2008).

Norms are also classified as either formal or informal. **Formal norms** generally have been written down and specify strict punishments for violators. In the United States we often formalize norms into laws, which are very precise in defining proper and improper behavior. Sociologist Donald Black (1995) defined *law* as "governmental social control"; that is, **laws** are formal norms enforced by the state. But laws are just one example of formal norms. The requirements for a college major and the rules of a card game are also considered formal norms.

By contrast, **informal norms** are generally understood but not precisely recorded. We follow largely

5 Movies on U.S. CULTURE

Revolutionary Road
A look at the social isolation and gender roles of 1950s America.

The Invention of Lying
What would society be like if we never told a lie?

Whip It
A misfit finds her place on a Texas Roller Derby team.

Boys N' the Hood
A portrait of the 1990s inner-city experience.

Good Hair
Chris Rock's documentary about the culture of hair in the Black community.

unspoken rules for all kinds of everyday interactions, such as how to ride on an elevator, how to pass someone on a sidewalk, and how to behave in a college classroom. Knowledge of such norms is often taken for granted.

In many societies around the world, norms reinforce patterns of male dominance. For example, various folkways reveal men's hierarchical position above women within the traditional Buddhist areas of Southeast Asia. In the sleeping cars of trains, women do not sleep in upper berths, above men. Hospitals that house men on the first floor do not place female patients on the second floor. Even on clotheslines, folkways in Southeast Asia dictate male dominance: women's attire is hung lower than that of men (Bulle 1987).

Acceptance of Norms People do not follow norms, whether mores or folkways, in all situations. In some cases they can evade a norm because they know it is weakly enforced. For instance, it is illegal for American teenagers to drink alcoholic beverages, yet drinking by minors is common throughout the nation. In fact, teenage alcoholism is a serious social problem.

In some instances behavior that appears to violate society's collective norms may actually represent adherence to the norms of a particular group. Teenage drinkers are often conforming to the standards of their peer group when they violate norms that condemn underage drinking. Similarly, business executives who use shady accounting techniques may be responding to a corporate culture that demands the maximization of profits at any cost, including the deception of investors and government regulatory agencies.

Norms are violated in some instances because one norm conflicts with another. For example, suppose you live in an apartment building and one night hear the screams of the woman next door, who is being beaten by her husband. If you decide to intervene by knocking on their door or calling the police, you are violating the norm of minding your own business while at the same time following the norm of assisting a victim of domestic violence.

Even if norms do not conflict, there are exceptions to any norm. The same action, under different circumstances,

> ## Strangers in a new culture see only what they know.
>
> **Anonymous**

Break-a-Norm Day

- Wearing formal clothes in an informal setting
- Eating with the wrong utensil or none at all
- Responding to friends or family the same as to a boss or teacher
- Having long gaps in speech when talking with someone

- Standing just a little too close to or far from someone when talking with him or her
- Facing the back of an elevator instead of getting in and turning around

Norms provide us with rules that guide our everyday behavior. All we need to do is step outside the lines even a little bit to see the influence they have over our lives. These are some examples of how people violate norms. How would you feel about violating any of these norms? How might others respond to you?

can cause one to be viewed as either a hero or a villain. For instance, secretly taping telephone conversations is normally considered not just intrusive but illegal. However, it can be done with a court order to obtain valid evidence for a criminal trial. We would heap praise on a government agent who used such methods to convict an organized crime figure. In our culture we tolerate killing another human being in self-defense, and we actually reward killing in warfare.

Acceptance of norms is subject to change as the political, economic, and social conditions of a culture are transformed. Until the 1960s, for example, formal norms throughout much of the United States prohibited the marriage of people from different racial groups. Over the past half century, however, such legal prohibitions have been cast aside. The process of change can be seen today in the increasing acceptance of single parents and the growing support for the legalization of marriage for same-sex couples.

When circumstances require the sudden violation of longstanding cultural norms, the change can upset an entire population. In Iraq, where Muslim custom strictly forbids touching by strangers for men and especially for women, the war that began in 2003 has brought numerous daily violations of the norm. Outside mosques, government offices, and other facilities likely to be targeted

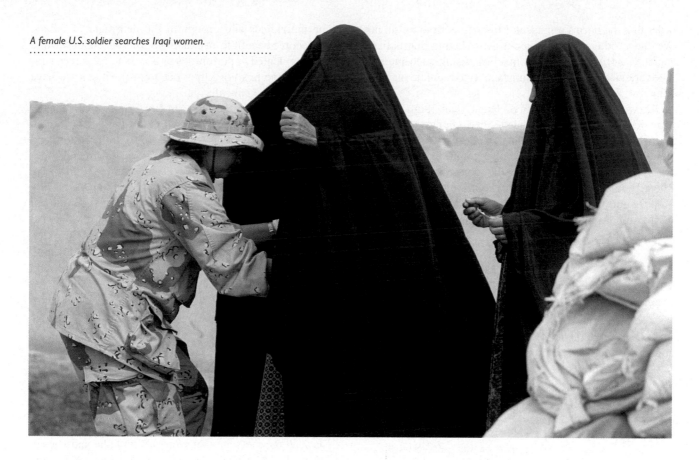

A female U.S. soldier searches Iraqi women.

by terrorists, visitors must now be patted down and have their bags searched by Iraqi security forces. To reduce the discomfort caused by the procedure, women are searched by female guards and men by male guards. Despite that concession, and the

fact that many Iraqis admit to or even insist on the need for such measures, people still wince at the invasion of their personal privacy. In reaction to the searches, Iraqi women have begun to limit the contents of the bags they carry or simply to leave them at home (Rubin 2003).

SANCTIONS

When norms are violated, we can usually expect a response designed to bring our behavior back into line. If a basketball coach sends a sixth player into the game, we count on the referee to call a foul. If a candidate shows up for a formal job interview in shorts and a T-shirt, we predict that no job offer will follow. If we park without putting money into the meter, we should expect a ticket. In each of these cases, some form of negative repercussion results from our failure to abide by expected norms.

Sanctions are penalties and rewards for conduct concerning a social norm. They include both negative and positive responses to behavior; their purpose is to influence future behavior. Adhering to norms can lead to positive sanctions such as a pay raise, a medal, a word of gratitude, or a pat on the back. Negative sanctions might include fines, threats, imprisonment, and stares of contempt. In this way sanctions work to enforce the

> **sanction** A penalty or reward for conduct concerning a social norm.

order that the norms represent. Most of the time we do not even need others to sanction our acts. Having internalized society's norms, we police ourselves, using such internal motivations as guilt or self-satisfaction to regulate our own behavior.

As we saw with the "Free Hugs" campaign, norms provide order, but norms change, and change can result in chaos. As social scientist Gustave Le Bon said in 1895, "Civilization is impossible without traditions, and progress impossible without the destruction of those traditions. The difficulty, and it is an immense difficulty, is to find a proper equilibrium between stability and variability." In a world of norms, we constantly face this tension: to obey or not to obey.

>> Culture and the Dominant Ideology

Together the elements of culture provide us with social coherence and order. Culture clarifies for us what we think is good and bad, and right and wrong, giving us a sense of direction. That is not to say, however, that there is universal agreement on values and norms or that culture works on behalf of all for the greater good. Culture helps to unify and provide meaning, but it also serves the interests of

dominant ideology A set of cultural beliefs and practices that legitimates existing powerful social, economic, and political interests.

Agricultural strikes in the 1960s and 1970s alerted the nation to the harsh economic plight of migrant workers.

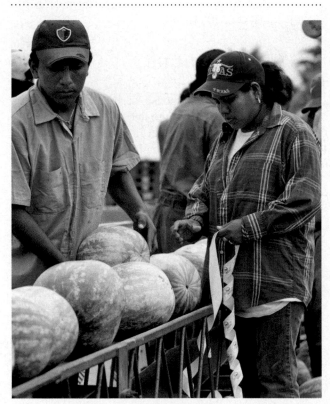

some individuals and groups to the detriment of others. Some people benefit from existing norms and values, while others are denied opportunities or access to resources simply due to the positions they occupy—positions we have culturally defined as inferior.

One of the ways culture can function to maintain the privileges of certain groups is through the establishment of a **dominant ideology**—the set of cultural beliefs and practices that legitimate existing powerful social, economic, and political interests. The dominant ideology helps to explain and justify who gets what and why in a way that supports and maintains the status quo. Dominant ideas can even squelch alternative expressions of what might be, casting such alternatives as threats to the existing order. This concept was first proposed by Hungarian Marxist Georg Lukács (1923) and Italian Marxist Antonio Gramsci (1929), but it did not gain an audience in the United States until the early 1970s. In Karl Marx's view, a capitalist society has a dominant ideology that serves the interests of the ruling class.

A society's most powerful groups and institutions control wealth and property. Armed with a dominant ideology, they can also shape beliefs about reality through religion, education, and the media. In so doing, they can influence what we come to accept as true. For example, feminists would argue that if all of society's most important institutions send the message that women should be subservient to men, this dominant ideology will help to control and subordinate women.

One of the limitations of the dominant ideology thesis is that, in the United States, it is not easy to identify a singular, all-inclusive "core culture." Studies report a lack of consensus on national values and a wide range of cultural traits from a variety of cultural traditions. In addition, as we saw in the surveys of young people's values, significant shifts in cultural values can occur. Yet there is no denying that certain expressions of values have greater influence than others, even in so complex a society as the United States. For example, the value of competition in the marketplace—a cornerstone of any capitalist economy—remains powerful, and we often look down on those who we suspect might be lazy.

>> Cultural Variation

Although societies can be defined in part by the culture their inhabitants share, culture varies both between and within societies. Inuit tribes in northern Canada, clad in furs and dieting on whale blubber, have little in common with farmers in Southeast Asia, who dress for the heat and subsist mainly on the rice they grow in their paddies. Cultures adapt to meet specific sets of circumstances, such as climate, level of technology, population, and geography. This adaptation to different conditions shows up in differences in all elements of culture, including language, values, norms, and sanctions.

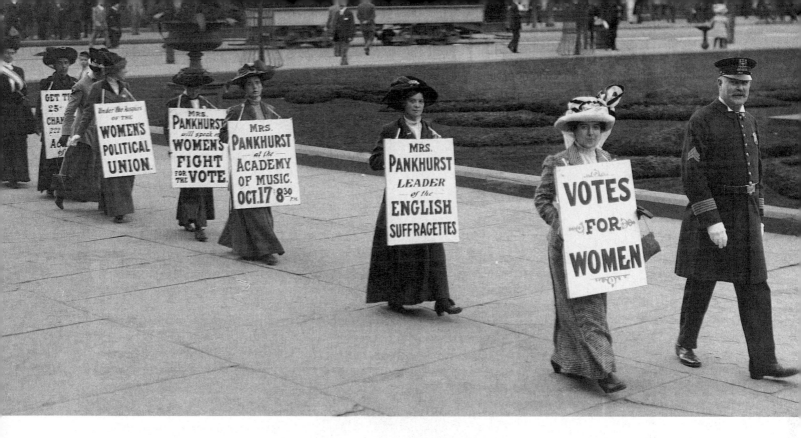

Thus, despite the presence of cultural universals such as courtship and religion, great diversity exists among the world's many cultures. Moreover, even within a single nation, certain segments of the populace develop cultural patterns that differ from the patterns of the dominant society.

ASPECTS OF CULTURAL VARIATION

Subcultures Rodeo riders, residents of a retirement community, workers on an offshore oil rig—all are examples of what sociologists refer to as *subcultures*. A **subculture** is a segment of society that shares a distinctive pattern of mores, folkways, and values that differs from the pattern of the larger society. In a sense, a subculture can be thought of as a culture existing within a larger, dominant culture. The existence of many subcultures is characteristic of complex societies such as the United States.

> ### SOCTHINK
> Are people who participate in *World of Warcraft* or *Second Life* part of subcultures? What are some characteristics of these groups that typify subcultures?

Members of a subculture participate in the dominant culture while at the same time engaging in unique and distinctive forms of behavior. Frequently, a subculture

will develop its own slang known as **argot**—specialized language that distinguishes it from the wider society. For example, back in the 1940s and 1950s, New York City's sanitation workers developed a humorous argot used to this day to describe the dirty and smelly aspects of their job. They call themselves *g-men* (a term more typically applied to government agents); a garbage scow or barge is known as a *honey boat;* and trash thrown from an upper-story window is called *airmail*. More recent coinages include *disco rice* (maggots) and *urban whitefish* (used condoms). Administrators at the Sanitation Department practice a more reserved humor than those who work on the trucks. When they send a *honey boat* to New Jersey, they are not dumping the city's garbage; they're *exporting* it. Policy makers at the department have also invented some novel acronyms to describe New Yorkers' attitude toward the construction of new sanitation facilities: *banana* (build absolutely nothing anywhere near anyone) and *nope* (not on planet earth) (Urbina 2004).

> **subculture** A segment of society that shares a distinctive pattern of mores, folkways, and values that differs from the pattern of the larger society.
>
> **argot** Specialized language used by members of a group or subculture.

Such argot allows insiders—the members of the subculture—to understand words with special meanings and establishes patterns of communication that outsiders cannot understand. In so doing, it clarifies the boundary between "us" and "them" and reinforces a shared identity. We see something like this in the taken-for-granted words and acronyms in the instant-messaging

Subculture Slang

Anime and Manga Fans

Chibi eyes: the characteristic, big childlike eyes used in anime

Majoko: a girl anime character with magical powers who must save the world

Con Artists & Scammers

Grifter: a person who steals through deception

Phishing: sending out emails seeking personal information that appear to be from legitimate companies

Graffiti Writers

Bite: to copy another graffiti write's work

Burner: a stylistically impressive, brilliantly colored piece of graffiti, usually written in a complex pattern of interlocking letters and other visual elements

Toy: an inexperienced or unskilled graffiti writer

Kill: to saturate an area with one's graffiti

Bikers (Motorcyclists)

Brain bucket: a helmet

Ink slinger: a tattoo artist

Pucker factor: the degree of panic felt during a near-accident

Yard shark: a dog that races out to attack passing motorcyclists

Skateboarders

Deck: a skateboard platform

Face plant: a face-first crash

Sketchy: in reference to a trick, poorly done

Subcultures often produce their own unique jargon. The words may be appropriate in those subcultures, but they have the effect of drawing a line between insiders and the rest of us.
Source: Reid 2006.

and text-messaging world. There, abbreviations come fast and furious, from the well-known, such as *lol* (laughing out loud), *brb* (be right back), and *g2g* (got to go), to the more obscure, such as *1337* (meaning "elite" and referring to symbolic language or "leet-speak") or *pwned* (leet term meaning "defeated").

In India a new subculture has developed among employees at the international call centers established by multinational corporations. To serve customers in the United States and Europe, the young men and women who work there must be fluent speakers of English. But the corporations that employ them demand more than proficiency in a foreign language; they expect their Indian employees to adopt Western values and work habits, including the grueling pace that U.S. workers take for granted. In return, the corporations offer perks such as Western-style dinners and dances and coveted consumer goods. Ironically, they allow employees to take the day off only on American holidays like Labor Day and Thanksgiving—not on Indian holidays like Diwali, the Hindu festival of lights. While most Indian families are home celebrating, call center employees see mostly each other; when they have the day off, no one else is free to socialize with them. As a result, these employees have formed a tight-knit subculture based on hard work and a taste for Western luxury goods and leisure-time pursuits. Increasingly, they are the object of criticism from Indians who live a more conventional Indian lifestyle centered on family and holiday traditions (Kalita 2006).

Countercultures Sometimes a subculture can develop that seeks to set itself up as an alternative to the dominant culture. When a subculture conspicuously and deliberately opposes certain aspects of the larger culture, it is known as a **counterculture.** Countercultures typically thrive among the young, who have the least investment in the existing culture.

The 1960s, now often characterized by the phrase "sex and drugs and rock 'n' roll," provide a classic case of an extensive counterculture. Largely composed of young people, members of this counterculture were turned off by a society they believed was too materialistic and technological. It included many political radicals and "hippies" who had "dropped out" of mainstream social institutions, but its membership was extensive and diverse. The young people expressed in their writings, speeches, and songs their visions, hopes, and dreams for a new society. As was reflected in the 1966 survey of first-year college students, these young women and men rejected the pressure to accumulate more expensive cars, larger homes, and an endless array of material goods. Instead, they expressed a desire to live in a culture based on more humanistic values, such as sharing, love, and coexistence with the environment. As a political force, they worked for peace—opposing U.S. involvement in the war in Vietnam and encouraging draft resistance—as well as racial and gender equality (Anderson 2007; Gitlin 1993).

In the wake of the attacks of September 11, 2001, people around the United States learned of the existence of terrorist groups operating as a counterculture within their own country. In Northern Ireland, Israel, the Palestinian territory, and other parts of the world, many generations have lived in such circumstances. But terrorist cells are not necessarily fueled only by outsiders. Frequently, people become disenchanted with the policies of their own country, and a few take very violent steps (Juergensmeyer 2003).

Culture Shock Today we are more and more likely to come into contact with and even immerse ourselves in cultures unlike our own. For example, it has become increasingly common for students to study abroad. Though they may well have predeparture orientation sessions, when they get in-country, they often have a difficult time adjusting because so many of the little things that they took for granted, things they barely noticed before, no longer apply. Anyone who feels disoriented, uncertain, out of place, or even fearful when

they encounter unfamiliar cultural practices may be experiencing **culture shock.** For example, a resident of the United States who visits certain areas in Cambodia and wants meat for dinner may be stunned to learn that a local specialty is rat meat. Similarly, someone from a strict Islamic culture may be shocked upon first seeing the comparatively provocative dress styles and open displays of affection that are common in the United States and other Western cultures.

Interestingly, once students who study abroad return home, they may experience a kind of reverse culture shock. Their time away has changed them, often in ways they were unaware of, and they find that they cannot so easily slip back into the old routines that those who remained at home expect of them. Culture shock reveals to us both the power and the taken-for-granted nature of culture. The rules we follow are so ingrained that we barely notice that we were following them until they are no longer there to provide the structure and order we assume as a given.

All of us, to some extent, take for granted the cultural practices of our society. As a result, it can be surprising and even disturbing to realize that other cultures do not follow our way of life. The fact is, customs that seem strange to us are considered normal and proper in other cultures, which may view our own mores and folkways as odd.

counterculture A subculture that deliberately opposes certain aspects of the larger culture.

culture shock The feelings of disorientation, uncertainty, and even fear that people experience when they encounter unfamiliar cultural practices.

ethnocentrism The tendency to assume that one's own culture and way of life represent what's normal or are superior to all others.

ATTITUDES TOWARD CULTURAL VARIATION

Ethnocentrism Because we are now more likely to encounter people from a whole range of cultural backgrounds than we were in the past, we are also more likely to struggle with what we think about the beliefs, values, and practices of others. When we hear people talking about "our" culture versus "their" culture, we are often confronted with statements that reflect the attitude that "our" culture is best. Terms such as *underdeveloped, backward,* and *primitive* may be used to refer to other societies. What "we" believe is a religion; what "they" believe is superstition and mythology.

It is tempting to evaluate the practices of other cultures on the basis of our own perspectives. Sociologist William Graham Sumner (1906) coined the term **ethnocentrism** to refer to the tendency to assume that one's own culture and way of life represent what's normal or are

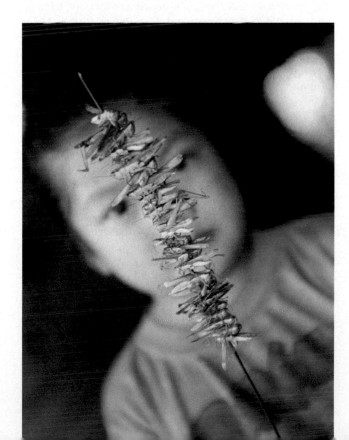

superior to all others. The ethnocentric person sees his or her own group as the center or defining point of culture and views all other cultures as deviations from what is "normal." Thus, Westerners who see cattle as a food source might look down on the Hindu religion and culture, which view the cow as sacred. People in one culture may dismiss as unthinkable the mate selection or child-rearing practices of another culture.

Ethnocentric value judgments have complicated U.S. efforts at democratic reform of the Iraqi government. Prior to the 2003 war in Iraq, U.S. planners had assumed that Iraqis would adapt to a new form of government in the same way the Germans and Japanese did following World War II. But in the Iraqi culture, unlike the German and Japanese cultures, loyalty to the family and the extended clan comes before patriotism and the common good. In a country in which almost half of all people, even those in the cities, marry a first or second cousin, citizens are predisposed to favor their own kin in government and business dealings. Why trust a stranger from outside the family? What Westerners would criticize as nepotism, then, is actually an acceptable, even admirable, practice to Iraqis (J. Tierney 2003).

One of the reasons ethnocentrism develops is because it contributes to a sense of solidarity by promoting group

cultural relativism The viewing of people's behavior from the perspective of their own culture.

> You never really understand a person until you consider things from his point of view . . . until you climb into his skin and walk around in it.
>
> **Harper Lee, *To Kill a Mockingbird***

pride. Denigrating other nations and cultures can enhance our own patriotic feelings and belief in our way of life. Yet this type of social stability is established at the expense of other peoples. One of the negative consequences of ethnocentric value judgments is that they serve to devalue groups and to deny equal opportunities.

Of course, ethnocentrism is hardly limited to citizens of the United States. Visitors from many African cultures are surprised at the disrespect that children in the United States show their parents. People from India may be repelled by our practice of living in the same household with dogs and cats. Many Islamic fundamentalists in the Arab world and Asia view the United States as corrupt, decadent, and doomed to destruction. All these people may feel comforted by membership in cultures that in their view are superior to ours (Juergensmeyer 2003).

Cultural Relativism Whereas ethnocentrism means evaluating foreign cultures using the familiar culture of the observer as a standard of correct behavior, **cultural relativism** means viewing people's behavior from the perspective of their own culture. It places a priority on understanding other cultures, rather than dismissing them as "strange" or "exotic." Unlike ethnocentrists, cultural relativists seek to employ the kind of value neutrality that Max Weber saw as so important.

Cultural relativism stresses that different social contexts give rise to different norms and values. Thus, we must examine practices such as polygamy, bullfighting, and monarchy within the particular contexts of the cultures in which they are found. Cultural relativism is not the same as moral relativism and thus does not suggest that we must unquestionably accept every cultural variation. But it does require a serious and unbiased effort to evaluate norms, values, and customs in light of their distinctive culture.

Practicing the sociological imagination calls for us to be more fully aware of the culture we as humans have created for ourselves and to be better attuned to the varieties of culture other people have established for themselves. Culture shapes our everyday behaviors all the time, and we select from the tools it provides. For the most part, we are not aware of the degree to which we are immersed in a world of our own making. Whether that includes the capacity to read a book, make a meal, or hug a stranger on the street, it is through culture that we establish our relationship to the external world and with each other.

Learn about another culture. One of the most effective ways is to immerse yourself in one. Seek out opportunities for deep and prolonged interaction with a group of people from a culture unlike your own. Contact your school's service learning program or study abroad office to find out what possibilities exist.

get involved!

For REVIEW

I. **Why do humans create culture?**
- Humans lack the complex instincts present in other animals, and as such they must construct a relationship to nature and with each other. We do this through the construction of shared culture.

II. **What does culture consist of?**
- Culture can be broken down into two categories. The first is material culture, which consists of our modification of the physical environment and includes technology. The second is nonmaterial culture, which consists of a number of components including language, values, norms, and sanctions.

III. **How does culture both enable and constrain?**
- While culture provides us with the knowledge, rules, and artifacts we need to survive, it also limits our options. Words enable us to see, and tools enable us to make things, but both are designed for particular purposes and shield us from alternative possibilities. Further, with ethnocentrism, we cut ourselves off from new possibilities from different cultures.

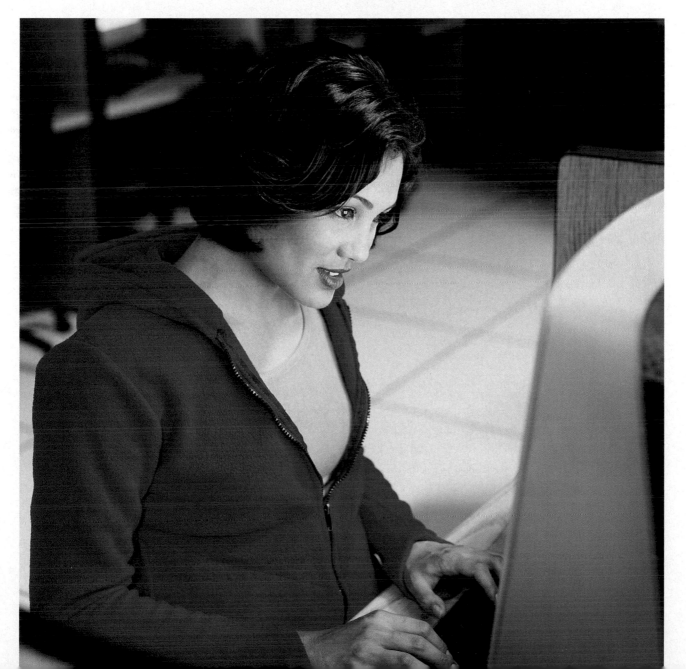

Functionalist View

Sharing a culture helps to define the society to which one belongs, establishing **social order.**

Society **preserves** its culture by transmitting shared language, norms, and values from one generation to the next, thus providing social **stability.**

The interests of **subgroups** within a culture are served by formation of **subcultures.**

PRESERVATION, FACILITATION, COMMUNICATION
KEY CONCEPTS

Conflict View

While a common culture helps to unify a society, it also **privileges** some to the detriment of others.

The **dominant ideology** in a culture justifies "who gets what."

The existence of subcultures reflects **unequal social arrangements,** as brought to light by the civil rights and feminist movements.

Language in a culture can be a source of conflict, as in the case of **sexist** language or language that transmits **racial stereotypes.**

KEY CONCEPTS
PRIVILEGE, DOMINANCE, INEQUALITY

MAKE THE CONNECTION

After reviewing the chapter, answer the following questions:

Interactionist View

Without social interaction, people would not be able to **construct their culture** or transmit it to others. In turn, having a common culture simplifies everyday transactions.

Cultural diffusion is enhanced by interactions involved in immigration, tourism, the Internet, and the mass media.

Both a culture's **language** and **nonverbal communication** facilitate day-to-day exchanges between people.

KEY CONCEPTS
SOCIAL CONSTRUCTION, NONVERBAL COMMUNICATION

1

How would each of the three perspectives make the case that "we need culture"?

2

How would each perspective explain the existence of ethnocentrism (p. 65)?

3

How would each perspective approach the role that dominant ideology (p. 62) performs in a culture?

4

How would you use the perspectives to describe one of the subcultures at your school?

Pop Quiz

1. What do sociologists refer to as the structure of relationships within which a culture is created and shared through regularized patterns of social interaction?
   a. culture
   b. diffusion
   c. globalization
   d. society

2. People's need for food, shelter, and clothing is an examples of what George Murdock referred to as
   a. norms.
   b. folkways.
   c. cultural universals.
   d. cultural practices.

3. What is an invention?
   a. introducing a new idea or object to a culture
   b. combining existing cultural items into a form that did not exist before
   c. making known or sharing the existence of an aspect of reality
   d. the physical or technological aspects of our daily lives

4. What term do sociologists use to refer to the process by which a cultural item spreads from group to group or society to society?
   a. diffusion
   b. globalization
   c. innovation
   d. cultural relativism

5. Which of the following statements is true according to the Sapir-Whorf hypothesis?
   a. Language simply describes reality.
   b. Language legitimates existing social, economic, and political interests.
   c. Language shapes our perception of reality.
   d. Language is not an example of a cultural universal.

6. Values represent shared _____, whereas norms provide guidelines for shared _____.
   a. rules; ideas
   b. beliefs; behaviors
   c. language; technologies
   d. actions; knowledge

7. What type of norms is deemed highly necessary to the welfare of a society, often because these norms embody the most cherished principles of a people?
   a. formal norms
   b. informal norms
   c. mores
   d. folkways

8. Which of the following terms describes the set of cultural beliefs and practices that help to maintain powerful social, economic, and political interests?
   a. mores
   b. dominant ideology
   c. consensus
   d. values

9. Terrorist groups are examples of
   a. cultural universals.
   b. subcultures.
   c. countercultures.
   d. dominant ideologies.

10. What is the term used when one seeks to understand another culture from its perspective, rather than dismissing it as "strange" or "exotic"?
    a. ethnocentrism
    b. culture shock
    c. cultural relativism
    d. cultural value

1 (d); 2 (c); 3 (b); 4 (a); 5 (c); 6 (b); 7 (c); 8 (b); 9 (c); 10 (c)

4

SOCIALIZATION

ISOLATION AND SOCIALIZATION

For the first six years of her life, Isabelle lived in almost total seclusion in a darkened room. She had little contact with other people, with the exception of her mother, who could neither speak nor hear. Isabelle's grandparents had been so deeply ashamed of Isabelle's illegitimate birth that they kept her hidden away from the world. Ohio authorities finally discovered Isabelle in 1938, when her mother escaped from her parents' home, taking Isabelle with her.

Six years old at the time of her rescue, Isabelle could not speak. Although she could make various croaking sounds, her only communication with her mother involved simple gestures. Isabelle had been largely deprived of the typical interactions and socialization experiences of childhood. Because she had seen few people, she initially showed a strong fear of strangers and reacted almost like a wild animal when confronted with an unfamiliar person. As she became accustomed to seeing certain individuals, her reaction changed to one of extreme apathy. At first, observers believed that Isabelle was deaf, but she eventually began to react to nearby sounds. On tests of her educational development, she scored at the level of an infant rather than a six-year-old.

Specialists developed a systematic training program to help Isabelle adapt to human relationships and socialization. After a few days of training, she made her first attempt to verbalize. Although she started slowly, Isabelle quickly passed through six years of development. In a little over two months, she was speaking in complete sentences. Nine months later, she could identify both words and sentences. Before Isabelle reached the age of nine, she was ready to attend school with other children. By her 14th year she was in sixth grade, doing well in school, and emotionally well adjusted.

Yet, without an opportunity to experience socialization in her first six years, Isabelle initially lacked what we often take for granted as natural human abilities. While we may be born with the propensity toward language and other social skills, Isabelle's inability to communicate at the time of her discovery—despite her physical and cognitive potential to learn—and her remarkable progress over the next few years underscore the importance of socialization in human development (K. Davis 1940, 1947).

As You READ

>>

- How do we become ourselves?
- Who shapes our socialization?
- How does our development change over time?

>> The Role of Socialization

What makes us who we are? Is it the genes we are born with or the environment in which we grow up? As we saw in Chapter 3, researchers have traditionally clashed over the relative importance of biological inheritance and environmental factors in human development—a conflict called the nature versus nurture debate. Although most social scientists today acknowledge the significance of the interaction between these factors in shaping human development, sociologists come down more strongly on the side of nurture. They argue that the rules we follow, the language we speak, and the values we believe in have less to do with our DNA than with the cultural context into which we emerge. Parents, teachers, friends, co-workers, and even television personalities provide us with the cultural tools we require to survive and thrive. We need to internalize the culture that has been constructed by others who came before us, and we do this through **socialization**—the

socialization The lifelong process through which people learn the attitudes, values, and behaviors appropriate for members of a particular culture.

SOC THINK

What skills that you learned before age two do you now take for granted? From whom did you learn them? In what contexts?

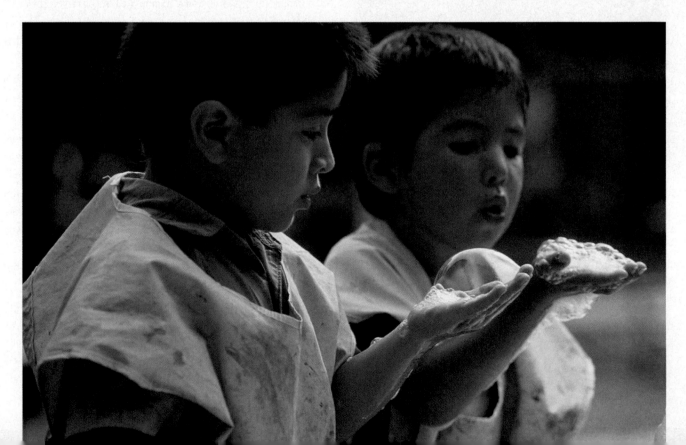

lifelong process through which people learn the attitudes, values, and behaviors appropriate for members of a particular culture.

SOCIAL ENVIRONMENT: THE IMPACT OF ISOLATION

We can better appreciate how heredity and environment interact and influence the socialization process by examining situations in which one factor operates almost entirely without the other (Homans 1979). As we saw above, Isabelle was able to proceed through the typical stages of socialization with the help of experts. Unfortunately, many other cases of children raised in extreme isolation demonstrate that missing out on these critical years of childhood socialization creates difficult obstacles to overcome. We want and need early intimacy and interaction with others.

Extreme Childhood Isolation Children who have been isolated or severely neglected typically have a difficult time recovering from the loss of early childhood socialization. For example, in 1970, California authorities discovered a 14-year-old girl named Genie locked in a room where she had been confined since she was 20 months old. During her years of isolation, no family member had spoken to her, nor could she hear anything other than swearing. Since there was no television or radio in her home, she had never heard the sounds of normal human speech. One year after beginning extensive therapy, Genie's grammar resembled that of a typical 18-month-old. Though she made further advances with continued therapy, she never achieved full language ability. Today Genie, now in her mid 50s, lives in a home for developmentally disabled adults in California (Curtiss 1977; James 2008; Rymer 1993).

While researchers know of only a few cases of children reared in near total isolation, they are aware of many cases of children raised in extremely neglectful social circumstances. Infants and young children in orphanages in the formerly communist countries of Eastern Europe often suffer from profound neglect. In many Romanian orphanages, babies once lay in their cribs for 18–20 hours a day, curled against their feeding bottles and receiving little adult care. Such minimal attention continued for the first five years of their lives.

Ten Modern Cases of Feral Children

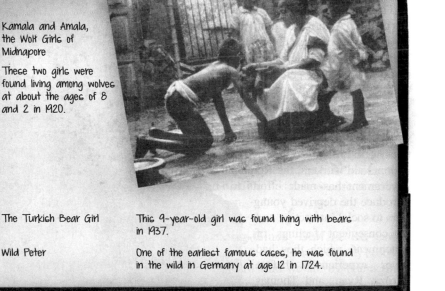

Shamdeo, the Sultanpur Wolf Boy	He was about 4 years old when discovered playing with wolves in 1974.
Memmie LeBlanc, the Wild Girl of Champagne	About 18 to 20 years old when found, she had learned language before having been abandoned.
John Ssebunya, the Ugandan Monkey Boy	Found living with a pack of monkeys in 1991 at age 6, he now gives talks about his experience.
The Syrian Gazelle Boy	An agile runner, he was found among gazelles at about the age of 10 in 1946.
Oxana Malaya, the Ukrainian Dog Girl	She was found living in the dog pen in her family's back yard in 1991 at the age of 8.
The Russian Bird Boy	Found in February 2008, he was cared for by his mother but never spoken to and chirps like a bird.
The Leopard Boy of Dihungi	He was found among leopards at age 5 in 1915 after having been in the wild three years.
Kamala and Amala, the Wolf Girls of Midnapore. These two girls were found living among wolves at about the ages of 8 and 2 in 1920.	
The Turkish Bear Girl	This 9-year-old girl was found living with bears in 1937.
Wild Peter	One of the earliest famous cases, he was found in the wild in Germany at age 12 in 1724.

Source: www.feralchildren.com.

we become who we are based on how we think others see us the **looking-glass self,** emphasizing the importance of social interaction on self-identity.

According to Cooley, the process of developing a self-identity, or self-concept, has three phases. First, we imagine how others see us—relatives, friends, even strangers on the street. Second, we imagine how others evaluate what we think they see—as intelligent, attractive, shy, or strange. Finally, we define our self as a result of these impressions—"I am smart" or "I am beautiful" (Cooley 1902). This process is ongoing; it happens during each and every one of our interactions. Our understanding of our self, then, involves a complex calculation in which we come to be who we are based not on how others actually see us or how they will judge us but on how we think they will see us and how we think they will judge us based on what we think they see.

According to Cooley, then, our self results from our "imagination" of how others view us. Because we never truly know what others think, we can develop self-identities based on *incorrect* perceptions of how others see us. We can develop a sense of confidence or a sense of doubt based on how we think others react to our performance, but we might be completely wrong. Imagine you are on a first date. All the cues you receive throughout the evening are positive— your companion smiles, laughs, and seems to be having a genuinely good time. You go home feeling happy, confident that the evening went really well. But your date never returns your calls, and there is no second date. You go from a feeling of elation and confidence to a sense of disappointment and doubt, perhaps even asking, "What's wrong with me?"

Mead: Stages of the Self George Herbert Mead (1863–1931), another American sociologist, sought to expand upon Cooley's theory that we become our self through interaction with others. He argued that there are two core components of the self: the "I" and the "Me." The **I** is our acting self. It is the part of us that walks, reads, sings, smiles, speaks, or performs any other action we might undertake. The **Me** is our socialized self. Based on the standards we have learned from others, the Me plans action and then judges our performance afterward.

For Mead the self represents an ongoing interaction between our socialized self and our acting self. The Me plans. The I acts. The Me judges. Take participating in classroom discussions as an example. Our Me may have something to say but fears that the words won't come out quite right, which could lead to embarrassment, so our I stays silent. Our Me then kicks our self afterwards when someone else says exactly what we planned to say and receives praise from the professor for having said it.

It is through our interactions with others that we get the social expectations of the Me into our heads. According to Mead (1964b), when we are young, we see ourselves as the center of the universe and find it difficult to consider the perspectives of others. For example, when shown a mountain scene and asked to describe what an observer on the opposite side of the mountain might see, young children describe only objects visible from their own vantage point. Although we always retain a certain level of self-centeredness, as we mature, the self changes and begins to reflect greater concern with the reactions of others.

Parents, friends, co-workers, coaches, and teachers are often among those who play a major role in shaping a person's self. The term **significant others** refers to individuals who are most important in the development of the self. Many young people, for example, choose the same occupational field as their parents

> I wanted to change the world. But I have found that the only thing one can be sure of changing is oneself.

Aldous Huxley

looking-glass self A theory that we become who we are based on how we think others see us.

I The acting self that exists in relation to the Me.

Me The socialized self that plans actions and judges performances based on the standards we have learned from others.

significant other An individual who is most important in the development of the self, such as a parent, friend, or teacher.

SOC THINK

What cues do you rely on to know if things are going well on a first date? How about on a job interview? To what extent do you think it is possible to fake such cues?

or adopt the same pop culture preferences as their friends (Sullivan [1953] 1968).

As we grow up, we develop a sense of who people are, how they fit together, and where we might fit into that map. Over time we begin to see that the positions these significant others occupy are part of a larger social network. Mead (1934, 1964a) described that transformation as a three-stage process of self-development: the preparatory stage, the play stage, and the game stage.

The Preparatory Stage During the *preparatory stage,* which lasts until about age three, children merely imitate the people around them, especially family members with whom they continually interact. Thus, a small child will bang on a piece of wood while a parent is engaged in carpentry work or will try to throw a ball if an older sibling is doing so nearby. This imitation is largely mindless—simple parroting of the actions of others.

As they grow older, children begin to realize that we attach meanings to our actions, and they become more adept at using symbols to communicate with others. **Symbols** are the gestures, objects, and words that form the basis of human communication. By interacting with family and friends, as well as by watching cartoons on television and looking at picture books, children in the preparatory stage begin to develop interaction skills they will use throughout their lives. They learn that they can use symbols to get their way, such as saying please and thank you, or perhaps throwing a tantrum in the candy aisle of the local supermarket.

The Play Stage As children develop skill in communicating through symbols, they gradually become more aware of social relationships out of which those symbols grow. During the *play stage,* from about ages three through five, they begin to pretend to be other people: a doctor, parent, superhero, or teacher. Such play need not make a lot of sense or be particularly coherent to adults, and children, especially when they are young, are able to move in and out of various characters with ease. For Mead, playing make-believe is more than just fun; it is a critical part of our self-development.

Mead, in fact, noted that an important aspect of the play stage is role playing. **Role taking** is the process of mentally assuming the perspective of another and responding from that imagined viewpoint. Through this process a young child internalizes the performances of other people and gradually learns, for example, when it is best to ask a parent for favors. If the parent usually comes home from work in a bad mood, the child might wait until after dinner, when the parent is more relaxed and approachable.

The Game Stage In Mead's third stage, the *game stage,* the child of about six to nine years of age no longer merely plays roles but now begins to consider several tasks and relationships simultaneously. At this point in development, children grasp not only their own social positions but also those of others around them. The transition from play to game is evident when teaching kids to play team sports such as T-ball or soccer. When they are little, you will often see a clump of kids chasing after a ball or moving up the field together. They have yet to learn that different people play different positions and that they will be more successful as a team if everyone plays the position to which they are assigned. When they do, they can take for granted that someone will be covering a base so they can throw a runner out or that a goalie will be there to make a save if the ball gets behind them. This map of who should be where and who should do what serves as a kind of blueprint for society, and internalizing it represents the final stage of development in Mead's model; the child can now respond to numerous members of the social environment.

Mead uses the term **generalized other** to refer to the attitudes, viewpoints, and expectations of society as a whole that a child takes into account in his or her behavior. Simply put, this concept suggests that when an individual acts, he or she takes into account an entire group of people. For example, a child will not act courteously merely to please a particular parent. Rather, the child comes to understand that courtesy is a widespread social value endorsed by parents, teachers, and religious leaders.

At the game stage, children can take a more sophisticated view of people and the social environment. They now understand what specific occupations and social positions are and no longer equate Mr. Williams only with the role of "librarian" or Ms. Sanchez only with "principal." It has become clear to the child that Mr. Williams can be a librarian, a parent, and a marathon runner at the same time and that Ms. Sanchez is one of many principals in our society. Thus, the child has reached a new level of sophistication in observations of individuals and institutions.

> **symbol** A gesture, object, or word that forms the basis of human communication.
>
> **role taking** The process of mentally assuming the perspective of another and responding from that imagined viewpoint.
>
> **generalized other** The attitudes, viewpoints, and expectations of society as a whole that a child takes into account in his or her behavior.

Goffman: Presentation of the Self Given that others play such a powerful role in shaping who we are and how we think about ourselves, the way we represent our self to others becomes a major concern for us and a significant interest to sociologists. Erving Goffman, a Canadian sociologist, provided a helpful model for better understanding how we go about constructing and maintaining our self through interactions with others. He suggested that each of us seeks to convey impressions of who we are to others even as those others are doing the same, creating a kind of performance that we can analyze and understand.

To study our everyday social interactions, Goffman offers the **dramaturgical approach,** which studies interaction as if we were all actors on a stage. All social encounters, according to Goffman, represent our attempts to carry out successful performances, equivalent to putting on a play. We perform front stage, largely following scripts, having already prepared for our performance backstage. We use appropriate props, including costumes, to make our performance believable. Although some improvisation is permissible, too much threatens the credibility of the character we are trying to play and may ruin the show. In order to give a successful performance, we also may need other cast members with whom we work as a team. Finally, our performance is carried out before an audience that judges how well we do. Whether in our role as students, restaurant servers,

> **dramaturgical approach** A view of social interaction in which people are seen as theatrical performers.
>
> **impression management** The altering of the presentation of the self in order to create distinctive appearances and satisfy particular audiences.
>
> **face-work** The efforts people make to maintain a proper image and avoid public embarrassment.

or even lovers, we all know that we have a part to play and that if we don't say the right lines or use the correct props the show will collapse, undermining our sense of self.

SOCTHINK

Imagine that going to class is like performing in a play. Who are the key players? What are some of their most-used lines? What props do people use to be convincing? How might the performance break down, and what steps might be taken to save the show?

Early in life, the individual learns to slant his or her presentation of the self in order to create distinctive appearances and satisfy particular audiences. Goffman (1959) referred to this altering of the presentation of the self as **impression management.** To maintain a proper image and avoid public embarrassment, we engage in **face-work.** How often do you initiate some kind of face-saving behavior when you feel flustered or rejected? In response to a rejection at a singles bar, a person may engage in face-work by saying, "There really isn't an interesting person in this entire crowd." Or, if we do poorly on an exam, we may say to a friend who did likewise, "This professor is incompetent." We feel the need to maintain a proper image of the self if we are to continue social interaction.

In some cultures, people engage in elaborate deceptions to avoid losing face. In Japan, for example, where lifetime employment has until recently been the norm, "company men" thrown out of work during a severe

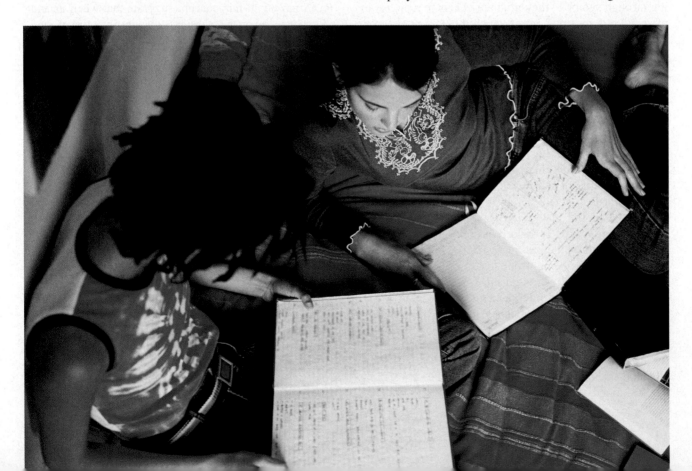

economic recession may feign employment, rising as usual in the morning, donning suit and tie, and heading for the business district. But instead of going to the office, they congregate at places such as Tokyo's Hibiya Library, where they pass the time by reading before returning home at the usual hour. Many of these men are trying to protect family members, who would be shamed if neighbors discovered that the family breadwinner was unemployed. Others are deceiving their wives and families as well (French 2000).

Goffman's work on the self represents a logical progression of sociological studies begun by Cooley and Mead on how personality is acquired through socialization and how we manage the presentation of our self to others. Cooley stressed the process by which we create a self; Mead focused on how the self develops as we learn to interact with others; Goffman emphasized the ways in which we consciously create images of ourselves for others.

PSYCHOLOGICAL APPROACHES TO THE SELF

Psychologists have shared the interest of Cooley, Mead, and other sociologists in the development of the self. Early work in psychology, such as that of Sigmund Freud (1856–1939), stressed the role of inborn drives—among them the drive for sexual gratification—in channeling human behavior. Later psychologists such as Jean Piaget emphasized the stages through which human beings progress as the self develops.

Like Cooley and Mead, Freud believed that the self is a social product and that aspects of one's personality are influenced by other people (especially one's parents). However, unlike Cooley and Mead, Freud suggested that the self has components that work in opposition to each other. According

to Freud, we have a natural instinct that seeks limitless pleasure, but this is at odds with our societal needs for order and constraint. By interacting with others, we learn the expectations of society and then select behavior most appropriate to our own culture.

Through his research on children, including newborns, the Swiss child psychologist Jean Piaget (1896–1980) underscored the importance of social interactions in developing a sense of self. In his well-known **cognitive theory of development,** Piaget (1954) identified four stages in the development of children's thought processes. In the first, or *sensorimotor,* stage, young children use their senses to make discoveries. For example, through touching they discover that their hands are actually a part of themselves.

> **cognitive theory of development** The theory that children's thought progresses through four stages of development.

During the second, or *preoperational,* stage, children begin to use words and symbols to distinguish objects and ideas. The milestone in the third, or *concrete operational,* stage is that children engage in more logical thinking. For example, they learn that even when a formless lump of clay is shaped into a snake, it is still the same clay. Finally, in the fourth, or *formal operational,* stage, adolescents become capable of sophisticated abstract thought and can deal with ideas and values in a logical manner.

Piaget suggested that moral development becomes an important part of socialization as children develop the ability to think more abstractly. When children learn the rules of a game such as hopscotch or Candy Land, they are learning to obey societal norms. Those under eight years of age display a rather basic level of morality: rules are rules, and there is no concept of "extenuating circumstances." As they mature, children become capable of greater autonomy, and they begin to experience moral dilemmas and doubts as to what constitutes proper behavior.

According to Piaget, social interaction is the key to development. As children grow older, they pay increasing attention to how other people think and why they act in particular ways. In order to develop a distinct personality, each of us needs opportunities to interact with others. As we saw earlier, Isabelle was deprived of the chance for normal social interactions, and the consequences were severe (Kitchener 1991).

>> Agents of Socialization

The people with whom we interact influence how we think about ourselves and how we represent ourselves to others, and the positions they occupy determine the kind of influence they have. Family, friends, schools, peers, the mass media, the workplace, religion, and the state are among the agents of socialization that play the most powerful roles in shaping the self.

FAMILY

The family is the most important agent of socialization, especially for children. We can see the power of family socialization among the Amish. Children in Amish communities are raised in a highly structured and disciplined manner, but they are not immune to the temptations posed by their peers in the non-Amish world. During a period of discovery called *rumspringa,* a term that means "running around," Amish young people attend barn dances where

taboos like drinking, smoking, and driving cars are commonly violated. Parents often react by looking the other way, sometimes literally, pretending not to notice. They remain secure in the knowledge that, after a lifetime of Amish socialization, their children almost always return to the traditional Amish lifestyle. Research shows that only about 20 percent of Amish youths leave the fold, and most of them join one of the only somewhat more modern Mennonite groups. Rarely does a baptized adult leave (Schachtman 2006; Zellner and Schaefer 2006).

Although the Amish provide what seems like an extreme case, the truth is that all families play a powerful role in shaping their children. Although peer groups and the media do influence us, research shows that the role of the family in socializing a child cannot be overestimated (McDowell and Parke 2009). The lifelong process of learning begins shortly after birth. Because newborns can hear, see, smell, and taste, and can feel heat, cold, and pain, they are constantly orienting themselves to the surrounding world. Human beings, especially family members, constitute an important part of their social environment. People minister to the baby's needs by feeding, cleaning, carrying, and comforting her or him. It is in the context of families that we learn to talk, walk, feed ourselves, go to the bathroom, and so on—basic skills that we take for granted as natural but that we learned thanks to our families.

Cross-Cultural Variation As both Cooley and Mead noted, the development of the self is a critical aspect of the early years of one's life. How children develop this sense of self, however, can vary from one society to another. For example, most parents in the United States do not send six-year-olds to school unsupervised. However, that is the norm in Japan, where parents push their children to commute to school on their own from an early age. In cities like Tokyo, first-graders must learn to negotiate buses, subways, and long walks. To ensure their safety, parents carefully lay out rules: never talk to strangers; check with a station attendant if you get off at the wrong stop; stay on to the end of the line, then call, if you miss your stop; take stairs, not escalators; don't fall asleep. Some parents equip the children with cell phones or pagers. One parent acknowledges that she worries, "but after they are 6, children are supposed to start being independent from the mother. If you're still taking your child to school after the first month, everyone looks at you funny" (Tolbert 2000:17).

Family structures also reproduce themselves through socialization. In the contexts of families, children learn expectations regarding marriage and parenthood. Children observe their parents expressing affection, dealing with finances, quarreling, complaining about in-laws, and so forth. Their learning represents an informal process of anticipatory socialization in which they develop a tentative model of what being married and being a parent are like.

The Impact of Race and Gender In the United States, social development includes exposure to cultural assumptions regarding gender and race. African American parents, for example, have learned that children as young as two years old can absorb negative messages about Blacks in children's books, toys, and television shows—the vast majority of which are designed primarily for White consumers. At the same time, African American children are exposed more often than others to the inner-city youth gang culture. Because most Blacks, even those who are middle class, live near very poor neighborhoods, their children are susceptible to these influences, despite their parents' strong family values (Benhorin and McMahon 2008; Kliewar and Sullivan 2009; Pattillo 2005).

The term **gender roles** refers to expectations regarding the proper behavior, attitudes, and activities of males and females. For example, we traditionally think of "toughness" as masculine—and desirable only in men—while we view "tenderness" as feminine. As we will see in Chapter 12, other cultures do not necessarily assign these qualities to each gender in the way that our culture does. As the primary agents of childhood socialization, parents play a critical role in guiding children into those gender roles deemed appropriate in a society.

Other adults, older siblings, the mass media, and religious and educational institutions also have a noticeable impact on a child's socialization into feminine and masculine norms. A culture or subculture may require that one sex or the other take primary responsibility for

> **gender role** Expectations regarding the proper behavior, attitudes, and activities of males and females.

the socialization of children, economic support of the family, or religious or intellectual leadership. In some societies girls are socialized mainly by their mothers and boys by their fathers—an arrangement that may prevent girls from learning critical survival skills. In South Asia, for example, fathers teach their sons to swim to prepare them for a life as fishermen; girls typically do not learn to swim. When the deadly tsunami hit the coast of South Asia in 2004, many more men than women survived.

While we consider the family's role in socialization, we need to remember, however, that children are not simply robots who lack agency. They do not play a passive role in their socialization. As Mead's "I" implies, they choose, sometimes to the consternation of their parents, and in so doing are active participants in their self-creation. Through the choices they make, they influence and alter the families, schools, and communities of which they are a part.

SCHOOL

In school we typically move beyond the more sheltered confines of our family and learn to become members of the larger social groups to which we belong. Schools teach us the taken-for-granted knowledge of the broader society—not only basic skills such as reading, writing, and 'rithmatic but also shared cultural knowledge such as the national anthem, the heroes of the American Revolution, and the pillars of good character. Like the family, schools have an explicit mandate to socialize people in the United States—and especially children—into the norms and values of U.S. culture.

Schools teach children the values and customs of the larger society because that shared culture provides the glue that holds us together as a society. If we did not transmit our knowledge and skills from one generation to the next, society would collapse. The knowledge we gain there, however, goes beyond just the official curriculum to include the more informal lessons we learn on the playground. We do learn the facts and figures of history, science, reading, math, and more, but we also learn how to stand up for ourselves when our parents or teachers are not there to hover over us or to bail us out.

In addition to providing social order, schools open doors for us as individuals. We are exposed to new ways of thinking and acting that allow us to make new choices about our future. While this can include training for careers that allow us to "get ahead," it also involves exposure to new cultures, ideas, practices, and possibilities. It might even lead us to an unexpected future such as a career in sociology!

Although schools provide both social order and individual opportunity, they can also reinforce existing inequality through the ways students are socialized. As economists Samuel Bowles and Herbert Gintis (1976) have observed, schools produce teachable students who become manageable workers. They argue that schools have less to do with transmitting academic content than with socializing students into the proper attitudes and behaviors of the workplace. Schools teach students how to work for rewards, how to work in teams, how to meet deadlines, how to take responsibility for a task or work product, how to comply with instructions, and so on. The students who internalize these skills best are rewarded with opportunities in the workplace while others are left behind.

These differential outcomes are compounded by the fact that the positions we occupy when we enter school shape where we end up. For example, higher education in the United States is costly despite the existence of public colleges and universities and financial aid programs. Students from affluent backgrounds, therefore, have an advantage in gaining access to universities and professional training. At the same time, less affluent young people may never receive the preparation that would qualify them for the best-paying and most prestigious jobs.

PEER GROUPS

Families and schools do shape us, but if you ask any 13-year-old who matters most in his or her life, the likely answer is "friends." As children grow older, the family becomes somewhat less important in social development. Instead, peer groups increasingly assume the role

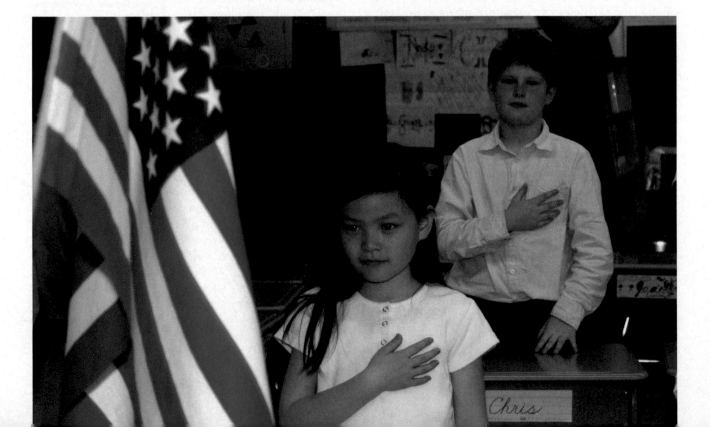

of Mead's significant other. Within the peer group, young people associate with others who are approximately their own age and who often enjoy a similar social status (Giordano 2003).

In the context of peer groups, a hierarchy often develops. Sociologists Patricia and Peter Adler conducted participant observation at elementary schools to investigate how popularity works among fourth- through sixth-grade students. They found that, even this early, a pecking order is established ranging from the "popular clique" at the top that includes the "cool kids" on down to what they call the "social isolates" at the bottom, whom other kids sometimes call "dweebs" or "nerds" (Adler and Adler 1996). Children get the message about where they fit and how they should behave.

In other research the Adlers also found that popularity reinforces gender stereotypes. To be popular as a boy is to be athletic, tough, and not too academic. To be popular as a girl is to be attractive, to be able to manipulate others using social skills, and to come from a family wealthy enough to permit shopping for the latest cool stuff (Adler, Kless, and Adler 1992). In similar research, college students were asked to reflect on what made people popular in high school. Researchers found that male and female students named many of the same paths to popularity—such as physical attractiveness, participation in sports, and grades/intelligence—but gave them different orders of importance. Neither men nor women named sexual activity, drug use, or alcohol use as one of the top five paths, but college men were much more likely than women to mention those behaviors as a means to becoming popular, for both boys and girls (Suitor et al. 2001). Other researchers have found that being considered popular early in high school increases the likelihood of using tobacco and

In the TV series *Glee*, the most popular couple in the high school loses face when Quinn, the head cheerleader, is revealed to be pregnant and joins the glee club with her boyfriend, Finn, the star quarterback. The respect from others that they took for granted quickly vanishes. In a meeting with the school counselor, Quinn gives voice to the power that people's perceptions of us can have in our lives: "Status is like currency. When your bank account is full, you can get away with doing just about anything. But right now, we're like toxic assets."

engaging in sexual activity later in high school (Mayeux, Sandstrom, and Cillessen 2008).

Though we value the importance of kids establishing themselves as individuals, the irony is that peer culture is not individualistic. Children, especially adolescents, run in packs and look, talk, and act alike (often in the name of individualism). Of course, although parents often lecture

High School Popularity

What makes high school girls popular?

According to college women:		According to college men:
1	Grades/intelligence	2
2	Participation in sports	3
3	General sociability	4
4	Physical attractiveness	1
	Popularity with boys	5
5	Clothes	

What makes high school boys popular?

According to college women:		According to college men:
1	Participation in sports	1
2	Grades/intelligence	2
	Popularity with girls	3
3	General sociability	4
4	Physical attractiveness	
5	School clubs/government	
	Car	5

Note: Students at the following universities were asked in which ways adolescents in their high schools had gained prestige with their peers: Cornell University, Louisiana State University, Southeastern Louisiana University, State University of New York at Albany, State University of New York at Stony Brook, the University of Georgia, and the University of New Hampshire.

Source: Suitor et al. 2001:445.

their kids about not giving in to peer pressure, they don't really mean it. What they mean is to not give in to the *wrong kinds* of peer pressure. They love peer pressure if it makes their children more like the "good kids" or, even better, if the form of social pressure they give in to is parental pressure.

MASS MEDIA AND TECHNOLOGY

In the past 80 or so years, media innovations—radio, motion pictures, recorded music, television, and the Internet—have become important agents of socialization. One national survey indicates that 71 percent of U.S. children have a television in their bedroom, and 70 percent of all youths ages 8–18 use the Internet every day (Rideout, Foehr, and Roberts 2010; Wartella et al. 2009). We are spending more and more of our time interacting with technology, which has an inevitable impact on our interactions with each other. Adding up totals from television, radio, print media, phones, computers, movies, and music—and taking multitasking (doing more than one task at a time) into account—Americans consume the equivalent of 11.8 hours of information per day outside of work (Bohn and Short 2010).

Television programs and even commercials can introduce young people to unfamiliar lifestyles and cultures. On PBS alone, children are exposed to life in the city, on the farm, and across the world. The same thing happens in other countries and regions. In the Palestinian-held Gaza Strip, for example, Hamas—a group better known for its suicide bombing campaigns—has launched a television program meant to familiarize children with

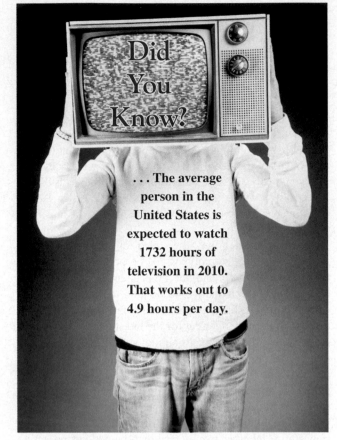

Did You Know?

... The average person in the United States is expected to watch 1732 hours of television in 2010. That works out to 4.9 hours per day.

Source: Bohn and Short 2010.

the Palestinian position on the disputed territories. In between lectures on revered sites such as Nablus and Al Aksa Mosque, the show's host, known as Uncle Hazim,

How Young People Use the Media

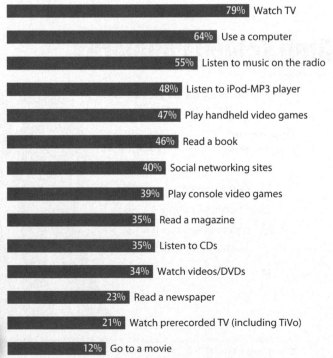

Percentage of 8- to 18-year-olds in a typical day

79%	Watch TV
64%	Use a computer
55%	Listen to music on the radio
48%	Listen to iPod-MP3 player
47%	Play handheld video games
46%	Read a book
40%	Social networking sites
39%	Play console video games
35%	Read a magazine
35%	Listen to CDs
34%	Watch videos/DVDs
23%	Read a newspaper
21%	Watch prerecorded TV (including TiVo)
12%	Go to a movie

Source: Rideout et al. 2010:44–45.

takes on-air phone calls from viewers and talks with animal characters reminiscent of those on *Sesame Street*. Designed with a child-age audience in mind, the show omits all mention of violence and armed conflict in pursuit of Hamas' goals (Craig Smith 2006b). On a different Palestinian network, an alternative called *Shara's Simsim* is affiliated with the official *Sesame Street* franchise and promotes its core values of optimism and tolerance (Shapiro 2009).

New technologies are changing how we interact with family, friends, and even strangers. Through email, cell phones, texting, and instant messaging, we can maintain close, almost constant, connections with family and friends both near and far. Through Facebook and MySpace, we can establish and extend networks with "friends" both known and unknown. But new technologies can also lead to narrowcasting, in which we interact mainly with people who are most like ourselves. This can limit the number of significant relationships we have with people with whom we might share fundamental differences, thus weakening our conflict resolution skills. Other skills, however, may be strengthened. Researchers studying technology use among families in northern California's Silicon Valley (a technology corridor) found that families are socialized into multi-tasking as the social norm; devoting one's full attention to one task—even eating or driving—is less and less common on a typical day (Silicon Valley Cultures Project 2004).

Around the world, including in Africa and other developing areas, people have been socialized into relying on new communications technologies. For instance, not long

ago, if Zadhe Iyombe wanted to talk to his mother, he had to make an eight-day trip from the capital city of Kinshasa (in the Democratic Republic of the Congo) up the Congo River by boat to the rural town where he was born. Now both he and his mother have access to a cell phone, and they send text messages to each other daily. And Iyombe and his mother are not atypical. Although cell phones aren't cheap, 2.5 billion owners in developing countries have come to consider them a necessity. Today, there are more cell phones in developing countries than in industrial nations—the first time in history that developing countries have outpaced the developed world in the adoption of a telecommunications technology (LeClaire 2009; K. Sullivan 2006).

Access to media can also increase social cohesion by presenting a common, more or less standardized view of culture through mass communication. Sociologist Robert Park (1922) studied how newspapers helped immigrants to the United States adjust to their environment by changing their

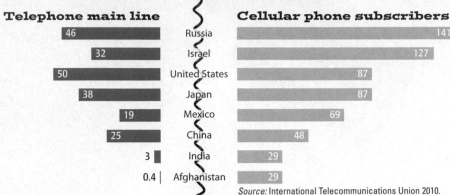

Telephones and Cell Phones by Country (rates per 100 people)

Telephone main line	Country	Cellular phone subscribers
46	Russia	141
32	Israel	127
50	United States	87
38	Japan	87
19	Mexico	69
25	China	48
3	India	29
0.4	Afghanistan	29

Source: International Telecommunications Union 2010.

customary habits and teaching them the values and views of people in their new home country. Unquestionably, the mass media play a significant role in providing a collective experience for members of society. Think about how the mass media bring together members of a community or even a nation by broadcasting important events and ceremonies (such as inaugurations, press conferences, parades, state funerals, and the Olympics) and by covering disasters.

Which media outlets did people turn to in the aftermath of the September 11, 2001, terrorist attacks? Television and telephone were the primary means by which people in the United States bonded. But the Internet also played a prominent role. About half of all Internet users—more than 53 million people—received some kind of news about the attacks online. Nearly three-fourths of Internet users communicated via email to show their patriotism, discuss events with their families, or reconnect with old friends. More than a third of Internet users read or posted material in online forums. In the first 30 days alone, the Library of Congress collected from one Internet site more than half a million pages having to do with the terrorist attacks. As a library director noted, "The Internet has become for many the public commons, a place where they can come together and talk" (D. L. Miller and Darlington 2002; Mirapaul 2001:E2; Rainie 2001).

THE WORKPLACE

Learning to behave appropriately in an occupation is a fundamental aspect of human socialization. In the United States, working full-time confirms adult status; it indicates that one has passed out of adolescence. In a sense, socialization into an occupation can represent both a harsh reality ("I have to work in order to buy food and pay the rent") and the realization of an ambition ("I've always wanted to be an airline pilot") (W. Moore 1968:862; Simmons 2009).

It used to be that our work life began with the end of our formal schooling, but that is no longer necessarily the case, at least not in the United States. More and more young people work today, and not just for a parent or relative. Adolescents generally seek jobs in order to earn spending money; 80 percent of high school seniors say that little or none of what they earn goes to family expenses. These teens rarely look on their employment as a means of exploring vocational interests or getting on-the-job training (Hirschman and Voloshin 2007).

Did You Know?

. . . May 7, 2011 is International Shutdown Day. This is an annual event to encourage people to turn off their computer for 24 hours and reflect on the impact computers have on our lives and our communities. Participants are urged to spend the time they save interacting with friends, going for a hike, or volunteering in the community.

Child Care Arrangements for Preschoolers

Relative care	Grandparent/other	29.9%
	Parent(s)	18.0%
	Sibling	2.2%
Nonrelative care	Organized care (including day care)	22.9%
	Other nonrelative	9.7%
Self-care		0.8%

Note: Organized care includes day care, Head Start, preschool, and school.

Source: U.S. Census Bureau 2009e:Table 1B.

Some observers feel that the increasing number of teenagers who are working earlier in life and for longer hours are finding the workplace to be almost as important an agent of socialization as school. In fact, a number of educators complain that time spent at work is adversely affecting students' schoolwork. The level of teenage employment in the United States is the highest among industrial countries, which may provide one explanation for why U.S. high school students lag behind those in other countries on international achievement tests.

Socialization in the workplace changes when it involves a more permanent shift from an after-school job to full-time employment. Occupational socialization can be most intense during the transition from school to job, but it continues throughout one's work history. Technological advances and corporate reorganization may alter the requirements of the position and necessitate new training. According to the Bureau of Labor Statistics (2008b), between the ages of 18 to 42 alone, the typical person holds 11 different jobs. We can no longer assume that we will have a job-for-life, so whether by choice or by necessity, we must be open to ongoing occupational socialization.

RELIGION AND THE STATE

Increasingly, social scientists are recognizing the growing importance of government ("the state") and the continued significance of religion as agents of socialization. Traditionally, family members served as the primary caregivers in U.S. culture, but in the 20th century, the family's protective function was steadily transferred to outside agencies such as public schools, hospitals, mental health clinics, and child care centers, many of which are run by the state. Historically, religious groups also provided such care and protection. Despite early sociological predictions that religion would cease to play a substantial role in modern society, these groups continue to play a significant role in identity formation and collective life (Warner 2005).

Preschool children in particular are often cared for by someone other than a parent. Eighty-eight percent of employed mothers depend on others to care for their children, and 29 percent of mothers who aren't employed have regular care arrangements. More than a third of children under age five are cared for by nonrelatives in nursery schools, Head Start programs, day care centers, family day care, and other providers. Children this age are also more likely to be cared for on a daily basis by grandparents than by their parents (U.S. Census Bureau 2008b).

Both government and organized religion act to provide markers representing significant life course transitions. For example, religious organizations continue to celebrate meaningful ritual

SOCTHINK

Should government play a larger role in socializing children by funding public education for all children starting at the age of two?

events—such as baptism, bismillah, or bar/bat mitzvah—that often bring together all the members of an extended family, even if they never meet for any other reason. Government regulations stipulate the ages at which a person may drive a car, drink alcohol, vote in elections, marry without parental permission, work overtime, and retire. Although these regulations do not constitute strict rites of passage— most

Leh Village, India school children.

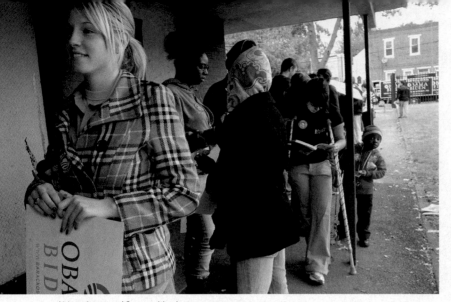

Although many 18-year-olds choose not to vote, voter turnout in the 2008 presidential election was the highest it had been in decades, causing long lines at some polling stations.

rite of passage A ritual marking the symbolic transition from one social position to another.

life course approach A research orientation in which sociologists and other social scientists look closely at the social factors that influence people throughout their lives, from birth to death.

socialization continues through all stages of the life cycle. In fact, some researchers have chosen to concentrate on socialization as a lifelong process. Sociologists and other social scientists who take such a **life course approach** look closely at the social factors, including gender and income, that influence people throughout their lives, from birth to death. They recognize that biological changes help mold but do not dictate human behavior.

In the transition from childhood to adulthood, we can identify certain markers that signify the passage from one life stage to the next. These milestones vary from one society and even one generation to the next.

In the United States, according to one national survey, completion of formal schooling has risen to the top, with 90 percent of people identifying it as an important rite of passage. On average, Americans expect this milestone to be attained by a person's 23rd birthday. Other major events in the life course, such as getting married or becoming a parent, are expected to follow three or four years later. Interestingly, the significance of these markers has declined, with only about one-third

Body painting is a ritual marking the passage to puberty in some cultures.

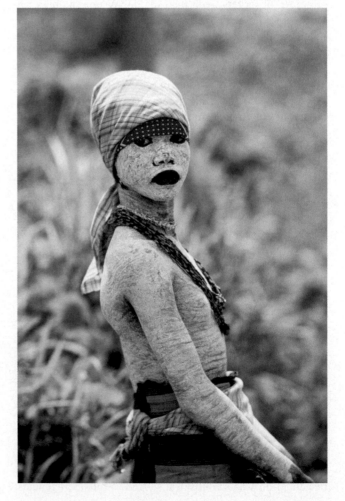

18-year-olds choose not to vote, and most people choose their age of retirement without reference to government dictates—they do symbolize the fact that we have moved on to a different stage of our life, with different expectations regarding our behavior.

>> Socialization Throughout the Life Course

Adolescents among the Kota people of the Congo in Africa paint themselves blue. Cuban American girls go on a day-long religious retreat before dancing the night away. These are both **rites of passage**—rituals that mark the symbolic transition from one social position to another, dramatizing and validating changes in a person's status.

In the Kota rite the color blue—the color of death—symbolizes the death of childhood and the passage to adulthood. For adolescent girls in Miami's Cuban American community, the *quinceañera* ceremony celebrating the attainment of womanhood at age 15 supports a network of party planners, caterers, dress designers, and the Miss Quinceañera Latina pageant. For thousands of years, Egyptian mothers have welcomed their newborns to the world in the Soboa ceremony by stepping over the seven-day-old infant seven times. And Naval Academy seniors celebrate their graduation from college by hurling their hats skyward.

THE LIFE COURSE

Such specific ceremonies mark stages of development in the life course. They indicate that the process of

Milestones in the Transition to Adulthood

Expected Age	Life Event	Percentage who view event as extremely/quite important
20.9	Financial independence from parents/guardians	80.9%
21.1	Separate residence from parents	57.2%
21.2	Full-time employment	83.8%
22.3	Completion of formal schooling	90.2%
24.5	Capability of supporting family	82.3%
25.7	Marriage	33.2%
26.2	Parenthood	29.0%

Source: T. Smith 2004.

of survey respondents identifying marriage and less than one-third identifying parenthood as important milestones representing adulthood (S. Furstenberg et al. 2004; T. Smith 2004).

One result of these staggered steps to independence is that in the United States, unlike some other societies, there is no clear dividing line between adolescence and adulthood. Nowadays, the number of years between childhood and adulthood has grown, and few young people finish school, get married, and leave home at about the same age, clearly establishing their transition to adulthood. The term *youthhood* has been coined to describe the prolonged ambiguous status that young people in their 20s experience (Côté 2000).

SOCTHINK

What are some of the markers of youthhood? When does it begin? When does it end? To what extent do you feel like an adult? What characteristics of our society contribute to ambiguity in our passage into adulthood?

ANTICIPATORY SOCIALIZATION AND RESOCIALIZATION

In our journey through our lives, we seek to prepare ourselves for what is coming and to adapt to change as necessary. To prepare, we undergo **anticipatory socialization,** which refers to processes of socialization in which a person "rehearses" for future positions, occupations, and social relationships. A culture can function more efficiently and smoothly if members become acquainted with the norms, values, and behavior associated with a social position before actually assuming that status. Preparation for many aspects of adult life begins with anticipatory socialization during childhood and adolescence and continues throughout our lives as we prepare for new responsibilities (Levine and Hoffner 2006).

High school students experience a bit of anticipatory socialization when they prepare for college. They begin to imagine what college life will be like and what kind of person they will be when they get there. They may seek out information from friends and family in order to get a better sense of what to expect, but increasingly, they also rely on campus websites and Facebook entries. To assist in this process and to attract more students, colleges are investing more time and money in websites through which students can take "virtual" campus tours, listen to podcasts, and stream videos of everything from the school song to a sample zoology lecture.

anticipatory socialization Processes of socialization in which a person "rehearses" for future positions, occupations, and social relationships.

resocialization The process of discarding former behavior patterns and accepting new ones as part of a transition in one's life.

total institution An institution that regulates all aspects of a person's life under a single authority, such as a prison, the military, a mental hospital, or a convent.

Occasionally, assuming a new social or occupational position requires that we *unlearn* an established orientation. **Resocialization** refers to the process of discarding old behavior patterns and accepting new ones as part of a life transition. Often resocialization results from explicit efforts to transform an individual, as happens in reform schools, therapy groups, prisons, religious conversion settings, and political indoctrination camps. The process of resocialization typically involves considerable stress for the individual—much more so than socialization in general, or even anticipatory socialization (Hart, Miller, and Johnson 2003).

Resocialization is particularly effective when it occurs within a total institution. Erving Goffman (1961) coined the term **total institution** to refer to an institution that regulates all aspects of a person's life under a single authority. Examples can be more or less extreme, from summer camp or boarding school to prison, the military, a mental hospital, or a convent. Because the total institution is generally cut off from the rest of society, it provides for all the needs of its members. In its extreme form, so elaborate are its requirements, and so all-encompassing its activities, that the total institution represents a miniature society.

Goffman (1961) identified several common traits of total institutions:

- All aspects of life are conducted in the same place under the control of a single authority.

- Any activities within the institution are conducted in the company of others in the same circumstances—for example, army recruits or novices in a convent.

- The authorities devise rules and schedule activities without consulting the participants.

- All aspects of life within a total institution are designed to fulfill the purpose of the organization. Thus, all activities in a monastery might be centered on prayer and communion with God (Malacrida 2005; Mapel 2007; Williams and Warren 2009).

degradation ceremony An aspect of the socialization process within some total institutions, in which people are subjected to humiliating rituals.

midlife crisis A stressful period of self-evaluation that begins at about age 40.

sandwich generation The generation of adults who simultaneously try to meet the competing needs of their parents and their children.

People often lose their individuality within total institutions. For example, a person entering prison may experience the humiliation of a **degradation ceremony** as he or she is stripped of clothing, jewelry, and other personal possessions. From that point on, scheduled daily routines allow for little or no personal initiative. The individual becomes secondary and

SOCTHINK

To what extent is summer camp, a cruise, or even life at a residential college similar to a total institution? In what ways is it different?

rather invisible in the overbearing social environment (Garfinkel 1956).

ROLE TRANSITIONS DURING THE LIFE COURSE

As we have seen, one of the key transitional stages we pass through occurs as we enter the adult world, perhaps by moving out of the parental home, beginning a career, or entering a marriage. As we age, we move into the midlife transition, which typically begins at about age 40. Men and women often experience a stressful period of self-evaluation, commonly known as the **midlife crisis,** in which they realize that they have not achieved basic goals and ambitions and may feel they have little time left to do so. This conflict between their hopes and their outcomes causes strain. Compounding such stresses that are often associated with one's career or partner is the growing responsibility for caring for two generations at once (Mortimer and Shanahan 2006; Wethington 2000).

During the late 1990s, social scientists began focusing on the **sandwich generation**—adults who simultaneously

Life in prison is highly regulated—even recreation time.

try to meet the competing needs of their parents and their children. Their caregiving goes in two directions: to children, who even as young adults may still require significant support and direction; and to aging parents, whose health and economic problems may demand intervention by their adult children.

Like the role of caring for children, that of caring for aging parents falls disproportionately on women. Overall, women provide 60 percent of the care their parents receive, and even more as the demands of the role grow more intense and time consuming. Increasingly, middle-aged women and younger are finding themselves on the "daughter track," as their time and attention are diverted by the needs of their aging mothers and fathers (Gross 2005; Taylor et al. 2009).

5 Movies on SOCIALIZATION

An Education
A middle-class British schoolgirl and her family are seduced by a slick older man.

In America
An Irish family adapts to life in New York City.

Children Underground
Documentary about children surviving in the subway systems of Romania.

Half Nelson
A young teacher in Brooklyn struggles in and out of the classroom.

Training Day
A day in the life of a rookie narcotics officer in the LAPD.

>> Aging and Society

Due to advances in areas such as health care, nutrition, and working conditions, life expectancy has risen significantly both in the Unites States and around the world. Someone born in 1900 in the United States had an average life expectancy of less than 50 years, but babies born in the U.S. in 2006 can anticipate living to 75 if they're boys and 80 if they're girls (Taylor et al. 2009:18). Globally, there are now more than 500 million people over the age of 65, composing approximately 8 percent of the world's population, a percentage that is expected to continue to rise (Population Reference Bureau 2009).

How societies deal with their elderly population varies significantly across cultures. One society may treat older people with reverence, whereas another sees them as unproductive and "difficult." The Sherpas—a Tibetan-speaking Buddhist people in Nepal—live in a culture that idealizes old age. Almost all elderly members of the Sherpa culture (picture above) own their homes, and most are in relatively good physical condition. Typically, older Sherpas value their independence and prefer not to live with their children. Among the Fulani of Africa, however, older men and women move to the edge of the family homestead. Since that is where people are buried, the elderly sleep over their own graves, for they are viewed socially as already dead (Goldstein and Beall 1981; Stenning 1958; Tonkinson 1978).

Understandably, all societies have some system of age stratification that associates certain social roles with distinct periods in life. Some of this age differentiation seems inevitable; it would make little sense to send young children off to war or to expect older citizens to handle physically demanding tasks, such as loading freight at shipyards.

In the United States, the proportion of the population that was 65 and older grew from 4.1 percent in 1900 to 13 percent in 2009; it is expected to rise to approximately 20 percent by 2050 (Taylor et al. 2009). These rates vary by race and ethnicity. In 2008, 15.7 percent of non-Hispanic Whites were older than 65, compared to 8.5 percent of African Americans, 9.6 percent of Asian Americans, and 5.7 percent of Hispanics. In part, these differences reflect the shorter life spans of the latter groups. They also stem from immigration patterns among Asians and Hispanics, who tend to be young when they enter the country (U.S. Census Bureau 2009f:Table 9).

The aging pattern in the United States also varies by state. Whereas Florida leads the country with 17.4 percent of its population over 65, Alaska comes in with the lowest U.S. rate at 7.3 percent. As of 2008, the top five states with the highest proportion of older people included Florida, West Virginia, Pennsylvania, Maine, and Iowa (Taylor et al. 2009). As a result of these trends, the development of retirement communities, along with various other amenities geared toward senior citizens, is particularly common in these states.

Aging Around the World

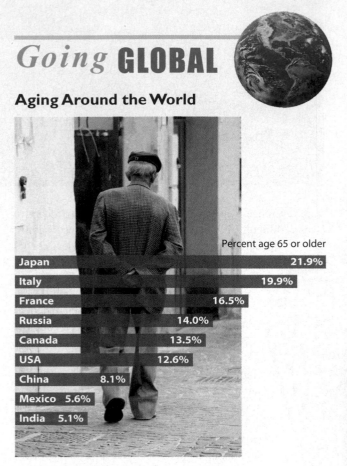

Percent age 65 or older

Japan	21.9%
Italy	19.9%
France	16.5%
Russia	14.0%
Canada	13.5%
USA	12.6%
China	8.1%
Mexico	5.6%
India	5.1%

Source: Taylor et al. 2009.

ADJUSTING TO RETIREMENT

Making the role transition into retirement can be a difficult process. Retirement is a rite of passage that typically marks a transition out of active participation in the full-time labor market. Symbolic events are associated with this rite of passage, such as retirement gifts, a retirement party, and special moments on the last day on the job. The preretirement period itself can be emotionally charged, especially if the retiree is expected to train his or her successor (Reitzes and Mutran 2004).

Gerontologist Robert Atchley (1976) has identified several phases of the retirement experience:

- *Preretirement,* a period of anticipatory socialization as the person prepares for retirement.

- *The near phase,* when the person establishes a specific departure date from his or her job.

- *The honeymoon phase,* an often euphoric period in which the person pursues activities that he or she never had time for before.

- *The disenchantment phase,* in which retirees feel a sense of letdown or even depression as they cope with their new lives, which may include illness or poverty.

- *The reorientation phase,* which involves the development of a more realistic view of retirement alternatives.

- *The stability phase,* in which the person has learned to deal with life after retirement in a reasonable and comfortable fashion.

- *The termination phase,* which begins when the person can no longer engage in basic, day-to-day activities such as self-care and housework.

Retirement is not a single transition, then, but a series of adjustments that varies from one person to another. The length and timing of each phase will differ for each individual, depending on such factors as financial and health status. In fact, a person will not necessarily go through all the phases identified by Atchley. For example, people who are forced to retire or who face financial difficulties may never experience a honeymoon phase. And many retirees continue to be part of the paid labor force of the United States, often taking part-time jobs to supplement their pensions, either because they want to or because they need to.

Actual and Projected Growth of the Elderly Population of the United States

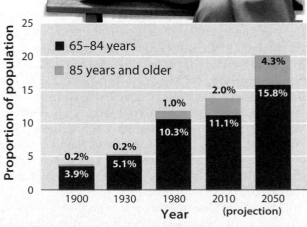

Proportion of population

- 65–84 years
- 85 years and older

Year	1900	1930	1980	2010	2050 (projection)
85 years and older	0.2%	0.2%	1.0%	2.0%	4.3%
65–84 years	3.9%	5.1%	10.3%	11.1%	15.8%

Source: He et al. 2005:9; U.S. Census Bureau 2008g:Table 1.

"Good news, honey—seventy is the new fifty."

>> Perspectives on Aging

Aging is an important aspect of socialization throughout the life course. The particular problems of the elderly have become the focus of a specialized field of research and inquiry known as **gerontology**—the study of the sociological and psychological aspects of aging and the problems of the aged. It originated in the 1930s, as an increasing number of social scientists became aware of the plight of the elderly.

Gerontologists rely heavily on sociological principles and theories to explain the impact of aging on the individual and society. They also draw on psychology, anthropology, physical education, counseling, and medicine in their study of the aging process. Three perspectives on aging—disengagement theory, activity theory, and age discrimination—arise out of these studies.

SOC THINK

What do you think about getting old? Can you picture yourself at age 65? What might your life look like?

DISENGAGEMENT THEORY

After studying elderly people in good health and relatively comfortable economic circumstances, Elaine Cumming and William Henry (1961) introduced their **disengagement theory,** which implicitly suggests that society and the aging individual mutually sever many of their relationships. Highlighting the significance of social order in society, disengagement theory emphasizes that passing social roles on from one generation to another ensures social stability.

According to this theory, the approach of death forces people to drop most of their social roles—including those of worker, volunteer, spouse, hobby enthusiast, and even reader. Younger members of society then take on these

functions. The aging person, it is held, withdraws into an increasing state of inactivity while preparing for death. At the same time, society withdraws from the elderly by segregating them residentially (in retirement homes and communities), educationally (in programs designed solely for senior citizens), and recreationally (in senior citizens' centers). Implicit in disengagement theory is the view that society should help older people to withdraw from their accustomed social roles.

Since it was first outlined more than five decades ago, disengagement theory has generated considerable controversy. Some gerontologists have objected to the implication that older people want to be ignored and put away—and even more to the idea that they should be encouraged to withdraw from meaningful social roles. Critics of disengagement theory insist that society forces the elderly into an involuntary and painful withdrawal from the paid labor force and from meaningful social relationships. Rather than voluntarily seeking to disengage, older employees find themselves pushed out of their jobs—in many instances, even before they are entitled to maximum retirement benefits (Boaz 1987).

> **gerontology** The study of the sociological and psychological aspects of aging and the problems of the aged.
>
> **disengagement theory** A theory of aging that suggests that society and the aging individual mutually sever many of their relationships.

ACTIVITY THEORY

How important is it for older people to stay actively involved, whether at a job or in other pursuits? A tragic disaster in Chicago in 1995 showed that it can be a matter of life and death. An intense heat wave lasting more than a week—with a heat index exceeding 115 degrees on two consecutive days—resulted in 733 heat-related deaths. About three-fourths of the deceased were 65 or older. Subsequent analysis showed that older people who lived alone had the highest risk of dying, suggesting that support networks for the elderly literally help to save lives. Older Hispanics and Asian Americans had lower death rates from the heat wave than other racial and ethnic groups. Their stronger social networks probably resulted in more regular contact with family members and friends (Klinenberg 2002; Schaefer 1998a).

Often seen as the opposite of disengagement theory, **activity theory** suggests that those elderly people who remain active and socially involved will be best adjusted. Proponents of this perspective acknowledge that a 70-year-old person may not have the ability or desire to perform various social roles that he or she had at age 40. Yet they contend that old people have essentially the same need for social interaction as any other group.

The improved health of older people—sometimes overlooked by social scientists—has strengthened the arguments of activity theorists. Illness and chronic disease are no longer quite the scourge of the elderly that they once were. The recent emphasis on fitness, the availability of better medical care, greater control of infectious diseases, and the reduction in the number of fatal strokes and heart attacks have combined to reduce the traumas of growing old.

Accumulating medical research also points to the importance of remaining socially involved. Among those who decline in their mental capacities later in life, deterioration is most rapid in those who withdraw from social relationships

activity theory A theory of aging that suggests that those elderly people who remain active and socially involved will be best adjusted.

and activities. Fortunately, the aged are finding new ways to remain socially engaged, as evidenced by their increasing use of the Internet, especially to keep in touch with family and friends (Taylor et al. 2009; Williams et al. 2010).

Admittedly, many activities open to the elderly involve unpaid labor, for which younger adults may

5 Movies on AGING

Gran Torino
A widowed veteran confronts gang violence in his neighborhood.

Up
A cranky old man and a young boy embark on an unusual adventure.

Harold and Maude
Not your average couple.

Cocoon
Florida retirees meet E.T.

The Bucket List
Two men confront death by ticking off items on their to-do list.

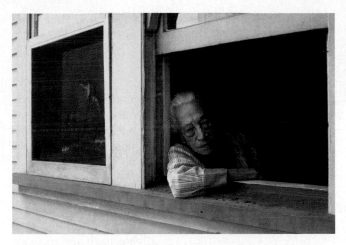

receive salaries. Unpaid elderly workers include hospital volunteers (versus aides and orderlies), drivers for charities such as the Red Cross (versus chauffeurs), tutors (as opposed to teachers), and craftspeople for charity bazaars (as opposed to carpenters and dressmakers). However, some companies have recently begun programs to hire retirees for full- or part-time work.

Continued engagement in the workforce has been a growing trend. In 2009, 26 percent of those aged 65–74 worked full- or part-time. Of those who consider themselves retired but who continue to work, almost 70 percent say they do so primarily because they want to, not because they need to for financial reasons. In fact, the percentage of those who choose to work after what we conventionally think of as retirement age continues to rise, even among the oldest in the population (Gendell 2008; Taylor et al. 2009:91). Though many continue to work into old age for social engagement, those who must do so for financial reasons often find their workforce experience to be a challenge.

In 2002, the Senate Special Committee on Aging convened a panel on the media's portrayal of older people and sharply criticized media and marketing executives for bombarding audiences with negative images of the aged. How many characters on top TV shows today can you think of who are over 65? How does that compare to the number of characters you can think of who are under 30?

Rising Labor Force Participation Rates Among the Elderly

Percentage change in labor force participation rates since 1994

	65–69 years	70–74 years	75 years and older
Women	43.6%	60.9%	37.1%
Men	28%	34.2%	11.6%

Source: Gendell 2008:47.

AGEISM AND DISCRIMINATION

Physician Robert Butler (1990) became concerned 30 years ago when he learned that a housing development near his home in metropolitan Washington, D.C., barred the elderly. Butler coined the term **ageism** to refer to prejudice and discrimination based on a person's age. For example, we may choose to assume that someone cannot handle a rigorous job because he is "too old," or we may refuse to give someone a job with authority because she is "too young."

In order to more fully understand issues regarding aging, it is important to also consider the impact of social structure on patterns of aging. Critics argue that neither disengagement nor activity theory answers the question of *why* social interaction must change or decrease in old age. The low status of older people is seen in prejudice and discrimination against them, in age segregation, and in unfair job practices—none of which are directly addressed by either disengagement or activity theory.

ageism Prejudice and discrimination based on a person's age.

Although firing people simply because they are old violates federal law, courts have upheld the right to lay off older workers for economic reasons. Critics contend that, later, the same firms hire young, cheaper workers to replace experienced older workers. When economic growth slows and companies cut back on their workforces, the number of complaints of age bias rises sharply as older workers begin to suspect they were bearing a disproportionate share of the layoffs. According to the Equal Employment Opportunity Commission, between 1999 and 2007, complaints of age discrimination rose more than 35 percent. However, evidence of a countertrend has emerged. To hang on to experienced workers, some firms have been giving larger raises to older workers, to encourage their retirement at the higher salary—a tactic that prompts younger workers to complain of age discrimination (EEOC 2008; Roscigno 2010).

A controlled experiment conducted by the AARP (formerly known as the American Association of Retired Persons) confirmed that older people often face discrimination when applying for jobs. Comparable résumés for two applicants—one 57 years old and the other 32 years old—were sent to 775 large firms and employment agencies around the United States. In situations for which positions were actually available, the younger applicant received a favorable response 43 percent of the time. By contrast, the older applicant received favorable responses only 17 percent of the time. One Fortune 500 corporation asked the younger applicant for more information while informing the older applicant that no appropriate positions were open (Bendick, Jackson, and Romero 1993; Neumark 2008).

> hospice care Treatment of the terminally ill in their own homes, or in special hospital units or other facilities, with the goal of helping them to die comfortably, without pain.

As a group, elderly people in the United States enjoy a standard of living that is much higher now than at any point in the nation's past. Class differences among the elderly remain evident but tend to narrow somewhat. Those older people who enjoyed middle-class incomes while younger tend to remain better off after retirement, but less so than before (Smith 2003).

To some extent, older people owe their overall improved standard of living to a greater accumulation of wealth—in the form of home ownership, private pensions, and other financial assets. But much of the improvement is due to more generous Social Security benefits. While modest when compared with other countries' pension programs, Social Security nevertheless provides 37 percent of all income received by older people in the United States. Still, in 2008, 9.7 percent of people age 65 or older lived below the poverty line (DeNavas-Walt 2009, Proctor and Smith 2009b; Social Security Administration 2008).

Members of groups who face a greater likelihood of income inequality earlier in their lives, including women and members of racial and ethnic minorities, continue to do so when they are older. For women aged 65 or older, the poverty rate is 11.9 percent compared to the rate for elderly men of 6.7 percent. Considering race and ethnicity, in 2008, 19.3 percent of Latinos aged 65 or older had incomes below the poverty level, which was more than twice the rate of 7.6 percent for non-Hispanic Whites. The 20.0 percent poverty rate for elderly African Americans was more than two-and-a-half times as high (DeNavas-Walt et al. 2009; U.S. Census Bureau 2008f:Table Pov01).

DEATH AND DYING

In the film *The Bucket List*, Morgan Freeman and Jack Nicholson play the two main characters, who are diagnosed with terminal cancer and have less than one year to live. They make a list of all the things they would like to do before they "kick the bucket." On the list are things they had never dared to do, such as traveling the world and skydiving, but it also includes reconciling broken relationships.

> First you are young; then you are middle-aged; then you are old; then you are wonderful.
>
> **Lady Diana Cooper**

Until recently, death was a taboo topic in the United States. Death represents a fundamental disruption that cannot be undone, so we often find it easier to live with a sense of denial about our mortality. In the words of sociologist Peter Berger, "Death presents society with a formidable problem . . . because it threatens the basic assumptions of order on which society rests" (1969:23). However, psychologist Elisabeth Kübler-Ross (1969), through her pioneering book *On Death and Dying,* greatly encouraged open discussion of the process of dying. Drawing on her work with 200 cancer patients, Kübler-Ross identified five stages of the experience: denial, anger, bargaining, depression, and finally acceptance.

While we may still be uncomfortable with the topic, *The Bucket List*'s portrayal of a "good death" represents one of the ways we have become more open about it. Gerontologist Richard Kalish (1985) laid out some of the issues people must face in order to prepare for a "good death." These included completing unfinished business, such as settling insurance and inheritance matters; restoring harmony to social relationships and saying farewell to friends and family; dealing with medical needs; and making funeral plans and other arrangements for survivors. In accomplishing these tasks, the dying person actively contributes to smooth intergenerational transitions, role continuity, compliance with medical procedures, and minimal disruption of the social system, despite the loss of a loved one.

We have also begun to create institutions to facilitate our wishes for a good death. The practice of **hospice care,** introduced in England in the 1960s, is devoted to easing this final transition. Hospice workers seek to improve the quality of a dying person's last days by offering comfort and by helping the person to remain at home, or in a homelike setting at a hospital or other special facility, until the end. Currently, there are more than 3200 hospice programs serving almost 1 million people a year.

Recent studies in the United States suggest additional ways in which people have broken through the historical taboos about death. For example, bereavement practices—once highly structured—are becoming increasingly varied and therapeutic. More and more people are actively addressing the inevitability of death by making wills, establishing "living wills" (health care proxies that explain their feelings about the use of life support equipment), donating organs, and providing instructions for family members about funerals, cremations, and burials. Given medical and technological advances and increasingly open discussion and negotiation regarding death and dying, it is possible that good deaths may become a social norm in the United States (Pew Research Center 2006).

We encounter some of the most difficult socialization challenges (and rites of passage) in these later years of life. Retirement undermines the sense of self we had that was based in our occupation, a particularly significant source of identity in the United States. Similarly, taking stock of our accomplishments and disappointments, coping with declining physical abilities, and recognizing the inevitability of death may lead to painful adjustments. Part of the difficulty is that potential answers to the "Now what?" question that we might have asked in previous life stages are dwindling, and we begin to face the end of our days.

And yet, as we reflect on the story of our lives, we can look back to see all the people who shaped us into becoming who we are. Such relationships play a crucial role in our overall self-concept and self-satisfaction. As we have already seen, we are interdependent. And, though the influences of others on our life can be both a blessing and a curse, we wouldn't be who we are without them.

Stop! Go on a "technology fast," and give up email, blogs, Facebook, MySpace, texting, computers, and even your cell phone for a day. Keep a journal of how you respond.

For REVIEW

I. **How do we become our self?**
- We are born with innate tendencies, but we depend upon the socializing influences of others with whom we interact to provide us with the cultural tools necessary for our survival.

II. **Who shapes our socialization?**
- Although almost anyone with whom we interact can have a significant influence on us, particularly important to our development are the family, school, peer group, mass media, religion, and the state.

III. **How does our development change over time?**
- We learn new things at various stages of our life course, experiencing significant transitions as we pass from childhood to adulthood and again from adulthood into retirement. At each stage, the kinds of things expected of us by others shift significantly.

FUNCTIONALIST VIEW

Socialization is a **lifelong process** that enables us to **learn the attitudes, values, and behaviors** appropriate for our culture.

Socialization promotes **integration** and **intimacy** with others and keeps us from being isolated.

The institutions of the family, school, mass media, workplace, government, and religion act as **agents of socialization** from childhood through adulthood.

INTEGRATION, AGENTS OF SOCIALIZATION
KEY CONCEPTS

Conflict View

We learn to accept a culture's dominant ideology as natural, which **reinforces existing inequalities.**

Alternative perspectives and experiences are often underrepresented and devalued.

Schools help reproduce the status quo in the way they socialize students into the proper attitudes and behaviors of the workplace.

KEY CONCEPTS
GENDER AND RACE, INEQUALITY

Interactionist View

Our **concept of the self,** who we are, emerges from our interactions with others.

Parents, friends, co-workers, coaches, teachers are among the **significant others** who play a major role in socialization and shaping a person's self.

Role taking, impression management, and face-work are concepts that convey the idea of social interactions as **performances.**

KEY CONCEPTS
CONCEPT OF SELF, PERFORMANCE

MAKE THE CONNECTION

After reviewing the chapter, answer the following questions:

1

How would each perspective approach the impact extreme isolation has on people (p. 73)?

2

How would each perspective explain the role socialization performs among children (pp. 75-78)?

3

How would a functionalist look at anticipatory socialization (p. 81)? How might this differ from a conflict approach (p. 90)?

4

Which agents of socialization have been most influential in your life? How does each perspective help shed light on those influences?

Pop Quiz

1. The nurture side of the nature–nurture debate argues that
   a. socialization plays a critical role in shaping our attitudes, values, and behaviors.
   b. our attitudes, values, and behaviors are largely inherited biologically through our DNA.
   c. sociology has a limited role in explaining our behaviors before age two.
   d. we cannot determine the degree to which our behaviors are shaped by heredity or environment.

2. According to Charles Horton Cooley, the process of developing a self-identity by imagining how others see us is known as
   a. socialization.
   b. the looking-glass self.
   c. the Me.
   d. the generalized other.

3. In George Herbert Mead's *play stage* of socialization, people mentally assume the perspectives of others, thereby enabling them to respond from that imagined viewpoint. This process is referred to as
   a. symbolization.
   b. the significant other.
   c. impression management.
   d. role taking.

4. Suppose a clerk tries to appear busier than he or she actually is when a supervisor happens to be watching. Erving Goffman would say this is a form of what?
   a. degradation ceremony
   b. impression management
   c. resocialization
   d. looking-glass self

5. Which social institution is considered to be the most important agent of socialization in the United States, especially for children?
   a. family
   b. school
   c. peer group
   d. mass media

6. The term *gender role* refers to
   a. the biological fact that we are male or female.
   b. a role that is given to us by a teacher.
   c. a role that is given to us in a play.
   d. expectations regarding the proper behavior, attitudes, and activities of males and females.

7. On the first day of basic training in the army, a male recruit has his civilian clothes replaced with army "greens," has his hair shaved off, loses his privacy, and finds that he must use a communal bathroom. All of these humiliating activities are part of
   a. becoming a significant other.
   b. impression management.
   c. a degradation ceremony.
   d. face-work.

8. What do sociologists call the symbolic representations of major change in a person's status throughout their life course?
   a. rites of passage
   b. anticipatory socialization
   c. impression management
   d. role taking

9. The process of discarding former behavior patterns and taking on new ones is known as what?
   a. resocialization
   b. impression management
   c. anticipatory socialization
   d. the I

10. Which theory argues that elderly people have essentially the same need for social interaction as any other group and that those who remain active and socially involved will be best adjusted?
    a. disengagement theory
    b. institutional discrimination theory
    c. activity theory
    d. ageism theory

1. (a); 2. (b); 3. (d); 4. (b); 5. (a); 6. (d); 7. (c); 8. (a); 9. (a); 10. (c)

5

SOCIAL

BECOMING AN INDIVIDUAL IN SOCIETY

"Tattooing had really never entered my awareness very much. When it did, the associations were always with sailors first, ex-convicts second, and various toughs and gangsters last. . . . I had read in some obscure novel about the three signs of 'badness'—socks rolled down to the ankle, long sideburns, and a tattoo showing on the wrist. Robert Mitchum's demented killer had *Love* and *Hate* tattooed on the fingers of each hand." So writes Samuel M. Steward (1990:8) of his perception of tattoos back in the 1950s, a perception widely shared by others at the time. Steward had been a college professor for 20 years, but he decided to walk away from that to become a tattoo artist. You might say he was ahead of his time.

Times change, and so do we. Nowadays almost 40 percent of people 18–40 years old have at least one tattoo. So many people have them—including society's trendsetters and major sports figures—that mainstream culture accepts tattoos. Yet, for those who grew up in an earlier era, perhaps the stigma remains: Only 10 percent of people aged 41–64 have tattoos.

In fact, knowing a person's age allows us to predict a variety of things about how they think and what they do. Research on "Millennials," the generation of people who are currently 18–29 years old, finds them to be more confident, self-expressive, and open to change than previous generations. They are more ethnically and racially diverse. They are more racially tolerant, more receptive of immigrants, and more accepting of homosexuality. They enthusiastically embrace technological advances and are more than twice as likely to have created a social networking profile, or to have used Twitter, than are those in the Baby Boom generation (ages 46–64). Millennials will likely be the most educated generation in American history (Pew Research Center 2010a).

Although we like to think of our preferences as a matter of our own individual choice, when we are born shapes our tastes. Like age, our gender, race, class, ethnicity, nationality, education, religious affiliation, occupation, and income all shape how we think, what we do, and even how we feel. Sociology investigates how those positions combine to form our social structure.

STRUCTURE &INTERACTION

As You READ >>

- What makes up society?
- How does social structure shape individual action?
- How do sociologists describe traditional versus modern societies?

>> Social Interaction

Whether we are working together to construct culture or learning from each other through socialization, we do so via **social interaction,** the shared experiences through which people relate to one another. Through this process we come to know what is expected of us. When parents discipline us or teachers praise us, we use those punishments and rewards to better inform how we might act in the future. The choices we make create patterns of behavior over time; thus our everyday interactions form the building blocks of society.

social interaction The shared experiences through which people relate to one another.

SELF AND SOCIETY

We come to be who we are through the daily interactions we have with others—whether going to class, working on the job, or driving in traffic. We seek to make sense of our interactions as they occur. Charles Horton Cooley, as we saw in Chapter 4, suggests that we interpret the responses others have to us, using them as a kind of mirror to inform our understanding of our self. Such an approach moves away from conceiving the self as an isolated, singular, unchanging object. In the words of George Herbert Mead (1934), "Selves can only exist in definite relationships to other selves. No hard-and-fast line can be drawn between our own selves and the selves of others" (p. 164). This social or relational conception of the self runs counter to the dominant sense of the self in the United States expressed in phrases such as "rugged individualism" or "I did it my way." But even these phrases are collective sentiments learned in the context of U.S. culture.

Over time we develop routine patterns of behavior that we take for granted—sitting in the same desk, having lunch with the same co-workers, traveling the same route. We do the same things and think many of the same thoughts, day after day. And so do others. Sometimes these practices are solidified into formal and informal norms, or institutionalized in the form of laws. The resulting predictability allows us to know what to do most of the time.

In time the positions we occupy relative to others (such as student, boss, or traffic cop) become common to others beyond our immediate sphere of experience, people with whom we do not directly interact. It then becomes possible to talk about the positions themselves, and the various relationships between them, apart from the individuals who occupy them. The end result is society—the structure of relationships within which culture is created and shared through regularized patterns of social interaction.

SOCIAL CONSTRUCTION OF REALITY

In working out the relationship between our self and society, we are engaged in the "social construction of reality." Sociologists Peter Berger and Thomas Luckmann (1966) use this phrase to describe the interdependent relationship in which we as individuals create society through our actions and, at the same time, become products of the society we construct. They present their argument in their three-part model of world construction. The three parts include

- *Constructing culture.* Our actions are not strictly determined by biological instincts. In order to survive, we must establish a relationship to nature and with each other. We do so by creating tools, language, ideas, beliefs, rules for behavior, and so on to establish order and meaning. Culture enables us to make sense of our experiences and to pattern our actions. (See Chapter 3 on culture.)
- *Constructing the self.* We become products of the worlds we create. Any time we enter into a new social world (for example, at birth, going away to college, the first day at a new job, marriage), we do not begin

from scratch. We are shaped by the tools, ideas, and rules for action that have been constructed by others who have gone before us. We learn how we should think and act through our interactions with others, sharing ideas and experiences. Through socialization, we are constrained by the very culture we construct. (See Chapter 4 on socialization.)

- *Constructing society.* Between these first two steps is an intervening stage in which we share the culture we create with others. Once it is shared, we lose control over it as individuals. It is no longer something "I" control; it is now in "our" hands. As a result of our shared acceptance, it comes to feel solid, real, or natural, even though we created it in the first place. One way to think of it is as an environment, a social world, or a structure within which we live. We come to take for granted that it simply "is."

In short, the social construction of reality is an ongoing process of constructing the objects, knowledge, and rules for behavior that we come to share collectively. These creations then shape or limit the ideas and actions that are available to us, but we then use them to create new culture. The result is predictability and order that is necessary for social interaction and collective action. Through social interaction, we are always creating and being created, producers and products.

The more we share culture with others, the more resistant it becomes to change. The ability to define social reality often reflects a group's power within a society. In fact, one of the crucial aspects of the relationship between dominant and subordinate groups is the ability of the former to set values and norms. Those who wield power and influence in a society are often reluctant to relinquish their positions of control. As a result, it is a struggle to change the meanings attached to the positions people occupy. Since the mid-1900s—starting with the civil rights movement of the 1950s and 1960s and continuing among women, the elderly, gays and lesbians, and people with disabilities—an important aspect of the process of social change has involved redefining or reconstructing social reality.

When members of subordinate groups challenge traditional social assumptions, they can raise our collective awareness about the consequences of group membership or social position and help us to perceive and experience reality in a new way. For example, when Olympic gold medalist Muhammad Ali began his professional boxing career in the early 1960s, he was much like any other young Black fighter. He was managed and sponsored by a White syndicate and went by his given name, Cassius Clay. Soon, however, the young boxer rebelled against the old stereotypes of the self-effacing Black athlete and began to define his own social role. He converted to Islam, becoming a member of the U.S.-based Nation of Islam, and abandoned his "slave name" to take the name Muhammad Ali. He insisted on expressing his own political views, including refusing to fight in the Vietnam War. Ali changed the terms of social interaction for Black athletes by rebelling against racist thinking and terminology. In redefining social reality, he helped open up greater opportunities for himself and for other African Americans in the world of sports and beyond.

>> Elements of Social Structure

Although not all sociologists accept the idea that society is a real, objective thing, the concepts of society and social structure provide tools useful when trying to make sense of why we act and think the way we do. **Social structure** consists of a series of predictable relationships composed of various positions people occupy. Structure, as the word implies, provides order. It appears to exist outside of us and precedes us. We learn to move into the social positions that already exist, usually taking their legitimacy for granted. We may not want to take the existence of "society" as an object too literally, but it does help us examine and understand the myriad ways that people act and interact. We can identify the following elements that make up social structure: statuses, social roles, groups, social networks, virtual worlds, and social institutions.

> **social structure** The way in which a society is organized into predictable relationships.

> **status** The social positions we occupy relative to others.

STATUSES

Status is perhaps the most basic component of social structure. It refers to the social positions we occupy relative to others. Such positions exist independent of the individuals who occupy them. Within our society, a person can occupy the status of student, fruit picker, son or daughter, violinist, teenager, resident of St. Louis, dental technician, or neighbor. A person can also occupy a number of different ent statuses at the same time.

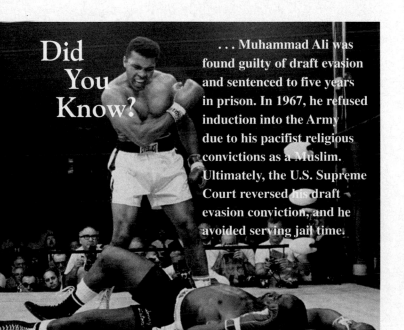

Did You Know?

... Muhammad Ali was found guilty of draft evasion and sentenced to five years in prison. In 1967, he refused induction into the Army due to his pacifist religious convictions as a Muslim. Ultimately, the U.S. Supreme Court reversed his draft evasion conviction, and he avoided serving jail time.

Social Statuses

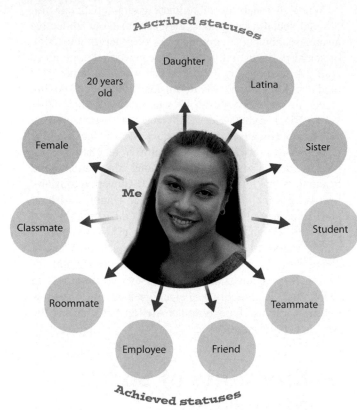

Ascribed statuses

Daughter · Latina · 20 years old · Sister · Female · Me · Classmate · Student · Roommate · Teammate · Employee · Friend

Achieved statuses

negative and confining stereotypes of the elderly. As a result of their work and that of other groups supporting older citizens, the ascribed status of "senior citizen" is no longer as difficult for millions of older people.

An ascribed status does not necessarily have the same social meaning in every society. In a cross-cultural study, sociologist Gary Huang (1988) confirmed the long-held view that respect for the elderly is an important cultural norm in China. There, in many cases, the prefix "old" is used respectfully: calling someone "old teacher" or "old person" is like calling a judge in the United States "your honor." Huang points out that such positive old-age-related language distinctions are uncommon in the United States; consequently, we view the term "old man" as more of an insult than a celebration of seniority and wisdom.

Unlike ascribed statuses, an **achieved status** is a social position that is within our power to change. Both bank president and prison guard are achieved statuses, as are lawyer, pianist, sorority member, convict, and social worker. We must do something to acquire an achieved status—go to school, learn a skill, establish a friendship, invent a new product, commit a crime, and so on. But our ascribed status can heavily influence our achieved status. Being male in the United States, for example, still decreases the likelihood that a person will consider child care as a career.

Master Status Each of us holds many different and sometimes conflicting statuses; some may connote a higher social position, and others a lower position. How, then, do others view our overall social position? According to sociologist Everett Hughes (1945), societies deal with inconsistencies by agreeing that certain statuses are more important than others. A **master status** is a status that dominates others and thereby determines a person's general position in society. For example, in 1998, Michael J. Fox revealed that he was diagnosed

Ascribed and Achieved Status Sociologists categorize statuses as either ascribed or achieved. An **ascribed status** is assigned to a person by society without regard for the person's unique talents or characteristics. Generally, the assignment takes place at birth; thus a person's age, race/ethnicity, and sex are all considered ascribed statuses. Though such characteristics are biological in origin, the key is the social meaning we attach to such categories. Ascribed statuses are often used to justify privileges or reflect a person's membership in a subordinate group, and we will analyze the impacts of race, ethnicity, and gender as ascribed statuses in Chapters 12 and 13.

In most cases, we can do little to change an ascribed status. We can, however, attempt to change the traditional constraints associated with it. For example, since its founding in 1971, the activist political group Gray Panthers has worked for the rights of older people and tried to modify society's

ascribed status A social position assigned to a person by society without regard for the person's unique talents or characteristics.

achieved status A social position that is within our power to change.

master status A status that dominates others and thereby determines a person's general position in society.

with Parkinson's disease. He had a remarkable career in films and television, but now his status as a well-known personality with Parkinson's may outweigh his statuses as actor, author, and political activist.

People with disabilities frequently observe that the nondisabled see them only as blind, or only as wheelchair users, and so on, rather than as complex human beings with individual strengths and weaknesses whose disability is merely one aspect of their lives. Often people with disabilities find that their status as "disabled" receives undue weight, overshadowing their actual ability to hold meaningful employment and contributing to widespread prejudice, discrimination, and segregation. For example, most voting places are inaccessible to wheelchair users and fail to provide ballots that can be used by the blind. Activists argue that such unnecessary and discriminatory barriers restrict people with disabilities more than do any biological limitations.

Ascribed statuses frequently influence our achieved status. The African American activist Malcolm X (1925–1965), an eloquent and controversial advocate of Black power and Black pride in the 1960s, recalled that his feelings and perspectives changed dramatically while in eighth grade. When his English teacher, a White man, advised him that his goal of becoming a lawyer was ridiculous and suggested he become a carpenter instead, Malcolm X (1964:37) found that his position as a Black man (ascribed status) was an obstacle to his dream of becoming a lawyer (achieved status). In the United States, the ascribed statuses of race and gender can function as master statuses that play an important part in one's efforts to achieve a desired professional and social status.

SOCIAL ROLES

The statuses we occupy imply both rights and responsibilities. A **social role** is a set of expectations for people who occupy a given social position or status. While we occupy a status, we play a role. Thus, in the United States, we expect that cab drivers will know how to get around a city, that receptionists will handle phone messages, and that police officers will take action if they see a citizen being threatened. With each distinctive social status—whether ascribed or achieved—come particular role expectations. However, actual performance varies from individual to individual. One secretary may assume extensive administrative responsibilities, whereas another may focus on clerical duties.

Roles are a significant component of social structure. Roles can contribute to a society's stability by enabling members to anticipate the behavior of others and to pattern their own actions accordingly. Yet social roles can also restrict people's interactions and relationships. If we view a person *only* as a police officer or a supervisor, it will be difficult to relate to him or her as a friend or neighbor.

Role Conflict Sometimes the statuses we occupy can clash. **Role conflict** occurs when incompatible expectations arise from two or more social statuses held by the same person. Fulfillment of the roles associated with one position may directly violate the roles linked to a second status.

Imagine the delicate situation of a woman who has worked for a decade on an assembly line in an electrical plant and has recently been named supervisor of her unit. She now must balance her status as a friend with her status as the boss. How should she treat her longtime friends and co-workers? Should she still have lunch with them? Should she recommend the firing of an old friend who cannot keep up with the demands of the assembly line? She will most likely experience a sharp conflict between her friendship and supervisory roles. Such role conflicts involve difficult ethical choices. The new supervisor will have to make a difficult decision about how much allegiance she owes her friend and how much she owes her employers, who have given her supervisory responsibilities.

social role A set of expectations for people who occupy a given social position or status.

role conflict The situation that occurs when incompatible expectations arise from two or more social statuses held by the same person.

Another type of role conflict occurs when individuals move into occupations that are not common among people with their ascribed status. Male preschool teachers and female police officers experience this type of role conflict. In the latter case, the women must strive to reconcile their workplace role in law enforcement with the societal view of a woman's proper role, which historically has not embraced many skills associated with police work. And even as female police officers encounter sexual harassment, as women do throughout the labor force, they must also deal with the "code of silence," an informal norm that precludes their implicating fellow officers in wrongdoing (Maher 2008; Pershing 2003).

Role Strain Role conflict describes the situation of a person dealing with the challenge of occupying two social positions simultaneously. However, even a single status can cause problems. Sociologists use the term **role strain** to describe the difficulty that arises when the same social status imposes conflicting demands and expectations.

People who belong to minority cultures may experience role strain while working in the mainstream culture. Criminologist Larry Gould (2002) interviewed officers of the Navajo Nation Police Department and found that they faced role strain when responding to the majority and minority communities. They were expected to follow the official policies and procedures defined by conventional law enforcement officials (sheriffs and FBI agents). At the same time, Navajo Nation officers practice an alternative form of justice known as Peacemaking, in which they seek reconciliation between the parties to a crime or grievance. The officers expressed great confidence in Peacemaking but worried that if they did not make arrests, other law enforcement officials would think they were too soft or were "just taking care of their own." All felt the strain of being considered "too Navajo" or "not Navajo enough."

role strain The difficulty that arises when the same social status imposes conflicting demands and expectations.

role exit The process of disengagement from a role that is central to one's self-identity in order to establish a new role and identity.

Role Exit Often, when we think of assuming a social role, we focus on the preparation and anticipatory socialization a person undergoes for that role. Such is true if a person is about to become an attorney, a chef, a spouse, or a parent. Yet, sociologists also pay attention to the adjustments involved in leaving social roles.

Sociologist Helen Rose Fuchs Ebaugh (1988) used the term **role exit** to describe the process of disengagement from a role that is central to one's self-identity in order to establish a new role and identity. Drawing on interviews—with, among others, ex-convicts, divorced men and women, recovering alcoholics, ex-nuns, former doctors, retirees, and transsexuals—Ebaugh (herself a former nun) studied the process of voluntarily exiting from significant social roles.

Ebaugh has offered a four-stage model of role exit. The first stage begins with doubt. The person experiences frustration, burnout, or simply unhappiness with an accustomed status and the roles associated with that social position. The second stage involves a search for alternatives. An individual who is unhappy with his or her career may take a leave of absence; an unhappily married couple may begin what they see as a trial separation.

The third stage of role exit is the action stage, or departure. Ebaugh found that the vast majority of her respondents could identify a clear turning point when it became essential to take final action and leave their jobs, end their marriages, or engage in some other type of role exit. Only 20 percent of respondents saw their role exit as

Sociologist Helen Rose Fuchs Ebaugh interviewed transsexuals (as pictured here) and others exiting from significant social roles in order to develop her four-stage model of role exit.

a gradual, evolutionary process that had no single turning point.

The last stage of role exit involves the creation of a new identity. Traditionally, students experience a form of role exit when they make the transition from high school to college. They may leave behind the role of a child living at home and take on the role of a somewhat independent college student living with peers in a dorm. Sociologist Ira Silver (1996) has studied the central role that material objects play in this transition. The objects students choose to leave at home (like stuffed animals and dolls) are associated with their prior identities. They may remain deeply attached to those objects but not want them to be seen as

SOC THINK

Whether from a sports team, a religious group, the military, or some other close-knit group, what experience, if any, have you had with role exiting? To what extent does your experience match the four stages Ebaugh describes?

While I love teaching, I hate grading. When I mention that to students they say I have no one to blame but myself; if I didn't assign things I wouldn't have to grade them. But I don't teach in a vacuum. If I didn't assign papers and tests students would focus their time and energy on their looming chemistry test or their literature paper instead of reading for, participating in, or even attending my course. It is not that students aren't interested or sincere; it's that they are forced to budget their time for which professors compete using assignments. Because we exist in social systems, the expectations of those systems limit the amount of innovation we might desire.

part of their new identities at college. The objects they bring with them symbolize how they now see themselves and how they wish to be perceived. iPods and wall posters, for example, are calculated to say, "This is me."

GROUPS

Statuses combine in various ways to form social groups. In sociological terms, a **group** is any number of people with shared norms, values, and goals who interact with one another on a regular basis. The members of a women's basketball team, a hospital's business office, a synagogue, or a symphony orchestra constitute a group. However, the residents of a suburb would not be considered a group, because they rarely interact with one another at one time.

> **group** Any number of people with shared norms, values, and goals who interact with one another on a regular basis.
>
> **primary group** A small group characterized by intimate, face-to-face association and cooperation.

We spend much of our time interacting in group settings. The type of group we are in influences our level of commitment and participation. Some groups demand our almost undivided attention and shape our core identity; others allow us to more easily accomplish specific goals.

Primary and Secondary Groups Charles Horton Cooley (1902) coined the term **primary group** to refer to a small group characterized by intimate, face-to-face association and cooperation. Such groups often entail long-term commitment and involve more of what we think of as our whole self. The members of a street gang can constitute a primary group; so can members of a family

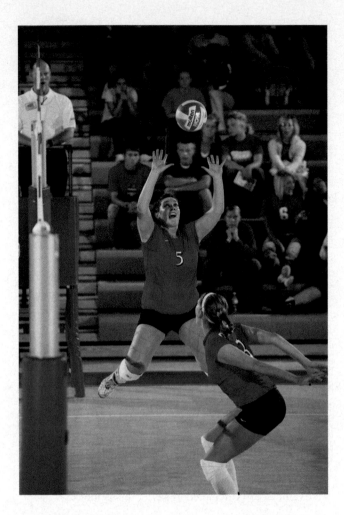

Comparison of Primary and Secondary Groups

Primary group	Secondary group
Generally small	Usually large
Relatively long period of interaction	Relatively short duration, often temporary
Intimate, face-to-face association	Little social intimacy or mutual understanding
Some emotional depth to relationships	Relationships generally superficial
Cooperative, friendly	More formal and impersonal

occupying the same household, or a group of "sisters" living in a college sorority.

Primary groups shape who we are and what we think about ourselves, thus playing a pivotal role both in the socialization process and in the development of our statuses and roles. Indeed, whether with family, friends, or teammates, primary groups can be instrumental in our day-to-day existence. When we find ourselves identifying closely with a group, it is probably a primary group.

We also participate in many groups that are not characterized by close bonds of friendship, such as large college classes and business associations. The term **secondary group** refers to a formal, impersonal group in which there is little social intimacy or mutual understanding. Participation in such groups is typically more instrumental or goal-directed, often involving only what we think of as one part of our self. Given these characteristics, we are more likely to move into and out of such groups as suits our needs.

The distinction between primary and secondary groups is not always clear-cut, however. Some social clubs may become so large and impersonal that they no longer

secondary group A formal, impersonal group in which there is little social intimacy or mutual understanding.

in-group Any group or category to which people feel they belong.

out-group A group or category to which people feel they do not belong.

function as primary groups; similarly, some work groups can become so close-knit that they are experienced as primary groups (Hochschild 1989). The accompanying table demonstrates some significant differences between primary and secondary groups.

In-Groups and Out-Groups In addition to degree of intimacy, groups can hold special meaning for members because of their relationship to other groups. For example, people in one group sometimes feel antagonistic toward or threatened by another group, especially if that group is perceived as being different either culturally or racially. To identify these "we" and "they" feelings, sociologists use two terms first employed by William Graham Sumner (1906): in-group and out-group.

An **in-group** can be defined as any group or category to which people feel they belong. Simply put, it comprises everyone who is regarded as "we" or "us." The in-group may be as narrow as a teenage clique or as broad as an entire society. The very existence of an in-group implies the existence of an out-group that is viewed as "they" or "them." An **out-group** is a group or category to which people feel they do not belong.

In-group members typically feel distinct and superior, seeing themselves as better than people in the out-group. Proper behavior for the in-group can be simultaneously viewed as unacceptable

Every society honors its live conformists,
and its dead troublemakers.

Mignon McLaughlin

behavior for the out-group. This double standard enhances the sense of superiority. Sociologist Robert Merton (1968) described this process as the conversion of "in-group virtues" into "out-group vices." We can see this differential standard operating in the context of terrorism. When a group or a nation takes aggressive actions, it usually justifies them as necessary even if civilians are hurt or killed. Opponents are quick to assign the emotion-laden label

of *terrorist* to such actions and to appeal to the world community for condemnation. Yet these same people may themselves retaliate with actions that hurt civilians, which the first group will then condemn as terrorist acts (Juergensmeyer 2003).

Reference Groups Both in-groups and primary groups can dramatically influence the way an individual thinks and behaves. Sociologists call any group that individuals use as a standard for evaluating themselves and their own behavior a **reference group.** For example, a high school student who aspires to join a social circle of hip-hop music devotees will pattern his or her behavior after that of the group. The student will begin

> **reference group** Any group that individuals use as a standard for evaluating themselves and their own behavior.

SOCTHINK

How do in-groups and out-groups function in a typical U.S. high school? What groups are common? How are boundaries separating insiders and outsiders maintained?

dressing like these peers, listening to the same downloads and DVDs, and hanging out at the same stores and clubs.

Reference groups have two basic purposes. They serve a normative function by setting and enforcing standards of conduct and belief. The high school student who wants the approval of the hip-hop crowd will have to follow the group's dictates, at least to some extent. Reference groups also perform a comparison function by serving as a standard against which people can measure themselves and others. An actor will evaluate him- or herself against a reference group composed of others in the acting profession (Merton and Kitt 1950).

coalition A temporary or permanent alliance geared toward a common goal.

social network A series of social relationships that links individuals directly to others and, through them, indirectly to still more people.

Often, two or more reference groups influence us at the same time. Our family members, neighbors, and co-workers all shape different aspects of our self-evaluation. In addition, reference group attachments change during the life cycle. A corporate executive who quits the rat race at age 45 to become a social worker will find new reference groups to use as standards for evaluation. We shift reference groups as we take on different statuses during our lives.

Coalitions As groups grow larger, coalitions begin to develop. A **coalition** is an alliance, whether temporary or permanent, geared toward a common goal. Coalitions can be broad-based or narrow and can take on many different objectives. Sociologist William Julius Wilson (1999) has reported on community-based organizations in Texas that include Whites and Latinos, working-class and affluent, who banded together to work for improved sidewalks, better drainage systems, and comprehensive street paving.

Out of this type of coalition building, Wilson hopes, will emerge better interracial understanding.

Some coalitions are intentionally short-lived. Short-term coalition building is a key to success in popular TV programs like *Survivor* and *Big Brother* in which players gain a strategic advantage by banding together to vote others off the island or out of the house. The political world is also the scene of many temporary coalitions. For example, in 2003, President George W. Bush established a "Coalition of the Willing": 45 nations dedicated to removing Saddam Hussein from power in Iraq and willing to provide troops to accomplish that goal. The Iraq invasion began in March 2003, and Hussein was captured in December 2003.

SOCIAL NETWORKS

Groups do not merely serve to define other elements of the social structure, such as roles and statuses; they also link the individual with the larger society. We all belong to a number of groups, and through our acquaintances, we connect with people in different social circles. Such connections comprise a **social network**—a series of social relationships that link individuals directly to others, and through them indirectly to still more people. Social networks can center on virtually any activity, from sharing job information to exchanging news and gossip. Some networks may constrain people by limiting the range of their interactions, yet networks can also empower people by making vast resources available to them (Watts 2004).

Sometimes the connections are intentional and public; other times networks can develop that link us together in ways that are not intentional or apparent. Sociologists Peter Bearman, James Moody, and Katherine Stovel (2004) investigated one such network, asking themselves this question: If you drew a chart of the romantic relationship network at a typical American high school, what would it look like? Using careful data collection techniques to enhance the validity of their findings, they found that 573 of the 832 students they surveyed had been either romantically or sexually involved in the previous 18 months. Of these, 63 couples connected only with each other as pairs with no other partners. Other students connected directly or indirectly with a handful of partners. One larger group, however, connected 288 students directly or indirectly into a single extended network (see the figure "Adolescent Sexual Networks"). Such an example points to the fact that the choices we make often link us with others both known and unknown.

Networks can also serve as a social resource that is every bit as valuable to us as economic resources when it comes to shaping our opportunities. Involvement in social networks—commonly known as "networking"—can be especially valuable in finding employment. For example, a 2009 survey of executives revealed that 73 percent found

Adolescent Sexual Networks

Each dot represents a boy or girl at "Jefferson High." The lines that link them represent romantic and sexual relationships that occurred over an 18-month period. Though most of the teenagers had had just one or two partners, 288 of the 832 students interviewed were linked in a giant sexual network. Another 90 students were involved in relationships outside the school (not shown on this chart).

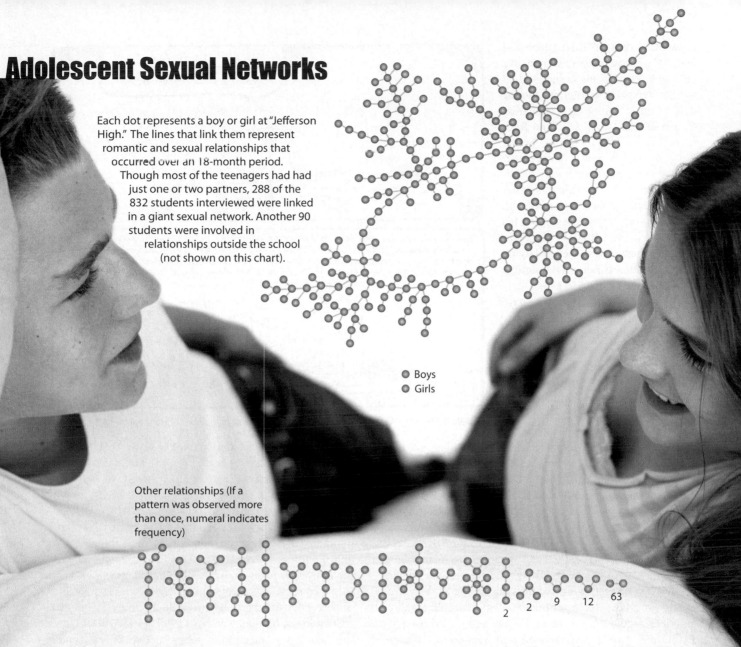

● Boys
● Girls

Other relationships (If a pattern was observed more than once, numeral indicates frequency)

2   2   9   12   63

Source: Bearman, Moody, and Stovel 2004:58.

job opportunities through network connections, compared to 14 percent by responding to job postings, and 9 percent by posting a résumé to a database or maintaining an online profile (ExecuNet 2009).

In the workplace, networking pays off more for men than for women because of the traditional presence of men in leadership positions. One survey of executives found that 63 percent of the men used networking to find new jobs, compared to 41 percent of the women. Thirty-one percent of the women used classified ads to find jobs, compared to only 13 percent of the men. Still, women at all levels of the paid labor force are beginning to make effective use of social networks. A study of women who were leaving the welfare rolls to enter the paid workforce found that networking was an effective tool in their search for employment. Informal networking also helped them to locate child care and better housing—keys to

successful employment (Benschop 2009; Carey and McLean 1997).

VIRTUAL WORLDS

Today, with recent advances in technology, people can maintain their social networks electronically; they don't need face-to-face contacts. Whether through text messaging, Blackberry devices, Skype, or social networking sites like Facebook, a significant amount of networking occurs online. Adolescents can now interact freely with distant friends, even under close scrutiny by parents or teachers. And employees with a taste for adventure can escape their work environments without leaving their cubicles.

The future of virtual networking and the effects it will have are difficult to predict. Consider Second Life (SL), a virtual world that included more than 15 million networked residents as of April 2010. More than 620,000 of those players were active per week. Participants in such virtual worlds typically create an **avatar** that is their online representation as a character, whether in the form of a 2-D or 3-D image or simply through text. The avatar that a player assumes may represent a very different looking-glass self from his or her actual identity. Once equipped with an avatar, the player goes about his or her life in the virtual world, establishing a business and even buying and decorating a home (Bainbridge 2007; Second Life 2010a).

In fact, virtual products have become a profitable business enterprise. Within the SL world, enterprising entrepreneurs sell a whole array of virtual products (land, houses, clothes, and even rainstorms) for real money. In 2009, $567 million USD were spent in user-to-user transactions within the SL world, and the top 25 SL avatars made a combined total of more than $12 million. Similarly, estimates are that Zynga, the company that produced the games Farmville and Mafia Wars for Facebook, has made more than $200 million selling virtual products including seeds, chickens, and crates (Fahmy 2010; Rosenwald 2010; Second Life 2010b).

> **avatar** A person's online representation as a character, whether in the form of a 2-D or 3-D image or simply through text.

Companies are increasingly taking advantage of the savings offered by conducting virtual meetings in the SL universe. Doing so allows for both increased global collaboration and decreased costs for travel. For example, IBM used SL for its past two annual Academy of Technology conferences, the most recent of which included 800 engineers and scientists, and saved hundreds of thousands of dollars as a result. Similarly, software engineering firm Agile

Dimensions estimates that it would have cost $35,695 to physically bring 35 people to its conference. Instead, its SL-based meeting cost $8,567 (mostly on software expenses), and the firm estimates savings of 27 tons of CO_2 emissions (Dodgson 2010; Machan 2010).

How will avatars affect our interactions in the future? A significant aspect of creating an avatar is the ability to control our virtual appearance. This change might take the emphasis away from physical or biological appearance and place it on social representation instead. Doing so may alter our perception of others and thus influence how we interact.

Sociologist Manuel Castells (1997, 1998, 2000) views these emerging electronic social networks as fundamental to new organizations and to the growth of existing businesses and associations; analysts such as Clay Shirky (2008) are trying to understand them. Shirky suggests that the Internet has radically transformed the possibilities for collective action. He argues that previous

As something of a spoof, CNET's online game review site, GameSpot, offered a tongue-in-cheek review of "Real Life." They gave it a 9.6 out of 10, saying that it features "believable characters, plenty of lasting appeal, and a lot of challenge and variety," and they described the game play as "extremely open-ended." They concluded that "if you take a step back and look at the big picture, you'll see that real life is an impressive and exciting experience, despite its occasional and sometimes noticeable problems" (Kasavin 2003). Part of what makes such a post amusing is that there is a sense that the boundary between the "real world" and virtual reality continues to blur. What happens, for example, when someone who is married in real life weds someone else's virtual-world character (Alter 2007)?

Shirky's Four Steps Toward Increased Internet Interaction

Step	Site
Sharing	Flikr; Bit Torrent; Del.icio.us
Conversation	Forums; MAKE; How To
Collaboration	Linux; Aegisub
Collective action	Flash Mob activism; NetRoots activisism

Source: Based on Shirky 2008.

technologies either allowed two-way communication that was small-scale because it was limited to individuals (e.g., the telephone), or facilitated large-scale group formation through broadcasting but was limited to one-way communication (e.g., talk radio listeners or fans of *Lost*). With the Internet, he suggests, "group action just got easier" because it supports interactive, large-scale group formation. He identifies a series of steps toward that end (see the accompanying table).

Finally, virtual networks can help to preserve real-world networks interrupted by war and other dislocations. In 2003, the deployment of U.S. troops in the Middle East increased many people's reliance on email. Today, digital photos and sound files accompany email messages between soldiers and their families and friends. GIs can even view siblings' graduations or children's birthday parties live, via webcams. And U.S. soldiers and Iraqi citizens have begun to post their opinions of the war in Iraq in online journals or blogs. Though critics are skeptical of the identity of some of the authors, these postings have become yet another source of news about the war (Faith 2005; O'Connor 2004; Sisson 2007).

SOCIAL INSTITUTIONS

Combinations of statuses, groups, and networks can coalesce to address the needs of a particular sector of society, forming what sociologists refer to as institutions. A **social institution** is an organized pattern of beliefs and behavior centered on basic social needs. Sociologists have tended to focus on five major institutions that serve as key elements of the larger social structure: family, education, religion, economy, and government. Though these institutions frequently overlap and interact, considering each institution individually provides us with a perspective within which we can analyze the larger social system. We will look in depth at all five in future chapters, but we begin here by considering the contributions each makes to the social structure.

> **social institution** An organized pattern of beliefs and behavior centered on basic social needs.

How we organize social interaction within each of these institutions helps contribute to social order. If a society is to survive, certain functions must be performed, and focusing on these institutions allows us to see how different societies fulfill these needs (Aberle et al. 1950). It is within the context of families, for example, that we ensure the society's continued existence by producing the next generation. Families carry out both biological reproduction (having children) and social reproduction (teaching them the culture they need for survival). Families also provide care and protection for members. Through education we teach the more formal and public culture necessary to be members of the larger society. This includes the formal curriculum (history, math, science, etc.) but also includes learning to interact with others outside our immediate families. We rely on religion to be the glue that holds society together by establishing a clear identity with shared beliefs and practices, answering basic questions about meaning, and enforcing both individual and collective discipline. Government helps to maintain internal order through laws, policing, and punishment and seeks to establish stable relations with other

In February 2010, an Austin man flew his plane into the city's IRS building.

societies through diplomacy. Finally, the economy regulates the production, distribution, and consumption of goods and services.

How societies choose to fulfill these functions can vary significantly, as can the degree to which these institutions overlap. For example, one society may protect itself from external attack by amassing a large arsenal of weaponry; another may make determined efforts to remain neutral in world politics and to promote cooperative relationships with its neighbors. No matter what its particular strategy, any society or relatively permanent group must address all these functional prerequisites for survival.

Focusing on the functions institutions fulfill can help us to better understand social order, but it often implies that the way things are is the way things should be. Sociologists who focus more on power, the consequences of difference, and resource distribution suggest that we must also look at the ways our construction of these institutions reinforces inequality. We can meet these functional needs in a variety of ways, so we must address the interest some groups have in maintaining the status quo.

SOCTHINK

How is it possible for education to represent both a path for opportunity and an instrument for maintaining inequality? Where in your experience have you seen both at work?

Major institutions, such as education, help to maintain the privileges of the most powerful individuals and groups within a society while contributing to the powerlessness of others. To give one example, public schools in the United States are financed largely through property taxes. This arrangement allows more affluent areas to provide their children with better-equipped schools and better-paid teachers than low-income areas can afford. As a result, children from prosperous communities are better prepared to compete academically than children from impoverished communities. The structure of the nation's educational system permits and even promotes such unequal treatment of schoolchildren (Kozol 2005).

bureaucracy A component of formal organization that uses rules and hierarchical ranking to achieve efficiency.

By focusing on everyday interactions within the contexts of these institutions, we can further understand why we think and act the way we do. Focusing on the economy, sociologist Mitchell Duneier (1994a, 1994b) studied the social behavior of the word processors, all women, who worked in the service center of a large Chicago law firm. Duneier was interested in the informal social norms that emerged in this work environment and the rich social network these female employees created.

Duneier learned that, despite working in a large office, these women found private moments to talk (often in the halls or outside the washroom) and shared a critical view of the firm's attorneys and day-shift secretaries. Expressing their frustration about their relative lack of power and respect, the word processors routinely suggested that their assignments represented work that the "lazy" secretaries should have completed during the normal workday. One word processor, seeking to reclaim a sense of personal power, reacted against the lawyers' superior attitude and pointedly refused to recognize or speak with any attorney who would not address her by name (Duneier 1994b).

Such approaches to viewing life in the contexts of social institutions allow us to better understand what it means to live in the world as it is structured today. Looking at society through the lens of social structure gives us a sense of what is going on with regard to both the "big picture" and the intimate details of our daily interactions. One of the ways that sociologists have characterized the structure of our modern world is in terms of bureaucracy.

"Frankly, at this point in the flow chart, we don't know what happens to these people..."

Cartoon by Chris Wildt, www.CartoonStock.com.

>> Bureaucracy

A **bureaucracy** is a component of a formal organization that uses rules and hierarchical ranking to achieve efficiency. The impressions we have of bureaucracies—rows of cubicles staffed with seemingly faceless people, endless waiting, complex language, and frustrating encounters with red tape—are often negative. But bureaucracy was established to provide fair and efficient means of organizing social life.

CHARACTERISTICS OF A BUREAUCRACY

Max Weber ([1913–1922] 1947) provided the first detailed sociological analysis of bureaucracy. He recognized that its underlying structure remained the same regardless of location, whether in religion, government, education, or business. Weber argued that bureaucracy was quite different from traditional forms of organization, such as those used to run a family business, and he set out to identify its core components. He did so by constructing what he called an **ideal type,** an abstract model of the essential characteristics of a phenomenon. In actuality, perfect bureaucracies do not exist; no real-world organization corresponds exactly to Weber's ideal type.

Weber proposed that whether the purpose is to run a church, a corporation, or an army, the ideal bureaucracy displays five basic characteristics: division of labor, hierarchy of authority, written rules and regulations, impersonality, and employment based on technical qualifications. Let's look at each in turn; the accompanying table provides a summary.

Division of Labor In bureaucracies, specialized experts perform specific tasks. In a college bureaucracy, for example, the admissions officer does not do the job of registrar; the academic advisor doesn't see to the maintenance of buildings. By working at a specific task, people are more likely to become highly skilled and carry out a job with maximum efficiency. This emphasis on specialization is so basic a part of our lives we may not realize that it is a fairly recent development in Western culture.

Division of labor has freed up people to specialize, enhancing their knowledge and skill and leading to significant advances and innovation. However, fragmenting work into smaller and smaller tasks can isolate workers from one another and weaken any connection they might feel to the overall objective of the bureaucracy. In *The Communist Manifesto* ([1847] 1955), Karl Marx and Friedrich Engels charged that capitalism's inherent drive toward increased efficiency and productivity reduces workers to a mere "appendage of the machine." Such a work arrangement, they wrote, produces extreme **alienation**—loss of control over our creative human capacity to produce, separation from the products we make, and isolation from our fellow producers. Restricting workers to very small tasks also can lessen their job security as new employees can easily be trained to replace them.

Another potential downside of the division of labor is that, even though it makes us more interdependent, our relative isolation can result in our failing to recognize our links with others. As we saw with the "hamburger as miracle" example in Chapter 1, we take other people's skills for granted and assume they will do their jobs, even though we are unaware of what most of those jobs are. In some cases this can lead to **trained incapacity**—a situation in which workers become so specialized that they develop blind spots and fail to notice potential problems. Even worse, workers can become so isolated that they may not care about what is happening in the next department. Some observers believe that such developments have caused

> **ideal type** An abstract model of the essential characteristics of a phenomenon.
>
> **alienation** Loss of control over our creative human capacity to produce, separation from the products we make, and isolation from our fellow producers.
>
> **trained incapacity** The tendency of workers in a bureaucracy to become so specialized that they develop blind spots and fail to notice potential problems.

Characteristics of a Bureaucracy

	Positive consequences	Negative consequences	
		For the individual	**For the organization**
Division of labor	Produces efficiency in a large-scale corporation	Produces trained incapacity	Produces a narrow perspective
Hierarchy of authority	Clarifies who is in command	Deprives employees of a voice in decision making	Permits concealment of mistakes
Written rules and regulations	Let workers know what is expected of them	Stifles initiative and imagination	Leads to goal displacement
Impersonality	Reduces bias	Contributes to feelings of alienation	Discourages loyalty to company
Employment based on technical qualifications	Discourages favoritism and reduces petty rivalries	Discourages ambition to improve oneself elsewhere	Inhibits innovative thinking

workers in the United States to become less productive on the job (Wais 2005).

In some cases, the bureaucratic division of labor can have tragic results. In the wake of the terrorist attacks on the World Trade Center and the Pentagon on September 11, 2001, many Americans wondered how the FBI and CIA could have failed to detect the terrorists' elaborately planned operation. The problem, in part, turned out to be the division of labor between the FBI, which focuses on domestic matters, and the CIA, which operates overseas. Officials at these intelligence-gathering organizations, both of which are huge bureaucracies, are well known for jealously guarding information from one another. Subsequent investigation revealed that they knew about Osama bin Laden and his al Qaeda terrorist network in the early 1990s. Unfortunately, five federal agencies—the CIA, FBI, National Security Agency, Defense Intelligence Agency, and National Reconnaissance Office—failed to share their information on the network. Although the hijacking of the four commercial airliners used in the massive attacks may not have been preventable, the bureaucratic division of labor definitely hindered efforts to defend against terrorism, undermining U.S. national security.

Hierarchy of Authority Bureaucracies follow the principle of hierarchy; that is, each position is under the supervision of a higher authority. A president heads a college bureaucracy; he or she selects members of the administration, who in turn hire their own staff. In the Roman Catholic Church, the pope is the supreme authority; under him are

goal displacement Overzealous conformity to official regulations of a bureaucracy.

The organizations of major corporations can be complex but most typically have a single CEO. Debra Lee, pictured here, is president and CEO of Black Entertainment Television.

performance. If situations arise that are not covered by the rules, bureaucracies are self-correcting. They have rules in place to ensure that new rules are established that make work expectations as clear and comprehensive as possible. Because bureaucracies are hierarchical systems of interrelated positions, such procedures provide a valuable sense of continuity for the organization. Individual workers may come and go, but the structure and past records of the organization give it a life of its own that outlives the services of any one particular person.

cardinals, bishops, and so forth. In businesses, the most basic relation is between boss and worker, but in large corporations there are various levels of authority. To track relationships, such companies map those connections using organizational charts that identify all the links of who answers to whom, ultimately leading up to the president or CEO at the top.

Written Rules and Regulations Through written rules and regulations, bureaucracies generally offer employees clear standards for an adequate (or exceptional)

Of course, rules and regulations can overshadow the larger goals of an organization to the point that they become dysfunctional. What if a hospital emergency room physician failed to treat a seriously injured person because he or she had no valid proof of U.S. citizenship? If blindly applied, rules no longer serve as a means to achieving an objective but instead become important (perhaps too important) in their own right. Robert Merton (1968) used the term **goal displacement** to refer to overzealous conformity to official regulations in which we lose sight of the larger principle from which the rule was created.

─SOC THINK─

Why do we tend to associate bureaucracies with red tape and inefficiency when they are explicitly organized to be the opposite? To what extent is our desire to be treated as an individual at odds with the principles of bureaucracies?

Impersonality Max Weber wrote that, in a bureaucracy, work is carried out "without hatred or passion." Bureaucratic norms dictate that officials judge people based on performance rather than personality. The intent is to ensure equal treatment for each person. But it can also contribute to the cold, uncaring feeling often associated with modern organizations.

We typically think of big government and big business when we think of impersonal bureaucracies, and bureaucratic impersonality often produces frustration and disaffection. Whether it involves registering for college classes or getting tech support for a malfunctioning computer, most people have had some experience of feeling like a number and longing for some personal attention. The larger the organization or society, however, the less possible such personal care becomes because attending to individual wants and needs is inefficient.

Employment Based on Technical Qualifications Within the ideal bureaucracy, hiring is based on technical qualifications rather than on favoritism, and performance is measured against specific standards. Written personnel policies dictate who gets promoted, and people often have a right to appeal if they believe that particular rules have been violated. In combination with the principle of impersonality, the driving personnel principle is supposed to be that it is "what you know, not who you know" that counts. Such procedures protect workers against

> Bureaucracy is . . . the most rational known means of exercising authority over human beings.
>
> Max Weber

arbitrary dismissal, provide a measure of security, and encourage loyalty to the organization.

Weber developed his five indicators of bureaucracy almost 100 years ago, and they continue to describe the ideal type. Not every formal organization will fully realize all of Weber's characteristics. The underlying logic they represent, however, points toward a way of doing things that is typical of life in modern societies.

BUREAUCRATIZATION AS A WAY OF LIFE

Bureaucracy for Weber was an indicator of a larger trend in modern society toward rational calculation of all decision making using efficiency and productivity as the primary standards of success. We recognize this pattern first at the level of businesses and organizations. More companies seek greater efficiency through **bureaucratization**—the process by which a group, organization, or social movement increasingly relies on technical-rational decision making in the pursuit of efficiency. Over time, however, the technical-rational approach pervades more and more areas of our lives.

The Spread of Bureaucratization One example of the expansion of bureaucratization is found in the spread of what sociologist George Ritzer (2008) calls **McDonaldization**—the process by which the principles of efficiency, calculability, predictability, and control shape organization and decision making, in the United States and around the world. Ritzer argues that these principles, which are at the heart of the McDonald's fast-food chain's success, have been emulated by many organizations, ranging from medical care to wedding planning to education. Even sporting events reflect the influence of McDonaldization. Around the world, stadiums are becoming increasingly similar, both physically and in the way they present the sport to spectators. Swipe cards, "sports city" garages and parking lots, and automated ticket sales maximize efficiency. All seats offer spectators an unrestricted view, and a big screen guarantees them access to instant replays. Scores, player statistics, and attendance figures are updated by computer and displayed on an automated scoreboard. Spectator enthusiasm is manufactured through video displays urging applause or rhythmic chanting. At food counters, refreshments

> **bureaucratization** The process by which a group, organization, or social movement increasingly relies on technical-rational decision making in the pursuit of efficiency.
>
> **McDonaldization** The process by which the principles of efficiency, calculability, predictability, and control shape organization and decision making, in the United States and around the world.

. . . The U.S. Census Bureau identifies 472 distinct occupational categories, such as Chief Executive and Crossing Guard, each of which contains at least 10,000 workers. They break these down into 14 occupational groups with 9 job categories.

Did You Know?

include well-known brands whose customer loyalty has been nourished by advertisers for decades. And, of course, the merchandising of teams' and even players' names and images is highly controlled.

Normally, we think of bureaucratization in terms of large organizations, but bureaucratization also takes place within small-group settings. Sociologist Jennifer Bickman Mendez (1998) studied domestic houseworkers employed in central California by a nationwide franchise. She found that housekeeping tasks were minutely defined, to the point that employees had to follow 22 written steps for cleaning a bathroom. Complaints and special requests went not to the workers but to an office-based manager.

Weber predicted that eventually even the private sphere would become rationalized. That is, we would turn to rational techniques in an effort to manage our self in order to handle the many challenges of modern life. A trip to any bookstore would seem to prove his point: We find countless self-help books, each with its own system of steps to help us solve life's problems and reach our goals.

Weber was concerned about the depersonalizing consequences of such rationalization, but he saw no way out.

> ## Civilization degrades the many to exalt the few.
>
> ———
>
> **Amos Bronson Alcott**

Because it is guided by the principle of maximum efficiency, the only way to beat bureaucratization, he thought, was to be more bureaucratic. He argued that, unfortunately, something human gets lost in the process. Culture critic Mike Daisey describes something like this through his experience working at Amazon.com. His job performance was measured based on five factors: time spent on each call, number of phone contacts per hour, time spent on each customer email, number of email contacts per hour, and the sum total of phone and email contacts per hour. Of these calculations, he writes, "Those five numbers are who you are. They are, in fact, all you are. . . . Metrics will do exactly what it claims to do: It will track everything your employees do, say, and breathe, and consequently create a measurable increase in their productivity" (Daisey 2002:114). Metrics do work, but they do so by dehumanizing the worker. "The sad thing," Daisey continues, "is that metrics work so well precisely because it strips away dignity—it's that absence that makes it possible to see precisely who is pulling his weight and who is not" (p. 114). When workers' performance is measured only in numbers, the only part of the self that counts is that part that produces those numbers. Weber predicted that those parts of the self deemed not necessary to the job, such as emotional needs and family responsibilities, would be dismissed as irrelevant.

From Bureaucracy to Oligarchy One of the dangers, then, is that bureaucratization overwhelms other values and principles, that how we

Office Space
Comedy about the social structure and culture of office work in the United States.

The Truman Show
In this postmodern tale, a man unknowingly lives his life on television.

Born into Brothels
True life stories of children growing up in the red-light district of Calcutta.

The Lives of Others
Communist bureaucracy turns on its citizens in East Berlin.

Mean Girls
Social cliques run amok at a suburban American high school.

5 Movies on SOCIAL STRUCTURE AND INTERACTION

organize to accomplish our goals overwhelms and alters the goals themselves. Sociologist Robert Michels ([1915] 1949) studied socialist parties and labor unions in Europe prior to World War I and found that such organizations were becoming increasingly bureaucratic. The emerging leaders of the organizations—even some of the most egalitarian—had a vested interest in clinging to power. If they lost their leadership posts, they would have to return to full-time work as manual laborers.

Through his research, Michels originated the idea of the **iron law of oligarchy,** the principle that all organizations, even democratic ones, tend to develop into a bureaucracy ruled by an elite few (called an oligarchy). Why do oligarchies emerge? People who achieve leadership roles usually have the skills, knowledge, or charisma to direct, if not control, others. Michels argued that the rank and file of a movement or organization look to leaders for direction and thereby reinforce the process of rule by a few. In addition, members of an oligarchy are strongly motivated to maintain their leadership roles, privileges, and power.

In such instances, actions that violate the core principles of bureaucracy can seep in. Ascribed statuses such as gender, race, and ethnicity can influence how people are treated in formal organizations. For example, a study of women lawyers in the nation's largest law firms found significant differences in the women's self-images, depending on the relative presence or absence of women in positions of power. In firms in which fewer than 15 percent of partners were women, the female lawyers were likely to believe that "feminine" traits were strongly devalued and that masculinity was equated with success. As one female attorney put it, "Let's face it: This is a man's environment, and it's sort of Jock City, especially at my firm." Women in firms where female lawyers were better represented in positions of power had a stronger desire for and higher expectations of promotion (Ely 1995:619).

BUREAUCRACY AND ORGANIZATIONAL CULTURE

Weber's model also predicted that bureaucratic organizations were self-correcting and would take steps to remedy worker concerns. Faced with sabotage and decreasingly productive workers, for example, early bureaucratic managers realized that they could not totally dismiss workers' emotional needs as irrelevant. As a result, new management philosophies arose to counter the negative effects of depersonalization.

According to the **classical theory** of formal organizations, also known as the **scientific management approach,** workers are motivated almost entirely by economic rewards. This theory stresses that only the physical constraints on workers limit their productivity. Therefore, workers may be treated as a resource, much like the machines that began to replace them in the 20th century. Under the scientific management approach, management attempts to achieve maximum work efficiency through scientific planning, established performance standards, and careful supervision of workers and production. Planning involves efficiency studies but not studies of workers' attitudes or job satisfaction.

Not until workers organized unions—and forced management to recognize that they were not objects—did theorists of formal organizations begin to revise the classical approach. Along with management and administrators, social scientists became aware that informal groups of workers have an important impact on organizations (Perrow 1986). An alternative

iron law of oligarchy The principle that all organizations, even democratic ones, tend to develop into a bureaucracy ruled by an elite few.

classical theory An approach to the study of formal organizations that views workers as being motivated almost entirely by economic rewards.

scientific management approach Another name for the classical theory of formal organizations.

management philosophy, the **human relations approach,** emphasizes the role of people, communication, and participation in a bureaucracy. This type of analysis reflects the significance of interaction and small-group behavior. Unlike planning under the scientific management approach, planning based on the human relations perspective focuses on workers' feelings, frustrations, and emotional need for job satisfaction. Today, many workplaces—primarily for those in higher-status occupations—have been transformed to family-friendly environments. To the extent that managers are convinced that helping workers meet all their needs increases productivity, care and concern are instituted as a result of rational calculation.

human relations approach An approach to the study of formal organizations that emphasizes the role of people, communication, and participation in a bureaucracy and tends to focus on the informal structure of the organization.

Gemeinschaft A close-knit community, often found in rural areas, in which strong personal bonds unite members.

Gesellschaft A community, often urban, that is large and impersonal, with little commitment to the group or consensus on values.

mechanical solidarity Social cohesion based on shared experiences, knowledge, and skills in which things function more or less the way they always have, with minimal change.

>> Social Structure in Global Perspective

Principles of bureaucratization may influence more and more spheres of our lives today, but it has not always been thus. In fact, sociology arose as a discipline in order to better understand and direct the transition from traditional to modern society. Early sociologists sought to develop models that described the basic differences between the two. They hoped that by better understanding how traditional societies operate, we might more effectively identify the underlying factors that shape core concerns in modern society, such as social order, inequality, and interaction.

GEMEINSCHAFT AND GESELLSCHAFT

Ferdinand Tönnies (1855–1936) was appalled by the rise of industrial cities in his native Germany during the late 1800s. In his view, the city marked a dramatic change from the ideal of a close-knit community, which Tönnies termed a *Gemeinschaft,* to that of an impersonal mass society, or *Gesellschaft* (Tönnies [1887] 1988).

The **Gemeinschaft** (pronounced "guh-MINE-shoft") is typical of rural life. It is a small community in which people have similar backgrounds and life experiences. Virtually everyone knows one another, and social interactions are intimate and familiar, almost like an extended family. In this community there is a sense of commitment to the larger social group and a sense of togetherness among members. People relate to others in a personal way, not just as, say, clerk or manager. However, with such personal interaction comes little privacy and high expectations of individual sacrifice.

Social control in the *Gemeinschaft* is maintained through informal means such as moral persuasion, gossip, and even gestures. These techniques work effectively because people genuinely care how others feel about them. Social change is relatively limited in the *Gemeinschaft;* the lives of members of one generation may be quite similar to those of their parents, grandparents, and so on.

In contrast, the **Gesellschaft** (pronounced "guh-ZELL-shoft") is characteristic of modern urban life. In modern societies, most people are strangers who feel little in common with other residents. Relationships are governed by social roles that grow out of immediate tasks, such as purchasing a product or arranging a business meeting. Self-interest dominates, and there is little consensus concerning values or commitment to the group. As a result, social control must rest on formal techniques, such as laws and legally defined sanctions. Social change is a normal part of life in the *Gesellschaft,* with substantial shifts evident even within a single generation.

Sociologists have used these two terms to compare social structures that stress close relationships with those that feature less personal ties. It is easy to view the *Gemeinschaft* with nostalgia, as a far better way of life than the rat race of contemporary existence. However, the more intimate relationships of the *Gemeinschaft* come at a price. The prejudice and discrimination found there can be quite confining; ascribed statuses such as family background often outweigh a person's unique talents and achievements. In addition, the *Gemeinschaft* tends to distrust individuals who are creative or simply different.

SOCTHINK

How would you classify the communities with which you are familiar? Are they more *Gemeinschaft* or *Gesellschaft*?

MECHANICAL AND ORGANIC SOLIDARITY

While Tönnies looked nostalgically back on the *Gemeinschaft,* Émile Durkheim was more interested in the transition to modern society, which he felt represented the birth of a new form of social order. Durkheim hoped to use sociology as a science to better understand this transition. In his book *The Division of Labor in Society* ([1893] 1933), Durkheim, not unlike Weber, highlighted the significance of the degree to which jobs are specialized in society. For Durkheim, however, the amount of division of labor that exists in a society shapes the degree to which people feel connected with each other.

In societies in which there is minimal division of labor, a shared way of thinking develops that emphasizes group solidarity. Durkheim termed this collective frame of mind **mechanical solidarity.** It involves a sense of social cohesion based on shared experiences, knowledge, and skill, in which things function more or less the way they always have, with minimal change. Most individuals perform the same basic tasks, and they do so together. In this type of society, no one needs to ask, "What do your parents do?" since all are engaged in similar work. Each person hunts, prepares food, makes clothing, builds homes, and so forth. As we see among the Amish, there is little concern for individual needs when people have few options regarding what to do with their lives. Instead, the group is the dominant force in society. Both social interaction and negotiation are based on close, intimate, face-to-face social contacts. Since there is little specialization, there are few social roles (Kraybill 2001).

As societies become more advanced technologically, they rely on greater division of labor. The person who cuts down timber is not the same person who puts up your roof. With increasing specialization, many different tasks must be performed by many different individuals—even in manufacturing a single item, such as a radio or stove. In general, social interactions become less personal than in societies characterized by mechanical solidarity. People begin relating to others on the basis of their social positions (butcher, nurse, and so on) rather than on their distinctive human qualities. Because the overall social structure of the society continues to change, statuses and social roles are in perpetual flux.

As we saw in the "hamburger as miracle" example in Chapter 1, once society has become more complex and division of labor is greater, no individual can go it alone. Dependence on others becomes essential for group survival. In Durkheim's terms, mechanical solidarity is replaced by **organic solidarity**—a collective consciousness resting on the need a society's members have for one another. Durkheim chose the term *organic solidarity* because he believed that role specialization forces individuals to become interdependent in much the same way as the various organs of the human body: Each performs a vital function, but none can exist alone. Also, like a living organism, society can grow and adapt to change.

TECHNOLOGY AND SOCIETY

Some sociologists focus more explicitly on technology than on social organization, expressed as division of labor, to understand distinctions between traditional and modern societies. In sociologist Gerhard Lenski's view, a society's level of technology is critical to the way it is organized. As we saw in Chapter 3, Lenski defines technology as "cultural information about the ways in which the material resources of the environment may be used to satisfy human needs and desires" (Nolan and Lenski 2006:361). As technology changes, new social forms arise, from preindustrial, to industrial, to postindustrial. The available technology does not completely define the form that a particular society and its social structure will take. Nevertheless, a low level of technology may limit the degree to which a society can depend on such things as irrigation or complex machinery.

organic solidarity A collective consciousness that rests on mutual interdependence, characteristic of societies with a complex division of labor.

hunting-and-gathering society A preindustrial society in which people rely on whatever foods and fibers are readily available in order to survive.

horticultural society A preindustrial society in which people plant seeds and crops rather than merely subsist on available foods.

Preindustrial Societies Perhaps the earliest form of preindustrial society to emerge in human history was the **hunting-and-gathering society,** in which people simply rely on whatever foods and fibers are readily available. Such groups are typically small and widely dispersed, and technology in such societies is minimal. Organized into groups, people move constantly in search of food. There is little division of labor into specialized tasks because everyone is engaged in the same basic activities. Because resources are scarce, there is relatively little inequality in terms of material goods.

In **horticultural societies,** people plant seeds and crops rather than merely subsist on available foods. Members of horticultural societies are much less nomadic than hunter-gatherers. They place greater emphasis on the production of tools and household objects. Yet technology remains rather limited in these societies, whose members cultivate crops with the aid of digging sticks or hoes (Wilford 1997).

The third type of preindustrial development is the **agrarian society.** As in horticultural societies, members of agrarian societies are engaged primarily in the production of food, but technological innovations such as the plow allow farmers to dramatically increase their crop yields and cultivate the same fields over generations. As a result it becomes possible for larger, more permanent settlements to develop.

agrarian society The most technologically advanced form of preindustrial society. Members are engaged primarily in the production of food, but they increase their crop yields through technological innovations such as the plow.

industrial society A society that depends on mechanization to produce its goods and services.

postindustrial society A society whose economic system is engaged primarily in the processing and control of information.

postmodern society A technologically sophisticated, pluralistic, interconnected, globalized society.

Agrarian societies continue to rely on the physical power of humans and animals (as opposed to mechanical power). Division of labor increases because technological advances free up some people from food production to focus on specialized tasks, such as the repair of fishing nets or blacksmithing. As human settlements become stabler and more established, social institutions become more elaborate and property rights more important. The comparative permanence and greater surpluses of an agrarian society allow members to specialize in creating artifacts such as statues, public monuments, and art objects and to pass them on from one generation to the next.

Industrial Societies The Industrial Revolution transformed social life in England during the late 1700s, and within a century its impact on society had extended around the world. An **industrial society** is one that depends on mechanization to produce its goods and services. The strength and stamina humans gained from new inventions such as the steam engine opened up a new world of possibilities by applying nonanimal (mechanical) sources of power to most labor tasks. As such, industrialization significantly altered the way people lived and worked, and it undercut taken-for-granted norms and values.

During the Industrial Revolution, many societies underwent an irrevocable shift from an agrarian-oriented economy to an industrial base. Specialization of tasks and manufacture of goods increasingly replaced the practice of individuals or families making an entire product in a home workshop. Workers, generally men but also women and even children, left their family homesteads to work in central locations such as urban factories.

The process of industrialization had distinctive social consequences. Families and communities could not continue to function as self-sufficient units. Individuals, villages, and regions began to exchange goods and services and to become interdependent. As people came to rely on the labor of members of other communities, the family lost its unique position as the main source of power and authority. The need for specialized knowledge led to formalized schooling, and education emerged as a social institution distinct from the family.

Postindustrial Societies Mechanized production continues to play a substantial role in shaping social order, relationships, and opportunities, but technological innovation once again has reshaped social structure by freeing up some people from the demands of material production. This has led to the rise of the service sector of the economy in many technologically advanced countries. In the 1970s, sociologist Daniel Bell wrote about the technologically advanced **postindustrial society,** whose economic system is engaged primarily in the processing and control of information. The main output of a postindustrial society is services rather than manufactured goods. Large numbers of people become involved in occupations devoted to the teaching, generation, or dissemination of ideas. Jobs in fields such as advertising, public relations, human resources, and computer information systems are typical of a postindustrial society (Bell 1999).

Some sociologists, including Bell, view this transition from industrial to postindustrial society as largely a positive development. Others, however, point to the often hidden consequences that result from differential access to resources in postindustrial society. For example, Michael Harrington (1980), who alerted the nation to

Did You Know?

... TV talk-show host Regis Philbin was a sociology major. He graduated from the University of Notre Dame with a B.A. in sociology in 1953. Sociology, he says, "gave me a great insight into human nature."

the problems of the poor in his book *The Other America,* questions the significance that Bell attaches to the growing class of white-collar workers. Harrington concedes that scientists, engineers, and economists are involved in important political and economic decisions, but he disagrees with Bell's claim that they have a free hand in decision making, independent of the interests of the rich. Harrington follows in the tradition of Marx by arguing that conflict between social classes will continue in the postindustrial society.

POSTMODERN LIFE

Sociologists recently have gone beyond discussion of the postindustrial society to contemplate the emergence of postmodern society. A **postmodern society** is a technologically sophisticated, pluralistic, interconnected, globalized society. Although it is difficult to summarize what a whole range of thinkers have said about postmodern

Going **GLOBAL**

International U.S. Favorability Ratings

Bottom eight nations | | **Top eight nations**

Bottom eight nations		Top eight nations	
China	47%	Kenya	90%
Russia	44%	Nigeria	79%
Argentina	38%	South Korea	78%
Egypt	27%	India	76%
Jordan	25%	France	75%
Pakistan	16%	Israel	71%
Palestinian Territories	15%	Britain	69%
Turkey	14%	Mexico	69%

Note: Data are for 2009.
Source: Pew Research Center 2009b.

Because we exist in an interdependent global network, the consequences of our actions, both large and small, reverberate throughout the world. In a global survey of 25 nations conducted in 2009, the Pew Research Center looked at international favorability ratings for the United States. How favorably do other nations view the United States? The average national score was 56.6 percent, a 10-point increase over 2008, largely attributed to the election of Barack Obama.

life, four elements provide a sense of the key characteristics of such societies today: stories, images, choices, and networks.

Stories Because postmodern societies are pluralistic and individualistic, people hold many different, often competing, sets of norms and values. Fewer people assume that a single, all-inclusive story—whether a particular religious tradition, or an all-encompassing scientific theory of everything, or even the faith many early sociologists had in the inevitability of modern progress—can unite us all under a common umbrella. Instead, we embrace the various individual and group stories that help us to make sense of the world and our place in it. We do so in the full knowledge that others out there are doing exactly the same thing and often coming to dramatically different conclusions. This multiplicity of stories undercuts the authority that singular accounts of reality have had in the past.

Images Postmodern society is also characterized by the explosion of the mass media, which emphasizes the importance of images. As we saw in Chapter 4, the average person in the United States watches almost five hours of television per day (Bureau of the Census 2008a). This works out to the equivalent of more than 71 full days per year. We are bombarded by images everywhere we turn, but in postmodern theory, the significance of the image goes much deeper than television and advertisements; it impacts our taken-for-granted notion of material reality itself. Theorists argue that we do not confront or interact with the material world directly. Just as language shapes our perception of reality according to the Sapir-Whorf hypothesis, our experience of "reality" is always mediated through representations of reality in the form of signs, symbols, and words. According to postmodernists, our images or models of reality come before reality itself. Postmodern theorists use a geography metaphor to illuminate this concept: "The map precedes the territory" (Baudrillard [1981] 1994). In other words, the images we construct draw our attention to certain features that we might not otherwise single out. A road map, for example, highlights different features, and for different purposes, than does a topographical map or political map. In so doing, it shapes what we see. We cannot step around or look through such cultural constructs to approach the thing itself, and so our knowledge of what is real is always constrained by the images we construct.

Choices In a postmodern world, reality is not simply given; it is negotiated. We pick and choose our reality from the buffet of images and experiences presented to us. In fact, we *must* choose. In contrast to societies characterized by mechanical solidarity, where one's life path is virtually set at birth, members of postmodern societies must make life choices all the time. Assuming we have access to sufficient resources, we choose what to eat, what to wear, and what to drive. Shopping, which in the past would have been viewed primarily as an instrumental necessity to provide for our basic needs, becomes an act of self-creation. As advertising professor James B. Twitchell (2000) put it, "We don't buy things, we buy meanings" (p. 47). An iPhone, a Coach purse, and a MINI Cooper are more than just a phone, a handbag, and a car. They are statements about the kind of person we are or want to be. The significance of choice goes much deeper than just consumer products. We also choose our partners, our schools, our jobs, our faith, and even our identities. As individuals, we may choose to affirm traditions, language, diet, and values we inherited from our family through socialization, but we can also choose to pursue our own path.

Networks Members of postmodern societies live in a globally interconnected world. The food we eat, the clothes we wear, the books we read, and the products we choose often come to us from the other side of the world. The computer technician we talk to for assistance in the United States may be located in India. McDonald's has even experimented with centralized drive-through attendants—who might even be located in another state—who take your order and transmit it to the restaurant you are ordering from (Richtel 2006). Increasingly, all corners of the globe are linked into a vast, interrelated social, cultural, political, and economic system. A rural Iowa farmer, for example, must be concerned with more than just the local weather and community concerns; he or she must know about international innovations in farming technology, including biotech, as well as the current and future state of international markets.

Whether in the form of traditional, modern, or postmodern society, social structure provides order, shaping the options that are available to us. It provides the context within which we interact with others. The statuses we occupy shape the roles we perform. What we think and do is influenced by the relationships we have with others in the contexts of groups, networks, and institutions. Sociology as a discipline is committed to making sense of our structural context and the impact it has on our lives.

Still, society and social structure are not singular things. Though we are, in many respects, products of society, socialized to think and act in appropriate ways, we always have the option to think and act in new ways and to construct new culture. The possibility for such change may be more apparent in our pluralistic world. Ours is a world not of "the" structure, "the" family, and "the" religion, but of structures, families, and religions. We have the possibility for more contact with more people who have more ways of thinking and acting than at any time in the past. As such, we can become aware of more alternatives for how we might think and act that might lead us to change our worlds.

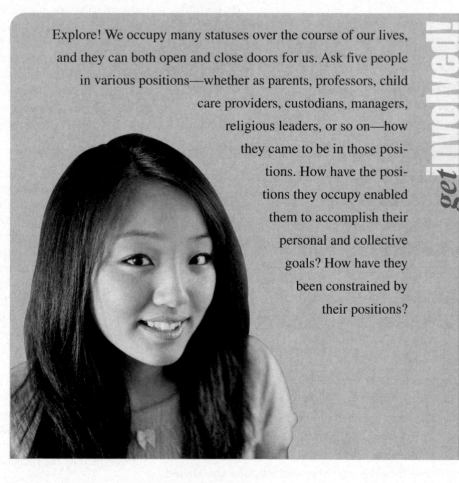

get involved!

Explore! We occupy many statuses over the course of our lives, and they can both open and close doors for us. Ask five people in various positions—whether as parents, professors, child care providers, custodians, managers, religious leaders, or so on—how they came to be in those positions. How have the positions they occupy enabled them to accomplish their personal and collective goals? How have they been constrained by their positions?

For REVIEW

I. **What makes up society?**
   - Society provides a structure that is built up out of the statuses we occupy; the roles we perform; and the groups, networks, and institutions that connect us.

II. **How does social structure shape individual action?**
   - The positions we occupy shape our perceptions, the resources to which we have access, and the options that are available. For example, in the context of bureaucracies, our social position, connections, and performance expectations are clearly defined.

III. **How do sociologists describe traditional versus modern societies?**
   - Sociologists highlight the impact that division of labor and technological development have on the organization of community, work, and social interaction in traditional and modern societies.

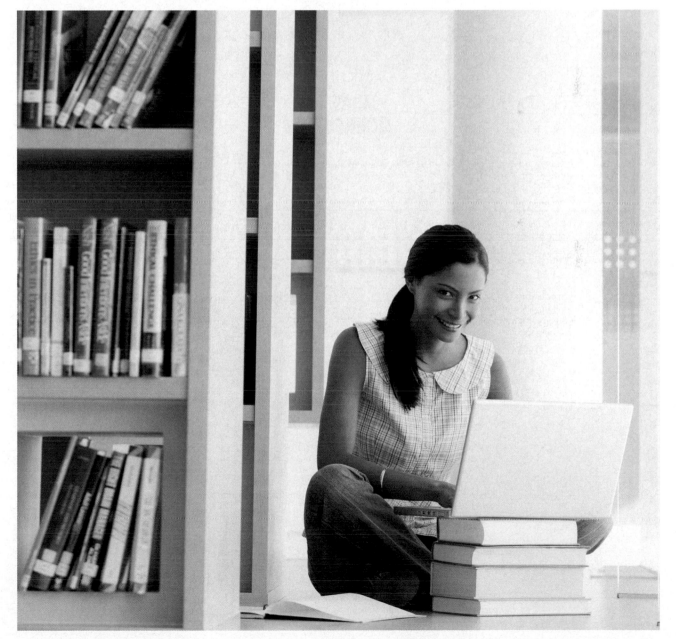

Functionalist view

The **elements of social structure**—statuses, groups, social networks, and social institutions—provide order, shape our options, and give context to our lives.

Social roles create a **stable society** by allowing people to anticipate the behavior of others and to act accordingly.

Institutions contribute to **social order** by performing **vital functions**, whether it is producing children (family), teaching them (schools), establishing order (government), or distributing goods and services (economy).

STRUCTURE, ORDER
KEY CONCEPTS

Conflict view

The elements of the social structure justify and reinforce existing systems of inequality and unequal distributions of resources.

Ascribed statuses, often conferred at birth, can be used to justify **privileges** for some while limiting opportunities for others by consigning them to a **subordinate group.**

In-groups and out-groups serve to highlight **differences** between people and can foster antagonism.

SUBORDINATION, INEQUALITY, PRIVILEGE
KEY CONCEPTS

MAKE THE CONNECTION

After reviewing the chapter, answer the following questions:

Interactionist view

It is through social interaction—the **shared experiences** through which we relate to others—that the elements of social structure are constructed.

Our social roles are governed by a set of expectations, but how we actually **perform** those roles can vary from individual to individual.

A **micro, bottom-up perspective** of social structure reinforce the significance of our actions, and can thus help us appreciate how we can think and act in new ways to bring about social change.

SHARED EXPERIENCES, MICRO PERSPECTIVE
KEY CONCEPTS

1
How does Berger and Luckmann's social construction of reality model integrate elements of functionalist, conflict, and interactionist perspectives?

2
Briefly describe how a functionalist, a conflict theorist, and an interactionist would view institutions (pp. 113–114).

3
Sociologists Daniel Bell and Michael Harrington have differing views of postindustrial society. Which perspectives do you think their views reflect (p. 122)?

4
Have you ever been part of an in- or out-group (p. 108)? If so, how might each perspective shed light on your experience?

Pop Quiz

1. The three stages of Berger and Luckmann's model describing the interdependent relationship between the individual and society are
   a. statuses, groups, and institutions.
   b. telling stories, making choices, and establishing networks.
   c. constructing culture, constructing the self, and constructing society.
   d. role conflict, role strain, and role exit.

2. In the United States, we expect that cab drivers will know how to get around a city. This expectation is an example of which of the following?
   a. role conflict
   b. role strain
   c. social role
   d. master status

3. What occurs when incompatible expectations arise from two or more social positions held by the same person?
   a. role conflict
   b. role strain
   c. role exit
   d. both a and b

4. In sociological terms, what do we call any number of people with similar norms, values, and expectations who interact with one another on a regular basis?
   a. a category
   b. a group
   c. an aggregate
   d. a society

5. Primary groups are characterized by
   a. a series of relationships that link individuals directly to others and, through them, indirectly to still more people.
   b. formal, impersonal relationships with minimal social intimacy or mutual understanding.
   c. social positions that are within our power to change.
   d. intimate, face-to-face association and cooperation.

6. The U.S. Postal Service, Def Jam Records, and the college or university in which you are currently enrolled as a student are all examples of
   a. primary groups.
   b. reference groups.
   c. formal organizations.
   d. *Gemeinschaft.*

7. The principle of bureaucracy that establishes that work should be carried out "without hatred or passion" is known as
   a. impersonality.
   b. hierarchy of authority.
   c. written rules and regulations.
   d. division of labor.

8. What type of society did Ferdinand Tönnies describe as a close-knit community in which members have strong personal bonds?
   a. *Gesellschaft*
   b. mechanical
   c. *Gemeinschaft*
   d. organic

9. Sociologist Daniel Bell uses which of the following terms to refer to a society whose economic system is engaged primarily in the processing and control of information?
   a. postmodern
   b. horticultural
   c. industrial
   d. postindustrial

10. What characteristic of postmodern life emphasizes the importance of consumption on identity creation?
    a. stories
    b. images
    c. choices
    d. networks

1. (c); 2. (c); 3. (a); 4. (b); 5. (d); 6. (c); 7. (a); 8. (c); 9. (d); 10. (c)

6

DEVIANCE

LIVING THE GANG LIFE

Sociology student Sudhir Venkatesh (2008), wanting to better understand the lives of poor African Americans, ventured into the housing projects in inner-city Chicago. After a rocky beginning, his naïveté and genuine curiosity helped to open the door to what became a seven-year, in-depth participation research project about gangs, drugs, crime, public housing, and more.

Venkatesh's commitment to going beyond what W.E.B. Du Bois dismissed as "car-window sociology" ultimately provided him access to information about crime and deviance that he could never have found through a survey. Through his research he learned that gangs have a highly organized structure, with those at the top of the gang hierarchy doing well financially, and the foot soldiers at the bottom, who make up 95 percent of the membership, averaging only $3.30 per hour (Levitt and Dubner 2005). They also have an astonishingly high death rate. These two facts together led one of Venkatesh's collaborators to say that selling drugs for a gang is perhaps "the worst job in all of America."

Although it may not yield much money, dealing drugs does allow gang members to help support their families. Venkatesh argued that their willingness to work these jobs, even in the face of minimal return and high risk, demonstrated their desire to work, but they found so few viable options that some actually worked at McDonald's to supplement their drug-dealing income.

Venkatesh also found that gangs seek to contribute to the local community, giving money to women who work in the buildings looking after children and the elderly. They require their young members to stay in school, and prohibit members from using hard drugs—in part because they cannot be good at business if they are high, and in part because it is bad for the image of the gang.

Through research like Venkatesh's, sociologists can better understand crime and deviance. The gang Venkatesh studied tried to create a level of stability in their neighborhood, but they relied on crime and violence as tools of their trade. What social factors lead to such outcomes, and can those factors or outcomes be changed? In this chapter we will look at these questions and more.

As You READ >>

- How do groups maintain social control?
- What is the difference between deviance and crime?
- How do sociologists explain deviance and crime?

>> Social Control

At some point all of us have wondered, "Should I do what *they* want or should I do what *I* want?" The tension between the individual and society is at the heart of sociology. To better understand the power that others wield over us, sociologists study social control, deviance, and crime.

As we saw in Chapter 3, we create norms—dress codes, game rules, dining etiquette—to provide social order and make our lives predictable. We enforce them through **social control**—the techniques and strategies for preventing deviant human behavior in any society. Social control occurs on all levels of society. In the family, we are socialized to obey our parents simply because they are our parents. Peer groups introduce us to informal norms, such as dress codes, that govern the behavior of their members. Colleges establish the standards they expect of students. In bureaucratic organizations, workers encounter a formal system of rules and regulations. Finally, the government of every society legislates and enforces social norms.

Most of us respect and accept basic social norms and assume that others will do the same. Even without thinking, we usually obey the instructions of police officers, follow the day-to-day rules at our jobs, and move to the rear of elevators when people enter. Such behavior reflects an effective process of socialization to the dominant standards of a culture. At the same time, we are well aware that others expect us to act "properly" and that failure to do so will result in consequences. **Sanctions** are the penalties and rewards we face for conduct concerning a social norm. For example, if we fail to live up to expectations at work, we might get fired. If we do a good job, we might get a promotion.

Sanctions point to the power that societies, institutions, and groups have over our lives. On the one hand, we want people to respect social norms so that the group or society can survive. Society is defined in part by people's willingness to accept shared beliefs and practices, even if doing so sometimes constrains their selfish pursuits. On the other hand, society can be oppressive, limiting individual freedom and advancing the interests of some at the expense of others. Entrenched interests seek to maintain the status quo and use their power over sanctions to do so. In fact, positive social change often comes through resistance to the status quo, with individuals and groups rejecting existing norms and following new paths. Such attempts may meet with significant opposition, as was evident in the civil rights movement. Similar struggles were necessary in America to win independence from England, to overturn the institution of slavery, to earn women the vote, and to force an end to the war in Vietnam.

CONFORMITY AND OBEDIENCE

Techniques for social control operate on both the group and the societal level. People we think of as peers or equals influence us to act in particular ways; the same is true of people who hold authority over us or whose positions we respect. Social psychologist Stanley Milgram (1975) made a useful distinction between these two levels of social control.

According to Milgram, **conformity** means going along with peers—individuals of our own status who have no special right to direct our behavior. **Obedience,** on the other hand, is compliance with higher authorities in a hierarchical structure. A recruit entering military service will typically conform to the habits and language of other recruits and obey the orders of superiors. Students will conform to the drinking behavior of their peers and obey the requests of campus security officers.

In a classic experiment, Milgram (1963, 1975) sought to test how far people would go when obeying authority. Would they administer increasingly painful electric shocks to another person if asked to do so by a scientific researcher? Contrary to what we might believe about ourselves, Milgram found that most of us would obey the researcher. In his words, "Behavior that is unthinkable in an individual . . . acting on his own may be executed without hesitation when carried out under orders" (1975:xi).

To set up his experiment, Milgram placed ads in local newspapers to

recruit subjects for an experiment at Yale University. His participants included postal clerks, engineers, high school teachers, and laborers. They were told that the purpose of the research was to investigate the effects of punishment on learning. The scientist, dressed in a gray technician's coat, explained that in each test, one subject would be randomly selected as the "learner"and another would function as the "teacher." However, the experiment was rigged so that the "real" subject would always be the teacher while an associate of Milgram's served as the learner.

> **social control** The techniques and strategies for preventing deviant human behavior in any society.
>
> **conformity** The act of going along with peers—individuals of our own status who have no special right to direct our behavior.
>
> **obedience** Compliance with higher authorities in a hierarchical structure.

To begin, each teacher was given a sample shock of 45 volts to convince him or her of the authenticity of the experiment. A learner was then strapped to an electric apparatus, and the teacher was taken to an electronic "shock generator" with 30 switches labeled from 15 to 450 volts. The experimenter then instructed the teacher to apply shocks of increasing voltage each time the learner gave an incorrect answer on a memory test. Teachers were told that "although the shocks can be extremely painful, they cause no permanent tissue damage." In reality, the learner did not receive any shocks.

In a prearranged script, the learner deliberately gave incorrect answers and pretended to be in pain when "shocked." For example, at 150 volts, the learner would cry out, "Get me out of here!" At 270 volts, the learner would scream in agony. When the shock reached 350 volts, the learner would fall silent. If the teacher wanted to stop the experiment, the experimenter would insist that the teacher continue, using such statements as "The experiment requires

Did You Know?

. . . Some prosecutors have sought to bring charges against college fraternities as gangs. They argued that the fraternity as an organization systematically promotes criminal behavior, including underage drinking and abusive actions toward women. Venkatesh suggests that, if you define a gang as "an established organization whose members come together for solidarity reasons and who engage in delinquent and/or criminal activities," then perhaps those prosecutors might be onto something (Dubner 2007).

that you continue" and "You have no other choice; you *must* go on" (Milgram 1975:19–23).

The results of this unusual experiment stunned and dismayed Milgram and other social scientists. A sample of psychiatrists had predicted that virtually all subjects would refuse to shock innocent victims. In their view, only a "pathological fringe" of fewer than 2 percent would continue administering shocks up to the maximum level. Yet almost two-thirds of participants fell into the category of "obedient subjects."

Why did these subjects obey? Why were they willing to inflict seemingly painful shocks on innocent victims who had never done them any harm? There is no evidence that these subjects were unusually sadistic; few seemed to enjoy administering the shocks. Instead, in Milgram's view, the key to obedience was the experimenter's social role as "scientist" and "seeker of knowledge."

Milgram pointed out that in the modern industrial world, we are accustomed to submitting to impersonal authority figures whose status is indicated by a title (professor, lieutenant, doctor) or by a uniform (the technician's coat). Because we view the authority as more important than the individual, we shift responsibility for our behavior to the authority figure. Afterward, Milgram's subjects frequently stated, "If it were up to me, I would not have administered shocks." They saw themselves as merely doing their duty (Milgram 1975).

Milgram launched his experimental study of obedience in part to better understand the involvement of Germans in the murder of 6 million Jews and millions of other people during World War II. In an interview conducted long after the publication of his study, he suggested that "if a system of death camps were set up in the United States of the sort we had seen in Nazi Germany, one would be able to find sufficient personnel for those camps in any medium-sized American town" (CBS News 1979:7–8). Though many people questioned this statement, the revealing photos taken at Iraq's Abu Ghraib prison in 2004, showing U.S. military guards humiliating if not torturing Iraqi prisoners, recalled the experiment Milgram had done two generations earlier. Under conducive circumstances, otherwise normal people can and often do treat one another inhumanely (Hayden 2004; Zimbardo 2007).

INFORMAL AND FORMAL SOCIAL CONTROL

The sanctions that society uses to encourage conformity and obedience—and to discourage violation of social norms—are carried out through both informal and formal social control. As the term implies, people use **informal social control** casually to enforce norms. Examples include smiles, laughter, a raised eyebrow,

A participant in the Milgram experiment.

and ridicule. We seek to read such cues in new situations such as a first date or a job interview so that we might adjust our behavior accordingly.

SOC THINK

All groups must use some form of social control if they are to maintain any sense of order. What mechanisms of formal and informal social control are evident in your college classes and in day-to-day life and social interactions at your school?

Formal social control is carried out by authorized agents, such as police officers, judges, school administrators, employers, military officers, and managers. It can serve as a last resort when socialization and informal sanctions do not bring about desired behavior. An increasingly significant means of formal social control in the United States is imprisonment. In 2008, more than 7.3 million adults underwent some form of correctional supervision—jail, prison, probation, or parole. Put another way, 1 out of every 31 adult Americans was subject to this very formal type of social control (Glaze and Bonczar 2009).

In 2007, in the wake of the mass shootings at Virginia Tech, many college officials reviewed security measures on their campuses. Administrators were reluctant to end or even limit the relative freedom of movement students on their campuses enjoyed. Instead, they concentrated on improving emergency communications between campus police and students, faculty, and staff. Reflecting a reliance on technology to maintain social control, college leaders called for replacement of the "old" technology of email with instant alerts that could be sent to people's cell phones via instant messaging.

Six years earlier, in the aftermath of the terrorist attacks of September 11, 2001, new measures of social control became the norm in the United States. Some of them, such as stepped-up security at airports and high-rise buildings, were highly visible to the public. The federal government has also publicly urged citizens to engage in informal social control by watching for and reporting people whose actions seem suspicious. But many other measures taken by the government have increased the covert surveillance of private records and communications.

Only a month and a half after September 11, and with virtually no debate, Congress passed the USA PATRIOT Act of 2001. It was reauthorized in 2005 and 2006, and extended by the Obama administration in 2010. Sections of this sweeping legislation revoked legal checks on the power of law enforcement agencies. Without a warrant or probable cause, the FBI can now secretly access most private records, including medical histories, library accounts, and student registrations. In 2002, for example, the FBI searched the records of hundreds of dive shops and scuba organizations. Agents had been directed to identify every person who had taken diving lessons in the past three years

because of speculation that terrorists might try to approach their targets underwater (Moss and Fessenden 2002).

Many people think that this kind of social control goes too far. Civil rights advocates also worry that the government's request for information on suspicious activities may encourage negative stereotyping of Muslims and Arab Americans. Clearly, there is a trade-off between the benefits of surveillance and violation of the right to privacy.

informal social control Social control that is carried out casually by ordinary people through such means as laughter, smiles, and ridicule.

formal social control Social control that is carried out by authorized agents, such as police officers, judges, school administrators, and employers.

The interplay between formal and informal social control can be complicated because we sometimes have to balance one source of control against another. College students, for example, receive conflicting messages about the acceptability of binge drinking. On the one hand, it represents deviance from the standards of conduct expected of those in an academic context. On the other hand, binge drinking shows conformity to the peer culture, especially in the context of sororities and fraternities (see the figure "Binge Drinking on Campus"). Increasingly, colleges and universities are taking steps to exert greater social control by instituting rules banning kegs, closing

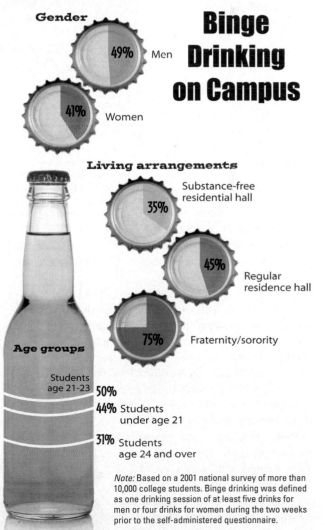

Binge Drinking on Campus

Gender
49% Men
41% Women

Living arrangements
35% Substance-free residential hall
45% Regular residence hall
75% Fraternity/sorority

Age groups
Students age 21-23 — 50%
44% Students under age 21
31% Students age 24 and over

Note: Based on a 2001 national survey of more than 10,000 college students. Binge drinking was defined as one drinking session of at least five drinks for men or four drinks for women during the two weeks prior to the self-administered questionnaire.

Source: Wechsler et al. 2002:208.

fraternities and sororities, expelling students after multiple alcohol-related violations, and working with local liquor retailers to discourage high-volume sales to students (Wechsler and Nelson 2008).

LAW AND SOCIETY

Some norms are so important to a society that they are formalized into laws limiting people's behavior. **Law** may be defined as governmental social control (Black 1995). Some laws, such as the prohibition against murder, are directed at all members of society. Others, such as fishing and hunting regulations, primarily affect particular categories of people. Still others govern the behavior of social institutions (for instance, corporate law and laws regarding the taxing of nonprofit enterprises).

Sociologists see the creation of laws as a social process. Because laws are passed in response to a perceived need for formal social control, sociologists have sought to explain how and why such a perception arises. In their view, law is not merely a static body of rules handed down from generation to generation. Rather, it reflects continually changing standards of what is right and wrong, of how violations are to be determined, and of what sanctions are to be applied (Schur 1968).

In diverse societies, the establishment of laws inevitably generates conflicts over whose values should prevail. As such, the creation of civil and criminal laws can be controversial. For example, should it be against the law to employ illegal immigrants? To have an abortion? To allow prayer in public schools? To smoke on an airplane? Such issues have been bitterly debated because they require a choice among competing values. Not surprisingly, unpopular laws—such as the 18th Amendment, which prohibited the manufacture and sale of alcohol (ratified in 1919), or the nationwide 55-mile-per-hour speed limit that was imposed in 1974—become

difficult to enforce when there is no consensus supporting the norms. In both cases, the public commonly violated the stated government policy, and the laws proved unenforceable; the states repealed Prohibition in 1933, and Congress overturned the national speed-limit policy in 1987.

The current debate over whether to allow people to use marijuana legally for medical purposes illustrates the difficulty in crafting laws that govern private behavior. Although approximately 70 percent of adults support such use, federal law prohibits all uses of marijuana (ProCon.org 2009). Nevertheless, as the map below shows, 14 states have granted citizens the right to use marijuana for medical purposes. In May 2009, the U.S. Supreme Court upheld the right of states to pass such statutes, despite existing federal laws.

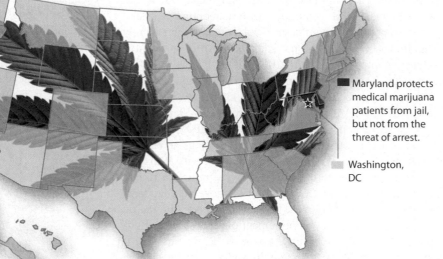

Maryland protects medical marijuana patients from jail, but not from the threat of arrest.

Washington, DC

14 states have laws that allow the cultivation of medical marijuana and that protect patients who possess medical marijuana (with their doctor's recommendations or certifications) from criminal penalties.

17 states and the District of Columbia have laws that recognize marijuana's medical value, but these laws are ineffective because they rely on federal cooperation.

Source: Marijuana Policy Project 2008.

Medical Marijuana Laws

Socialization is the primary vehicle for instilling conforming and obedient behavior, including obedience to law. Generally, it is not external pressure from a peer group or authority figure that makes us go along with social norms. Rather, we have internalized such norms as valid and desirable and are self-policing. In a profound sense, we want to see ourselves (and to be seen) as loyal, cooperative, responsible, and respectful of others. In the United States and other societies around the world, people are socialized both to want to belong and to fear being viewed as different or deviant.

Control theory suggests that our connection to other members of society leads us to conform systematically to society's norms. According to sociologist Travis Hirschi and other control theorists, our bonds to family members, friends, and peers induce us to follow the mores and folkways of our society. We give little conscious thought to whether we will be sanctioned if we fail to conform. Socialization develops our self-control so well that we don't need further pressure to obey social norms. Although control theory does not explain the rationale for every conforming act, it nevertheless reminds us that while the media may focus on crime and disorder, most members of most societies conform to and obey basic norms most of the time (Gottfredson and Hirschi 1990; Hirschi 1969).

>> Deviance

The flip side of social control is deviance. **Deviance** is behavior that violates the standards of conduct or expectations of a group or society (Wickman 1991:85). In the United States, most people classify those who are alcoholics, compulsive gamblers, or mentally ill as deviant. Being late for class is categorized as a deviant act, as is wearing jeans to a formal wedding. On the basis of the sociological definition, we are all deviant from time to time. Each of us violates common social norms in certain situations.

WHAT BEHAVIOR IS DEVIANT?

Because deviance involves violation of some group's norms, defining an act as deviant depends on the context. File sharing on the Internet—including MP3s, movies, computer games, books, and almost anything else that can be digitized—provides an example of how deviance can be in the eye of the beholder. Sharing files, whether through BitTorrent, LimeWire, or eMule, has become widespread. New movies are sometimes available online even before they have been released in the theater. Because the "property" these files represent is not physical, it can be reproduced for virtually no cost. Anyone with a computer and an Internet connection can grab them from people who are willing to share, then pass them along to others. Just how deviant is this? Record and movie companies take it very seriously; they have actively pursued lawsuits against those who share files in

> **deviance** Behavior that violates the standards of conduct or expectations of a group or society.

part to scare those who might think of doing it. However, the widespread availability of these files suggests that many people do not view this practice as particularly deviant. Some even view it as an act of protest against what they consider unfair prices charged by big corporations.

In most instances, those individuals and groups with the greatest status and power define what is acceptable and what is deviant. For example, serious medical warnings of the dangers of tobacco appeared as early as 1964, yet cigarette smoking continued to be accepted for decades—in good part because of the power of tobacco farmers and cigarette manufacturers. Only after public health and anticancer activists led a long campaign against cigarette smoking did smoking become more of a deviant activity. Today, many state and local laws limit where people can smoke.

Of course, deviation from norms is not always negative, let alone criminal. A member of an exclusive social club who speaks out against a traditional policy of excluding women, Blacks, and Jews from admittance is deviating from the club's norms. So is a police officer who blows the whistle on corruption or brutality within the department.

DEVIANCE AND SOCIAL STIGMA

Some people are unwillingly cast in negative social roles because of physical or behavioral characteristics. Whole groups of people—for instance, "short people" or "blondes"—may be labeled in this way. Once individuals

Present-day fans of bullfighting, which has a long and rich history in Spain and elsewhere, are now often stigmatized for their admiration of a sport that can result in pain and death for the bulls.

... In 2006, the **Spanish Association of Fashion Designers banned overly thin models—those with a** *body mass index* **score under 18—from the runway during Madrid Fashion Week. Similarly, in 2009, Germany's most popular women's magazine,** *Brigitte*, **banned professional models from its pages, replacing them with "real life" women. Both groups established these policies to encourage healthier practices for the models, and in response to protests that such ultrathin images of women contribute to eating disorders.**

that the beauty myth makes many women feel uncomfortable with themselves, men too lack confidence in their appearance. The number of males who choose to undergo cosmetic procedures has risen sharply over the years; in 2009, men accounted for 15 percent of such surgeries (American Academy of Cosmetic Surgery 2010).

Often people are stigmatized for deviant behaviors that they may no longer practice. The labels "former gambler," "ex-convict," "recovering alcoholic," and "ex–mental patient" can stick to a person for life. Goffman draws a useful distinction between a prestige symbol that calls attention to a positive aspect of one's identity, such as a wedding band or a badge, and a stigma symbol that discredits or debases one's identity, such as a conviction for child molestation. While stigma symbols may not always be obvious, they can become a matter of public knowledge. Starting in 1994, many states required convicted sex offenders to register with local police departments. Some communities publish the names and addresses, and in some instances even the pictures, of convicted sex offenders on the Web.

A person need not be guilty of a crime to be stigmatized. Homeless people often have trouble getting a job because employers are wary of applicants who cannot give a home address. Moreover, hiding one's homelessness is difficult because agencies generally use the telephone to contact applicants about job openings. If a homeless person has access to a telephone at a shelter, the staff generally answers the phone by announcing the name of the institution—a sure way to discourage prospective employers. Even if a homeless person surmounts these obstacles and manages to get a job, she or he is often fired when the employer learns of the situation. Regardless of a person's positive attributes, employers regard the negative connotation of homelessness as sufficient reason to dismiss an employee.

have been assigned a deviant role, they can have trouble presenting a positive image to others and may even experience lowered self-esteem. Sociologist Erving Goffman coined the term **stigma** to describe the labels society uses to devalue members of certain social groups (Goffman 1963).

We face pressure not to deviate too far from expected norms. To avoid stigma, for example, women can feel pressured to approximate what Naomi Wolf (1992) refers to as the "beauty myth"—an exaggerated ideal of beauty, beyond the reach of all but a few females. As a result, many of the 14.8 million cosmetic procedures performed by physicians on women in 2009 were performed on women who would be defined objectively as having a normal appearance. Although feminist sociologists have accurately noted

>> Crime

If deviance means breaking group norms, **crime** is a violation of law for which some governmental authority applies formal penalties. It is a type of deviance representing a violation of social norms administered by the state. Laws divide crimes into various categories, depending on the severity of the offense, the age of the offender, the potential punishment, and the court that holds jurisdiction over the case.

OFFICIAL CRIME REPORTS

When we think of crime, the categories most likely to come to mind involve what we might think of as street crimes. The FBI breaks such crimes into two major categories: violent crimes and property crimes. They do not include all types of crime in these reports, focusing only on four major types within each category. Violent crimes include murder, forcible rape, robbery, and aggravated assault; property crimes include burglary, larceny-theft, motor vehicle theft, and arson. The FBI provides an annual account of the number of these crimes in their *Uniform Crime Reports* (UCR), which is available online. Because they are tracked so closely by the FBI and have been for a long time, these crimes have come to be known as **index crimes.**

As we can see in the accompanying table, property crimes occur at a much higher rate than do violent crimes. In fact, according to the "crime clock" that the FBI provides as part of its report, a property crime occurs on average every 3.2 seconds. The most frequent property crime is larceny-theft, which includes incidents such as shoplifting and stealing items from cars. By contrast, a violent crime occurs every 22.8 seconds. Robbery, which involves the use or threat of force, is the most frequent violent crime, with one occurring every 1.2 minutes. Murder is the least frequent of the index crimes, with one occurring every 32.3 minutes (U.S. Department of Justice 2009b).

Trends in Crime Analysis of crime data reports reveals a significant decline in violent crime nationwide during the late 1990s after consistently high rates over many years.

Sociologists have offered a number of explanations for this, including

- a booming economy and falling unemployment rates through most of the 1990s;
- community-oriented policing and crime prevention programs;
- new gun control laws; and
- a massive increase in the prison population, which at least prevents inmates from committing crimes outside prison.

In the past five years, rates have held relatively steady, but even with the previous declines, rates of reported crime remain well above both those of other nations and those of the United States just 20 years earlier. Feminist scholars draw our attention to one significant variation: the proportion of major crimes committed by women has increased. Between 1999 and 2008, female arrests for major reported crimes increased 11.6 percent, while comparable male arrests declined 3.1 percent (U.S. Department of Justice 2009a: Table 33).

> **stigma** A label used to devalue members of certain social groups.
>
> **crime** A violation of criminal law for which some governmental authority applies formal penalties.
>
> **index crimes** The eight types of crime reported annually by the FBI in the *Uniform Crime Reports*: murder, forcible rape, robbery, aggravated assault, burglary, larceny-theft, motor vehicle theft, and arson.

National Crime Rates and Percentage Change

Offenses in 2008		Number reported	Rate per 100,000 inhabitants	Percent change in rate Since 1999	Percent change in rate Since 2004
Violent crimes	Murder	16,272	5.4	0.8	4.8
	Forcible rape	89,000	29.3	-6.4	-0.5
	Robbery	441,855	145.3	10.1	7.9
	Aggravated assault	834,885	274.6	-1.5	-8.4
	Total	1,382,012	454.5	1.6	-3.1
Property crimes	Burglary	2,222,196	730.8	3.6	5.8
	Larceny-theft	6,588,873	2,167.0	-5.0	-5.3
	Motor vehicle theft	956,846	314.7	-22.7	-16.9
	Total	9,767,915	3,212.5	-5.3	-4.3

= 10,000 Offenses

Notes: Arson was designated an index offense beginning in 1979; data on arson were still incomplete as of 2004. Because of rounding, the offenses may not add to totals.

Source: U.S. Department of Justice 2009a: Tables 1, 1A.

Crimes Reported to Police

Percent reported to police

47.1%	Total violent crime
62.0%	Aggravated assault
60.5%	Robbery
41.4%	Rape/sexual assault
40.3%	Total property crime
79.6%	Motor vehicle theft
56.2%	Burglary
33.6%	Larceny-theft

Note: Percentages based on the National Crime Victimization Survey for 2008.
Source: Rand 2008, 2009.

Limitations of Crime Statistics There are limitations to official crime statistics, the most serious of which is that they include only those crimes reported to law enforcement agencies. In addition, because members of racial and ethnic minority groups often distrust law enforcement agencies, they may not contact the police when they are victimized. Further, feminist sociologists and others have noted that many women do not report rape or spousal abuse out of fear they will be blamed for the crime.

Partly because of such deficiencies in official statistics, the U.S. Department of Justice initiated the National Crime Victimization Survey in 1972 (Rand 2009). In compiling this annual report, the department's Bureau of Justice Statistics not only gathers information from law enforcement agencies but also interviews more than 75,000 individuals in 42,000 households to determine if they were victims of a specific set of crimes during the preceding year. In general, those who administer **victimization surveys** question ordinary people, not police officers, to determine whether they have been victims of crime.

Even using such surveys, the likelihood of underreporting the actual number of crimes remains. Surveys require that victims understand what has happened to them and

SOCTHINK

The Clery Act, passed in 1990, requires schools to provide students with timely reports of campus crimes. How reliable do you think such reports are? Why might reports of crime on college campuses underestimate the actual number of incidents?

that they be willing to disclose such information to interviewers. People are particularly reluctant to report crimes such as fraud, income tax evasion, and blackmail in victimization studies. Nevertheless, 90 percent of all households have been willing to cooperate with investigators for the National Crime Victimization Survey. As shown in the figure "Crimes Reported to Police," victimization surveys reveal that a significant percentage of crimes are not reported to the police, varying by type of crime, thus demonstrating that official UCR statistics underreport actual crime levels (Rand 2009).

Another limitation of the UCR official statistics is that they exclude many offenses that we would count as criminal. In so doing, they minimize the degree to which we see perpetrators of other types of crime as criminal in the same way as violators of the index crimes. We turn next to several such categories, including white-collar crime, victimless crimes, and organized crime.

WHITE-COLLAR CRIME

Income tax evasion, stock manipulation, consumer fraud, bribery and extraction of kickbacks, embezzlement, and misrepresentation in advertising—these are all examples of **white-collar crime,** or illegal acts committed in the course of business activities, often by affluent, "respectable" people. Historically, we have viewed such crimes differently because they

"I swear I wasn't looking at smut—I was just stealing music."

are often perpetrated through respected occupational roles (Sutherland 1949, 1983).

Edwin Sutherland (1940) coined the term *white-collar crime* in 1939 to refer to acts by individuals, but the term is now used more broadly to include offenses by businesses and corporations as well. Corporate crime, or any act by a corporation that is punishable by the government, takes many forms and includes individuals, organizations, and institutions among its victims. Corporations may engage in anticompetitive behavior, environmental pollution, medical fraud, tax fraud, stock fraud and manipulation, accounting fraud, the production of unsafe goods, bribery and corruption, and health and safety violations (J. Coleman 2006).

5 Movies on CRIME

The Silence of the Lambs
A cannibal holds the key to finding a serial killer.

Capote
Writer Truman Capote explores a gruesome murder case.

City of God
When crime is the culture.

No Country for Old Men
A violent cat-and-mouse game between a witness, a hit man, and a sheriff.

Ocean's Eleven
Eleven men make theft an art form.

The downfall of Bernie Madoff represents the largest case of white-collar crime of its type in history. Madoff, an American businessman who managed people's financial investments, promised investors annual returns of 15 to 20 percent and delivered on that promise for years. This enabled him to attract extremely wealthy clients from around the world, even charitable organizations. In the end, he was just running a scam. Madoff had provided investors with false statements showing nonexistent trades and profits. Estimates are that he defrauded his clients out of $65 billion in purported assets. Life savings and family fortunes were gone in an instant (Gaviria and Smith 2009).

The scheme collapsed in December 2008, after Madoff confessed to his sons that his investment company was a "giant Ponzi scheme." After consulting an attorney, they

SOC THINK

Should gambling, prostitution, and recreational drugs be legalized? What are the potential consequences, both positive and negative, of doing so?

reported their father to the FBI. Madoff was arrested the next day. In a Ponzi scheme, the fraudulent investor uses money from new investors to pay off old ones rather than investing the money. The payoff is at higher-than-average rates of return, which encourages new investors who are attracted by the profits. The whole system topples if current investors want to pull their money out, or if there aren't enough new investors to cover profits and payouts to existing investors. Both happened with the economic collapse in late 2008. On March 12, 2009, Madoff pled guilty to 11 felony counts, including securities fraud, mail fraud, money laundering, and perjury. He was sent directly to jail and was sentenced to the maximum of 150 years in prison (Henriques and Healy 2009).

What is particularly interesting about the Madoff case is that officials at the Securities and Exchange Commission (SEC) were tipped off numerous times to the possibility that Madoff's investments were a scam. Finally, after receiving documented accusations that he was running a Ponzi scheme, the SEC launched an official investigation in 2006. Two years later they concluded that there was "no evidence of fraud." The SEC failed to see what analysts now say should have been obvious. Red flags were ignored, but why? Sociologists suggest that white-collar criminals are often given the benefit of the doubt. In fact, during each previous investigation, Madoff deliberately and successfully used his status as a respected businessman as evidence of his innocence. He might have avoided detection had it not been for his own confession (Berenson and Henriques 2008).

VICTIMLESS CRIMES

Another category of crimes that raises questions about how we define deviance consists of so-called victimless crimes. **Victimless crime** refers to the willing exchange among adults of widely desired, but illegal, goods and services, such as drugs or prostitution (Schur 1965, 1985). The fact that the parties involved are willing participants has led some people to suggest that such transactions should not constitute crimes.

Some activists are working to decriminalize many of these illegal practices. Supporters of decriminalization are troubled by the attempt to legislate a moral code for adults. In their view, prostitution, drug use, gambling, and other victimless crimes are impossible to prevent. The already overburdened criminal justice system should instead devote its resources to "street crimes" and other offenses with obvious victims.

victimization survey A questionnaire or interview given to a sample of the population to determine whether people have been victims of crime.

white-collar crime Illegal acts committed by affluent, "respectable" individuals in the course of business activities.

victimless crime A term used by sociologists to describe the willing exchange among adults of widely desired, but illegal, goods and services.

Despite widespread use of the term *victimless crime,* however, many people object to the notion that there is no victim other than the offender in such crimes. Excessive drinking, compulsive gambling, and illegal drug use contribute to an enormous amount of personal and property damage. A person with a drinking problem can become abusive to a spouse or children; a compulsive gambler or drug user may steal to pursue his or her obsession. Feminist sociologists contend that prostitution, as well as the more disturbing aspects of pornography, reinforce the misconception that women are "toys" who can be treated as objects rather than people. According to critics of decriminalization, society must not give tacit approval to conduct that has such harmful consequences (Farley and Malarek 2008; Meier and Geis 1997).

> Where there are rules there will always be violations of those rules.
>
> Joel M. Charon

organized crime The work of a group that regulates relations among criminal enterprises involved in illegal activities, including prostitution, gambling, and the smuggling and sale of illegal drugs.

transnational crime Crime that occurs across multiple national borders.

ORGANIZED CRIME

When it comes to organized crime, the name Tony Soprano is the first that comes to mind for many people. He was the fictional boss of the DiMeo crime family on HBO's hit series *The Sopranos.* In real life, examples of

The HBO series *The Wire* has been widely praised for its realistic portrayal of urban life in Baltimore including its coverage of drugs, gangs, and law enforcement. A growing number of sociologists teach courses based on the show to demonstrate lessons about community, crime, poverty, and corruption. Sociologist William Julius Wilson, who teaches such a course at Harvard, maintains, "Although *The Wire* is fiction, not a documentary, its depiction of [the] systemic urban inequality that constrains the lives of the urban poor is more poignant and compelling [than] that of any published study, including my own" (Bennett 2010).

organized crime groups go beyond the Mafia to include the Japanese Yakuza, the Russian Organization, Colombian drug cartels, and many other international crime syndicates. For our purposes, we will consider **organized crime** to be the work of a group that regulates relations among criminal enterprises involved in illegal activities, including prostitution, gambling, and the smuggling and sale of illegal drugs (National Institute of Justice 2007).

Organized crime dominates the world of illegal business, just as large corporations dominate the conventional business world. It allocates territory, sets prices for goods and services, and acts as an arbiter in internal disputes. A secret, conspiratorial activity, organized crime generally evades law enforcement. It takes over legitimate businesses, gains influence over labor unions, corrupts public officials, intimidates witnesses in criminal trials, and even "taxes" merchants in exchange for "protection" (Federal Bureau of Investigation 2009).

Historically, organized crime has provided a means of upward mobility for groups of people struggling to escape poverty. Sociologist Daniel Bell (1953) used the term *ethnic succession* to describe the sequential passage of leadership from Irish Americans in the early 1900s to Jewish Americans in the 1920s and then to Italian Americans in the early 1930s. Recently, ethnic succession has become more complex, reflecting the diversity of the nation's latest immigrants. Colombian, Mexican, Russian, Chinese, Pakistani, and Nigerian immigrants are among those who have begun to play a significant role in organized crime activities (Friman 2004; Kleinknecht 1996).

There has always been a global element in organized crime. However, law enforcement officials and policy makers now acknowledge the emergence of a new form of organized crime that takes advantage of advances in electronic communications. International organized crime includes drug and arms smuggling, money laundering, and trafficking in illegal immigrants and stolen goods (Lumpe 2003; Office of Justice Programs 1999).

INTERNATIONAL CRIME

In the past, international crime was often limited to the clandestine shipment of goods across the border between two countries. Increasingly, however, crime is no more restricted by such borders than is legal commerce. Rather than concentrating on specific countries, international crime now spans the globe.

Transnational Crime More and more, scholars and law enforcement officials are turning their attention to **transnational crime,** or crime that occurs across multiple national borders. Historically, probably the most dreaded example of transnational crime has been slavery. At first, governments did not regard slavery as a crime but merely

International Incarceration Rates

Rank
out of 217 nations

International incarceration rates
(prison population rates per 100,000 of the national population)

Rank	Country	Rate
1	United States of America	753
3	Russian Federation	610
25	South Africa	325
25	Israel	325
57	Mexico	204
89	England and Wales	152
116	China	119
119	Kenya	117
120	Canada	116
166	Sweden	74
178	Japan	63
204	India	32

Source: International Centre for Prison Studies 2010.

International Crime Rates Taking an international perspective on crime reinforces one of the key sociological lessons about crime and deviance: Place matters. Although cross-national data comparison can be difficult, we can offer insight about how crime rates differ around the world.

During the 1980s and 1990s, violent crimes were much more common in the United States than in the nations of western Europe. Murders, rapes, and robberies were reported to the police at much higher rates in the United States. Yet the incidence of certain other types of crime appears to be higher elsewhere. For example, England, Italy, Australia, and New Zealand all have higher rates of car theft than the United States. Developing nations have significant rates of reported homicide due to civil unrest and political conflict among civilians (van Dijk, van Kesteren, and Schmit 2007; World Bank 2003a). But when it comes to putting offenders in jail, the United States tops them all. On a typical day, the United States imprisons 753 of every 100,000 adults, compared to 610 in Russia, fewer than 204 in Mexico, and 116 in Canada (International Centre for Prison Studies 2010).

Why are rates of violent crime so much higher in the United States than in western Europe? Sociologist Elliot Currie (1985, 1998) has suggested that our society places greater emphasis on individual economic achievement than other societies. At the same time, many observers have noted that the culture of the United States has long tolerated, if not condoned, many forms of violence. Coupled with sharp disparities between poor and affluent citizens, significant unemployment, and substantial alcohol and drug abuse, these factors combine to produce a climate conducive to crime.

However, disturbing increases in violent crime are evident in other Western societies. For example, crime has skyrocketed in Russia since the overthrow of Communist Party rule (with its strict controls on guns and criminals) in 1991. In 1998 there were fewer than 260 homicides in Moscow; now there are more than 1000 homicides a year. Organized crime has filled the power vacuum in Moscow: One result is that gangland shootouts and premeditated "contract hits" have become more common. Some prominent reformist politicians have been targeted as well. Russia incarcerates an extremely high proportion of its citizens—almost as high as the United States (Bush 2006; Pridemore 2003).

regulated it as they would trade in any other good. In the 20th century, transnational crime grew to embrace trafficking in endangered species, drugs, and stolen art and antiquities.

Transnational crime is not exclusive of some of the other types of crime we have discussed. For example, organized criminal networks are increasingly global. Technology definitely facilitates their illegal activities, such as trafficking in child pornography. Beginning in the 1990s, the United Nations began to categorize transnational crimes, such as hijacking, illegal drug trade, sea piracy, and terrorism.

One way to fight such crime has been through multilateral cooperation in which countries cooperate to pursue border-crossing crime. The first global effort to control international crime was the International Criminal Police Organization (Interpol), a cooperative network of European police forces founded to stem the movement of political revolutionaries across borders. While such efforts to fight transnational crime may seem lofty—an activity with which any government would want to cooperate—they are complicated by sensitive legal and security issues. Most nations that have signed protocols issued by the United Nations, including the United States, have expressed concern over potential encroachments on their national judicial systems, as well as concern over their national security. Thus, they have been reluctant to share certain types of intelligence data. The terrorist attacks of September 11, 2001, increased both the interest in combating transnational crime and sensitivity to the risks of sharing intelligence data (Deflem 2005; Felson and Kalaitzidis 2005).

>> Sociological Perspectives on Deviance and Crime

Why do people violate social norms? We have seen that deviant acts are subject to both informal and formal social control. The nonconforming or disobedient person may face disapproval, loss of friends, fines, or even imprisonment. Why, then, does deviance occur?

Sociologists have been interested in crime and deviance from the very beginning and have generated numerous theories of deviance and crime. Though we might wish otherwise, there is no one, simple, universal theory that explains all such acts. Here we will look to just a few of the theories that sociologists have offered in order to identify significant factors that we must consider in our attempt to understand deviance and crime more fully.

SOCIAL ORDER, DEVIANCE, AND CRIME

Émile Durkheim's ([1895] 1964) emphasis on the importance of social order led him to investigate the nature and causes of deviance and crime. He wondered why deviance, which would seem to undermine order, is found in all societies. For Durkheim the answer rested with how such actions were perceived by others.

Durkheim's Theory of Deviance Durkheim argued that there is nothing inherently deviant or criminal in any act; the key is how society responds to the act. He put it this way: "We must not say that an action shocks the common consciousness because it is criminal, but rather that it is criminal because it shocks that consciousness" ([1895] 1964:123–24). In other words, nothing is criminal or worthy of condemnation unless we decide it is. For example, we do not regard killing in self-defense or in combat in the same way we view killing in cold blood. At least, that is the case until we change our minds about how we view wartime killing, as has happened at various times in our past. When it comes to war, for example, our attitudes about what is appropriate can shift. In both Vietnam and Iraq, strong public support gave way to serious misgivings about U.S. involvement in these nations. In both cases, this was driven in part by images from the conflict, including, for example, the treatment of prisoners at Abu Ghraib. In this way, our understanding of what constitutes deviance and crime are tied to issues of social solidarity.

In fact, Durkheim concluded that deviance and crime actually can have a positive impact on society in a variety of ways. For example, identifying acts as deviant clarifies our shared beliefs and values and thus brings us closer together. We say, in effect, "This is who we are, and if you want to be one of us you cannot cross this line. Some things we might let go, but if you push the limits too far you will face sanctions." Punishment, too, can draw a group together, uniting members in their opposition to the offender. Sanctions also discourage others from similar violations, thus increasing conformity. When we see a driver receiving a speeding ticket, a department store cashier being fired for yelling at a customer, or a college student getting a failing grade for plagiarizing a term paper, we are reminded of our collective norms and values and of the consequences of their violation.

5 Movies on DEVIANCE

Trainspotting
Scottish youths struggle with unemployment, dissatisfying relationships, and addiction.

Girl, Interrupted
A young girl enters a mental institution during the 1960s.

A Clockwork Orange
The success and failure of rehabilitating a delinquent.

The Devil and Daniel Johnston
The true story about a young musician who suffers from schizophrenia.

Ghost World
A prank by two outcast teenagers takes an unexpected turn.

Finally, Durkheim did recognize that deviant acts might also force us to recognize the limits of our existing beliefs and practices, opening up new doors and leading to cultural innovation.

Based on Durkheim's analysis, it is possible to conclude that all societies identify criminals for the sake of social order. No matter how much unity a society might appear to have, there will always be some who push the limits. Regardless of how "good" such people may appear to be to outsiders, they may face sanction within the group for the good of the whole.

SOCTHINK

Durkheim argues that increased division of labor results in fewer shared experiences and thus a weakened sense of community. Might this imply that we need ever-more shocking violations of our remaining shared values in order to bring us together?

Durkheim did, however, also recognize that some social circumstances increase the likelihood of turning toward deviance and crime. As we have already seen, Durkheim ([1897] 1951) introduced the term **anomie** into the sociological literature to describe the loss of direction felt in a society when social control of individual behavior has become ineffective. Anomie is a state of normlessness that typically occurs during a period of profound social change and disorder, such as a time of economic collapse, political or social revolution, or even sudden prosperity. The power of society to constrain deviant action at such times is limited because there is no clear consensus on shared norms and values. Just as we saw with Durkheim's analysis of suicide, at times when social integration is weak, people are freer to pursue their own deviant paths.

Merton's Theory of Deviance Sociologist Robert Merton (1968) took Durkheim's theory a step further. He realized that sometimes members of a society share collective values or goals and other times they do not. He also realized that some people accept the means to attain those goals and others don't. To understand deviance and crime, he felt it was necessary to go beyond the general state of society to look more closely at where people fit in relationship to both goals and means.

We can better understand Merton's model by looking at economic success as an important goal in the United States. In addition to providing this goal for people, our society offers recommended pathways on how to pursue success—go to school, work hard, do not quit, take advantage of opportunities, and so forth. A mugger and a merchant may share the common goal of economic success, but their means of attaining it are radically different. What happens to individuals in a society with a heavy emphasis on wealth as a basic symbol of success? Merton reasoned that people adapt in certain ways, either by conforming to or by deviating from such cultural expectations. His **anomie theory of deviance** posits five basic forms of adaptation.

Conformity to social norms, the most common adaptation in Merton's typology, is the opposite of deviance. The "conformist" accepts both the overall societal goal (for example, to become wealthy) and the approved means (hard work). In Merton's view, there must be some consensus regarding accepted cultural goals and the legitimate means for attaining them. Without such a consensus, societies could exist only as collectives of people rather than as unified cultures, and they might experience continual chaos.

The other four types of behavior all involve some departure from conformity. The "innovator" accepts the goals of society but pursues them with means that are regarded as improper. For instance, a safecracker may steal money to buy consumer goods and take expensive vacations.

Every office has its ritualist.
....

> ## Law and justice are not always the same.
>
> ──────
>
> **Gloria Steinem**

In Merton's typology, the "ritualist" has abandoned the goal of material success and become compulsively committed to the institutional means. Work becomes simply a way of life rather than a means to the goal of success. An example would be the bureaucratic official who blindly applies rules and regulations without remembering the larger goals of the organization. Certainly, that would be true of a welfare caseworker who refuses to assist a homeless family because their last apartment was in another district.

> **anomie theory of deviance** Merton's theory of deviance as an adaptation of socially prescribed goals or of the means governing their attainment, or both.

The "retreatist," as described by Merton, has basically withdrawn (or retreated) from both the goals and the means of society. In the United States, drug addicts and vagrants are typically portrayed as retreatists. Concern has been growing that adolescents who are addicted to alcohol will become retreatists at an early age.

DWIGHT SCHRUTE

DETERMINED WORKER INTENSE GOOD WORKER HARD WORKER TERRIFIC

The final adaptation identified by Merton reflects people's attempts to create a *new* social structure. The "rebel" feels alienated from the dominant means and goals and may seek a dramatically different social order. Members of a revolutionary political organization, such as a militia group, can be categorized as rebels according to Merton's model.

Merton's theory, though popular, does not fully account for patterns of deviance and crime. While it is useful in explaining certain types of behavior, such as illegal gambling by disadvantaged "innovators," it fails to explain key differences in crime rates. Why, for example, do some disadvantaged groups have lower rates of reported crime than others? Why do many people in adverse circumstances reject criminal activity as a viable alternative? Merton's theory does not easily answer such questions (Clinard and Miller 1998). In order to more fully appreciate such nuances, we must add to what we can learn from Merton by turning to additional theories that seek to better understand deviance and crime at an interpersonal level.

> **cultural transmission** A school of criminology that argues criminal behavior is learned through social interactions.
>
> **differential association** A theory of deviance that holds violation of rules results from exposure to attitudes favorable to criminal acts.

INTERPERSONAL INTERACTION AND LOCAL CONTEXT

Perhaps the likelihood of committing deviant acts is not solely shaped by social integration or the acceptance of society's larger goals and means to attain them. Maybe parents around the world were right all along that it really does depend on who your friends

Did You Know?

... In a 2006 survey of more than 5000 students at 32 graduate schools, 56 percent of master of business administration (MBA) students admitted to cheating within the past academic year. This contrasted with 47 percent of nonbusiness students (McCabe Butterfield and Treviño 2006). Considering goals and means, into which category of Merton's model might those MBA students belong?

are. If we are to understand and explain such acts, we must also consider the importance of social interaction and the local context.

Cultural Transmission As humans, we learn how to behave in social situations, whether properly or improperly. Sociologist Edwin Sutherland (1883–1950) proposed that, just as individuals are socialized to conform to society's basic norms and values, so also are they socialized to learn deviant acts. It's not that we are born to be wild; we learn to be wild.

Sutherland drew on the **cultural transmission** school, which emphasizes that individuals learn criminal behavior by interacting with others. Such learning includes not only the techniques of lawbreaking (for example, how to break into a car quickly and quietly), but also the motives, drives, and rationalizations of the criminal. The cultural transmission approach can also be used to explain the behavior of those who habitually abuse alcohol or drugs.

Sutherland maintained that through interactions with a primary group and significant others, people acquire definitions of proper and improper behavior. He used the term **differential association** to describe the process through which exposure to attitudes favorable to criminal acts leads to the violation of rules. Research suggests that this view of differential association also applies to noncriminal deviant acts, such as smoking, binge drinking, and cheating (Higgins, Tewksbury, and Mustaine, 2007; Nofziger and Hye-Ryeon 2006; Vowell and Chen 2004).

To what extent will a given person engage in an activity that is regarded as proper or improper? For each individual, it will depend on the frequency, duration, and importance of two types of social interaction—those experiences that endorse deviant behavior and those that promote acceptance of social norms. People are more likely to engage in norm-defying behavior if they are part of a group or subculture that stresses deviant values, such as a street gang.

Sutherland offers the example of a boy who is sociable, outgoing, and athletic and who lives in an area with a high rate of delinquency. The youth is very likely to come into contact with peers who commit acts of vandalism, fail to attend school, and so forth, and he may come to adopt such behavior. However, an introverted boy who lives in the same neighborhood may stay away from his peers and avoid delinquency. In another community, an outgoing and athletic boy may join a Little League baseball team or a scout troop because of his interactions with peers. Thus, Sutherland views improper behavior as the result of the types of groups to which one belongs and the kinds of friendships one has (Sutherland, Cressey, and Luckenbill 1992).

Although the cultural transmission approach may not explain the conduct of the first-time, impulsive shoplifter or the impoverished person who steals out of necessity, it does help to explain the deviant behavior of juvenile delinquents or graffiti artists. It directs our attention to the paramount role of social interaction and context in increasing a person's motivation to engage in deviant behavior (Morselli, Tremblay, and McCarthy 2006; Sutherland et al. 1992).

Social Disorganization Theory The relative strength of social relationships in a community or neighborhood influences the behavior of its members. Social psychologist Philip Zimbardo (2007) studied the effect of these communal relationships by conducting the following experiment. He abandoned a car in each of two different neighborhoods, leaving its hood up and removing its hub caps. In one neighborhood, people started to strip the car for parts even before Zimbardo had finished setting up a remote video camera to record their behavior. In the other neighborhood, weeks passed without the car being touched, except for a pedestrian who stopped to close the hood during a rainstorm.

Social disorganization theory attributes increases in crime and deviance to the absence or breakdown of communal relationships and social institutions, such as the family, school, church, and local government. The lack of such local community connections, with their associated cross-age relationships, makes it difficult to exert informal control within the community, especially of children. Without community supervision and controls, playing outside becomes an opportunity for deviance, and

older violators socialize children into inappropriate paths. Crime becomes a normal response to a local context.

This theory was developed at the University of Chicago in the early 1900s to describe the apparent disorganization that occurred as cities expanded with immigrants from abroad and migrants from rural areas. Using the latest survey techniques, Clifford Shaw and Henry McKay (1969) literally mapped the distribution of social problems in Chicago. They found high rates of social problems in neighborhoods where buildings had deteriorated and the population had declined. Interestingly, the patterns persisted over time, despite changes in the neighborhoods' ethnic and racial composition.

> **social disorganization theory** The theory that attributes increases in crime and deviance to the absence or breakdown of communal relationships and social institutions, such as the family, school, church, and local government.

Labeling Theory Sometimes when it comes to deviance, what you see determines what you get. The Saints and Roughnecks were two groups of high school males who were continually engaged in excessive drinking, reckless driving, truancy, petty theft, and vandalism. There the similarity ended. None of the Saints was ever arrested, but every Roughneck was frequently in trouble with police and townspeople. Why the disparity in their treatment? On the basis of observation research in their high school, sociologist William Chambliss (1973) concluded that how they were seen, as rooted in their social class positions, played an important role in the varying fortunes of the two groups.

The Saints hid behind a facade of respectability. They came from "good families," were active in school organizations, planned on attending college, and received good grades. People generally viewed their delinquent acts as a

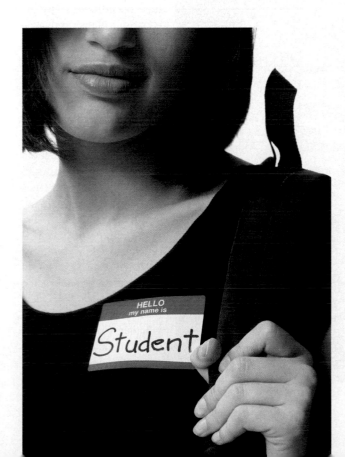

HELLO
my name is

Student

few isolated cases of sowing wild oats. The Roughnecks had no such aura of respectability. They drove around town in beat-up cars, were generally unsuccessful in school, and aroused suspicion no matter what they did.

We can understand such discrepancies by using an approach to deviance known as **labeling theory,** which emphasizes how a person comes to be labeled as deviant or to accept that label. Unlike Sutherland's work, labeling theory does not focus on why some individuals come to commit deviant acts. Instead, it attempts to explain why society views certain people (such as the Roughnecks) as deviants, delinquents, bad kids, losers, and criminals, while it sees others whose behavior is similar (such as the Saints) in less harsh terms. Sociologist Howard Becker (1963:9; 1964), who popularized this approach, summed up labeling theory with this statement: "Deviant behavior is behavior that people so label."

> **labeling theory** An approach to deviance that attempts to explain why certain people are viewed as deviants while others engaged in the same behavior are not.
>
> **societal-reaction approach** Another name for labeling theory.

Labeling theory is also called the **societal-reaction approach,** reminding us that it is the response to an act, not the act itself, that determines deviance. Traditionally, research on deviance has focused on people who violate social norms. In contrast, labeling theory focuses on police, probation officers, psychiatrists, judges, teachers, employers, school officials, and other regulators of social control. These agents, it is argued, play a significant role in creating the deviant identity by designating certain people (and not others) as deviant (Bernburg, Krohn, and Rivera 2006). An important aspect of labeling theory is the recognition that some individuals or groups have the power to define labels and apply them to others. This view ties into the conflict perspective's emphasis on the social significance of power.

In recent years, the practice of racial profiling, in which people are identified as criminal suspects purely on the basis of their race, has come under public scrutiny. Studies confirm the public's suspicion that in some jurisdictions, police officers are much more likely to stop African American males than White males for routine traffic violations, in the expectation of finding drugs or guns in their cars. Civil rights activists refer to these cases sarcastically as DWB (Driving While Black) violations (Warren et al. 2006). Beginning in late 2001, profiling took a new turn as people who appeared to be Arab or Muslim came under special scrutiny.

Although the labeling approach does not fully explain why certain people accept a label and others manage to reject it, labeling theorists do suggest that the power an individual has relative to others is important in determining his or her ability to resist an undesirable label. It opens the door to additional emphasis on the undeniably important actions of people with power who can shape what counts as deviance.

POWER AND INEQUALITY

In addition to its significance for labeling theory, the story of the Saints and Roughnecks points toward the role that power and control over valued resources can play in defining deviance. Sociologist Richard Quinney (1974, 1979, 1980) is a leading proponent of the view that the criminal justice system serves the interests of the powerful; people with power protect their own interests and define deviance to suit their own needs. Crime, according to Quinney (1970), is defined as such by legislators who may be influenced by the economic elites to advance their interests.

Race and Class Looking at crime from this perspective draws our attention to the effects that power and position might have throughout the criminal justice system in the United States. Researchers have found that the system treats suspects differently based on their racial, ethnic, or social class background. In many cases, officials using their own discretion make biased decisions about whether to press charges or drop them, whether to set bail and how much, and whether to offer parole

Executions by State Since 1976

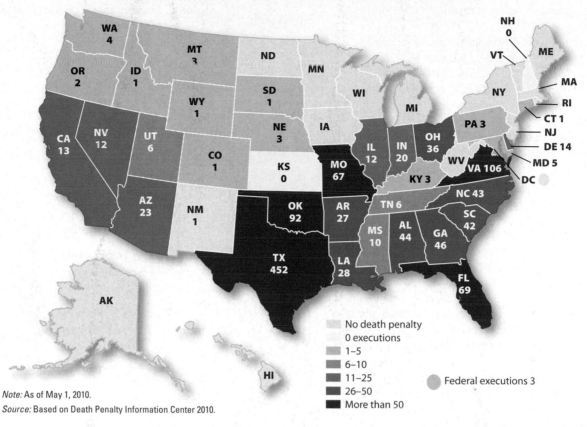

Legend	
	No death penalty
	0 executions
	1–5
	6–10
	11–25
	26–50
	More than 50

WA 4, OR 2, ID 1, MT 3, ND, MN, WI, MI, NH 0, VT, ME, MA, NY, PA 3, RI, CT 1, NJ, DE 14, MD 5, DC

CA 13, NV 12, UT 6, WY 1, SD 1, NE 3, IA, IL 12, IN 20, OH 36, WV, VA 106

AZ 23, NM 1, CO 1, KS 0, MO 67, KY 3, NC 43, SC 42

OK 92, AR 27, TN 6, MS 10, AL 44, GA 46

TX 452, LA 28, FL 69

AK, HI

Federal executions 3

Note: As of May 1, 2010.

Source: Based on Death Penalty Information Center 2010.

or deny it. Researchers have found that this kind of **differential justice**—differences in the way social control is exercised over different groups—puts African Americans and Latinos at a disadvantage in the justice system, both as juveniles and as adults. On average, White offenders receive shorter sentences than comparable Latino and African American offenders, even when prior arrest records and the relative severity of the crime are taken into consideration (Brewer and Heitzeg 2008; Quinney 1974).

We see this pattern of differential justice at work with death penalty cases. Simply put, poor people cannot afford to hire the best lawyer and often must rely on court-appointed attorneys, who typically are overworked and underpaid. With capital punishment in place, these unequal resources may mean the difference between life and death for poor defendants. Indeed, the American Bar Association (2009) has repeatedly expressed concern about the limited defense most defendants facing the death penalty receive. Through mid-2010, DNA analysis and other new technologies had exonerated 17 death row inmates and 252 inmates overall (Innocence Project 2010).

> Whenever you find yourself on the side of the majority, it is time to pause and reflect.
>
> **Mark Twain**

Various studies show that defendants are more likely to be sentenced to death if their victims were White rather than Black. About 77 percent of the victims in death penalty cases are White, even though about half of *all* murder victims are White. There is some evidence that Black defendants, who constituted 42 percent of all death row inmates in 2010, are more likely to face execution than Whites in the same legal circumstances. About 70 percent of those who have been exonerated by DNA testing were members of minority groups. Evidence exists, too, that capital defendants receive poor legal services because of the racist attitudes of their own defense counsel. Apparently, discrimination and racism do not end even when the stakes are life and death (Death Penalty Information Center 2010; Innocence Project 2010; D. Jacobs et al. 2007).

Differential justice is not limited to the United States. In 2007, the people of India were alarmed to learn that police had never investigated a series of killings in the slums of New Delhi. Only after residents found 17 bodies of recently murdered children in a sewer drain on the edge

> **differential justice** Differences in the way social control is exercised over different groups.

of a slum were police moved to act. For many onlookers, it was just the latest example of the two-tier justice system found in India and many other countries (Gentleman 2007).

Such dramatic differences in social treatment may lead to heightened violence and crime. People who view themselves as the victims of unfair treatment may lash out, not against the powerful so much as against fellow victims. In studying crime in rural Mexico, Andrés Villarreal (2004) found that crime rates were high in the areas where land distribution was most inequitable. In areas where land was distributed more equally, communities appeared to suffer less violence and to enjoy greater social cohesion.

Gender Feminist criminologists such as Meda Chesney-Lind (with Lisa Pasko 2004) and Gillian Balfour (2006) have suggested that many of the existing approaches to deviance and crime were developed with only men in mind. For example, in the United States, for many years any husband who forced his wife to have sexual intercourse—without her consent and against her will—was not legally considered to have committed rape. The law defined rape as pertaining only to sexual relations between people who were not married to each other, reflecting the overwhelmingly male composition of state legislatures at the time.

It took repeated protests by feminist organizations to get changes in the criminal law defining rape. It was not until 1993 that husbands in all 50 states could be prosecuted under most circumstances for the rape of their wives. However, significant exceptions remain in no fewer than 30 states. For example, the husband is exempt when he does not need to use force because his wife is asleep, unconscious, or mentally or physically impaired. These interpretations rest on the notion that the marriage contract entitles a husband to have sex (Bergen 2006).

5 Movies on ORGANIZED CRIME/ CORPORATE CRIME

Gomorrah
The story of contemporary organized crime in Italy.

The Departed
Police corruption and the Irish Mob in Boston.

The Corporation
Documentary about the modern-day corporation.

The Informant!
An eccentric employee blows the whistle on his corporation's price-fixing scheme.

Eastern Promises
The inner workings of the Russian mafia.

When it comes to crime and to deviance in general, society tends to treat women in a stereotypical fashion. For example, consider how women who have many and frequent sexual partners are more likely to be viewed with scorn than men who are promiscuous. Cultural views and attitudes toward women influence how they are perceived and labeled. The feminist perspective also emphasizes that deviance, including crime, tends to flow from economic relationships. Traditionally, men have had greater earning power than their wives. As a result, wives may be reluctant to report acts of abuse to the authorities and thereby lose what may be their primary or even sole source of income. In the workplace, men have exercised greater power than women in pricing, accounting, and product control, giving them greater opportunity to engage in such crimes as embezzlement and fraud. But as women have taken more active and powerful roles both in the household and in business, these gender differences in deviance and crime have narrowed (Bisi 2002; Chesney-Lind 1989; Kruttschnitt and Carbone-Lopez 2010).

Together, sociological perspectives on crime and deviance help us to better understand and explain such acts. No single explanation is sufficient. We

get involved!

Observe! If possible, visit your local courthouse to observe a trial in action. Most court proceedings are open to the public, so take advantage of that opportunity to learn more about how our system works.

must consider multiple factors from a variety of perspectives including: the extent to which deviance exists for the sake of social order; the degree of opportunity to attain both means and ends; the role of socialization in deviance; the strength of local community networks; the power to administer labels and make them stick; and differential access to valuable resources based on class, race, and gender. As Sudhir Venkatesh found in his research on gangs, if we are to fully understand something, we need to dig deep enough and consider what is going on from enough angles and with sufficient care, concern, and curiosity.

For REVIEW

I. How do groups maintain social control?
   • They use positive and negative sanctions in both formal and informal ways to bring about conformity and obedience.

II. What is the difference between deviance and crime?
   • Deviance involves violating a group's expected norms, which may lead the offender to be stigmatized. Crime is a form of deviance that involves violating the formal norms administered by the state for which the offender may receive formal sanctions.

III. How do sociologists explain deviance and crime?
   • Sociologists offer up a number of theories of crime, each of which provides additional factors to be considered—such as the need for social order, the significance of interpersonal relationships and local context, and the importance of power and access to resources—that help us to better understand why deviance and crime occur.

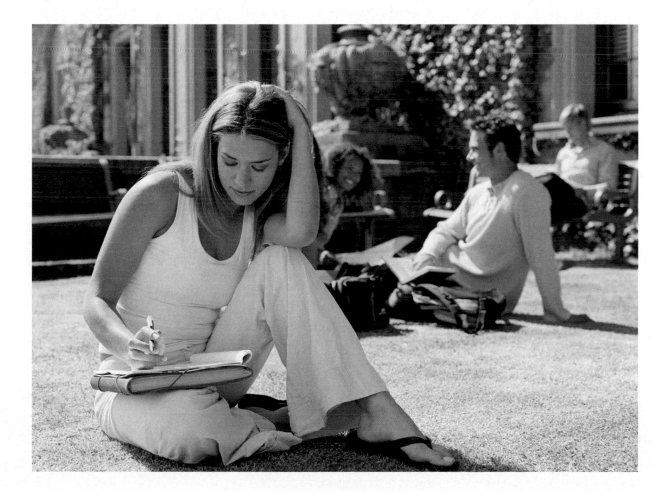

Functionalist View

Agents of **social control** aim to limit deviant social behavior by enforcing norms and providing negative sanctions for disobedience. Government exerts formal social control through its **laws.**

Deviance can actually contribute to social stability by defining the limits of proper behavior and encouraging **conformity** to laws and rules.

Social **integration** constrains deviant acts because it provides a clear **consensus** on shared norms and values.

CONFORMITY, OBEDIENCE, LAW, ORDER
KEY CONCEPTS

Conflict View

In diverse societies, the process of making laws generates conflicts over whose values should prevail.

Individuals and groups with the greatest **status and power** generally define who or what is deviant in a society.

The criminal justice system **treats suspects differently** based on their racial, ethnic, or class background, which leads to distrust in the criminal system.

POWER, DIFFERENTIAL JUSTICE
KEY CONCEPTS

Interactionist View

People learn what is proper and improper behavior through their interactions with others—an idea known as **cultural transmission.**

Informal social control is achieved through casual interactions—a smile, a raised eyebrow, ridicule—that prompt us to adjust our behavior.

A breakdown in interpersonal social relationships in a local community can lead to increases in crime and deviance.

LABELING, CULTURAL TRANSMISSION
KEY CONCEPTS

MAKE THE CONNECTION

After reviewing the chapter, answer the following questions:

1

How would each perspective approach the conclusions of Venkatesh's study of gang life in Chicago (p. 129)?

2

What perspective do you think provides the best explanation for the results of Milgram's experiment on obedience (p. 132)? Why?

3

Describe victimless crime from the point of view of each of the three perspectives, using one of the following examples in your response: drug use, gambling, or prostitution (p. 139).

4

Which perspective best describes the way you learned proper social behavior? Were social norms socialized and internalized (functionalist), imposed by powerful authority figures (conflict), or learned from observing others (interactionist)? Provide examples.

Pop Quiz

1. Society brings about acceptance of basic norms through techniques and strategies for preventing deviant human behavior. This process is termed
   a. stigmatization.
   b. labeling.
   c. law.
   d. social control.

2. The penalties and rewards we face for conduct concerning a social norm are known as
   a. informal social controls.
   b. stigmas.
   c. sanctions.
   d. conformities.

3. Stanley Milgram used the word *conformity* to mean
   a. going along with peers.
   b. compliance with higher authorities in a hierarchical structure.
   c. techniques and strategies for preventing deviant behavior in any society.
   d. penalties and rewards for conduct concerning a social norm.

4. According to Hirschi's control theory,
   a. deviance involves acceptance and/or rejection of society's goals and means.
   b. our connection to members of society leads us to systematically conform to society's norms.
   c. we come to view ourselves as deviant based on how others view us.
   d. power and access to resources shape whose norms and values determine individual action.

5. Which of the following statements is true of deviance?
   a. Deviance is always criminal behavior.
   b. Deviance is behavior that violates the standards of conduct or expectations of a group or society.
   c. Deviance is perverse behavior.
   d. Deviance is inappropriate behavior that cuts across all cultures and social orders.

6. The FBI reports which two major categories of crime in its annual Uniform Crime Reports?
   a. violent crime and property crime
   b. organized crime and white-collar crime
   c. victimless crime and transnational crime
   d. transnational crime and victimization crime

7. Which type of crime involves the willing exchange among adults of widely desired, but illegal, goods and services?
   a. index crimes
   b. white-collar crime
   c. victimless crime
   d. organized crime

8. Which of the following is *not* one of the basic forms of adaptation specified in Robert Merton's anomie theory of deviance?
   a. conformity
   b. innovation
   c. ritualism
   d. hostility

9. Which of the following theories contends that criminal victimization increases when communal relationships and social institutions break down?
   a. labeling theory
   b. conflict theory
   c. social disorganization theory
   d. differential association theory

10. Even though they committed the same deviant acts, the Saints and the Roughnecks did not receive the same treatment from authorities. Sociologist William Chambliss suggests this was due to the fact that authorities viewed members of the groups differently. Which theory supports that conclusion?
    a. Merton's anomie theory
    b. culture transmission theory
    c. differential association theory
    d. labeling theory

1. (d); 2. (c); 3. (a); 4. (b); 5. (b); 6. (a); 7. (c); 8. (d); 9. (c); 10. (d)

7

FAMILIES

LOVE AND MARRIAGE

Janis Spindel is a modern-day matchmaker. She has arranged more than 900 marriages since 1993, but her services don't come cheap. She charges a $20,000 initiation fee, a $1,000 per year membership fee that includes 12 dates, and expects a $75,000–$250,000 bonus upon marriage. When it comes to selecting dates, she doesn't leave the choice up to her clients. Rather than allowing them to choose from a list of candidates, she selects particular individuals from her database for each date. In spite of these high costs and constrained choices, her business is thriving.

Though the goal is the same, modern-day matchmakers are quite different from their historical counterparts. We get a glimpse of the role traditional matchmakers played in communities in the classic musical *Fiddler on the Roof.* In it, the local matchmaker arranged the marriage of Tevye and Golde, two of the main characters. The couple met for the first time on their wedding day. As they approach their 25th anniversary, their three oldest daughters want to reject the matchmaker tradition, choosing husbands based on love instead. As Tevye reflects on what changing attitudes mean for his daughters, his family, and his community, asks Golde, seemingly for the first time "Do you love me?" It is as if they never thought to ask in all their years together.

In the story, the daughters' breaks with convention are tied to the larger social, economic, and historical upheavals in their early-1900s Russian village. Tradition has always ruled in the community; thus, Tevye and Golde struggle to accept their daughters' relationships and even to understand their own. Tevye and Golde decide that they do, in fact, love each other. But their affirmation of love emerges only upon the decline of traditions that have guided village life for generations.

The practice of matchmaking, whether traditional or modern, grows out of the social context of the times (Thernsrom 2005). We often think that the way things are is the way things have always been, but when it comes to love, marriage, and families, there has been significant variation over time and across cultures.

As You READ >>

- What is the family?
- How do people pick partners?
- How do families vary?

>> Global View of the Family

Families vary around the world. Among Tibetans, a woman may be married simultaneously to more than one man, usually brothers. This system allows sons to share the limited amount of good land. Among the Betsileo of Madagascar, a man has multiple wives, each one living in a different village where he cultivates rice. Wherever he has the best rice field, that woman is considered his first or senior wife. Among the Yanomami of Brazil and Venezuela, it is considered proper to have sexual relations with one's opposite-sex cousins if they are the children of one's mother's brother or father's sister. But if one's opposite-sex cousins are the children of one's mother's sister or father's brother, the same practice is considered to be incest (Haviland et al. 2005; Kottak 2004).

Did You Know?

More than 2 million couples get married in the United States every year. That works out to almost 6000 per day. In 2008, Nevada had by far the highest marriage rate with 112,185 couples tying the knot, so perhaps not everything that happens in Vegas stays in Vegas.

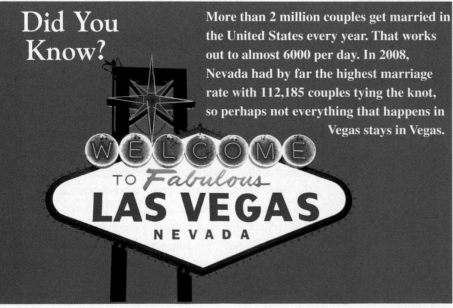

Source: Tejada-Vera and Sutton 2009.

In the United States, the family of today is not what it was a century or even a generation ago. New roles, new gender distinctions, and new child-rearing patterns have all combined to create new forms of family life. Today, for example, more and more women are taking the breadwinner's role, whether as a spouse or as a single parent. Blended families—the result of divorce and remarriage—are common. And many people are seeking intimate relationships outside marriage, whether in gay or lesbian partnerships or in cohabiting arrangements.

We see such changes reflected in popular culture representations of families. The 1950s U.S. family members talk about their lives—and about ancestors who lived and died long before we were born. Yet a person's lineage is more than simply a personal history; it also reflects societal traditions that govern descent. In every culture, children encounter relatives to whom they are expected to show an emotional attachment. The state of being related to others is called **kinship.** Kinship is culturally learned, however, and is not totally determined by biological or marital ties. For example, adoption creates a kinship tie that is legally acknowledged and socially accepted.

was epitomized on television by shows such as *Leave It to Beaver* and *Father Knows Best* with a stay-at-home mom, working dad, and assorted kids. Times have changed. *Two and a Half Men* features a father, son, and uncle; *Parenthood* depicts families across three generations; and then there's *Desperate Housewives*. Perhaps the closest you get these days to the 1950s family is *The Simpsons* with Homer, Marge, Lisa, Bart, and Maggie. This shift in how families are portrayed is consistent with changes we have seen both in practice and in our understanding of what constitutes a family.

Because families as we experience them are varied in structure and style, we need a sociological approach that is sufficiently broad to encompass all those things we experience as family. We will look at two different definitional approaches. The first is a substantive definition that focuses on what a family *is,* and the second is a functional definition that focuses on what families *do.*

SUBSTANCE: WHAT A FAMILY IS

Perhaps the most conventional approach to defining family is the **substantive definition,** which focuses on blood and law. Blood, in this case, means that people are related because they share a biological heritage passed on directly from parent to child, linking people indirectly to grandparents, aunts and uncles, and other biological relatives. Law means the formal social recognition and affirmation of a bond as family, particularly in the form of marriage and adoption.

The primary advantage of this definitional approach is that boundaries are clear; we can tell who is in and who is out. This makes it easier to count such families, so perhaps it is no surprise that the U.S. Census relies on a substantive approach: "A family is a group of two people or more (one of whom is the householder) related by birth, marriage, or adoption and residing together" (U.S. Census Bureau 2008a). It also allows us to track who is related to whom over time.

Kinship Patterns Many of us can trace our roots by looking at a family tree or by listening to elderly family

The family and the kin group are not necessarily one and the same. Whereas the family is a household unit, kin do not always live together or function as a collective body on a daily basis. Kin groups include aunts, uncles, cousins, in-laws, and so forth. In a society such as the United States, the kinship group may come together only rarely, for a wedding or funeral. However, kinship ties frequently involve obligations and responsibilities. We may feel compelled to assist our kin, and we feel free to call upon them for many types of aid, including loans and babysitting.

How do we identify kinship groups? The principle of descent assigns people to kinship groups according to their relationship to a mother or father. There are three primary ways of determining descent. The United States follows the system of **bilateral descent,** which means that both sides of a person's family are regarded as equally important. For example, no higher value is given to the brothers of one's father than to the brothers of one's mother. However, most societies—according to anthropologist George Murdock, 64 percent of societies— give preference to one side of the family or the other in tracing descent. In **patrilineal** (from the Latin *pater,* "father") **descent,** only the father's relatives are significant

> **substantive definition of the family** A definition of the family based on blood, meaning shared genetic heritage, and law, meaning social recognition and affirmation of the bond including both marriage and adoption.
>
> **kinship** The state of being related to others.
>
> **bilateral descent** A kinship system in which both sides of a person's family are regarded as equally important.
>
> **patrilineal descent** A kinship system in which only the father's relatives are significant.

SOCTHINK

How important are intergenerational kinship networks and extended family members in your family? How has this changed since your parents' and grandparents' generations?

in terms of property, inheritance, and emotional ties. Conversely, in societies that favor **matrilineal** (from the Latin *mater,* "mother") **descent,** only the mother's relatives are significant.

Family Types The substantive approach also shapes what we traditionally view as common family types. If we assume that we are connected through blood and law, we can analyze how we structure those relationships. Families might place greater emphasis on immediate family members or on extended family networks. They also are shaped by the number of partners deemed appropriate.

Historically, family connections served as a valuable resource, providing us with access to material, social, and cultural resources. We depended on relatives for food, shelter, opportunities, and knowledge. In fact, historian Stephanie Coontz (2005) argues that, historically, the primary reason to get married was to obtain not a partner but in-laws, thus extending one's network of cooperative relationships. This was the logic of the matchmaker tradition that not only brought Tevye and Golde together in *Fiddler on the Roof* but brought their families together as well. The matchmaker, as a member of the community, sought to maximize social network connections for the good of the whole.

> **matrilineal descent** A kinship system in which only the mother's relatives are significant.
>
> **extended family** A family in which relatives—such as grandparents, aunts, or uncles—live in the same household as parents and their children.
>
> **nuclear family** A married couple and their unmarried children living together.
>
> **monogamy** A form of marriage in which one woman and one man are married only to each other.
>
> **serial monogamy** A form of marriage in which a person may have several spouses in his or her lifetime but only one spouse at a time.
>
> **polygamy** A form of marriage in which an individual may have several husbands or wives simultaneously.

A family in which relatives—such as grandparents, aunts, or uncles—live in the same household as parents and their children is known as an **extended family.** Although not common, such living arrangements do exist in the United States. The structure of the extended family offers certain advantages over that of the nuclear family. Crises such as death, divorce, and illness put less strain on family members because more people can provide assistance and emotional support. In addition, the extended family constitutes a larger economic unit than the nuclear family. If the family is engaged in a common enterprise—a farm or a small business—the additional family members may represent the difference between prosperity and failure.

With the advent of the Industrial Revolution, the economy shifted away from agricultural production and its corresponding small-town life and toward industrial production in urban areas. Families became smaller and more mobile in response to these structural changes. The obligations of the extended family could hold individuals back, and so we saw a move toward a smaller family unit that came to be known as the nuclear family.

The **nuclear family** includes a married couple and their unmarried children living together. The concept of nuclear family builds on the essence or nucleus of the substantive definition of blood and law, including as it does both the parent-to-child and the marriage relationship.

Most people in the United States assume that the nuclear family is by far the most common arrangement. In fact, married couples with children under 18 make up 32 percent of total families. The breadwinner father and stay-at-home mom model idealized in 1950s television makes up only 9.8 percent of total families and 21 percent of families with children under 18 (Bureau of Labor Statistics 2009c:Table 4). In contrast, the percentage of single-parent and nonfamily households has risen steadily over the past 50 years.

Types of Marriage In considering these different family types, we have limited ourselves to the form of marriage that is characteristic of the United States—monogamy. The term **monogamy** describes a form of marriage in which one woman and one man are married only to each other. Individuals in the United States are more likely to move into and out of a number of serious romantic relationships, what sociologist Andrew Cherlin (2009) refers to as the "marriage-go-round." Termed **serial monogamy,** a person may have several spouses in his or her lifetime, but only one spouse at a time.

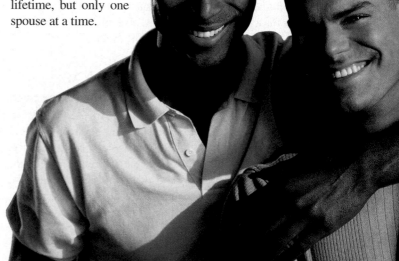

Some cultures allow an individual to have several husbands or wives simultaneously. This form of marriage is known as **polygamy.** In fact, most societies throughout the world, past and present, have preferred polygamy to monogamy. Anthropologist George Murdock (1949, 1957) sampled 565 societies and found that in more than 80 percent, some type of polygamy was the preferred form. While polygamy declined steadily through most of

U.S. Households by Family Type

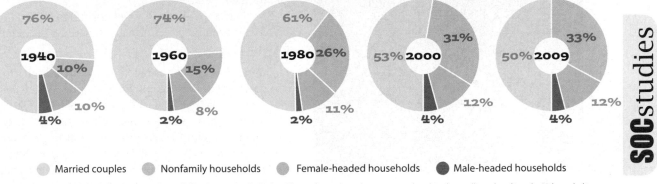

- ⬤ Married couples
- ⬤ Nonfamily households
- ⬤ Female-headed households
- ⬤ Male-headed households

Note: Nonfamily households include women and men living alone or exclusively with people to whom they are not related, as in a college dormitory, homeless shelter, or military base.

Source: U.S. Census Bureau 2010a:Table HH-1.

the 20th century, in 28 sub-Saharan African countries, at least 10 percent of men still have polygamous marriages (Tertilt 2005).

There are two basic types of polygamy. The most common is **polygyny,** which refers to the marriage of a man to more than one woman at the same time. Less common is **polyandry,** in which a woman may have more than one husband at the same time. Such is the case, for example, in the Nyinba culture of Nepal and Tibet, in which brothers share a common wife. This arrangement provides a sufficient number of physical laborers in the difficult farming environment yet minimizes the number of offspring.

Most people assumed that polygamy was a thing of the past in the United States. However, in April 2008, law enforcement officials in Texas received an anonymous phone call purported to be from a 16-year-old girl who claimed that she had been forced into a polygamous marriage with an adult man. The girl also complained of having been beaten. Shortly thereafter, officials raided the Yearning for Zion ranch where the girl was living, taking a total of 462 children from the ranch and placing them into temporary legal custody. The ranch was run by members of the Fundamentalist Church of Jesus Christ of Latter Day Saints (FLDS), a group that practices polygamy even though it is illegal in the United States and was banned by the mainstream LDS denomination more than 100 years ago. The state ordered DNA testing to ascertain who was related to whom. Ultimately, the children were returned

to their families as there was insufficient evidence to demonstrate abuse or the immediate risk of abuse. However, the case did raise awareness of the fact that polygamy continues to exist in the United States.

> **polygyny** A form of polygamy in which a man may have more than one wife at the same time.
>
> **polyandry** A form of polygamy in which a woman may have more than one husband at the same time.

SOC THINK

Why do you think that polygamy was the most common form of marriage historically? Why has it given way to monogamy in modern societies?

Once we begin to look at the varieties of family types around the world, we see the main limitation of the substantive definition: There are people who seem to be family but who do not fit neatly into blood or law. For example, the biological parent-to-child tie was expanded by including adoption as part of law. We accept stepparents and stepsiblings as family members even when the children have not been formally adopted by the stepparent. We are currently debating whether to grant same-sex couples legal standing as families. But what about pushing the definition of family still further? Is dad's college

Big Love, Long Life?

In 2008, the HBO television series *Big Love* was nominated for a Golden Globe award as the year's best television series, drama. It portrays a fictionalized account of a polygamous family, telling the story of Bill Henrickson, his three wives (Barb, Nicki, and Margene), and their eight children. It was a surprise success given its unconventional storyline. While uncommon in the United States, more than 50 percent of men in Cameroon have multiple wives. One study found that men in nations that practice polygyny tend to have a longer life span, perhaps because their multiple wives bear the burden to lighten the workload of daily life (Callaway 2008; Tertilt 2005).

functionalist definition of families A definition of families that focuses on what families do for society and for their members.

friend "Uncle" Bob part of the family? New forms of reproductive technology, involving donated sperm and eggs and surrogate parents, also challenge conventional thinking. Any substantive definition we might come up with runs the risk of excluding those whom we think of as family members. In response, sociologists turn toward the more inclusive functionalist definition of families to address such limitations.

FUNCTIONS: WHAT FAMILIES DO

People in the United States seem to agree that traditional definitions of family are too restrictive. When they are asked how they would define family, their conception is much more inclusive than the substantive definition implies. In one survey, only 22 percent of the respondents defined family in the same way as the U.S. Census Bureau. Instead,

74 percent considered a family to be "any group whose members love and care for one another" (Coontz 1992:21).

We need a definition of family that is inclusive enough to encompass the broad range of intimate groups that people form, such as extended families, nuclear families, single-parent families, blended or reconstituted or step-families, gay and lesbian families, child-free families, racially and ethnically mixed families, commuter marriage families, surrogate or chosen families, and more. One way to avoid getting trapped into overly narrow conceptions of families and to embrace their diversity is to shift focus from a substantive definition of what families *are* to a **functionalist definition** of what families *do* for society and for their members.

Sociologist William F. Ogburn (Ogburn and Tibbits 1934) identified six primary functions that families perform for us:

- *Reproduction.* For a society to maintain itself, it must replace dying members. Families provide the context within which biological reproduction takes place.
- *Socialization.* Parents and other family members monitor a child's behavior and transmit the norms, values, and language of their culture to the child.
- *Protection.* Unlike the young of other animal species, human infants need constant care and economic security. In all cultures, the family assumes the ultimate responsibility for the protection and upbringing of children.
- *Regulation of sexual behavior.* Sexual norms are subject to change both over time (for instance, in the customs for dating) and across cultures (compare strict Saudi Arabia to the more permissive Denmark). However, whatever the time period or cultural values of a society, standards of sexual behavior are most clearly defined within the family circle.
- *Affection and companionship.* Ideally, families provide members with warm and intimate relationships, helping them to feel satisfied and secure. Of course, a family member may find such rewards outside the family—from peers, in school, at work—and may even perceive the home as an unpleasant or abusive setting. Nevertheless, we expect our relatives to understand us, to care for us, and to be there for us when we need them.

Personal Sociology

Pets As Family

When discussing families in terms of what they do instead of what they are, students inevitably ask, "Do pets count as family?" Some strongly agree, while others think it is the most ridiculous thing they have ever heard. More and more students are coming down on the side of pets as family. When we "adopted" Jessie, our Pembroke Welsh corgi, I better understood why. Owners develop strong emotional bonds with their pets and some refer to them as their "fur kids." Pets provide a source of comfort and companionship. They give us someone to care about, and they care for us in their own ways. Isn't that what we want from family?

- *Provision of social status.* We inherit a social position because of the family background and reputation of our parents and siblings. For example, the race, ethnicity, social class, education level, occupation, and religion of our parents all shape the material, social, and cultural resources to which we have access and therefore the options we might have.

No matter how it is composed, any group that fulfills these functions is family to us. We might count teammates, close college dorm mates, or a long-term circle of friends as family. We look to such groups in moments of need for all kinds of support, including care and affection, guidance in how to think and act, dating advice, and sometimes even material support, whether borrowing a car or just some money for pizza. We may use the expression that they are "like family" to convey that sense, or we may even refer to such significant people in our lives as our sister, brother, mom, or dad. In fact, given the survey results above, people may already be defining as family any group that provides sufficient love and care for each other. According to this functionalist definition, a family *is* what a family *does.*

AUTHORITY PATTERNS: WHO RULES?

Regardless of what a family looks like, within the context of any group we define as family, we will inevitably have to address issues of power. Imagine, for example, that you have recently married and must begin to make decisions about the future of your new family. You and your partner face many questions: Where will you live? How will you furnish your home? Who will do the cooking, shopping, and cleaning? Whose friends will be invited to dinner? Each time a decision must be made, an issue is raised: Who has the power to make the decision? In simple terms, who rules the family?

Societies vary in the way that power is distributed within the family; historically, however, the answer to that question has largely been shaped by gender. A society that expects males to dominate in all family decision making is termed a **patriarchy.** In patriarchal societies, such as Iran, the eldest male often wields the greatest power, although wives are expected to be treated with respect and kindness. An Iranian woman's status is typically defined by her relationship to a male relative, usually as a wife or daughter. In many patriarchal societies, women find it more difficult to obtain a divorce than a man does (Farr 1999). In contrast, in a **matriarchy,** women have greater authority than men. Formal matriarchies, which are uncommon, emerged among Native American tribal societies and in nations in which men were absent for long periods because of warfare or food-gathering expeditions.

> **patriarchy** A society in which men dominate in family decision making.
>
> **matriarchy** A society in which women dominate in family decision making.

More than a century ago, Friedrich Engels ([1884] 1959), a colleague of Karl Marx, went so far as to say that the family is the ultimate source of social inequality because of its role in the transfer of power, property, and privilege. Historically, he argues, the family has legitimized and perpetuated male dominance. It has contributed to societal injustice, denied women opportunities that are extended to men, and limited freedom in sexual expression and mate selection. In the United States, it was not until the first wave of contemporary feminism, in the mid-1800s, that there was a substantial challenge to the historical status of wives and children as the legal property of husbands and fathers.

Due in part to the efforts of women and men in similar movements over the years, we have seen the rise of a third type of authority pattern. In the **egalitarian family,** spouses are regarded as equals. This shift has been driven at least in part by occupational and financial opportunities for women that previously had been denied them (Wills and Risman 2006). That does not mean, however, that all decisions are shared in such families. Wives may hold authority in some spheres, and husbands in others. For example, sociologists have found that, in terms of paid and unpaid labor in two-parent families, the total hours worked by mothers and fathers is roughly equal at about 65 hours per week, though the distribution of tasks varies (Bianchi, Robinson, and Milkie 2006).

egalitarian family An authority pattern in which spouses are regarded as equals.

Historian Stephanie Coontz (2008) suggests that, when it works, marriage today is better than ever. She writes that it "delivers more benefits to its members—adults and children—than ever before. A good marriage is fairer and more fulfilling for both men and women than couples of the past could ever have imagined." She points to shared decision making and housework, increases in time spent with children, and declines in violence and sexual coercion and in the likelihood of adultery.

Although the egalitarian family has become a more common pattern in the United States in recent decades, male dominance over the family has hardly disappeared. Sociologists have found that although married men are increasing their involvement in child care, their wives still perform a disproportionate amount of it. Furthermore, with 11 million stay-at-home moms versus 290,000 stay-at-home dads, the dominant practice reinforces normative expectations (U.S. Census Bureau 2010a:Table SHP-1). And unfortunately, many husbands reinforce their power and control over wives and children through acts of domestic violence.

In addition to such internal power struggles, families also continue to provide a foundation for power within the larger society. Family serves as the basis for transferring power, property, and privilege from one generation to the next. Although the United States is widely viewed as a land of opportunity, social mobility is restricted in important ways. Children inherit the privileged or less-than-privileged social and economic status of their parents (and in some cases, of earlier generations as well). The social class of parents significantly influences children's socialization experiences and the degree of protection they receive. Thus, the socioeconomic status of a child's family will have a marked influence on his or her nutrition, health care, housing, educational opportunities, and in many respects, life chances as an adult. In many ways the family helps to maintain inequality.

>> Marriage and Family

Despite concerns about power and inequality in the family sphere, people's faith in marriage persists. Currently, more than 95 percent of all men and women in the United States marry at least once during their lifetimes. Though people wait a bit longer to marry now than in the past, the most historically consistent aspect of family life in this country has been the high rate of marriage. In the United States, the median age at first marriage is 25.9 years for women and 28.1 years for men. Since 1960, this represents an increase of 5.6 years for women and 5.3 years for men (Cherlin 2009; U.S. Census Bureau 2010a:Table MS-2).

SOCTHINK

Why might people turn to matchmaking services today? What are the disadvantages of relying on our own contacts and judgment when it comes to finding a romantic partner?

COURTSHIP AND MATE SELECTION

There are many ways that we might go about finding someone to marry. Historically, it was not uncommon for marriages to be arranged by families or matchmakers. This is a practice that continues in many cultures today. In the Asian nation of Uzbekistan, for example, courtship is largely orchestrated by the couple's parents. A young Uzbekistani woman is socialized to eagerly anticipate her marriage to a man whom she has met only once, at the final inspection of her dowry (Kamp 2008; Rand 2006).

Ten Questions Couples Should Ask (or Wish They Had) Before Marrying

Do you want to have children?

Who will do what when it comes to housework?

What are your expectations regarding sex?

What do you think about having a television in the bedroom?

What do you expect regarding religious training for our children?

How much money do you owe?

Do you like and respect my friends?

What do you really think about my parents?

What does my family do that annoys you?

Are there some things you are not willing to give up in the marriage?

Source: New York Times 2006.

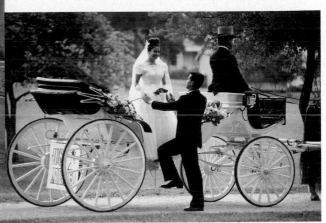

When it comes to marriage in the United States, most of us assume that true love will guide the way. We can't imagine allowing others, including parents and matchmakers, to select partners for us through arranged marriages. Many are surprised to hear that this practice continues today in some subcultures in the United States. We often take for granted that we are best suited to make this personal and

Going GLOBAL

Percentage of People Aged 20–24 Ever Married, Selected Countries

Country	Men	Women
Niger	32.2	89.7
India	34.8	77.0
Mexico	37.8	52.3
Haiti	19.9	60.1
China	21.4	42.6
Canada	13.5	24.4
United States	13.0	22.6
Australia	4.6	10.4
France	2.0	6.2

Source: United Nations 2009; U.S. Census Bureau 2010a:Table A1.

intimate selection. We may look to advice from family and friends, but the deciding factor is how we feel about the other person. We assume that the pool of potential partners is wide open so long as they get our heart racing.

In practice, however, our pool of potential partners is substantially reduced by our social location. We are sometimes blind to the basic social rules that inevitably narrow our choices (Kalmijn 1998):

- We are limited to those who are available and with whom we have contact.
- We are heavily influenced by opinions of family, friends, and the organizations to which we belong (including religious groups and the workplace).
- We are most attracted to people like ourselves.

In the first case, our position in the social structure influences the degree to which we have the opportunity to establish a relationship with someone. Second, partner selection involves more than just the happy couple; those close to us play a significant role in shaping which characteristics we perceive as acceptable. As a result, as the saying goes, like attracts like (or at least it tends to).

When sociologists analyze social factors that shape our selection of partners, they pay particular attention to the balance between endogamy and exogamy. **Endogamy** (from the Greek *endon,* "within") specifies the groups within which a spouse must be found and prohibits marriage with outsiders. For example, in the United States, many people are expected to marry within their own racial, ethnic, or religious group and are strongly discouraged or even prohibited from marrying outside the group. Endogamy is intended to reinforce the cohesiveness of the group by suggesting to young people that they should marry someone "of their own kind."

In contrast, **exogamy** (from the Greek *exo,* "outside") requires mate selection outside certain groups, usually one's own family or certain kinfolk. The **incest taboo,** a social norm common to virtually all societies, prohibits sexual relationships between certain culturally specified

> **endogamy** The restriction of mate selection to people within the same group.
>
> **exogamy** The requirement that people select a mate outside certain groups.
>
> **incest taboo** The prohibition of sexual relationships between certain culturally specified relatives.

relatives. In the United States, this taboo means that we must marry outside the nuclear family. We cannot marry our siblings, and in most states, we cannot marry our first cousins.

Endogamy influences a number of social location variables. We tend to pick partners who are the same age, race, ethnicity, education, and religion. Though the degree of influence of these variables has shifted over time, each continues to play a significant role. For example, in one study researchers found that the average age difference between spouses was 3.8 years, though the significance of the age gap decreases as we get older. A five-year age difference is more significant when someone is 18 than when the person is 38 or 58. Age is one of the factors for which third-party pressure can exert significant influence; people tend to look suspiciously at relationships in which the age difference is perceived to be too large (Blossfeld 2009; Rosenfeld 2008; Sherkat 2004; Thomas and Sawhill 2002).

homogamy The conscious or unconscious tendency to select a mate with personal characteristics and interests similar to one's own.

The role of race in selecting partners demonstrates how social norms can both change and remain the same. For a time, interracial marriage was illegal in the United States. This was still the case in some states until a 1967 Supreme Court ruling overturned these laws. In the past 50 years, the number of marriages between African Americans and Whites in the United States has increased more than tenfold, jumping from 51,000 in 1960 to 550,000 in 2009. Including all racial groups, the percentage of interracial marriages rose from 0.4 percent in 1960 to 4.1 percent in 2009 (U.S. Census Bureau 1998:Table 1; 2010a:Table FG4).

Despite the overall increase in the acceptance and practice of interracial marriage, most married people continue to select a partner of the same race. As we can see from the accompanying table, however, there is some variation both by race and by gender. Those who are White are the most likely to practice racial endogamy; almost 98 percent of both men and women select a marital partner of the same race. Among African Americans, men are slightly more likely than women to be involved in interracial marriages. For those who are Asian, however, there is a more significant gender difference; women are much more likely to be in an interracial marriage than men. Still, more than 80 percent of Asian women select a partner of the same race. Such patterns demonstrate the continued significance endogamy plays in partner selection (U.S. Census Bureau 2010a:Table FG4).

Even within these broader endogamous social categories, we tend to pick people like ourselves. This is known as **homogamy**—the conscious or unconscious tendency to select a mate with personal characteristics and interests similar to one's own. Internet dating services depend upon this principle to help find matches. Sociologist Pepper Schwartz, who works as a consultant for PerfectMatch.com, has developed a 48-question survey that covers everything from decision-making style to degree of impulsivity. Internet dating service eHarmony claims that its technique of matching people on the basis of similar characteristics, interests, and abilities—that is, relying on the principles of endogamy and homogamy—results in 236 marriages per day (Gottlieb 2006; Logue 2009; Peel 2008).

In theory, Cupid's arrow could strike anyone on our behalf. But love is not blind. Love is a product of the social and cultural forces that shape the choices we make. Of course, knowledge of the ways our choices are patterned can free us up to follow different paths.

Patterns of Interracial Marriage

	White wife	Black wife	Asian wife
White husband	50,863	196	534
Black husband	354	4,150	39
Asian husband	200	10	2,752

Number in thousands

Percent husbands with same race wife
- 97.6% White
- 90.2% Black
- 92.1% Asian

Percent wives with same race husband
- 97.9% White
- 94.8% Black
- 81.8% Asian

Note: Numbers in thousands. Table does not show data for Other Race husbands and wives.
Source: U.S. Census Bureau 2010a:Table FG4.

VARIATIONS IN FAMILY LIFE AND INTIMATE RELATIONSHIPS

Within the United States, social class, race, and ethnicity create variations in family life. Studying these variations will give us a more sophisticated understanding of contemporary family styles in our country. The desire to avoid having to negotiate such differences also helps to explain why people often practice homogamy.

Social Class Differences Social class differences matter when it comes to parenting. Historically, poor and working-class families were more authoritarian, and middle-class families were more permissive and less

SOCTHINK

How important are factors such as age, education, race, ethnicity, social class, gender, and religion in whom you might choose for a serious relationship? To what extent are or were you conscious of such influences when you pick someone to date?

5 Movies on MARRIAGE AND FAMILIES

Far From Heaven
Subverting the ideal 1950s marriage.

Monsoon Wedding
An Indian wedding celebration.

The Squid and the Whale
How divorce affects children.

It's Complicated
A divorced couple with adult children reunite with mixed results.

A Home at the End of the World
An alternative marriage and family.

were below the official poverty line. The rate for married couples was only 5.5 percent (DeNavas-Walt, Proctor, and Smith 2009a:14). Racial and class factors are often closely related. In examining family life among racial and ethnic minorities, keep in mind that certain patterns may result from class as well as cultural factors.

Racial and Ethnic Differences The subordinate status of racial and ethnic minorities in the United States profoundly affects their family lives. For example, the lower incomes of African Americans, Native Americans, most Hispanic groups, and selected Asian American groups make creating and maintaining successful marital unions a difficult task. The economic restructuring of the past 50 years, described by sociologist William Julius Wilson (1996) and others, in which blue-collar jobs disappeared from urban areas as companies moved production facilities abroad, has especially affected people living in inner cities and desolate rural areas. Furthermore, the immigration policy of the United States has complicated the successful relocation of intact families from Asia and Latin America.

The African American family suffers from many negative and inaccurate stereotypes. It is true that in a significantly higher proportion of Black than White families, no husband is present in the home. Yet Black single mothers often belong to stable, functioning kin networks, which mitigate the pressures of sexism and racism. Members of these networks—predominantly female kin such as mothers, grandmothers, and aunts—ease financial strains by sharing goods and services. In addition to these strong kinship bonds, Black family life has emphasized deep religious commitment and high aspirations for achievement (F. Furstenberg 2007; Stack 1974).

Like African Americans, Native Americans draw on family ties to cushion many of the hardships they face. On the Navajo reservation, for example, teenage parenthood is not regarded as the crisis that it is elsewhere in the United States. The Navajo trace their descent matrilineally. Traditionally, couples reside with the wife's family after marriage, allowing the grandparents to help with the child rearing. While the Navajo do not approve of teenage parenthood, the deep emotional commitment of their extended families provides a warm home environment for fatherless children (Dalla and Gamble 2001).

Sociologists also have taken note of differences in family patterns among other racial and ethnic groups. For example, although Mexican American men have been

likely to use physical punishment. Starting in the 1950s, exposure to common child-rearing advice in books, magazines, and on television reduced the extremes by creating a shared understanding of appropriate parenting techniques, but recent research shows that parenting practices still differ. For example, middle-class parents provide more structure through participation in organized activities, and working-class parents allow their children greater freedom so long as they don't overstep disciplinary bounds. The material, social, and cultural resources children inherit from their parents (whether in the form of money, connections, language, tastes, attitudes, or experience) help to reproduce social class across generations (Kronstadt and Favreault 2008; Lareau 2003).

Among people who are poor, women often play a significant role in the economic support of the family. Men may earn low wages, may be unemployed, or may be entirely absent from the family. In 2008, 29 percent of all families headed by women with no husband present

> The goal in marriage is not to think alike, but to think together.

Robert C. Dodds

described as exhibiting a sense of virility, personal worth, and pride in their maleness that is called **machismo,** Mexican Americans are also described as being more familistic than many other subcultures. **Familism** refers to pride in the extended family, expressed through the mainte-

machismo A sense of virility, personal worth, and pride in one's maleness.

familism Pride in the extended family, expressed through the maintenance of close ties and strong obligations to kinfolk outside the immediate family.

nance of close ties and strong obligations to kinfolk outside the immediate family. Traditionally, Mexican Americans have placed proximity to their extended families above other needs and desires.

These family patterns are changing, however, in response to changes in Latinos' social class standing, educational achievements, and occupations. Like other Americans, career-oriented Latinos in search of a mate but short on spare time are turning to the Internet. As Latinos and other groups assimilate into the dominant culture of the United States, their family lives take on both the positive and the negative characteristics associated with non-Hispanic White households (Landale and Orapesa 2007).

CHILD-REARING PATTERNS

Caring for children is a universal function of the family, yet the ways in which different societies assign this function to family members can vary significantly. The Nayars of southern India acknowledge the biological role of fathers, but the mother's eldest brother is responsible for her children. In contrast, uncles play only a peripheral role in child care in the United States. Even within the United States, child-rearing patterns are varied. Just as our conception of families has changed, so also has our practice of child rearing.

Parenthood and Grandparenthood The socialization of children is essential to the maintenance of any culture. Consequently, parenthood is one of the most important (and most demanding) social roles in the United States. Sociologist Alice Rossi (1968, 1984) has identified four factors that complicate the transition to parenthood and the role of socialization. First, there is little anticipatory socialization for the social role of caregiver. The normal school curriculum gives scant attention to the subjects most relevant to successful family life, such as child care and home maintenance. Second, only limited learning occurs during the period of pregnancy itself. Third, the transition to parenthood is quite abrupt. Unlike adolescence, it is not prolonged; unlike the transition to work, the duties of caregiving cannot be taken on gradually. Finally, in Rossi's view, our society lacks clear and helpful guidelines for successful parenthood. There is little consensus on how parents can produce happy and well-adjusted offspring—or even on what it means to be well adjusted. For these reasons, socialization for parenthood involves difficult challenges for most men and women in the United States.

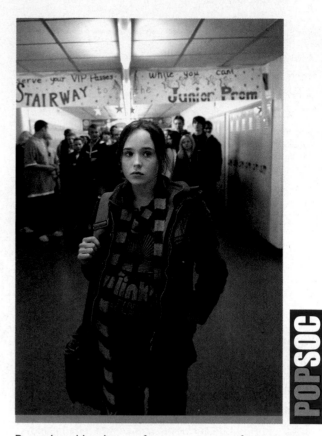

POPSOC

Parenthood has been a frequent source of entertainment in the movies. Examples of such films include *Mr. Mom, Parenthood, Finding Nemo, Freaky Friday, Cheaper by the Dozen, Daddy's Little Girls, Juno, Baby Mama, The Blind Side,* and even *Alvin and the Chipmunks.* They all convey messages of what it means to be a parent. What lessons might we learn from an analysis of how mothers and fathers are portrayed in such films? What recurring images and themes occur? How common is the bungling dad or the career mom who wonders if she is making the right choices? What are the consequences of such films for how we practice parenting?

One recent development in family life in the United States has been the extension of parenthood, as adult children continue to live at home or return home after college. In 2009, 57 percent of men and 49 percent of women aged 18–24 lived with their parents compared to 52 and 35 percent, respectively, in 1960 (U.S. Census Bureau 2010a:Table AD-1). Some of these adult children were still pursuing an education, but in many instances, financial difficulties underlay these living arrangements. While rents and real estate prices have skyrocketed, salaries for younger workers have not kept pace, and many find themselves unable to afford their own homes. Moreover, with many marriages now ending in divorce, divorced sons and daughters often return to live with their parents, sometimes with their own children.

In some homes, child-rearing responsibilities fall to grandparents. In 2004, 6.5 million children, or 9 percent of all children in the United States, lived in a household with a grandparent (Kreider 2008). In about a third of these homes, no parent was present to assume responsibility for the youngsters. Special difficulties are inherent in such relationships, including legal custodial concerns, financial issues, and emotional problems for adults and youths alike. Perhaps not surprisingly, support groups such as Grandparents as Parents have emerged to provide assistance.

Adoption In a legal sense, **adoption** is a "process that allows for the transfer of the legal rights, responsibilities, and privileges of parenthood" to a new legal parent or parents (E. Cole 1985:638). In many cases, these rights are transferred from a biological parent or parents (often called birth parents) to an adoptive parent or parents.

About 4 percent of all people in the United States are adopted, and about 2 percent by persons not related to them at birth. There are two legal methods of adopting an unrelated person: (1) the adoption may be arranged through a licensed agency, or (2) in some states it may be arranged through a private agreement sanctioned by the courts. Adopted children may come from the United States or from abroad. In 2009, more than 12,753 children entered the United States as the adopted children of U.S. citizens. Although the number of international adoptions remains substantial, it has declined in recent years, down from 23,000 in 2004. China, the source for about one-fourth of overseas adoptions, recently began

to tighten the rules for foreigners. Applicants who are single, obese, or older than 50 may now be disqualified automatically (Carr 2007; Gross 2007; U.S. Department of State 2009).

In the United States, one of the limitations historically was that only married couples could adopt. In 1995, an important court decision in New York held that a couple does not have to be married to adopt a child. Under this ruling, unmarried heterosexual couples, lesbian couples, and gay couples can all legally adopt children in New York. Writing for the majority, Chief Justice Judith Kaye argued

> **adoption** In a legal sense, a process that allows for the transfer of the legal rights, responsibilities, and privileges of parenthood to a new legal parent or parents.

that by expanding the boundaries of who can be legally recognized as parents, the state may be able to assist more children in securing "the best possible home." With this ruling, New York became the third state (after Vermont and Massachusetts) to recognize the right of unmarried couples to adopt children (Dao 1995; Human Rights Campaign 2009).

For every child who is adopted, many more remain the wards of state-sponsored child protective services. In 2007, 491,000 children in the United States were living in foster care. Approximately 132,000 of these children were waiting for adoption (U.S. Census Bureau 2009f:Table 567).

Dual-Income Families The idea of a family consisting of a wage-earning husband and a stay-at-home wife has largely given way to the dual-income household. Among married couples with children under 6, 55 percent have both husband and wife in the labor force (Bureau of Labor Statistics 2009c:Table 4).

—**SOC**THINK—

What are the advantages and disadvantages of the dual-income model for women, for men, for children, and for society as a whole?

Both opportunity and need have driven the rise in the number of dual-income couples. Women now have the chance to pursue opportunities in a way that previously had been closed due to cultural expectations regarding gender. This has resulted in increased education levels for women and increased participation in occupational fields that had been largely closed. At the same time, however, couples find it harder to make it on a single income. Evidence of this trend can be found in the rise of married couples living apart for reasons other than marital discord. The 3.6 million couples who now live apart represent 1 out of every 33 marriages. More than half live farther than 100 miles apart, and half of those live 1000 or more miles apart. Of course, couples living apart are nothing new; men have worked at transient jobs for generations as

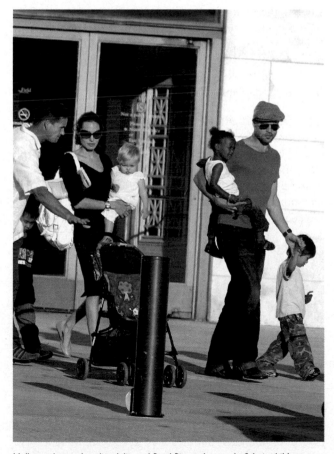

Hollywood stars Angelina Jolie and Brad Pitt and several of their children, many from overseas adoptions.

soldiers, truck drivers, or traveling salesmen. The existence of such household arrangements reflects an acceptance of the egalitarian family type (L. Cullen 2007; Holmes 2006).

Single-Parent Families The 2004 *American Idol* winner Fantasia Barrino's song "Baby Mama" offers a tribute to young single mothers—a subject she knows about. Barrino was 17 when she became pregnant with her daughter. Though critics charged that the song sends the wrong message to teenage girls, Barrino says it is not about encouraging teens to have sex. Rather, she sees the song as an anthem for young mothers courageously trying to raise their children alone (Cherlin 2006).

single-parent family A family in which only one parent is present to care for the children.

In recent decades, the stigma attached to unwed mothers and other single parents has significantly diminished. **Single-parent families,** in which only one parent is present to care for the children, can hardly be viewed as a rarity in the United States. In 2004, a single parent

headed about 20 percent of White families with children under age 18, 29 percent of Hispanic families, 59 percent of African American families, and 11 percent of Asian/Pacific Islander families (as we can see in the figure on page 168; Kreider 2008).

The life of single parents and their children is not inevitably more difficult than that of a traditional nuclear family. It is as inaccurate to assume that a single-parent family is necessarily deprived as it is to assume that a two-parent family is always secure and happy. Nevertheless, to the extent that such families have to rely on a single income or a sole caregiver, life in the single-parent family can be extremely stressful. A family headed by a single mother faces especially difficult problems when the mother is a teenager, especially when she lacks access to significant social and economic resources (Sawhill 2006).

Why might low-income teenage women wish to have children and face the obvious financial difficulties of motherhood? Some theorists argue that these women tend to have low self-esteem and limited options; a child may provide a sense of motivation and purpose for the teenager whose economic worth in our society is limited at best. Given the barriers that many young women face because of their gender, race, ethnicity, and class, many teenagers may believe they have little to lose and much to gain by having a child.

Although 87 percent of single parents in the United States are mothers, the number of households headed by single fathers more than tripled between 1970 and 2000. Single mothers often develop social networks, but single fathers are typically more isolated. In addition, they must deal with schools and social service agencies that are more accustomed to women as custodial parents (U.S. Census Bureau 2010a:Table CH1).

Stepfamilies As a result of single parents who marry or divorced parents who remarry, approximately 15 percent of children under 18 live in a married stepfamily. But stepfamilies can involve more than just young children in these relationships. Sociologist Susan Stewart (2007) recommends expanding our definition of stepfamilies to include cohabitating couples with children from previous relationships, families whose stepchildren do not live with them full-time, gay or lesbian couples with children from former heterosexual relationships, and stepfamilies with adult children. The expanded definition highlights the fact that stepfamily membership extends throughout the life course. The exact nature of blended families has social significance for adults and children alike.

> What greater thing is there for human souls than to feel that they are joined for life—to be with each other in silent unspeakable memories.
>
> **George Eliot**

Comedians Tina Fey and Amy Poehler starred in the 2008 film Baby Mama, in which Fey played a would-be single mother.

Family members in stepfamilies must deal with resocialization issues when an adult becomes a stepparent or a child becomes a stepchild and stepsibling. In evaluating these stepfamilies, some observers have assumed that children would benefit from remarriage because they would be gaining a second custodial parent and would potentially enjoy greater economic security. However, after reviewing many studies of stepfamilies, sociologist Andrew J. Cherlin (2008b:800) concluded that "the well-being of children in stepfamilies is no better, on average, than the well-being of children in divorced, single-parent households."

Stepparents can and do play valuable and unique roles in their stepchildren's lives, but their involvement does not guarantee an improvement in family life. In fact, standards may decline. Studies suggest that children raised in families with stepmothers are likely to have less health care, education, and money spent on their food than children raised by biological mothers. The measures are also negative for children raised by stepfathers, but only half as negative as in the case of stepmothers. This may be due to the stepmother holding back out of concern for seeming too intrusive or relying on the biological father to carry out parental duties (Schmeeckle 2007; Schmeeckle et al. 2006).

>> Diverse Lifestyles

Marriage is no longer the presumed route from adolescence to adulthood. In fact, it has lost much of its social significance as a rite of passage. Now, establishing oneself through education and a career has taken precedence (Cherlin 2004, 2009). The nation's marriage rate has declined since 1970 because people are postponing marriage until later in life and because more couples, including same-sex couples, are deciding to form partnerships without marriage.

COHABITATION

In the United States, testing the relationship waters by living together before marriage is an increasingly common

Rise of Single–Parent Families in the United States

2009
78%
89%
1970
Whites
9%
2%
18%
4%

2009
68%
1970
African Americans
42%
28%
55%
4%
4%

2009
72%
81%
1970
Hispanics
15%
26%
4%
3%

2009
87%
84%
1980
Asians or Pacific Islanders
11%
5%
11%
3%

1970/80   2009

Two-parent families

One-parent families, maintained by mother

One-parent families, maintained by father

Note: "Children" refers to children under 18. Early data for Asian Americans are for 1980. Hispanics can be of any race. Not included are unrelated people living together with no children present. All data exclude the 4 percent of children in nonparental households.

Source: U.S. Census Bureau 1994:62; 2010a:Table C9.

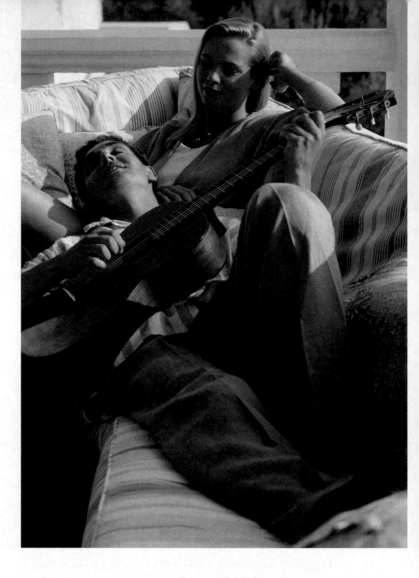

practice. Researchers found that, while close to half of women and men aged 15–44 were married, almost 10 percent were instead cohabiting. **Cohabitation** is conventionally defined as the practice of a man and a woman living together in a sexual relationship without being married (Goodwin, Mosher, and Chandra 2010).

About half of all currently married couples in the United States say that they lived together prior to marriage. And this percentage is likely to increase. The number of unmarried-couple households in the United States rose sixfold in the 1960s and increased another 72 percent between 1990 and 2000. Presently, more than 8 percent of opposite-sex couples are unmarried. Cohabitation is more common among African Americans and American Indians than among other racial and ethnic groups; it is least common among Asian Americans. The figure on page 169 shows how cohabitation varies by region (Goodwin et al. 2010; Peterson 2003; T. Simmons and O'Connell 2003).

In much of Europe, cohabitation is so common that the general sentiment seems to be "Love, yes; marriage, maybe." In Iceland, 62 percent of all children are born to single mothers; in France, Great Britain, and Norway, the proportion is about 40 percent. Government policies in these countries make few legal distinctions between

Unmarried-Couple Households by State

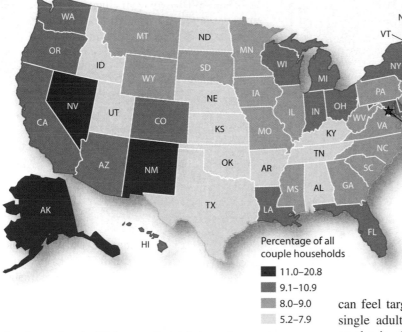

Percentage of all couple households

- 11.0–20.8
- 9.1–10.9
- 8.0–9.0
- 5.2–7.9

Note: Data are from the 2000 Census and include both opposite-sex and same-sex partners. U.S. average is 9.1 percent.

Source: T. Simmons and O'Connell 2003:4.

married and unmarried couples or households (Lyall 2002; M. Moore 2006; Thomson and Bernhardt 2010).

People commonly associate cohabitation only with younger couples, but according to a study done in Los Angeles, working couples are almost twice as likely to cohabit as college students. And census data show that in 2003, 45 percent of unmarried couples had one or more children present in the household. These cohabitants are more like spouses than dating partners. Moreover, in contrast to the common perception that people who cohabit have never been married, researchers report that about half of all people involved in cohabitation in the United States have been previously married. Cohabitation serves as a temporary or permanent alternative to matrimony for many men and women who have experienced their own or their parents' divorces (Fields 2004; Popenoe and Whitehead 1999).

REMAINING SINGLE

As noted earlier, more and more people in the United States are postponing entry into a firstmarriage. The trend toward maintaining a single lifestyle for a longer period

is related to the growing economic independence of young people. This trend is especially significant for women. Freed from financial needs, women don't necessarily need to marry to enjoy a satisfying life. Divorce, late marriage, and longevity also figure into this trend. Even so, among those who lived to be 65 or older, only 4 percent of women and men in the United States remained single throughout their lives (U.S. Census Bureau 2009f:Table 34).

There are many reasons a person may choose not to marry. Some singles do not want to limit their sexual intimacy to one lifetime partner. Some men and women do not want to become highly dependent on any one person—and do not want anyone depending heavily on them. In a society that values individuality and self-fulfillment, the single lifestyle can offer certain freedoms that marriage may not.

Remaining single represents a clear departure from societal expectations and can feel targeted in a society that presumes marriage. A single adult must confront the inaccurate view that he or she is always lonely, is a workaholic, or is immature. These stereotypes help to support the traditional assumption in the United States and most other societies that to be truly happy and fulfilled, a person must get married and raise a family. To counter these societal expectations, singles have formed numerous support groups (Hertz 2006; Lundquist 2006).

> **cohabitation** The practice of a man and a woman living together in a sexual relationship without being married.

MARRIAGE WITHOUT CHILDREN

There has also been a significant increase in childlessness in the United States. According to census data, approximately 17 percent of women will now complete their childbearing years without having borne any children, compared to 10 percent in 1980. As many as 20 percent of women in their 30s expect to remain childless (Clausen 2002).

Childlessness within marriage has generally been viewed as a problem that can be solved through such means as adoption and artificial insemination. More and more couples today, however, choose not to have children and regard themselves as child-free rather than childless. They do not believe that having children automatically follows from marriage, nor do they feel that reproduction is the duty of all married couples. Childless couples have formed

> Call it a clan, call it a network, call it a tribe, call it a family. Whatever you call it, whoever you are, you need one.
>
> Jane Howard

Percentage of Marriages to Reach Milestones*

Men, year of first marriage	Anniversary (percentage still married)*							
	5th	10th	15th	20th	25th	30th	35th	40th
1955–59	96.4	88.3	80.3	73.8	70.4	67.3	64.7	61.4
1960–64	95.1	85.0	75.2	69.7	65.0	62.4	59.7	52.5
1965–69	90.5	76.9	67.4	62.3	58.6	55.5	48.2	
1970–74	88.5	74.4	64.6	58.1	53.8	46.2		
1975–79	88.1	73.0	65.2	59.6	49.5			
1980–84	88.7	73.7	65.3	53.8				
1985–89	89.3	76.4	60.6					
1990–94	89.4	70.0						

*Counts marriages ended by divorce, separation, and death

Women, year of first marriage	Anniversary (percentage still married)*							
	5th	10th	15th	20th	25th	30th	35th	40th
1955–59	94.0	86.8	79.4	72.4	67.2	63.5	58.9	54.7
1960–64	92.8	82.3	72.7	66.5	60.4	56.1	52.7	44.9
1965–69	89.5	74.9	65.7	60.0	55.1	51.3	43.8	
1970–74	87.1	71.6	61.4	55.4	50.6	42.1		
1975–79	85.3	70.0	61.4	55.7	46.4			
1980–84	86.5	70.7	63.1	52.4				
1985–89	85.7	73.0	56.9					
1990–94	87.2	69.2						

Source: U.S. Census Bureau 2004:Table 2.

In the United States and many other countries, overall divorce rates began to increase in the late 1960s but then leveled off; since the late 1980s, the divorce rate has declined by 30 percent. This trend is due partly to the aging of the baby boomer generation and the corresponding decline in the proportion of people of marriageable age. But it also indicates an increase in marital stability in recent years (Coontz 2006).

Getting divorced obviously does not sour people on marriage. About 63 percent of all divorced people in the United States have remarried. However, women are less likely than men to remarry because many retain custody of their children after a divorce, which complicates a new adult relationship (Bianchi and Spain 1996; Saad 2004). Some people regard the nation's high rate of remarriage as an endorsement of the institution of marriage, but it does lead to the new challenges of a kin network characterized by both current and prior marital relationships. Such networks can be particularly complex if children are involved or if an ex-spouse remarries.

FACTORS ASSOCIATED WITH DIVORCE

One of the major factors shaping the increase in divorce over the past 100 years has been the greater social acceptance of divorce. It is no longer considered necessary to endure an unhappy marriage. Even major religious groups have relaxed what were often negative attitudes toward divorce, commonly having treated it as a sin in the past.

The growing acceptance of divorce is a worldwide phenomenon. Only a decade ago, Sunoo, South Korea's foremost matchmaking service, had no divorced

Did You Know?

... For women, the likelihood of getting a divorce decreases for each year she waits to get married. Women who got married at age 35 or older have the lowest chance of getting divorced.

clients. Few Koreans divorced, and those who did felt social pressure to resign themselves to the single life. In one recent seven-year period, South Korea's divorce rate doubled. Now, 15 percent of Sunoo's membership is divorced (Onishi 2003).

In the United States, a variety of factors have contributed to the growing social acceptance of divorce. For instance, most states have adopted less restrictive divorce laws in the past three decades. No-fault divorce laws, which allow a couple to end their marriage without assigning blame (by specifying adultery, for instance), accounted for an initial surge in the divorce rate after they

Trends in Marriage and Divorce in the United States

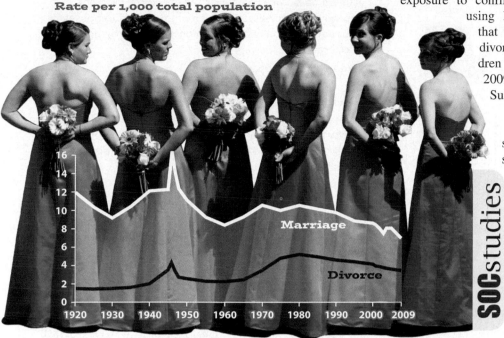

Rate per 1,000 total population

Sources: Bureau of the Census 1975:64; Tejada-Vera and Sutton 2010.

dysfunctional relationship. A national study conducted by sociologists Paul R. Amato and Alan Booth (1997) showed that in about a third of divorces, the children actually benefited from parental separation because it lessened their exposure to conflict. Additional researchers, also using larger samples, have concluded that the long-term harmful effects of divorce affect only a minority of children (Booth and Amato 2001; Cherlin 2009; Hetherington and Kelly 2002; Sun and Li 2008).

The debates surrounding issues such as divorce, cohabitation, and same-sex families highlight many of the issues sociologists seek to address in their investigation of family life. What families are, what they do, how they do it, and what obstacles they face are issues relevant for all families. In our modern, pluralistic world, the singular traditions of the past can no longer be taken for granted, as Tevye and Golde discovered in *Fiddler on the Roof.* People come from many different cultures with multiple taken-for-granted assumptions. Sociology investigates such complexity, providing us with tools so that we might better understand how we think and act in the context of families.

were introduced in the 1970s, though these laws appear to have had little effect beyond that. Additionally, a general increase in family incomes, coupled with the availability of free legal aid to some poor people, has meant that more couples can afford costly divorce proceedings. Also, as society provides greater opportunities for women, more and more wives are becoming less dependent on their husbands, both economically and emotionally. They may feel more able to leave a marriage if it seems hopeless.

IMPACT OF DIVORCE ON CHILDREN

Divorce is traumatic for all involved, but it has special meaning for the more than 1 million children whose parents divorce each year. There is significant sociological debate on the effects divorce has on children. One major study tracked 131 children of divorce over a 25-year period. It concluded that the impacts of divorce are substantial and long-lasting, including higher rates of drug and alcohol abuse, limited resources for college, and fear of intimacy in adulthood (Wallerstein, Lewis, and Blakeslee 2000). These researchers recommended that parents should stay together in a "good enough" marriage for the sake of the children. One of the limitations of this research is the relatively small sample size, raising questions about the degree to which the results can be generalized.

Other sociologists have concluded that, for many children, divorce signals the welcome end to a highly

Volunteer! There are numerous organizations designed to assist children in situations of need, including Big Brothers and Big Sisters, CASA (Court Appointed Special Advocates), and school tutoring programs. Such programs can fulfill some of the functions of families. Seek out one of these organizations, and find out ways that you can help.

For REVIEW

I. What is the family?

- Sociologists define the family in terms of both what a family is, with an emphasis on blood and law, and what families do or what functions they perform, including reproduction, socialization, protection, regulation of sexual behavior, affection and companionship, and provision of social status.

II. How do people pick partners?

- Social factors shape the pool of potential partners from which individuals select. People balance selection, favoring someone who is from within their group (endogamy) but not too close (exogamy). People tend to pick people with similar social characteristics (homogamy), including age, education, class, race, and ethnicity.

III. How do families vary?

- There is significant variation in terms of proximity (extended versus nuclear), authority (patriarchal, matriarchal, and egalitarian), duration (divorce), and structure (dual-income, single-parent, stepfamilies, cohabitation, singlehood, child-free, and same-sex).

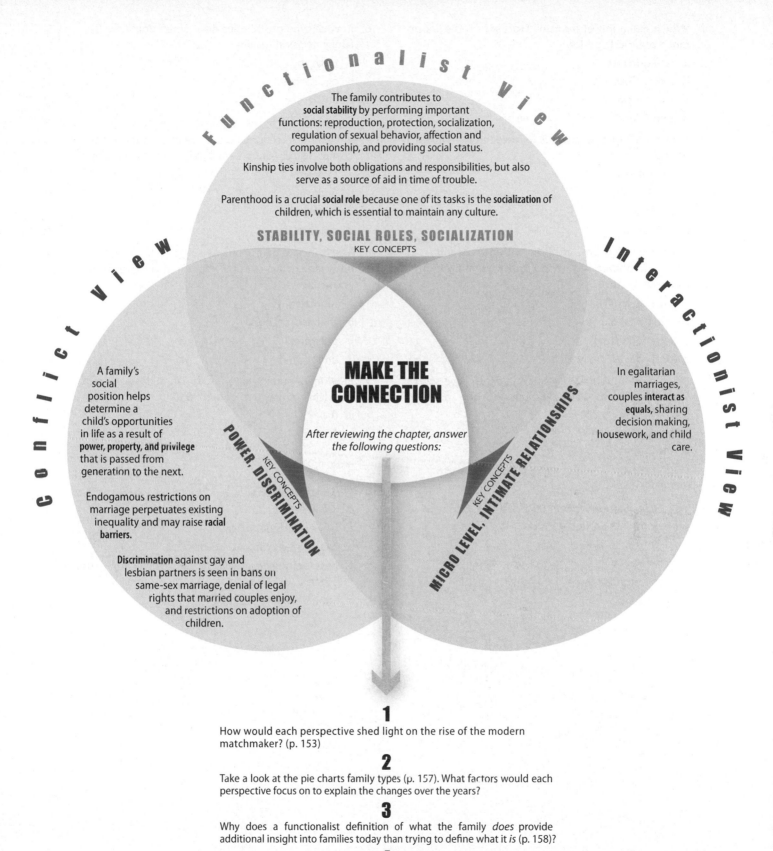

Functionalist View

The family contributes to **social stability** by performing important functions: reproduction, protection, socialization, regulation of sexual behavior, affection and companionship, and providing social status.

Kinship ties involve both obligations and responsibilities, but also serve as a source of aid in time of trouble.

Parenthood is a crucial **social role** because one of its tasks is the **socialization** of children, which is essential to maintain any culture.

STABILITY, SOCIAL ROLES, SOCIALIZATION
KEY CONCEPTS

Conflict View

A family's social position helps determine a child's opportunities in life as a result of **power, property, and privilege** that is passed from generation to the next.

Endogamous restrictions on marriage perpetuates existing inequality and may raise **racial barriers.**

Discrimination against gay and lesbian partners is seen in bans on same-sex marriage, denial of legal rights that married couples enjoy, and restrictions on adoption of children.

KEY CONCEPTS
POWER, DISCRIMINATION

Interactionist View

In egalitarian marriages, couples **interact as equals**, sharing decision making, housework, and child care.

KEY CONCEPTS
MICRO LEVEL, INTIMATE RELATIONSHIPS

MAKE THE CONNECTION

After reviewing the chapter, answer the following questions:

1
How would each perspective shed light on the rise of the modern matchmaker? (p. 153)

2
Take a look at the pie charts family types (p. 157). What factors would each perspective focus on to explain the changes over the years?

3
Why does a functionalist definition of what the family *does* provide additional insight into families today than trying to define what it *is* (p. 158)?

4
Who rules in your family? Would a functionalist, conflict, or interactionist perspective best describe your family dynamics?

Pop Quiz

1. Which definition of the family focuses on the importance of blood and law?
   a. functionalist
   b. matrilineal
   c. substantive
   d. extended

2. Which system of descent is followed in the United States?
   a. matrilineal
   b. patrilineal
   c. bilateral
   d. unilateral

3. Alice, age seven, lives at home with her parents, her grandmother, and her aunt. Alice's family is an example of a(n)
   a. nuclear family.
   b. patrilineal family.
   c. extended family.
   d. polygynous family.

4. In which form of marriage may a person have several spouses in his or her lifetime but only one spouse at a time?
   a. serial monogamy
   b. monogamy
   c. polygamy
   d. polyandry

5. The marriage of a woman to more than one man at the same time is referred to as
   a. polygyny.
   b. monogamy.
   c. serial monogamy.
   d. polyandry.

6. In what type of societies do women dominate in family decision making?
   a. polygyny
   b. egalitarian
   c. patriarchy
   d. matriarchy

7. Which norm requires mate selection outside certain groups, usually one's own family or certain kinfolk?
   a. exogamy
   b. endogamy
   c. matriarchy
   d. patriarchy

8. The principle that prohibits sexual relationships between certain culturally specified relatives is known as
   a. monogamy.
   b. the incest taboo.
   c. polygamy.
   d. endogamy.

9. How many states guaranteed gay and lesbian couples the right to marry as of mid-2010.
   a. 0
   b. 5
   c. 23
   d. 41

10. Overall, the divorce rate in the United States in the past 30 years
    a. has risen dramatically.
    b. has risen slowly but steadily.
    c. has declined after having risen significantly in the 1960s and 1970s.
    d. shows no clear pattern.

1. (c); 2. (c); 3. (c); 4. (a); 5. (d); 6. (d); 7. (a); 8. (b); 9. (b); 10. (c)

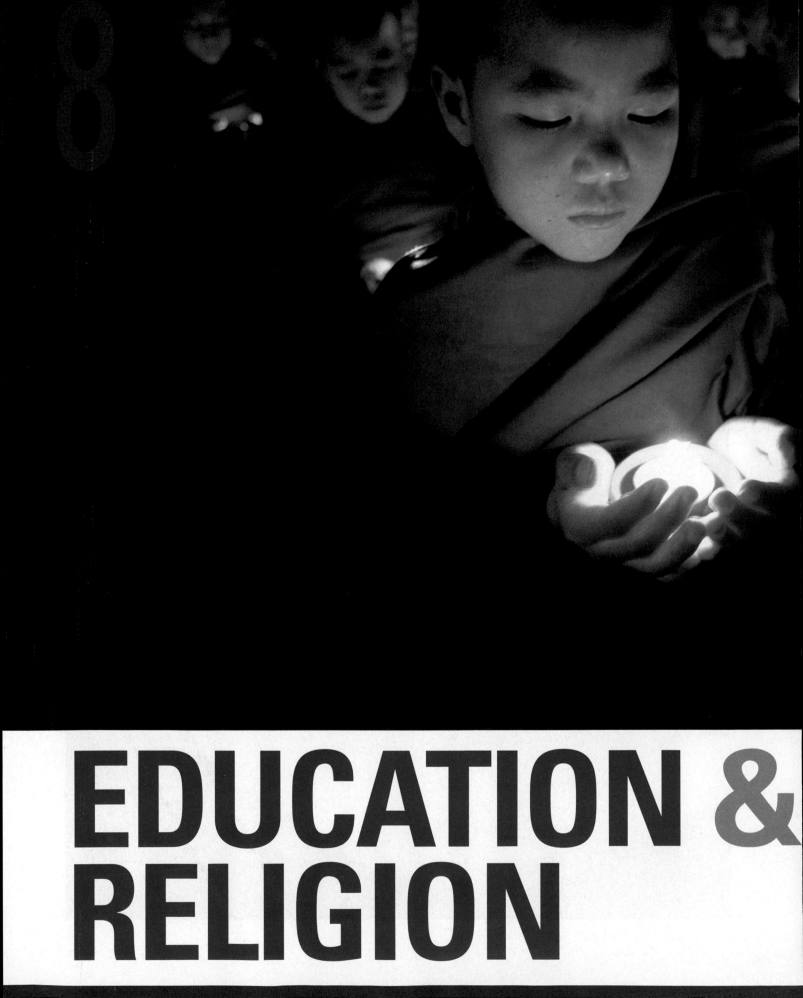

8

EDUCATION & RELIGION

FAITH AND LEARNING

Patrick Henry College, located near Washington, D.C., was founded in 2000 with the explicit intention of competing with Ivy League schools. The elite students it pursues, however, come from a particular niche: Approximately 80 percent of them were homeschooled, and they all share a strong commitment to evangelical Christian faith.

In keeping with the school's expectation of a high level of religious commitment, students must sign a "Statement of Faith" that sets out a series of Christian beliefs, including the virgin birth of Jesus Christ, the existence of Satan, and eternal punishment in hell for non-Christians. Students are required to abide by a strict dress code, attend daily chapel, and abstain from alcohol, smoking, and premarital sex.

The students by and large take these commitments quite seriously. As journalist Hannah Rosin (2007) recounts in her book on Patrick Henry College titled *God's Harvard,* "To them, a 'Christian' keeps a running conversation with God in his or her head . . . and believes that at any moment God might in some palpable way step in and show He either cares or disapproves" (p. 5).

Student Elisa Muench was something of a trailblazer at Patrick Henry College. She was the first woman to run for a leadership position in student government, in the face of disapproval by students who thought it inappropriate that a woman should serve in such an office. As a junior, she had an internship in the White House. Yet she found herself fearing that what counted as success in the eyes of the dominant society, including a professional career, might conflict with success in the eyes of God (Rosin 2007:85). Elisa struggled to be true to both her educational and religious teachings.

It is within such educational and religious communities that we learn what to believe and how to act. All of us are, in some respects, like Elisa, seeking to balance the sometimes conflicting demands of the various spheres of our lives, including family, education, religion, work, and politics. In this chapter, we focus on the roles education and religion play both for individuals and for society as a whole.

- How does education help to maintain social order?
- How does education support the existing system of inequality?
- How do sociologists define religion?

>> Education in Society

Historically, we counted on families to be significant agents of socialization, teaching us the basic knowledge, values, and norms we needed to survive. As societies became more diverse and the division of labor increased, however, our educational needs expanded, and we placed a greater emphasis on more formal socialization. To do so we turned to **education,** the formal process of instruction in which some people consciously teach while others adopt the social role of learner.

education A formal process of instruction in which some people consciously teach while others adopt the social role of learner.

As a society, we invest a significant amount of time and money in education because we believe the individual and collective benefits are worth it. On the one hand, we value education as a path to knowledge and understanding. We investigate the deeper mysteries of life—truth, beauty, wisdom—so that we might have a better understanding of ourselves and our world. As sociologist W.E.B. Du Bois ([1903] 1994) put it, "The true college will ever have one goal,—not to earn meat, but to know the end and aim of that life which meat nourishes" (p. 51). On the other hand, we see education as a means of ensuring fairness and opportunity; we count on schools to provide us all with the knowledge and the tools we need to achieve better circumstances in life, including good jobs.

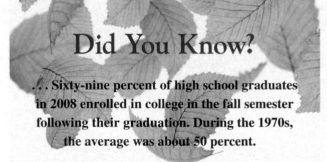

Did You Know?

. . . Sixty-nine percent of high school graduates in 2008 enrolled in college in the fall semester following their graduation. During the 1970s, the average was about 50 percent.

Source: Bureau of Labor Statistics 2009d.

In the United States, this commitment to education goes back to a belief that our outcomes should not be determined by birth, but by ability and effort. According to this value, being born to aristocratic parents should not ensure economic and social privilege any more than being born to parents with limited means should consign one to a life of poverty. Early American political leaders such as Benjamin Franklin and Thomas Jefferson advocated public education as an essential component of democratic societies because it provides individuals with opportunities and society with informed citizens. Horace Mann, "the father of public education," wrote in 1848, "Education, beyond all other devices of human origin, is the great equalizer of the conditions of men" ([1848] 1957). Mann hoped that public education would ensure that children without means would share classrooms, curriculum, and experiences with children of the well-off, and thus have a chance to get ahead in society.

The history of education in the United States is one of expansion and institutionalization. Initially, public schools were open only to White males. Over time, due in part to the efforts of sociologists like Du Bois and Jane Addams, public education expanded to include everyone regardless of race, ethnicity, sex, or national origin. Expansion is further

Who most influenced you to go to college? Considering people you know who did not go to college, what influenced them to make that choice? How powerful are socialization and social networks in making such decisions?

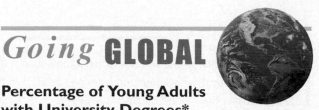

Going GLOBAL

Percentage of Young Adults with University Degrees*

- Iceland: 63%
- Australia: 50%
- Poland: 49%
- United Kingdom: 39%
- Japan: 39%
- OECD average: 39%
- United States: 37%
- Czech Republic: 35%
- Spain: 32%
- Canada: 31%
- Germany: 23%
- Greece: 18%

Note: Young adult typically means age 22–25, but different countries report data for slightly different ranges. University degree is the equivalent of a BA or BS. The Organization for Economic Cooperation and Development (OECD) is an international organization composed of 30 democratic nations.

Source: OECD 2009:Table A3.2.

and individuals need this know-how to survive and prosper. Schools teach students how to read, speak foreign languages, repair automobiles, and much more. Sociologists have identified five positive functions that education serves for both individuals and society.

Transmitting Culture As a social institution, education preserves and transmits the dominant culture. Each generation of young people learns the basic knowledge and skills necessary both for their survival and for the survival of society itself. As part of the formal curriculum, students learn "the three R's" (reading, 'riting, and 'rithmetic), as well as history, science, and much more. The school curriculum increasingly includes formal socialization into core social values, sometimes taking up functions traditionally carried out by families. For example, a school program called Character Counts articulates six Pillars of Character: trustworthiness, respect, responsibility, fairness, caring, and citizenship.

A school education can transform a child's world, allowing entry into a whole new universe of experience and thought. Imagine what our lives would be like without the ability to read (an obstacle many around the world still face). Education connects us with others beyond our immediate circumstances, thus expanding our ability to understand. Throughout grade school, high school, and college, we add new material to our shared knowledge. By and large, we have schools and teachers to thank for transmitting all that knowledge.

In addition to the formal curriculum, schools create social space for children to transmit unofficial culture among their peers and to establish themselves as individuals separate from their families. Parents aren't hovering over their shoulders to ensure their children say the right things or keep their coats on at recess, and they can't protect children from getting hurt. School is the place where children learn to stand on their own and to establish relationships with their peer group (Adler and Adler 1996). As children get older, peer relationships grow stronger, and the distance from the parental world grows greater.

Promoting Social Integration Why do we need to know things like $2 + 2 = 4$, "in 1492 Columbus sailed the ocean blue," or $a^2 + b^2 = c^2$? The answer is simple: There's a certain stock of knowledge, collectively deemed important, that we assume all members of society should possess. It represents our common culture, providing a foundation that allows us to interact, as well as to change. Even if no one individual possesses it all—and even if

reflected in the growing percentage of Americans staying in school longer. From 1940 to 2008, the proportion of people with a high school diploma increased from 25 to 87 percent, and the number with a college degree rose from 5 to 29 percent (U.S. Census Bureau 2009b:Table A-2). This growth has resulted in greater institutionalization as education has become more formalized—and a distinct part of the public sphere. Educational organizations have become more professional and bureaucratic in their attempt to provide services efficiently to the whole population.

>> Sociological Perspectives on Education

Sociologists have closely examined the degree to which education actually succeeds in providing social order and individual opportunity. They have found that while it does offer opportunity and helps to establish social order, it also perpetuates inequality. Fulfilling the hopes of Jefferson, Franklin, and Mann, it has produced an educated citizenry equipped to take on the challenges of modern life. At the same time, however, it reinforces existing beliefs, values, and norms that justify the status quo and its inequalities. Sociologists seek to understand how education can do both at the same time.

EDUCATION AND SOCIAL ORDER

Society needs people with the knowledge and skills to perform the tasks necessary for its continued existence, any single item seems necessary only for contestants on *Jeopardy!*—taken together, such knowledge represents who we are and what we believe is important. To put it in Durkheim's terms, it is part of our collective conscience and therefore is part of what binds us together as a society (Durkheim [1925] 1961).

SOCTHINK

Why do you think there has been a move toward character education in schools? What changes in society might contribute to that perceived need?

In an effort to promote social integration, many colleges and universities have established learning communities within which students share common experiences, or they may require first- and second-year students to live on campus.

Such programs become more important when students come from diverse backgrounds with different cultural expectations. The goal is to provide experiences that will unify a population composed of diverse racial, ethnic, and religious groups into a community whose members share—to some extent—a common identity. The social integration fostered by education contributes to societal stability and consensus.

In the past, the integrative function of education was most obvious in its emphasis on promoting a common language. Immigrant children were expected to learn

SOCTHINK

Does offering bilingual education to accommodate non-English-speaking students undermine social integration in the United States?

English. In some instances, they were even forbidden to speak their native language on school grounds. More recently, bilingualism has been defended both for its educational value and as a means of encouraging cultural diversity. However, critics argue that bilingualism undermines the social and political integration that education traditionally has promoted.

Training and Social Control In schools, students learn general behaviors that are expected of them as members of society and specialized skills they will need in the workforce. In the early grades in particular, significant time and effort are spent getting students to do what the teacher wants them to do, when and how the teacher wants them to do it. Through the exercise of social control, schools teach students various skills essential to their future positions in society. Norms provide us with the order and stability we need to make our individual and collective lives predictable, and schools help us internalize normative expectations. Students learn manners, punctuality, creativity, discipline, and responsibility, skills and abilities we need well beyond the classroom. In effect, schools serve as a transitional agent of social control, bridging the gap between childhood and entry into the labor force and wider society.

In a society with a complex division of labor, we especially count on schools to select and train students so that they can become effective workers in specialized jobs. We expect schools to choose those with the most ability to pursue degrees in fields that demand the greatest skill. For example, we want students with aptitude in math and science to become engineers. We use grades as an indicator of such ability and provide degrees to certify that the graduate has sufficient training to perform the job well. We hold out the promise of higher pay to reward those who make the sacrifices that higher education calls for in terms of time

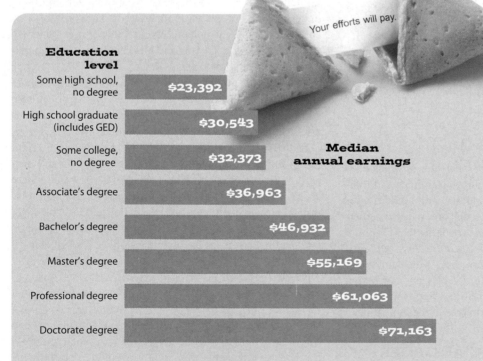

Education Pays

Your efforts will pay.

Median annual earnings

Education level	
Some high school, no degree	$23,392
High school graduate (includes GED)	$30,543
Some college, no degree	$32,373
Associate's degree	$36,963
Bachelor's degree	$46,932
Master's degree	$55,169
Professional degree	$61,063
Doctorate degree	$71,163

* Includes full-time, full-year wage and salary for workers aged 25–34.

Source: U.S. Census Bureau 2009g:Part 46.

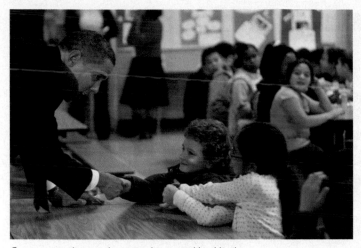

Government policies at the national, state, and local levels all influence what happens within the classroom.

and money. As we will see below, however, many people are concerned about the degree to which this ideal is achieved.

Stimulating Cultural Innovation While schools do preserve and transmit existing culture, education can also stimulate social change. In response to the soaring pregnancy rate among teenagers, for example, public schools began to offer sex education classes. As a means of countering discrimination based on sex or race, many schools turned to affirmative action in admissions—giving priority to females or minorities. Project Head Start, an early-childhood program that serves more than 908,000 children annually, has sought to compensate for the disadvantages in school readiness experienced by children from low-income families (U.S. Census Bureau 2009f:Table 562). To ensure school readiness, it provides classes for preschool children from families below a certain income level, working with them on letter recognition, vocabulary, nutrition, and other basic skills.

Colleges and universities are particularly committed to cultural innovation. Faculty members, especially at large universities, must pursue research and publish articles and books. In so doing, they produce new technology, techniques, knowledge, and practices. Cultural innovation on campuses goes beyond such concrete results, however, because college provides a context within which we can challenge existing ideas and try out new practices. Such experimentation sometimes leads people to accuse professors, especially those with innovative or unpopular ideas, of being out of touch or out of line, but we need people to experiment with new ideas so that our culture does not stagnate.

Campuses also provide an environment in which students from around the world with widely divergent ideas and experiences can interact. In 2007–2008, U.S. campuses hosted just more than 624,000 international students. Such exposure provides opportunities for cultural innovation as people from various cultures are exposed to and experiment with new and different cultural norms and values (Planty et al. 2009).

Child Care Historically, family members had the primary responsibility to teach and care for their children until adulthood. Increasingly, we expect schools and teachers to do more of the job—and at younger and younger ages. The movement toward day care and preschool is driven in part by changes in the economy. While this shift does provide children with a head start in learning the skills they will need in a globally competitive world, working parents have come to depend on schools to essentially babysit their kids, making sure they are cared for and protected. Because they take responsibility for the children during the schoolday, schools effectively free up parents to participate in the paid labor force.

EDUCATION AND INEQUALITY

What if, instead of leveling the playing field, schools reinforce existing systems of inequality? We rely on schools to provide a fair chance of success for all but researchers have found that the social positions students occupy when they start school are often reproduced when they finish. Take, for example, the impact a parent's education level can have on a child's success in school, as described by sociologist Annette Lareau (2003):

> Children of highly educated mothers continue to outperform children of less educated mothers throughout their school careers. By the time young people take the SAT examinations for admission to college, the gap is dramatic, averaging 150 points (relative to an average score of 500 points) between children of parents who are high school dropouts, and those with parents who have a graduate degree. (p. 29)

This example points to one of our basic sociological insights: Social position matters, shaping both the resources available to us and our likely outcomes. It clashes with our faith that schools will provide a fair chance for mobility in which, regardless of social position, smart, hardworking kids have an opportunity to flourish and unqualified or unmotivated kids will fail. We don't expect our education systems to perpetuate a system of inequality, serving the

The Influence of Parents' Education on Students' Test Performance

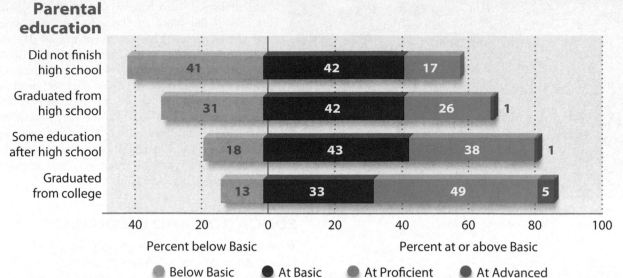

Parental education

Did not finish high school	41	42	17	
Graduated from high school	31	42	26	1
Some education after high school	18	43	38	1
Graduated from college	13	33	49	5

40   20   0   20   40   60   80   100

Percent below Basic   Percent at or above Basic

● Below Basic ● At Basic ● At Proficient ● At Advanced

Note: Percentage distribution of 12th-grade students across NAEP economics achievement levels, by highest level of parental education, 2006.

Source: Planty et al. 2008:25.

interests of those who already have economic, social, and cultural resources. But sociologists point to a number of ways in which this very thing can happen.

One of the ways we see education systems perpetuate inequality is through school funding. Jonathan Kozol (2005:321), who has studied educational inequality for decades, reports that, in the same year, Chicago public schools spent $8482 per student while the wealthy northern suburban Highland Park and Deerfield school district spent $17,291. Throughout his work he provides many such examples from across the country. Schools in well-off areas have the funding to offer programs and facilities that poor districts cannot hope to match, including high-tech labs; athletic facilities; and elective classes in art, music, and languages. As a former New York City principal, in an interview with Kozol, puts it, "I'll believe money doesn't count the day the rich stop spending so much on their own children" (Kozol 2005:59). In this section, we look at a number of such ways that the experience of and outcomes from education are not equal for everyone.

SOC THINK

Only about 9 percent of funding for public schools comes from the federal government. In most states, a significant percentage of funding comes from local property taxes. What are the consequences of this model for equitable funding of education? Why might some districts resist changing this model?

The Hidden Curriculum One of the ways that schools reinforce the existing system of inequality is through the teaching of what sociologists call the **hidden curriculum**—standards of behavior that society deems proper and that teachers subtly communicate to students (Langhout and Mitchell 2008; Thornberg 2008). It prepares students to submit to authority. For example, children learn not to speak until the teacher calls on them, and they learn to regulate their activities according to the clock

In the classic comic strip *Calvin and Hobbes,* Calvin is a first-grader who often struggles with balancing what he wants to do versus doing what is expected of him. That is especially true when it comes to school. He gives voice to the experience many of us have had as we are socialized to accept the institutional expectations of the larger society at the cost of our individual freedom.

or bells. A classroom environment that is overly focused on obedience rewards students for pleasing the teacher and remaining compliant rather than for creative thought and academic learning. In this way, schools socialize students to submit to authority figures, including bosses and political leaders.

Teacher Expectancy Student outcomes can also become a self-fulfilling prophecy based on how teachers perceive students. Psychologist Robert Rosenthal and school principal Lenore Jacobson (1968) documented what they referred to as a **teacher-expectancy effect**—the impact that a teacher's expectations about a student's performance may have on the student's actual achievements. They conducted experiments to document this effect.

Rosenthal and Jacobson informed teachers that they were administering a verbal and reasoning pretest to children in a San Francisco elementary school. After administering the tests, the researchers told the teachers that some of the students were "spurters"—children who showed particular academic potential. However, rather than using the actual test scores to make this determination, the researchers randomly selected the 20 percent of the students they identified as spurters. When the students were later retested, the spurters scored not only significantly higher than they had in previous tests, but also significantly higher than their peers. Moreover, teachers evaluated the spurters as more interesting, more curious, and better adjusted than their classmates. This is a classic case of a self-fulfilling prophecy at work. Teachers expected some students to do well, and so they did. Such effects are of particular concern if factors such as race, ethnicity, class, or gender shape teachers' perceptions. Recent research continues to affirm the significant role that teacher expectations have on student performance, and also finds that students' race and ethnicity can shape those expectations and, therefore, outcomes (McKown and Weinstein 2008; Rubie-Davies 2010; van den Bergh et al. 2010).

Bestowal of Status As we saw above, part of the public school ideal was that education would contribute to the creation of opportunity and the establishment of a more open society. In a classic sociology study, Kingsley Davis and Wilbert E. Moore (1945) argued that all societies have positions that are more important for the society's survival or that require greater skill or knowledge to perform. Ideally, the institution of education selects those with ability and trains them for such positions. We reward people in such positions with social prestige and high pay, Davis and Moore claim, because we value such skills and

PRINCIPAL

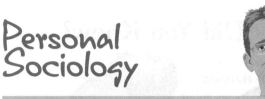

respect the fact that these individuals sacrificed the time and energy necessary to acquire those skills. For example, not everyone has the skill necessary to become a medical doctor, and in order to encourage people who do have the potential to pursue that path, we promise them sufficient social and economic compensation.

The problem with this model is that, in practice, factors other than potential and ability shape outcomes such as social class, race, ethnicity, and gender. Although the educational system helps certain poor children to move into middle-class professional positions, it denies most disadvantaged children the same educational opportunities afforded to children of the affluent. In this way, schools tend to preserve social class inequalities in each new generation (Giroux 1988; Pinkerton 2003).

One way schools reinforce class differences is by putting students in tracks. The term **tracking** refers to the practice of placing students in specific curriculum groups on the basis of their test scores and other criteria. Tracking begins very early, often in first-grade reading groups. The practice can

> **hidden curriculum** Standards of behavior that are deemed proper by society and are taught subtly in schools.
>
> **teacher-expectancy effect** The impact that a teacher's expectations about a student's performance may have on the student's actual achievements.
>
> **tracking** The practice of placing students in specific curriculum groups on the basis of their test scores and other criteria.

in admissions. And women have made the most of this opportunity. Starting in the late 1960s, the percentage of women earning college degrees began rising dramatically. In 1980 women earned 49 percent of degrees conferred, and the 2008 rate is 57 percent. Women students are also more likely to be taught by women professors, who now comprise 45 percent of total faculty (Corbett, Hill, and St. Rose 2008; Snyder and Dillow 2010:Table 188).

SOCTHINK

Women's participation in college athletics has increased more than 500 percent since 1972, from 31,852 then to 178,084 in 2007–2008. And high school rates rose from 294,015 in 1972 to 3.1 million participants in 2009 (NFHS 2009). To what extent would we have seen such an increase had it not been for a law that mandated increased opportunity? How might increased opportunity for women in athletics have an impact on increased opportunity in other areas?

The fact that schools can actually reinforce existing patterns of inequality has led some educators to wonder whether schools should discourage members of disadvantaged groups from even attempting college. They fear that the long-term emotional toll of failure would be too great. Sociologists John R. Reynolds and Chardie L. Baird (2010) sought to answer the question "Do students who try but fail to achieve their educational dreams experience long-term frustration and anxiety?" Based on research from two national longitudinal studies, they concluded that the answer to this question is no. Those who fail to fulfill their aspirations develop "adaptive resilience," allowing them to cope with their lack of college success. Reynolds summarizes it this way: "Aiming high and failing is not consequential for mental health, while trying may lead to higher achievements and the mental

and material benefits that go along with those achievements" (quoted in Elish 2010). As a result of their research, Reynolds and Baird recommend encouraging students to aim higher because it significantly increases students' chances of getting ahead, as the experience of women in higher education demonstrates. In fact, researchers have found that those with characteristics making them least likely to pursue a college degree—such as coming from low-income families, having parents with less education,

or being African American or Latino—are most likely to benefit from obtaining one (Brand and Xie 2010).

Education does establish social order and provide opportunities for individuals to get ahead. At the same time, in preserving the existing order, it reproduces practices of inequality. Sociology allows us to better understand how these seemingly contradictory outcomes can be accomplished through education. As the experience with Title IX demonstrates, positive social change is possible. Having a better appreciation of how education functions enables us to more effectively work toward realizing the initial goal of education: to provide opportunity and a more open society.

>> Schools as Formal Organizations

The early advocates of public education would be amazed at the scale of the education system in the United States in the 21st century. In many respects, today's schools, when viewed as an example of a formal organization, are similar to factories, hospitals, and business firms. Instead of producing cars, patients, or profits, they pump out millions of students per year. In doing so, schools must be responsive to the various constituencies outside of the student body, including parents, employers, neighborhoods, and politicians. To handle their complex mission, schools have had to become increasingly institutionalized.

THE BUREAUCRATIZATION OF SCHOOLS

It simply is not possible for a single teacher to transmit all the necessary culture and skills to children who will enter many diverse occupations. The growing number of students being served by school systems and the greater degree of specialization required within a technologically complex society have combined to bureaucratize schools.

In many respects, schools put into practice all of Max Weber's principles of bureaucracy that we considered in Chapter 5. When it comes to the division of labor, teachers specialize in particular age levels and specific subjects. Schools are hierarchically organized, with teachers reporting to principals, who are themselves answerable to the superintendent of schools and the board of education. In terms of written rules and regulations, teachers must submit written lesson plans, and students, teachers, and administrators must all adhere to established policies and procedures or face sanctions for not doing so. As schools grow, they become increasingly impersonal, and teachers are expected to treat all students in the same way, regardless of their distinctive personalities and learning needs. Finally, hiring and promotion—and even grading—are based on technical qualifications alone, and standards are established and rubrics created in an effort to ensure this practice (Vanderstraeten 2007).

Average Salaries for Teachers

More than $54,000
$47,000–53,999
$43,000–46,999
Under $43,000

Source: American Federation of Teachers 2008.

Teacher Turnover

21%
High-poverty

11%

Leavers

2% | 3% | 1% | 3% | 1%

15%
Low-poverty

6%

Leavers

3% | 4% | 1%

0.5% 0.5%

Transferred to another school
Retired
Took other job
Pursued further education
Left for family reasons
Other

Note: Percentage of public K–12 teachers who did not teach in the same school the following year, by poverty level of school and the reason teachers left.

Source: Planty et al. 2008:51.

The trend toward more centralized education particularly affects disadvantaged people, for whom education promises to be a path to opportunity. The standardization of educational curricula, including textbooks, generally reflects the values, interests, and lifestyles of the most powerful groups in our society, and may ignore those of racial and ethnic minorities. In addition, in comparison to the affluent, the resource poor often lack the time, financial resources, and knowledge necessary to sort through complex educational bureaucracies and to organize effective lobbying groups. As a result, low-income and minority parents will have even less influence over citywide and statewide educational administrators than they have over local school officials (Kozol 2005).

TEACHING AS A PROFESSION

As schools become more bureaucratic, teachers increasingly encounter the conflicts inherent in serving as a professional within the context of a bureaucracy. Teachers must work within the system, submitting to its hierarchical structure and abiding by its established rules. At the same time, teachers want to practice their craft as professionals with some degree of autonomy and respect for their judgment. Conflicts arise from having to serve simultaneously as instructor, disciplinarian, administrator, and employee of a school district.

As professionals, teachers feel pressure from a number of directions. First, the level of formal schooling required for teaching remains high, and the public has begun to call for new competency examinations. Second, teachers' salaries are significantly lower than those of many comparably educated professionals and skilled workers. Finally, the overall prestige of the teaching profession has declined over the past decade. Many teachers, disappointed and frustrated, have left the educational world for careers in other professions. In fact, between a quarter and a third of new teachers quit within their first three years, and as many as half leave poor urban schools within their first five years (Wallis 2008). Even within a single year, teacher turnover is significant; in high-poverty areas, more than 20 percent of teachers did not teach in the same school the following year.

STUDENT SUBCULTURES

Schools also provide an arena for students' social and recreational needs. Education helps toddlers and young children develop interpersonal skills that are essential during adolescence and adulthood. In their high school and college years, students may meet future spouses and establish lifelong friendships.

School leaders often seek to develop a sense of school spirit and collective identity, but student subcultures are complex and diverse. As we saw in Chapter 4, school cliques and social groups may crop up according to race, social class, physical attractiveness, academic placement, athletic ability, and leadership roles in the school and community (Adler and Adler 1996; Milner 2006; Suitor, Minyard, and Carter 2001). In his classic community study of "Elmtown," sociologist August B. Hollingshead (1975) found some 259 distinct cliques in a single high school. The cliques, whose average size was five, were centered on the school itself, on recreational activities, and on religious and community groups.

Amid these close-knit and often rigidly segregated cliques, some students get left out. Historically, gay and lesbian students have been particularly vulnerable to such exclusion. Many have organized to establish their own stronger sense of collective identity, including through the establishment of gay–straight alliances (GSAs)—school-sponsored support groups that bring gay teens together with sympathetic straight peers. Begun in Los Angeles in 1984, these programs numbered more than 4000 nationwide in 2010.

We can find a similar diversity of student groups at the college level. Sociologists have identified four distinctive subcultures among college students (Clark and Trow 1966; Horowitz 1987):

- The *collegiate* subculture focuses on having fun and socializing. These students define what constitutes a "reasonable" amount of academic work (and what amount of work is "excessive" and leads to being labeled as a "grind"). Members of the collegiate subculture have little commitment to academic pursuits. Athletes often fit into this subculture.

- The *academic* subculture identifies with the intellectual concerns of the faculty and values knowledge for its own sake.
- The *vocational* subculture is interested primarily in career prospects and views college as a means of obtaining degrees that are essential for advancement.
- The *nonconformist* subculture is hostile to the college environment and seeks out ideas that may or may not relate to academic studies. This group may find outlets through campus publications or issue-oriented groups.

Each college student is eventually exposed to these competing subcultures and must determine which (if any) seems most in line with his or her feelings and interests.

SOCTHINK

To what extent do you fit into one of the four college subcultures? What background influences, including friends, teachers, or parents, might have contributed to your following that path instead of the others?

The typology used by the researchers reminds us that the school is a complex social organization—almost like a community with different neighborhoods. Of course, these four subcultures are not the only ones evident on college campuses in the United States. For example, one might find subcultures of Iraq or Afghanistan war veterans or former full-time homemakers, or students may gather together on the basis of race, ethnicity, or nationality.

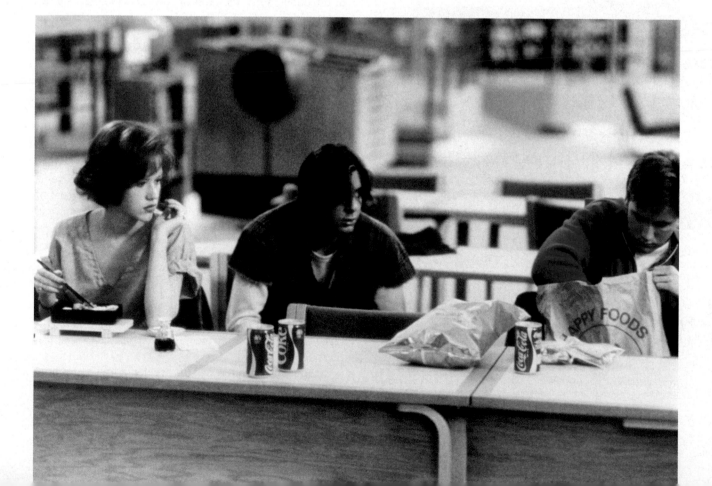

Projected Public High School Graduates by Race and Ethnicity, 2020

Source: WICHE 2008:59.

Black, non-Hispanic
13.2%

Asian/Pacific Islander
7.8%

American Indian/ Alaska Native
1.2%

Hispanic
24.2%

White, non-Hispanic
53.7%

percent increase in students since 1963. These students are more likely to be older, female, Black, Hispanic, low-income, and part-time, compared to their peers at four-year schools. In fact, the more income and education a student's parents have, the less likely she or he is to attend a community college. This highlights the role these schools play in providing opportunity for those with limited resources. Enrollment at community colleges raises the aspirations of students. Whether they initially expected to take only a few courses or to finish with a two-year degree, almost one-half of these students later aspired to more education, including a four-year degree or beyond (Provasnik and Planty 2008).

One of the concerns raised about community colleges is persistence—the degree to which students pursue an education. The rate at which such students leave community college without completing a degree or certificate program (45 percent) is significantly higher than that for students at four-year schools (16 to 17 percent). Even those who had initially enrolled intending to pursue a four-year degree left school early at a rate of 39 percent. Such high rates led some theorists to suggest that community colleges serve a "cooling out" function. They argue that the limited number of good jobs in society is a given, so not everyone can succeed in obtaining one. Because community colleges appear to provide opportunities for anyone to succeed, failure to do so is perceived to be the individual's responsibility alone. As such, students are more likely to blame themselves than to develop a critique of the social structure that shaped their likely outcomes. In other words, community colleges do provide opportunity for some, but they also help to justify the existing system of inequality (Bahr 2008; Clark 1960, 1980).

COMMUNITY COLLEGES

Community colleges exist as a testament to the ideals put forth by Jefferson, Franklin, and Mann. The GI bill in the 1940s and Pell Grants in the 1960s provided significant college financial aid for those with limited means, opening wide the doors to college. However, availability of financial aid, especially in the form of grants, has declined significantly in recent years. Community colleges continue to give students a chance to prove themselves, however, and their relatively low cost and open enrollment lower the barriers to success. As a result, an increasing number of students have turned to community colleges, including a surge in fall 2009 enrollments due to a weak economy.

There are now more than 6 million community college students in the United States, making up 35 percent of all postsecondary students. This represents an almost 750

HOMESCHOOLING

Some parents view formal schooling as a path to opportunity; others have decided to opt out altogether. More than 1.5 million students are now being educated at home—about 2.9 percent of the K–12 school population. Homeschooled families are more likely to be White, have two parents in the household with only one in the labor force, have parents with a bachelor's degree, and have three or more children (Planty et al. 2009).

In a sense this represents a return to the pre–public school days of American education, in which the primary responsibility for teaching rested with parents. When asked to identify the most important reason for choosing this path, 36 percent of parents said they were motivated by a desire to provide religious or moral instruction (the most common response), and 83 percent overall identified that as an important factor. A concern about the environment of schools—safety, drugs, and negative peer pressure—was most important to 21 percent, and 17 percent attributed their decision primarily to dissatisfaction with the school's academic instruction (Planty et al. 2009). In addition, some immigrants choose homeschooling as a way to ease their children's transition to a new society. For example, increasing numbers of the nation's growing Arab American population have joined the movement toward homeschooling (Cooper and Sureau 2007; MacFarquhar 2008). Other parents see it as a good alternative for children who suffer from attention deficit hyperactivity disorder (ADHD) and learning disorders (LDs). A study by the Home School Legal Defense Association (2005), a homeschool advocacy organization, found that homeschooled students score higher than others on standardized exams in every subject and in every grade.

> **substantive definition of religion** The idea that religion has a unique content or substance relating to the sacred that separates it from other forms of knowledge and belief.
>
> **sacred** Elements beyond everyday life that inspire respect, awe, and even fear.

The rise in homeschooling points toward a growing dissatisfaction with the institutionalized practice of education. Early public school advocates argued for the importance of a common curriculum rooted in a shared sense of values. Homeschooling, on the other hand, points toward pluralism and the desire to retain the unique subcultural values of a community. Although new forms of schooling may meet the individual needs of diverse groups in today's society, they also undermine the historical commitment to public education as a means of fostering unity within society.

SOCTHINK

What do you think are the advantages and disadvantages of being homeschooled? How might it contribute to a stronger sense of identity? How might it threaten the social order?

>> Defining Religion

Education plays a major role in socializing members of society into shared values and norms, and religion helps to cement those beliefs and practices into people's hearts and minds. Religion contributes to social order, provides a sense of shared identity, and offers believers meaning and purpose. Though levels of religious participation vary from place to place, religion continues to be a major force both on the world stage and in the lives of individuals. To fully understand its various forms, sociologists take two basic approaches to defining religion. The first focuses on what religion is, and the second focuses on what it does.

SUBSTANCE: WHAT RELIGION IS

According to a **substantive definition of religion,** religion has a unique content or substance that separates it from other forms of knowledge and belief. Most commonly, this unique focus involves some conception of a supernatural realm, such as heaven, but it does not have to be outside the physical world. The key is that religion centers around something that goes above and beyond the mundane realities of our everyday existence, that points to something larger, and that calls for some response from us in terms of how we think and act. Sociologist Peter Berger (1969) provided a substantive definition of religion as "the human enterprise by which a sacred cosmos is established" (p. 25). The sacred here refers to that extraordinary realm that becomes the focus of religious faith and practice. It provides believers with meaning, order, and coherence. In describing that sacred realm, people might touch on concepts such as gods and goddess, angels and demons, heaven and hell, nirvana, or other beings or realms. A society with broad agreement about the nature and importance of this sacred realm is, by definition, more religious.

Sociologists that follow a substantive approach focus on the ways in which religious groups rally around what they define to be sacred. The **sacred** encompasses elements beyond everyday life that inspire respect, awe, and even fear. People interact with the sacred realm through

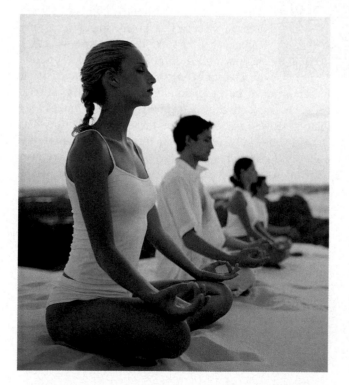

ritual practices, such as prayer or sacrifice. Because believers have faith in the sacred, they accept what they cannot understand. The sacred realm exists in contrast to the **profane,** which includes the ordinary and commonplace.

Different religious groups define their understanding of the sacred or profane in different ways. For example, who or what constitutes "god" varies between Muslims, Christians, and Hindus. Even within a group, different believers may treat the same object as sacred or profane, depending on whether it connects them to the sacred realm. Ordinarily, a piece of bread is profane, but it becomes sacred for Christians during their practice of communion because through it believers enter into connection with God. Similarly, a candelabrum becomes sacred to Jews if it is a menorah. For Confucians and Taoists, incense sticks are not mere decorative items, but highly valued offerings to the gods in religious ceremonies that mark the new and full moons.

SOC THINK

Do you think it is appropriate for religious leaders, such as pastors, priests, rabbis, or imams, to discuss political issues during religious services? Why or why not?

FUNCTION: WHAT RELIGIONS DO

A functionalist approach focuses less on what religion is than on what religions do, with a particular emphasis on how religions contribute to social order. According to a **functionalist definition of religion,** religion unifies believers into a community through shared practices and a common set of beliefs relative to sacred things. The emphasis here is on the unifying dimension of religion rather than on the substance of that which unifies. For functionalists, the supernatural or something like it is not an essential part of religion. Religion need not have gods or goddesses, an afterlife, or other such conventional elements. In fact, any social practices that strongly unite us, such as being a sports fan, can function like religion for the individual and for society.

The functional approach to defining religion has roots in the work of Émile Durkheim. He defined religion as "a unified system of beliefs and practices relative to sacred things, that is to say things set apart and forbidden—beliefs and practices which unite into a single moral community, called a 'church,' all those who adhere to them" ([1887] 1972:224). This definition points to three aspects sociologists focus on when studying religion: a unified system of beliefs and practices, involving sacred things, in the context of community.

The first element of Durkheim's functional approach is the unified system of beliefs and practices. What those beliefs and practices are matters less than the fact that they are shared. Terms historically used to describe religious beliefs include *doctrine, dogma, creeds,* and *scripture,* all representing principles believers share through faith. Practices refer to shared rituals such as attendance at services, prayer, meditation, and fasting. Because beliefs and practices are central to religion, we look at them in more detail below.

Unlike the substantive approach, Durkheim's emphasis on sacred things focuses less on the objects themselves than on the believers' attitude toward those objects. Sacred objects and sacred places convey a sense of awe, and religion calls upon believers to treat them with reverence and care. Roman Catholics, for example, treat the bread and wine of communion with respect because they believe that the sacrament transforms those elements into the body and blood of Christ. For Muslims, the Qur'an is a sacred object, and the Kaaba in Mecca is a sacred place. In the functional approach to religion, however, sacredness is in the eyes of the beholders. Any object can be sacred so long as people define it as such and treat it accordingly.

profane The ordinary and commonplace elements of life, as distinguished from the sacred.

functionalist definition of religion The idea that religion unifies believers into a community through shared practices and a common set of beliefs relative to sacred things.

The most important component of Durkheim's definition is this third part: community. It is not the church, mosque, or temple as a building that matters, but the unification of a body of believers into a shared community. What they believe, what they practice, or what they view as sacred is less important than that they have these beliefs, practices, and shared sacred things in common.

lives and societal conditions in political terms—for example, by obscuring the overriding significance of conflicting economic interests. Marxists suggest that by inducing a "false consciousness" among the disadvantaged, religion lessens the possibility of collective political action that could end capitalist oppression and transform society. Sociological analysis in this tradition seeks to reveal the ways in which religion serves the interests of the powerful at the expense of others.

Gender and Religion Drawing on the feminist approach, researchers and theorists point to the fundamental role women play in religious socialization. Women play a critical role in the functioning of religious organizations, yet when it comes to positions of leadership, women generally take a subordinate role in religious governance. Indeed, most faiths have a long tradition of exclusively male spiritual leadership. Furthermore, because most religions are patriarchal, religious

beliefs tend to reinforce men's dominance in secular as well as spiritual matters. Women are more likely than men to say religion is important in their lives, more likely to pray daily, and more likely to attend weekly services. Women play a vital role as volunteers, staff, and religious educators, but even today, religious decision making and leadership typically falls to men. Exceptions to this rule, such as the Shakers and Christian Scientists, as well as Hinduism with its long goddess heritage, are rare (Pew Research Center 2009d; Schaefer and Zellner 2007).

In the United States, women compose 14.8 percent of the clergy, even though they account for 51 percent of students enrolled in theological institutions. Female clerics typically have shorter careers than men and are often relegated to fields that do not involve congregational leadership, such as counseling. In faiths that restrict leadership positions to men, women still serve unofficially. For example, about 4 percent of Roman Catholic congregations are led by women who hold non-ordained pastoral positions—a necessity in a church that faces a shortage of male priests (Adams 2007; Banerjee 2006; U.S. Census Bureau 2009f: Table 603).

In this chapter, we have looked at both education and religion. In both cases we find institutions that play a powerful role in shaping how we think and act. Each provides opportunity and reinforces the status quo, including its system of inequality. Sociologists believe that by having a better appreciation for both the opportunities and constraints such institutions

present, we can better act both individually and collectively to bring about positive social change.

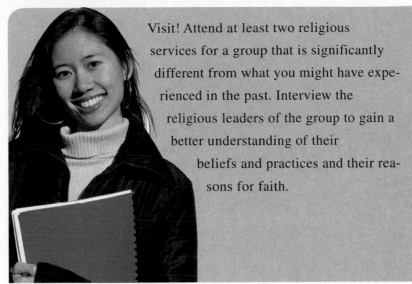

Visit! Attend at least two religious services for a group that is significantly different from what you might have experienced in the past. Interview the religious leaders of the group to gain a better understanding of their beliefs and practices and their reasons for faith.

get involved!

For REVIEW

I. How does education help to maintain social order?

- Education transmits culture, promotes social integration, provides training and social control, and contributes to cultural innovation.

II. How does education support the existing system of inequality?

- Education reinforces the status quo, and therefore its existing inequalities, through the hidden curriculum, teacher expectancy, bestowal of status, and credentialism.

III. How do sociologists define religion?

- One approach focuses on the substance of what religion is, defining religion as knowledge and beliefs relating to the sacred realm. The other approach looks at what religions do for society in terms of social order and integration. Both approaches analyze common components including belief, ritual, experience, and community.

Functionalist View

Education serves five positive functions: transmitting culture, promoting **social integration**, training and social control, stimulating cultural innovation, and childcare.

As societies have become more diverse, education has taken on more of the task of formal **socialization.**

Religion provides **social order,** a sense of **shared identity,** and meaning and purpose in people's lives.

SOCIAL INTEGRATION, SOCIALIZATION, SOCIAL ORDER
KEY CONCEPTS

Conflict View

The education system helps reproduce the existing system of **inequality.**

Unequal funding, tracking, the *hidden curriculum* and *credentialism* serve to reinforce the status quo.

According to Marx, religion can function like a drug that blinds people to their true interests, prompting them instead to accept **submission to authority,** thereby reinforcing the interests of those in power.

INEQUALITY, SUBMISSION TO AUTHORITY
KEY CONCEPTS

MAKE THE CONNECTION

After reviewing the chapter, answer the following questions:

Interactionist View

Students from grade school through graduate school learn formal and informal norms, values, and interpersonal skills through classroom interactions.

A teacher's **expectations** about a student impacts on student performance and achievement.

Religious rituals generally involve important **face-to-face interactions** with fellow at services.

EXPECTATIONS, INTERACTIONS
KEY CONCEPTS

1

The graph on p. 182 shows one way that "education pays." Using each perspective, how does education pay? Who benefits?

2

How do educational institutions bestow status from both the functionalist and conflict perspectives (p. 185)?

3

Using the conflict perspective, describe how women experience (or have experienced) discrimination in both the educational and religious spheres (pp. 187, 204).

4

Which perspective do you think best describes the dynamics of a typical classroom setting? Explain including examples.

Pop Quiz

1. Horace Mann, often referred to as the "father of public education," refers to education as
   a. the great equalizer.
   b. the opiate of the masses.
   c. an instrument for social control.
   d. an opportunity engine.

2. One of the ways education contributes to social order is by providing an environment within which we can challenge existing ideas and experiment with new norms and values. This is known as
   a. transmitting culture.
   b. promoting social integration.
   c. training and social control.
   d. cultural innovation.

3. Samuel Bowles and Herbert Gintis have argued that capitalism requires a skilled, disciplined labor force and that the educational system of the United States is structured with that objective in mind. Citing numerous studies, they offer support for what they call
   a. tracking.
   b. credentialism.
   c. the correspondence principle.
   d. the teacher-expectancy effect.

4. Fifty years ago, a high school diploma was the minimum requirement for entry into the paid labor force of the United States. Today, a college diploma is the bare minimum. This change reflects the process of
   a. tracking.
   b. credentialism.
   c. the hidden curriculum.
   d. the correspondence principle.

5. The college student subculture that focuses on having fun and socializing and doesn't take its studies too seriously is the
   a. collegiate subculture.
   b. academic subculture.
   c. vocational subculture.
   d. nonconformist subculture.

6. The approach to defining religion that emphasizes the significance of the sacred, most often supernatural, realm is known as the
   a. functionalist approach.
   b. component approach.
   c. substantive approach.
   d. ecclesiae approach.

7. Religious rituals are
   a. statements to which members of a particular religion adhere.
   b. the feelings or perceptions of being in direct contact with the ultimate reality, such as a divine being.
   c. the religious structures through which faith communities organize themselves.
   d. practices required or expected of members of a faith.

8. Looking at world religions, the religion with the most followers around the world is
   a. Buddhism.
   b. Islam.
   c. Judaism.
   d. Christianity.

9. Sociologist Max Weber pointed out that the followers of John Calvin emphasized a disciplined work ethic, worldly concerns, and a rational orientation to life. Collectively, this point of view has been referred to as
   a. capitalism.
   b. the Protestant ethic.
   c. the sacred.
   d. the profane.

10. The use of a church, primarily Roman Catholic, in a political effort to eliminate poverty, discrimination, and other forms of injustice evident in a secular society is referred to as
    a. creationism.
    b. ritualism.
    c. religious experience.
    d. liberation theology.

1. (a); 2. (d); 3. (c); 4. (b); 5. (a); 6. (c); 7. (d); 8. (d); 9. (b); 10. (d)

9

GOVERNMENT AND ECONOMY

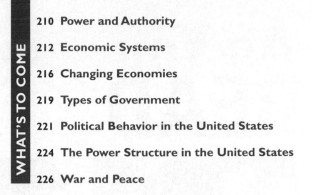
ADAPTING AND SURVIVING IN A MULTINATIONAL WORLD

In 2002, Jim Wier headed to Wal-Mart's corporate headquarters in Bentonville, Arkansas, to tell its executives that he would no longer be selling his company's Snapper lawn mowers in Wal-Mart stores. This was highly unusual for a Wal-Mart supplier. Most would go to great lengths to get their products on Wal-Mart shelves because, with 127 million U.S. customers per week, the possibilities for high-volume sales are immense. In fact, when Snapper pulled its mowers from Wal-Mart, Snapper's sales dropped 20 percent (Fishman 2006).

Wal-Mart began as a single store in 1962, and there are now 3702 U.S. stores and 4112 in 14 countries. In fact, Wal-Mart is the largest corporation in the world, with a total of $405 billion in revenues in fiscal year 2010. It is also the world's largest private employer, with 1.4 million U.S. workers and 600,000 abroad.

Wier understood the appeal of gaining access to all those Wal-Mart customers, but as he put it, "Once you get hooked on the volume, it's like getting hooked on cocaine" (Fishman 2006:117). The need to maintain volume, he argued, would change the character of the company, requiring it to cut corners and change operating procedures. He opted instead to sell to a different kind of customer, one who wants quality, durability, and service more than up-front savings.

Ironically, to compete with Wal-Mart, Snapper had to adopt similar business techniques. To maximize efficiency, Wal-Mart measures everything. Snapper, too, now tracks every step of the production process to increase efficiency. Its productivity is three times what it was a decade ago with a workforce half the size. Though it continues to thrive, Snapper still faces an uphill fight.

Companies and workers have no choice but to adapt to compete with huge multinational corporations such as Wal-Mart and with firms and workers globally. When a company's revenues are greater than the gross national income for the majority of the world's nations—Wal-Mart would rank 25th out of 210 nations—it cannot help but have economic and political consequences (World Bank 2009c). In this chapter we look at both the economy and politics to better understand how both shape our lives.

As You READ

> >

- How is economic and political power organized?
- How does power operate?
- How has the economy changed over time?

>> Power and Authority

On January 20, 2009, Barack Obama was sworn in as the 44th president of the United States of America. It marked a major milestone in U.S. history. All 43 presidents before him had been White men, so his election as the first African American symbolized greater opportunity for all.

Sociologists have always been interested in how power, presidential or otherwise, is achieved and maintained. In the midst of major political and economic shifts, early sociologists developed theories of power intended to be sufficiently broad to explain the rise of democracy or the expansion of market-based capitalism, yet sufficiently narrow to explain who gets their way within interpersonal relationships.

POWER

According to Max Weber, **power** is the ability to exercise one's will over others, even if they resist. To put it another way, if you can make people do what you want them to do—whether that is to go to war, coordinate a business meeting, clean their room, or even take an exam—you have power. Power

relations can involve large organizations, small groups, or even people in intimate relationships.

There are three basic sources of power within any political system: force, influence, and authority. **Force** is the actual or threatened use of coercion to impose one's will on others. When leaders imprison or even execute political dissidents, they are applying force; so, too, are terrorists when they seize or bomb an embassy or assassinate a political leader. **Influence,** on the other hand, refers to the exercise of power through a process of persuasion. A citizen may change his or her view of a Supreme Court nominee because of a newspaper editorial, the expert testimony of a law school dean before the Senate Judiciary Committee, or a stirring speech by a political activist at a rally. In each case, sociologists would view such efforts to persuade people as examples of influence.

TYPES OF AUTHORITY

Authority, the third source of power, refers to institutionalized power that is recognized by the people over whom it is exercised. Sociologists commonly use the term in connection with those who hold legitimate power through elected or publicly acknowledged positions. A person's authority is often limited by her or his position. Thus, a referee has the authority to decide whether a penalty should be called during a football game but has no authority over the price of tickets to the game.

Max Weber ([1913] 1947) developed a classification system for authority that has become one of the most useful

Personal Sociology

Because I Said So

My daughters, Emily and Eleanor, mostly do what I ask, accepting my authority as legitimate. The fact that I am their father is usually enough to get them to obey. As they grew, however, they sometimes disobeyed, creating a power struggle. In such instances, they faced the prospect of "sitting in the green chair" until I said they could get out. Just the threat of being sent there usually did the trick. It was not much of a punishment, really. Our green rocking chair sits in the living room, in full view of the television, and is not isolated from the rest of the family. But having to just sit there had the desired effect of reinforcing my traditional authority as a parent.

SOC THINK

Which of these three forms of power do parents, bosses, or professors most rely on? Are there times when each of those groups use each of the three types of power?

and frequently cited contributions of early sociology. He identified three ideal types of authority: traditional, rational-legal, and charismatic. Weber did not insist that only one type applies to a given society or organization. All can be present, but their relative importance will vary. Sociologists have found Weber's typology valuable in understanding different manifestations of legitimate power within a society.

Traditional Authority Until the middle of the 20th century, Japan was ruled by a revered emperor whose absolute power was passed down from generation to generation. In a political system based on **traditional authority,** legitimate power is conferred by custom and

accepted practice. The past is a justification of the present. A king or queen is accepted as ruler of a nation simply by virtue of inheriting the crown; a tribal chief rules because that is the accepted practice. The ruler may be loved or hated, competent or destructive; in terms of legitimacy, that does not matter. For the traditional leader, authority rests in custom, not in personal characteristics, technical competence, or even written law. People accept the ruler's authority because that is how things have always been done. Traditional authority is absolute when the ruler has the ability to determine laws and policies.

Rational-Legal Authority

The U.S. Constitution gives Congress and the president the authority to make and enforce laws and policies. Power made legitimate by law is a form of rational-legal authority. **Rational-legal authority** involves formally agreed-upon and accepted rules, principles, and procedures of conduct that are established in order to accomplish goals in the most efficient manner possible. Such authority extends beyond governments to include any organization. Bureaucracies are the purest form of rational-legal authority. Generally, in societies based on rational-legal authority, leaders are thought to have specific areas of competence and authority, but are not thought to be endowed with divine inspiration, as in certain societies with traditional forms of authority.

power The ability to exercise one's will over others even if they resist.

force The actual or threatened use of coercion to impose one's will on others.

influence The exercise of power through a process of persuasion.

authority Institutionalized power that is recognized by the people over whom it is exercised.

traditional authority Legitimate power conferred by custom and accepted practice.

rational-legal authority Authority based on formally agreed-upon and accepted rules, principles, and procedures of conduct that are established in order to accomplish goals in the most efficient manner possible.

charismatic authority Power made legitimate by a leader's exceptional personal or emotional appeal to his or her followers.

Charismatic Authority Joan of Arc was a simple peasant girl in medieval France, yet she was able to rally the French people and lead them into major battles against English invaders despite having no formally recognized position of power. How was this possible? As Weber observed, power can be legitimized by the charisma of an individual. **Charismatic authority** refers to power made legitimate by a leader's exceptional personal or emotional appeal to his or her followers.

Charisma lets a person such as Joan of Arc lead or inspire without relying on set rules or traditions. In fact, charismatic authority is derived more from the beliefs of followers than from the actual qualities of leaders. So long as people perceive a charismatic leader such as Jesus, Joan of Arc, Gandhi, Malcolm X, or Martin Luther King Jr. as having qualities that set him or her apart from ordinary citizens, that leader's authority will remain secure and often unquestioned (Adair-Toteff 2005; Potts 2009). That unfortunately is also the case with malevolent figures such as Adolf Hitler, whose charismatic appeal turned people toward violent and destructive ends in Nazi Germany.

Political leaders increasingly depend on television, radio, and the Internet to establish and maintain charismatic authority. This practice took hold with President Franklin D. Roosevelt's use of fireside chats over the radio to calm a nation that faced the Great Depression and World War II. News coverage of Barack Obama's presidency frequently mentions his capacity to charm; early approval ratings reflect significant faith in his leadership (Bligh and Kohles 2009). Public opinion can shift, however, as President George W. Bush learned. His approval ratings after the September 11, 2001, terrorist attacks soared to 85 percent, but by the end of his second term they hovered around 25 percent (among the lowest recorded for a president), making it difficult for him to advance his legislative agenda.

Did You Know?

. . . FDR gave 30 fireside chats during his presidency on topics ranging from the banking crisis of the Great Depression to the war effort during World War II. These broadcasts were extremely popular and drew large audiences. For the first time ever, people had a sense that the president was speaking directly to them, and the warm, simple manner of the presentation encouraged this feeling.

>> Economic Systems

In many ways the economy has become the primary institution of our time. An **economic system** is the social institution dedicated to the production, distribution, and consumption of goods and services. We depend on it to coordinate and provide for our wants and needs, and in turn, the economic system reflects the core values of a given society. Our economic position has a powerful impact on our families, it shapes our educational opportunities and choices (including the decision to go to college), it influences our political preferences, and it even affects our religious beliefs and practices.

economic system The social institution through which goods and services are produced, distributed, and consumed.

capitalism An economic system based on private property, in which profit-seeking individuals, companies, and corporations compete in the marketplace.

Sociology developed as a discipline in part to come to terms with the economic transition from a preindustrial to an **industrial society,** one that depends on mechanization to produce its goods and services (as discussed in Chapter 5). At the heart of this shift, the Industrial Revolution changed where we live (from rural to urban settings) and the type of work we do (from agricultural to industrial jobs). The mechanization of production gave rise to factories (especially in the textile industries) and contributed to the decline of home-based or craft production. The steam engine provided the early power necessary to expand industrial production on a large scale. It did so by effectively enhancing workers' strength and stamina. Workers were then able to exert superhuman amounts of power for superhuman amounts of time. In pursuit of greater productivity, and guided by bureaucratic principles, work became increasingly specialized and routinized. Out of this transition from preindustrial to industrial society, two major economic systems arose: capitalism and socialism.

CAPITALISM

Capitalism is an economic system based on private property, in which profit-seeking individuals, companies, and corporations compete in the marketplace. Value under capitalism is determined based on what people are willing and able to pay for available goods and services. The basic principles of capitalism were laid out by Adam Smith in 1776 in his book *The Wealth of Nations,* including four key concepts: pursuit of profit, competition in the market, the law of supply and demand, and laissez-faire.

- *Pursuit of profit.* One of the basic presuppositions of capitalism is that, in our exchanges with others, human beings naturally seek to get the greatest return on their investments. This extends beyond economic exchanges (i.e., making a financial profit) to include social and cultural exchanges (in which even a conversation represents an exchange of symbolic resources such as status or attention). Pursuit of personal profit is not just morally acceptable; it is at the core of our identity as humans.
- *Competition in the market.* The marketplace is the context in which we exchange goods and services (such

Did You Know?

... The average annual sales for Wal-Mart equal $2060.36 per household in the United States.

SOCTHINK

Why is competition essential to capitalism? Why might capitalists seek to establish monopolies?

as shoes, cell phones, and college degrees); we do so in competition with other producers and consumers. Competition keeps prices in check. The marketplace must be open to whoever has the ability to compete so that no individual or firm controls a disproportionate share of the market.

- *Law of supply and demand.* In a competitive marketplace, a natural balance will be reached between production and consumption at the appropriate price. If the demand for a good or service is high and the supply is low, prices will go up, and vice versa. If a producer charges too much, another producer will step in to provide the good or service at a more reasonable price. Adam Smith described this process as the "invisible hand" of the marketplace through which prices reach their natural level. Companies that don't respond to the prompting of the invisible hand—for example, by charging too much or too little—will ultimately fail.

- *Laissez-faire.* The expression **laissez-faire** means "let them do [as they please]," and in this context it means that outside entities, especially the government, should not intervene in the marketplace. Instead, the market should be allowed to function free from external influence. Ideally, markets self-correct using the invisible hand. Though governments may mean well, they cannot bring about a better result for society as a whole than can individuals who are allowed to compete on their own. In capitalism, the greatest

> Nowadays people know the price of everything and the value of nothing.
>
> Oscar Wilde

social good is attained through the competition of profit-seeking individuals.

In practice, capitalism struggles to stick to these ideals due to contradictions that inevitably arise. On the one hand, capitalism tends toward the establishment of **monopolies,** in which a single business firm controls the market. Though the system needs competition, capitalists, in their pursuit of profits, seek to dominate the market to the point of monopolizing it. This violates the principle of competition. On the other hand, governments often respond by intervening in the marketplace—through policies such as antitrust legislation—to ensure sufficient competition, thus violating the principle of laissez-faire. In addition, some goods and services (such as police, fire protection, roads, national defense, and public education) are deemed important enough for the public good to be provided for all, even at the expense of government intervention.

SOCIALISM

Socialism is an economic system in which the means of production and distribution in a society are collectively rather than privately owned. Value under socialism is determined by the amount of work it takes to produce products and the use we get out of those products. The basic principles of socialism were laid out by Karl Marx in the middle- to late 1800s in a variety of publications, including *The Communist Manifesto.* Marx believed socialism to be inevitable for the following reasons: Humans must produce, production makes us uniquely human, we pour ourselves into our products, economy determines society, and scarcity and distribution are obstacles to the good society.

- *Humans must produce.* Unlike animals, humans lack the complex instincts

laissez-faire The principle that people should be able to compete freely, without government intervention, in the capitalist marketplace.

monopoly Control of a market by a single business firm.

socialism An economic system under which the means of production and distribution are collectively owned.

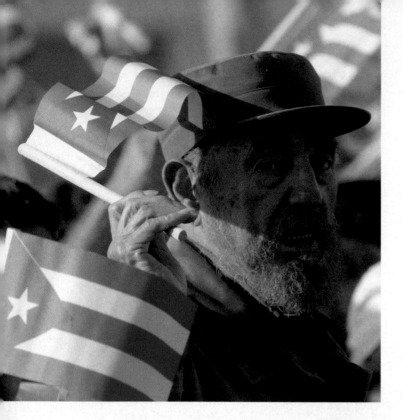

that direct how we provide for our basic human needs (food, shelter, and clothing) from nature. Therefore, we must fulfill those basic needs through technological innovation and culture creation.

- *Production makes us uniquely human.* Our capacity to produce distinguishes humans from the rest of the natural world. It is this free and creative productive ability, what Marx referred to as labor power, that must be protected, nourished, and valued because it is at the core of our identity as humans.

- *We pour ourselves into our products.* For Marx, when we make something, we put part of who we are into each product; this is most apparent in craft labor. For example, a handmade bookshelf inspires pride because our labor power is the difference between the original stack of lumber and the finished shelf. To put it in an equation: *Raw materials + Labor power = Products.* According to Marx, we naturally find joy in labor and take pleasure in sharing both the process and products with others.

- *Economy determines society.* Marx argued that, because our capacity and need to produce is at the core of who we are, it serves as the foundation for society. In essence, how we organize the economy determines all other forms of social relations, such as government, family, education, and religion. In most agrarian societies, production is rooted in the land, so ownership and control of land becomes the foundation of power. Social institutions may reinforce the privileged position of landowners, for example, by rooting a king's "divine right" to rule in religious authority. Over time, this foundation shifts as our capacity to produce

mixed economy An economic system that combines elements of both capitalism and socialism.

evolves through technological innovation. Eventually, the systems of social relations that grew out of that particular set of economic relations no longer match the new economic base, and a revolution to a new set of social relations occurs. Marx contended that this shift brought about the transition from feudalism to capitalism—when the agricultural power base that gave rise to royalty gave way to the industrial power base of capitalists and corporations—and he predicted it will shift again from capitalism to communism.

- *Scarcity and distribution are obstacles to the good society.* For Marx, the ideal society is one in which we as humans have control over, and reap the full benefits of, our labor power. Until this point in history, however, no large-scale society has fully attained this ideal because we lacked the technological capacity to produce enough for everyone. This has resulted in social systems that divide the haves and have-nots: slavery's separation between masters and slaves, feudalism's separation between lords and peasants, capitalism's separation between owners and workers. Thanks to technological innovation—a consequence of our creative capacity to produce—we can eventually solve the problem of inadequate production. In fact, Marx praised capitalism because it ultimately solves this problem by placing pressure on producers for constant innovation. Once we are technically capable of producing enough for all, any continued poverty, hunger, or extreme inequality is due to how we choose to distribute the products we make, rather than to our inability to produce enough. In other words, it's a social problem, solvable by the establishment of a new set of social relations that ensures equitable distribution. According to Marx, people will eventually decide that it doesn't make sense to maintain such economic extremes in the face of material abundance; thus a revolution in social relations toward socialism is inevitable.

In practice, the socialist ideal of collective ownership has been difficult to attain. The grand experiment in what was known as the Soviet Union—uniting Russia and neighboring countries as one large socialist bloc—ultimately collapsed in 1989. It did so under the weight of bureaucratic inefficiency, political corruption, and insufficient productivity—problems that seem endemic to socialist states. In addition, crackdowns on dissidents by the totalitarian socialist governments in both the Soviet Union and communist China have led to the murders of millions of their own people, purportedly for the good of the state. Recent surveys show that majorities in almost all of the former Soviet-bloc nations approve of the steady transition from socialism to democracy and free markets (Pew 2009e).

THE MIXED ECONOMY

In practice, national economic systems combine elements of both capitalism and socialism. A **mixed economy** features elements of more than one economic system. Starting from a socialist ideal and moving toward a mixed economy

Fifty Years of Growth, 1970–2020

Percent GDP increases (trillions of dollars)

Chart showing values for: United Kingdom, Japan, United States, Canada, Spain, Mexico, Brazil, India, China — with vertical axis from 0 to 3000 (in increments of 500).

■ Percent GDP increase, 1970–2007   ■ Percent GDP increase, 2007–2020 (projected)

Source: U.S. Department of Agriculture 2007.

(as China has done in recent years) involves opening up some aspects of the state-controlled economy to competition and the free market. Conversely, moving from a capitalist ideal toward a mixed economy removes some goods and services from the competitive free market and provides them for all or subsidizes them to assure broader access. In the United States, we are provided with goods and services such as police and fire protection, roads, and public schools. Most agree that we should all have access to such public goods without regard for our ability to pay. There is currently a debate under way about whether health care should be considered a similar public good.

There has long been a debate in the United States about the degree to which the government should be involved in the economy, but with the severe economic downturn starting in late 2008, the U.S. government took a more active role. The situation looked grim. The housing-market bubble burst, major banking and investment companies failed, and the stock market plummeted 40 percent from October 1, 2008, to March 9, 2009. Retail sales fell, production levels dropped, and unemployment rates spiked. Comparisons were being drawn to events leading up to the Great Depression, and elected officials moved toward a more mixed economy in hopes of avoiding an even greater collapse.

Government officials decided that some companies were "too big to fail," meaning that the domino effect of their failure would be greater than the cost of violating the laissez-faire ideal. The Bush administration, itself a strong proponent of free market principles, took the first steps toward this recent government intervention in the economy. In September 2008, it pushed the Troubled Assets Relief Program (TARP) through Congress to provide up to $700 billion to buy mortgage-backed securities and to prop up the financial sector. The Obama administration continued along the same lines. For example, in an effort to kick-start the U.S. economy, Congress passed the American Recovery and Reinvestment Act in February 2009, providing almost $800 billion for infrastructure projects, education and health care funding, and tax cuts. And in June 2009, General Motors, which for years was the world's largest company, went bankrupt. The U.S. government became its majority stockholder, owning 60 percent of its shares. These funds helped many firms survive that otherwise would have failed. Now that they are back on their feet, some companies have paid back the loans they received from the government. For example, General Motors has paid back its $8.4 billion of government loans in full, with interest, and five years early. The U.S. government remains its single largest shareholder.

Though critics charged that Presidents Bush and Obama were moving the nation toward socialism, most people were willing to accept such actions in hopes that they would minimize the negative impacts the economic downturn had on their lives. Families were already feeling the pinch: One quarter had a member of their household lose a job within the past year, and almost half saw 20 percent or more of a retirement account or other investments disappear. One-fifth struggled to meet mortgage or rent payments, and the national average for credit card debt rose to $5729 per user (Morin and Taylor 2009). In hopes of hanging onto jobs and keeping the economy functioning, the majority of citizens accepted these huge government expenditures as a means to save capitalism from its own excesses.

SOC THINK

Should the U.S. government let companies fail regardless of apparent economic consequences?

THE INFORMAL ECONOMY

An informal economy operates within the confines of the dominant macroeconomic system in many countries, whether capitalist or socialist. In this **informal economy,** transfers of money, goods, or services take place but are not reported to the government. Examples of the informal economy include bartering in which people trade goods and services with someone (say, exchanging a haircut for a computer lesson), selling goods on the street, and engaging in illegal transactions, such as gambling or drug deals. Participants in this type of economy avoid taxes and government regulations.

> **informal economy** Transfers of money, goods, or services that are not reported to the government.

In the developing world, governments often create burdensome business regulations that overworked bureaucrats must administer. When requests for licenses and permits pile up, delaying business projects, legitimate entrepreneurs find that they need to "go underground" to get anything done. Despite its apparent efficiency, this type of informal economy is dysfunctional for a country's overall political and economic well-being. Because informal firms typically operate in remote locales to avoid detection, they cannot easily expand when they become profitable. And given the limited protection for their property and contractual rights, participants in the informal economy are less likely than others to save and invest their income.

SOC THINK

When doing jobs in the informal economy such as babysitting, lawn mowing, housecleaning, or construction, it can be nice to get cash under the table without having to pay taxes, Social Security, and so on. What are the long-term disadvantages of doing so for the individual? What about for society? Why might someone opt to do so anyway?

Informal economies can also be dysfunctional for workers. Working conditions in these businesses are often unsafe or dangerous, and the jobs rarely provide any benefits to those who become ill or cannot continue to work. Perhaps more significant, the longer a worker remains in the informal economy, the less likely he or she is to make the transition to the regular economy. No matter how efficient or productive a worker may be, employers expect to see experience in the formal economy on a job application. Experience as a successful street vendor or self-employed cleaning person does not carry much weight with interviewers (Venkatesh 2006).

>> Changing Economies

As recent economic upheaval demonstrates, economies are not static. Just as they changed due to the impact of the Industrial Revolution, economies continue to adapt to new contexts. The current changes are part of an ongoing shift in the workplace. Technological innovation and globalization have reduced the number of traditional blue-collar jobs through deindustrialization. Microfinancing has opened up opportunities for poor people, especially women, around the world.

THE CHANGING FACE OF THE WORKFORCE

The workforce in the United States constantly adapts to circumstances. During World War II, when men were mobilized to fight abroad, women entered the workforce in large numbers. With the coming of the civil rights movement in the 1960s, minorities found numerous job opportunities opening to them. Although predictions are not always reliable, sociologists and labor specialists foresee a workforce increasingly composed of women and racial and ethnic minorities. In 1960 there were twice as many men in the labor force as women. As of March 2009, the labor force was 49.7 percent female, due in part to the fact that men have received 80 percent of recent layoffs (Boushey 2009). The dynamics for minority group workers are even more dramatic, as the number of Black, Latino, and Asian American workers continues to increase at a faster rate than the number of White workers.

More and more, then, the workforce reflects the diversity of the population, as ethnic minorities enter the labor force and immigrants and their children move from marginal jobs or employment in the informal economy to

Workforce Diversity: Past, Present, and Future

Percentage of the workforce

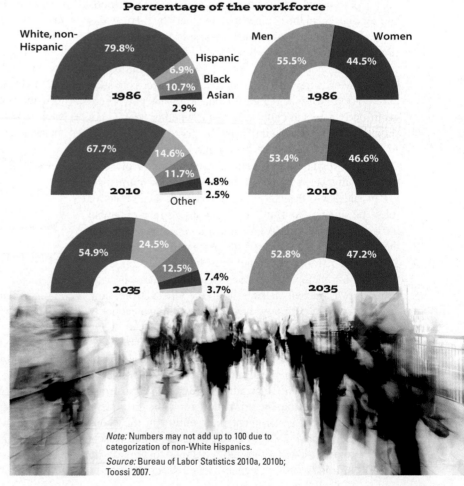

White, non-Hispanic

1986
79.8%
Hispanic 6.9%
Black 10.7%
Asian 2.9%

2010
67.7%
14.6%
11.7%
4.8%
Other 2.5%

2035
54.9%
24.5%
12.5%
7.4%
3.7%

Men — Women

1986
55.5% — 44.5%

2010
53.4% — 46.6%

2035
52.8% — 47.2%

Note: Numbers may not add up to 100 due to categorization of non-White Hispanics.

Source: Bureau of Labor Statistics 2010a, 2010b; Toossi 2007.

positions of greater visibility and responsibility. A sociological study of workplace programs designed to increase managerial diversity found that 39 percent of employers had diversity training programs. Researchers discovered that relying solely on education programs designed to reduce managerial bias was not particularly effective. The most successful approach is to have a point person, task force, or affirmative action plan that holds people responsible for change (Kalev, Dobbin, and Kelly 2006).

DEINDUSTRIALIZATION

In recent decades, the U.S. economy has moved away from its industrial base through the process of **deindustrialization,** which refers to the systematic, widespread withdrawal of investment in basic aspects of productivity, such as factories and plants. Giant corporations that deindustrialize are not necessarily refusing to invest in new economic opportunities. Rather, the targets and locations of investment change, and the need for labor decreases as advances in technology

The effects of the economic downturn have been widespread. Recent college graduates have found a difficult job market. Many people have expressed frustration that large corporations have received billions while individual workers struggle.

> Majority rule only works if you're also considering individual rights. Because you can't have five wolves and one sheep voting on what to have for supper.

Larry Flynt

continue to automate production. First, companies may move their plants from the nation's central cities to the suburbs. The next step may be relocation from suburban areas of the Northeast and Midwest to the South, where labor laws place more restrictions on unions. Finally, a corporation may simply relocate outside the United States to a country with a lower rate of prevailing wages. General Motors, for example, decided to build a multibillion-dollar plant in China rather than in Kansas City or even in Mexico (Lynn 2003).

> **deindustrialization** The systematic, widespread withdrawal of investment in basic aspects of productivity, such as factories and plants.

Although deindustrialization often involves relocation, it can also take the form of corporate restructuring known

SOC THINK

If you were the CEO of an American manufacturing company that was facing declining profits due to international competition, and Wal-Mart insisted that you reduce the price of your products another 5 percent this year, what would you do? To what extent does the system within which companies operate shape the choices that are available to them?

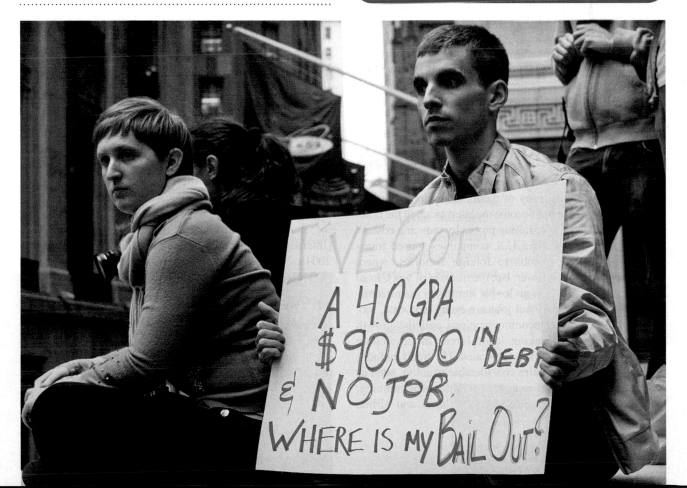

right to rule. Typically, they governed on the basis of traditional forms of authority, sometimes accompanied by the use of force. By the beginning of the 21st century, however, monarchs held genuine governmental power in only a few nations, such as Monaco. Most monarchs, such as Queen Elizabeth II in England, now have little practical power; they serve primarily ceremonial roles.

oligarchy A form of government in which a few individuals rule.

dictatorship A government in which one person has nearly total power to make and enforce laws.

totalitarianism Virtually complete government control and surveillance over all aspects of a society's social and political life.

democracy In a literal sense, government by the people.

OLIGARCHY

An **oligarchy** is a form of government in which a few individuals rule. A venerable method of governing that flourished in ancient Greece and Egypt, oligarchy now often takes the form of military rule. In developing nations in Africa, Asia, and Latin America, small factions of military officers may forcibly seize power, either from legally elected regimes or from other military cliques (Michels [1915] 1949).

Strictly speaking, the term *oligarchy* is reserved for governments that are run by a few selected individuals. However, the People's Republic of China can be classified as an oligarchy if we stretch the meaning of the term. In China, power rests in the hands of a large but exclusive ruling *group,* the Communist Party. In a similar vein, we might argue that many industrialized nations of the West should be considered oligarchies (rather than democracies), because only a powerful few—leaders of big business, government, and the military—actually rule. Later in this chapter, we will examine the "elite model" of the U.S. political system in greater detail.

DICTATORSHIP AND TOTALITARIANISM

A **dictatorship** is a government in which one person has nearly total power to make and enforce laws. Dictators rule primarily through the use of coercion, which often

SOC THINK

In 2001, expressing a sentiment shared by many past presidents, George W. Bush joked that, when it came to working with Congress, "a dictatorship would be a heck of a lot easier." In what ways is the U.S. system of government intentionally inefficient? Why might that be on purpose?

includes imprisonment, torture, and executions. Typically, they *seize* power rather than being freely elected (as in a democracy) or inheriting power (as in a monarchy). Some dictators are quite charismatic and manage to achieve a certain popularity, although their supporters' enthusiasm is almost certainly tinged with fear. Other dictators rely on force and are often bitterly hated by their people.

Frequently, dictators develop such overwhelming control over people's lives that their governments are called totalitarian. (Monarchies and oligarchies may also achieve this type of dominance.) **Totalitarianism** involves virtually complete government control and surveillance over all aspects of a society's social and political life. Germany during Hitler's reign, the Soviet Union under Stalin in the 1930s, and North Korea today are classified as totalitarian states.

DEMOCRACY

In a literal sense, **democracy** means government by the people. The word comes from two Greek roots— *demos,* meaning "the populace" or "the common people," and *kratia,* meaning "rule." Of course, in large, populous nations such as the United States, government by the people is impractical at the national level. Americans cannot vote on every important issue.

SOC THINK

The United States is commonly classified as a representative democracy, because the elected members of Congress and state legislatures make our laws. However, critics have questioned how representative our democracy really is. Do Congress and the state legislatures genuinely represent the masses? Are the people of the United States legitimately self-governing, or has our government become a forum for powerful elites?

Percent turnout of registered voters at parliamentary elections since 1945

Country	Percent
Australia	94.7
Italy	88.3
Germany	83.9
Cambodia	83.6
Canada	70.3
United States	64.1
Russian Federation	59.3
India	59.1
Mexico	59.1
Colombia	44.0
Egypt	40.5
Mali	25.6

Note: Includes national elections to the legislative body.

Source: International Institute for Democracy and Electoral Assistance 2010.

Consequently, popular rule is generally maintained through **representative democracy,** a form of government in which certain individuals are selected to speak for the people.

>> Political Behavior in the United States

Citizens of the United States take for granted many aspects of their political system. They are accustomed to living in a nation with a Bill of Rights, two major political parties, voting by secret ballot, an elected president, state and local governments distinct from the national government, and so forth. Because it is, in principle, a representative democracy, the system depends on all individuals having equal access to and input into the political process in order to be fully responsive. In practice, two particular concerns—voter participation and race and gender representation—raise questions about the degree to which this is happening.

VOTER PARTICIPATION

In a democratic system, voters have the right to select their political leaders. They are free to vote for whom they choose, and political parties seek to persuade voters to support their positions. In April 2010, 33 percent of registered voters in the United States saw themselves as Democrats, 25 percent as Republicans, and 34 percent as independents (Pollster.com 2010).

Historically, voter participation rates in the United States were highest from 1848 to 1896, during which an average of about 80 percent of eligible voters participated in presidential elections. The rate declined steadily until it reached 48.9 percent in 1928. It fluctuated throughout the rest of the 20th century, rising to more than 60 percent in 1940 and 1960 and falling to around 50 percent in 1948, 1988, and 1996. Concerns about voter apathy were expressed going into the 21st century, so the increases in the new millennium were greeted as a welcome trend (McDonald 2009).

> **representative democracy**
> A form of government in which certain individuals are selected to speak for the people.

In the 2008 presidential election, voter turnout hit a 40-year high, representing the third straight presidential election with an increase in voter participation. In the battle between Barack Obama and John McCain, 61.7 percent of eligible voters participated. Compare this to 60.1 percent in the race between George W. Bush and John Kerry in 2004 and 54.2 percent in the 2000 election, which pitted George W. Bush against Al Gore (McDonald 2009).

While a few nations still command high voter turnout, it is increasingly common to hear national leaders of

Did You Know?

... Young voters were much more likely to vote for Obama in 2008 than any other age group. Of voters aged 18–29, 66 percent voted for Obama. This compares to 52 percent among 30–44 year-olds and 50 percent for those aged 45–64. People 65 and older preferred McCain; only 45 percent of that age group chose Obama.

other countries complain of voter apathy. Still, among the 166 countries that have held parliamentary elections since 1945, the United States ranked only 147th in voter turnout in 2006 and 109th in 2008 (International Institute for Democracy and Electoral Assistance 2009).

Political participation makes government accountable to the voters. If participation declines, government operates with less of a sense of accountability to society. This issue is most serious for the least powerful individuals and groups in the United States. Historically, voter turnout has been particularly low among members of racial and ethnic minorities, although in the 2008 presidential election participation rates increased 9 percent among African Americans and 5 percent among Hispanics (Lopez and Taylor 2009). The poor—whose focus understandably is on survival—are also traditionally underrepresented among voters. The low turnout found among these groups is due at least in part to their common feeling of powerlessness. By the same token, by declining to vote, they encourage political power brokers to continue to ignore the interests of the less affluent and the nation's minorities. The segment of the voting population that has shown the most voter apathy is the 18- to 24-year-olds (Holder 2006).

RACE AND GENDER IN POLITICS

Because politics is synonymous with power and authority, we should not be surprised that marginalized groups lack political strength. Nationally, women did not get the vote until 1920. Most Chinese Americans were turned away from the polls until 1926. American Indians did not win

Reasons for Not Voting, 18- to 24-Year-Olds

Reason	Percent
Too busy, conflicting schedule	21.0
Out of town	14.2
Not interested	12.1
Other reason	11.6
Don't know or refused	11.2
Registration problems	9.0
Did not like candidates or campaign issues	8.0
Forgot to vote	4.5
Illness or disability	3.2
Inconvenient polling place	2.6
Transportation problems	2.4
Bad weather conditions	0.2

Percent

Source: U.S. Census Bureau 2009h:Table 12.

Women in National Legislatures, Selected Countries

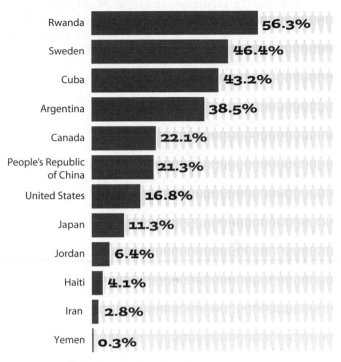

Country	Percent
Rwanda	56.3%
Sweden	46.4%
Cuba	43.2%
Argentina	38.5%
Canada	22.1%
People's Republic of China	21.3%
United States	16.8%
Japan	11.3%
Jordan	6.4%
Haiti	4.1%
Iran	2.8%
Yemen	0.3%

Note: Data are for lower legislative houses only, as of February 28, 2010; data on upper houses, such as the U.S. Senate or the U.K. House of Lords, are not included.

Source: Inter Parliamentary Union 2010.

the right to vote until 1954. And African Americans were disenfranchised until 1965, when national voting rights legislation was passed. Predictably, it has taken these groups some time to develop their political power and begin to exercise it fully.

Progress toward the inclusion of minority groups in government has been slow as well. As of early 2010, only 17 out of 100 U.S. senators were women. One senator was an African American, 1 was a Latino, 1 was an Asian American, and 1 was a Native Hawaiian/Pacific Islander, leaving 79 White non-Hispanic men. Among the 435 members of the U.S. House of Representatives, 305

were White non-Hispanic men. Seventy-six were women, 39 were African Americans (including 14 women), 28 were Latinos (including 6 Latinas), 8 were Asian Americans or Native Hawaiian/Pacific Islanders, and 1 was an American Indian. These numbers, though low, represent a high-water mark for these groups.

Many critics within minority communities decry what they term "fiesta politics." This refers to the tendency of White power brokers to visit racial and ethnic minority communities only when they need electoral support, making a quick appearance on a national or ethnic holiday to get their picture taken and then vanishing. When the election is over, they too often forget to consult the residents who supported them about community needs and concerns.

Female politicians may be enjoying more electoral success now than in the past, but there is evidence that the media cover them differently from male politicians. A content analysis of newspaper coverage of gubernatorial races showed that reporters wrote more

(Under) Representation in Congress Compared to Overall Population

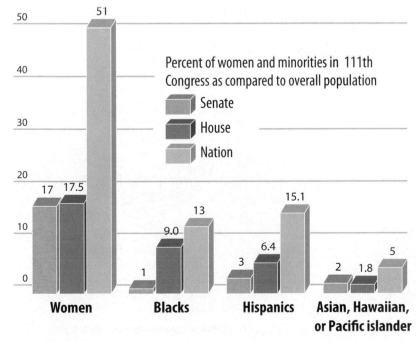

Percent of women and minorities in 111th Congress as compared to overall population

- Senate
- House
- Nation

Women — Senate 17, House 17.5, Nation 51
Blacks — Senate 1, House 9.0, Nation 13
Hispanics — Senate 3, House 6.4, Nation 15.1
Asian, Hawaiian, or Pacific islander — Senate 2, House 1.8, Nation 5

Source: Manning 2010.

often about a female candidate's personal life, appearance, or personality than a male candidate's, and less often about her political viewpoints and voting record. Furthermore, when political issues were raised in newspaper articles, reporters were more likely to illustrate them with statements made by male candidates than by female candidates (Devitt 1999; Jost 2008; Paxton Kunovich, and Hughes 2007).

Whereas the proportion of women in national legislatures has increased in the United States and many other nations, women account for at least half the members of the national legislature in only one country. The African Republic of Rwanda ranks the highest, with 56.3 percent of its legislative seats held by women. Overall, the United States ranked 100th among 196 nations in the proportion of women serving as national legislators in 2010 (Inter-Parliamentary Union 2010).

> **elite model** A view of society as being ruled by a small group of individuals who share a common set of political and economic interests.
>
> **power elite** A small group of military, industrial, and government leaders who control the fate of the United States.

To remedy this situation, many countries have adopted quotas for female representatives. In some, the government sets aside a certain percentage of seats for women, usually 10–30 percent. In others, political parties have decided that 20–40 percent of their candidates should be women. Thirty-two countries now have some kind of quota system (Vasagar 2005).

>> The Power Structure in the United States

The issue of power extends beyond just politics and the people who occupy formally recognized offices. Over the years, sociologists repeatedly have sought to discover who really holds power in the United States. Do "we the people" genuinely run the country through our elected representatives? Or does a small elite behind the scenes control both the government and the economic system? It is difficult to determine the location of power in a society as complex as the United States. In exploring this critical question, social scientists have developed two basic views of our nation's power structure: the power elite and the pluralist models.

POWER ELITE MODELS

Karl Marx believed that 19th-century representative democracy was essentially a sham. He argued that industrial societies were dominated by relatively small numbers of people who owned the factories and controlled natural resources. In Marx's view, government officials and military leaders were essentially servants of this capitalist class and followed their wishes. Therefore, any key decisions made by politicians inevitably reflected the interests of the dominant business owners. Like others who hold an **elite model** of power relations, Marx believed that society is ruled by a small group of individuals who share political and economic interests.

Mills' Model Sociologist C. Wright Mills, who developed the concept of the sociological imagination that we looked at in Chapter 1, put forth a model similar to Marx's in his pioneering work *The Power Elite* ([1956] 2000). Mills described a small group of military, industrial, and government leaders who controlled the fate of the United States—the **power elite.** Power rested in the hands of a few, both inside and outside government.

A pyramid illustrates the power structure of the United States in Mills' model. The power elite rests at the top

Power Elite Models

SOCstudies

THE POWER ELITE

Corporate rich
Executive branch
Military leaders

Interest group leaders
Legislators
Local opinion leaders

Unorganized, exploited masses

C. Wright Mills' model, 1956

Social upper class

THE POWER ELITE

Corporate community

Policy-formation organizations

G. William Domhoff's model, 2006

Source: Left, based on C. W. Mills (1956) 2000; right, Domhoff 2006:105.

Public Trust in Government

Source: Pew Research Center 2010c.

and includes the corporate rich, leaders of the executive branch of government, and heads of the military (whom Mills called the "warlords"). Directly below are local opinion leaders, members of the legislative branch of government, and leaders of special-interest groups. Mills contended that these individuals and groups basically follow the wishes of the dominant power elite. At the bottom of the pyramid are the unorganized, exploited masses.

A fundamental element in Mills' thesis is that the power elite not only includes relatively few members but also operates as a self-conscious, cohesive unit. Although not necessarily diabolical or ruthless, the elite comprises similar types of people who interact regularly with one another and have essentially the same political and economic interests. Mills' power elite represents not a conspiracy but rather a community of interest and sentiment among a small number of influential people (Jenness, Smith, and Stepan-Norris 2006).

Critics claim that Mills failed to clarify when the elite opposes protests and when it tolerates them, making it difficult to test his model. Furthermore, they say, he failed to provide detailed case studies that would substantiate the interrelationships among members of the power elite. Nevertheless, his challenging theories forced scholars to look more critically at the democratic political system of the United States.

In analyzing the scandals that have rocked major corporations such as Enron and Arthur Andersen over the past decade, observers have noted that members of the business elite are closely interrelated. In a study of the members of the boards of directors of Fortune 1000 corporations, researchers found that each director can reach *every* other board of directors in just 3.7 steps. That is, by consulting acquaintances of acquaintances, each director can quickly reach someone who sits on each of the other 999 boards. Furthermore, the face-to-face contact directors regularly have in their board meetings makes them a highly cohesive elite.

Finally, the corporate elite not only is wealthy, powerful, and cohesive but also is overwhelmingly White and male (G. Davis 2003, 2004; Kentor and Jang 2004; Mizruchi 1996; Strauss 2002).

pluralist model A view of society in which many competing groups within the community have access to government, so that no single group is dominant.

war Conflict between organizations that possess trained combat forces equipped with deadly weapons.

Domhoff's Model Sociologist G. William Domhoff (2006, 2009) agrees with Mills that a powerful elite runs the United States. Domhoff stresses the role played by elites from within networks of organizations including the corporate community; policy formation organizations such as think tanks, chambers of commerce, and labor unions; and the social upper class. Membership in these groups overlaps, and members with connections in more than one of these spheres have more power and influence. Domhoff finds that those in this latter group are still largely White, male, and upper class, but he notes the presence of a small number of women and minority men in key positions—groups that were excluded from Mills' top echelon and are still under-represented today (Zweigenhaft and Domhoff 2006).

─SOC THINK─

Is there a relatively small and unified group of powerful people in the United States who, in effect, rule the country through their power and influence?

Although the three groups in Domhoff's power elite model do overlap, they do not necessarily agree on specific policies. Domhoff notes that in politics, two different coalitions have exercised influence. A corporate-conservative coalition has played a large role in both political parties, generating support for particular candidates through direct-mail appeals. A liberal-labor coalition is based in unions, local environmental organizations, a segment of the minority group community, liberal churches, and the university and arts communities (Zweigenhaft and Domhoff 2006). This suggests that the interests of members of the power elite are not always singular or uniform but that overall they do work together to advance their larger interests.

THE PLURALIST MODEL

Other theorists argue that power in the United States is shared more widely, that there is no core group at the top who are able to advance their common interests. In their view, a pluralist model more accurately describes the nation's power structure. According to the **pluralist model,** many competing groups within the community have access to government so that no single group is dominant.

The pluralist model suggests that a variety of groups play a significant role in decision making. Typically, pluralists make use of intensive case studies or community studies based on observation research. One of the most famous—an investigation of decision making in New Haven, Connecticut—was reported by Robert Dahl (1961). Dahl found that, although the number of people involved in any important decision was rather small, community power was nonetheless diffuse. Few political actors exercised decision-making power on all issues, and no one group got its way all the time. One individual or group might be influential in a battle over urban renewal but have little impact on educational policy.

The pluralist model, too, has its critics. Domhoff (1978, 2006) reexamined Dahl's study of decision making in New Haven and argued that Dahl and other pluralists had failed to trace how local elites who were prominent in decision making belonged to a larger national ruling class. In addition, studies of community power, such as Dahl's work in New Haven, can examine decision making only on issues that become part of the political agenda. They fail to address the potential power of elites to keep certain matters entirely out of the realm of political debate.

Dianne Pinderhughes (1987) has criticized the pluralist model for failing to account for the exclusion of African Americans from the political process. Drawing on her studies of Chicago politics, Pinderhughes points out that the residential and occupational segregation of Blacks and their long political disenfranchisement violate the logic of pluralism—which would hold that such a substantial minority should always have been influential in community decision making. This critique applies to many cities across the United States, where other large racial and ethnic minorities, among them Asian Americans, Puerto Ricans, and Mexican Americans, are relatively powerless.

Historically, pluralists have stressed ways in which large numbers of people can participate in or influence governmental decision making. New communications technologies like the Internet are increasing the opportunity to be heard, not just in countries like the United States but in developing countries the world over. The ability to communicate with political leaders via email, for example, increases the opportunity for the average citizen to have a voice in politics.

>>War and Peace

When it comes to political power, perhaps no decision is as weighty as the decision to go to war. Conflict is a central aspect of social relations. Sociologists Theodore Caplow and Louis Hicks (2002:3) have defined **war** as conflict between organizations that possess trained combat forces equipped with deadly weapons. This meaning is broader than the legal definition, which typically requires a formal declaration of hostilities.

U.S. Public Opinion on the Necessity of War, 1971–2007

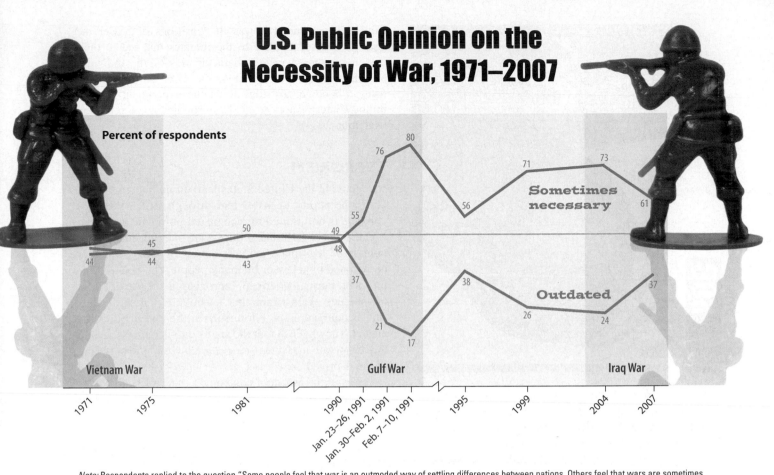

Percent of respondents

Sometimes necessary: 44, 45, 50, 49, 55, 76, 80, 56, 71, 73, 61

Outdated: 44, 44, 43, 48, 37, 21, 17, 38, 26, 24, 37

Vietnam War   Gulf War   Iraq War

1971, 1975, 1981, 1990, Jan. 23–26, 1991, Jan. 30–Feb. 2, 1991, Feb. 7–10, 1991, 1995, 1999, 2004, 2007

Note: Respondents replied to the question "Some people feel that war is an outmoded way of settling differences between nations. Others feel that wars are sometimes necessary to settle differences. With which point of view do you agree?"

Source: Gallup 2009.

WAR

Sociologists approach war in three different ways. Those who take a global view study how and why two or more nations become engaged in military conflict. Those who take a nation-state view stress the interaction of internal political, socioeconomic, and cultural forces. And those who take a micro view focus on the social impact of war on individuals and the groups to which they belong.

Analysis at the global level focuses on macro issues such as the distribution of resources, struggles over political philosophies, and debates about boundaries. Often it involves nations with competing political and economic systems, as was the case in World War I, World War II, and the Cold War. Some have argued that the conflict in Iraq is about bringing freedom and democracy to the Middle East, and others argue it was motivated by oil and profits.

Sociologists have devoted much effort to studying the internal decision-making process that leads to war. During the Vietnam War, Presidents Johnson and Nixon both misled Congress, painting a falsely optimistic picture of the likely outcome. Based on their intentional distortions, Congress appropriated the military funds the two administrations requested. However, in 1971, the *New York Times* published a set of classified documents now known as "The Pentagon Papers," which revealed that many members of both administrations had knowingly distorted the real prospects for the war. Two years later— over Nixon's veto—Congress passed the War Powers Act, which requires the president to notify Congress of the reasons for committing combat troops to a hostile situation (Patterson 2003).

Even though government leaders make the decision to go to war, public opinion plays a significant role in its execution. By 1971, the number of U.S. soldiers killed in Vietnam had surpassed 50,000, and antiwar sentiment was strong. Surveys done at that time showed that the public was split roughly equally on the question of whether war was an appropriate way to settle differences between nations (see the figure above). This division in public opinion continued until the United States led the charge in the Gulf War following Iraq's invasion of Kuwait in 1990. Since then, however, support for war has declined.

A major change relating to the conduct of war involves the composition of the U.S. military. Women represent a growing presence among the troops. Almost 200,000 women, or about 20 percent of U.S. military forces, are now in uniform, serving not just as support personnel but as an integral part of combat units. The first casualty of the war in Iraq, in fact, was Private First Class Lori Piestewa,

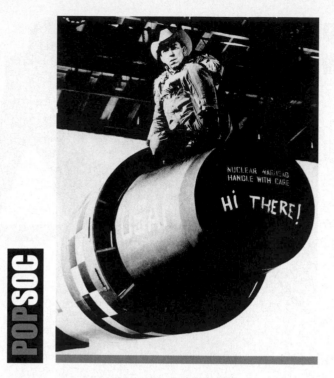

NUCLEAR WARHEAD
HANDLE WITH CARE

HI THERE!

During World War II, the U.S. government sponsored films to garner support for the war effort, boost people's morale, and even demonize the enemy. From cartoons featuring Mickey Mouse and Donald Duck to films including *This Is the Army* (which starred Ronald Reagan), Hollywood cooperated in getting the message out in the 1940s. In more recent years, antiwar films have also raised difficult questions that governments would sometimes rather not be aired. During the Cold War, *Dr. Strangelove* called into question the insanity of the nuclear standoff; in 1970, the film version of *M*A*S*H*, though set in Korea, raised questions about the conflict in Vietnam. More recently, there have been numerous films about the war in Iraq, including Michael Moore's *Fahrenheit 9/11, No End in Sight, Stop-Loss,* and *War, Inc.*

a member of the Hopi tribe and a descendant of Mexican settlers in the Southwest (Bureau of the Census 2007a:Table 503).

At the level of interpersonal interaction, war can bring out the worst as well as the best in people. In 2004, graphic images of the abuse of Iraqi prisoners by U.S. soldiers at Iraq's Abu Ghraib prison shocked the world. For social scientists, the deterioration of the guards' behavior brought to mind psychology professor Philip Zimbardo's mock prison experiment at Stanford University, in which volunteer guards in a simulated prison acted sadistically toward volunteer prisoneers.

Zimbardo concluded it was the positions of power the guards occupied relative to the inmates that led to their behavior rather than the characteristics of the individuals themselves. In July 2004, the U.S. military began using a documentary film about the experiment to train military interrogators to avoid mistreatment of prisoners (Zarembo 2004).

TERRORISM

As people in the United States learned on September 11, 2001, the ability to instill fear through large-scale violent acts is not limited to recognized political states, and it can involve political groups that operate outside the bounds of legitimate authority. Acts of terror, whether perpetrated by a few or by many people, can be a powerful force. Formally defined, **terrorism** is the use or threat of violence against random or symbolic targets in pursuit of political aims. For terrorists, the end justifies the means. They believe that the status quo is oppressive and that desperate measures are essential to end the suffering of the deprived.

An essential aspect of contemporary terrorism involves use of the media. Terrorists may wish to keep secret their individual identities, but they want their political messages and goals to receive as much publicity as possible. The purpose of many acts of terrorist violence is more symbolic than strategic or tactical. These attacks represent a statement made by people who feel that the world has gone awry, that accepted political paths to problem resolution are ineffective or blocked, and that there is a larger or cosmic struggle going on, raising the stakes and so justifying the means (Juergensmeyer 2003). Whether through calls to the media, anonymous manifestos, or other means, terrorists typically admit responsibility for and defend their violent acts.

Terrorism is a global concern. In 2008, there were 11,000 terrorist attacks worldwide resulting in 15,000

Aftermath of a 2009 suicide blast attack of a five-star hotel in Pakistan.

deaths (National Counterterrorism Center 2010). Since September 11, 2001, governments around the world have renewed their efforts to fight terrorism. Even though the public generally regards increased surveillance and social control as a necessary evil, these measures have nonetheless raised governance issues. For example, some citizens in the United States and elsewhere have expressed concern that measures such as the USA PATRIOT Act of 2001 threaten civil liberties. Citizens also complain about the heightened anxiety created by the vague "terror alerts" the federal government issues from time to time. Worldwide, immigration and the processing of refugees have slowed to a crawl, separating families and preventing employers from filling job openings. As these efforts to combat political violence illustrate, the term *terrorism* is an apt one (R. Howard and Sawyer 2003).

> **terrorism** The use or threat of violence against random or symbolic targets in pursuit of political aims.
>
> **peace** The absence of war or, more broadly, a proactive effort to develop cooperative relations among nations.

PEACE

Sociologists have considered **peace** both as the absence of war and as a proactive effort to develop cooperative relations among nations. It is important to note, however, that armed conflict involves more than just warring nations. From 1945 to the end of the 20th century, the 25 major wars that occurred between countries killed a total of

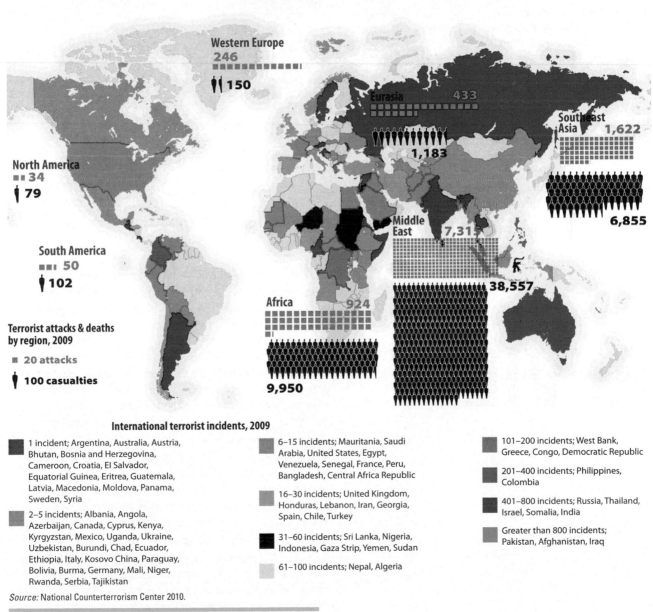

Going **GLOBAL**

Terrorist Attacks

Western Europe 246 ⋮ 150

North America 34 79

South America 50 102

Eurasia 433 1,183

Southeast Asia 1,622 6,855

Middle East 7,31_ 38,557

Africa 924 9,950

Terrorist attacks & deaths by region, 2009

■ 20 attacks

i 100 casualties

International terrorist incidents, 2009

1 incident; Argentina, Australia, Austria, Bhutan, Bosnia and Herzegovina, Cameroon, Croatia, El Salvador, Equatorial Guinea, Eritrea, Guatemala, Latvia, Macedonia, Moldova, Panama, Sweden, Syria

2–5 incidents; Albania, Angola, Azerbaijan, Canada, Cyprus, Kenya, Kyrgyzstan, Mexico, Uganda, Ukraine, Uzbekistan, Burundi, Chad, Ecuador, Ethiopia, Italy, Kosovo China, Paraguay, Bolivia, Burma, Germany, Mali, Niger, Rwanda, Serbia, Tajikistan

6–15 incidents; Mauritania, Saudi Arabia, United States, Egypt, Venezuela, Senegal, France, Peru, Bangladesh, Central Africa Republic

16–30 incidents; United Kingdom, Honduras, Lebanon, Iran, Georgia, Spain, Chile, Turkey

31–60 incidents; Sri Lanka, Nigeria, Indonesia, Gaza Strip, Yemen, Sudan

61–100 incidents; Nepal, Algeria

101–200 incidents; West Bank, Greece, Congo, Democratic Republic

201–400 incidents; Philippines, Colombia

401–800 incidents; Russia, Thailand, Israel, Somalia, India

Greater than 800 incidents; Pakistan, Afghanistan, Iraq

Source: National Counterterrorism Center 2010.

3.3 million people. While this is significant, the 127 civil wars that occurred in the same time period resulted in 16 million deaths. In other words, five times as many people died as a result of conflicts *within* nations than died in wars *between* nations (Fearon and Laitin 2003).

Sociologists and other social scientists who draw on sociological theory and research have tried to identify conditions that deter war. One of their findings is that international trade may act as a deterrent to armed conflict. As countries exchange goods, people, and then cultures, they become more integrated and less likely to threaten each other's security. Viewed from this perspective, not just trade but also immigration and foreign exchange programs have a beneficial effect on international relations.

Another means of fostering peace is the activity of international charities and activist groups, or nongovernmental organizations (NGOs). The Red Cross and Red Crescent, Doctors Without Borders, and Amnesty International donate their services wherever they are needed, without regard to nationality. In the past decade or so, these NGOs have been expanding in number, size, and scope. By sharing news of local conditions and clarifying local issues, they often prevent conflicts from escalating into violence and war. Some NGOs have initiated ceasefires, reached settlements, and even ended warfare between former adversaries.

Finally, many analysts stress that nations cannot maintain their security by threatening violence. Peace, they contend, can best be maintained by developing strong mutual security agreements among potential adversaries (Etzioni 1965; Shostak 2002). Following this path involves active diplomacy and, to the extent that it involves negotiations with countries viewed as enemies, can be controversial.

From Snapper mowers to microloans to peace movements, stories such as these provide hope. Even though large-scale economic trends can have negative impacts on companies, communities, and individuals, as well as shaping political outcomes, positive social change is possible. Sociological analysis helps us to see the underlying processes at work in the economy and politics, and in so doing can assist us in recognizing places in those systems where opportunities for bringing about such change exist.

Investigate! Who contributed and how much to the senators and representatives in your state? What interests do those contributors represent? OpenSecrets.org provides an easily searchable database to track down who gives what to whom.

get **involved!**

For
REVIEW

I. **How is economic and political power organized?**

- The two major economic systems are capitalism and socialism, though in practice most economies are some mix of the two. Political systems of government include monarchy, oligarchy, dictatorship, totalitarianism, and democracy. A debate exists when looking at formal power in the United States about the degree to which there is a small, cohesive group of power elites who effectively rule or if leadership is more diverse and pluralistic, operating through democratic processes.

II. **How does power operate?**

- Power involves the capacity to get others to do what you want, which can involve force, influence, and authority. In the case of authority, followers accept your power as legitimate, whether based on a traditional, rational-legal, or charismatic foundation.

III. **How has the economy changed over time?**

- The rise of a global economy has brought with it a changing composition of the national and international workforce, deindustrialization, and in the form of microfinancing, economic opportunities for people who are poor.

Functionalist View

Power and authority are exercised in society to maintain social order for the good of the whole.

The economic system is a social institution that organizes the production, distribution, and consumption of goods and services.

The political system maintains **order** in society through internal policing and diplomatic relations with outsiders.

ORDER, SYSTEMS, ALLOCATION OF RESOURCES
KEY CONCEPTS

Conflict View

Power and authority are exercised to preserve and extend the integrity of the elites in society.

Capitalism primarily benefits the owners of the means of production; **socialism** allows workers to benefit from their own **labor power.**

The **power elite**, a small group of military, industrial, and government leaders, shape the direction of society.

KEY CONCEPTS
COERCION, POWER ELITE, LABOR POWER

Interactionist View

Power and authority are **socially constructed** through interactions with others.

Authority depends upon followers accepting the legitimacy of their leader's right to rule.

In the U.S. political system, leaders are selected by those who **vote**; the political parties try to **persuade** the voters to support their positions.

KEY CONCEPTS
AUTHORITY, PERSUASION

MAKE THE CONNECTION

After reviewing the chapter, answer the following questions:

1

How would each perspective explain Jim Wier's decision to no longer sell lawn mowers through Wal-Mart (p. 209)?

2

How might each perspective seek to explain charismatic authority (p. 211)?

3

How might theorists from each perspective explain war (p. 227)?

4

Are you an active or an apathetic voter? What factors influence your approach? Which perspective best describes the way you participate in the political world?

Pop Quiz

1. Which source of power depends primarily on persuasion to achieve its goals?
   a. oligarchy
   b. influence
   c. force
   d. authority

2. Which of the following is *not* part of the classification system of authority developed by Max Weber?
   a. traditional authority
   b. pluralist authority
   c. legal-rational authority
   d. charismatic authority

3. Under capitalism, laissez-faire means that
   a. the means of production and distribution in a society are collectively held.
   b. people should compete freely, with minimal government intervention in the economy.
   c. a single business firm controls the market.
   d. society depends on mechanization to produce its goods and services.

4. Transfers of money, goods, and services that take place but are not reported to the government are best described as
   a. globalization.
   b. the mixed economy.
   c. laissez-faire capitalism.
   d. the informal economy.

5. The systematic, widespread withdrawal of investment in basic aspects of productivity such as factories and plants is called
   a. deindustrialization.
   b. downsizing.
   c. postindustrialization.
   d. gentrification.

6. Political scientist Harold Lasswell defined *politics* as
   a. the struggle for power and authority.
   b. the allocation of valued resources.
   c. who gets what, when, and how.
   d. a cultural universal.

7. The type of government in which a few individuals rule is known as
   a. a monarchy.
   b. a democracy.
   c. a dictatorship.
   d. an oligarchy.

8. Comparing voter turnout in the United States to that of other nations, the United States ranks
   a. first with the highest level of turnout.
   b. in the top 10 internationally.
   c. in about the top third of all nations.
   d. in the bottom half of all nations.

9. According to C. Wright Mills, power rests in the hands of the
   a. people.
   b. power elite.
   c. aristocracy.
   d. representative democracy.

10. The use or threat of violence against random or symbolic targets in pursuit of political aims is referred to as
    a. politics.
    b. power.
    c. terrorism.
    d. authority.

1. (b); 2. (b); 3. (b); 4. (d); 5. (a); 6. (c); 7. (d); 8. (d); 9. (b); 10. (c)

SOCIAL CLASS

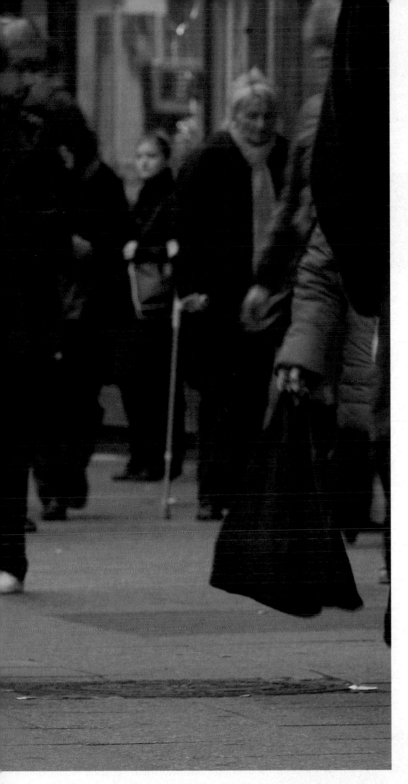

LIVING THE GOOD LIFE—OR NOT

Grayer is four years old. He takes lessons in French, Latin, music, swimming, ice skating, karate, and physical education—in addition to attending preschool. When he failed to get into the elite kindergarten of her choice, his mother hired a grief counselor for him. He lives on Park Avenue in Manhattan with his mother and father, but the person with whom he spends most of his time is his nanny.

Grayer's fictional character was drawn from the real-life experiences of Emma McLaughlin and Nicola Kraus (2002), who worked as nannies to help pay their way through college. They told their stories in the book *The Nanny Diaries,* which later became a film (2007). They depict a world in which, like ours, social class matters.

Sima, one of the nannies in the novel, was an engineer in her home country of El Salvador. She came to the United States with her husband and children, but when he was unable to obtain a green card her husband went back to El Salvador with the kids. Nan, the main nanny character in the book, refers to Sima as "a woman who has a higher degree than I will ever receive, in a subject I couldn't get a passing grade in, and who has been home [to see her husband and children] less than one month in the last twenty-four" (p. 173).

In her book, *Just Like Family,* Tasha Blaine (2009) found that the story of immigrant women leaving their own families for months or years at a time to raise the children of others is hardly unique. After interviewing more than 100 nannies, she observed that women like Sima often felt guilty about leaving their children behind but did so in hopes of providing a better life for them. She also found that nannies often are caught between being treated as an employee and "like family," increasing the possibility that nannies will be taken advantage of in the workplace. In this chapter we see how the social class positions we occupy, from corporate executive to nanny, shape our hopes, dreams, and likely outcomes.

As You READ

>>

- What is social class?
- How does social class operate?
- What are the consequences of social class?

>> Understanding Stratification

Social class was among the earliest interests of sociologists and remains of interest to this day. Marx, Weber, and Durkheim all highlighted the significance of class differences and sought to understand both their causes and consequences. Du Bois and Addams carried this a step further, actually working to ameliorate the excesses of social stratification.

In the United States, however, social class has long been a touchy subject (DeMott 1990). When the topic of social class does come up here, many people's first response is to deny that it exists. Some even angrily argue that opportunity is open to everyone and that individual effort alone determines one's life outcome. From a sociological perspective, however, we must understand the consequences of social class differences if we are to understand why we think and act the way we do. This is especially true in capitalist societies, in which the significance of economic position is heightened. To provide context, we begin by considering the varieties of ways in which societies are stratified.

SYSTEMS OF STRATIFICATION

Ever since people first began to speculate about the nature of human society, they have focused on the differences between individuals and groups within society. The term **social inequality** describes a condition in which members of society have different amounts of wealth, prestige, or power. Some degree of social inequality characterizes every society. Sociologists refer to social inequality that is built

into the structure of society as **stratification**—the structured ranking of entire groups of people that perpetuates unequal economic rewards and power in a society.

Stratification shapes individual opportunity based on the layer or stratum that one occupies in the system. Certain groups of people stand higher in social rankings, control scarce resources, wield power, and receive special treatment. Unequal rewards include income and wealth, but they are also related to the power conveyed by social networks (who you know) and knowledge (what you know). Control over such resources enables one generation to pass on social advantages to the next, producing groups of people arranged in rank order, from low to high.

Sociologists focus on four major systems of stratification: slavery, caste, estate, and class. In order to understand how we end up on the level we do, it is helpful to recall the distinction between achieved status and ascribed status from Chapter 5. **Ascribed status** is a social position assigned to a person by society without regard for his or her unique talents or characteristics. In contrast, **achieved status** is a social position that a person attains largely through his or her own efforts. The nation's most affluent families generally inherit wealth and status, whereas many members of racial and ethnic minorities inherit disadvantaged status. Age and gender are additional ascribed statuses that influence a person's wealth and social position.

Slavery The most extreme form of legalized social inequality for individuals and groups is **slavery.** Enslaved individuals are the property of other people, who have the right to treat them as they please, as if they were tools or draft animals.

Did You Know?

... Slavery continues to be practiced around the world. Approximately 12.3 million people worldwide—80 percent of whom are female and about half of whom are children—are in bondage to forced labor in areas such as agriculture, mining, textiles, and sex trafficking.

Source: Andrees and Belser 2009.

The practice of slavery has varied over different times and places. Most of the slaves in ancient Greece were prisoners of war or individuals captured and sold by pirates. Although succeeding generations could inherit slave status, it was not necessarily permanent. A person's status might change, depending on which city-state happened to triumph in a military conflict. In effect, all citizens had the potential to become slaves or gain freedom, depending on the historical circumstances. By contrast, slavery in the United States and Latin America was an ascribed status, and slaves faced racial and legal barriers to freedom.

Today, the Universal Declaration of Human Rights, which is binding on all members of the United Nations, prohibits slavery in all its forms. According to the United Nations (2010), contemporary forms of slavery include debt bondage, forced labor, child labor and child servitude, sexual slavery, sale of children, forced marriage, and the sale of wives. In many developing countries, bonded laborers are imprisoned in lifetime employment. Though slavery is outlawed in the United States and Europe, guest workers and illegal immigrants have been forced to labor for years under terrible conditions, either to pay off debts or to avoid being turned over to immigration authorities. In 2007 a wealthy couple from New York was convicted of holding two Indonesian women as slaves in their home for four years (Eltman 2007; Greenhouse 2007).

> **stratification** A structured ranking of entire groups of people that perpetuates unequal economic rewards and power in a society.
>
> **achieved status** A social position that a person attains largely through his or her own efforts.
>
> **slavery** A system of enforced servitude in which some people are owned by others as property.
>
> **caste** A hereditary rank, usually religiously dictated, that tends to be fixed and immobile.

Castes Castes are hereditary ranks, usually dictated by religion, that tend to be fixed and immobile. The caste system is generally associated with Hinduism in India and other countries. In India there are four major castes, or *varnas:* priests (*Brahman*), warriors (*Kshatriya*), merchants (*Vaishya*), and artisans/farmers (*Shudra*). A fifth category of outcastes, referred to as the *dalit,* or untouchables, is considered to be so lowly and unclean as to have no place within this system of stratification. There are also many minor castes. Caste membership is an ascribed status (at birth, children automatically assume the same position as their parents). Each caste is sharply defined, and members are expected to marry within that caste.

the landowner, who in return offered the peasants military protection against bandits and rival nobles. The basis for the system was the nobles' ownership of land, which was critical to their superior and privileged status. As in systems based on slavery and caste, inheritance of one's position largely defined the estate system. The nobles inherited their titles and property; the peasants were born into a subservient position within an agrarian society.

As the estate system developed, it became more differentiated. Nobles began to achieve varying degrees of authority. By the 12th century, a priesthood had emerged in most of Europe, along with classes of merchants and artisans. For the first time, there were groups of people whose wealth did not depend on land ownership or agriculture. This economic change had profound social consequences as the estate system ended and a class system of stratification came into existence.

Social Classes A **class system** is a social ranking based primarily on economic position in which achieved characteristics can influence social mobility. In contrast to slavery and caste systems, in a class system the boundaries between classes are imprecisely defined, and one can move from one stratum, or level, of society to another. Even so, the various layers of social classes are fairly stable over time; a person's position within them shapes her or his access to material, social, and cultural resources. Class standing, though it can be improved, is heavily dependent on ascribed characteristics including family background, race, and ethnicity.

Sociologists commonly use a five-class model to describe the class system in the United States: upper, upper-middle, lower-middle, working, and lower class (Beeghley 2007; Rossides 1997). Although the lines separating social classes are not as sharp as the divisions between castes, there are differences between the five classes in terms of key resources. Among these are income, occupation, bureaucratic authority, educational attainment, social networks, and political connections.

The *upper class,* or capitalist class, is the smallest and most exclusive, including 1–2 percent of the U.S. population. Members are wealthy, well respected, and politically powerful. On the other end of the spectrum is the *lower class,* also known as the underclass, or the poor. This class, 15–20 percent of the population, has limited access to the paid labor force, lacks wealth, and is too weak politically to exert significant power. It consists of a disproportionate number of Blacks, Hispanics, single mothers with dependent children, and recent immigrants.

Sandwiched between these two classes are the upper-middle, lower-middle, and working classes. The *upper-middle class* is composed of business executives and upper-level management (a subset called the corporate class),

In 1950, after gaining independence from Great Britain, India adopted a new constitution that formally outlawed the caste system. Over the past decade or two, however, urbanization and technological advances have brought more change to India's caste system than the government has in more than half a century. The anonymity of city life tends to blur caste boundaries, allowing the *dalit* to pass unrecognized in temples, schools, and workplaces. The globalization of high technology also has opened up India's social order, bringing new opportunities to those who possess the skills and ability to capitalize on them, regardless of caste.

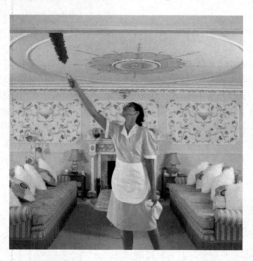

estate system A system of stratification under which peasants were required to work land leased to them by nobles in exchange for military protection and other services. Also known as feudalism.

class system A social ranking based primarily on economic position in which achieved characteristics can influence social mobility.

Estates A third type of stratification system developed within the feudal societies of medieval Europe. Under the **estate system,** or feudalism, nobles owned the land, which they leased to peasants who worked it and lived on it. The peasants turned over a portion of what they produced to doctors, lawyers, architects, and other professionals. Comprising about 15 percent of the population, they participate extensively in politics and take leadership roles in voluntary associations. The *lower-middle class,* sometimes simply referred to as the middle class, includes less affluent professionals (such as elementary school teachers and nurses), owners of small businesses, and a sizable number of clerical workers. Although not all members of this varied class hold a college degree, they typically hope to send their children to college. They make up 30–35 percent of the population.

Members of the *working class,* who make up the remaining 30–35 percent of population, usually hold jobs that involve manual labor. Some blue-collar members of this class, such as electricians, may have higher incomes than people in the middle class. Yet, even if they have achieved some degree of economic security, they tend to identify with manual workers and have a long history of involvement in the labor movement. Of the five classes, the working class faces the greatest declines in the United States as jobs that once required physical labor are taken over by machines or sent abroad where labor is cheaper.

SOCIAL MOBILITY

A key component of each of these systems of stratification is **social mobility**—the degree to which one can change the social stratum into which one is born. The ascent of a person from a poor background to a position of prestige, power, or financial reward—such as in the 2002 movie *Maid in Manhattan*—is an example of social mobility. In the film, Jennifer Lopez plays a chambermaid in a big-city hotel who rises to become a company supervisor and the girlfriend of a well-to-do politician. While stories in which the commoner marries the prince truly were fairy tales in the era of the estate system, today they are metaphors for the potential permeability of modern class boundaries.

> **social mobility** Movement of individuals or groups from one position in a society's stratification system to another.
>
> **open system** A social system in which the position of each individual is influenced by his or her achieved status.
>
> **closed system** A social system in which there is little or no possibility of individual social mobility.

Open Versus Closed Stratification Systems

Sociologists distinguish between stratification systems that are open versus closed to indicate the degree of social mobility in a society. An **open system** implies that a person's achieved status influences his or her social position. Such a system encourages competition among members of society. The United States has sought to move toward this ideal by removing once-legal barriers faced by women, racial and ethnic minorities, and people born in lower social classes.

At the other extreme is the **closed system,** which allows little or no possibility of individual social mobility. Caste systems are examples of closed systems. In such societies, social placement is based on ascribed statuses, such as race or family background, which cannot be changed.

Types of Social Mobility Sociologists also distinguish between mobility *within* a strata versus movement *between* levels. For example, a bus driver who becomes a hotel clerk moves from one social position to another of approximately the same rank. Sociologists call this kind of movement

horizontal mobility The movement of an individual from one social position to another of the same rank.

vertical mobility The movement of an individual from one social position to another of a different rank.

intergenerational mobility Changes in the social position of children relative to their parents.

intragenerational mobility Changes in social position within a person's adult life.

horizontal mobility. However, if the bus driver were to become a lawyer, he or she would experience **vertical mobility**—the movement of an individual from one social position to another of a different rank (Sorokin [1927] 1959). Vertical mobility can involve moving upward or downward in a society's stratification system.

Sociologists also contrast the significance of mobility across an individual's career or lifetime versus movement that spans generations. **Intergenerational mobility** involves changes in the social position of children relative to their parents. Thus, a plumber whose father was a physician provides an example of downward intergenerational mobility. A film star whose parents were both factory workers illustrates upward intergenerational mobility. Because education contributes significantly to upward mobility, any barrier to the pursuit of advanced degrees limits intergenerational mobility (Isaacs, Sawhill, and Haskins 2008).

Intragenerational mobility, on the other hand, involves changes in social position within a person's adult life. Thus, a woman who enters the paid labor force as a teacher's aide and eventually becomes superintendent of the school district experiences upward intragenerational mobility. A man who becomes a cab driver after his accounting firm goes bankrupt undergoes downward intragenerational mobility.

SOCIOLOGICAL PERSPECTIVES ON STRATIFICATION

From early on in the discipline, sociologists have examined the role that control over valued resources plays in social stratification. As we saw in Chapter 9, Karl Marx was critical of capitalism because the social class system prevented workers from receiving the full benefits of their labor power. Max Weber, who sought to extend Marx's model and make it more broadly applicable, argued that three primary resources shape social position: class, status, and party. More recently, Pierre Bourdieu has highlighted the significance of culture as an additional resource. We will look at each of their models in turn.

5 Movies on SOCIAL CLASS

Bread and Roses
Poorly paid janitors struggle to unionize in Los Angeles.

Capitalism: A Love Story
Michael Moore questions the capitalist system in this documentary.

Water
An Indian widow attempts to escape the social restrictions of her position.

Trouble the Water
Two street hustlers become heroes in the aftermath of Hurricane Katrina.

Pride and Prejudice
Social class dictates young women's lives in 19th-century English society.

SOCTHINK

What is the story of social mobility in your family? To what extent have there been shifts both across and within generations? What factors, such as family connections or historical events, contributed to the social mobility that occurred?

In the United States, one way to define the "American Dream" is as upward vertical mobility that is intragenerational. In other words, a person could experience a significant shift in social class position over the course of her or his career, from a relatively low-level position to one of significant wealth and power. Though this does happen, as we will see below, the "American reality" is that we tend to end up in positions relatively close to where we began.

Marx on Class In Karl Marx's view, social relations during any period of history depend on who owns the means of production such as land, factories, machines, and tools. Control over production was important to Marx because people cannot produce—the very ability that he placed at the center of what makes us unique—without access to such resources (see Chapter 9). For Marx, the group that owns the material means of production possesses the most significant source of power in a society. Under the feudal estate system, for example, most production was agricultural and the nobility owned the land. Peasants had little choice but to work according to terms dictated by the landowners.

As we saw in Chapter 9, Marx argued that so long as scarcity exists, there will always be a divide between the haves and the have-nots. Under capitalism, the two main classes are the bourgeoisie and the proletariat. The **bourgeoisie,** or capitalist class, owns the means of

... CEO pay rose 167 percent from 1989 to 2007 while median worker pay rose 10 percent. The average CEO makes more in one workday than the typical worker does in one year.

Source: Mishel, Bernstein, and Shierholz 2009.

production, such as factories and machinery; the **proletariat,** or working class, lacks such ownership.

The competition that is at the heart of capitalism initially pits capitalists against each other in their pursuit of profit in the marketplace. Their success, however, also depends on competition between the bourgeoisie and the proletariat. In order to succeed against their competitors, individual capitalists seek to reduce production costs so that they can lower prices, increase sales, and maintain profits. One of their major expenses is the cost of labor. They reduce these costs through mechanization (inventing new machines capable of taking over more of the labor), de-skilling (simplifying the work process by breaking it down into its most basic steps so that minimal knowledge is required), and offshoring (finding labor in other parts of the world capable of doing the work for less money). It's not that capitalists are personally greedier than others or have a particular desire to exploit their workers; they act based on the principles inherent in the system. If they don't take these steps, competing capitalists will, threatening the very survival of the firm.

Marx argued that this downward pressure on workers' wages and working conditions is unrelenting. It ultimately leads to the development of a massive global working class of largely poor, unskilled workers competing against each other for low-wage jobs, resulting in racial, ethnic, and nationalistic conflict among the proletariat. Ironically, it is the technological innovation of capitalism that makes a better future possible. Marx praised this aspect of capitalism because it solves the problem of production like no other previous economic system. Capitalism, he writes, was "the first to show what man's activity can bring about. It has accomplished wonders far surpassing Egyptian pyramids, Roman aqueducts, and Gothic cathedrals" (Marx and Engels [1848] 1998:38). As a result, we no longer face inevitable scarcity. We can now produce enough so that no one in the world needs to go hungry.

Once this technological obstacle to providing for all our needs was solved, Marx felt that the only obstacle to an equitable society would be the capitalist system of social relations. Its emphasis on private property enabled the few at the top, the bourgeoisie, to own and control much more than they could ever hope to need or want while the majority at the bottom, the proletariat, struggled. Eventually, Marx argued, the proletariat would see that they had no real interest in the existing set of social relations. They would develop **class consciousness**—a subjective awareness of common vested interests and the need for collective political action to bring about social change. This would lead to the overthrow of capitalism in favor of a system of more equitable distribution in the form of socialism and then communism.

A question that often arises in response to Marx's work is this: Why hasn't that revolution happened? One answer is that Marx thought capitalists would work against the development of such class consciousness by shaping society's accepted values and norms. The term **dominant ideology** describes a set of cultural beliefs and practices that helps to maintain powerful social, economic, and political interests. Private property is a core principle of this ideology, but our failure to recognize the collective efforts that go into the production of any products and services contributes as well. For Marx, the bourgeoisie controlled not only material resources, but also the means of producing beliefs about reality through religion, education, and the media (Abercrombie, Hill, and Turner 1980, 1990; Marx [1845] 2000). As a result, workers had to overcome what Marx termed **false consciousness**—an attitude held by members of a class that does not accurately reflect their objective position. A worker with false consciousness may adopt an individualistic viewpoint toward capitalist exploitation ("*I* am being exploited by *my* boss"). In contrast, the class-conscious worker realizes that all workers are being exploited by the bourgeoisie and have a common stake in revolution.

Weber's Multidimensional Model

Unlike Marx, Max Weber insisted that class does not totally define a person's position within the stratification system. Instead, he identified three distinct components of stratification: class, status, and party (Weber [1916] 1958a). These three point to the importance of material, social, and organizational resources in shaping how much power people have.

Weber used the term **class** to refer to a group of people who have a similar level of

bourgeoisie Karl Marx's term for the capitalist class, comprising the owners of the means of production.

proletariat Karl Marx's term for the working class in a capitalist society who lack ownership of the means of production.

class consciousness In Karl Marx's view, a subjective awareness held by members of a class regarding their common vested interests and need for collective political action to bring about social change.

false consciousness A term used by Karl Marx to describe an attitude held by members of a class that does not accurately reflect their objective position.

class A group of people who have a similar level of economic resources.

capital is inherited. Parents teach their children linguistic patterns and cultural tastes, from the use of double negatives to the appreciation of literature (Rothstein 2009). Cultural capital is also reproduced in the next generation in the context of schools, where class distinctions within the community shape the curriculum and patterns of discipline. Jonathan Kozol (2005), who has studied educational inequality for years, told the story of an inner-city high school student who wanted to take an AP class in preparation for college but was placed in a sewing class instead. As a friend of hers put it, the factory owners need workers, and it won't be their kids: "You're ghetto—so you sew!" (p. 180). Such transmission increases the likelihood that social advantage will be passed from one generation to the next.

Social mobility from this perspective involves more than just acquiring more money and better social connections. Winning the lottery, for example, does not transform a person at the bottom of the hierarchy into one at the top, or, as Bourdieu put it, "Having a million does not in itself make one able to live like a millionaire" (1984:374). Such movement requires a social and cultural transformation as well. For mobility to happen, individuals must earn and learn a different set of knowledge and skills, as well as a whole new lifestyle: new tastes, attitudes, language, and thoughts.

Material, Social, and Cultural Resources Combining insights from these perspectives, we can point to three critical categories of resources that shape the positions we occupy and influence our likelihood for social mobility. Material resources refer to economic resources that we own or control, including money, property, and land. Social resources include prestige based on the position we occupy and connections based on the social networks we are a part of. It turns out that the old saying "It's not what you know; it's who you know" has some truth to it. Position and connections make it possible for us to increase the likelihood of accomplishing our goals. Finally, cultural resources include our tastes, language, and way of looking at the world. They represent our knowledge of cognitive, normative, and material elements of culture that we can draw on when acting to accomplish our goals. A simple but classic example involves knowing which fork to use for the various courses of a formal dinner. But it also includes knowing how to respond when we are put on the spot, whether in a business meeting, at a rock concert, or in class. Viewing social class in terms of material, social, and cultural resources makes social class a much more useful concept when trying to map our social lives or figure out why we think and act as we do.

All societies have some degree of stratification, and tracking these three resources helps us to better understand how stratification works. Even if we accept the

principle that a certain degree of inequality is inevitable, however, questions remain about the extent of inequality that is practiced. In addition, if inequality is to be tied to ability and effort, we need to investigate the degree to which positions are earned versus inherited. We turn next to an analysis of the degree of inequality that exists in the United States.

Did You Know?

...Swiss watchmaker Romain Julien produced a watch that doesn't tell the time; it only indicates whether it is day or night. Cost? $300,000. The company only produced nine and they sold out within 48 hours.

>> Social Class in the United States

Social class dividing lines in the United States are not as clear-cut or firm as they were historically in, say, England. When we take a step back, however, we see that social class differences do impact our everyday lives. We may not label them as such, and we might want to dismiss their significance. Nevertheless, looking through the lens of class as highlighted by these three resources brings to the surface differences that we already recognize as important.

CULTURAL CAPITAL

In some ways it is helpful to look first at cultural resources because, while we recognize that such differences exist, we may not recognize how significant they can be. If one person likes Chopin while another likes Kenny Chesney, what difference does that make? As indicated above, however, such tastes do not exist in isolation; rather, they are tied to social and material resources and can serve as a means of exclusion (Halle 1993; Wilson 2007). Looking at just a few examples, we can appreciate the degree to which we already see class, even if we don't usually identify it as such.

We can recognize class in the clothes we wear, and even in the terms we use to describe them, such as "business casual" or "blue collar." Some people would not be caught dead wearing a suit and tie (or maybe that's the only way they will wear them), whereas others are incapable of being comfortable in blue jeans and a T-shirt. And brands can matter, whether it's Lilly Pulitzer, Sean Jean, J. McLaughlin, Gap, Rocawear, H&M, Free People, Baby Phat, Juicy Couture, Wrangler, Calypso, Abercrombie & Fitch, Coach, or Gucci. Even the fabrics clothes are made of suggest class differences, with higher classes more likely to wear clothes made out of organic materials (such as wool, silk, or cotton) and lower classes more likely to wear synthetic fabrics (including nylon, rayon, and orlon). This is likely driven not only by the initial cost differences for such materials, but also by the long-term care costs for dry-cleaning.

SOCTHINK

Paul Fussell (1992), in his book *Class: A Guide Through the American Status System,* argued that the writing on our clothes says a lot about our social class. What story do the logos, brands, and writing on your clothes tell about you? How might your clothing choices have differed had you been in a different class position?

We also see class differences when it comes to houses. Just driving through neighborhoods, we recognize class indicators of houses: the distance they are located from the street; the composition of a driveway, if there is one; the fastidiousness of lawn care; the existence of flamingoes, gnomes, or gazing balls; and the presence of pillars or fountains. When it comes to where we live, expressions such as "the wrong side of the tracks," "snob hill," and "McMansion" point to our recognition that class matters.

Similarly, class makes a difference when it comes to vacations. Elites might head to Martha's Vineyard or the Hamptons, or they might "summer" in Nepal or Istanbul. Middle-class people are more likely to head to Disney World or perhaps go on a cruise, though either dream vacation may be possible only after having saved for some time or going into debt. Because money and vacation time are often limited, working-class families are more likely to go on a one-week trip, probably not too far from home, to which they are more likely to drive, and it might involve camping.

prestige The respect and admiration that an occupation holds in a society.

esteem The reputation that a specific person has earned within an occupation.

We could look at other areas too, including what we eat (fast food versus haute cuisine), what we drink (Bud Light versus fine wine), and what sports we watch (NASCAR and professional wrestling versus tennis and America's Cup yachting). In all kinds of ways, our preferences are shaped by our social class positions. Yet we seldom take seriously the source of such preferences or their effect on the choices we make and the doors that these choices may open or close to us.

STATUS AND PRESTIGE

We have a sense of where people fit relative to each other. Some we see as higher, while others we see as lower. We have seen as much already with regard to cultural preferences, but when it comes to status, it is not just what people like that we rank, but who they are. Sociologists seek to describe those systems of ranking and the advantages and disadvantages they convey.

Occupational Prestige One way sociologists describe the relative social class positions people occupy is by focusing on their occupational prestige. The term **prestige** refers to the respect and admiration that an occupation holds in a society. Fairly or not, "my daughter, the physicist" connotes something very different from "my daughter, the waitress." Prestige is independent of the particular individual who occupies a job, a characteristic that distinguishes it from esteem. **Esteem** refers to the reputation that a specific person has earned within an occupation. Therefore, we can say that the position of president of the United States has high prestige even though it has been occupied by people with varying degrees of esteem. A hairdresser may have the esteem of his clients, but he lacks the prestige of a corporate executive.

Using the results from a series of national surveys, sociologists have identified prestige rankings for more than 700 occupations. They created a scale with 0 as the lowest possible score and 100 as

Did You Know?

... According to Harris polls, the status of teachers has risen more than any other occupational category they have tracked over the past 30 years. In 2008, 51 percent of respondents identified teachers as having "very great prestige" compared with 29 percent in 1977.

Prestige Rankings of Occupations

Occupation	Score		Occupation	Score
Physician	86		Farmer	40
Lawyer	75		Correctional officer	40
College professor	74		Receptionist	39
Architect	73		Carpenter	39
Dentist	72		Barber	36
Psychologist	69		Child care worker	36
Clergy	69		Hotel clerk	32
Pharmacist	68		Bus driver	32
Registered nurse	66		Auto body repairer	31
High school teacher	66		Truck driver	30
Accountant	65		Salesworker (shoes)	28
Athlete	65		Garbage collector	28
Elementary school teacher	64		Waiter and waitress	28
Banker	63		Bartender	25
Veterinarian	62		Bill collector	24
Legislator	61		Farm worker	23
Airline pilot	61		Janitor	22
Police officer or detective	60		Maid	20
Actors and Directors	58		Newspaper vendor	19
Librarian	54		Car washer	19
Firefighter	53			
Social worker	52			
Dental hygienist	52			
Electrician	51			
Funeral director	49			
Farm manager	48			
Mail carrier	47			
Secretary	46			
Insurance agent	45			
Bank teller	43			
Nurse's aide	42			

Note: 100 is the highest and 0 the lowest possible prestige score.

Source: J. Davis, Smith, and Marsden 2007.

do confer status to people based on the positions they occupy. Someone with a higher status is more likely to get the benefit of the doubt because of the position she or he occupies, regardless of her or his individual characteristics, whereas the reverse is true for someone from a lower position.

Socioeconomic Status

As a single variable, occupation provides us with a sense of where people stand, but status involves more than just occupational prestige. In their research, sociologists add variables to the mix to gain a more complete picture of social class standing. These include such things as the value of homes, sources of income, assets, years in present occupations, neighborhoods, and considerations regarding dual careers. Adding these variables will not necessarily paint an alternative picture of class differentiation in the United States, but it does allow sociologists to measure class in a more complex and multidimensional way. When researchers use multiple measures, they typically speak of **socioeconomic status (SES),** a measure of social class that is based on income, education, occupation, and related variables.

One of the lessons we learn from SES research is that society often undervalues, in terms of prestige and pay, work that is essential for our individual and collective survival. In an effort to make the value of women's contribution to the economy more visible, for example, the International Women Count Network, a global grassroots feminist organization, has sought to give a monetary value to women's unpaid work. Besides providing symbolic recognition of women's contributions to society, it proposes that this value also be used to calculate pension and other benefits that are based on wages received. The United Nations has placed an $11-*trillion* price tag on unpaid labor by women, largely in child care, housework, and agriculture. In March 2009, in order to ensure the full integration of women into

the highest, and ranked the occupations based on the results of their surveys. Physician, lawyer, dentist, and college professor were among the most highly regarded occupations, whereas bartender, farmworker, janitor, maid, and car washer were near the bottom. Sociologists have found a significant amount of stability in such rankings from 1925 to the present (J. Davis, Smith, and Marsden 2007). This suggests that we not fully convey the income disparities in our society. We get some sense of income inequality by contrasting the median (middle) score with the mean (arithmetic average), which in 2008 was $68,424. The mean is so much higher because some people make a lot more money than others, which draws the mean up, making it a less useful statistic for describing "average" or typical income (DeNavas-Walt, Proctor, and Smith 2009).

socioeconomic status (SES) A measure of class that is based on income, education, occupation, and related variables.

income Wages and salaries measured over some period, such as per hour or year.

wealth The total of all a person's material assets, including savings, land, stocks, and other types of property, minus his or her debt at a single point in time.

We gain additional insight into this inequality by looking at the relative placement of households from bottom to top.

Mean Household Income by Quintile

$294,709

$171,057

$79,760

$50,132

$29,517

$11,655

| Lowest quintile | Second quintile | Middle quintile | Fourth quintile | Highest quintile | Top 5% |

Source: U.S. Census Bureau 2009i: Table H-3.

the formal economy and to have their economic contributions considered in policy making, the United Nations Commission on the Status of Women called on governments to incorporate the value of unpaid work in the household into policies and budgets.

INCOME AND WEALTH

Cultural capital and status provide a clearer picture of how we perceive social class, but income and wealth serve as its material foundation. **Income** refers to wages and salaries measured over some period, such as per hour or year. **Wealth** encompasses all of a person's material assets, including savings, land, stocks, and other types of property, minus his or her debts at a single point in time. If you were to sell everything you own and pay off all your debts, what you had left would be the value of your wealth. These material resources make our class-based lifestyles possible (Bourdieu 1986). As such, if we are to understand social class in the United States, we need a clear picture of their distribution.

Income Income inequality is a basic characteristic of a class system. In 2008, the median household income in the United States was $50,303, a decline of 3.6% from 2007. In other words, half of all households had higher incomes in that year, and half had lower incomes. But this fact does

The Income Pie: Percent Share of Total Income

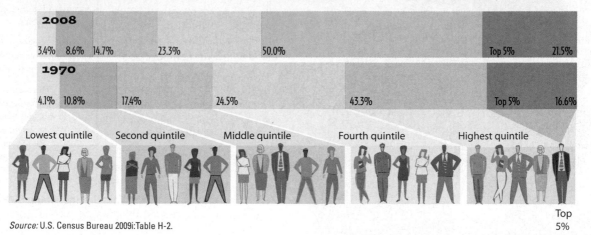

2008						
3.4%	8.6%	14.7%	23.3%	50.0%	Top 5%	21.5%

1970						
4.1%	10.8%	17.4%	24.5%	43.3%	Top 5%	16.6%

Lowest quintile Second quintile Middle quintile Fourth quintile Highest quintile

Top 5%

Source: U.S. Census Bureau 2009i:Table H-2.

One of the most common ways to present income dispersion is to line up all income-earning households from low to high and then break them into quintiles, or blocks of 20 percent. There are approximately 117 million households in the United States, so each quintile would include an equal number of about 23.4 million households. Doing so allows us to get a sense of what the average income is within each of these quintiles, along with the percentage of the total income pie that each quintile earns.

As we can see in the accompanying graphs, looking at the population in this way shows a significant degree of income inequality. Focusing on the extremes, the mean income for households in the lowest quintile is $11,656, while households in the top quintile average $171,057. Those households in the top 5 percent, the ones most responsible for bringing up the arithmetic mean, average $294,709. Those in the bottom quintile earn just 3.4 percent of the nation's total income, while those in the top quintile earn 50.0 percent. In fact, the top 5 percent earns a significantly greater percent of total income than the bottom 40 percent combined (DeNavas-Walt et al. 2009).

By all measures, income in the United States is distributed unevenly. The 14,988 families in the top 0.01 percent had average incomes of $35 million, and the top 400 taxpayers averaged $345 million, an increase of $80 million over the previous year. On the other end of the scale, almost 29 million households reported incomes under $15,000 (Internal Revenue Service 2009; Piketty and Saez 2009). Nobel Prize–winning economist Paul Samuelson described the situation in the following way: "If we made an income pyramid out of building blocks, with each layer portraying $500 of income, the peak would be far higher than Mount Everest, but most people would be within a few feet of the ground" (Samuelson and Nordhaus 2005:383).

Income inequality has increased steadily since 1970. Former Federal Reserve Board Chair Alan Greenspan was referring to this trend when he told Congress that the rising gap between the rich and the poor in the United States is a "very disturbing trend" that threatens democratic society (Greenspan 2005). Just how dramatic has this growth in inequality been? As the "Income Pie" chart shows, the share earned by each of the bottom quintiles has decreased since 1970, while the top quintile now earns almost one-half of total income. This represents the greatest degree of income inequality since before the Great Depression.

Americans do not appear to be seriously concerned about income and wealth inequality in the United States. In a comparison of opinions about social inequality in 27 different countries, respondents in the United States were less aware than those in other countries of the extent of inequality of the income distribution. Americans would prefer to "level down" the top of the nation's earning distribution, but compared to people in other countries, they are less concerned about reducing income differentials at the bottom of the distribution (Osberg and Smeeding 2006).

SOC THINK

Why do you think that most Americans do not seem to be aware of or concerned about the degree of income inequality in the United States? To what extent might it be due to the power of the American Dream, the influence of the media, or the working of the dominant ideology?

Wealth Wealth in the United States is much more unevenly distributed than income. The median wealth for families in 2007 was $120,300. Contrast this with the mean of $556,300 and, just as with income, we see significant inequality. Comparing the top end to the bottom, we get a sense of the scale of difference. On the low end, the bottom 25 percent of wealth-holding families had a median wealth of $1200 and mean wealth of –$2300, meaning that, on average, they owed more than they owned. The top 10 percent, on the other hand, had a median wealth of $1.9 million and a mean wealth of $4.0 million (Bucks et al. 2009:A11).

Percentage of Wealth Owned, by Percentile

Wealth owned

Percentile of population

Wealth owned	Percentile of population
33.8%	99–100th / 95–99th / 90–95th
26.6%	50–90th
11.1%	
26.0%	0–50th
2.5%	

Source: Kennickell 2009:35.

We can get a better sense of the degree of difference by looking at how total wealth is distributed. As the accompanying chart shows, the top 1 percent owns 33.8 percent of all wealth in the United States. By contrast, the bottom 50 percent owns just 2.5 percent. In fact, the top 1 percent owns more than the bottom 90 percent combined. The concentration of ownership is even more extreme when it comes to stocks, with the top 1 percent owning 51.9 percent of their total value, and business assets, of which they own 62.7 percent. In fact, the only place where the bottom 50 percent comes close to matching its share of wealth relative to its portion of the population is with debt. The bottom 50 percent owes 52.8 percent of all installment debt and 43.1 percent of outstanding credit card debt (Kennickell 2009).

Middle Class Struggles Even in an era of overall prosperity, those in the middle class often struggle just to make ends meet. Middle incomes have remained steady or even fallen over the past 40 years while the income shares of those in the top quintile, and especially the top 5 percent, increased substantially. Health care costs have risen dramatically, and the cost of a college education, a critical resource for social mobility, has gone up even faster. As a result of the recent economic downturn, many middle-class employees lost their jobs and the ripple effect led to increased bankruptcies and mortgage foreclosures. Whereas in the 1950s a single-income family could earn sufficient income to provide a middle-class lifestyle, most families now find they must rely on two incomes, an option not available for all families (Bucks et al. 2009; DeNavas-Walt et al. 2009c; Lewin 2008).

Sociologists and other scholars have identified several factors that have contributed to the struggles middle-class families face:

- *Disappearing opportunities for those with little education.* Today, increasing numbers of jobs require formal schooling, yet fewer than a third of adults aged 25–29 have a college degree.

- *Global competition and rapid advances in technology.* These two trends, which began several decades ago, have rendered workers more replaceable than they once were. Increasingly, these trends are affecting the more complex jobs that were once the bread and butter of middle-class life.

- *Growing dependence on the temporary workforce.* For those workers who have no other job, these positions are tenuous at best, because they rarely offer health care coverage or retirement benefits.

- *The rise of new-growth industries and nonunion workplaces.* In the past, workers in heavy industry were able to achieve middle-class incomes through the efforts of strong labor unions. But today, the growth areas in the economy are in service jobs and large retail outlets. Though these industries have added employment opportunities, they are often at the lower end of the wage scale.

In response to these concerns, observers note that living standards in the United States are improving. Middle-class families want large homes, college degrees for their children, and high-quality health care—the cost of which

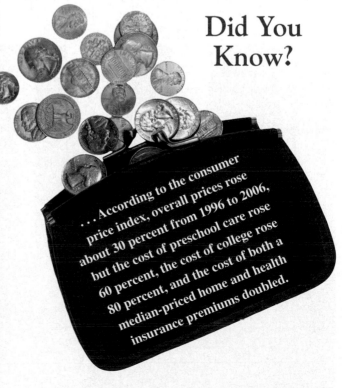

Did You Know?

...According to the consumer price index, overall prices rose about 30 percent from 1996 to 2006, but the cost of preschool care rose 60 percent, the cost of college rose 80 percent, and the cost of both a median-priced home and health insurance premiums doubled.

has been rising faster than inflation. Accomplishing these goals, however, has often meant becoming a dual-income family, working longer hours, or taking multiple jobs (Leonhardt 2007; Massey 2007).

POVERTY

In 2008, 39.8 million people in the United States—13.2 percent of the population—were living in poverty. Based on official calculations, a family consisting of two adults and two children with a combined annual income of $21,027 or less fell below the poverty line. By contrast, a single person under the age of 65 must earn less than $10,787 annually to be officially considered poor (DeNavas-Walt et al. 2009c).

Defining Poverty Such figures make it seem like a simple matter to define who is living in poverty: You are either above the threshold or below it. Sociologists have found, however, that our conceptions of poverty vary. For example, we can define poverty in either absolute or relative terms.

Absolute poverty refers to a minimum level of subsistence that no family should be expected to live below. According to this definition, someone who is below the poverty level ultimately lacks sufficient resources to survive. Many nations, including the United States, use this criterion as the basis of their definition of poverty. As we can see in the accompanying graph, a comparatively high proportion of children in U.S. households are poor, meaning that their families are unable to afford basic consumer goods (food, shelter, and clothing). This

> **absolute poverty** A minimum level of subsistence that no family should be expected to live below.

Going **GLOBAL**

The Poverty Rate in Households with Children, Selected Countries

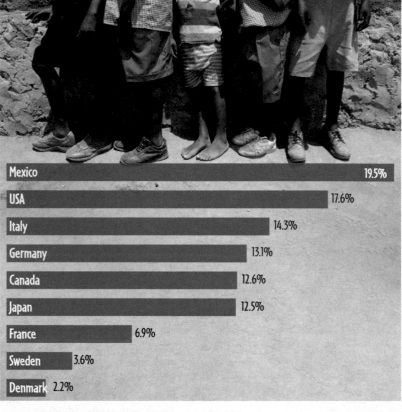

Country	Rate
Mexico	19.5%
USA	17.6%
Italy	14.3%
Germany	13.1%
Canada	12.6%
Japan	12.5%
France	6.9%
Sweden	3.6%
Denmark	2.2%

Source: OECD 2009:Table EQ3.2.

cross-national comparison actually understates the extent of poverty in the United States because U.S. residents are likely to pay more for housing, health care, child care, and education than residents of other countries, where such expenses are often subsidized.

In contrast, **relative poverty** is a floating standard of deprivation by which people at the bottom of a society, whatever their lifestyles, are judged to be disadvantaged in comparison with the nation as a whole. For example, people who have sufficient food, clothing, and shelter might nonetheless be considered poor if they live in a wealthy nation such as the United States, because they can't afford to buy things the culture defines as important but are not essential for survival. Similarly, someone who would be considered poor by U.S. standards would be well-off by global standards of poverty; hunger and starvation are daily realities in many regions of the world. In addition, when viewed in historical terms, someone currently defined as poor may be better-off in absolute terms than a poor person in the 1930s or 1960s.

The poverty line in the United States is calculated based on a formula established in 1964. President Lyndon B. Johnson had recently declared a War on Poverty, but at the time, no official measure of poverty existed. To enact an official measure, the Johnson administration turned to the work of Mollie Orshansky, a food economist at the research bureau of the Social Security Administration. Orshansky proposed combining two facts to establish a general

> ## Civilization is unbearable, but it is less unbearable at the top.
>
> ———————————
>
> **Timothy Leary**

poverty threshold. The first came from a study that found that families spend approximately one-third of their budget on food. The second was the estimated cost of a minimally nutritious diet established by U.S. Department of Agriculture dieticians. Orshansky combined these two pieces of information to establish the poverty threshold as three times the cost of the USDA diet. She assumed that families facing poverty would cut back on both food and nonfood expenditures at approximately the same rate so that the 3-to-1 ratio would hold (Fisher 1992, 2008; Orshansky 1965).

There has been a long-standing debate about whether this approach to defining poverty in the United States measures the true nature of poverty. For example, critics argue that the measure is too simplistic, or that the multiplier should be higher because families now spend one-fourth or one-fifth of their budget on food. Recognizing the limits of the official definition, the U.S. government will start calculating a supplemental measure of poverty in the fall of 2011. This more complex measure will take into account the actual costs of food, clothing, shelter, utilities, taxes, work expenses, and out-of-pocket medical costs. In addition to income, it will count food stamps and tax credits as available resources. And it will be adjusted to reflect price differences across geographic regions (U.S. Census Bureau 2010b).

relative poverty A floating standard of deprivation by which people at the bottom of a society, whatever their lifestyles, are judged to be disadvantaged in comparison with the nation as a whole.

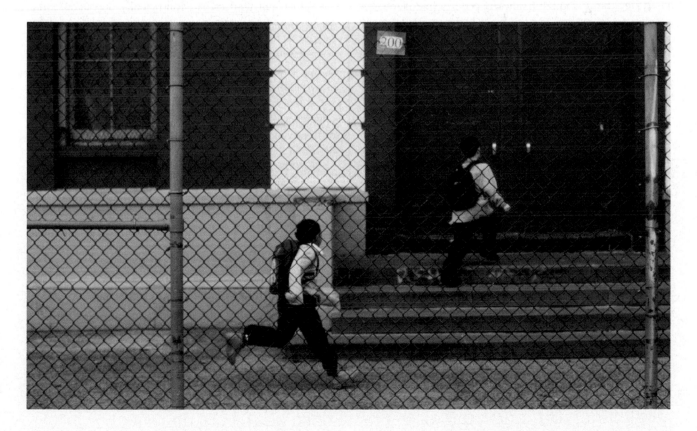

Who Are the Poor in the United States?

	Percentage of the population of the United States	Percentage of the poor of the United States
Age		
Under 18 years old	25	35
18 to 64 years old	63	55
65 years and older	13	9
Race/Ethnicity		
Whites (non-Hispanic)	65	43
Blacks	13	24
Hispanics	16	28
Asians and Pacific Islanders	4	4
Families		
Married couples	75	40
Female householder, no husband present	18	51
Male householder, no wife present	7	9

Note: Age and race ethnicity percents are based on total persons. Families percents are based on total families.

Source: DeNavas-Walt et al. 2009c.

Who Are the Poor? One of the lessons we learn by analyzing those who fall below the poverty line is that our stereotypes about poverty are flawed. For example, many people in the United States believe that the vast majority of the poor are able to work but will not. Yet, of the 39.8 million people in poverty, 45 percent are either under age 18 or 65 years old or older. Many working-age adults who are poor do work outside the home, although often in part-time positions. In 2008, about 10 percent of all poor adults worked full-time, compared to 44 percent of all adults. Of those poor adults who do not work, most are ill or disabled, or are occupied in maintaining a home. As we can see in the accompanying table, the likelihood of being in poverty is also shaped by factors such as age, race, ethnicity, and family type (DeNavas-Walt et al. 2009c; U.S. Census Bureau 2009g:Table Pov 24).

underclass The long-term poor who lack training and skills.

Since World War II, an increasing proportion of the poor people of the United States have been women, many of whom are divorced or never-married mothers. In 1959, female householders accounted for 23 percent of the nation's poor families; by 2008, that figure had risen to 51 percent. This alarming trend, known as the feminization of poverty, is evident not just in the United States but around the world (DeNavas-Walt et al. 2009c).

About half of all women living in poverty in the United States are in transition, coping with an economic crisis caused by the departure, disability, or death of a husband. The other half tend to be economically dependent either on the welfare system or on friends and relatives living nearby. A major factor in the feminization of poverty has been the increase in families with women as single heads of household. In 2008, 28.7 percent of families headed by single mothers lived in poverty, compared to 13.8 percent for single-father households and 5.5 percent for married couples. Contributing to such rates are factors such as the difficulty in finding affordable child care and sex discrimination in the labor market (DeNavas-Walt et al. 2009c).

In 2008, 43 percent of poor people in the United States were living in big cities. These urban residents are the focus of most governmental efforts to alleviate poverty. Yet, according to many observers, the plight of the urban poor is growing worse, owing to the devastating interplay of inadequate education and limited employment prospects. Traditional employment opportunities in the industrial sector are largely closed to the unskilled poor. Past and present discrimination heightens these problems for those low-income urban residents who are Black and Hispanic (DeNavas-Walt et al. 2009c).

Along with other social scientists, sociologist William Julius Wilson (1987, 1996, 2008, 2009), used the term **underclass** to describe the long-term poor who lack training and skills. According to an analysis of census data, 7.9 million people live in high-poverty neighborhoods.

About 30 percent of the population in these neighborhoods is Black, 29 percent Hispanic, and 24 percent White. In central cities, about 49 percent of the underclass is African American, 29 percent Hispanic, 17 percent White, and 5 percent "other" (Jargowsky and Yang 2006).

Analyses of people who are poor in general reveal that they are, however, not a static social class. The overall composition of the poor changes continually; some individuals and families move above the poverty level after a year or two, while others slip below it. Still, hundreds of thousands of people remain in poverty for many years at a time. African Americans and Latinos are more likely than Whites to be persistently poor. Over a 21-year period, 15 percent of African Americans and 10 percent of Latinos were persistently poor, compared to only 3 percent of Whites. Both Latinos and Blacks are less likely than Whites to leave the welfare rolls as a result of welfare reform (Mangum, Mangum, and Sum 2003).

In 1996, in a historic shift in federal policy, Congress passed the Personal Responsibility and Work Opportunity Reconciliation Act, ending the long-standing federal guarantee of assistance to every poor family that meets eligibility requirements. The law sets a lifetime limit of five years of welfare benefits and requires all able-bodied adults to work after receiving two years of benefits (although hardship exceptions are allowed). The federal government gives block grants to the states to use as they wish in assisting poor and needy residents, and it permits states to experiment with ways to move people off welfare.

SOC THINK

Should welfare recipients be required to work? If so, should the government subsidize preschool and afterschool care for their children while they are at work?

Other countries vary widely in their commitment to social service programs. But most industrialized nations devote higher proportions of their expenditures to housing, social security, welfare, health care, and unemployment compensation than the United States does. For example, in Cuba, 96 percent of health care expenditures are paid for by the government, compared to 82 percent in the United Kingdom and 70 percent in Canada. The U.S. government pays out 45 percent of expenditures, ranking close to Mexico and China (World Bank 2010a).

The issue of poverty is ultimately about more than just money. It is also tied to social and cultural resources. Poor

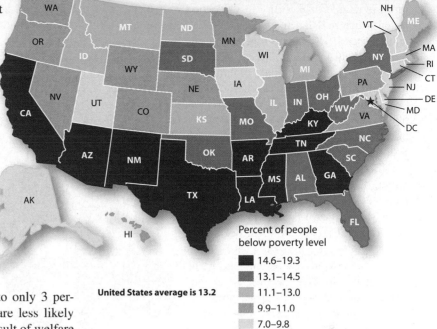

People Below Poverty Level

Percent of people below poverty level

- 14.6–19.3
- 13.1–14.5
- 11.1–13.0
- 9.9–11.0
- 7.0–9.8

United States average is 13.2

Source: U.S. Census Bureau 2009g:Table Pov46.

people often lack the social network connections to help them get good jobs, not to mention having to overcome the negative prestige associated with being poor. When it comes to cultural capital, they also often lack the same kind of educational credentials that can serve as a valuable cultural resource. Journalist David Shipler (2004), in his in-depth study titled *The Working Poor: Invisible in America*, referred to the combination of factors that poor people must overcome as the "interlocking deficits of poverty." As Shipler put it, "Breaking away and moving a comfortable distance from poverty seems to require a perfect lineup of favorable conditions. A set of skills, a good starting wage, and a job with the likelihood of promotion are prerequisites. But so are clarity of purpose, courageous self-esteem, a lack of substantial debt, freedom from mental illness or addiction, a functional family, a network of upstanding friends, and the right help from private or governmental agencies" (2004:4–5). To deal with poverty as a social problem, we must address all three of the major resource areas because mobility out of poverty is a difficult task. The truth is, however, most of us end up near where we start.

SOCIAL MOBILITY

The belief in upward mobility is an important value in the United States. As we saw above, social class systems are more open than other stratification systems, but this does not mean that the principle of opportunity necessarily matches the practice of mobility. For such mobility to be possible, ascribed statuses and inherited positions, along with the resources to which they provide access, should not play a significant role in shaping outcomes.

Occupational Mobility Two classic sociological studies conducted a decade apart offered insight into the degree of mobility in the nation's occupational structure (Blau and Duncan 1967; Featherman and Hauser 1978). Taken together, these investigations lead to several noteworthy conclusions. First, occupational mobility (both intergenerational and intragenerational) has been common among males. Approximately 60–70 percent of sons are employed in higher-ranked occupations than their fathers. Second, although there is a great deal of mobility in the United States, much of it is minor. That is, people who reach an occupational level above or below that of their parents usually advance or fall back only one or two out of a possible eight occupational levels. Thus, the child of a laborer may become an artisan or a technician, but he or she is less likely to become a manager or professional. The odds of reaching the top are extremely low unless one begins from a relatively privileged position.

Income and Wealth More recent studies focusing on income and wealth mobility show much the same results (Corak 2010). Mobility does occur, but most people do not move very far. In comparing father's and son's income, researchers found that sons of low-income fathers have almost a 60 percent chance of rising above the lowest quintile, but only a 22.5 percent chance of reaching the median and a 4.5 percent chance of breaking into the top quintile (Mishel, Bernstein, and Shierholz 2009). Similarly, as we can see in the accompanying graph, when looking at wealth, 36 percent of children with parents in the lowest quintile end up there themselves while only 7 percent make it to the top quintile. On the other end of the scale, 36 percent of children with parents in the top wealth quintile stay there while only

11 percent drop down into the bottom quintile (Haskins 2008:8). In fact, the likelihood of ending up in the same position as your parents has been rising since about 1980 (Aaronson and Mazumder 2007).

Education Studies also conclude that education plays a critical role in mobility. The impact of formal schooling on adult status is even greater than that of family background (although, as we have seen, family background influences the likelihood that one will receive higher education). Furthermore, education represents an important means of intergenerational mobility. A person who was born into a poor family but who graduates from college has a one in five chance of entering the top quintile of all income earners as an adult (Isaacs et al. 2008).

Education is a critical factor in the development of cultural capital. As such, access to higher education plays an important role in social mobility. In 2007, 58 percent of high school students in the lowest income quintile enrolled in college the following fall compared to 78 percent of those from the highest quintile (Planty et al. 2009). For students from families with the lowest incomes, the cost can be prohibitive. Only 11 percent of children from the poorest families in the United States have earned college degrees, compared to 53 percent of children from the top fifth of the population. Those moderate-income students who do graduate, and even those who fail to complete their degrees, are often saddled with heavy postgraduate debt (Isaacs et al. 2008).

Did You Know?

...Although 67 percent of families make more money than their parents, only half of those earn enough to jump them into the next income quintile.

─**SOC**THINK─

The percentage of financial aid in the form of grants has gone down while the percentage of loan aid has increased. Why do you think that has occurred? What are the consequences of such a shift for social mobility?

The impact of education on mobility has diminished somewhat over the past decade. An undergraduate degree—a BA or BS—serves less as a guarantee of upward mobility now than it did in the past, simply because more and more entrants into the job market hold such a degree. Moreover, intergenerational mobility is declining because there is no longer such a stark difference between generations. In earlier decades, many high school–educated parents managed to send their children to college, but today's college students are increasingly likely to have college-educated parents (Economic Mobility Project 2007).

Child wealth quintile

■ Top
■ Fourth
■ Middle
■ Second
■ Bottom

Source: Haskins 2008.

Chart labels:

Child wealth quintile bars by Parental wealth quintile:

Bottom quintile: 7%, 12%, 16%, 29%, 36%
Second quintile: 12%, 15%, 24%, 24%, 26%
Middle quintile: 15%, 24%, 25%, 21%, 16%
Fourth quintile: 26%, 26%, 20%, 13%, 15%
Top quintile: 36%, 24%, 14%, 16%, 11%

Parental wealth quintile

Wealth Mobility: Percentage of Children in Each Wealth Quintile Compared to Parental Wealth Quintile

Race and Ethnicity Sociologists have long documented the fact that the class system is more rigid for African Americans than it is for members of other racial groups. Black men who have good jobs, for example, are less likely than White men to see their adult children attain the same status. The cumulative disadvantage of discrimination plays a significant role in the disparity between the two groups' experiences. Compared to White households, the relatively modest wealth of African American households means that adult Black children are less likely than adult White children to receive financial support from their parents. Indeed, young Black couples are much more likely than young White couples to be assisting their parents—a sacrifice that hampers their social mobility (Isaacs 2007c).

The African American middle class has grown over the past few decades due to economic expansion and the benefits of the civil rights movement of the 1960s. Yet many of these middle-class households have little savings, a fact that puts them in danger during times of crisis. Studies have consistently shown that downward mobility is significantly higher for Blacks than it is for Whites (Isaacs 2007c; Oliver and Shapiro 1995).

The Latino population is not doing much better. The typical Hispanic has less than 10 percent of the wealth that a White person enjoys. A 2004 study suggests that in recent years Latinos have even lost ground. Their continuing immigration accounts for part of the disparity: Most of the new arrivals are destitute. But even the wealthiest 5 percent of Latino households have only a third as much net worth as the top 5 percent of White households (Bucks et al. 2009; Kochhar 2004).

Gender Studies of mobility, even more than those of class, have traditionally ignored the significance of gender, but some research findings are now available that explore the relationship between gender and mobility. Women's employment opportunities are much more limited than

men's. Moreover, according to recent research, women whose skills far exceed the jobs offered them are more likely than men to withdraw entirely from the paid labor force. Their withdrawal violates an assumption common to traditional mobility studies: that most people will aspire to upward mobility and seek to make the most of their opportunities.

In contrast to men, women have a rather large range of clerical occupations open to them. But the modest salary ranges and limited prospects for advancement in many of these positions reduce the possibility of upward mobility. Self-employment as shopkeepers, entrepreneurs, independent professionals, and the like—an important road to upward mobility for men—is more difficult for women, who find it harder to secure the necessary financing. Although sons commonly follow in the footsteps of their fathers, women are less likely to move into their fathers' positions. Consequently, gender remains an important factor in shaping social mobility. Women in the United States (and in other parts of the world) are especially likely to be trapped in poverty, unable to rise out of their low-income status (Heilman 2001).

> **life chances** The opportunities people have to provide themselves with material goods, positive living conditions, and favorable life experiences.

On the positive side, although today's women lag behind men in employment, their earnings have increased faster than their mothers' did at a comparable age so that their incomes are substantially higher. The one glaring exception to this trend involves the daughters of low-income parents. Because these women typically care for children—many as single parents—and sometimes for other relatives as well, their mobility is severely restricted (Isaacs 2007b).

>> Life Chances

One of the lessons we learn from sociology is that class matters. Max Weber saw class as being closely related to people's **life chances**—that is, their opportunities to provide themselves with material goods, positive living conditions, and favorable life experiences (Weber [1916] 1958a). Life chances are reflected in measures such as housing, education, and health. Occupying a higher position in a society improves individuals' life chances and brings greater access to social rewards. In contrast, people in the lower social classes are forced to devote a larger proportion of their limited resources to the necessities of life.

In fact, our very survival can be at stake. When the supposedly unsinkable British ocean liner *Titanic* hit an iceberg in 1912, it was not carrying enough lifeboats to accommodate all passengers. Plans had been made to evacuate only first- and second-class passengers. About 62 percent of the first-class passengers survived the disaster. Despite a rule that women and children would go first, about a third of those passengers were male. In contrast, only 25 percent of the passengers in third class survived. The first attempt to alert them to the need to abandon ship came well after other passengers had been notified (D. A. Butler 1998; Crouse 1999).

Class position also affects people's vulnerability to natural disasters. When Hurricane Katrina hit the Gulf Coast of the United States in 2005, affluent and poor people alike became its victims. However, poor people who did not own automobiles (100,000 of them in New Orleans alone) were less able than others to evacuate in advance of the storm. Those who survived its fury had no nest egg to draw on, and thus were more likely than others to accept relocation wherever social service agencies could place them—sometimes hundreds or even thousands of

digital divide The relative lack of access to the latest technologies among low-income groups, racial and ethnic minorities, rural residents, and the citizens of developing countries.

Education Pays: Full-Time, Year-Round Workers, Ages 25–64

Education level	Median annual earnings
Professional degree	$100,000
Doctorate degree	$91,720
Master's degree	$67,180
Bachelor's degree	$55,729
Associate's degree	$42,040
Some college, no degree	$39,660
High school grad (includes GED)	$33,809
Some high school, no degree	$25,689

Source: U.S. Census Bureau 2009f:Part 28.

miles from home (Department of Homeland Security 2006; Fussell 2006).

Some people have hoped that the Internet revolution would help to level the playing field by making information and markets uniformly available. Unfortunately, however, not everyone can get onto the information superhighway, so yet another aspect of social inequality has emerged—the **digital divide.** The poor, minorities, and those who live in rural communities and inner cities are not getting connected at home or at work. For example, 63 percent of households in the United States have broadband Internet access from home, but Internet access varies significantly by income. Only 35 percent of households making $20,000 or less have broadband access, compared to 88 percent of those with incomes of more than $100,000. Among the 7 percent of households still using dial-up, 25 percent make less than $30,000 per year; cost was cited as the most significant reason for not upgrading to broadband. And, finally, of people who identified themselves as non–Internet users two-thirds made less than $30,000 per year (Horrigan 2009).

Wealth, status, and power may not ensure happiness, but they certainly provide additional ways of coping with problems and disappointments. For this reason, the opportunity for advancement—for social mobility—is of special significance to those at the bottom of society. People with limited resources want the chance to attain the rewards and privileges that are granted to high-ranking members of a culture.

If we are to better understand why we think and act the way we do, we must consider the impact of social class. The positions we occupy shape our access

What factors have shaped your life chances? What kinds of resources have you inherited from others? What resources might you have lacked access to?

to material, social, and cultural resources, which in turn shapes our future positions. In the United States, part of the American Dream is that anyone who is willing to work hard can get ahead. The principle of meritocracy—that we earn our positions—is at the heart of that faith, which represents a rejection of aristocracy in which positions are inherited. Class patterns in the United States call into question the degree to which principle and practice meet.

. . . Researchers found that, by the age of three, children whose parents have professional jobs have heard 500,000 instances of praise and 80,000 of disapproval. In families receiving welfare, the ratio reverses; children have been praised 75,000 times and reprimanded 200,000 times.

Did You Know?

Source: Hart and Risley 1995.

Calculate! Figure out what it takes to get by in your community using the Basic Family Budget Calculator at the Economic Policy Institute website: www.epi.org/content.cfm/datazone_fambud_budget. Contrast that amount with the official poverty line. Compare your results with those from other communities.

get **Involved!**

For
REVIEW

I. **What is social class?**
- Like slavery, caste, and estate, it is a stratification system in which people and groups are ranked, but it places them based primarily on economic position.

II. **How does social class operate?**
- Three categories of resources are key: material, including income and wealth; social, including social networks and prestige; and, cultural, including tastes, education, and knowledge. Power is based on access to and control over these resources.

III. **What are the consequences of social class?**
- While class-based systems are more open than the others, our life chances are shaped by our inherited class position and the material, social, and cultural resources that go with it. For most people, the social mobility that does occur, whether in terms of occupation, income, or wealth, is of a relatively short distance.

Functionalist View

All societies have some degree of stratification in order to ensure that all of society's needs are met.

In a society with a complex **division of labor,** some positions will inevitably be more important or require more skill than others.

Those with more talent and determination fill the higher-paid and more prestigious positions, whereas those who do not develop their talents take the low-ranking jobs.

DIVISION OF LABOR, SOCIAL MOBILITY
KEY CONCEPTS

Conflict View

Stratification systems perpetuate unequal economic rewards and facilitate exploitation.

Social class standing is largely an **ascribed status.**

People in power maintain and spread their interests and influence through their hold on the **dominant ideology** in a society.

Income and wealth are **distributed unequally** in U.S. society, and the gap between the rich and the poor is steadily increasing.

STRATIFICATION, INEQUALITY, DOMINANT IDEOLOGY
KEY CONCEPTS

Interactionist View

Social mobility results from interactions in which people attempt to better their place in the class system (for example, getting degrees, **networking,** acquiring cultural capital).

When we interact with others, we **exchange** our cultural capital resources, such as knowledge, tastes, attitudes, and ways of thinking.

Our social class helps determine our taste in clothes, food, music, TV shows, and many other everyday preferences.

NETWORKING, EXCHANGE
KEY CONCEPTS

MAKE THE CONNECTION

After reviewing the chapter, answer the following questions:

1

Analyze social mobility from the point of view of the three perspectives (pp. 253–255). In what way might mobility be functional? How would conflict theory explain it? What role does interaction play?

2

How do the conflict and the interactionist perspectives intersect in Marx's concept of "false consciousness" (p. 241)?

3

How would a theorist from each perspective explain the distribution of material, social, and cultural resources in society?

4

Think about your own "life chances" (p. 255). Which perspective(s) helps you to see factors that shaped your opportunities and outcomes?

Pop Quiz

1. Social inequality refers to
   a. the structured ranking of entire groups of people that perpetuates unequal economic rewards and power in a society.
   b. social ranking based primarily on economic position.
   c. the positive or negative reputation an individual has in the eyes of others.
   d. a condition in which members of society have different amounts of wealth, prestige, or power.

2. The stratification system in which hereditary ranks are usually religiously dictated is the
   a. class system.
   b. estate system.
   c. caste system.
   d. slave system.

3. A plumber whose father was a physician is an example of
   a. downward intergenerational mobility.
   b. upward intergenerational mobility.
   c. downward intragenerational mobility.
   d. upward intragenerational mobility.

4. According to Karl Marx, the class that owns the means of production is the
   a. nobility.
   b. proletariat.
   c. Brahman.
   d. bourgeoisie.

5. Which of the following were viewed by Max Weber as distinct components of stratification?
   a. conformity, deviance, and social control
   b. class, status, and party
   c. class, caste, and age
   d. class, prestige, and esteem

6. According to Pierre Bourdieu, our tastes, our education, the way we talk, and the things we like all represent forms of
   a. social capital.
   b. esteem.
   c. cultural capital.
   d. intelligence.

7. The term sociologists use to describe multiple measures of social position including income, education, and occupation is
   a. prestige.
   b. esteem.
   c. socioeconomic status.
   d. ranking.

8. Approximately how much wealth does the top 1 percent of families own in the United States?
   a. 20 percent
   b. 33 percent
   c. 50 percent
   d. 80 percent

9. Approximately what percentage of the U.S. population lived in poverty in 2008?
   a. 2.1 percent
   b. 8.6 percent
   c. 13.2 percent
   d. 19.4 percent

10. What term do sociologists use to describe the opportunities people have to provide themselves with material goods, positive living conditions, and favorable life experiences?
    a. esteem
    b. wealth
    c. social mobility
    d. life chances

1. (d); 2. (c); 3. (a); 4. (d); 5. (b); 6. (c); 7. (c); 8. (b); 9. (c); 10. (d)

11

GLOBAL INEQ

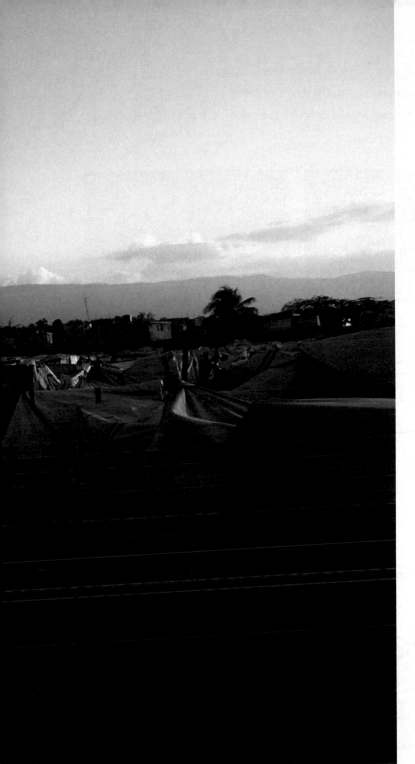

STRUGGLING TO SURVIVE IN A WORLD OF PLENTY

In spring of 2008, riots broke out in countries around the world in response to a global food crisis. From sub-Saharan African nations to countries including Egypt, India, and Yemen, people took to the streets in response to skyrocketing prices and food shortages. Hit hardest by the effects of this crisis were people in the poorest countries, where the margin between survival and starvation is razor-thin.

In Haiti, even before the January 2010 earthquake, three-quarters of the population lived on less than $2 a day. Like many others, Georges Jean Wesner gets up every day at 4:00 A.M. to walk two hours to get two small pails of rice and beans from a charity food kitchen—his only available source of food for his family. There are no jobs to earn a living. People have even turned to eating patties made of mud, oil, and sugar, about which Olwich Louis Jeune, 24, says, "It's salty and it has butter, and you don't know you're eating dirt. . . . It makes your stomach quiet down" (Lacey 2008; Williams 2008). Since the earthquake, despite large-scale charitable efforts, Haitians continue to struggle for survival.

In the Darfur region of Sudan, Khamisa Tafaela worried because her 10-month-old son was vomiting and suffering from diarrhea. She had already lost one son who had the same symptoms. She, along with her husband and their five children, had been living in a camp in West Darfur for more than four years with thousands of others forced from their homes in Sudan. For the second month in a row, she had been living on halved food rations, not because there was insufficient food, but because it was too dangerous to get the food from the warehouses to the camps (*Sudan Tribune* 2008).

We see in this Darfur story that the food crisis may be due not only to insufficient food, but also to insufficient access to food. Dominique Strauss-Kahn, the managing director of the International Monetary Fund, says, "There is enough food to feed the world . . . the problem is that prices have risen and many people cannot afford food. So we need to get food—or the money to buy food—to those most in need" (IMF 2008). In other words, we produce enough globally so that everyone can have enough, but we do not allocate resources in such a way that people now facing starvation can gain access to the food they need to survive.

UALITY

As You READ >>

- How did the global divide develop?
- How significant is global stratification?
- Why did the global movement for universal human rights develop?

>> The Global Divide

When it comes to resources, the global divide is immense. Millions of people struggle on the very edge of survival even as others around the world lead lives of relative comfort and leisure. A few centuries ago, most people were poor. There was a significant divide between the few who were extremely wealthy and the many who lacked significant resources, with little concept of a middle class between the nobility and the peasants. In much of Europe, life was as difficult as it was in Asia or South America. This was true until the Industrial Revolution and increased agricultural productivity resulted in explosive economic growth. However, the ensuing rise in living standards was not evenly distributed across the world.

We get a glimpse of the relative share of resources, and their consequences, by looking at splits between developing and industrial nations. For example, the likelihood of dealing with the death of a child or the burden of disease is much greater for those in developing nations. At the same time, the industrial nations of the world, with a much smaller share of the total population, have much higher incomes and many more exports than the developing nations. People in industrial nations also receive better health care and have greater security due to what those nations spend on health care and the military (Sachs 2005a; Sutcliffe 2002). As we will see, the divide within countries in terms of income, wealth, poverty, and social mobility is also significant.

Average income varies significantly across the nations of the world along a continuum from those that are the richest in natural resources to those that are the poorest. The contrast between those at the top and those at the bottom is stark. For example, in 2008, per capita gross

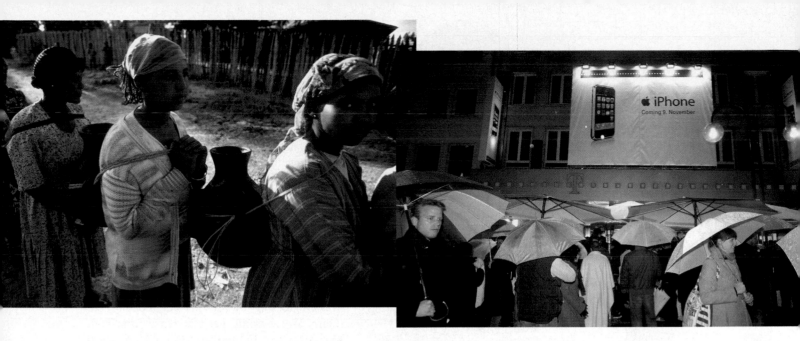

Before you finish eating breakfast in the morning, you've depended on more than half of the world.

Martin Luther King Jr.

Gross National Income per Capita

Gross National Income per capita 2008
Calculated using purchasing power parity in international dollars

- Low income ($975 or less)
- Lower middle income ($976–$3,855)
- Upper middle income ($3,856–$11,905)
- High income ($11,906 or more)
- Data not available

Note: 2008 data with a few exceptions from 2007.
Source: World Bank 2010b.

	Developing nations		Industrial nations
Deaths of children	99%	1%	
Rural population	94%	6%	
Total births	94%	6%	
The burden of disease	93%	7%	
TOTAL POPULATION	85%	15%	
Cultivated land	74%	26%	
Urban population	73%	27%	
Income	46%	54%	
CO$_2$ emissions	36%	64%	
Health spending	24%	76%	
Exports	22%	78%	
Military spending	12%	88%	

Note: In this comparison, industrial nations include the United States and Canada, Japan, western Europe, and Australasia. Developing nations include Africa, Asia (except Japan), Latin America, eastern Europe, the Caribbean, and the Pacific.

Source: Adapted from Sutcliffe 2002:18.

national income (the total value of goods and services produced per citizen) in the industrialized countries of the United States, Canada, Switzerland, France, and Norway was more than $40,000. By comparison, more than 20 countries, including Malawi, Ethiopia, Nepal, Rwanda, and Afghanistan, had a per capita gross national income of $900 or less (World Bank 2010b).

>> Perspectives on Global Stratification

Theorists have taken a step back to look at this global system from a top-down, macro perspective. In so doing, they provide us with insights into how the world system developed and how the various parts fit together.

We will focus on three areas of analysis: the rise of modernization, the legacy of colonialism, and the growth of multinational corporations.

THE RISE OF MODERNIZATION

Early sociologists often assumed that society was progressing toward some common positive future. We certainly get that sense from both Karl Marx and Émile Durkheim, who believed that societies would all inevitably evolve along a similar path, ending up in some shared version of the good society. For Durkheim this meant a natural balance between interdependence and individual freedom; for Marx it meant some form of socialism. Max Weber was not as hopeful, though he believed that all societies would move toward a rational-legal form of authority.

SOCTHINK

Early sociologists were optimistic that positive social change was inevitable. To what extent do you think people today share this vision of the inevitable rise of the good society? How might cynicism about the possibility for change contribute to the maintenance of the status quo?

This notion that the present was superior to the past, with its petty tyrannies and irrational superstitions, and that the future would unite us all, shaped how people viewed the world throughout much of the 20th century. Many people supposed that, through **modernization,** nations would move from traditional forms of social organization toward forms characteristic of post–Industrial Revolution societies. Features of the latter include a complex division of labor in which work is specialized; the separation of institutions including family, economy, government, education, and religion into specialized spheres, each with their own experts; the decline of the local and the rise of a societal or global orientation; the rise of rational decision making in the public sphere and a corresponding decline in public religious authority; and the spread of both cultural diversity, as more peoples from different backgrounds come into contact with each other, and a corresponding growth in

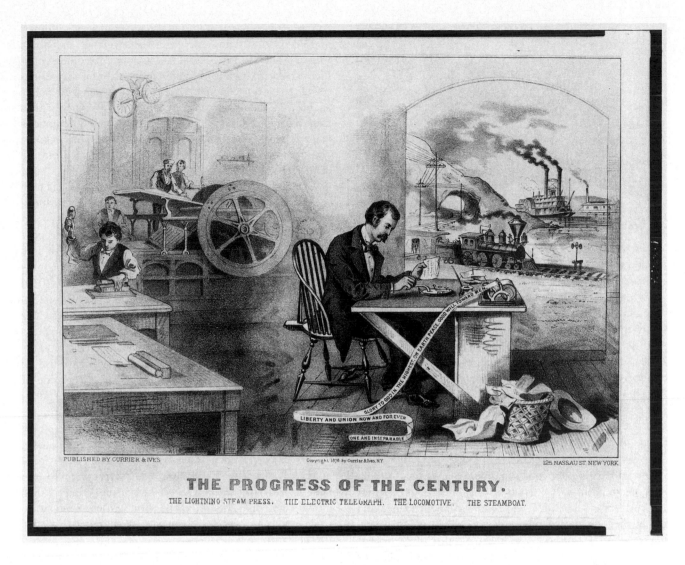

THE PROGRESS OF THE CENTURY.
THE LIGHTNING STEAM PRESS.   THE ELECTRIC TELEGRAPH.   THE LOCOMOTIVE.   THE STEAMBOAT.

egalitarianism as a value that embraces such diversity (Bruce 2000).

From this modernization perspective, countries such as China and India are in the process of becoming modern societies. Even if the transition from traditional to modern is difficult for many, the presupposition is that their people will benefit in the long term. According to these theorists, just as many people in the United States and Europe experienced displacement and poverty in the early years of the Industrial Revolution, only later to lead more comfortable lives, the same future awaits people in developing nations.

Many sociologists today are quick to note that terms such as *modernization* and even *development* contain an ethnocentric bias. There is an implicit sense in this model that people in such nations are more "primitive" and that modern Western culture is more advanced, more "civilized." The unstated assumption is that what "they" (people living in developing countries) really want is to become more like "us" (people in modern industrialized nations). According to this vision, they want both our economic development and our cultural values including democracy, freedom, and consumerism. Such modernization, then, represents a form of cultural imperialism. Many groups around the world reject this path, viewing such "development" as an attack on their way of life including their core values and norms.

THE LEGACY OF COLONIALISM

An alternative perspective to modernization focuses on colonialism as a model for better understanding the expansion of our interconnected world. **Colonialism** occurs when a foreign power maintains political, social, economic, and cultural domination over a people for an extended period. In simple terms, it is rule by outsiders. The long reign of the British Empire over much of North America, parts of Africa, and India is an example of colonial domination. The same can be said of French rule over Algeria, Tunisia, and other parts of North Africa. Relations between the colonial nation and the colonized people are similar to those between the dominant capitalist class and the proletariat, as described by Marx.

> **modernization** The far-reaching process by which nations pass from traditional forms of social organization toward those characteristic of post–Industrial Revolution societies.
>
> **colonialism** The maintenance of political, social, economic, and cultural dominance over a people by a foreign power for an extended period.

When it comes to U.S. media portrayals of people from around the world, we frequently see negative stereotypes reinforced, perpetuating a sense of U.S. cultural superiority. In an analysis of more than 1000 films, communications professor Jack Shaheen (2006, 2009) found that only 5 percent of Arab and Muslim characters were presented in a positive light. Arabs were repeatedly caricatured as villains, buffoons, lechers, incompetents, and terrorists. For example, Shaheen argues that Disney's *Aladdin* recycles Arab stereotypes, describing the fictional city of Agrabah as barbaric but home. The good news, he said, is that positive representations have risen to about 30 percent, thanks to films such as *Syriana* and *Babel*.

By the 1980s, such global political empires had largely disappeared. Most of the nations that were colonies prior to World War I had achieved political independence and established their own governments. However, for many of these countries, the transition to genuine self-rule was not yet complete. Colonial domination had established patterns of economic exploitation that continued even after nationhood was achieved—in part because the former colonies were unable to develop their own industry and technology. Their dependence on more industrialized nations, including their former colonial masters, for managerial and technical expertise, investment capital, and manufactured goods kept the former colonies in a subservient position. Such continuing dependence and foreign domination are referred to as **neocolonialism.**

neocolonialism Continuing dependence of former colonies on foreign countries.

world systems analysis A view of the global economic system as one divided between certain industrialized nations that control wealth and developing countries that are controlled and exploited.

dependency theory An approach contending that industrialized nations continue to exploit developing countries for their own gain.

Sociologist Immanuel Wallerstein (2000, 2004, 2010) views the global economic system as being divided between nations that control wealth and nations from which resources are taken. Through his **world systems analysis,** Wallerstein has described the unequal economic and political relationships in which certain industrialized nations (among them the United States, Japan, and Germany) and their global corporations dominate the core of this system.

At the semiperiphery of the system are countries with marginal economic status, such as Israel, Ireland, and South Korea. Wallerstein suggests that the poor developing countries of Asia, Africa, and Latin America are on the periphery of the world economic system. The key to Wallerstein's analysis is the exploitative relationship of core nations toward noncore nations. Core nations and their corporations control and exploit noncore nations' economies. Unlike other nations, they are relatively independent of outside control (Hardt and Negri 2009).

The division between core and periphery nations is both significant and remarkably stable. A study by the International Monetary Fund (2000) found little change over the past century for the 42 economies studied. The only changes were Japan's movement up into the group of core nations and China's movement down toward the margins of the semiperiphery nations. Yet Wallerstein (2000, 2010) speculates that the world system as we currently understand it may soon undergo unpredictable changes. The world is becoming increasingly urbanized, a trend that is gradually eliminating the large pools of low-cost workers in rural areas. In the future, core nations will have to find other ways to reduce their labor costs. The exhaustion of land and water resources through clear-cutting and pollution is also driving up the costs of production.

Wallerstein's world systems analysis is the most widely used version of **dependency theory.** According to this theory, even as developing countries make economic advances, they remain weak and subservient to core nations and corporations in an increasingly intertwined global economy. This interdependency allows industrialized nations to continue to exploit developing countries for their own gain.

World Systems Analysis at the Beginning of the 21st Century

Core	Semiperiphery	Periphery
Canada	China	Afghanistan
France	India	Bolivia
Germany	Ireland	Chad
Japan	Mexico	Dominican Republic
United Kingdom	Pakistan	Egypt
United States	Panama	Haiti
		Philippines
		Vietnam

Note: Figure shows only a partial listing of countries.

SOCstudies

Big Mac Index

Global average

City	Minutes
Nairobi	
Jakarta	
Mexico City	
Budapest	
São Paulo	
Singapore	
Doha	
Shanghai	
Rome	
Johannesburg	
Moscow	
Paris	
Sydney	
Frankfurt	
New York	
London	
Toronto	
Tokyo	
Chicago	

Minutes (0, 20, 40, 60, 80, 100, 120, 140, 160)

Note: Number of minutes it takes a worker with an average net wage to earn sufficient income to purchase a Big Mac, March 2009.

Sources: http://www.economist.com/daily/chartgallery/displayStory.cfm?story_id=14288808 and http://boingboing.net/2009/08/21/how-many-minutes-do.html.

According to world systems analysis and dependency theory, a growing share of the human and natural resources of developing countries is being redistributed to the core industrialized nations. This redistribution happens in part because developing countries owe huge sums of money to industrialized nations as a result of foreign aid, loans, and trade deficits. The global debt crisis has intensified the Third World dependency rooted in colonialism, neocolonialism, and multinational investment. International financial institutions are pressuring indebted countries to take severe measures to meet their interest payments. The result is that developing nations may be forced to devalue their currencies, freeze workers' wages, increase privatization of industry, and reduce government services and employment.

These trends are part of the larger process of **globalization**—the worldwide integration of government policies, cultures, social movements, and financial markets through trade and the exchange of ideas. Because the forces of world financial markets transcend governance by conventional nation-states, international organizations such as the World Bank and the International Monetary Fund have emerged as major players in the global economy. The function of these institutions, which are heavily funded and influenced by core nations, is to encourage trade and development and to ensure the smooth operation of international financial markets. As such, they are seen as promoters of globalization and defenders primarily of the interests of core nations. Critics call attention to a variety of related issues, including violations of workers' rights, the destruction of the environment, the loss of cultural identity, and discrimination against minority groups in periphery nations.

THE GROWTH OF MULTINATIONAL CORPORATIONS

Worldwide, corporate giants have played a key role in the rise of globalization. The term **multinational corporations** refers to commercial organizations that are headquartered in one country but do business around the world. Such private trade and lending relationships are not new; merchants have conducted business abroad for hundreds of years, trading gems, spices, garments, and other goods. Today's multinational giants are not merely buying and selling overseas; they are also producing goods all over the world (Wallerstein 1974, 2004). Through deindustrialization, corporate executives also have relocated production jobs around the globe.

Increasingly, it is not just production jobs that are being relocated. Today's global factories may now have the "global office" alongside them. Multinationals based in core nations are beginning to establish reservation services and centers for processing data and insurance claims in the periphery nations. As service industries become a more important part of the international marketplace, many companies are concluding that the low costs of overseas operations more than offset the expense of transmitting information around the world.

> **multinational corporation**
> A commercial organization that is headquartered in one country but does business throughout the world.

SOCTHINK

How has the rise of multinational corporations and the trend toward globalization affected you, your family, and your community, both positively and negatively?

These multinational corporations are huge, with total revenues on a par with the total value of goods and services exchanged in entire nations. Foreign sales represent an important source of profit for multinational corporations, encouraging them to expand into other countries (in many cases, the developing nations). The U.S. economy is heavily dependent on foreign commerce, much of which is conducted by multinationals. More than one-fourth of all goods

Going GLOBAL

Multinational Corporations Compared to Nations

Rank	Corporate revenue / Gross domestic product	Millions of dollars	
1		$458,361	Royal Dutch Shell
23		468,800	Saudi Arabia
2		$442,851	Exxon Mobil
24		451,830	Norway
3		$405,607	Wal-Mart Stores
25		413,503	Austria
4		$367,053	BP
26		355,876	Greece
5		$263,159	Chevron
34		267,576	Ireland
6		$234,674	Total
35		243,765	Colombia
7		$230,764	Conoco Phillips
36		243,497	Portugal
8		$226,577	ING Group
37		221,773	Malaysia
9		$207,814	Sinopec
40		207,118	Nigeria
10		$204,352	Toyota Motor
41		202,101	Israel

Note: Corporations are paired with comparably sized countries.
Sources: For corporate data, *Fortune* 2009; for GDP data, World Bank 2010c.

SOC THINK

Multinational corporations have become so big that they have more economic resources than do some nations. What consequences arise from the fact that they can relocate their headquarters, offices, and production facilities anywhere in the world? How might this affect a nation's political power?

and services in the United States involve either the export of goods to foreign countries or the import of goods from abroad (U.S. Trade Representative 2003).

Modernization Consistent with the modernization approach, some analysts believe that the relationship between the corporation and the developing country is mutually beneficial. Multinational corporations can help the developing nations of the world by bringing industries and jobs to areas where subsistence agriculture once served as the only means of survival. Multinationals also promote rapid development through the diffusion of inventions and innovations from industrial nations. The combination of skilled technology and management provided by multinationals and the relatively cheap labor available in developing nations benefits the corporation. Multinationals can take maximum advantage of technology while reducing costs and boosting profits. Through their international ties, multinationals also make the nations of the world more interdependent. These ties may inhibit certain disputes from reaching the point of serious conflict. A country cannot afford to sever diplomatic relations or engage in warfare with a nation that is the headquarters for its main business suppliers or a key market for its exports.

Dependency Critics of multinational expansion challenge this favorable evaluation of the impact of corporations. They argue that multinationals exploit local workers to maximize profits. For example, Starbucks—the international coffee retailer based in Seattle—gets some of its coffee beans from farms in Ethiopia. It sells its "Black Apron Exclusives" coffee in a fancy black box for $26 per pound, but it paid Ethiopian workers who picked the beans 66 cents per day (Knudson 2007).

The pool of cheap labor in the developing world prompts multinationals to move factories out of core countries. Workers in these developing countries do not have the same kinds of legal protections and also lack unions to fight on their behalf. In industrialized countries, organized labor insists on decent wages and humane working conditions, but governments seeking to attract or keep multinationals may develop a "climate for investment," including repressive antilabor laws that restrict union activity and collective bargaining. If labor's demands become too threatening, the multinational firm will simply move its plant elsewhere, leaving a trail of unemployment behind. Nike, for example, has moved its factories from the United States to Korea to Indonesia to Vietnam in search of the lowest labor costs.

Workers in the United States and other core countries are beginning to recognize that their own interests are served by helping to organize workers in developing nations. As long as multinationals can exploit cheap labor abroad, they will be in a strong position to reduce wages and benefits in industrialized countries. With this in mind, starting in the 1990s, labor unions, religious organizations, campus groups, and other activists began to mount public relations campaigns to pressure companies such as Nike, Starbucks, Reebok, Gap, and Wal-Mart to improve wages and working conditions in their overseas operations (Radovich 2006; Solidarity Center 2009).

Sociologists studying the effects of foreign investment by multinationals have found that, although it initially may contribute to a host nation's wealth, such investment eventually increases economic inequality within developing nations. This finding holds for both income and ownership. The upper and middle classes benefit most from economic expansion; the lower classes are less likely to benefit. And because multinationals invest in limited economic sectors and restricted regions of a nation, only some sectors benefit. The expansion of such sectors of the host nation's economy, such as hotels and high-end restaurants, appears to retard growth in agriculture and other economic sectors. Moreover, multinational corporations often buy out or force out local entrepreneurs and companies, thereby increasing economic and cultural dependence (Kerbo 2009; Wallerstein 1979b, 2004).

Governments in developing nations are not always prepared to deal with the sudden influx of foreign capital and its effects on their economies. One particularly striking example of how unfettered capitalism can harm developing nations is found in the Democratic Republic of Congo (formerly Zaire). The Congo has significant deposits of the metal columbite-tantalite—coltan, for short—which is used in the production of electronic circuit boards. Until the market for cell phones, pagers, and laptop computers heated up recently, U.S. manufacturers obtained most of their coltan from Australia. But at the height of

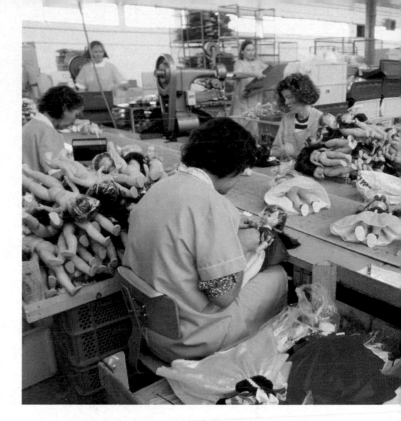

consumer demand, they turned to miners in the Congo to increase their supply.

Predictably, the escalating price of the metal—as much as $400 per kilogram at one point, or more than three times the average Congolese worker's yearly wages—attracted undesirable attention. Soon the neighboring countries of Rwanda, Uganda, and Burundi, at war with one another and desperate for resources to finance the conflict, were raiding the Congo's national parks, slashing and burning to expose the coltan underneath the forest floor. Indirectly, the sudden increase in the demand for coltan was financing war and the rape of the environment. U.S. manufacturers have since cut off their sources in the

Congo in an effort to avoid abetting the destruction. How-ever, their action has only penalized legitimate miners in the impoverished country (Lasker 2008; Lovgren 2006).

>> Stratification Around the World

As these economic investments by multinationals suggest, at the same time the gap between rich and poor nations is widening, so too is the gap between rich and poor citizens within nations. As discussed earlier, stratification in developing nations is closely related to their rela-tively weak and dependent position in the global economy. Local elites work hand in hand with mul-tinational corporations and prosper from such alliances. At the same time, the economic system creates and perpetuates the exploitation of industrial and agricultural workers.

INCOME AND WEALTH

Global inequality is staggering, as these two graphs suggest. In at least 20 nations around the world, the most affluent 10 percent of the population receives at

Percent Shares of Global Household Wealth

Source: Davies et al. 2009.

Distribution of Income in Nine Nations

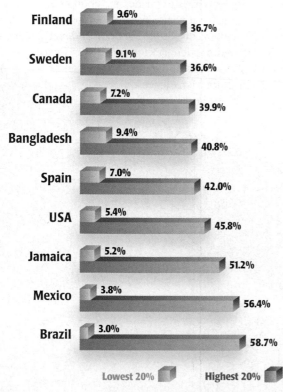

Note: Data are considered comparable although based on statistics covering 2000 to 2008.

Source: World Bank 2009d, 2010e.

least 40 percent of all income. Among these countries are the African nation of Namibia (the leader, at 65 percent of all income) as well as Colombia, Brazil, Mexico, and South Africa (Davies et al. 2009).

When it comes to wealth, the top 10 percent of the world's population own 85 percent of global household wealth, and the top 1 percent own 40 percent. On the other end of the spectrum, the bottom 50 percent of the world's population combined own 1 percent of global wealth. Median household wealth globally is estimated to be $8635 per adult. To make it into the top 1 percent takes $518,364. Analyzing the distribution globally, the bulk of the wealth is held by countries in North America, Europe, and the rich Asia-Pacific nations. The United States has 4.7 percent of the world's population but owns 25.1 percent of global household wealth. Contrast this with India, which has 16.9 percent of the world's popula-tion but only 4.2 percent of global wealth. In addition, the entire continent of Africa has 13.4 percent of the world's population but only 2.2 percent of global wealth (Davies et al. 2009).

Looking in more detail at the world's top 10 percent of wealth holders, 19 percent come from the United States; 14 percent come from Japan; and Germany, Italy, Britain, France, and Spain combine for 26 percent. Within nations, the amount of wealth held by the top 10 percent varies. Denmark demonstrates the most significant amount of wealth inequality, with the top 10 percent of wealth holders there owning 76.4 percent of household wealth—significantly

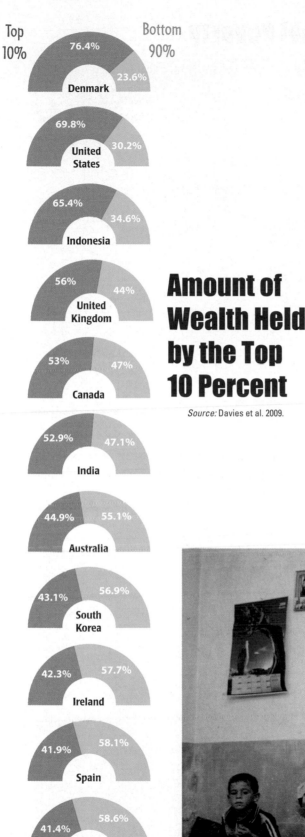

Top 10%   Bottom 90%

76.4% **23.6%**
Denmark

69.8% **30.2%**
United States

65.4% **34.6%**
Indonesia

56% **44%**
United Kingdom

53% **47%**
Canada

52.9% **47.1%**
India

44.9% **55.1%**
Australia

43.1% **56.9%**
South Korea

42.3% **57.7%**
Ireland

41.9% **58.1%**
Spain

41.4% **58.6%**
China

39.3% **60.7%**
Japan

Amount of Wealth Held by the Top 10 Percent

Source: Davies et al. 2009.

more than Japan, where the top 10 percent hold 39.3 percent of the wealth (Davies et al. 2009).

Women in developing countries often face significant obstacles, making it difficult for them to attain economic assets. Karuna Chanana Ahmed, a sociologist from India who has studied women in developing nations, calls women "the most exploited among the oppressed" (Anderson and Moore 1993). Beginning at birth, women face sex discrimination. They are commonly fed less than male children, are denied educational opportunities, and often are hospitalized only when they are critically ill. In countries such as the United States, France, the United Kingdom, Russia, Azerbaijan, and Ethiopia, the proportion of the nonagricultural labor force made up by women approaches or exceeds 50 percent. In other nations the rate can be significantly lower: Bahrain 9.8 percent,

Mapping Global Poverty

Note: The size of each country shows the proportion of the world population living in poverty there.

Source: www.worldmapper.org.

Pakistan 13.2 percent, Saudi Arabia 14 percent, Iran 16.1 percent, Egypt 18.1 percent, Bangladesh 20.1 percent, and Zimbabwe 21.9 percent. In Afghanistan, it is illegal for a wife to step out of the house without her husband's permission. In Saudi Arabia, women are prohibited from driving, walking alone in public, and socializing with men other than their families (International Labour Organization 2008; World Bank 2010f).

SOC THINK

What are the major obstacles to accomplishing the Millennium Project's goals? To what extent are they economic, social, and/or cultural? Is it simply a matter of will?

POVERTY

In developing countries, any deterioration in the economic well-being of the least well-off threatens their very survival. Using the global poverty line established by the World Bank of $1.25 per day, 1.4 billion people in the world are considered poor, and 2.6 billion people consume less than $2 a day. In fact, 80 percent of the world's population lives on less than $10 a day (Chen and Ravallion 2008; Shah 2010).

Though poverty is a worldwide problem affecting billions of people, it is distributed unequally. As the world map above

Millennium Project Goals by 2015

Eradicate extreme poverty and hunger

Achieve universal primary education

Promote gender equality and empower women

Reduce child mortality

Improve maternal health

Combat HIV/AIDS, malaria, and other diseases

Ensure environmental sustainability

Develop a global partnership for development

Source: www.unmillenniumproject.org.

Percent of Population Living on Less than $1.25 a Day

Country	Percent
Dominican Republic	5%
China	15.9%
Kenya	19.7%
Pakistan	22.6%
South Africa	26.2%
India	41.6%
Bangladesh	49.6%
Haiti	54.9%
Nigeria	64.4%
Malawi	73.9%
Rwanda	76.6%
Liberia	83.7%

Source: United Nations Development Programme 2009: Table 1.

demonstrates, if we drew each country to scale based on its number of poor people, Africa and Asia would appear huge. The relatively affluent areas of North America and Europe would be quite small.

In an effort to reduce global poverty, the United Nations passed the Millennium Declaration in 2000, promising to "spare no effort to free our fellow men, women, and children from the abject and dehumanizing conditions of extreme poverty." They established 2015 as the target date for reaching specific, measurable goals to alleviate hunger and improve education, gender equality, and child mortality.

Significant progress on reaching these goals has already been made. The percentage of the population in developing countries living on $1.25 per day fell from 52 percent to 26 percent between 1981 and 2005. Though the global economic downturn is expected to slow the pace of progress, the global poverty rate is expected to continue to fall. In fact, the goal of cutting the developing world's poverty rate in half is on track. This was driven primarily by the reduction of extreme poverty in East Asia, which saw its rate fall from almost 80 percent in 1981 to 18 percent by 2005. In China alone there are 600 million fewer people living below the global poverty line.

> **gross national income (GNI)** The total value of a nation's goods and services.

Over that same period, rates in Africa have changed less dramatically, though there was a decline from 58 to 50 percent between 2000 and 2005. Current projections are that, by 2015, China will make it to 5.1 percent and Sub-Saharan Africa will make it to 38.0 percent. As of 2010, goals for achieving gender parity in education, promoting gender equality, and access to clean water are also estimated to be on track. Significant challenges remain in the areas of child mortality, maternal mortality, and access to sanitation (Chen and Ravallion 2008, 2009; United Nations 2008; World Bank 2010g).

To accomplish the project's goals, planners estimate that industrial nations must set aside 0.7 percent of their **gross national income (GNI)**—the total value of a nation's goods and services—for aid to developing nations. In 2009, only five countries were giving at least that much: Denmark, Luxembourg, the Netherlands, Norway, and Sweden. The average level of official development assistance from developed countries was 0.48 percent, with the United States contributing 0.20 percent. Although the U.S. government delivers far more total aid dollars than any other nation, the rate of GNI it contributes puts it ahead of Korea, Italy, and Japan among 22 industrialized nations such as the United Kingdom, France, and Germany (OECD 2010:Table 1).

5 Movies on GLOBAL INEQUALITY

Babel
Four stories on hardship from around the globe.

Slumdog Millionaire
A boy from the slums of Mumbai is accused of cheating on a game show.

Life and Debt
The IMF exploits Jamaica.

Maria Full of Grace
A factory worker is forced to transport heroin to the United States.

The Girl in the Cafe
An unlikely couple meets in the midst of a G8 summit.

SOCIAL MOBILITY

Although there is significant global inequality, perhaps sufficient social mobility exists to provide hope for those born without significant access to resources. As we saw in the previous chapter, mobility can and does happen in the United States, though the majority of such movement is over only short distances. Here we will look at the possibility for mobility in both industrial nations and developing nations, as well as consider the impact gender has on mobility.

Intergenerational Mobility Across Nations Intergenerational mobility varies across countries; for example, the amount of income advantage passed from fathers to sons is significantly higher in the United Kingdom, the United States, and France than in Denmark, Norway, or Finland (Corak 2006). What this means, in contrast to the classic vision of the American Dream, is that there is less chance for intergenerational mobility in the United States than in those Scandinavian countries.

Foreign Aid per Capita in Eight Countries

Per capita aid in dollars

	Total aid in millions of dollars	Per capita aid in dollars
Japan	9.6	$63
USA	26.8	$79
Australia	3.0	$130
Canada	4.8	$131
Germany	14.0	$154
France	10.9	$161
United Kingdom	11.5	$182
Norway	4.0	$772

Note: Data for bilateral aid in 2008 released by World Bank in 2010.
Source: Deutscher 2010:182, 187.

Intergenerational Earnings Mobility by Country

Country	Percentage of earning advantage passed from fathers to sons
Denmark	15
Norway	17
Finland	18
Canada	19
Sweden	27
Germany	32
France	41
United States	47
United Kingdom	50

Source: Corak 2006.

In developing nations, macrolevel social and economic changes often overshadow microlevel movement from one occupation to another. For example, there is typically a substantial wage differential between rural and urban areas, which leads to high levels of migration to the cities. Yet the urban industrial sectors of developing countries generally cannot provide sufficient employment for all those seeking work.

In large developing nations, the most socially significant mobility is the movement out of poverty. This type of mobility is difficult to measure and confirm, however, because economic trends can differ from one area of a country to another. For instance, China's rapid income growth has been accompanied by a growing disparity in income between urban and rural areas and among different regions. Similarly, in India during the economic development of the 1990s, poverty declined in urban areas but may have remained static at best in rural areas. Around the world, social mobility is also dramatically influenced by catastrophes such as crop failure and warfare (World Bank 2006).

Gender Differences and Mobility Only recently have researchers begun to investigate the impact of gender on the mobility patterns of developing nations. Many aspects of the development process—especially modernization in rural areas and the rural-to-urban migration just described—may result in modification or abandonment of traditional cultural

Did You Know?

... Working 14 hours a day at 13 cents an hour, it would take seamstress Robin Akther of the Western Dresses factory in Dhaka, Bangladesh, 50 years to earn $16,200.

Source: Fishman 2006.

practices and even marital systems. The effects on women's social standing and mobility are not necessarily positive. As a country develops and modernizes, women's vital role in food production deteriorates, jeopardizing both their autonomy and their material well-being. Moreover, the movement of families to the cities weakens women's ties to relatives who can provide food, financial assistance, and social support.

In the Philippines, however, women have moved to the forefront of the indigenous peoples' struggle to protect their ancestral land from exploitation by outsiders. Having established their right to its rich minerals and forests, members of indigenous groups had begun to feud among themselves over the way in which the land's resources should be developed. Aided by the United Nations Partners in Development Programme, women volunteers established the Pan-Cordillera Women's Network for Peace and Development, a coalition of women's groups dedicated to resolving local disputes. The women mapped boundaries, prepared development plans, and negotiated more than 2000 peace pacts among community members. They have also run in elections, campaigned on issues related to social problems, and organized residents to work together for the common good (United Nations Development Programme 2000:87).

SOCIAL STRATIFICATION IN MEXICO

To get a more complete picture of these global stratification issues, it helps to look at a particular case. Here we will focus on the dynamics of stratification in Mexico, a country of 111 million people.

In May 2003, on a stretch of highway in southern Arizona, the open doors of an abandoned tractor trailer revealed the dead bodies of 19 Mexicans. The truck had been carrying a group of about 75 men, women, and children across the Sonoran Desert illegally into the United States when the people hidden inside began to suffer from the intense desert heat. Their story is not unusual. In recent years, as many as 500 people per year have died trying to cross the U.S.–Mexican border. From October 2008 through April 2009, according to border patrol officials in Arizona, 72 died in the Tucson sector alone (McCombs 2009).

Why do Mexicans risk their lives crossing the dangerous desert that lies between the two countries? The answer to this question can be found primarily in the income disparity between the two nations—one an industrial giant and the other a partially developed country still recovering from a history of colonialism and neocolonialism. Since the early 20th century, there has been a close cultural, economic, and political relationship between Mexico and the United States, one in which the United States is the dominant party. According to Immanuel Wallerstein's analysis, the United States is at the core while neighboring Mexico is still on the semiperiphery of the world economic system.

Mexico's Economy If we compare Mexico's economy to that of the United States, differences in the standard of living and in life chances are quite dramatic, even though Mexico is considered a semiperiphery nation. Gross national income is a commonly used measure of an average resident's economic well-being. In 2008, the gross national income per person in the United States came to $47,930; in Mexico, it was a mere $9990. About 36 percent of adults in the United States have a bachelor's degree, compared to only 18 percent of those in Mexico. And fewer than 6.7 of every 1000 infants in the United States die in the first year of life, compared to about 15 per 1000 in Mexico (Snyder and Dillow 2010; World Bank 2010b, 2010h).

Did You Know?

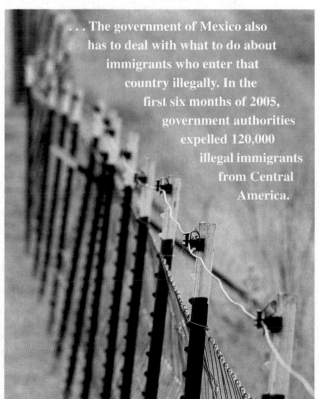

... The government of Mexico also has to deal with what to do about immigrants who enter that country illegally. In the first six months of 2005, government authorities expelled 120,000 illegal immigrants from Central America.

Not only is Mexico unquestionably a poor country, but the gap between its richest and poorest citizens is one of the widest in the world. The top quintile earns 55.1 percent of total income while the bottom earns just 4.3 percent. The World Bank reports that, in 2008, 3.3 percent of Mexico's population survived on just $2 per day. At the same time, the wealthiest 10 percent of Mexico's people accounted for 41 percent of the nation's income. According to *Forbes* magazine, Mexico's Carlos Slim Helú edged out Bill Gates to become the world's richest person in 2010 with a fortune of $53.5 billion (Kroll and Miller 2010; World Bank 2010d).

Political scientist Jorge Castañeda (1995:71), who later served as Mexico's foreign minister, called Mexico a "polarized society with enormous gaps between rich and poor, town and country, north and south, white and brown (or *criollos* and *mestizos*)." He added that the country is also divided along lines of class, race, religion, gender, and age. To better understand the nature of the stratification within Mexico, we will examine race relations and the plight of Mexican Indians, the status of Mexican women, and immigration to the United States and its impact on the U.S.–Mexican borderlands.

Race Relations in Mexico: The Color Hierarchy

Mexico's indigenous Indians account for an estimated 14 percent of the nation's population. According to a United Nations report, more than 90 percent of Mexico's indigenous people (the ethnic group historically native to a region) live in extreme poverty. The literacy rate in Mexico as a whole is 92 percent, but it hovers around 50 percent among the indigenous population (Cevallos 2009; Minority Rights Group International 2007; United Nations Development Programme 2008).

The subordinate status of Mexico's Indians is but one reflection of the nation's color hierarchy, which links social class status to the appearance of racial purity. At the top of this hierarchy are the *criollos,* the 10 percent of the population who are typically White, well-educated members of the business and intellectual elites, with familial roots in Spain. In the middle is the large, impoverished *mestizo* majority, most of whom have brown skin and a mixed racial lineage as a result of intermarriage. At the bottom of the color hierarchy are the destitute, full-blooded Mexican Indian minority and a small number of Blacks, some descended from 200,000 African slaves brought to Mexico. This color hierarchy is an important part of day-to-day life—enough so that some Mexicans in the cities use hair dyes, skin lighteners, and blue or green contact lenses to appear White and European. Ironically, however, nearly all Mexicans are considered part Indian

SOC THINK

How might racial categories in Mexico differ from those in the United States? Why might such differences arise?

because of centuries of intermarriage (Castañeda 1995; Standish and Bell 2009).

Many observers take note of widespread denial of prejudice and discrimination against people of color in Mexico. Schoolchildren are taught that the election of Benito Juárez, a Zapotec Indian, as president of Mexico in the 19th century proves that all Mexicans are equal. Yet there has been a marked growth in the past decade of formal organizations and voluntary associations representing indigenous Indians (Escárcega 2008; Stavenhagen 1994; Utne 2003).

The Status of Women in Mexico

Though the United Nations convened the first international conference on the status of women in Mexico in 1975, and opportunities there have improved, women still face significant obstacles. Women now constitute 45 percent of the labor force—an increase from 31 percent in 1980. Unfortunately, Mexican women are even more mired in the lowest-paying jobs than their counterparts in industrial nations, on average earning 42 percent less than men. Men are still typically viewed as heads of the household, making it difficult for women to obtain credit and technical assistance in many parts of the country and to inherit land in rural areas. As for education, the literacy rate for women in Chiapas (71 percent) and Oaxaca (73 percent), states with high levels of indigenous populations, is well below the national average (INEGI 2009; United Nations Development Programme 2008).

In the political arena, though they rarely occupy top decision-making positions, women have significantly increased their representation in the national legislature to 28 percent. Mexico now ranks 29th among 196 nations in female representation. In spite of this, the struggle for enforcement of legal rights continues. In February 2007, Mexico passed the General Law on Women's Access to a Life Free from Violence. States have not followed through with implementation of the law's basic requirements, such as establishing protocols to follow when claims of abuse are filed or constructing shelters for domestic violence victims. In fact, there are only 60 such shelters in all of Mexico (Amnesty International 2009a; Inter-Parliamentary Union 2010).

In recent decades, Mexican women have organized to address an array of economic, political, and health issues. For example, as far back as 1973, women in Monterrey—the nation's third-largest city—protested the continuing disruptions of the city's water supply. Through coordinated efforts, including delegations of politicians, rallies, and public demonstrations, they succeeded in improving Monterrey's water service, a major concern in developing nations. After being denied the opportunity to run for mayor in her hometown in 2007, Eufrosina Cruz organized QUIEGO (Queremos Unir Integrando por Equidad y Gé-nero en Oaxaca, meaning "we want to come together for equity and gender in Oaxaca") to raise awareness about political rights for women in her home state and ultimately throughout Mexico (Bennett, Dávila-Poblete, and Rico 2005; Cevallos 2009).

Personal Sociology

Central College, where I teach, started its first international program in 1965. It was a leader in establishing study abroad programs for students. It now operates programs around the world in places such as Merida in Mexico, Bangor in Wales, and Hangzhou in China. Central instituted these programs to provide students with a prolonged experience in another country in hopes that such exposure would enable them to go beyond being just a tourist and achieve a deeper understanding of another culture. I always encourage my students to go abroad because I find that those who do come back changed. They return to campus with a deeper understanding, not only of the world but of themselves.

The Borderlands Growing recognition of the borderlands reflects the increasingly close and complex relationship between Mexico and the United States. The term **borderlands** refers to the area of common culture along the border between Mexico and the United States. Legal and illegal emigration from Mexico to the United States, day laborers crossing the border regularly to go to work in the United States, the implementation of the North American Free Trade Agreement (NAFTA), the exchange of media across the border—all make the notion of separate Mexican and U.S. cultures obsolete in the borderlands.

The economic position of the borderlands is rather complicated, as demonstrated by the emergence of *maquiladoras.* These are foreign-owned factories, often located just across the border in Mexico, that are allowed to import parts and materials without tariffs. Typical jobs include manufacturing electronics, transportation equipment, electrical machinery, and textiles and apparel, as well as service jobs in call centers and coupon processing operations. The chief appeal for U.S. companies is less expensive labor. As of 2006, hourly compensation costs (including salary and benefits) for maquiladora manufacturing production workers was $2.64. This compares to $29.98 per hour in the United States (Bureau of Labor Statistics 2009a, 2009b; Cañas and Gilmer 2009).

> **borderlands** The area of common culture along the border between Mexico and the United States.

Maquiladoras now employ more than 1.2 million workers. They account for about 40 percent of all Mexico's exports. Overall, 80 percent of Mexico's exports go to the United States. This makes Mexico's economy more sensitive to U.S. fluctuations, a significant problem with the recent economic downturn. Maquiladoras estimate a job loss of 163,000 for 2009, a rate two to four times higher than in other Mexican firms (Black 2009; Bogan et al. 2008).

The Borderlands

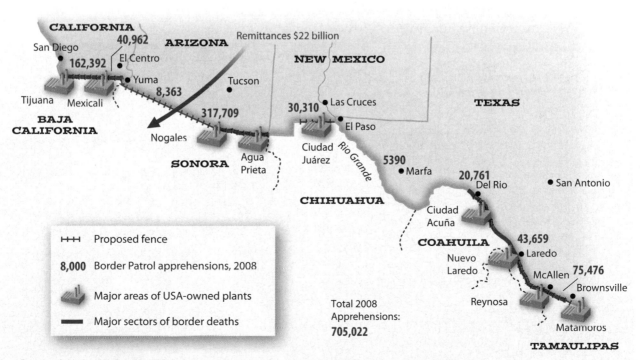

Source: Based on Schaefer 2009. Data from U.S. Department of Homeland Security 2009:Table 35. Coronado and Cañas 2010.

Though the maquiladora program was established in 1965, it really took off after the North American Free Trade Agreement (NAFTA) was implemented in 1994, removing most barriers to trade between Mexico, the United States, and Canada. Things changed, however, with China's entry into the World Trade Organization in 2001. Labor costs were even lower there. As a result, jobs that had moved from the United States to Mexico, especially those requiring minimal skills, are now being transferred to China (Cañas and Gilmer 2009; Sargent and Matthews 2009).

Emigration to the United States From the Mexican point of view, the United States too often regards Mexico simply as a reserve pool of cheap labor, encouraging Mexicans to cross the border when workers are needed but discouraging and cracking down on them when they are not. Some people, then, see immigration more as a labor market issue than a law enforcement issue. Viewed from the perspective of Wallerstein's world systems analysis and dependency theory, it is yet another example of a core industrialized nation exploiting a developing country.

remittances The monies that immigrants return to their families of origin. Also called *remesas*.

The social impact of immigration to the United States is felt throughout Mexico. According to sociological research, the earliest emigrants were typically married men of working age from the middle of the stratification

-SOCTHINK-

How do U.S. consumers benefit from the buildup of factories along the U.S.–Mexican border? What impact might they have on U.S. workers?

Mass grave site in Srebrenica, Bosnia-Herzegovina.

system. They had sufficient financial resources to afford the costs and risks of immigration, yet were experiencing enough financial strain that entering the United States was attractive to them. Over time, kinship ties to emigrants multiplied, and immigration became less class-selective, with entire families making the trek to the United States (Massey 1998, 2008).

Many Mexicans who have come to the United States send a portion of their earnings back across the border to family members in Mexico. This substantial flow of money, referred to as **remittances** (or *remesas*), amounted to $22 billion in 2009. It is second only to oil as a source of foreign revenue for Mexico. After years of growth, remittances sent to Mexico fell 3.6 percent in 2008, due to the economic downturn in the United States. The decline was more dramatic in 2009, falling 15 percent for the year. Though remittances still totaled $21.5 billion, it meant a loss of $3.8 billion to the Mexican economy for that month alone. As a result of the weak economy, more Mexicans left the United States to head back to Mexico than entered the United States in the first quarter of 2009, a dramatic reversal of events (Barta and Millman 2009; Coronado and Cañas 2010; Passel and Cohn 2009).

>> Universal Human Rights

As globalization has spread, affecting more and more peoples around the world, a movement toward ensuring universal human rights has arisen. Recognizing the harmful effects of such global expansion, activists in this movement fight to preserve and protect the interests of people who lack significant power or access to resources. The sheer

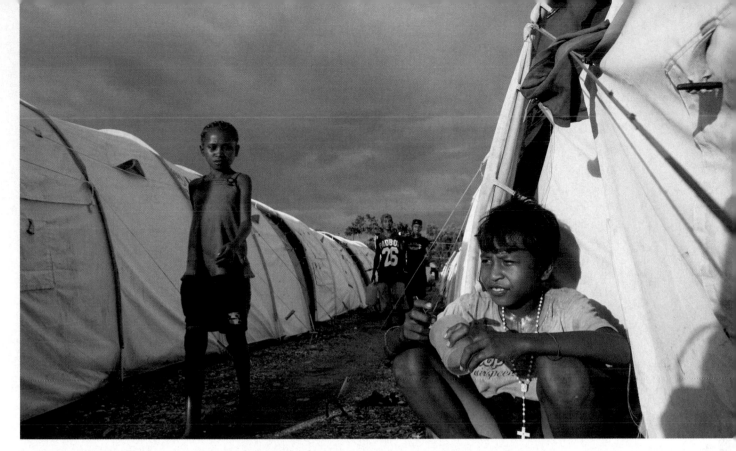

Ongoing violence in East Timor has driven children like these to seek safety in refugee camps in the country.

size and economic might of multinational corporations, along with their freedom to move jobs and plants around the world without regard for the impact on national populations, encouraged the establishment of universal human rights as a countervailing source of power. The goal of human rights activists is to establish a nonnegotiable and inviolable foundation of rights that applies no matter where people are or which governments or multinational corporations are involved.

DEFINING HUMAN RIGHTS

The term **human rights** refers to universal moral rights that all people possess by virtue of being human. The most important elaboration of human rights appears in the Universal Declaration of Human Rights, adopted by the United Nations (UN) in 1948. This declaration prohibits slavery, torture, and degrading punishment; grants everyone the right to a nationality and its culture; affirms freedom of religion and the right to vote; proclaims the right to seek asylum in other countries to escape persecution; and prohibits arbitrary interference with one's privacy and the arbitrary seizure of a person's property. It also emphasizes that mothers and children are entitled to special care and assistance.

At first, the United States opposed a binding obligation to the Universal Declaration of Human Rights. The government feared loss of national sovereignty—the right to rule over its people without external interference. This concern was driven in part by the existence of racial segregation

laws that were still common at the time the UN issued the Universal Declaration and that violated the human rights principles. By the early 1960s, however, the United States had begun to use the declaration to promote democracy abroad (Forsythe 1990).

In the 1990s, concerns about human rights brought the term *ethnic cleansing* into the world's vocabulary as a euphemism for forcible expulsion and murder. In the former Yugoslavia, Serbs initiated a policy intended to "cleanse" Muslims from parts of Bosnia-Herzegovina and

> **human rights** Universal moral rights possessed by all people because they are human.

ethnic Albanians from the province of Kosovo. Hundreds of thousands of people were killed in fighting there, while many others were uprooted from their homes. Moreover, reports surfaced of Serbian soldiers raping substantial numbers of Muslim, Croatian, and Kosovar women. Regrettably, ethnic cleansing has since spread to other parts of the world, including East Timor, Iraq, Kenya, and Sudan.

An ongoing human rights concern is the transnational crime of trafficking in humans. Each year an estimated 600,000–800,000 men, women, and children are transported across international borders for slavery or sexual exploitation. In 2000, Congress passed the Trafficking Victims Protection Act, which established minimum standards for the elimination of human trafficking. The act requires the State Department to monitor other countries' efforts to vigorously investigate, prosecute, and convict individuals who participate in trafficking—including government officials. Each year the department reports its findings, dividing countries into three groups, or tiers, depending on their level of compliance. Tier-1 countries

Human Trafficking Report

Tier 1 Full Compliance	Tier 2 Significant Effort	Tier 2 Watch List Some Effort, but Trafficking Remains a Concern	Tier 3 Noncompliant, No Effort
Australia	Afghanistan	Azerbaijan	Burma
Canada	Bahamas	Bahrain	Chad
Columbia	Brazil	Cambodia	Cuba
Denmark	Greece	China	Fiji
France	Hong Kong	Dominican Republic	Iran
Germany	Israel	Egypt	Kuwait
Italy	Japan	Ghana	Malaysia
Nigeria	Mexico	India	Niger
Norway	Romania	Iraq	North Korea
Poland	Rwanda	Pakistan	Saudi Arabia
South Korea	Turkey	Russia	Sudan
Spain	Vietnam	Senegal	Syria
	Zambia	Ukraine	Zimbabwe

Note: Table is incomplete; each tier lists only sample nations.

Source: U.S. Department of State 2010.

are thought to be largely in compliance with the act. Tier-2 nations are making a significant effort to comply, while tier-2 "watch" nations are making efforts to comply, though trafficking remains a real concern. Tier-3 countries are not compliant (Kapstein 2006; Kempadoo and Doezema 1998; Ribando 2008).

PRINCIPLE AND PRACTICE

When it comes to human rights, the balance between principle and practice can be problematic. In the wake of the terrorist attacks of September 11, 2001, increased police personnel and surveillance at U.S. airports and border crossings caused some observers to wonder whether human rights were not being jeopardized in the name of security. At the same time, thousands of noncitizens of Arab and south Asian descent were questioned for no other reason than their ethnic and religious backgrounds. A few were placed in custody, sometimes without access to legal assistance. And as the war on terror moved overseas, human rights concerns escalated. In 2005, then Secretary-General Kofi Annan of the UN criticized the United States and Britain for equating people who were resisting the presence of foreign troops in Afghanistan and Iraq with terrorists (Parker 2004; Steele 2005).

What this points to is the significance of perspective even when it comes to something that appears to be a fundamental principle. Cultural insiders and outsiders can disagree about what constitutes a violation. For example, was India's caste system an inherent violation of human rights? What about the many cultures of the world that view the subordinate status of women as

—SOC THINK—

To what extent do you think violations of human rights are excusable in a time of war? At such times, how might our perception of the balance between rights and security alter what we think of as universal?

an essential element in their traditions? Should human rights be interpreted differently in different parts of the world?

We can consider, as an example, female genital mutilation, a practice that is common in more than 30 countries around the world but that has been condemned in Western nations as a human rights abuse. This controversial practice often involves removal of the clitoris, in the belief that its excision will inhibit a young woman's sex drive, making her chaste and thus more desirable to her future husband. Though some countries have passed laws against the practice, they have gone largely unenforced. Emigrants from countries where genital mutilation is common often insist that their daughters undergo the procedure, to protect them from Western cultural norms that allow premarital sex (Religious Tolerance 2008). To what extent should outside nations have the power to dictate such internal laws? In this sense, the movement for universal human rights also represents a form of cultural imperialism.

In 1993, the United States opted for an absolute definition of human rights, insisting that the Universal

SOC THINK

How active should the U.S. government be in addressing violations of human rights in other countries? At what point, if any, does concern for human rights turn into ethnocentrism through failure to respect the distinctive norms, values, and customs of another culture?

Declaration of Human Rights set a single standard for acceptable behavior around the world. In practice, however, interpretation still plays a role. Some human rights activists have argued that the United States practices selective enforcement of human rights. Critics contend, for example, that officials in the United States are more likely to become concerned about human rights abuses when oil is at stake, as in the Middle East, or when military alliances come into play, as in Europe.

HUMAN RIGHTS ACTIVISM

Efforts to protect and ensure human rights seldom come from inside governments but arise out of social movements that organize to generate economic, social, and political pressure in an effort to force change. For example, in June 2008, Human Rights Watch (www.hrw.org), a premier international human rights organization, called for other African nations to impose sanctions on Zimbabwe after what they called the sham reelection of President Robert Mugabe. They monitor human rights abuses around the world, including calling upon U.S. officials to end abuses against prisoners in the Guantanamo Bay detention camps.

In Sudan, the Save Darfur Coalition (www.savedarfur.org) fights for justice and relief for refugees who were attacked, driven off their land and out of the country, and often killed by the Janjaweed, a group of armed gunmen backed by the Sudanese government. Their cause was helped significantly with the release of the film *The Devil Came on Horseback*—translated from the Janjaweed—in which ex-marine Brian Steidle, who was hired as a human rights observer by the African Union, documented genocide in Darfur with photos and video. He ultimately testified before Congress and at the UN, providing his documentation to support the genocide claims. In addition to numerous other organizational efforts, the Save Darfur Coalition also coordinated an agreement on May 28, 2008, in which presidential candidates Barack Obama, John McCain, and Hillary Clinton issued a joint statement demanding an end to the violence in Darfur. Though the Sudanese government maintains that the war is officially over, violence continues. In May 2010, Ibrahim Gambari, the head of UNAMID, the joint African Union–UN Mission in Darfur, put it this way: "Results have been mixed despite our best efforts. . . . In the area of security and the protection of civilians some progress has been made, but pockets of instability remain" (UN News Service 2010).

Médecins sans Frontières (Doctors Without Borders), the world's largest independent emergency medical aid organization, won the 1999 Nobel Peace Prize for its work in countries worldwide. Founded in 1971 and based in Paris, on any given day the organization has 27,000 doctors, nurses, and other expert volunteers working in more than 65 countries. "Our intention is to highlight current upheavals, to bear witness to foreign tragedies and reflect on the principles of humanitarian aid," explains Dr. Rony Brauman, the organization's president (Doctors Without Borders 2010).

SOC THINK

Should outside nations, including the UN, have the power to force the United States to change its laws to comply with human rights principles?

In recent years, awareness has been growing of lesbian and gay rights as an aspect of universal human rights. In 1994, Amnesty International (1994:2) published a pioneering report in which it acknowledged that "homosexuals in many parts of the world live in constant fear of government persecution." The report examined abuses in Brazil, Greece, Mexico, Iran, the United States, and other countries, including cases of torture, imprisonment, and extrajudicial execution. Later in 1994, the United States issued an order that would allow lesbians and gay men to seek political asylum in the United States if they could prove they had suffered government persecution in their home countries solely because of their sexual orientation (Amnesty International 2009b; Johnston 1994). One result of this policy change was that dozens of homosexual men and women from Mexico and other Latin American nations were granted asylum in the United States each year. As treatment of homosexuals has

> There can be no peace as long as there is grinding poverty, social injustice, inequality, oppression, environmental degradation, and as long as the weak and small continue to be trodden by the mighty and powerful.
>
> **the Dalai Lama**

improved in those nations, the likelihood of receiving asylum has declined (Connolly 2008).

One of the things we learn from sociology is that we are embedded in larger networks in which decisions and events that happen far away, and about which we may know little or nothing, shape our daily life experiences. Ethnic cleansing in the former Yugoslavia, human rights violations in Iraq and Afghanistan, increased surveillance in the name of counterterrorism, violence against women inside and outside the family, governmental torture of lesbians and gay men—all of these are vivid reminders that social inequality can have life-and-death consequences. In each case, people recognized the consequences of global inequality, and individuals, groups, and nations took steps to address the problems. By developing a more fully formed sociological imagination, we can more readily see such issues and take necessary steps toward addressing them.

Donate! Give of your time and your money. It can be something as simple as going to www.freerice.com to donate rice to the UN World Food Program or giving clothes to a local shelter. Or perhaps it might include volunteering time at a local organization that works with international immigrants or donating money to organizations that seek to alleviate global poverty, such as OxFam.

get involved!

For REVIEW

I. How did the global divide develop?

- Theorists emphasizing modernization argue that it is part of the natural evolution of societies as they pass through the effects of the Industrial Revolution and beyond. Dependency theorists argue that it is due to a fundamental power struggle between wealthy nations at the core and developing nations at the periphery.

II. How significant is global stratification?

- Analyses of wealth, income, poverty, and social mobility demonstrate a wide gap both within and between nations.

III. Why did the global movement for universal human rights develop?

- As global inequality became more apparent, activists worked to establish a foundational set of human rights that would protect people regardless of who or where they were.

SOCVIEWS on Global Inequality

Functionalist View

Through **modernization**, nations make the transition from traditional forms of organization to postindustrial societies for the benefit of all.

Globalization involves the worldwide **integration** of government policies, cultures, social movements, and financial markets through trade and exchange of ideas.

Multinational organizations create jobs and industries in developing countries, foster innovation, and make nations of the world **interdependent.**

Conflict View

There is significant **inequality** between the rich and the poor within as well as across nations, but the scourge of poverty is most evident in Africa and Asia.

According to world system analysis, modernization can result in political, economic, and cultural **imperialism.**

The economic success of core nations depends upon the extraction of raw materials and cheap labor from periphery nations.

Interactionist View

People undergoing modernization often experience a dramatic change in the established ways of working and interacting.

Encounters with people from different cultures open us up to alternative ways of thinking and acting.

Many women in developing nations face inequality in employment opportunities, education and health care, thus limiting their **social interaction** in the community.

MAKE THE CONNECTION

After reviewing the chapter, answer the following questions:

KEY CONCEPTS **IMPERIALISM, INEQUALITY**

KEY CONCEPTS **SOCIAL INTERACTION, ENCOUNTERS**

1

How might each perspective seek to better understand the situation in countries such as Haiti and Sudan (p. 261)?

2

How do the modernization and world systems theories fit with the functionalist and conflict perspectives (p. 264–266)

3

How would each perspective provide insight into situation of immigration between the United States and Mexico (p. 278)?

4

What ties do you have to a developing nation—perhaps as a tourist, or a second-generation immigrant, or an activist? Which perspective best fits those ties? Why?

Pop Quiz

1. Which of the following terms is used by contemporary social scientists to describe the far-reaching process by which nations pass from traditional forms of social organization toward those characteristic of post–Industrial Revolution societies?
   a. dependency
   b. globalization
   c. industrialization
   d. modernization

2. The maintenance of political, social, economic, and cultural domination over a people by a foreign power for an extended period of time is referred to as
   a. globalization.
   b. government-imposed stratification.
   c. colonialism.
   d. dependency.

3. Immanuel Wallerstein's world systems analysis focuses on
   a. the unequal access to and control of resources between core and periphery nations.
   b. the natural evolutionary development of all societies toward the modern ideal.
   c. the rise of multinational corporations.
   d. the global pattern of inequality faced by women.

4. Companies that are headquartered in one country but do business throughout the world are known as
   a. global corporations.
   b. multinational corporations.
   c. maquiladoras.
   d. international agencies.

5. Approximately how much of global household wealth is owned by households in North America?
   a. about one-tenth
   b. about one-quarter
   c. about one-third
   d. about one-half

6. How much of total global wealth do the bottom 50 percent of the world's population own?
   a. 1 percent
   b. 6 percent
   c. 23 percent
   d. 47 percent

7. Globally, approximately how many people subsist on less than $1.25 per day?
   a. 500 million
   b. 1.4 billion
   c. 3.2 billion
   d. 5 billion

8. Karuna Chanana Ahmed, a sociologist from India who has studied developing nations, calls which group the most exploited of oppressed people?
   a. children
   b. women
   c. the elderly
   d. the poor

9. Which of the following terms refers to the foreign-owned factories established just across the border in Mexico, where the companies that own them don't have to pay taxes or high wages, or provide insurance or benefits for their workers?
   a. *maquiladoras*
   b. *hombres*
   c. *mujeres*
   d. *remesas*

10. In what year did the United Nations adopt the Universal Declaration of Human Rights?
    a. 1865
    b. 1919
    c. 1948
    d. 1993

1. (d); 2. (c); 3. (a); 4. (b); 5. (b); 6. (a); 7. (b); 8. (b); 9. (a); 10. (c)

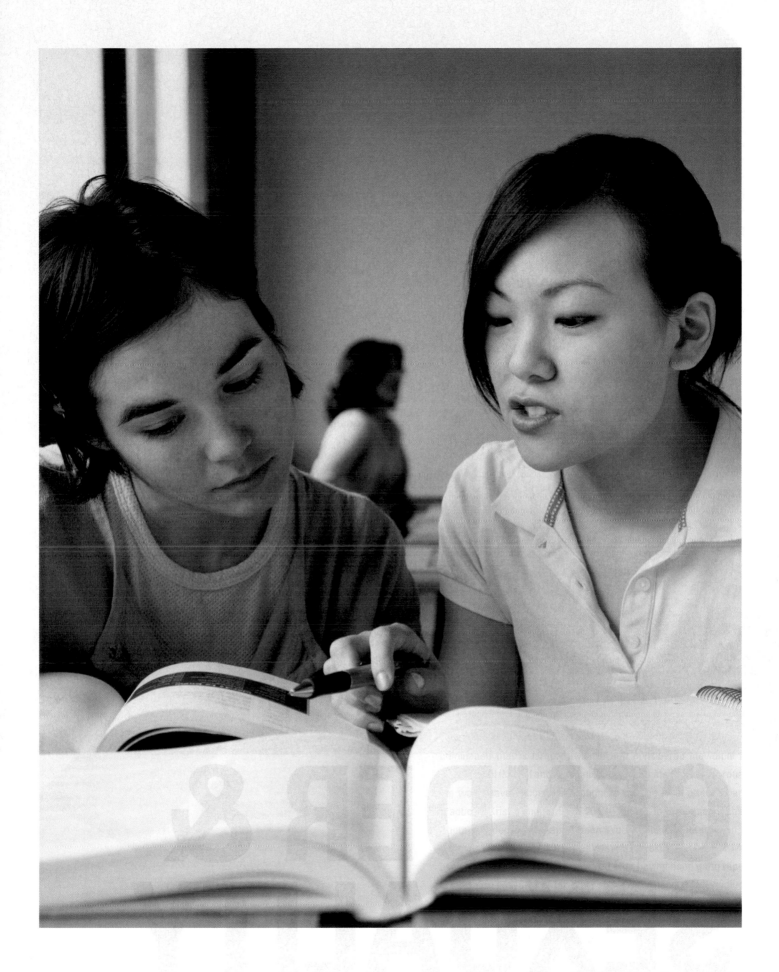

as helpless, passive, incompetent, and in need of a strong male caretaker. Starting in the 1970s, publishers made explicit attempts to provide more balanced representations of gender roles for both women and men. However, recent research continues to find sex-based stereotypes at work. Children's books still show females primarily in traditional roles, such as mother, grandmother, or volunteer— even if they also hold nontraditional roles, such as working professional. Another study of children's picture books found that fathers were significantly less likely to touch, hug, kiss, talk to, or feed children (Anderson and Hamilton 2005; Etaugh 2003; Hamilton et al. 2006).

Men's Gender Roles

Conventional gender-role expectations also exist for men. For example, stay-at-home fathers are still relatively uncommon. For every stay-at-home dad, there are 32 stay-at-home moms. Although it is still rare for men to stay home to care for their children, there is evidence that attitudes are changing. In a nationwide survey, 69 percent of respondents said that if one parent stays home with the children, it makes no difference whether that parent is the mother or the father. Only 30 percent thought that the mother should be the one to stay home (Robison 2002; U.S. Census Bureau 2010a:Table FG8).

While attitudes toward parenting may be changing, traditional gender-role expectations continue to have a significant impact. Men, too, receive messages from family, peers, and the media about what it means to be masculine. One of the most powerful expectations is to be tough, both physically and emotionally, in sports, at work, and even in relationships. Males who fail to conform to such gender norms face criticism and even humiliation. Boys, for example, run the risk of being called a "chicken," "sissy," or "fag" even by fathers or brothers (Katz 1999; Pascoe 2007). Such name-calling represents a form of social control that limits the likelihood of new gender norms being established.

We also see the impact of gendered expectations demonstrated by men in nontraditional occupations, such as preschool teacher or nurse. They may lie about their occupations when introduced to others in order to avoid negative reactions. For example, researchers interviewed a 35-year-old male nurse who reported that he would claim to be "a carpenter or something like that" when he "went clubbing," because women weren't interested in getting to know a male nurse. Subjects of the

multiple masculinities The idea that men learn and play a full range of gender roles.

study made similar accommodations in casual exchanges with other men (Bagilhole and Cross 2006; Cross and Bagilhole 2002).

There may be a price to pay for such narrow conceptions of manhood. Boys who successfully adapt to cultural standards of masculinity may

Did You Know?

. . . Women are more likely to perform unpaid volunteer work in the United States. A total of 36 million women volunteer, which includes 30 percent of all women. This compares to 23 percent for men.

Source: Rotolo and Wilson 2007.

grow up to be inexpressive men who cannot share their feelings with others. They remain forceful and tough, but they are also closed and isolated. These traditional gender roles may be putting men at a disadvantage. Today girls outdo boys in high school, grabbing a disproportionate share of the leadership positions, from valedictorian to class president to yearbook editor—everything, in short, except captain of the boys' athletic teams. And their advantage continues after high school. In the 1980s, girls in the United States became more likely than boys to go to college. By 2008, women accounted for 57 percent of college students nationwide. And in 2006–2007, for the first time, more women than men in the United States earned doctoral degrees (Aud et al. 2010).

Increasing numbers of men in the United States have criticized the restrictive aspects of the traditional male gender role. Australian sociologist R. W. Connell (2002, 2005) has written about **multiple masculinities,** meaning that men learn and play a range of gender roles. These may include a nurturing-caring role, an effeminate-gay role, or their traditional role. Sociologist Michael Kimmel gave voice to this broader conception of what it means to be a man when he was sitting with his newborn son in the park. When a woman came up to him and said that he was expressing his "feminine side," he responded, "I'm not expressing anything of the sort, ma'am. I'm being tender and loving and nurturing toward my child. As far as I can tell, I'm expressing my *masculinity*" (Kimmel 2004:290–91).

GENDER ACROSS CULTURES

Though socialization into gender roles can narrow what we come to think of as appropriate behavior, examples such as Kimmel's suggest that what we define as appropriate does change over time. Gender expectations also differ across cultures. The fact that gender expectations and performance vary across time and place suggests that masculinity and femininity are not strictly determined by our genes.

As we saw in the case of Woineshet Zebene at the beginning of the chapter, women face significant oppression, violence, and discrimination in nations around the globe. Whether in the form of sex trafficking, socially condoned rape, or denial of medical services, the simple fact of being a women is enough to justify such practices in some countries. Quotidian cruelties exist in these cultures because women are not seen as fully human (Kristof and WuDunn 2009).

Other cultures take dramatically different approaches toward gender. Some assume the existence of three or four gender categories. Judith Lorber (1994) notes that "male women," biological males who live for the most part as women, and "female men," biological females who live for the most part as men, can be found in various societies. "Female men" can be found in some African and Native American societies, where they take on male work and family roles. "Male women" include the *berdaches* of the Native Americans of the Great Plains and *hijras* of India (Nanda 1997; Reddy 2005). Michael Kimmel (2004) describes the *xanith* of Oman in the Middle East:

> They work as skilled domestic servants, dress in men's tunics (but in pastel shades more associated with feminine colors), and sell themselves in passive homosexual relationships. They are permitted to speak with women on the street (other men are prohibited). At sex-segregated public events, they sit with the women. However, they can change their minds. (p. 65)

These gender categories are a well-accepted part of their social lives. Individuals who fill them are not simply tolerated or viewed as deviant. The *berdache,* for example, have high status because they are thought to have special powers (Kimmel, 2004; Roscoe 1997).

Beginning with the path-breaking work of Margaret Mead ([1935] 2001) and continuing through contemporary fieldwork, scholars have shown that gender roles can vary greatly from one physical environment, economy, and political system to the next. Peggy Reeves Sanday's

(2002, 2008) work in West Sumatra, Indonesia, for example, describes the 4-million-member Minangkabau society as one in which men and women are not competitors but partners for the common good. This society is characterized by a nurturing approach to the environment, blended with Islamic religious ethics. Women control the land through inheritance; in the event of a divorce, the ex-husband leaves with only his clothes. The larger community may be governed by men, women, or both men and women working together. Sanday's findings, together with Mead's, confirm the influential role of culture and socialization in gender-role differentiation.

REIMAGINING SEX AND GENDER

When it comes to gender, many people assume that the patterns we observe are a given, that biology, as the old saying goes, is destiny. Or, more specifically, that our sex defines our experience as men and women in obvious and predictable ways. We hear echoes of this sentiment in places such as John Gray's best-selling book, *Men Are from Mars, Women Are from Venus* (1992). This powerful analogy presents men and women as aliens from different planets, implying that the chasm between them is natural, inevitable, and difficult, if not impossible, to bridge. A man behaves in certain ways because he is biologically male, and the same goes for women. There are, however, signs that this assumption about the relationship between sex and gender is being called into question; sociologists have, in fact, identified numerous ways in which sex and gender are social constructions.

Recognizing the limitations of a simple, dimorphic model of sex can then open up opportunities for both men and women. It suggests that the line between what anthropologist Lisa Peattie and sociologist Martin Rein refer to as the natural and the artificial shifts over time. When we say something is *natural,* what we mean is that it should be accepted as given and cannot be changed. For example, when people say that "men are more rational," or that "women are more nurturing," the assumption is that these stereotypes are determined by our biology and thus immutable. Analysis of how gender is expressed across cultures and over time suggests, however, that many such characteristics are really *artificial*—that is, they are social constructions subject to change (Peattie and Rein 1983).

Some major shifts in social life have been brought about by challenging what is considered "natural." Even into the 20th century it was thought that women's biological makeup justified their exclusion from schools, the workplace, and politics—social locations in which women's participation is now taken for granted. For example, women were once banned from colleges and universities in the United States because it was presumed that they were biologically incapable of succeeding. At the Jefferson Medical College in Philadelphia in 1847, Professor Charles Meigs, in a famous speech delivered to an all-male class of gynecology students, said of women, "She has a head almost too small for intellect and just big

SOCTHINK

Given that our understandings of gender vary across time and place, why are we so committed to the notion that gender differences are narrowly determined by biology?

"How It Works"

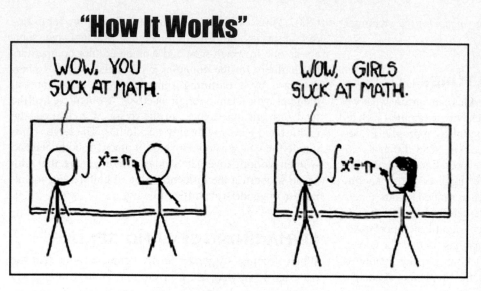

enough for love. . . . She reigns in the heart . . . the household altar is her place of worship and service" (quoted in Collins 2003:89–90). In 1874, at Harvard University, Dr. Edward Clarke, a member of its board of overseers, wrote that women were too delicate to handle the rigors of college education. The increased effort needed for thinking would sap energy from a woman's uterus and ovaries, leading these reproductive organs to shrink (Clarke 1874). In fact, Harvard did not formally admit women to its undergraduate program until the early 1970s. When women were finally given the opportunity to attend college, a right they had to fight hard for to win, they excelled. They now have a higher overall grade point average, and they outnumber men among college graduates. What was once thought to be natural is now recognized to have been a social construction. It turns out that the problem wasn't biology; it was the socially constructed culture that denied opportunity.

On the flip side, the notion that men just aren't as nurturing as women persists. It appears to grow out of the presumption that women, because they give birth and nurse babies, are naturally better at providing love, care, and protection. Yet research demonstrates that when men have the primary responsibility for raising children, they do the same things conventionally associated with "mothering." For example, sociologist Barbara Risman conducted research on single fathers and concluded that "when males take full responsibility for child care, when they meet expectations usually confined to females, they develop intimate and affectionate relationships with their children. Despite male sex-role training, fathers

feminism The belief in social, economic, and political equality for women.

respond to the nontraditional role of single parent with strategies stereotypically considered feminine" (Risman 1986:101). Similarly, researchers looking at response patterns for nearly 30,000 parents found no significant differences between North American mothers and fathers on factors including nurturance, warmth, responsiveness, encouragement, interaction, or disciplinary strictness. Thus it is not strictly biology that determines nurturing; it is the social structure and a person's position within it (Barnett and Rivers 2004; Lytton and Romney 1991; Risman and Johnson-Sumerford 1998).

Identifying some aspect of our definitions of sex and gender as artificial reveals the complex relationship between the two. Questioning our conceptions of the natural, however, is never easy, as women who have worked for the right to vote and equal opportunity have discovered. Confronting these notions can look like an attempt to defy reality itself, but such defiance is necessary to enact significant social change.

>> Working for Change: Women's Movements

One of the lessons we learn from research on gender is that change is possible. As we saw with college education for women, past norms need not determine future practices. Change, however, seldom comes without conflict. People have fought against existing cultural assumptions about what is natural in order to advance opportunity for women in politics, the economy, and other spheres of public and private life. **Feminism** is the term for this belief in social, economic, and political equality for women.

> Gender equality is more than a goal in itself. It is a precondition for meeting the challenge of reducing poverty, promoting sustainable development and building good governance.
>
> **Kofi Annan**

THE FIRST WAVE

The feminist movement in the United States was born in upstate New York, in the town of Seneca Falls, in the summer of 1848. On July 19, the first women's rights convention began, attended by Elizabeth Cady Stanton, Lucretia Mott, and other pioneers in the struggle for women's rights. This first wave of feminists faced ridicule and scorn as they fought for legal and political equality for women. They were not

WOMAN MAY WEAR TROUSERS.

Attorney General of Kansas Rules There Is No Law Against It.

TOPEKA. Kan.. April 28.—Gov. Stubbs received a letter yesterday from a widow at Oswego asking permission to wear men's trousers while at work at her home. It said she was supporting a large family. which necessitated outside work, and that in wearing skirts she was badly handicapped.

The letter was turned over to the Attorney General, who ruled there was no law prohibiting a woman from wearing men's trousers, especially if she were the head of the house.

Source: Published: April 29, 1910. Copyright © The New York Times.

afraid to risk controversy on behalf of their cause; in 1872, Susan B. Anthony was arrested for attempting to vote in that year's presidential election.

Ultimately, the early feminists won many victories. The pinnacle accomplishment of the first wave was the passage and ratification of the 19th Amendment to the Constitution, which granted women the right to vote in national elections beginning in 1920. After this peak, however, suffrage did not lead to other reforms related to women's social and economic position, and in the early and mid-20th century, the women's movement became a much less powerful force for social change.

THE SECOND WAVE

The second wave of feminism in the United States emerged in the 1960s and came into full force in the 1970s. Betty Friedan's book *The Feminine Mystique* played a crucial part, as did two other pioneering books that argued for women's rights: Simone de Beauvoir's *The Second Sex* (1952) and Kate Millett's *Sexual Politics* (1970). Friedan was an upper-middle class, White, suburban housewife who worked part-time as a freelance journalist in the 1950s. As part of a story she planned to write, she surveyed her college classmates about their lives. What she heard repeatedly from women like herself was that they shared a sense of nameless, aching dissatisfaction that she famously labeled "the problem that has no name." Even though they were living what many considered the American Dream, something was missing. They mostly blamed themselves for this feeling of emptiness or incompleteness, and when they sought help, doctors and psychiatrists prescribed charity work, community activities, or perhaps tranquilizers.

In *The Feminine Mystique*, Friedan argued that the problem was not with women as individuals, but with the position they occupied in American society at the time. Friedan's realization that this was not a private trouble but a public issue represents a classic case of using the sociological imagination. Women were cut off from the public sphere, and their lack of access to valued economic, social, and cultural resources—including money and power in the workplace—was the real problem. (Friedan herself attributed part of her relative happiness to the fact that she retained dual status as both journalist and housewife.) In order to challenge this structural problem, women had to take on the cultural assumption that the primary and most "natural" goal for women was to be a wife and mother in the private sphere. As Friedan put it, "We can no longer ignore that voice within women that says, 'I want something more than my husband and my children and my home'" (1963:32).

In 1966, Friedan helped found the National Organization for Women (NOW) in order to fight for equality for women; she served as its president until 1970. In addition to

... When the 19th Amendment finally passed in 1920, it did so by a single vote. Having passed the House and Senate in 1919, it still needed to win approval in 36 state legislatures. It reached this milestone when Tennessee legislator Harry T. Burn switched his vote and broke the tie after receiving a letter from his mother that said, "Don't forget to be a good boy and help Mrs. [Carrie Chapman] Catt put the 'Rat' in ratification."

Did You Know?

of social life. Feminists fought to open up structural opportunity and to ensure that women could make choices about going to college, pursuing a career based on ability rather than gender expectations, getting married or staying single, having children or remaining childless, and so on.

The question of whether women should have control over their reproductive rights and their bodies has also played a significant role in this movement. In the United States, most people support a woman's right to a legal abortion, but with reservations. According to a 2009 national survey, 18 percent oppose a woman's right to a legal abortion under all circumstances. However, 21 percent feel that abortion should be legal under any circumstances and 57 percent agree under certain circumstances. These findings have held fairly steady for the past 35 years (Gallup 2010).

As more and more women identified existing cultural practices as sexist attitudes and practices—including attitudes they themselves had accepted through socialization into traditional gender roles—they began to challenge male dominance. A sense of sisterhood, much like the class consciousness that Marx hoped would emerge in the proletariat, became evident. Individual women identified their interests with women as a whole, and they rejected the principle that their happiness depended on their acceptance of submissive and subordinate roles.

SOC THINK

What does it mean to be a feminist?

THE THIRD WAVE

In the 1980s, partially due to second-wave successes in opening up opportunities and earning greater respect for women, a sense developed that the central goals of feminism had largely been accomplished. Some scholars argued that we had entered a postfeminist era. In the early 1990s, however, a new style of feminism arose that went beyond fighting the structural obstacles that motivated the first and second waves. It ventured into the cultural sphere to embrace a multiplicity of voices, expressions, and experiences. This third wave was part of a conceptual shift away from a singular focus on equality of persons, which it takes as a given, to a celebration of difference (Brooks 1997; Lotz 2007; Showden 2009).

The third wave arose in part as a generational shift; younger women were

Nancy Pelosi, Democrat from California, and the first female Speaker of the U.S. House of Representatives.

political and legal battles, one of the organization's tools was "consciousness-raising groups." Among other things, these groups sought to elevate awareness among women of the degree to which they shared "the problem that has no name." This shared consciousness could then lead to collective action and the development of a new structure with enhanced opportunities. Choice was a core value at the center of these efforts. The existing system limited options for women in many areas

A Woman's Proper Place?

Percent of first-year college students who agree or strongly agree that "the activities of married women are best confined to the home and the family."

Source: Pryor et al. 2007.

dissatisfied with the dominant image of feminism as stodgy and uptight. It also represented a shift in message toward a more varied and pluralistic understanding of what feminism is. This was evident in two early anthologies that played a pivotal role presenting the multiplicity of voices this movement represents: Rebecca Walker's *To Be Real: Telling the Truth and Changing the Face of Feminism* (1995) and Barbara Findlen's *Listen Up: Voices from the Next Feminist Generation* (1995). Previously, feminists were characterized as White, upper-middle class, and heterosexual. Third-wave feminists place greater emphasis on agency and subjectivity; are committed to personal empowerment; are more open about sexuality and sexual exploration; and celebrate diversity of gender, race, ethnicity, and class. Embracing a multiplicity of identities led to a commitment to social justice and a global perspective so that other voices have the opportunity to be heard (Baumgardner and Richards 2000; Groeneveld 2009; Lotz 2007; Zimmerman, McDermott, and Gould 2009).

There is in the third wave a bit of the postmodern idea of self-creation, according to which we can choose our identities from a buffet of possibilities and create our own realities. This fits with the notion that our sex is not narrowly determined by biology and that our expression of our gender need not be singular in nature, but is open to our creativity and control. One result is a more playful or ironic element to the movement, especially when it comes to so-called girlie feminism, which seeks to reclaim things like lipstick, high heels, and more sexualized images of women as viable emblems of feminist empowerment. Critics have argued that this rhetoric of choice diminishes the continued power of racial, sexual, and class positions in society (Munford

2007; Renegar and Sowards 2009; Showden 2009).

One of the outgrowths of this new feminist perspective was the recognition that defining others primarily by any one position may diminish the importance of the multiple positions we all occupy. To look at the social location of Hispanic women, for example, we must pay mind to both their gender and ethnicity (as well as other factors). Two significant theoritical developments arising out of this multiple-identity approach are standpoint theory and intersectionality. Standpoint theory maintains that our understanding of reality is shaped by the positions we occupy and the experiences we have. Given that the views of some (based on their gender, sexuality, race, ethnicity, or class) are privileged over others, this theory emphasizes the importance of listening to the voices of those who are in some way considered outsiders. Doing so provides a deeper and richer understanding of social systems (Collins 2000; Harding 2004; Hartsock 1983; Smith 1987). Intersectionality represents a second major development. According to this approach, we cannot speak of gender or race or

> **sexuality** Denotes our identities and activities as sexual beings.

class or sexuality as if they exist in isolation from each other. Rather, these combine within us in ways that make it difficult to separate the effects of each. As such, research must analyze the intermingled effects of multiple social statuses on identity, knowledge, and outcomes (Alimahomed 2010; Harding 2004; Shields 2008). For both standpoint theory and intersectionality, a narrative approach in research, in which we hear the voices of those who are other to us, is critical.

>> The Social Construction of Sexuality

The shifts that occur in how sex and gender are defined—as more complex than simple binary categories of male and female or masculine and feminine—also apply to sexuality. In the United States, as a consequence of the dimorphic model of sex, the dominant ideology presumed heterosexual relationships, in which the idealized norm was chastity until marriage followed by lifelong faithfulness to a single partner. This vision reached perhaps its zenith in the 1950s television portrayal of families in programs such as *Leave It To Beaver* and *Father Knows Best*. Times have changed.

Sexuality denotes our identities and activities as sexual beings. In terms of identity, our sexuality represents an expression of who we are in a way similar to gender, race,

sexual orientation The categories of people to whom we are sexually attracted.

heterosexual A category of sexual orientation that includes those who are sexually attracted to members of the opposite sex.

homosexual A category of sexual orientation that includes those who are attracted to members of the same sex.

bisexual A category of sexual orientation that includes those who are attracted to both men and women.

transgender People who appear to be biologically one sex but who identify with the gender of another.

ethnicity, and class. In terms of our sexual practices, sexuality shapes what we do (or do not do) and with whom.

SEXUALITY AND IDENTITY

Sexual expression is not simply a result of biological urges and instincts. It is situated within, and an outgrowth of, existing social, cultural, and historical processes. Though alternative expressions of sexuality have a long history in the United States, their existence and practice has not always been acknowledged (Duberman, Vicinus, and Chauncy 1989; Escoffier 1997). During the 1960s, experimentation with "free love" helped open the door to more widespread recognition of such expressions. At the same time, organizations arose, such as the Gay Liberation Front in 1969 and the Gay Activist Alliance in 1970, which raised awareness that alternatives existed and sought to establish the legitimacy of alternative sexualities in the public consciousness. As a result, people became more aware

of the concept of **sexual orientation**—the categories of people to whom we are sexually attracted—as a form of personal and community identity. Initially, in keeping with the dimorphic model of sex, the two major subcategories included **heterosexual,** those who were sexually attracted to members of the opposite sex, and **homosexual,** those who were attracted to members of the same sex. Homosexual men were identified as gay and homosexual women were identified as lesbian. **Bisexual** was later added to these subcategories to include those who were attracted to both men and women.

This model of sexuality, even though it extended awareness of sexuality beyond the 1950s version, still presents the dividing lines as clear-cut and absolute. Classifying where you or others belong is presumed to be a simple matter of identifying your sexual practices and selecting the appropriate category. But people's experiences of sexuality are more complex and varied than that. For example, what about those who have had occasional homosexual experiences in their past but are now practicing heterosexuals? Or those who engage in same-sex practices but do not identify themselves as gay, lesbian, or bisexual? In an attempt to clarify just one of these definitions, historian David Halperin (2009) identified 13 different formulations of bisexuality, thus highlighting the ambiguity in drawing these lines.

Over time, in response to the limitations of this approach, a new model presented sexuality as a continuum rather than an either-or designation. A key component of this approach is the recognition of people who are **transgender**—those who appear to be biologically one sex but who identify with the gender of another—as an additional category. Doing so highlights the socially constructed nature of sexuality as opposed to its biological element, and creates more space for alternative expressions of sexuality. This is particularly true if transgender is defined even more broadly, as historian Susan Stryker (2007) suggests, "as anything that disrupts or denaturalizes normative gender, and which calls our attention to the process through which normativity is produced" (p. 60). From this perspective, transgender involves transgressions of dominant gender norms in ways that enable us to recognize their existence and power (Brooks and Quina 2009; Crabtree 2009; Kinsey, Pomeroy, and Martin 1948; Kinsey, Pomeroy, and Gebhardt 1953; Waites 2009).

Though awareness of alternative forms of sexuality has increased, a cultural expectation of heterosexuality remains dominant in the United States. Sociologists use the term

First-Year College Students' Attitudes About Homosexuality Laws

Men

Women

70
60
50
40
30
20
10
0

'76 '78 '80 '82 '84 '86 '88 '90 '92 '94 '96 '98 2000 '02 '04 '06

"It is important to have laws prohibiting homosexual relationships," percent of first-year college students who agree strongly or somewhat.
Source: Pryor et al. 2007.

Thomas Beatie was born female and underwent sexual reassignment surgery to become male. He kept his female reproductive organs in hopes one day of becoming a parent. When his wife could not become pregnant, he conceived and gave birth to their first child in 2008.

heteronormativity to describe the cultural presupposition that heterosexuality is the appropriate standard for sexual identity and practice and that alternative sexualities are deviant, abnormal, or wrong (Chambers 2007; Elia 2003). As an example of heteronormativity, a 1957 survey found that "four out of five people believed that anyone who preferred to remain single was 'sick,' 'neurotic,' or 'immoral' " (Coontz 2005:230). Additionally, homosexuality was categorized as a psychological disorder until 1972 in the American Psychiatric Association's official *Diagnostic and Statistical Manual of Mental Disorders* (DSM). A new edition of the DSM is due out in 2012, and debate centers around what are now called "gender identity disorders," including those who are transgender and transsexual. Some psychological professionals prefer not to identify these as disorders because doing so stigmatizes these identities. Others argue that it is important to maintain these diagnoses because transgender people who seek gender reassignment surgery might not get proper diagnosis and treatment without such a designation (Drescher 2010; Melby 2009).

Heteronormativity is a form of ethnocentrism that generalizes a particular cultural ideal (heterosexuality) onto all other populations, thus denying legitimacy to those outside it (Chambers 2007). It can be maintained in subtle, often invisible ways during our everyday interactions. The television series *Glee* captured just such a moment in an encounter between Kurt, a gay high school student, and his father, Burt, who is generally understanding and supportive of Kurt's sexuality. Kurt was saddened at the seeming ease with which his dad talked sports with Finn, the school's star quarterback. His father tries to reassure him by saying,

SOC THINK

How is heteronormativity reinforced in the current top-rated songs and television programs? Can you think of any exceptions?

"Kurt, I love you. And I am sympathetic to all your stuff. But come on, buddy, we've got a deal here, right? I don't try to change you; you don't try to change me. You are my son, and a little guy talk with some other kid isn't going to change that." Kurt replies, "Guy talk? I'm a guy." It is precisely at moments such as this, when a person becomes invisible as a guy because he does not conform to the dominant gender expectations, that heteronormativity is at work.

Socialization plays a key role in determining our sexual identity (Parker 2009). Just as was the case with gender, we face significant pressure to obey dominant norms for masculinity and femininity. In her book *Dude You're a Fag,* sociologist C. J. Pascoe (2007) set out to understand how heteronormativity is reproduced. She conducted an ethnographic study of boys in a working-class high school. She found that one of the ways they reinforced existing masculinity norms was by casually using the term "fag" to call out anyone who deviates from the dominant masculine ideal. According to Pascoe, calling someone a fag was not so much an anti-gay act (though she admits it was that too) as it was a means of keeping guys in line. Whereas it was possible to be a homosexual and still be masculine, being a fag represented a form of failed masculinity. The threat of being a fag hangs over them like a specter or ghost that could possess them at any time; only eternal vigilance keeps it at bay. Pascoe argues that rejecting this role also represented a repudiation of femininity. So not only did this discourse support existing heteronormative standards,

> **heteronormativity** A term that sociologists use to describe the cultural presupposition that heterosexuality is the appropriate standard for sexual identity and practice and that alternative sexualities are deviant, abnormal, or wrong.

it also reinforced traditional conceptions of gender. Other researchers found similar results in a study of "hogging" in which men have sex with overweight or obese women not as a means of establishing a relationship with them but, rather, as a game to prove their masculinity to other guys (Prohaska and Gailey 2010).

Such examples point to the fact that differences in sexuality are not just matters of orientation and alternative preferences; they are connected to larger systems of power in which some statuses are privileged over others (Brickell 2009). We construct our sexual identities, making sense of who we are, within the contexts of our social structures. Within these worlds, not all paths are accepted as equally legitimate. In the United States, establishing a sexual identity as something other than heterosexual has been diffi-

---

SOCTHINK

How does gendered name-calling, such as joking that a guy is a fag, function to maintain clear-cut gender boundaries? What consequences does it have for gays, lesbians, or heterosexual girls?

---

cult due to the meanings attached to such identities and the lack of broader cultural support for them. These power differences contribute to discrimination and threats of violence. According to the FBI, for example, 17 percent of the 7780 hate crime incidents reported in 2008 involved sexual orientation (U.S. Department of Justice 2009a).

In an effort to ensure the civil, political, and social rights of those in lesbian, gay, bisexual, and transgender (LGBT) communities around the world, a group of human rights experts gathered in Indonesia in 2006 to establish the Yogyakarta Principles (www.yogyakartaprinciples.org/). The principles are built on the supposition of universal human rights and seek to extend these rights to include sexual orientation and gender identity. They identify 29 basic principles including the right to equality and nondiscrimination, the right to work, and the right to found a family. This movement arose in part because homosexuality remains a crime in many nations; in some it is punishable by death.

In places where there has been more openness about sexuality, increasingly, sexual preference may not necessarily be the primary mode of identification, but it exists in combination with gender, race, ethnicity, nationality, and class (Stein 2010). As alternative expressions of sexuality become more accepted and less alternative, their role as master status through which all identity is filtered may become less powerful. Instead, in keeping with the intersectionality perspective, sexuality may become but one significant piece of identity that shapes who we are and the paths we are likely to pursue (Gomez 1997).

SEXUALITY IN ACTION

While our sexuality shapes our conception of who we are, it also has consequences for what we do. In sociological terms,

as suggested by the Thomas theorem (see p. 15), we come to perceive ourselves and others through interaction and socialization. We then act on the basis of those perceptions. In our everyday lives, our perceptions of ourselves and our sexual practices often reinforce each other. Working out our sexuality in practice includes the types of sex acts we perform and the types of sexual relationships we establish with others.

Because such topics are generally considered to be taboo, people are often both ignorant and curious about actual sexual practices. The Kinsey Reports (*Sexual Behavior in the Human Male* [1948] and *Sexual Behavior in the Human Female* [1953]) provided the earliest in-depth research studies on people's sexual practices. Their results, particularly their finding that 8 percent of men had been in predominantly homosexual relationships for at least three years between ages 16 and 55, were considered shocking at the time. Both volumes became best sellers. Their studies opened the door for others to conduct additional research (Bullough 1998; Laumann et al. 1994; Smith 2006).

The National Survey of Family Growth (NSFG) provides recent data and includes detailed information on actual sexual practices. It is conducted by the National Center for Health Statistics (NCHS) and the Centers for Disease

Alfred C. Kinsey

Control and Prevention (CDC), and is based on a national sample of more than 12,500 respondents (Mosher, Chandra, and Jones 2005). Summarizing the results of heterosexual relationship patterns, the NSFG researchers report:

> Among adults 25–44 years of age, 97 percent of men and 98 percent of women have had vaginal intercourse; 90 percent of men and 88 percent of women have had oral sex with an opposite-sex partner; and 40 percent of men and 35 percent of women have had anal sex with an opposite-sex partner. (p. 1)

They also investigated the numbers of opposite-sex partners people had in their lifetime, finding that, among women, 32 percent report they have had 1 or 2 male partners, 36 percent say 3 to 6, and 11 percent report they have had 15 or more. For men the numbers are 17 percent with 1 or 2 partners, 28 percent say 3 to 6, and 29 percent report 15 or more. Within the previous 12 months, 68 percent of women and 63 percent of men reported only one opposite-sex partner, while approximately 15 percent of women and men reported zero partners. Among married couples, 2.5 percent of married men and 3.8 percent of married women reported more than one opposite-sex partner in the previous 12 months. Among those cohabitating, 16 percent of men and 15 percent of women reported more than one opposite-sex partner within the previous year.

One contentious question in such studies is the percentage of homosexuals in the U.S. population. A commonly used figure (derived from the Kinsey Reports) estimates that approximately 10 percent of the population is homosexual. The NSFG study distinguished between having had same-sex experiences and identifying with particular sexual orientations. The researchers found that, among men aged 25–44, 6.5 percent have had same-sex sexual contact in their lifetime and 3 percent reported having had such experiences in the previous 12 months. Among women of the same age, 10.5 percent have had same-sex sexual contact in their lifetime and 3.4 percent reported having had such contact within the previous 12 months. The researchers also investigated bisexual practices, finding that 1 to 2 percent of men and women have had both male and female partners within the past 12 months.

Simply having had same-sex experiences does not necessarily result in a same-sex identity. The NSFG researchers asked, "Do you think of yourself as a heterosexual, homosexual, bisexual, or something else?" As the accompanying table demonstrates (see p. 302), 90 percent of both men and women identify themselves as heterosexual. The numbers of people who identify as homosexual and bisexual are lower than the numbers of those who have engaged in such practices. Overall, the percentage of men and women aged 18–44 who identify themselves as either homosexual or bisexual is approximately 4.1 percent. This finding is consistent with other more recent national studies on sexual behavior in the United States (Laumann et al. 1994; Mosher et al. 2005; Smith 2006).

Relationship Values by Gender and Sexual Identity

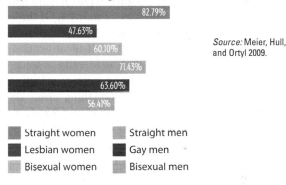

Importance of love
- 91.15%
- 73.09%
- 85.74%
- 81.59%
- 82.14%
- 79.02%

Importance of faithfulness
- 93.36%
- 79.78%
- 83.66%
- 85.02%
- 80.53%
- 73.87%

Importance of lifelong commitment
- 82.79%
- 47.63%
- 60.10%
- 71.43%
- 63.60%
- 56.41%

Straight women — Straight men
Lesbian women — Gay men
Bisexual women — Bisexual men

Source: Meier, Hull, and Ortyl 2009.

The age at which people have their first sexual experiences has historically been an additional interest of researchers. In terms of opposite-sex experiences, the percentage of teens who have had sexual intercourse rises with each subsequent year. Before the age of 14, 6 percent of girls and 8 percent of boys have had vaginal sexual intercourse; by age 16, it is 27 percent for girls and 25 percent for boys; at age 18, it is 59 percent for girls and 54 percent for boys. Among those aged 15–17, approximately 11 percent of females and 13 percent of males had engaged in oral sex but had not had vaginal intercourse (Abma, Martinez, Mosher, and Dawson 2004).

One of the concerns about those who have sex at a young age is sexual coercion. In fact, among girls who had their first sexual intercourse before age 14, 27 percent said that they really didn't want it to happen at the time. Another 55 percent had mixed feelings about whether they wanted sex or not. For boys who were the same age, 5 percent didn't want it to happen and 28 percent had mixed feelings. For those who had sex before age 20, 13 percent of females and 6 percent of males didn't want it to happen (Abma et al. 2004).

When it comes to same-sex experiences among those who are younger, females have a higher likelihood of having

Labor Force Participation The labor market has opened up significantly since Betty Friedan published *The Feminine Mystique* in 1963. Today, millions of women—married or single, with or without children, pregnant or recently having given birth—are in the labor force. Overall,

> **glass ceiling** An invisible barrier that blocks the promotion of a qualified individual in a work environment because of the individual's gender, race, or ethnicity.

59.5 percent of adult women in the United States were in the labor force in 2008, compared to 41 percent in 1970. By contrast, in 2008, 73 percent of adult men in the United States were in the labor force, compared to 76 percent in 1970. Overall, 67 percent of women who are pregnant with their first child work full-time, compared to 44 percent in

the early 1960s. Among married mothers, 62 percent of those with children under age 6 were in the labor force in 2008, compared to 30 percent in 1970 (T. Johnson 2008; U.S. Census Bureau 2009f:Tables 576, 585).

Still, women entering the job market find their options restricted in important ways. Particularly damaging is occupational segregation, or confinement to sex-typed "women's jobs." For example, in 2008, women accounted for 98 percent of all dental hygienists and 84 percent of all librarians. Entering such sex-typed occupations often places women in "service" roles that parallel the traditional gender-role standard (U.S. Census Bureau 2009f:Table 603).

Women are underrepresented in occupations historically defined as "men's jobs," which often offer much greater financial rewards and prestige than women's jobs. For example, in 2008, women accounted for approximately 47 percent of the paid labor force of the United States, yet they constituted only 10 percent of civil engineers, 27 percent of all dentists, 22 percent of all computer programmers, and 31 percent of physicians. Sixty-eight percent of professional women are in health care or education (Bureau of Labor Statistics 2009e; U.S. Census Bureau 2009f:Table 603).

When it comes to getting promotions, women sometimes encounter attitudinal or organizational bias that prevents them from reaching their full potential. The term **glass ceiling** refers to an invisible barrier that blocks the promotion of a qualified individual in a work environment because of the individual's gender, race, or ethnicity. A 2007 study showed that women held less than 15 percent of the seats on the boards of directors of the 500 largest corporations in the United States. In 2010, only 15 of those corporations had a female CEO while 485 had a male in that post (Angelo 2010; Catalyst 2007; Guerrera and Ward 2007).

U.S. Women as a Percentage of All Workers in Select Occupations

Underrepresented		Overrepresented	
Aircraft pilots	2.6	High school teachers	56.0
Firefighters	4.8	Cashiers	75.5
Civil engineers	10.4	Social workers	79.4
Police officers	14.7	Elementary teachers	81.2
Clergy	14.8	Librarians	83.5
Chefs and head cooks	17.0	File clerks	83.8
Printers	19.8	Tellers	90.1
Dentists	27.2	Registered nurses	91.7
Computer systems analysts	27.5	Word processors and typists	92.9
Physicians	30.5	Receptionists	93.6
Mail carriers	33.0	Child care workers	95.6
Lawyers	34.4	Dental hygienists	97.7

Note: Women constitute 47 percent of the entire labor force.

Source: Data for 2008 reported in U.S. Census Bureau 2009f:Table 603.

Income Today we claim to value "equal pay for equal work," meaning that someone's sex (along with race, ethnicity, or age) shouldn't matter in determining what the person earns; the only characteristic that should matter is job performance. But in practice, women do not earn as much on average as men, even in the same occupations. When comparing individuals who worked full-time, year-round in 2008, the median income for men was $46,367, and the median for women was $35,745 (DeNavas-Walt et al. 2009). In other words, women earned 77 cents for every dollar that men earned overall.

Taking occupational segregation into account does not explain away the wage gap. Although women are often more concentrated in occupations with lower average wages than men (child care worker or receptionist versus physician or civil engineer), a detailed analysis by researchers at the Census Bureau found only 9 out of 509 occupational categories within which women earned at least 95 percent of men's earnings (Weinberg 2004). Significant wage gaps exist within occupations across the board. For example, wage gaps persist in the three occupations for which women receive the highest average pay: pharmacist (86 percent of men's earnings), lawyer (81 percent), and chief executive (80.2 percent). Of course, in some occupations the wage gap is significantly wider, including insurance agent (66 percent), retail sales (71 percent), and physician/surgeon (64 percent) (Bureau of Labor Statistics 2009e).

Even in occupations where women are more likely to be concentrated, they still earn less on average than do men in the same field. Examples include receptionist (94 percent), elementary or middle school teacher (88 percent), and registered nurse (87 percent). Observers of the labor force have termed this advantage for men in female-dominated occupations the "glass escalator," in contrast to the glass ceiling (Bureau of Labor Statistics 2009e; Cognard-Black 2004).

What accounts for these wage gaps between men and women in the same occupation? The Census Bureau studied the following characteristics of men and women in the same occupation:

- Age and degree of formal education
- Marital status and the presence of children at home
- Specialization within the occupation (for example, family practice versus surgical practice)
- Years of work experience
- Hours worked per year

Taking all these factors into consideration reduced the pay gap between men and women by only 2 cents. Even taking such factors into account, women still earned 79 cents for every dollar earned by men. In sum, the disparity in pay between men and women cannot be explained by pointing to women's career choices (Correll, Benard, and Paik 2007; Government Accountability Office 2003; Weinberg 2007).

> **second shift** The double burden—work outside the home followed by child care and housework—that many women face and few men share equitably.

Home and Work Today, many women face the challenge of trying to juggle work and family. Who does the housework when women become productive wage earners? In households where both work full-time, wives do on average 28 hours of housework while husbands do 16. This approximate 2:1 ratio holds across social class levels. Even in households where she works and he does not, wives still do more housework (Belkin 2008).

Sociologist Arlie Hochschild (1989, 1990, 2005) has used the phrase **second shift** to describe the double burden—work outside the home followed by child care and housework—that many women face and few men share equitably. On the basis of interviews with and observations of 52 couples over an eight-year period, Hochschild reported that the wives (and not their husbands) drive home from the office while planning domestic schedules and playdates for children—and then begin their second shift. Drawing on national studies, she concluded that women spend 15 fewer hours each week in leisure activities than their husbands. In a year, these women work an extra month of 24-hour days because of the second shift; over a dozen years, they work an extra year of 24-hour days. Hochschild found that the married couples she studied were fraying at the edges, and so were their careers and their marriages. With such reports in mind, many feminists

Actual and Projected Wage Gaps Between Male and Female Earnings

	1994	2001	2011	2031
Percentage gap between men's and women's earnings				
All ages	27.5	29.2	26.5	21.9
Ages 25–44	20.9	21.3	17.6	16.9
Ages 45–64	42.9	43.6	38.8	29.0

Source: Kelly Rathie, "Male Versus Female Earnings—Is the Gender Gap Converging?" *Economist Ltd.,* Spring 2002, vol. 7, no. 1.

power women possess in society. As Kristof and WuDunn (2009) put it, "People get away with enslaving village girls for the same reason that people got away with enslaving blacks two hundred years ago: The victims are perceived as discounted humans" (p. 24). Increased education and opportunity for women, they suggest, leads to a curtailing of violence. In the United States, the fight for self-determination by women has had a substantial effect on opportunity for women in politics, the workplace, and relationships.

WOMEN AROUND THE WORLD

Opportunities for women vary significantly around the world. In an attempt to quantify the degree of gender inequality, the World Economic Forum releases an annual global gender gap index. It ranks 130 nations in four categories, including economic participation and opportunity, educational attainment, health and survival, and political empowerment. Researchers then combine these rankings into a single value intended to measure the inequality gap

Somalian-born author Ayaan Hirsi Ali, now a Dutch feminist and activist, and named by TIME magazine in 2005 as one of the 100 most influential people in the world.

Going **GLOBAL**

Gender Inequality in Industrial Nations

Striking differences exist in women's empowerment—that is, the percentage of women in leadership positions—from one country to the next (right). Yet there is much less difference in the division of housework, even in the same countries (left).

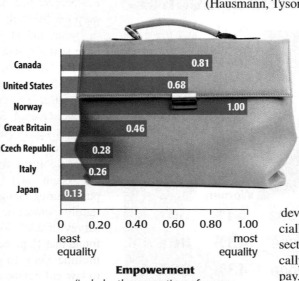

	Division of Housework	Empowerment
Canada	3.70	0.81
United States	3.72	0.68
Norway	3.73	1.00
Great Britain	3.92	0.46
Czech Republic	4.07	0.28
Italy	4.24	0.26
Japan	4.49	0.13

5   4   3   2   1
wife   husband
always does   always does

Division of Housework
(includes laundry, grocery shopping, dinner preparation, and care for sick family members)

0   0.20   0.40   0.60   0.80   1.00
least   most
equality   equality

Empowerment
(includes the proportions of women in parliament, in management, and in professional/technical positions)

Source: Adapted from Fuwa 2004:757.

that exists between men and women in each country, with a score of 100 percent indicating equality. In 2009, only four countries—Iceland, Norway, Finland, and Sweden—scored above 80 percent. The United States ranked 31st, with a score of 72 percent, behind nations such as the Philippines, the United Kingdom, South Africa, and Cuba. The bottom 10 nations, including countries such as Saudi Arabia, Turkey, Pakistan, and Chad, had scores below 60 percent (Hausmann, Tyson, and Zahidi 2009).

When it comes to the economy, it is estimated that women grow half the world's food, but they rarely own land. They constitute one-third of the world's paid labor force but are generally found in the lowest-paying jobs. Women perform much of the exploited labor in developing nations, especially in the nonindustrial sector. Female workers typically toil long hours for low pay, but they still contribute significantly to their families' incomes (Quisumbing, Meinzen-Dick, and Bassett 2008; UNCTAD 2009).

Single-parent households headed by women, which appear to be on the rise in many nations, are typically found in the poorest sections of the population. The feminization of poverty has become a global phenomenon.

As is the case in the United States, women in other industrialized nations also experience occupational segregation. In Great Britain, for example, only 29 percent of computer analysts are women, while 81 percent of cashiers and 90 percent of nurses are women (Cross and Bagilhole 2002; Women and Work Commission 2006). Worldwide, women hold less than 1 percent of corporate managerial positions.

In recognition of the underrepresentation of women on boards of directors, the Norwegian legislature established minimum quotas for the number of female board members. As the architects of the plan put it, "Instead of assuming what people *can't* do at work, provide opportunities for employees to prove what they can do." The goal was not complete equity for women, but 40 percent representation by 2008. The percentage in Norway in 2010 stood at 40—much higher than Europe's average of 21 percent (Inter-Parliamentary Union 2010; Norwegian Ministry of Children and Equality 2009).

Women in other industrial nations also struggle with the balance between home and work, especially regarding housework. According to one survey, 30 percent of the couples in U.S. households share most of the housework, compared to 4 percent in Japan, 25 percent in Great Britain, 27 percent in Sweden, and 32 percent in Canada (C. Geist 2005). Sociologist Makiko Fuwa (2004) analyzed gender inequality in 22 industrial countries using data from the International Social Survey Programme. Fuwa compared how couples divided their housework to society-wide measures of women's presence in high-status occupations, as well as their wages relative to men's. A pattern emerged in which those countries that placed greater emphasis on empowerment for women tended to have more balanced housework loads between men and women.

Sociology often confronts us with things that can make us uncomfortable, such as gender inequality. The point of doing so is a more complete understanding of what we do and why we do it. Such knowledge can lead us to new and better practices that provide greater understanding, fairness, equality, and opportunity. Through practicing the sociological imagination, as Betty Friedan did in the case of gender, we can make the world a better place.

For REVIEW

I. How has our understanding of sex and gender shifted over time?

- The presumption that gender and sexuality are narrowly determined by our biology has given way to an understanding of both as socially constructed, complex, and multidimensional.

II. How has opportunity for women in the United States changed over time?

- In the 1950s, women's primary roles were wife and mother. Since that time, largely due to the efforts of the second wave of the women's movement, their labor force participation and income have risen significantly.

III. To what extent does gender still shape access to resources?

- Women continue to be paid less than men in the same occupations, tend to be segregated into a narrower range of female-dominated occupations, bear greater responsibility for housework, and are underrepresented as elected officials.

Functionalist View

Gender roles establish the proper behavior, attitudes, and activities expected of men and women for a stable society.

Shifts in sexuality are a consequence of changes in what modern societies need, especially in terms of reproduction, to maintain social order.

Families need both an **instrumental leader** and an **expressive leader**; historically, women's natural gravitation to expressive goals freed men for instrumental tasks, and vice versa.

GENDER ROLES, INSTRUMENTAL LEADER, EXPRESSIVE LEADER
KEY CONCEPTS

Conflict View

The presumption that gender is determined by nature results in a belief that biology is destiny, an ideology that reinforces the existing system of gender inequality.

Heteronormativity is a form of power that limits alternative expressions of sexuality and contributes to discrimination.

Even after the feminist movements produced substantial changes, women still face significant **discrimination** in wages, occupations, and politics.

KEY CONCEPTS
IDEOLOGY, DISCRIMINATION, SEXISM

Interactionist View

Our conceptions of gender and sexuality are not determined by biology but, rather, are the consequences of historical, social, and cultural practices over time.

Male–female differences and heterosexual preferences get reinforced through **everyday interaction**, such as giving trucks to boys and dolls to girls.

The negative responses people have when gender and sexuality norms are broken—reinforce existing dominant roles.

KEY CONCEPTS
SOCIAL CONSTRUCTION, GENDER NORMS, ROLES

MAKE THE CONNECTION

After reviewing the chapter, answer the following questions:

1

How would each of the perspectives seek to explain the experiences of women around the world, like Woineshet Zebene, who face significant violence and discriminations (pp. 293–294)?

2

How would each of the three perspectives look at the supposition that differences between men and women are "natural" and always have been?

3

How would the macro approaches of the conflict and functionalist perspectives study gender and sexuality differently than the micro approach of the interactionist perspective?

4

How does each perspective contribute to your understanding of your own gender-role socialization?

Pop Quiz

1. What term do sociologists use to describe the biological differences between males and females?
   a. gender
   b. sexism
   c. anatomy
   d. sex

2. What term does geneticist Anne Fausto-Sterling use to describe those who have biological characteristics typically associated with both males and females?
   a. sex
   b. gender
   c. intersexual
   d. gender displays

3. When college students conducted an experiment in which they violated expected gender norms, they demonstrated the power of
   a. gender-role socialization.
   b. biological determinism.
   c. instrumental leadership.
   d. the glass ceiling.

4. What is the expression used when claiming that gender for men is not narrowly limited to traditional conceptions of masculinity?
   a. intersexual
   b. gender modification
   c. sex
   d. multiple masculinities

5. What do groups such as the *berdaches, hijras,* and *xanith* reveal about the nature of sex and gender?
   a. All societies share the same dimorphic, male–female model of sex.
   b. The number of sex and gender categories varies across cultures.
   c. Socialization plays a significant role in modern societies, but a more limited role in traditional societies.
   d. Sex categories vary across cultures, but expressions of gender are universal.

6. The primary accomplishment of the first wave of the women's movement was
   a. making women citizens.
   b. gaining the right to an abortion.
   c. earning the right to nondiscrimination in the workplace.
   d. winning the right to vote.

7. What term describes the categories of people to whom we are sexually attracted?
   a. heteronormativity
   b. sexual orientation
   c. sexuality
   d. sexual displays

8. According to early sociologists Talcott Parsons and Robert Bales, which type of leader bears responsibility for completion of tasks, focuses on more-distant goals, and manages the external relationship between the family and other social institutions?
   a. expressive
   b. charismatic
   c. instrumental
   d. traditional

9. Overall, when comparing full-time, year-round workers, how much do women earn compared to every dollar men earn?
   a. 42 cents
   b. 63 cents
   c. 77 cents
   d. 92 cents

10. The expression "second shift" refers to
    a. doing the emotional work of maintaining family relationships.
    b. maintaining the household including housework in addition to a job outside the home.
    c. having a work shift ranging approximately between 4:00 P.M. and midnight.
    d. doing paid labor at the workplace.

1. (d); 2. (c); 3. (a); 4. (d); 5. (b); 6. (d); 7. (b); 8. (c); 9. (c); 10. (b)

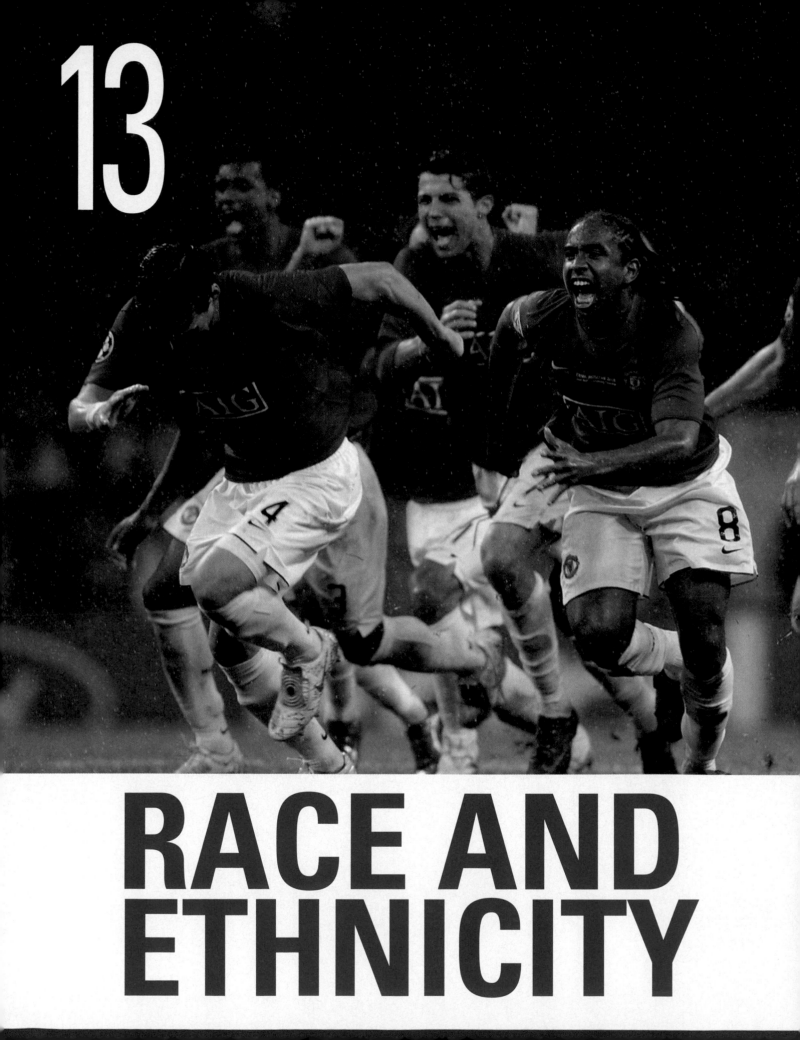

13

RACE AND ETHNICITY

COMING TO AMERICA

On May 12, 2008, Santiago Cordero was on a high school field trip when he got an urgent text message. The Immigration and Customs Enforcement agency (ICE) had raided the meat processing plant where his mother worked. ICE had arrested 389 people, and his mother was one of them (Fuson 2008).

The raid occurred at Agriprocessors, Inc., in Postville, a rural Iowa town with a population of about 2500. It was the largest such raid in U.S. history. The plant employed 968 people, and ICE agents had warrants for the arrest of 697 of them.

Santiago's immigration story is not uncommon. His dad was the first in the family to come from Mexico. He gained legal work documentation and now serves as a custodian in the local school district. Santiago arrived a year later, and his mom and siblings arrived after that. They had no such papers.

In high school, Santiago served as an interpreter for student–teacher conferences, started on the varsity football team, and organized the school's first soccer team, which included 28 students from five nationalities. As a senior he won the class volunteer award and received two scholarships. He graduated on May 25 and faced the possibility of arrest and deportation as soon as he walked across the stage to receive his diploma (Fuson 2008).

The Postville workers represented the latest in a long line of immigration stories. Earlier immigrants arrived from Germany, Italy, Poland, Lithuania, China, Vietnam, or Laos, but the obstacles and opposition they faced were similar. A decade before, the Postville workers would have likely been from Mexico or Bosnia. Now many of those workers had moved on to better jobs. Of the 389 workers arrested, 295 were from Guatemala. Other processing plants were employing increasing numbers of immigrants from Somalia and Sudan. People immigrate because conditions in their homelands are so poor. Like every other immigration stream in U.S. history, they are looking for opportunity (Leys 2008).

Postville represents a microcosm of the United States. It has a diverse population from around the world, both rich and poor. In a small community like this, face-to-face interaction with people from other cultures is inevitable. Such contact can break down some barriers and lead to greater understanding on all sides. As Postville's school superintendent, David Strudthoff, put it, "It's harder than hell to hate people when you get to know them" (quoted in Fuson 2008).

- How do sociologists define race and ethnicity?
- What are prejudice and discrimination, and how do they operate?
- What are the consequences of race and ethnicity for opportunity?

>> Racial and Ethnic Groups

The election of Barack Obama as president marked a watershed moment in American history. Every president who served before him was a White, non-Hispanic male. From all over the country, there were reports of children from various racial and ethnic backgrounds, both boys and girls, saying that anyone could grow up to be president. Once Obama took office, what had seemed unthinkable only a generation ago gave way to a new sense of possibility, opening the door for greater opportunity for all throughout the nation.

Since European colonists established their first settlement in Jamestown in 1607 with the help of the native Powhatan tribe, intergroup relations based on ethnic and racial background have played a powerful role in shaping both interaction and opportunity. One of the factors shaping opportunity was access to valued material, social, and cultural resources, a factor strongly influenced by the social status of the group to which one belonged. A **minority group** is a subordinate group whose members have significantly less control or power over their own lives than the members of the dominant or majority group have over theirs. Sociologists consider groups that lack power to be minority groups even if they represent a numeric majority of the population in a society.

Race and ethnicity historically have served as markers of minority group status. The term **racial group** describes a group that is set apart from others because of physical

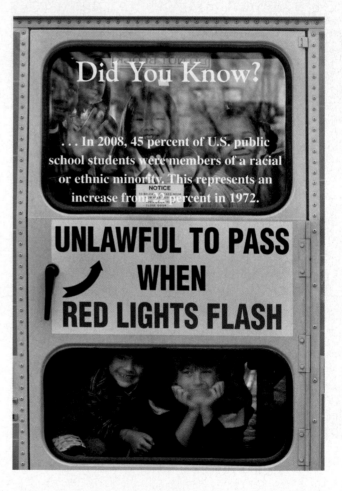

Did You Know?

. . . In 2008, 45 percent of U.S. public school students were members of a racial or ethnic minority. This represents an increase from 22 percent in 1972.

UNLAWFUL TO PASS WHEN RED LIGHTS FLASH

differences that have taken on social significance. Whites, African Americans, and Asian Americans are all considered racial groups in the United States. Although the construct of race emphasizes the significance of external physical differences, it is the culture of a particular society that identifies and attaches social significance to those differences. An **ethnic group** is one that is set apart from others primarily because of its national origin or distinctive

minority group A subordinate group whose members, even if they represent a numeric majority, have significantly less control or power over their own lives than the members of a dominant or majority group have over theirs.

racial group A group that is set apart from others because of physical differences that have taken on social significance.

ethnic group A group that is set apart from others primarily because of its national origin or distinctive cultural patterns.

Racial and Ethnic Groups in the United States

Classification	Number in Thousands	Percentage of Total Population
Racial Groups		
Whites (non-Hispanic)	198,943	65.4%
Blacks/African Americans	37,546	12.4
Asian American	13,414	4.4
Chinese	3,078	1.0
Asian Indians	2,496	0.8
Filipinos	2,426	0.8
Vietnamese	1,432	0.5
Koreans	1,344	0.4
Japanese	710	0.2
Pacific Islanders and other	428	0.1
Native Americans, Alaskan Native	2,443	0.8
Ethnic Groups		
White ancestry (single or mixed, non-Hispanic)		
Germans	50,272	16.5
Irish	36,278	11.9
English	27,516	9.0
Italians	17,749	5.8
Poles	9,887	3.3
French	9,447	3.1
Scottish and Scotch-Irish	9,365	3.1
Jews	6,489	2.1
Hispanic (or Latinos)	46,891	15.4
Mexican Americans	30,739	10.1
Puerto Ricans	4,217	1.4
Cubans	1,617	0.5
Salvadorans	1,592	0.5
Dominicans	1,328	0.4
Other Hispanics	7,400	2.4
Total (all groups)	**304,060**	

Note: Percentages do not total 100 and subtotals do not add up to totals in major categories because of overlap between groups (for example, Polish American Jews or people of mixed ancestry, such as Irish and Italian).

Source: U.S. Census Bureau 2009f:Table 77; 2009j:Tables B03001, DP-2, DP-5.

cultural patterns. In the United States, Puerto Ricans, Jews, and Polish Americans are all categorized as ethnic groups. As a nation composed primarily of immigrants and their descendants, the United States has a significant amount of racial and ethnic diversity.

RACE

Historically in the United States, it was presumed that racial categorization was a simple matter: Race was biologically determined in straightforward ways, and the dividing lines between groups were clear. It was also assumed that, for the most part, a person's parents would both be of the same race, so identifying a child's racial makeup was also a simple matter. Of course there were times when people from different racial groups had children. In the 19th century, potential ambiguity was resolved in the United States by establishing the "one-drop rule." In that case, if a person had any ancestors who were Black, no matter how many generations back, the person was labeled Black, even if he or she appeared to be White.

The one-drop rule represented an attempt at keeping racial classification simple and pure, but biological analysis demonstrates that no clear boundaries exist between the entrenched racial categories. When considering race, it's not a question of whether or not biological variation exists—it certainly does. The key is whether or not such differences justify the division of the human population into clear and distinct groups.

When it comes to genetic variation, the biological differences within what we think of as racial groups are actually greater than the differences between those groups. Genetic researchers Luca Cavalli-Sforza, Paolo Menozzi, and Alberto Piazza (1994), for example, point out that people from northeast China are genetically closer to Europeans, Eskimos, and North American Indians than they are to people from south China (p. 84). In fact, the overall degree of human genetic variation is quite small when compared with genetic variation among other large mammals—due primarily to the fact that communities of human beings have always interacted and reproduced, even across great distances (MacEachern 2003:20).

Scientists working on the Human Genome Project (HGP) have mapped our entire genetic code, providing us with the most detailed description of our biological makeup available. They concluded that race as we understand it does not exist. Craig Venter (2000), one of the project's lead scientists, declared in his presentation of the HGP results that "the concept of race has no genetic or scientific basis," and in a later interview, he said, "Race is a social concept, not a scientific one" (quoted in Angier 2000). The researchers found that all humans share the same basic genetic material, and physical manifestations such as skin color represent different combinations, in greater or lesser degrees, of the same shared genes.

Social Construction of Race To understand race, we must move beyond biology to understand the ways in which we socially construct racial categories. If we look cross-culturally, we see that different groups define racial categories in different ways at different times. Each society defines which differences are important while ignoring other characteristics that could serve as a basis for social differentiation. In the United States, we see differences in both skin color and hair color, yet people learn that differences in skin color have a dramatic social and political meaning whereas differences in hair color do not.

When observing skin color, many people in the United States tend to lump others rather casually into the traditional categories of "Black," "White," and "Asian." More-subtle differences in skin color often go unnoticed. In many nations of Central America and South America, by contrast, people recognize color gradients on a continuum from light to dark skin color. Brazil has approximately 40 color groupings, and in other countries people may be described as "Mestizo Honduran," "Mulatto Colombian," or "African Panamanian." What people see as "obvious" differences, then, are subject to each society's social definitions.

We develop our understanding of racial categories through the process of what sociologists Michael Omi and Howard Winant (1994) have called **racial formation**—a sociohistorical process in which racial categories are created, inhibited, transformed, and destroyed. Omi and Winant argue that race is neither fundamentally biological nor an illusion that can simply be ignored. To understand race, one must pay careful attention to the social, economic, and political forces that have established it as a basic distinction among human beings. Historically, those in positions of power have categorized whole groups of people as fundamentally distinct from each other (e.g., when the one-drop rule was instituted) and then used their control over resources to treat people differently based on those distinctions. The result is a social structure that reinforces presumed racial differences and justifies unequal treatment

racial formation A sociohistorical process in which racial categories are created, inhibited, transformed, and destroyed.

stereotype An unreliable generalization about all members of a group that does not recognize individual differences within the group.

on the basis of race. The creation of a reservation system for Native Americans in the late 1800s is one example of racial formation. Federal officials combined what were distinctive tribes into a single racial group, which we refer to today as Native Americans.

Did You Know?

. . . In a 2007 survey of African Americans, 37 percent said that, due to increased diversity within their community, Blacks should no longer be thought of as a single race. Just over half—53 percent—thought that they still should be.

Given that our understanding of race was rooted in particular historical circumstances, it has shifted over time as those circumstances changed. For example, the massive influx of immigrants in the 19th century, from places like Ireland, Germany, China, Italy, and eastern Europe, complicated the supposed simplicity of the Black–White divide. These immigrant groups were often judged to be biologically beneath White citizens. For example, both the Irish and the Italians were regarded as members of another race inferior to Whites. Many African Americans of the time regarded being Irish as lower socially than being Black. Over time, both the Irish and the Italians came to be seen as two White ethnic groups. This was accomplished in part by positioning themselves as distinct from African Americans in order to identify more closely with the White majority (Guglielmo 2003; Ignatiev 1995; Roediger 2005).

Even though these differences are socially constructed, their consequences are no less real. Race is often used to justify unequal access to economic, social, and cultural resources based on the assumption that such inequality is somehow "natural." This can happen through the use of **stereotypes,** for example, which are unreliable generalizations about all members of a group that do not recognize individual differences within the group. Anthropologist Ashley Montagu (1997), who was at the forefront of the movement to use scientific evidence to demonstrate the socially constructed nature of race, suggested that "the

Like many Americans, champion golfer Tiger Woods is of mixed racial heritage. His father's ancestry was African American, Chinese, and Native American, and his mother is of Thai, Chinese, and Dutch descent.

very word (*race*) is racist; that the idea of 'race,' implying the existence of significant biologically determined mental differences rendering some populations inferior to others, is wholly false" (p. 35).

SOC THINK

To what extent do race and ethnicity influence the opportunities you have and obstacles you face? How conscious are you of your race and ethnicity and their possible influences on your life?

Multiple Identities As the number of people who are biracial or multiracial grows, the limits of our racial categories are becoming increasingly apparent. Prominent figures have helped to bring this trend into the limelight. Tiger Woods, the world's best-known golfer, provides a classic example. Woods created his own racial category, referring to himself as "Cablinasian," a combination of his Caucasian, Black, American Indian, and Asian (Chinese and Thai) ancestry. Other examples include President Barack Obama, who had a Black father originally from Kenya and a White mother originally from Kansas, and Academy Award–winning actress Halle Berry, who had an African American father and a White, British-born mother.

In recognition of the growing diversity of the U.S. population, and the growing numbers of interracial marriages,

the 2000 and 2010 Census allowed people to select more than one category when identifying their race. People can choose from five major race categories—White, Black, Asian, Native American, and Native Hawaiian or Other Pacific Islander—in addition to "Some other race." Considering all the combinations people might select, a total of 63 race categories are now possible (U.S. Census Bureau 2010c).

More than 7 million people in the United States (or about 2.6 percent of the population) reported that they were of two or more races. Half of the people classified as multiracial were under age 18, suggesting that this segment of the population will grow in the years to come. People who claimed both White and American Indian ancestry were the largest group of multiracial residents (Bonilla-Silva 2004; N. Jones 2005).

This expansion of possible racial categories is part of the Census Bureau's ongoing effort to provide a snapshot of race as it is understood at various points in U.S. history. As the table on p. 318 demonstrates, racial categories used by the Census Bureau have shifted over time. The most recent expansion to allow multiracial identification is a direct consequence of the limitations of using fewer categories to reflect an increasingly diverse society. In order to get an accurate count, the Census Bureau needs categories that are mutually exclusive, meaning that each individual fits in one place and one place only. To do so, it must expand the number of available options beyond the three- or five-race models that often seemed, by common sense, to be sufficient.

ETHNICITY

An ethnic group is set apart from others explicitly because of its national origin or cultural patterns. Distinctive characteristics can include language, diet, sports, and religious beliefs, along with various traditions, norms, and values. Among the ethnic groups in the United States are peoples with a Spanish-speaking background, referred to collectively as Latinos or Hispanics, such as Puerto Ricans, Mexican Americans, and Cuban Americans. Other ethnic groups in this country include Jewish, Irish, Italian, and Norwegian Americans.

Puerto Rican Day Parade, New York City.

U.S. Race Categories, 1790–2010

Year	Race Categories
1790	Free white males Free white females All other free persons Slaves
1890	White Black Mulatto Chinese Indian
1940	White Negro Indian Chinese, Japanese, Filipino, Hindu, Korean Other
1990	White Black or Negro American Indian Eskimo Aleut Asian or Pacific Islander, Chinese, Filipino, Hawaiian, Korean, Vietnamese, Japanese, Asian Indian, Samoan, Guamanian, other Asian or Pacific Islander Other race
2010	White Black, African American, or Negro American Indian or Alaskan Native (print name of tribe) Asian: Asian Indian, Chinese, Filipino, Japanese, Korean, Vietnamese, Other Asian Native Hawaiian, Guamanian or Chamorro, Samoan, or Other Pacific Islander Some other race (print race)

Source: Nobles 2000:1739.

The distinction between race and ethnicity is not always clear-cut. While the conventional approach views race as biological and ethnicity as cultural, racial groups express their identity in cultural ways (including language, norms, values, diet, etc.). Alternatively, ethnic groups may self-identify as a race. The Census Bureau runs into this difficulty in its attempt to catalog each. It treats race and ethnicity as separate items, but in its ethnicity question, the only category recognized is "Hispanic, Latino, or Spanish origin." This creates difficulties for groups that see themselves as a distinct ethnicity and find the race options inadequate to describe who they are. In such circumstances, many people choose "Some other race" and then write in an ethnicity or nationality (such as Mexican, Iranian, or Saudi Arabian) as their race. In the 2000 Census, of those who selected "other," 97 percent also selected Hispanic as their ethnicity. In fact, 42 percent of those who self-identified as Hispanic also selected "Some other race" (U.S. Commission on Civil Rights 2009:4).

The Census has continued to try to make these categories clear. In an attempt to clarify confusion about the relationship between race and ethnicity, the 2010 Census included the line "For this census, Hispanic origins are not races" (U.S. Census Bureau 2010c). It also considered, but did not implement, collapsing race and ethnicity into a single question, effectively making Hispanic into a racial category (consistent with the way many Hispanics, especially Mexican Hispanics, view themselves). It also contemplated dropping the "Some other race" category to reduce confusion, effectively forcing people to choose from the existing categories. To address the limitations of the ethnicity question, the 2010 Census also studied the possibility of expanding it to include additional options (e.g., German, French, Italian) to more fully reflect people's self-identified ethnic origin (U.S. Commission on Civil Rights 2009). As currently practiced, the Census further

Did You Know?

... Of the Muslims in the United States, 65 percent are foreign born. Of those who were born here, about one-half are African American. Approximately one-fourth of all U.S. Muslims are third generation.

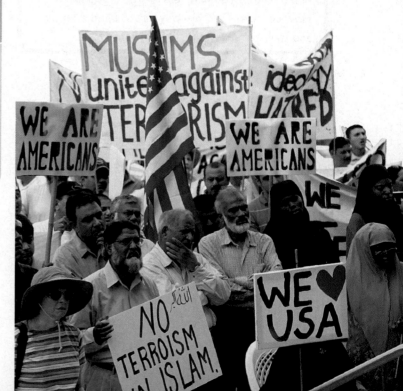

complicates things by including some ethnic nationalities as examples within racial categories (e.g., Japanese and Chinese as examples in the Asian category) but does not do so for others (e.g., White or Black). Such examples highlight the fact that race and ethnicity are more complex in practice than the commonsense models we may believe.

Although we will look at various ethnic and racial groups in more detail later in the chapter, it is important to understand the significance such categories have in society. As we have already seen, often they are used to justify exclusion from critical resources. This exclusion is rooted in both values and norms, that is, in how we think and how we act. When it comes to race and ethnicity, the terms that describe such practices are *prejudice* and *discrimination*.

>> Prejudice and Discrimination

In recent years, college campuses across the United States have been the scene of bias-related incidents. Student-run newspapers and radio stations have ridiculed racial and ethnic minorities; threatening literature has been stuffed under the doors of minority students; and graffiti endorsing the views of White supremacist organizations such as the Ku Klux Klan have been scrawled on university walls. In some cases, there have even been violent clashes between groups of White and Black students (Schmidt 2008). Such acts grow out of attitudes people have about other groups.

PREJUDICE

Prejudice is a negative attitude toward an entire category of people, often an ethnic or racial minority. If you resent your roommate because he or she is sloppy, you are not necessarily guilty of prejudice. However, if you immediately stereotype your roommate on the basis of such characteristics as race, ethnicity, or religion, that is a form of prejudice. Prejudice tends to perpetuate false definitions of individuals and groups.

Sometimes prejudice results from **ethnocentrism**—the tendency to assume that one's own culture and way of life represent the norm or are superior to all others. Ethnocentric people judge other cultures by the standards of their own group without taking into account the perspectives and experiences of others. This often leads to prejudice against cultures they view as inferior.

One important and widespread ideology that reinforces prejudice is **racism**—the belief that one race is supreme and

> **prejudice** A negative attitude toward an entire category of people, often an ethnic or racial minority.
>
> **racism** The belief that one race is supreme and all others are innately inferior.

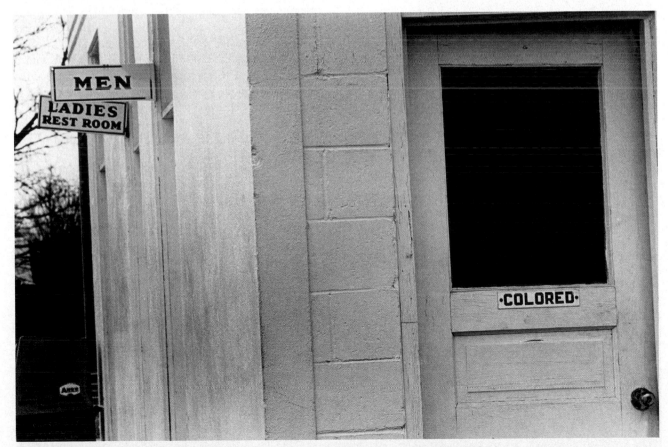

Before passage of the Civil Rights Act in 1964, segregation of public accommodations was the norm throughout the South.

Categorization of Reported Hate Crimes

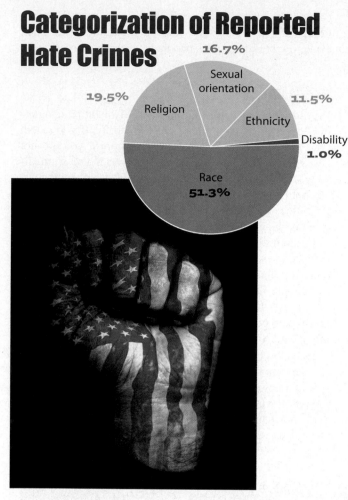

- Sexual orientation 16.7%
- Ethnicity 11.5%
- Disability 1.0%
- Religion 19.5%
- Race 51.3%

Source: U.S. Department of Justice 2009a.

hate crime A criminal offense committed because of the offender's bias against an individual based on race, religion, ethnicity, national origin, or sexual orientation.

color-blind racism The use of race-neutral principles to perpetuate a racially unequal status quo.

discrimination The denial of opportunities and equal rights to individuals and groups because of prejudice or other arbitrary reasons.

all others are innately inferior. When racism prevails in a society, members of subordinate groups generally experience prejudice, discrimination, and exploitation. In 1990, as concern mounted about racist attacks in the United States, Congress passed the Hate Crimes Statistics Act. A **hate crime** is a criminal offense committed because of the offender's bias against an individual based on race, religion,

ethnicity, national origin, or sexual orientation. In 2008 alone, more than 7700 hate crimes were reported to authorities. More than 60 percent of those crimes against persons involved racial or ethnic bias.

Over the past three generations, nationwide surveys have consistently shown growing support among Whites for integration, interracial dating, and the election of minority group members to public office—including even the presidency of the United States. Nevertheless, there are persistent patterns of unequal treatment. People claim not to be prejudiced, affirming principles such as equal opportunity, yet many fail to put these ideals into practice.

Some sociologists suggest that **color-blind racism,** which uses the principle of race neutrality to perpetuate a racially unequal status quo, is at work (Bonilla-Silva 2010). In such cases, commitment to the principle of equality actually serves to perpetuate inequality. In a system where inequality based on race and ethnicity is built into the structure of society, unwillingness to address these issues explicitly in those terms serves to perpetuate the status quo. Although it might seem counter to the principle of equality, some nations have established quotas in political representation and hiring to force the social structure to provide greater opportunity, a practice that is controversial in the United States.

DISCRIMINATION

Prejudice often leads to **discrimination**—the denial of opportunities and equal rights to individuals and groups because of prejudice or other arbitrary reasons. Whereas prejudice is a way of thinking, discrimination involves action. Imagine that a White corporate president with a prejudice against Asian Americans has to fill an executive position and that the most qualified candidate for the job is a Vietnamese American. If the president refuses to hire this candidate and instead selects an inferior White candidate, she or he is engaging in an act of racial discrimination.

Discriminatory Behavior Prejudiced attitudes should not be equated with discriminatory behavior. Although the two are generally related, they are not identical; either condition can be present without the other. A prejudiced person does not always act on his or her biases. The White president, for example, might choose—despite her or his prejudices—to

Members of the Ku Klux Klan, masked in white robes and hoods, used nighttime cross-burnings to instill terror.

hire the Vietnamese American because that person is the most qualified. That would be prejudice without discrimination. On the other hand, a White corporate president with a completely respectful view of Vietnamese Americans might refuse to hire them for executive posts out of fear that biased clients would take their business elsewhere. In that case, the president's action would constitute discrimination without prejudice.

Sometimes, racial and ethnic discrimination is overt. Internet forums like Craigslist.org or Roommate.com feature classified ads that state "African Americans and Arabians tend to clash with me" or "Clean, Godly Christian men only." Although, antidiscrimination laws prevent such notices from being published in the newspapers, existing law has not caught up with online bigotry in hiring and renting (Liptak 2006).

In sociologist Devah Pager's 2003 experiment investigating racial discrimination in hiring (see Chapter 2), a White job applicant with a prison record received slightly more callbacks than a Black applicant with no criminal record. Over time, the cumulative impact of such differential behavior contributes to significant differences in access to critical resources. For example, income varies significantly based on race and ethnicity in the United States (Pager and Shepherd 2008).

The Glass Ceiling Discrimination persists even for the most educated and qualified minority group members from the best family backgrounds. Despite their talent and experience, they sometimes encounter attitudinal or organizational bias that prevents them from reaching their full potential. Recall that the term *glass ceiling* refers to an invisible barrier that blocks the promotion of a qualified individual in a work environment because of the individual's gender, race, or ethnicity (Jackson and O'Callaghan 2009; Schaefer 2006).

In early 1995, the federal Glass Ceiling Commission issued the first comprehensive study of barriers to promotion in the United States. The commission found that glass ceilings continue to block women and minority group men from top management positions in the

U.S. Median Income by Race, Ethnicity, and Gender

Median income (thousands of dollars)

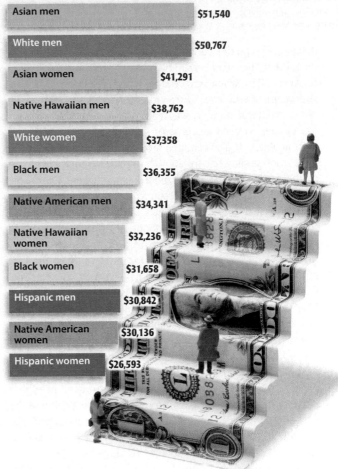

Asian men	$51,540
White men	$50,767
Asian women	$41,291
Native Hawaiian men	$38,762
White women	$37,358
Black men	$36,355
Native American men	$34,341
Native Hawaiian women	$32,236
Black women	$31,658
Hispanic men	$30,842
Native American women	$30,136
Hispanic women	$26,593

Note: Includes only people working full-time, year-round, 16 years and older. White refers to non-Hispanic Whites.

Source: U.S. Census Bureau 2009j:Table B20017.

nation's industries. For example, in 2006, 72 percent of the members on the boards of directors for Fortune 100 companies were White men, compared to 13 percent White women, 11 percent minority males, and 4 percent minority females (Catalyst 2008). In fact, the glass ceiling appears to harm firms. Researchers have found that having more diversity increases performance in groups; firms with more diverse boards also are more profitable than those that are more homogeneous (Phillips, Liljenquist, and Neale 2009; Virtcom 2009).

Federal troops were needed to support the Supreme Court decision that led to the integration of schools in the 1950s.

Racial Profiling Another form of discrimination involves **racial profiling,** which is any arbitrary action initiated by an authority based on race, ethnicity, or national origin rather than on a person's behavior. Generally, racial profiling occurs when law enforcement officers, including customs officials, airport security, and police, assume that people who fit a certain description are likely to engage in illegal activities. Concerns about racial profiling were raised in April 2010 when Arizona passed the Support Our Law Enforcement and Safe Neighborhoods Act, designed to crack down on illegal immigration from Mexico. The law requires immigrants to carry documents validating their legal immigration status. It also requires law enforcement officials who have stopped someone for another offense to request evidence of the person's legal immigration status "where reasonable suspicion exists that the person is an alien who is unlawfully present in the United States" (State of Arizona 2010). Concerns were also expressed about the effect the law would have on the ability of local police officers to conduct effective investigations in Hispanic communities. To protest the law, numerous groups and organizations—such as the National Council of La Raza, the Service Employees International Union, and the Los Angeles City Council—decided not to do further business in Arizona, resulting in millions of dollars in lost revenue for the state.

> **racial profiling** Any police-initiated action based on race, ethnicity, or national origin rather than on a person's behavior.

Today, authorities continue to rely on racial profiling despite overwhelming evidence that race is not a valid predictor of criminal behavior. A recent study showed that African Americans are still more likely than Whites to be frisked and handled with force when they are stopped. Yet Whites are more likely than Blacks to possess weapons, illegal drugs, and stolen property (Ridgeway 2007).

Research on the ineffectiveness of racial profiling, coupled with complaints by minority communities about the stigmatization it fosters, has led to growing demands

Did You Know?

... Blacks and Whites have significantly different perceptions of local law enforcement. In a 2007 survey, when asked how much confidence they had in local police, 42 percent of Whites and 14 percent of Blacks had a "great deal," while 31 percent of Blacks and 10 percent of Whites had "very little."

to end the practice. However, these efforts came to an abrupt halt after the September 11, 2001, terrorist attacks on the United States, in the face of widespread suspicion toward Muslim and Arab immigrants. Federal authorities subjected foreign students from Arab countries to special questioning, and they scrutinized legal immigrants identified as Arab or Muslim for possible illegal activity. They also prosecuted Arab and Muslim detainees for violations that were routinely ignored among immigrants of other ethnicities and faiths (Withrow 2006).

THE PRIVILEGES OF THE DOMINANT

One often-overlooked aspect of discrimination is the privileges that dominant groups enjoy at the expense of others. For instance, we tend to focus more on the difficulty women have balancing career and family than on the ease with which men avoid household chores and advance in the workplace. Similarly, we concentrate more on discrimination against racial and ethnic minorities than on the advantages members of the White majority enjoy. Indeed, most White people rarely think about their "Whiteness," taking their status for granted. However, sociologists and other social scientists are becoming increasingly interested in what it means to be "White," for White privilege is the other side of the proverbial coin of racial discrimination (Painter 2010).

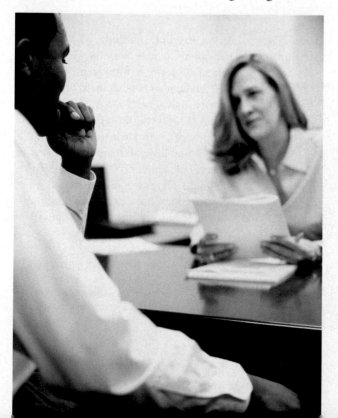

Feminist scholar Peggy McIntosh (1988) became interested in White privilege after noticing that most men would not acknowledge the privileges attached to being male—even if they would agree that being female had its disadvantages. She wondered whether White people suffer from a similar blind spot regarding their own racial privilege. Intrigued, McIntosh began to list all the ways in which she benefited from her Whiteness. She soon realized that the list of unspoken advantages was long and significant.

McIntosh found that as a White person, she rarely needed to step out of her comfort zone, no matter where she went. If she wished to, she could spend most of her time with people of her own race. She could find a good place to live in a pleasant neighborhood, buy the foods she liked to eat from almost any grocery store, and get her hair styled in almost any salon. She could attend a public meeting without feeling that she did not belong or that she was different from everyone else.

McIntosh discovered, too, that her skin color opened doors for her. She could cash checks and use credit cards without suspicion, and she could browse through stores without being shadowed by security guards. She could be seated without difficulty in a restaurant. If she asked to see the manager, she could assume he or she would be of her own race. If she needed help from a doctor or a lawyer, she could get it.

McIntosh also realized that her Whiteness made the job of parenting easier. She did not need to worry about protecting her children from people who didn't like them due to their race. She could be sure that their books would show pictures of people who looked like them and that their history texts would describe White people's achievements. She knew that the television programs they watched would include White characters.

Finally, McIntosh had to admit that others did not constantly evaluate her in racial terms. When she appeared in public, she didn't need to worry that her clothing or behavior might reflect poorly on White people. If she was recognized for an achievement, it was seen as her own accomplishment, not that of an entire race. And no one ever assumed that the personal opinions she voiced should be those of all White people. Because

McIntosh blended in with the people around her, she wasn't always onstage.

These are not all the privileges White people take for granted as a result of their membership in the dominant racial group in the United States. As Devah Pager's study showed, White job seekers enjoy a tremendous advantage over equally well-qualified—even better-qualified—Blacks. Whiteness *does* carry privileges—to a much greater extent than most White people realize.

> Whites of course have the privilege of not caring, of being colorblind. Nobody else does.
>
> **Ursula K. LeGuin**

INSTITUTIONAL DISCRIMINATION

Such persistent patterns of inequality suggest that discrimination is practiced not only by individuals in one-to-one encounters but also by institutions in their daily operations. Social scientists are particularly concerned with the ways in which structural factors, such as employment, housing, health care, and government operations, maintain the social significance of race and ethnicity. **Institutional discrimination** refers to the denial of opportunities and equal rights to individuals and groups that results from the normal operations of a society. This kind of discrimination consistently affects certain racial and ethnic groups more than others.

The response to the September 11, 2001 terrorist attacks on the United States provides an example of institutional, discrimination. Under pressure to prevent terrorist takeovers of commercial airplanes, Congress passed the Aviation and Transportation Security Act, which was intended to strengthen airport screening procedures. The law stipulated that all airport screeners must be U.S. citizens. Nationally, 28 percent of all airport screeners were legal residents but not citizens of the United States; as a group, they were disproportionately Latino, Black, and Asian. Many observers noted that other airport and airline workers, including pilots, cabin attendants, and even armed National Guardsmen stationed at airports, need not be citizens. Though a Circuit Court of Appeals judge issued a court order in 2002 allowing qualified noncitizen airport screeners to retain or reapply for their jobs, in 2003 a California district court dismissed the case. Even well-meant legal measures can have disastrous consequences for racial and ethnic minorities (H. Weinstein 2002).

SOCTHINK

McIntosh recommends that we all step back and consider unearned advantages we inherit due to the positions we may occupy. What would be on your list? What disadvantages might you inherit?

SOCTHINK

Why might institutional discrimination be an even greater concern than interpersonal discrimination?

In some cases, even seemingly neutral institutional standards can have discriminatory effects. African American students at a midwestern state university protested a policy under which fraternities and sororities that wished to use campus facilities for a dance were required to post a $150 security deposit to cover possible damages. The Black students complained that the policy had a discriminatory impact on minority student organizations. Campus police countered that the university's policy applied to all student groups interested in using the facilities. However, because the overwhelmingly White fraternities and sororities at the school had their own houses, which they used for dances, the policy indeed affected only African American and other minority organizations.

Attempts have been made to eradicate or compensate for discrimination in the United States. The 1960s saw the passage of many pioneering civil rights laws, including the landmark 1964 Civil Rights Act, which prohibits discrimination in public accommodations and publicly owned facilities on the basis of race, color, creed, national origin, and gender. In two important rulings in 1987, the Supreme Court held that federal prohibitions against racial discrimination protect members of all ethnic minorities—including Hispanics, Jews, and Arab Americans—even though they may be considered White.

For more than 40 years, government, schools, and industry have instituted affirmative action programs to overcome past discrimination. **Affirmative action** refers to positive efforts to recruit minority group members or women for jobs, promotions, and educational opportunities. Many people resent these programs, arguing that advancing one group's cause merely shifts the discrimination to another group. By giving priority to African Americans in admissions, for example, schools may deny more academically qualified White candidates. In many parts of the country and many sectors of the economy, affirmative action is being rolled back, even though it was never fully implemented.

Discriminatory practices continue to pervade nearly all areas of life in the United States. In part, that is because various individuals and groups actually benefit from racial and ethnic discrimination in terms of money, status, and influence. Discrimination permits members of the

affirmative action Positive efforts to recruit minority group members or women for jobs, promotions, and educational opportunities.

exploitation theory A belief that views racial subordination in the United States as a manifestation of the class system inherent in capitalism.

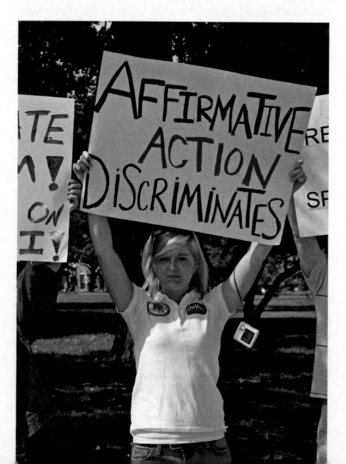

majority to enhance their wealth, power, and prestige at the expense of others. Less qualified people get jobs and promotions simply because they are members of the dominant group. Such individuals and groups will not surrender these advantages easily.

>> Sociological Perspectives on Race and Ethnicity

Sociologists seek to understand and explain why prejudice and discrimination develop and persist and what might be done to address them. As we have seen, often such negative characteristics exist because they serve certain interests. Here we look at how prejudice and discrimination contribute to the maintenance of the existing social order by reinforcing the dominant culture.

SOCIAL ORDER AND INEQUALITY

One of the ways we see such beliefs and practices perpetuated is through acceptance of the dominant ideology that supports them. Prejudice and discrimination are rooted in fundamental beliefs about the natural order of the world. Such values provide a moral justification for maintaining an unequal society that routinely deprives minority groups of their rights and privileges. In the 19th century, Southern Whites, for example, justified slavery by asserting that Africans were physically and spiritually subhuman and devoid of souls. It is easy in retrospect to find such beliefs appalling, but they became part of what people assumed was natural and were therefore difficult to challenge.

This does not mean, however, that certain groups do not intentionally promote such beliefs at the expense of others. Prejudice and discrimination help to preserve the existing system of inequality. **Exploitation theory,** for example, argues that such practices are a basic part of the capitalist economic system (Blauner 1972; Cox 1948; Hunter 2000). Racism keeps minorities in low-paying jobs, thereby supplying the capitalist ruling class with a pool of cheap labor. Moreover, by forcing racial minorities to accept low wages, capitalists can restrict the wages of all members of the proletariat. Business owners can always replace workers from the dominant group who demand higher wages with minorities who have no choice but to accept low-paying jobs. This increases the likelihood that working-class members of the majority group will develop racist attitudes

SOCTHINK

What are the cost and benefits of establishing hiring quotas based on race, ethnicity, or gender to ensure greater opportunity?

Perceptions of Discrimination

Black respondents

Hispanic respondents

White respondents

How often do Blacks face discrimination when . . . ?

Applying to a college or university

Applying for a job

Almost always/frequently

Renting an apartment or buying a house

Eating at a restaurant or shopping in a retail store

Not often/hardly ever

Source: Pew Research Center 2007:30.

toward working-class members of minority groups, whom they view as threats to their jobs. As a result, they direct their hostilities not toward the capitalists but toward other workers, thereby not challenging the structure of the existing system.

Maintaining these practices, however, comes at significant cost to society. For example, a society that practices discrimination fails to use the resources of all individuals.

Discrimination limits the search for talent and leadership to the dominant group. Advocates for the children whose parents were caught up in the Postville immigration raid, for example, bemoaned the loss of creativity and talent that those kids would take with them when they left the country with their deported parents. Discrimination also aggravates social problems such as poverty, delinquency, and crime. Such effects require the investment of a good deal of time and money in which the primary goal is to maintain barriers to the full participation of all members (Rose 1951).

Challenging prejudice and discrimination, however, involves questioning taken-for-granted views of the world in which people have invested their faith and trust. Women in the 1950s in the United States had to do just that. They challenged the idea that it was "natural" for women to stay at home and have babies rather than get an education and enter the paid labor force. During the same time, workers in the civil rights movement faced a similar challenge in confronting social attitudes that represented barriers to the full participation of African Americans in U.S. society.

THE CONTACT HYPOTHESIS

At its heart, racism is about division, separating the human population into us versus them. As society becomes more global and interdependent, more people from diverse cultural backgrounds have increased opportunities to interact with others unlike themselves on a daily basis. This is precisely what the school superintendent from Postville gave voice to. When people interact with others as people, rather than as stereotypes or distant others, the possibility arises for prejudice and discrimination to decrease.

contact hypothesis The theory that in cooperative circumstances interracial contact between people of equal status will reduce prejudice.

genocide The deliberate, systematic killing of an entire people or nation.

Take, for example, a Hispanic woman who is transferred from a job on one part of an assembly line to a similar position working next to a White man. At first, the White man may be patronizing, assuming that she must be incompetent. For her part, the Latina is cold and resentful; even when she needs assistance, she refuses to admit it. After a week, the growing tension between the two leads to a bitter quarrel. Yet over time, each slowly comes to appreciate the other's strengths and talents. A year after they begin working together, these two workers become respectful friends. This example represents an example of the contact hypothesis in action.

The **contact hypothesis** states that in cooperative circumstances, interracial contact between people of equal status will cause them to become less prejudiced and to abandon old stereotypes. People begin to see one another as individuals and to discard the broad generalizations characteristic of stereotyping. Note the phrases "equal status" and "cooperative circumstances." In our assembly-line example, if the two workers had been competing for one vacancy as a supervisor, the racial hostility between them might have worsened, highlighting the significance of power and position when it comes to the issue of racism (Allport 1979; Fine 2008).

As Latinos and other minorities slowly gain access to better-paying and higher-responsibility jobs, the contact hypothesis may take on even greater significance. The trend in our society is toward increasing contact between individuals from dominant and subordinate groups. That may be one way of eliminating—or at least reducing—racial and ethnic stereotyping and prejudice. Another may be the establishment of interracial coalitions, an idea suggested by sociologist William Julius Wilson (1999). To work, such coalitions would obviously need to provide an equal role for all members.

PATTERNS OF INTERGROUP RELATIONS

The possibility of equal status, however, is shaped by how societies handle racial and ethnic differences. Some societies are more open to diverse groups maintaining their cultural traditions. Others pressure groups to abandon their beliefs and practices in favor of those of the dominant society. We will focus on six characteristic patterns of intergroup relations: genocide, expulsion, amalgamation, assimilation, segregation, and pluralism. Each pattern defines the dominant group's actions and the minority group's responses. The first two are relatively rare, though their consequences are extreme; the final four are more common.

Genocide The most devastating pattern of intergroup relations is **genocide**—the deliberate, systematic killing of an entire people or nation. This is precisely what happened when Turkish authorities killed 1 million Armenians beginning in 1915. The term is most commonly associated with Nazi Germany's extermination of 6 million European Jews, along with gays, lesbians, and the Romani people ("Gypsies"), during World War II. The term also describes the United States' policies toward Native Americans in the 19th century. In 1800, the Native American (or American

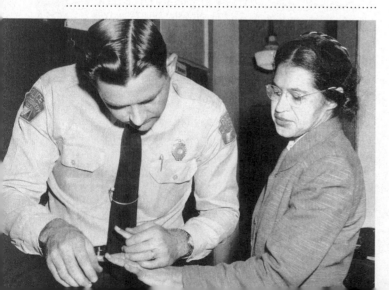

Civil rights activist Rosa Parks being fingerprinted upon her arrest in 1955 for her act of civil disobedience in refusing to give up her seat on a bus to a White man.

Indian) population of the United States was about 600,000; by 1850, warfare with the U.S. cavalry, disease, and forced relocation to inhospitable environments had reduced it to 250,000.

Expulsion Another extreme response is **expulsion**—the systematic removal of a group of people from society. In 1979, Vietnam expelled nearly 1 million ethnic Chinese, partly as a result of centuries of hostility between Vietnam and neighboring China. Similarly, Serbian forces began a program of "ethnic cleansing" in 1991, in the newly independent states of Bosnia and Herzegovina. Throughout the former Yugoslavia, the Serbs drove more than 1 million Croats and Muslims from their homes. Some they tortured and killed; others they abused and terrorized, in an attempt to "purify" the land (Cigar 1995; Petrovic 1994). More recently, the government of Sudan has pushed people off their land and out of the country in Darfur (Steidle 2007).

Amalgamation When a majority group and a minority group combine to form a new group, **amalgamation** results. This often occurs through intermarriage over several generations. This pattern can be expressed as $A + B + C \rightarrow D$, where A, B, and C represent different groups in a society, and D signifies the end result, a unique cultural-racial group unlike any of the initial groups (Newman 1973).

The belief in the United States as a "melting pot" became compelling in the early 20th century, particularly since that image suggested that the nation had an almost

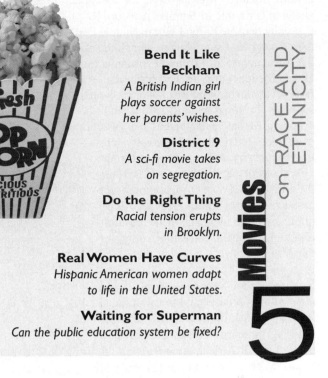

Movies on RACE AND ETHNICITY

5

Bend It Like Beckham
A British Indian girl plays soccer against her parents' wishes.

District 9
A sci-fi movie takes on segregation.

Do the Right Thing
Racial tension erupts in Brooklyn.

Real Women Have Curves
Hispanic American women adapt to life in the United States.

Waiting for Superman
Can the public education system be fixed?

divine mission to amalgamate various groups into one people. In actuality, however, many residents were not willing to include Native Americans, Jews, Blacks, Asians, and Irish Roman Catholics in the melting pot. Therefore, this pattern does not adequately describe dominant-subordinate relations in the United States.

Assimilation In India, many Hindus complain about Indian citizens who emulate the traditions and customs of the British. In France, people of Arab and African origin, many of them Muslim, complain they are treated as second-class citizens—a charge that provoked riots in 2005. In Australia, Aborigines who have become part of the dominant society refuse to acknowledge their darker-skinned grandparents on the street. All of these cases are examples of the effects of **assimilation**—the process through which a person forsakes his or her own cultural tradition to become part of a different culture. Generally, it is practiced by minority group members who want to conform to the standards of the dominant group. Assimilation can be described as a pattern in which $A + B + C \rightarrow A$. The majority, A, dominates in such a way that members of minorities B and C imitate it and attempt to become indistinguishable from it (Newman 1973).

Assimilation can strike at the very roots of a person's identity. In the United States, some immigrants have changed their ethnic-sounding family names to names that better fit into the dominant White Protestant

expulsion The systematic removal of a group of people from society.

amalgamation The process through which a majority group and a minority group combine to form a new group.

assimilation The process through which a person forsakes his or her own cultural tradition to become part of a different culture.

POPSOC

In a survey about media portrayals of African Americans, the majority of Whites and Hispanics felt that the way Blacks are portrayed in television and films is better today than it was 10 years ago. Among African Americans, however, only 43 percent agreed. Blacks were also more likely than the other groups to say that negative portrayals have a negative impact on society's views of Blacks. Both Blacks and Whites agreed, at almost identical levels, that hip-hop and rap have a bad influence on society today.

culture. Jennifer Anastassakis, for example, changed her name to Jennifer Aniston, Ralph Lipschitz became Ralph Lauren, Natalie Portman switched from Natalie Hershlag, and the Academy Award–winning British actress Helen Mirren gave up her birth name of Ilyena Vasilievna Mironova. Name changes, switches in religious affiliation, and the dropping of native languages can obscure one's roots and heritage. Especially across generations, assimilation can lead to the virtual death of a culture in that family's history. It is not uncommon for grandchildren of immigrants who have not learned the language or the cultural traditions of their ancestors to regret this loss.

Segregation Separate schools, separate seating on buses and in restaurants, separate washrooms, even separate drinking fountains—these were all part of the lives of African Americans in the South when segregation ruled early in the 20th century. **Segregation** refers to the physical separation of two groups of people in terms of residence, workplace, and social events. Generally, a dominant group imposes this pattern on a minority group. Segregation is rarely complete, however. Intergroup contact inevitably occurs, even in the most segregated societies.

From 1948 (when it received its independence) to 1990, the Republic of South Africa severely restricted the movement of Blacks and other non-Whites by means of a wide-ranging system of segregation known as **apartheid.**

Former South African President Nelson Mandela oversaw that country's transition from a segregated society.

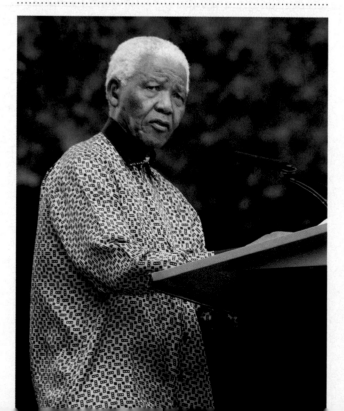

Composition of Neighborhoods by Racial and Ethnic Groups June 6–25, 2005			
	% of non-Hispanic Whites who say there are "many" of each group in area	% of Blacks who say there are "many" of each group in area	% of Hispanics who say there are "many" of each group in area
Whites	86%	45%	52%
Blacks	28%	66%	32%
Hispanics	32%	26%	61%
Asians	12%	6%	13%
Recent immigrants	14%	18%	30%

Source: Who Are the People in Your Neighborhood? Gallup Organization July 12, 2005.

Apartheid even included the creation of separate homelands where Blacks were expected to live. However, decades of local resistance to apartheid, combined with international pressure, led to marked political changes in the 1990s. In 1994, a prominent Black activist, Nelson Mandela, became South Africa's president in the first election in which Blacks (the majority of the nation's population) were allowed to vote. Mandela had spent almost 28 years in South African prisons for his anti-apartheid activities. His election was widely viewed as the final blow to South Africa's oppressive policy of segregation.

Long-entrenched social patterns are difficult to change, however. A recent analysis of living patterns in U.S. metropolitan areas shows that, despite federal laws that forbid housing discrimination, residential segregation is still the norm. Even though 65 percent of Americans say they prefer to live in a racially diverse community, across the nation, neighborhoods remain divided along both racial and ethnic lines. The average White person lives in an area that is at least 83 percent White, while the average African American lives in a neighborhood that is mostly Black. The typical Latino lives in an area that is 42 percent Hispanic. Overall, segregation flourishes at the community and neighborhood levels, despite the increasing diversity of the nation as a whole (Bolt, Ozuekren, and Phillips 2010; Taylor and Morin 2008).

Pluralism In a pluralistic society, a subordinate group does not have to forsake its lifestyle and traditions. **Pluralism** is based on mutual respect for one another's cultures among the various groups in a society. This pattern allows a minority group to express its own culture and still participate without prejudice in the larger society. Earlier, we described amalgamation as

A + B + C → D, and assimilation as A + B + C → A. Using this same approach, we can conceive of pluralism as A + B + C → A + B + C; that is, all the groups coexist in the same society (Newman 1973).

In the United States, pluralism is more of an ideal than a reality. There are distinct instances of pluralism—the ethnic neighborhoods in major cities, such as Koreatown, Little Tokyo, Andersonville (Swedish Americans), and Spanish Harlem—yet there are also limits to cultural freedom. To survive, a society must promote a certain consensus among its members regarding basic ideals, values, and beliefs. Thus, if a Romanian immigrant to the United States wants to move up the occupational ladder, he or she cannot avoid learning English.

Switzerland exemplifies the modern pluralistic state. There the absence of both a national language and a dominant religious faith leads to a tolerance for cultural diversity. In addition, various political devices safeguard the interests of ethnic groups in a way that has no parallel in the United States. By contrast, Great Britain has had difficulty achieving cultural pluralism in a multiracial society. East Indians, Pakistanis, and Blacks from the Caribbean and Africa experience prejudice and discrimination within the dominant White society there. Some British advocate cutting off all Asian and Black immigration, and a few even call for expulsion of those non-Whites currently living in Britain.

>> Race and Ethnicity in the United States

Few societies have a more diverse population than the United States; the nation is truly a multiracial, multiethnic society. Of course, this has not always been the case.

The population of what is now the United States has changed dramatically since the arrival of European settlers in the 1600s. Immigration, colonialism, and, in the case of Blacks, slavery determined the racial and ethnic makeup of our present-day society.

RACIAL GROUPS

The largest racial minorities in the United States are African Americans, Native Americans, and Asian Americans.

segregation The physical separation of two groups of people in terms of residence, workplace, and social events; often imposed on a minority group by a dominant group.

apartheid A former policy of the South African government, designed to maintain the separation of Blacks and other non-Whites from the dominant Whites.

pluralism Mutual respect for one another's cultures among the various groups in a society, which allows minorities to express their own cultures without experiencing prejudice.

African Americans "I am an invisible man," wrote Black author Ralph Ellison in his novel *Invisible Man* (1952:3). "I am a man of substance, of flesh and bone, fiber and liquids—and I might even be said to possess a mind. I am invisible, understand, simply because people refuse to see me."

Almost six decades later, many African Americans still feel invisible. Despite their large numbers, they have long been treated as second-class citizens. As of 2008, according to official government statistics, 24.7 percent of African Americans were in poverty compared to 8.2 percent for non-Hispanic Whites (DeNavas-Walt et al. 2009).

Contemporary institutional discrimination and individual prejudice against African Americans are rooted in the history of slavery in the United States. Many other subordinate groups had little wealth and income, but as sociologist W.E.B. Du Bois (1909) and others have noted,

Racial and Ethnic Groups in the United States, 1790–2050 (Projected)

1790
African Americans 19%
White 81%

1880
12%
88%

1970
11%
Hispanic 5%
All others 2%
White non-Hispanic 83%

2008
15%
12%
Asian and other 4%
65%

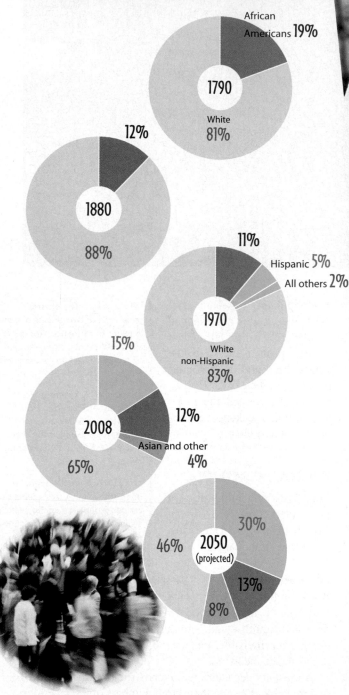

2050 (projected)
30%
46%
13%
8%

Note: U.S. Census categories vary over time.

Source: Gibson and Jung 2002:Table 1; Ortman and Guarneri 2008; U.S. Census Bureau 2009j:Table DP-5.

enslaved Blacks were in an even more oppressive situation because they could not own property legally and could not pass on the benefits of their labor to their children. In spite of generations of slavery with its long-term economic

consequences, African Americans never received slave reparations to compensate for the historical injustices of forced servitude (Williams and Collins 2004).

The end of the Civil War did not bring genuine freedom and equality for Blacks. Whites were able to maintain their dominance formally through legalized segregation and informally by means of vigilante terror and violence. The southern states passed "Jim Crow" laws to enforce official segregation, and the Supreme Court in the case of *Plessy v. Ferguson* upheld them as constitutional in 1896. In addition, Blacks faced the danger of lynching campaigns, often led by the Ku Klux Klan, during the late 1800s and early 1900s (Franklin and Moss 2000).

During the 1950s and 1960s, a vast civil rights movement emerged, with many competing factions and strategies for change. The Southern Christian Leadership

Poverty Rates by Race and Ethnicity

Hispanic, any race	23.2%
Black	21.7%
Asian	11.8%
White, non-Hispanic	8.6%

Source: DeNavas-Walt et al. 2009:Table 4.

Conference (SCLC), founded by Dr. Martin Luther King Jr., used nonviolent civil disobedience to oppose segregation. The National Association for the Advancement of Colored People (NAACP) favored use of the courts to press for equality for African Americans.

Many younger Black leaders, most notably Malcolm X, turned toward an ideology of Black power. Proponents of **Black power** rejected the goal of assimilation into White middle-class society. They defended the beauty and dignity of Black and African cultures and supported the creation of Black-controlled political and economic institutions (Ture and Hamilton 1992).

Despite numerous courageous actions to achieve Black civil rights, Black and White citizens are still separate, still unequal. The median household income for African American households is $34,218, compared to $55,530 for Whites. The majority of Black children from middle-income families end up earning less than their parents, whereas 68 percent of children in middle-income White families earn more. And due in part to unequal access to health care, the life expectancy of African Americans is shorter than that of Whites (DeNavas-Walt et al. 2009; Isaacs 2008).

Some African Americans—especially middle-class men and women—have made economic gains over the past 50 years. For example, data compiled by the Department of Labor show that the number of African Americans in management increased nationally from 2.4 percent of the total in 1958 to 7.5 percent in 2007. Yet Blacks still represent only 6 percent or less of all biologists, civil engineers, chemists, lawyers, chief executives, and financial analysts. In another occupation important to developing role models, African Americans account for 5.4 percent of all in the United States full-time college professors (U.S. Census Bureau 2009f:Table 603; Snyder and Dillow 2010:Table 246).

In politics, though African Americans remain underrepresented, progress in the number of elected officials has improved over time. Between 1969 and 2010, the number of African Americans in Congress rose from 6 to 40, and the election of Barack Obama as president represents a major breakthrough in the glass ceiling. However, African Americans still make up only 7.5 percent of Congress. Such lack of progress is especially distressing in view of sociologist W.E.B. Du Bois' observation over a century ago that Blacks could not expect to achieve equal social and

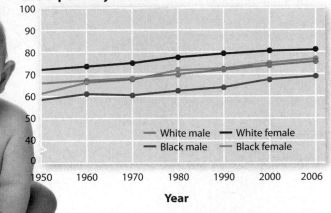

Life Expectancy by Race and Sex, 1950–2006

Life expectancy at birth

Legend: White male — White female — Black male — Black female

Source: National Center for Health Statistics 2009:Table 24.

economic opportunity without first gaining political rights (Manning 2010).

Native Americans Today about 2.4 million Native Americans represent a diverse array of cultures distinguishable by language, family organization, religion, and livelihood. The outsiders who came to the United States—European settlers and their descendants—came to know these native peoples' forebears as "American Indians." By the time the Bureau of Indian Affairs (BIA) was organized as part of the War Department in 1824, Indian–White relations had featured three centuries of hostility that had led to the virtual elimination of native peoples. During the 19th century, many bloody wars wiped out a significant part of the nation's Indian population. By the end of the century, schools for Indians—operated by the BIA or by church missions—prohibited the practice of Native American cultures. Yet at the same time, such schools did little to make the children effective competitors in White society (U.S. Census Bureau 2009j:Table B02005).

Today, life remains difficult for members of the 562 tribal groups in the United States, whether they live in urban

> **Black power** A political philosophy, promoted by many younger Blacks in the 1960s, that supported the creation of Black-controlled political and economic institutions.

Did You Know?

. . . With the release of *The Princess and the Frog* in December 2009, Princess Tiana became Disney's first African American princess in a feature film. At the same time, Disney was criticized for drawing on racial stereotypes of 1920s New Orleans in the film.

Major Asian American Groups in the United States

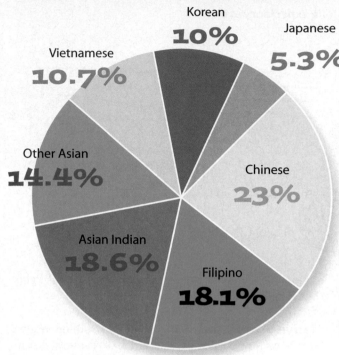

Korean **10%**

Japanese **5.3%**

Vietnamese **10.7%**

Other Asian **14.4%**

Chinese **23%**

Asian Indian **18.6%**

Filipino **18.1%**

Source: U.S. Census Bureau 2009j:Table DP-5.

areas or on reservations. For example, one Native American teenager in six has attempted suicide—a rate four times higher than the rate for other teenagers. Over time, some Native Americans have chosen to assimilate and abandon all vestiges of their tribal cultures to escape certain forms of prejudice. However, by the 1990s, an increasing number of people in the United States were openly claiming a Native American identity. Since 1960, the federal government's count of Native Americans has tripled. According to the 2000 Census, the Native American population increased 26 percent during the 1990s. Demographers believe that more and more Native Americans who previously concealed their identity are no longer trying to pass as White (Grieco and Cassidy 2001).

model or ideal minority
A subordinate group whose members supposedly have succeeded economically, socially, and educationally despite past prejudice and discrimination.

The introduction of gambling on Indian reservations has transformed the lives of some Native Americans. Native Americans got into the gaming industry in 1988, when Congress passed the Indian Gambling Regulatory Act. The law stipulates that states must negotiate agreements with tribes interested in commercial gaming; they cannot prevent tribes from engaging in gambling operations even if state law prohibits such ventures. The income from these lucrative operations is not evenly distributed, however. About two-thirds of recognized Indian tribes are not involved in gambling ventures. And those tribes that earn substantial revenues from gambling constitute only a small fraction of Native Americans (J. Taylor and Kalt 2005).

Asian Americans Asian Americans are a diverse group, one of the fastest-growing segments of the U.S. population. Among the many groups of Americans of Asian descent are Vietnamese Americans, Chinese Americans, Japanese Americans, and Korean Americans.

Asian Americans are often held up as a **model** or **ideal minority** group, supposedly because they have succeeded economically, socially, and educationally despite past prejudices and discrimination. Yet this picture minimizes the degree of diversity among Asian Americans. There are rich and poor Japanese Americans, rich and poor Filipino Americans, and so on. In fact, Southeast Asians living in the United States have the highest rate of welfare dependency of any racial or ethnic group. Even though Asian Americans have substantially more schooling than other ethnic groups, their median income is only slightly higher than that of Whites, and their poverty rate is higher as well. For example, in 2008, 32 percent of Asian households had incomes over $100,000 per year. This compares to 23 percent for White (non-Hispanic), 10 percent for Black, and 12 percent for Hispanic households (DeNavas-Walt et al. 2009:Table A-1).

The fact that as a group Asian Americans work in the same occupations as Whites suggests that they have been successful—and many have. However, there are some differences between the two groups. Asian immigrants, like other minorities and immigrants, are found disproportionately in low-paying service occupations. At the same time, better-educated Asian Americans are concentrated near the top in professional and managerial positions, although they rarely reach the pinnacle. Instead, they hit the glass ceiling, or try to "climb a broken ladder," as some put it. In 2007, only 1.5 percent of the 5563 people who served on the boards of the nation's 500 largest corporations were Asian American (Yoong and Young 2007).

Vietnamese Americans Each Asian American group has its own history and culture. Vietnamese Americans, for instance, came to the United States primarily during and after the Vietnam War—especially after the U.S. withdrawal from the region in 1975—and currently number 1.5 million. Assisted by local agencies, refugees from communist Vietnam settled throughout the United States, tens of thousands of them in small towns. Over time, Vietnamese Americans have gravitated toward the larger urban areas, establishing ethnic enclaves featuring Vietnamese restaurants and grocery stores.

In 1995, the United States resumed normal diplomatic relations with Vietnam. Gradually, the *Viet Kieu,* or Vietnamese living abroad, began to return to their old country to visit, but usually not to take up permanent residence. Today, almost 40 years after the end of the Vietnam War, sharp differences of opinion remain among Vietnamese Americans, especially the older ones, concerning the war and the present government of Vietnam (Pfeifer 2008).

Chinese Americans Unlike African slaves and Native Americans, the Chinese were initially encouraged to immigrate to the United States. From 1850 to 1880, thousands of Chinese immigrated to this country, lured by job opportunities created by the discovery of gold. However, as employment possibilities decreased and competition for mining jobs grew, the Chinese became the target of a bitter campaign to limit their numbers and restrict their rights. Chinese laborers were exploited, then discarded.

In 1882, Congress enacted the Chinese Exclusion Act, which prevented Chinese immigration and even forbade Chinese in the United States to send for their families. As a result, the Chinese population declined steadily until after World War II. More recently, the descendants of the 19th-century immigrants have been joined by a new influx from Hong Kong and Taiwan. These groups may contrast sharply in their degree of assimilation, desire to live in Chinatowns, and feelings about this country's relations with the communist People's Republic of China.

Currently, 3.1 million Chinese Americans live in the United States. Some Chinese Americans have entered lucrative occupations, yet many immigrants struggle to survive under living and working conditions that belie the model minority stereotype. In major U.S. cities, including New York and San Francisco, Chinatown districts contain illegal sweatshops in which recent immigrants—many of them Chinese women—work for minimal wages. Even in legal factories in the garment industry, hours are long and rewards are limited. A seamstress typically works 11 hours per day, 6 days a week, and earns $10,000–15,000 a year (Greenhouse 2008; Louie 2001; Shi 2008; Shipler 2004).

> One day our descendants will think it incredible that we paid so much attention to things like the amount of melanin in our skin or the shape of our eyes or our gender instead of the unique identities of each of us as complex human beings.
>
> Franklin Thomas

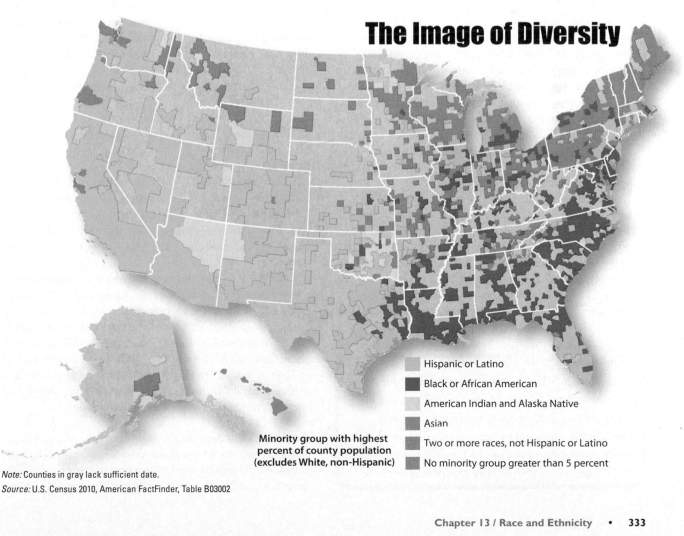

The Image of Diversity

Hispanic or Latino

Black or African American

American Indian and Alaska Native

Asian

Two or more races, not Hispanic or Latino

No minority group greater than 5 percent

Minority group with highest percent of county population (excludes White, non-Hispanic)

Note: Counties in gray lack sufficient date.

Source: U.S. Census 2010, American FactFinder, Table B03002

Japanese Americans Approximately 710,000 Japanese Americans live in the United States. As a people, they are relatively recent arrivals. In 1880, only 148 Japanese lived in the United States, but by 1920, there were more than 110,000. Japanese immigrants—called the *Issei*, or first generation—were usually males seeking employment opportunities. Many Whites saw them (along with Chinese immigrants) as a "yellow peril" and subjected them to prejudice and discrimination.

In 1941, the attack on Hawaii's Pearl Harbor by Japan had severe repercussions for Japanese Americans. The federal government decreed that all Japanese Americans on the West Coast had to leave their homes and report to "evacuation camps." Japanese Americans became, in effect, scapegoats for the anger that other people in the United States felt concerning Japan's role in World War II. By August 1943, 113,000 Japanese Americans had been forced into hastily built camps. In striking contrast, only a few German Americans and Italian Americans were sent to such camps (Neiwert 2005).

This mass detention was costly for Japanese Americans. The Federal Reserve Board estimates their total income and property losses at nearly half a billion dollars.

> A fully functional multiracial society cannot be achieved without a sense of history and open, honest dialogue.
>
> **Cornel West**

Moreover, the psychological effect on these citizens—including the humiliation of being labeled "disloyal"—was immeasurable. Eventually, children born in the United States to the *Issei*, called *Nisei*, were allowed to enlist in the army and serve in Europe in a segregated combat unit. Others resettled in the East and Midwest to work in factories.

In 1983, a federal commission recommended government payments to all surviving Japanese Americans who had been held in detention camps. The commission reported that the detention was motivated by "race prejudice, war hysteria, and a failure of political leadership." It added that "no documented acts of espionage, sabotage, or fifth-column activity were shown to have been committed" by Japanese Americans. In 1988, President Ronald Reagan signed the Civil Liberties Act, which required the federal government to issue individual apologies for all violations of Japanese Americans' constitutional rights

SOCTHINK

There is significant variation among numerous Asian nations and the billions of people they represent. Why do you think there is a tendency to lump people of Asian descent into a single category? How might factors such as geographic region and immigration history influence this perception?

and established a $1.6 billion trust fund to pay reparations to the approximately 82,250 surviving Japanese Americans who had been detained (U.S. Department of Justice 1999). Each person who applied and was eligible received $20,000 with payments starting in 1990.

Korean Americans At 1.3 million, the population of Korean Americans exceeds that of Japanese Americans. Yet Korean Americans are often overshadowed by other groups from Asia. Today's Korean American community is the result of three waves of immigration. The initial wave arrived between 1903 and 1910, when Korean laborers migrated to Hawaii. The second wave followed the end of the Korean War in 1953; most of those immigrants were wives of U.S. servicemen and war orphans. The third wave, continuing to the present, has reflected the admissions priorities established by the 1965 Immigration Act. These well-educated immigrants arrive in the United States with professional skills, though they often must settle, at least initially, for positions of lower responsibility than those they held in Korea.

In the early 1990s, the apparent friction between Korean Americans and another minority racial group, African Americans, attracted nationwide attention. In New York City, Los Angeles, and Chicago, Korean American merchants confronted Blacks who were allegedly threatening them or robbing their stores. Black neighborhoods responded with hostility to what they perceived as the disrespect and arrogance of Korean American entrepreneurs. In South Central Los Angeles, the only places to buy groceries, liquor, and gas were owned by Korean immigrants, who had largely replaced White businesspeople. African Americans were well aware of the dominant role that Korean Americans played in their local retail markets. During the 1992 riots in South Central, small businesses owned by Koreans were a particular target. More than 1800 Korean businesses were looted or burned during the riots (Kim 1999).

Conflict between the two groups was dramatized in Spike Lee's 1989 movie *Do the Right Thing*. The situation stems from Korean Americans' position as the latest immigrant group to cater to the needs of inner-city populations abandoned by those who have moved up the economic ladder. This type of friction is not new; generations of Jewish, Italian, and Arab merchants have encountered similar hostility from another oppressed minority that to outsiders might seem an unlikely source.

Arab Americans Arab Americans are immigrants and their descendants who hail from the 22 nations of the Arab world. As defined by the League of Arab States, these are the nations of North Africa and what is commonly known as the Middle East. Not all residents of those countries are Arab; for example, the Kurds of northern Iraq are not Arab. And some Arab Americans may have immigrated to the United States from non-Arab countries such as Great Britain or France, where their families have lived for generations.

The Arabic language is the single most unifying force among Arabs, although not all Arabs, and certainly not all Arab Americans, can read and speak Arabic. Moreover, the language has evolved over the centuries so that people in different parts of the Arab world speak different dialects. The fact that the Muslim holy book the Qur'an (or Koran) was originally written in Arabic gives the language special importance to Muslims.

Estimates of the size of the Arab American community differ widely. By some counts, up to 3.5 million people of Arab ancestry now reside in the United States. Among those who identify themselves as Arab Americans, the most common country of origin is Lebanon, followed by Syria, Egypt, and Palestine. In 2000, these four countries of origin accounted for two-thirds of all Arab Americans. As with other racial and ethnic groups, the Arab American population is concentrated in certain areas of the United States. Their rising numbers have led to the development of Arab retail centers in several cities, including Dearborn and Detroit, Michigan; Los Angeles; Chicago; New York City; and Washington, D.C. (David 2008).

As a group, Arab Americans are extremely diverse. Many families have lived in the United States for several generations; others are foreign born. Despite the stereotype, most Arab Americans are *not* Muslim, and not all practice religion. The majority of Arab Americans are Christian. Nor can Arab Americans be characterized as having a specific family type, gender role, or occupational pattern (Arab American Institute 2008; David 2004).

For years, airport personnel and law enforcement authorities used appearance and ethnic-sounding names to identify Arab Americans and search their belongings. After the terrorist attacks of September 2001, criticism of this practice declined as concern for the public's safety mounted.

ETHNIC GROUPS

Unlike racial minorities, members of subordinate ethnic groups may not be hindered by physical differences from assimilating into the dominant culture of the United States. However, members of ethnic minority groups still face many forms of prejudice and discrimination. Take, for instance, the country's largest ethnic groups—Latinos, Jews, and White ethnics.

Latinos Together, the various groups included under the general category Latinos represent the largest minority in the United States. In 2008, there were more than 46 million Hispanics in this country, including 31 million Mexican Americans, more than 4 million Puerto Ricans, 1.6 million Cuban Americans, and a smaller number of people of Central and South American origin. The latter group represents the fastest-growing and most diverse segment of the Hispanic community.

According to Census Bureau data, the Latino population now outnumbers the African American population in 8 of the 10 largest cities of the United States: New York City, Los Angeles, Houston, Phoenix, San Antonio, Dallas, San Diego, and San Jose. Hispanics are now the majority of residents in cities such as Miami, Florida; El Paso, Texas; and Santa Ana, California. The rise in the Hispanic population of the United States—fueled by comparatively high birthrates and levels of immigration—has intensified debates over public policy issues such as bilingualism and immigration (U.S. Census Bureau 2009j:Table DP-5).

The various Latino groups share a heritage of Spanish language and culture, which can cause serious problems in their assimilation. An intelligent student whose first language is Spanish may be presumed to be slow or even unruly by English-speaking schoolchildren, and frequently by English-speaking teachers as well. The labeling of Latino children as underachievers, as learning disabled, or as emotionally disturbed can act as a self-fulfilling prophecy for some children. Bilingual education aims at easing the educational difficulties experienced by Hispanic children and others whose first language is not English.

The educational challenges facing Latinos is reflected in the fact that 68 percent of Hispanics aged 25–29 have completed high school, compared to 88 percent for non-Hispanic Whites. At the college level, 37 percent of Whites

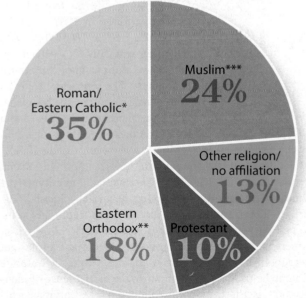

Arab American Religious Affiliation

Muslim*** 24%

Roman/ Eastern Catholic* 35%

Other religion/ no affiliation 13%

Eastern Orthodox** 18%

Protestant 10%

*Catholic includes Roman Catholic, Maronite, and Melkite (Greek Catholic).
**Orthodox includes Antiochian, Syrian, Greek, and Coptic.
***Muslim includes Sunni, Shi'a, and Druze.

Source: Arab American Institute 2008.

Cities with Large Numbers of Hispanics

Cities	Number of Hispanics	% of population Hispanic
New York	2,313,400	27.7
Los Angeles	1,867,861	49.1
Houston	865,085	42.7
San Antonio	794,073	61.4
Chicago	770,386	28.1
Phoenix	655,825	43.0
Dallas	547,781	44.6
El Paso	482,725	80.1
San Diego	351,447	27.7

Source: U.S. Census Bureau 2009j:Table DP-5.

Major Hispanic Groups in the United States

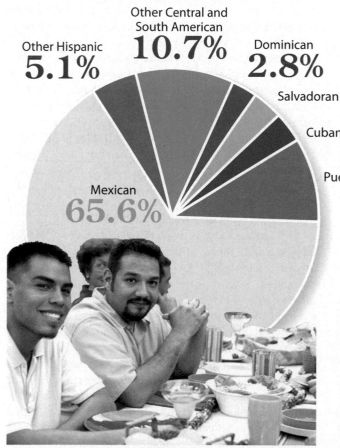

Other Hispanic **5.1%**

Other Central and South American **10.7%**

Dominican **2.8%**

Salvadoran **3.4%**

Cuban **3.4%**

Puerto Rican **9.0%**

Mexican **65.6%**

Source: U.S. Census Bureau 2009j:Table B03001.

have a bachelor's degree, whereas only 12.4 percent of Hispanics have the same. The average income for Hispanic households is $37,913, which is 68 percent as much as non-Hispanic White households. In terms of wealth, 49 percent of Hispanics own their own home, compared to 75 percent for Whites (DeNavas-Walt 2009; Kochhar, Gonzalez-Barrera, and Dockterman 2009; Planty et al. 2009).

Mexican Americans The largest Latino population is Mexican American (see the graph on the left). There were 12.7 million Mexican immigrants living in the United States in 2008, 17 times as many as the 760,000 in 1970. Approximately 55 percent of them are unauthorized immigrants. The opportunity for a Mexican to earn in one hour what it would take an entire day to earn in Mexico has pushed millions of immigrants, legal and illegal, north (Pew Hispanic Center 2009).

Aside from the family, the most important social institution in the Mexican American community is the church—specifically, the Roman Catholic Church. This strong identification with the Catholic faith has reinforced the already formidable barriers between Mexican Americans and their predominantly White and Protestant neighbors in the Southwest. At the same time, the Catholic Church helps many immigrants to develop a sense of identity and assists their assimilation into the dominant culture of the United States. The complexity of the Mexican American community is underscored by the fact that Protestant churches—especially those that endorse expressive, open worship—have attracted increasing numbers of Mexican Americans.

Puerto Ricans The second-largest segment of Latinos in the United States is Puerto Ricans. Since 1917, residents of Puerto Rico have held the status of American citizens; many have migrated to New York and other eastern cities. Puerto Ricans have experienced serious poverty both in the United States and on the island. Those who live in the continental United States earn barely half the family income of Whites. As a result, a reverse migration began in the 1970s, with more Puerto Ricans leaving for the island than coming to the mainland (Torres 2008).

Politically, Puerto Ricans in the United States have not been as successful as Mexican Americans in organizing for their rights. For many mainland Puerto Ricans—as for many residents of the island—the paramount political issue is the destiny of Puerto Rico itself. Should it continue in its present commonwealth status, petition for admission to the United States as the 51st state, or attempt to become an independent nation? This question has divided Puerto Rico for decades and remains a central issue in Puerto Rican elections. In a 1998 referendum, for example, voters supported a "none of the above" option, effectively favoring continuation of the commonwealth status over statehood or independence.

Cuban Americans Cuban immigration to the United States dates back as far as 1831, but it began in earnest following Fidel Castro's seizure of power in the Cuban revolution of 1959. The first wave of 200,000 Cubans included many professionals with relatively high levels of schooling; these men and women were largely welcomed as refugees from communist tyranny. However, more recent waves of immigrants have aroused growing concern, partly because they were less likely to be skilled professionals. After Castro's revolution, the United States severed formal relations with Cuba, preventing all trade and banning travel. In recent years there has been some softening of that relationship, and in April 2009, President Obama signed a bill easing both economic and travel restrictions.

Jewish Americans Jews constitute about 2.2 percent of the population of the United States. They play a prominent role in the worldwide Jewish community because the United States has the world's largest concentration of Jews. Like the Japanese, many Jewish immigrants came to this country and became white-collar professionals in spite of prejudice and discrimination.

Anti-Semitism—that is, anti-Jewish prejudice—has often been vicious in the United States, although rarely so widespread and never so formalized as in Europe. In many cases, Jews have been used as scapegoats for other people's failures. Given such attitudes, Jews continue to face discrimination. Despite high levels of education and professional training, they are still conspicuously absent from the top management of large corporations (except for the few firms founded by Jews). Until the late 1960s, many prestigious universities maintained restrictive quotas that limited Jewish enrollment. Private social clubs and fraternal groups frequently limit membership to gentiles (non-Jews), a practice upheld by the Supreme Court in the 1964 case *Bell v. Maryland.*

The Anti-Defamation League (ADL) of B'nai B'rith funds an annual tally of reported anti-Semitic incidents. Although the number has fluctuated, the 1994 tabulation reached the highest level in the 19 years the ADL had been recording them. In 2008, the total reported incidents of harassment, threats, vandalism, and assaults came to 1352, which represented a decline in incidents for a fourth straight year. Some incidents were inspired and carried out by neo-Nazi skinheads—groups of young people who champion racist and anti-Semitic ideologies. Such threatening behavior only intensifies the fears of many Jewish Americans, who remember the Holocaust—the extermination of 6 million Jews by Nazi Germany during World War II (Anti-Defamation League 2009).

As is true for other minorities in the United States, Jewish Americans face the choice of maintaining ties to their long religious and cultural heritage or becoming as indistinguishable as possible from gentiles. Many Jews have tended to assimilate, as is evident from the rise in the rate of marriages between Jews and Christians. A study of 50 Jewish communities in the United States found a median intermarriage rate of 33 percent. Many people in the Jewish community worry that intermarriage

> **anti-Semitism** Anti-Jewish prejudice.

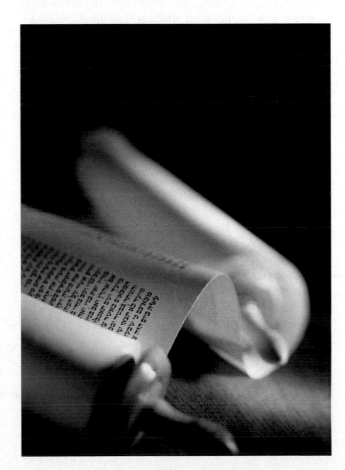

will lead to a rapid decline in those who identify themselves as "Jewish." Yet, when asked which was the greater threat to Jewish life in the United States—intermarriage or anti-Semitism—only 33 percent of respondents chose intermarriage; 62 percent selected anti-Semitism (American Jewish Committee 2005; Sheskin and Dashefsky 2007).

White Ethnics A significant segment of the population of the United States is made up of White ethnics whose ancestors arrived from Europe within the past century. The nation's White ethnic population includes about 50 million people who claim at least partial German ancestry, 36 million Irish Americans, almost 18 million Italian Americans, and 10 million Polish Americans, as well as immigrants from other European nations. Some of these people continue to live in close-knit ethnic neighborhoods, whereas others have largely assimilated and left the "old ways" behind (U.S. Census Bureau 2009j:Table DP-2).

Many White ethnics today identify only sporadically with their heritage. **Symbolic ethnicity** refers to an emphasis on concerns such as ethnic food or political issues rather than on deeper ties to one's ethnic heritage. It is reflected in the occasional family trip to an ethnic bakery, the celebration of a ceremonial event such as St. Joseph's Day among Italian Americans, or concern about the future of Northern Ireland among Irish Americans. Except in cases in which new immigration reinforces old traditions, symbolic ethnicity tends to decline with each passing generation (Anagnostou 2009a, 2009b; Gans 2009; Waters 2009).

symbolic ethnicity An ethnic identity that emphasizes concerns such as ethnic food or political issues rather than deeper ties to one's ethnic heritage.

White ethnics and racial minorities have often been antagonistic to one another because of economic competition. As Blacks, Latinos, and Native Americans emerge from the lower class, they must compete with working-class Whites for jobs, housing, and educational opportunities. In times of high unemployment or inflation, any such competition can easily generate intense intergroup conflict (Roediger 2005).

In many respects, the plight of White ethnics involves the same basic issues as that of other subordinate people in the United States. How ethnic can people be—how much can they deviate from an essentially White, Anglo-Saxon, Protestant norm—before society responds to their desire to be different? The United States does seem to reward people for assimilating. Yet, as we have seen, assimilation is no easy process. In the years to come, more and more people will face the challenge of fitting in, not only in the United States, but also around the world as the flow of immigrants from one country to another continues to increase.

>> Immigration

According to a United Nations report, there are 191 million international immigrants in the world, or 3 percent of the global population. This includes 38 million in the United States. Of these, 53 percent are from Latin America, 27 percent from Asia, 13 percent from Europe, and 4 percent from Africa (United Nations 2009; U.S. Census Bureau 2009j:Table DP-2). The constantly increasing numbers of immigrants and the pressure they put on employment opportunities and welfare capabilities in the countries they enter raise difficult questions for many of the world's economic powers. Who should be allowed in? At what point should immigration be curtailed (Bloemraad, Korteweg, and Yurdakal 2008)?

IMMIGRATION TRENDS

The migration of people is not uniform across time or space. At certain times, war or famine may precipitate large movements of people, either temporarily or permanently. Temporary dislocations occur when people wait until it is safe to return to their home areas. However, more and more migrants who cannot eke out an adequate living in their home nations are making permanent moves to developed nations. The major migration streams flow into North America, the oil-rich areas of

Going GLOBAL

World Immigration Since 1500

Source: J. Allen 2008.

the Middle East, and the industrial economies of western Europe and Asia. Currently, seven of the world's wealthiest nations (including Germany, France, the United Kingdom, and the United States) shelter about one-third of the world's migrant population but less than one-fifth of the world's total population. As long as disparities in job opportunities exist among countries, there is little reason to expect this international trend to reverse.

Even though the sending nation loses a significant source of labor and talent due to emigration, the process does contribute to its economy. For example, it reduces the size of the population that an economy with limited resources has a difficult time supporting, and it leads to an economic infusion in the form of remittances—monies that immigrants send back to their home nations. Worldwide, immigrants send more than $300 billion a year back home to their relatives—an amount that represents a major source of income for developing nations. In Guatemala, for example, the home country of the majority of workers at the Postville meat packing plant, $4.3 billion was sent back home in 2008, representing 11 percent of Guatemala's economy (*Guatemala Times* 2009; Leys 2008).

Immigrants continue to face obstacles due to their relative lack of resources. Immigrant women, for example, face all the challenges that immigrant men do, plus some additional ones. Typically, they bear the responsibility for obtaining services for their families, particularly their children. Women are often left to navigate the bureaucratic tangle of schools, city services, and health care, as well as the unfamiliar stores and markets they must shop at to feed

their families. Women who need special medical services or are victims of domestic violence are often reluctant to seek outside help. Finally, because many new immigrants view the United States as a dangerous place to raise a family, women must be especially watchful over their children's lives (Hondagneu-Sotelo 2003).

One consequence of global immigration has been the emergence of transnationals—people or families who move across borders multiple times in search of better jobs and education. The industrial tycoons of the early 20th century, whose power outmatched that of many nation-states, were among the world's first transnationals. Today, however, millions of people, many of very modest means, move back and forth between countries much as commuters do between city and suburbs. More and more of these people have dual citizenship. Rather than being shaped by allegiance to one country, their identity is rooted in

SOC THINK

Birthrates in the United States, as in many industrialized nations, are low. Populations in many states face natural decrease and will shrink without immigration to compensate for those low birthrates. Given this, why does immigration still cause such tension among many communities in the United States? Might this change as people in such states realize they need those immigrants?

Going GLOBAL

Legal Migration to the United States, 1820–2010

Millions of immigrants

1820s	1840s	1860s	1880s	1900s	1920s	1940s	1960s	1980s	2000s
0.1	0.6	1.7	2.3	3.7	4.1	0.5	2.5	4.2	10.2
		2.6	2.8	5.2	5.7	1.0	3.2	6.2	
					8.8			9.7	

Europe and Canada

All Others

Source: Author's estimates for the period 2000–2010; Office of Immigration Statistics 2007.

their struggle to survive—and in some instances prosper—by transcending international borders (Croucher 2004; Sassen 2005).

IMMIGRATION POLICIES

Countries that have long been a destination for immigrants, such as the United States, usually have policies to determine who has preference to enter. Often, clear racial and ethnic biases are built into these policies. In the 1920s, U.S. policy gave preference to people from western Europe while making it difficult for residents of southern and eastern Europe,

Asia, and Africa to enter the country. During the late 1930s and early 1940s, the federal government refused to loosen restrictive immigration quotas in order to allow Jewish refugees to escape the terror of Nazi Germany. In line with this policy, the SS *St. Louis,* with more than 900 Jewish refugees on board, was denied permission to dock in the United States in 1939. The ship was forced to sail back to Europe, where at least a few hundred of its passengers later died at the hands of the Nazis (Morse 1967; G. Thomas and Witts 1974).

Since the 1960s, U.S. policy has encouraged the immigration of relatives of U.S. residents and of people who have desirable skills. This policy has significantly altered the pattern of sending nations. Previously, Europeans dominated, but for the past 40 years, immigrants have come primarily from Latin America and Asia. Thus, an ever-growing proportion of the U.S. population will be Asian or Hispanic. To a large degree, fear and resentment of racial and ethnic diversity is a key factor in opposition to immigration. In many nations, people are concerned that the new arrivals do not reflect and will not embrace their own cultural and racial heritage.

The long border with Mexico provides ample opportunity for illegal immigration into the United States. Throughout the 1980s, the public perception grew that the United States had lost control of its borders. As indicated above, it was this sentiment that gave rise to Arizona's controversial immigration law in 2010. Feeling pressure to control immigration, Congress ended a decade of debate by approving the Immigration Reform and Control Act of 1986. The act marked a historic change in the nation's immigration policy. For the first time, the hiring of illegal aliens was outlawed, and employers caught violating the law became subject to fines and even prison. Just as significant a change was the extension of amnesty and legal status to many illegal immigrants already living in the United States. Over 20 years later, however, the act appears to have had mixed results. Substantial numbers of unauthorized immigrants continue to enter the country each year, with an estimated 12 million present now at any given time—a marked increase since 2000 (Passel and Cohn 2009).

Recently, immigrants have staged massive marches to pressure Congress to speed the naturalization process and develop ways for illegal immigrants to gain legal residency. Opponents of illegal immigration have called for more resources with which to track down and deport illegal immigrants and close up the U.S.–Mexican border. Numerous states are also considering legislation patterned after the 2010 Arizona law. Despite this widespread public dissatisfaction with the nation's immigration policy, little progress has been made. Congress has had difficulty reaching a bipartisan compromise that pleases both sides.

In the wake of the September 11, 2001, attacks on the World Trade Center and the Pentagon, immigration procedures were complicated by the need to detect potential terrorists. Illegal immigrants especially, but even legal immigrants, have faced increased scrutiny by government officials around the world. For would-be immigrants to many nations, the wait to receive the right to enter a country—even to join relatives—has increased substantially, as immigration officials scrutinize what were once routine applications more closely.

The intense debate over immigration reflects deep value conflicts in the cultures of many nations. One strand of our culture, for example, has traditionally emphasized egalitarian principles and a desire to help people in time of need. At the same time, hostility to potential immigrants and refugees—whether the Chinese in the 1880s, European Jews in the 1930s and 1940s, or Mexicans, Haitians, and Arabs today—reflects not only racial, ethnic, and religious prejudice but a desire to maintain the dominant culture of the in-group by excluding those viewed as outsiders.

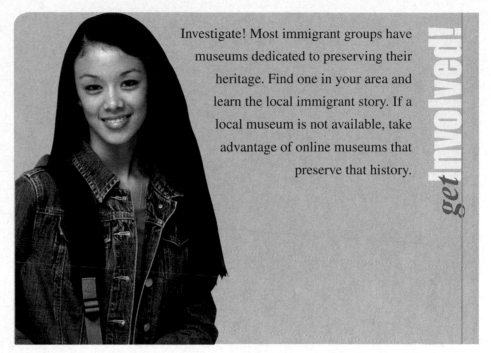

Investigate! Most immigrant groups have museums dedicated to preserving their heritage. Find one in your area and learn the local immigrant story. If a local museum is not available, take advantage of online museums that preserve that history.

get Involved!

For REVIEW

I. How do sociologists define race and ethnicity?

- Race is defined by the social significance that groups attach to external physical characteristics. Ethnicity is rooted in cultural and national traditions that define a population. Sociologists emphasize the significance of culture and its consequences for both.

II. What are prejudice and discrimination, and how do they operate?

- Prejudice involves attitudes and beliefs whereas discrimination involves actions. In both cases, they represent a negative response to a group of people that denies them full equality as persons. Institutional discrimination is built into the structure of society itself, systematically denying some groups access to key resources.

III. What are the consequences of race and ethnicity for opportunity?

- Racial and ethnic groups in the United States—including African Americans, Native Americans, Asian Americans, Latino Americans, Jewish Americans, and White ethnic Americans—face differing levels of opportunity based on their relative position in society. Groups within each of these categories continue to face significant structural inequality.

Functionalist View

Historically, race and ethnicity have contributed to **social integration** and **identity** by providing clear boundaries between groups.

Amalgamation, assimilation, and pluralism function to bring **order** to society. Immigration is functional for the host nation if it gains needed workers and for the sending nation when remittances are sent back.

INTEGRATION, IDENTITY, ORDER
KEY CONCEPTS

Conflict View

Prejudice, discrimination, ethnocentrism, stereotyping, racism, and hate crimes are all manifestations of perceived **superiority** of a dominant group over subordinate minority groups.

Institutional discrimination denies opportunities and equal rights to individuals and groups as part as the normal operations of society.

Exploitation theory holds that prejudice and discrimination help preserve inequality in the economic system as a whole.

KEY CONCEPTS
DISCRIMINATION, EXPLOITATION, RACISM

MAKE THE CONNECTION

After reviewing the chapter, answer the following questions:

Interactionist View

According to the **contact hypothesis**, interracial contact between people in cooperative circumstances will lessen prejudice and stereotyping.

Racial **profiling** occurs when arbitrary actions are taken by authorities based on a person's perceived racial or ethnic identity.

Being White in the United States represents an often unacknowledged form of privilege in everyday encounters.

KEY CONCEPTS
CONTACT, INTERACTION

1

Examine the story of the Postville immigrants from the point of view of each perspective (p. 313)?

2

How would each perspective explain stereotyping (p. 326)? How so?

3

How do the functionalist and conflict perspectives intersect in both color-blind racism (p. 320) and affirmative action (p. 324)?

4

Using the interactionist perspective, describe an example of interracial contact you have experienced along with its consequences.

Pop Quiz

1. A group that is set apart because of its national origin or distinctive cultural patterns is a(n)
   a. assimilated group.
   b. ethnic group.
   c. minority group.
   d. racial group.

2. According to the findings of the Human Genome Project, race
   a. determines intellectual ability.
   b. is a biological, not a social, concept.
   c. explains significant social outcomes.
   d. has no genetic or scientific basis.

3. Starting with the 2000 Census, there were a total of _____ possible race combinations you could choose from to identify yourself.
   a. 3
   b. 6
   c. 27
   d. 63

4. Suppose that a White employer refuses to hire a Vietnamese American and selects an inferior White applicant. This decision is an act of
   a. prejudice.
   b. ethnocentrism.
   c. discrimination.
   d. stigmatization.

5. The term that Peggy McIntosh uses to describe the unearned advantages that those in the majority take for granted is
   a. privilege.
   b. discrimination.
   c. racism.
   d. institutional discrimination.

6. Working together as computer programmers for an electronics firm, a Hispanic woman and a Jewish man overcome their initial prejudices and come to appreciate each other's strengths and talents. This scenario is an example of
   a. the contact hypothesis.
   b. a self-fulfilling prophecy.
   c. amalgamation.
   d. reverse discrimination.

7. Intermarriage over several generations, resulting in various groups combining to form a new group, would be an example of
   a. pluralism.
   b. assimilation.
   c. segregation.
   d. amalgamation.

8. Jennifer Anastassakis changed her name to Jennifer Aniston. Her action was an example of
   a. expulsion.
   b. assimilation.
   c. segregation.
   d. pluralism.

9. The largest racial minority group in the United States is
   a. Asian Americans.
   b. African Americans.
   c. Native Americans.
   d. Jewish Americans.

10. Which of the following is the largest overall minority group in the United States?
    a. African Americans
    b. Asian Americans
    c. Latinos
    d. Arab Americans

1. (b); 2. (d); 3. (d); 4. (c); 5. (a); 6. (a); 7. (d); 8. (b); 9. (b); 10. (c)

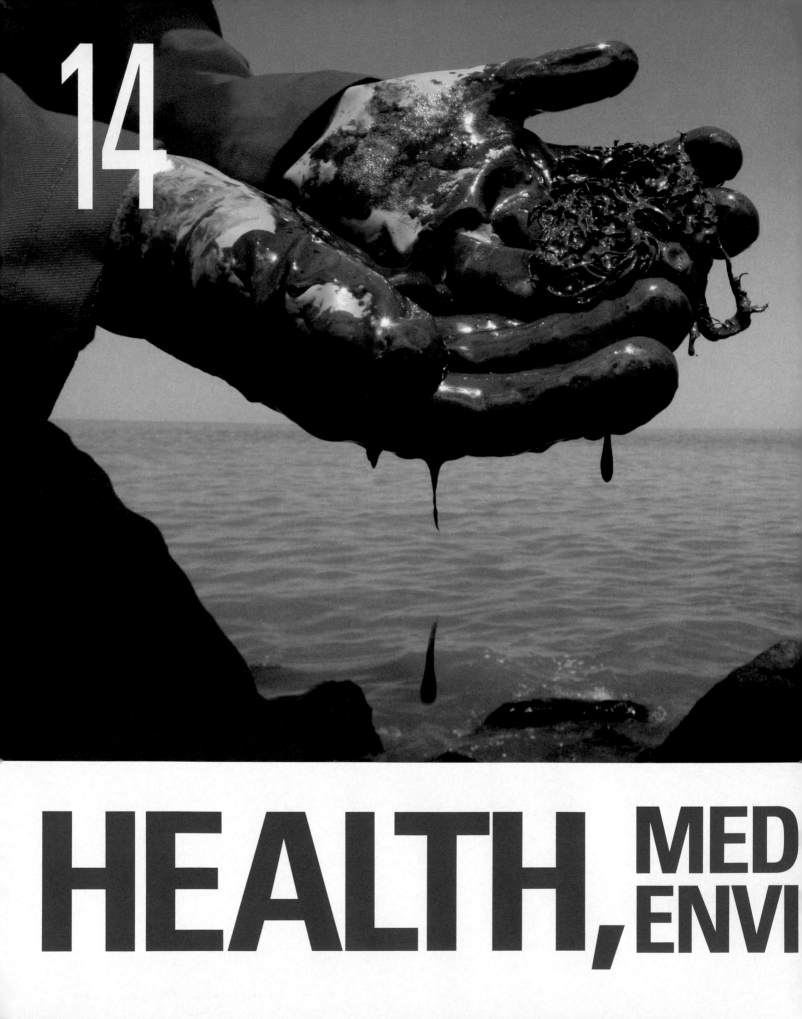

14

HEALTH, MED ENVI

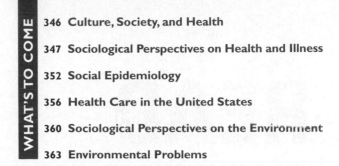

LIVING ON MOTHER EARTH

On April 20, 2010, an explosion at the Deepwater Horizon oil drilling platform approximately 40 miles off the coast of Louisiana in the Gulf of Mexico marked the beginning of an environmental catastrophe. Workers had just completed a series of pressure tests to ensure the well's integrity when methane gas entered the drill column and erupted out of the well. The blowout protector, designed to automatically seal the well in such cases, failed. Eleven members of the 126-person crew aboard the oil rig were killed in the resulting explosion. At the wellhead on the Gulf floor, more than 10,000 barrels of oil per day began gushing into the water.

A year earlier, as part of the oil-drilling approval process, BP, the corporation that owns the rights to the well, filed an exploration plan with the Minerals Management Service (MMS), an agency of the U.S. Department of the Interior. In that report, BP repeatedly minimized both the likelihood of an accident and any possible impact should one occur, reporting that, "in the event of an unanticipated blowout resulting in an oil spill, it is unlikely to have an impact" (BP Exploration & Production Inc. 2009). BP maintained that any effects would likely be "sublethal" to fish, marine mammals, turtles, and birds. It also argued that the well's distance from shore would ensure minimal impact on beaches, wildlife refuges, and wilderness areas in the event of an oil spill. And the corporation expressed confidence in its ability to contain, recover, and remove any spill. Having filed this report, BP received an exemption from the MMS, freeing it from conducting a detailed environmental impact analysis.

In the end, we will likely find that there wasn't a single cause to this catastrophe, though there may well have been a primary trigger. Instead, it was likely the convergence of several factors (technological failures, lax government oversight, corporate self-interest, etc.) that led to this disastrous result. Just as the natural environment consists of an interdependent web of relationships, so does the social environment. We must develop a more complete understanding of both to avoid catastrophic outcomes like this one in the future.

ICINE, AND RONMENT

- What does sociology contribute to something as seemingly biological as health?
- What is social epidemiology?
- What environmental lessons do we learn from sociology?

>> Culture, Society, and Health

When it comes to health and illness, we must take seriously the interdependent connections that shape our likely outcomes. To understand health, we cannot focus on biology alone. We must consider relationships, contexts, and the significance and impact of culture and society. The communities in which we live shape how we think about health and the body, as do our access to health care and our exposure to health risks.

We can begin, however, with a general definition of health from the preamble to the 1946 constitution of the World Health Organization (WHO). It defined **health** as a "state of complete physical, mental, and social well-being, and not merely the absence of disease and infirmity" (Leavell and Clark 1965:14). This absolute standard provides an ideal type of what constitutes health, although in practice most people fall somewhere along a continuum between this ideal on one extreme and death on the other.

Our culture influences where we place ourselves along that continuum. Different places present us with differing levels of health risk. The type of health care available and our access to it also influence what we come to count as essential care, as do the risks we face. In rural areas, for example, residents must travel many miles to see a doctor. On the other hand, people who live in the country may escape many of the stresses and strains, along with environmental risks, that plague people who live in cities. Similarly, in Japan, organ transplants are rare. The Japanese do not generally favor harvesting organs from brain-dead donors. As a result, they forgo the health benefits that such transplants provide.

Researchers have shown that diseases, too, are rooted in the shared meanings of particular cultures. The term

health As defined by the World Health Organization, a state of complete physical, mental, and social well-being, not merely the absence of disease and infirmity.

culture-bound syndrome A disease or illness that cannot be understood apart from some specific social context.

culture-bound syndrome refers to a disease or illness that cannot be understood apart from some specific social context. This means that there is something particular about the culture—how it is organized, what it believes, what is expected of members—that contributes to that

Anorexia is not a new disease, though it is discussed much more openly today. Seventies rock star Karen Carpenter died from anorexia in 1983.

Did You Know?

...The average American woman is 5 feet 4 inches tall, weighs 155 pounds, and wears a size 14 dress, while the average model is 5 feet 9 inches tall, weighs 110 pounds, and wears a size 0 or 2.

malady (Buckle et al. 2007; Nicolas et al. 2006; U.S. Surgeon General 1999).

In the United States, a culture-bound syndrome known as anorexia nervosa has received increasing attention in recent decades. First described in England in the 1860s, this condition is characterized by an intense fear of becoming obese and a distorted image of one's body. Those who suffer from anorexia nervosa (primarily young women in their teens or 20s) lose weight drastically through self-induced semistarvation. Anorexia nervosa is best understood in the context of Western culture, which typically views the slim, youthful individual as healthy and beautiful, and the fat person as ugly and lacking in self-discipline.

Throughout most of the 20th century, U.S. researchers dealt with the concept of culture-bound syndromes only in cross-cultural studies. However, recent increases in immigration, especially after the Immigration and Nationality Act of 1965 opened the doors to more immigrants, along with efforts by the medical establishment to reach out to immigrant communities, have led to a belated recognition that not everyone views medicine in the same way. Medical practitioners are now being trained to recognize cultural beliefs that are related to medicine. For example, people from Central America may consider pain a consequence of the imbalance of nature, and Muslim women are particularly concerned about personal modesty. Health care professionals are increasingly incorporating such knowledge into their practices.

Culture can also influence the relative incidence of a disease or disorder. In her book *The Scalpel and the Silver Bear,* Dr. Lori Arviso Alvord, the first Navajo woman to become a surgeon, writes of the depression and alcoholism that attend life on the reservation. These diseases, she says, are born from "historical grief": "Navajo children are told of the capture and murder of their forefathers and mothers, and then they too must share in the legacy." Not just for the Navajo, Alvord writes, but for African Americans as well, the weight of centuries of suffering, injustice, and loss too often manifests itself in despair and addiction. The rate of alcoholism mortality among Native Americans is more than three times that of the general U.S. population (Alvord and Van Pelt 1999:12; Heron et al, 2009).

>> Sociological Perspectives on Health and Illness

Whether we are considered "healthy" or "ill" is not our decision alone to make. Family, friends, co-workers, physicians, and others all shape how we perceive the state of our own and others' health. To fully understand the scope of health and illness in society, we have to consider how society defines illness, what the consequences of such definitions are, and how social position and access to resources shape health outcomes.

ILLNESS AND SOCIAL ORDER

Illness represents a threat to the social order. If too many people are sick at the same time, it not only presents a problem for those who are ill but also undercuts our collective ability to perform tasks necessary for the continued operation of society. This can result in debates over what constitutes being "sick enough" to be considered truly ill. At what point, for example, do we stay home from school or work due to illness, and who gets to decide? All of us have likely faced this dilemma, sometimes dragging ourselves out of bed and going anyway because we felt we needed to be there, whether for the sake of ourselves or for others.

When people cross the line into illness, they take on what sociologists call the **sick role,** a term that refers to societal expectations about the attitudes and behavior of a person labeled as ill (Parsons 1951, 1975). Fit members of society exempt those who are sick from typical, day-to-day responsibilities and generally do not blame them for their condition. Yet the sick members of society are obligated to attempt recovery, which includes seeking competent professional care. This obligation arises from the sense of responsibility we have to perform our normal roles in society, whether as student, worker, parent, or more. It also is motivated by the reality that we may well face sanctions from others for failing to return to those normal roles quickly. In fact, especially in the context of competitive work environments, we often look down on those who seem to get sick too easily or frequently, suspecting that they are either lazy or weak. Such attitudes present significant difficulties for those facing chronic health problems.

sick role Societal expectations about the attitudes and behavior of a person viewed as being ill.

SOCTHINK

What factors shape your likelihood of doing all you can to avoid "being sick"? How might the power others have over you influence your actions? What positions do they occupy relative to you?

Physicians and nurses have the power to label people as healthy or sick and, thus, to function as gatekeepers for the sick role. For example, instructors often require students to get a note from a health care professional to verify a claim of illness as a legitimate excuse for missing a paper or an exam. The ill person becomes dependent on the doctor or nurse, because physicians and nurses control the resources that patients need, whether it be a note for a professor or a prescription for medication. We look to such professionals to solve our health care needs, trusting that they have sufficient expertise and experience to diagnose and treat our problems.

Factors such as gender, age, social class, and ethnic group all influence patients' judgments regarding their own state of health. Younger people may fail to detect the warning signs of a dangerous illness, and the elderly may focus too much on the slightest physical malady. People who are employed are less willing to assume the sick role for fear of consequences they might face at work. Similarly, from an early age, athletes learn to define certain ailments as "sports injuries" and so do not regard themselves as "sick" when suffering from such maladies.

POWER, RESOURCES, AND HEALTH

The faith we place in physicians to heal what ails us has helped them attain significant levels of prestige and power.

Sociologist Eliot Freidson (1970:5) has likened the status of medicine today to that of state religions in the past—it has an officially approved monopoly on the right to define health and to treat illness. Theorists use the phrase "medicalization of society" to refer to the growing role of medicine as a major institution of social control (Conrad 2007; Zola 1972, 1983).

The Medicalization of Society Social control involves techniques and strategies for regulating behavior in order to enforce the distinctive norms and values of a culture. How does medicine manifest its social control? First, medicine has greatly expanded its domain of expertise in recent decades. Physicians now examine a wide range of issues in addition to basic health, among them sexuality, old age, anxiety, obesity, child development, alcoholism, and drug addiction. We tolerate this expansion of the boundaries of medicine because we hope that these experts can provide factual and effective cures to complex human problems, as they have to various infectious diseases.

The social significance of this expanding medicalization is that once a problem is viewed from a medical model framework—once medical experts become influential in proposing and assessing relevant public policies—it becomes more difficult for common people to join the discussion and exert influence on decision making. It also becomes more difficult to view these issues as being shaped by social, cultural, or psychological factors rather than simply by physical or medical factors (Caplan 1989; Davis 2006; Starr 1982).

A second way that medicine serves as an agent of social control is by retaining absolute jurisdiction over many

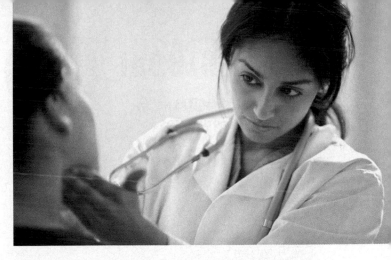

health care procedures. The medical industry has even attempted to guard its jurisdiction by placing health care professionals such as chiropractors and nurse-midwives outside the realm of acceptable medicine. Despite the fact that midwives first brought professionalism to child delivery, they have been portrayed by doctors as having invaded the "legitimate" field of obstetrics, in both the United States and Mexico. Nurse-midwives have sought licensing as a way to achieve professional respectability, but physicians continue to exert power to ensure that midwifery remains a subordinate occupation (Scharnberg 2007).

Inequities in Health Care Another serious concern regarding power and resources in the context of contemporary medicine involves the glaring inequities that exist in health care. Around the world, poor areas tend to be underserved because medical services concentrate where the wealth is. The United States, for example, has about 27 physicians per 10,000 people, whereas African nations average less than 2 per 10,000 (World Health Organization 2010).

The supply of health care in poorer countries is further reduced by what is referred to as **brain drain**—the immigration to the United States and other industrialized nations of skilled workers, professionals, and technicians who are needed in their home countries. As part of this brain drain, physicians, nurses, and other health care professionals have come to the United States from developing countries such as India, Pakistan, and various African states. Their emigration out of the Third World represents yet another way in which the world's core industrialized nations enhance their quality of life at the expense of developing countries (List 2009).

Such inequities in health care have clear life-and-death consequences. For example, there are dramatic differences in infant mortality rates between developing countries such as Afghanistan, Sierra Leone, and Pakistan and industrial nations like Iceland, Japan, and Australia. The **infant mortality rate** is the number of deaths of infants under one year old per 1000 live births in a given year. This measure is an important indicator of a society's level of health care; it reflects prenatal nutrition, delivery procedures, and infant screening measures. Such differences in infant mortality reflect unequal distribution of health care resources

> **brain drain** The immigration to the United States and other industrialized nations of skilled workers, professionals, and technicians who are needed in their home countries.
>
> **infant mortality rate** The number of deaths of infants under one year old per 1000 live births in a given year.

based on the wealth or poverty of various nations. Surprisingly, despite our national wealth and the huge amounts spent on health care in the United States, at least 45 nations have lower infant mortality rates including Canada, Cuba, and the United Kingdom. An additional way that developing countries suffer the consequences of health care inequality is in reduced life expectancy. Average life expectancy in African nations is 55 compared to 80 for western European nations. By comparison, in the United States it is 78 years (Population Reference Bureau 2009).

Labeling and Power Sometimes the power to label and the power to oppress go hand in hand. A historical example illustrates perhaps the ultimate extreme in labeling social behavior as a sickness. As enslavement of Africans in the United States came under increasing attack in the 19th century, medical authorities provided new rationalizations for the oppressive practice. Noted physicians published articles stating that the skin color of Africans deviated from "healthy" white skin coloring because Africans suffered from congenital leprosy. Moreover, physicians classified the continuing efforts of enslaved Africans to escape from their White masters as an example of the "disease" of drapetomania (or "crazy runaways"). In 1851, the prestigious *New Orleans Medical and Surgical Journal* suggested that the remedy for this "disease" was to treat slaves

5 Movies on HEALTH AND MEDICINE

The Diving Bell and the Butterfly
A man suddenly becomes completely paralyzed.

My Sister's Keeper
Cancer puts a strain on family relationships.

Philadelphia
One man's battle with AIDS and the society that shuns him.

Sicko
A documentary criticizing the U.S. health care system.

Life, Above All
A 12-year-old girl uncovers her community's unspoken struggle with AIDS.

Going GLOBAL

Infant Mortality Rates in Selected Countries

Infant deaths per 1,000 live births

Afghanistan 155

Somalia 111

Pakistan 67

Haiti 57

India 55

World 46

Mexico 19

United States 6.6

Canada 5.0

Australia 4.1

Japan 2.6

Luxembourg 2.1

Source: Population Reference Bureau 2009.

How will these people respond? People's intense fear of the disease has led to prejudice and discrimination—even social ostracism—against those who have (or are suspected of having) AIDS. A person who has AIDS must deal not only with the serious medical consequences of the disease, but also with the distressing social consequences associated with the label.

AIDS caught major social institutions—particularly the government, the health care system, and the economy—by surprise when it was first noticed by medical practitioners in the 1970s. It has since spread around the world, with the first U.S. cases of AIDS reported in 1981. Rather than being a distinct disease, AIDS is actually a predisposition to various diseases that is caused by a virus, the human immunodeficiency virus (HIV). The virus gradually destroys the body's immune system, leaving the carrier vulnerable to infections such as pneumonia that those with healthy immune systems generally can resist.

Although the numbers of new cases and deaths have recently shown some evidence of decline, more than a million people in the United States were living with AIDS or HIV as of December 2008. Globally, an estimated 33.4 million people are now infected; however, the disease is not evenly distributed. Those areas least equipped to deal with it—the developing nations of sub-Saharan Africa, where 5.2 percent of the adult population is infected—face the greatest challenge (UNAIDS 2009).

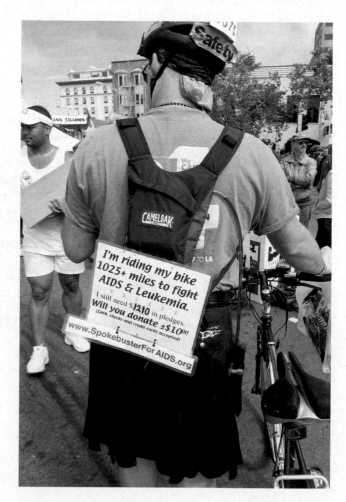

kindly, as one might treat children. Apparently, these medical authorities would not entertain the view that it was healthy and sane to flee slavery or join in a slave revolt (Szasz 1971).

Globally, the power of one particular label—"person with AIDS"—has become quite evident. This label often functions as a master status that overshadows all other aspects of a person's life. Once someone is told that he or she has tested positive for HIV, the virus associated with AIDS, that person is forced to confront immediate and difficult questions: Should I tell my family members? My sex partners? My friends? My co-workers? My employer?

Going GLOBAL

HIV/AIDS Cases

Eastern Europe/Central Asia
1.5 million
87,000

East Asia
850,000
59,000

North America
1.4 million
25,000

Western/Central Europe
850,000
13,000

Caribbean
240,000
12,000

North Africa/Middle East
310,000
20,000

South/Southeast Asia
3.8 million
270,000

Latin America
2.0 million
77,000

Sub-Saharan Africa
22.4 million
1.4 million

Oceania (Australia/New Zealand)
59,000
2,000

People living with HIV
Deaths from AIDS in 2008
100,000 people

Source: UNAIDS 2009.

Note: Total number of adults and children living with HIV, 33.4 million; total number of estimated adult and child deaths during 2008, 2.0 million.

In the United States, because those in high-risk groups—gay men and IV drug users—were comparatively powerless, and labeled as such, policy makers were slow to respond to the AIDS crisis. Over time, however, the response has improved, and today people with HIV or AIDS who receive appropriate medical treatment are living longer than they did in the past. The high cost of drug treatment programs has generated intensive worldwide pressure on the major pharmaceutical companies to lower the prices to patients in developing nations, especially in sub-Saharan Africa. Bowing to this pressure, several of the companies have agreed to make the combination therapies available at cost. As a result, the accessibility of HIV treatment has increased steadily, though inequalities remain. Globally, the proportion of adults and children with advanced HIV infection receiving antiretroviral therapy rose from 7 percent in 2003 to 42 percent in 2008, with the rate slightly higher at 44 percent in sub-Saharan Africa (Mahy et al. 2010; UNAIDS 2009).

According to labeling theorists, we can view a variety of life experiences as illnesses or not. Recently, the medical community has recognized premenstrual syndrome, posttraumatic disorders, and hyperactivity as medical disorders. Probably the most noteworthy medical example of labeling is the case of homosexuality. For years, psychiatrists classified being gay or lesbian not as a lifestyle but as a mental disorder subject to treatment. This official sanction by the psychiatry profession became an early target of the growing gay and lesbian rights movement in the United States. In 1974, members of the American Psychiatric Association voted to drop homosexuality from the standard manual on mental disorders (Conrad 2007).

NEGOTIATING CURES

In practice, we seek to strike a balance between the authority of the physician and the agency of the patient. Physicians use cues to reinforce their prestige and power. According to medical sociologist Brenda Beagan (2001, 2003), the technical language students learn in medical school becomes the basis for the script they follow as novice physicians. The familiar white coat and stethoscope is their costume—one that helps them to appear confident and professional at the same time that it identifies them as doctors to patients and other staff members. Beagan found that many medical students struggle to project the appearance of competence they think their role demands, but over time most become accustomed to expecting respect and deference.

Patients, on the other hand, are not passive. Sometimes, patients play an active role in health care by failing to follow a physician's advice. For example, some patients stop taking medications long before they should. Some decrease or increase the dosage on purpose (because they think they know better what they need), and others

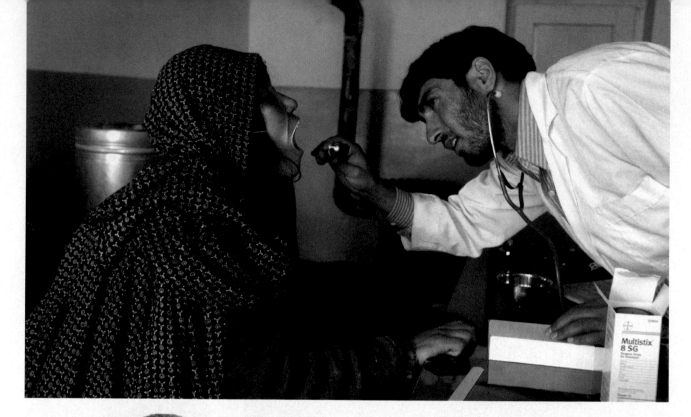

Did You Know?

... In research looking at how social class operates, sociologist Annette Lareau (2003) found that middle-class parents and children were more likely to engage with physicians, asking questions and questioning diagnoses. Working-class patients were more deferential to the doctor's authority.

Patients' active involvement in their health care can have very positive consequences. Some patients consult books, magazines, and websites about preventive health care techniques, attempt to maintain a healthful and nutritious diet, carefully monitor any side effects of medication, and adjust the dosage based on perceived side effects. Recognizing this change, pharmaceutical firms are advertising their prescription drugs directly to potential customers. For their part, medical professionals are understandably suspicious of these new sources of information. Studies, including one published in the *Journal of the American Medical Association,* found that health information on the Internet is often incomplete and inaccurate, even on the best sites. Nevertheless, there is little doubt that Internet research is transforming patient–physician encounters (Adams and de Bont 2007; Arora et al. 2008; Berland 2001).

>> Social Epidemiology

By looking at patterns of health and illness throughout society, we can better understand which factors are at work in shaping health outcomes. **Social epidemiology** is the study of disease distribution, impairment, and general health status across a population. Initially, epidemiology concentrated on the scientific study of epidemics, focusing on how they started and spread. Contemporary social epidemiology is much broader in scope, concerned not only with epidemics but also with nonepidemic diseases, injuries, drug addiction and alcoholism, suicide, and mental illness. In 2001, epidemiologists took on the new role of tracking bioterrorism. They mobilized to trace an anthrax outbreak and prepare for any terrorist use of smallpox or other lethal microbes. Epidemiologists draw on the work

never even fill their prescriptions. Such noncompliance results in part from the prevalence of self-medication in our society; many people are accustomed to self-diagnosis and self-treatment.

of a wide variety of scientists and researchers, among them physicians, sociologists, public health officials, biologists, veterinarians, demographers, anthropologists, psychologists, and meteorologists.

Researchers in social epidemiology commonly use two concepts: incidence and prevalence. **Incidence** refers to the number of new cases of a specific disorder that occur within a given population during a stated period, usually a year. For example, the incidence of AIDS in the United States in 2007 was 37,041 cases. In contrast, **prevalence** refers to the total number of cases of a specific disorder that exist at a given time. The prevalence of AIDS in the United States through 2007 was approximately 460,000 cases (Department of Health and Human Services 2007).

When disease incidence figures are presented as rates—for example, the number of reports per 100,000 people—they are called **morbidity rates.** This is distinct from the **mortality rate,** which refers to the incidence of death in a given population. Sociologists find morbidity rates useful because they can reveal whether a specific disease occurs more frequently among one segment of a population than another. As we shall see, social class, race, ethnicity, gender, and age can all affect a population's morbidity rates (Barr 2008).

SOCIAL CLASS

Social class is clearly associated with differences in morbidity and mortality rates. Studies in the United States and other countries have consistently shown that people in the lower classes have higher rates of mortality and disability than those in higher classes. One study concluded that Americans with 12 years or less of schooling could expect to die seven years sooner than those with more than 12 years of schooling (Meara, Richards, and Cutler 2008; Pear 2008).

A number of factors appear to influence the effect class has on health. Crowded living conditions, substandard housing, poor diet, and stress all contribute to the ill health of many low-income people in the United States. In certain instances, poor education may lead to a lack of awareness of measures necessary to maintain good health. Financial strains are certainly a major factor in the health problems of less affluent people.

People who are poor—many of whom belong to racial and ethnic minorities—are less able than others to afford quality medical care (see the accompanying graph). Not surprisingly, those with high incomes are significantly more likely to have health insurance, either because they can afford it or because they have jobs that provide it. The middle class has been particularly hard hit by the decision of companies to eliminate employer-provided coverage (the most common form of health insurance). Such rates declined steadily from 2000 to 2008 (DeNavas-Walt et al. 2009; E. Gould 2008).

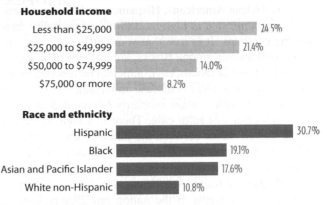

Percentage of People Without Health Insurance

Household income

Less than $25,000	24.5%
$25,000 to $49,999	21.4%
$50,000 to $74,999	14.0%
$75,000 or more	8.2%

Race and ethnicity

Hispanic	30.7%
Black	19.1%
Asian and Pacific Islander	17.6%
White non-Hispanic	10.8%

Source: DeNavas-Walt et al. 2009.

The ultimate price to pay for a lack of health insurance is the increased risk of early death. Uninsured women who develop breast cancer tend to be diagnosed later—when treatment is less effective—than insured women. Uninsured men who develop high blood pressure are more likely than others to forgo screenings and medication, a decision that jeopardizes their health. According to a 2009 Harvard Medical School study, approximately 45,000 deaths per year are associated with lack of health insurance (Wilper et al. 2009).

What is particularly troubling about social class differences is that they appear to be cumulative. Little or no health care in childhood or young adulthood is likely to mean more illness later in life. The longer that low income presents a barrier to adequate health care, the more chronic and difficult to treat illness becomes (Prus 2007).

Karl Marx would have argued, and some contemporary sociologists agree, that capitalist societies such as the United States care more about maximizing profits than they do about the health and safety of industrial workers. As a result, government agencies do not take forceful action to regulate conditions in the workplace, and workers suffer many preventable job-related injuries and illnesses. As we will see later in this chapter, research also shows that the lower classes are more vulnerable to environmental pollution, another consequence of capitalist production, than are the affluent, not only where they work but where they live as well.

social epidemiology The study of the distribution of disease, impairment, and general health status across a population.

Incidence The number of new cases of a specific disorder that occur within a given population during a stated period.

prevalence The total number of cases of a specific disorder that exist at a given time.

morbidity rate The incidence of disease in a given population.

mortality rate The incidence of death in a given population.

> It is a lot harder to keep people well than it is to just get them over a sickness.
>
> **DeForest Clinton Jarvis**

older. While some individuals with Alzheimer's exhibit only mild symptoms, the risk of severe problems resulting from this disease rises substantially with age (Alzheimer's Association 2010).

Due to their increased health risks, the rate at which older people in the United States (ages 75 and older) use health services is more than three times greater than that for younger people (ages 15–24). This heightened use level is tied to health insurance coverage, with people over age 65 the most likely to be covered (see the graph below). The disproportionate use of the U.S. health care system by older people is a critical factor in all discussions about the cost of health care and possible reforms of the health care system (U.S. Census Bureau 2009f: Table 162).

A person's odds of good health are shaped by her or his class, race and ethnicity, gender, and age. Even geography matters, as there are significant differences in the number of physicians from one state to the next. Health care professionals and program advisors need to take such differential effects into account when considering what constitutes equitable health care coverage. Any attempts to do so, however, are constrained by the cost of health care.

Availability of Physicians by State

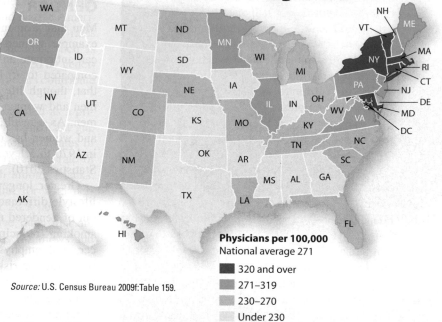

Source: U.S. Census Bureau 2009f:Table 159.

Physicians per 100,000
National average 271

- 320 and over
- 271–319
- 230–270
- Under 230

Total Health Care Expenditures in the United States, 1970–2019 (projected)

Total expenditure in billions of dollars

$4,483
$2,339
$714
$253
$75

| 1970 | 1980 | 1990 | 2008 | 2019 (projected) |

Source: Centers for Medicare and Medicaid Services 2010a:Table 1; 2010b:Table 1.

Health Insurance Rates by Age

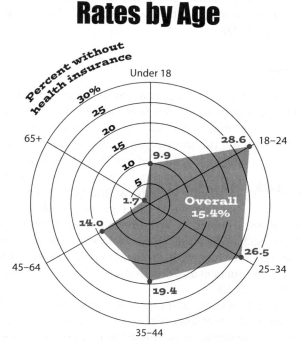

Percent without health insurance

Under 18 — 9.9
18–24 — 28.6
25–34 — 26.5
35–44 — 19.4
45–64 — 14.0
65+ — 1.7

Overall 15.4%

Source: DeNavas-Walt et al. 2009:Table 7.

>> Health Care in the United States

The costs of health care have skyrocketed in the past 40 years. In 1997, total expenditures for health care in the United States crossed the trillion-dollar threshold—more than four times the 1980 figure. In 2000, the amount spent on health care equaled what we spent on education, defense, prisons, farm subsidies, food stamps, and foreign aid combined. By the year 2018, total expenditures for health care in the United States are expected to exceed $4.4 trillion or $13,387 per person. The United States currently devotes a greater proportion of its spending (15.3 percent of GDP) to health care than do all other OECD (Organization for Economic Cooperation and Development) nations, including France (11.0 percent), Canada (10.0 percent), the United Kingdom (8.4 percent), and Japan (8.1 percent). Over time health care in the United States has evolved to become a big business (Centers for Medicare and Medicaid Services 2010a, 2010b; Kaiser Family Foundation 2009).

A HISTORICAL VIEW

Today, state licensing and medical degrees confer a widely recognized level of authority on medical professionals. This was not always the case. The "popular health movement" of the 1830s and 1840s emphasized preventive care and what is termed "self-help." It voiced strong criticism of "doctoring" as a paid occupation. New medical philosophies or sects established their own medical schools and challenged the authority and methods of traditional doctors. By the 1840s, most states

POPSOC

Our perception of doctors and health care is shaped by the media. For a long time, *E.R.* was the king of the hospital heap on television. In recent years, *Grey's Anatomy, Scrubs,* and *House* took off. If such programs were our only source of information about backstage life among doctors and nurses, what would we conclude about the nature of health care in the United States?

had repealed medical licensing laws, and the health care field was largely unregulated (Porter 1998, 2004).

In response, through the leadership of the American Medical Association (AMA), founded in 1848, "regular" doctors marginalized lay practitioners, sectarian doctors, and female physicians in general. They institutionalized their authority through standardized programs of education and licensing. Only those who successfully completed AMA programs gained legitimate authority as medical practitioners. The authority of the physician no longer depended on lay attitudes or on the person occupying the sick role; increasingly, it was built into the structure of the medical profession and the health care system.

As the institutionalization of health care proceeded, the medical profession gained control over both the market for its services and the various organizational hierarchies that govern medical practice, financing, and policy making. By the 1920s, physicians controlled hospital technology, the division of labor of health personnel, and indirectly, other professional practices such as nursing and pharmaceutical services (Coser 1984; Starr 1982; Whorton 2002).

THE ROLE OF GOVERNMENT

Not until the 20th century did health care receive federal aid in conjunction with the expansion of medicine as a social institution. The first significant government involvement was the 1946 Hill-Burton Act, which provided subsidies for building and improving hospitals, especially in rural areas. An even more important development was the enactment in 1965 of two wide-ranging government assistance programs: Medicare, which is essentially a compulsory health insurance plan for the elderly, and Medicaid, which is a noncontributory federal and state insurance plan for the poor. These programs greatly expanded federal involvement in health care financing for needy men, women, and children.

While health care costs were rising, a growing portion of the U.S. population (46.3 million in 2008) remained uninsured. An inability to afford coverage was a major factor. In 1993, the Clinton administration proposed health care reform designed to provide universal coverage, but the legislation failed to pass. Throughout the George W. Bush administration, the United States remained the only wealthy, industrialized nation that did not provide some form of universal coverage (DeNavas-Walt et al. 2009).

By 2009, there was widespread political agreement that the existing system, with its projected escalating costs, was not sustainable. From 1999 to 2008, for example, the cost of health insurance premiums rose 119 percent, while wages rose only 34 percent (Kaiser Family Foundation 2009). The Obama administration pledged to enact reform that would both contain costs and expand coverage. Though there was general consensus regarding these aims, there were significant disagreements on how best to accomplish them. Some supported a single-payer system in which the government is the primary source of health care funding. Others continued to support market-based reforms that minimize government involvement. A significant intervening position focused on whether or not the government should provide a "public option," allowing people to choose a government-funded plan among many private company plans.

In March 2010, Congress passed, and President Obama signed into law, the Patient Protection and Affordable Care Act and the Health Care and Education Reconciliation Act. Though implementation will take years to complete, key provisions include:

- Young adults will be able to stay on their parents' health care plans until age 26.
- Coverage for checkups and other preventive care will not require co-pays.
- Annual caps and lifetime limits on the cost of benefits patients can receive will be eliminated.
- People with preexisting conditions cannot be denied coverage, and companies will no longer be able to cut employees from a plan when they get sick.
- Most Americans will be required to purchase some form of health insurance.
- Tax credits for the purchase of insurance will be available for individuals and families between 100 and 400 percent of the poverty level.
- Companies with more than 50 employees will be required to provide an employer-sponsored health plan that provides a mandated level of minimal coverage.
- Small businesses will be eligible to receive tax credits to assist them in providing coverage.
- State-based insurance exchanges will offer a choice of plans for small businesses and people who lack employer-supplied coverage.
- Insurance companies will be required to provide greater transparency regarding spending on overhead costs.

The acts passed Congress with virtually no bipartisan support. Republicans continued to prefer market-based

Rising Medicare Expenses

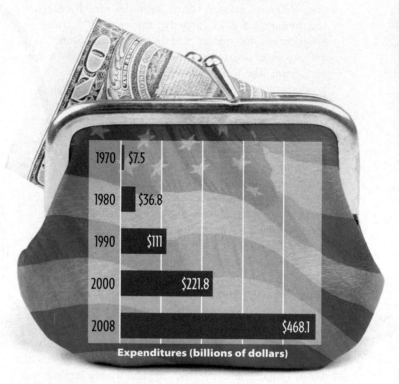

Year	Expenditure
1970	$7.5
1980	$36.8
1990	$111
2000	$221.8
2008	$468.1

Expenditures (billions of dollars)

Source: National Center for Health Statistics 2010:Table 142.

solutions arguing that free market capitalism would lead to greater efficiency and cost control. Though most liberal Democrats voted for the legislation, many of them were also critical of the bill. They argued that reform did not go far enough to ensure universal coverage and cost reduction, and they expressed displeasure about the lack of a public option. In the end, however, the legislation represented a substantial shift in the history of health care in the United States.

PHYSICIANS, NURSES, AND PATIENTS

The power of medicine and the prestige of doctors have risen together. As the occupation became more professional and training more standardized, some of the depersonalizing effects of working in a bureaucratic organization came to influence role performance. For example, when reflecting on the medical school training she received, Dr. Lori Arviso Alvord commented, "I had been trained by a group of physicians who placed much more emphasis on their technical abilities and clinical skills than on their abilities to be caring and sensitive" (Alvord and Van Pelt 1999:13). Though doctors were taught to treat patients like people, bureaucratic demands, including patient overload

SOCTHINK

Is the way doctors interact with patients and staff due more to the fact that they are mostly male or to their level of prestige and power?

and cost-cutting by hospitals, tended to undercut relationship building (Jaye, Egan, and Parker 2006).

Just as physicians maintain dominance in their interactions with patients, they often control interactions with nurses. Even when nurses may have more information about a patient, nurses must still defer to the physician's authority. Researchers have referred to this process as the "doctor–nurse game" (Reeves, Nelson, and Zwarenstein 2008; Stein 1967; Stein, Watts, and Howell 1990). In this game, the nurse should never openly disagree with the physician. When nurses have recommendations concerning a patient's care, they must communicate them indirectly, in a deferential tone. For example, if asked by a doctor, "What sleeping medication has been helpful to Mrs. Brown in the past?" (an indirect request for a recommendation), the nurse will respond with a disguised recommendation, such as "Pentobarbital 100 mg was quite effective night before last." This careful response allows the physician to authoritatively restate the same prescription as if it were his idea.

Traditionally, this power relationship between doctors and nurses has paralleled the male dominance of the United States. Like other women in subordinate roles, the nurses (mostly female) were expected to perform their duties without challenging the authority of the doctors (mostly male). More recently, however, increasing numbers of women are becoming physicians. In 2008, 48 percent of all new medical school students in the United States were female, up from 8 percent in 1965 and 31 percent in 1982. In nursing, however, the overwhelming majority continues to be female (Leadley 2009).

A study of male and female medical residents suggests that the increasing number of women physicians may alter the traditional doctor–patient relationship. The study found male residents to be more focused on the intellectual challenges of medicine and the prestige associated with certain medical specialties. In contrast, female residents were more likely to express a commitment to caring for patients and devoting time to them. As women continue to enter and move higher in the hierarchies of the medical profession, sociological studies will surely be done to see whether these apparent gender differences persist.

COMPLEMENTARY AND ALTERNATIVE MEDICINE

In modern forms of health care, people rely on physicians and hospitals for the treatment of illness. Yet a significant proportion of adults in the United States attempt to maintain good health or respond to illness through the use of

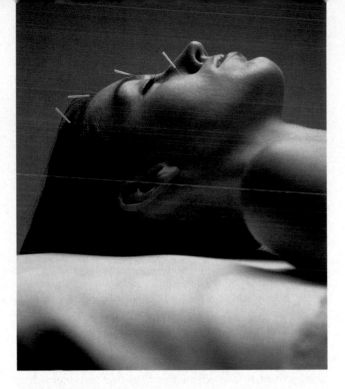

alternative health care techniques. For example, in recent decades, interest has been growing in holistic medical principles, first developed in China. **Holistic medicine** refers to therapies in which the health care practitioner considers the person's physical, mental, emotional, and spiritual characteristics. The individual is regarded as a totality rather than a collection of interrelated

> **holistic medicine** Therapies in which the health care practitioner considers the person's physical, mental, emotional, and spiritual characteristics.

Complementary and Alternative Medicine Use

Treatment	Percent
Homeopathic treatment	1.8
Guided imagery	2.2
Progressive relaxation	2.9
Diets	3.6
Yoga	6.1
Massage	8.3
Chiropractic	8.6
Meditation	9.4
Deep breathing	12.7
Natural products	17.7

Source: Barnes et al. 2008.

SOCTHINK

What do you think about alternative medicine? Would you be willing to get assistance from a holistic healer? What background factors, such as age, race and ethnicity, or gender, might play a role in your willingness or unwillingness to do so?

organ systems. Treatment methods include massage, chiropractic medicine, acupuncture, respiratory exercises, and the use of herbs as remedies. Nutrition, exercise, and visualization may also be used to treat ailments (Barnes, Bloom, and Nahin 2008; Stratton and McGivern-Snofsky 2008).

Practitioners of holistic medicine do not necessarily function totally outside the traditional health care system. Some have medical degrees and rely on X-rays and EKG machines for diagnostic assistance. Others who staff holistic clinics, often referred to as wellness clinics, reject the use of medical technology. The recent resurgence of holistic medicine comes amid widespread recognition of the value of nutrition and the dangers of overreliance on prescription drugs—especially those used to reduce stress, such as Valium (Baer and Coulter 2008).

The medical establishment—professional organizations, research hospitals, and medical schools—continues to zealously protect its authority. However, a major breakthrough occurred in 1992 when the federal government's National Institutes of Health (NIH)—the nation's major funding source for biomedical research—opened the National Center for Complementary and Alternative Medicine and empowered it to accept grant requests. A 2007 NIH-sponsored national study found that 38.3 percent of adults in the United States had used some form of complementary and alternative medicine within the previous year. Examples of practices include use of natural products (such as echinacea or omega-3 fatty acids), deep breathing, meditation, chiropractic treatment, massage, yoga, diet-based therapies (including vegetarian, macrobiotic, and Atkins), homeopathic treatment, and acupuncture. When private or communal prayer was included as part of the NIH-sponsored 2002 study, the number rose to 62.1 percent (Barnes et al. 2004; Barnes et al. 2008).

On the international level, the WHO has begun to monitor the use of alternative medicine around the world. According to the WHO, 80 percent of people in some African and Asian countries use alternative medicine, from herbal treatments to the services of a faith healer. In most countries, these treatments are largely unregulated, even though some of them can be fatal. For example, kava kava, an herbal tea used in the Pacific Islands to relieve anxiety, can be toxic to the liver in concentrated form. Other alternative treatments have been found to be effective in the treatment of serious diseases, such as malaria and sickle-cell anemia. The WHO's goal is to compile a list of such practices, as well as to encourage the development of universal training programs and ethical standards for practitioners of alternative medicine. To date, the organization has published findings on about 100 of the 5000 plants believed to be used as herbal remedies (World Health Organization 2005, 2008a).

Sociological analysis of health and illness suggests that if we are to understand sickness we must look

beyond biology. Society and culture, family and friends, the medical profession, and social position all help shape medical outcomes. Given the increasing costs of health care, and the fact that different groups experience different outcomes, this issue becomes one of equality and fairness. To what extent, for example, are we willing to accept that a child will live or die due to his or her income, race, or ethnicity? Or that one's life expectancy is shaped by such factors? It is precisely such concerns that drive debates about the expansion of health care coverage as a social right.

>> Sociological Perspectives on the Environment

We have seen that the environment people live in has a noticeable effect on their health. Those who live in stressful, overcrowded places suffer more from disease than those who do not. Likewise, people have a noticeable effect on their environment. Around the world, increases in population, together with the economic development that accompanies them, have had serious environmental consequences. We can see signs of despoliation almost everywhere: Our air, our water, and our land are being polluted, whether we live in St. Louis; Mexico City; or Lagos, Nigeria. Although environmental problems may be easy to identify, devising socially and politically acceptable solutions to them is much more difficult. Sociologists provide us with some models to better understand the issues we must consider (Sutton 2007).

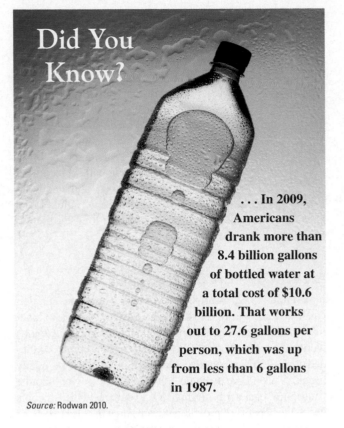

Did You Know?

... In 2009, Americans drank more than 8.4 billion gallons of bottled water at a total cost of $10.6 billion. That works out to 27.6 gallons per person, which was up from less than 6 gallons in 1987.

Source: Rodwan 2010.

HUMAN ECOLOGY

Human ecology is an area of study that is concerned with interrelationships between people and their environment. As biologist and environmentalist Barry Commoner (1971:39) put it during the early stages of the modern environmental movement, "Everything is connected to everything else." Human ecologists focus on how the physical environment shapes people's lives and on how people influence the surrounding environment.

In an application of the human ecological perspective, sociologists and environmentalists have identified several relationships between the environment and people. Among them are the following:

- *The environment provides the resources essential for life.* These include air, water, and materials used to create shelter, transportation, and needed products. If human societies exhaust these resources—for example, by polluting the water supply or cutting down rain forests—the consequences could be dire.
- *The environment serves as a waste repository.* More so than other living species, humans produce a huge quantity and variety of waste products—bottles, cans, boxes, paper, sewage, garbage, and so on. Various types of pollution have become more common because human societies are generating more wastes than the environment can safely absorb.
- *The environment "houses" our species.* It is our home, our living space, the place where we reside, work, and play. At times we take this truism for granted, but not

when day-to-day living conditions become unpleasant and problematic. If our air is "heavy," if our tap water turns brown, or if toxic chemicals seep into our neighborhood, we remember why it is vital to live in a healthful environment.

There is no shortage of illustrations of the interconnectedness of humans and the environment. For example, scientific research has linked pollutants in the environment to people's health and behavior. The increasing prevalence of asthma, lead poisoning, and cancer has been tied to human alterations to the environment. Similarly, the rise in melanoma (skin cancer) diagnoses has been linked to global climate change. And ecological changes in our food and diet have been related to childhood obesity and diabetes.

> **human ecology** The area of study concerned with the interrelationships between people and their environment.

With its view that "everything is connected to everything else," human ecology stresses the trade-offs inherent in every decision that alters the environment. In facing the environmental challenges of the 21st century, government policy makers and environmentalists must determine how they can fulfill humans' pressing needs for food, clothing, and shelter while preserving the environment as a source of resources, a waste repository, and a home.

POWER, RESOURCES, AND THE ENVIRONMENT

Analyzing environmental issues from a world systems approach allows us to better understand the global consequences of differential access to resources. This approach highlights the difference in relative

Did You Know?

An average of 17,454 square kilometers (4.3 million acres) of Brazilian rain forest was lost each year from 2001 to 2009. The rate has recently slowed with 7,464 square kilometers (1.8 million acres) lost in 2009.

Source: INPE 2010.

power between core nations, which control wealth and so dominate the global economy, and developing countries, which lack control and whose resources are exploited. This process only intensifies the destruction of natural resources in poorer regions of the world. Less affluent nations are being forced to exploit their mineral deposits, forests, and fisheries in order to meet their debt obligations. People in developing nations often end up turning to the only means of survival available to them, including plowing mountain slopes, burning sections of tropical forests, and overgrazing grasslands (Palm et al. 2005; Pollini 2009).

Brazil exemplifies this interplay between economic troubles and environmental destruction. Each year more than 4.3 million acres of rain forest are cleared for crops and livestock. The elimination of the rain forest affects worldwide weather patterns, heightening the gradual warming of the earth. These socioeconomic patterns, with their harmful environmental consequences, are evident not only in Central and South America, but also in many regions of Africa and Asia (INPF 2010).

Although destruction of the rain forest has long been a concern, only in the past few decades have policy makers begun to listen to the indigenous peoples who live in these areas. Preservation of the rain forests may make sense at the global level, but for many local peoples, it limits their ability to cultivate crops or graze cattle. Even though it harms the global environment, they feel they have no choice but to take advantage of their available resources. In 2008, native peoples from Brazil to the Congo to Indonesia convened to make the case that wealthier countries should compensate them for conservation of the tropical rain forests (Barrionuevo 2008).

There is, in fact, a certain amount of ethnocentrism involved when people in industrialized countries insist that those developing nations change their practices to save the planet. In calling for the poverty-stricken and "food-hungry" populations of the world to sacrifice, they should also consider the lifestyle consequences for the "energy-hungry" nations. The industrialized nations of North America and Europe account for only 12 percent of the world's population but are responsible for 60 percent of worldwide consumption. The money their residents spend on ocean cruises each year could provide clean drinking water for everyone on the planet. Ice cream expenditures in Europe alone could be used to immunize every child in the world. The global consumer represents a serious environmental threat, but it is often difficult to look in the mirror and blame ourselves because our individual contribution to the problem seems so small. Collectively, however, the choices we make have a significant global impact (Diamond 2008; Gardner, Assadourian, and Sarin 2004).

environmental justice
A legal strategy based on claims that racial minorities are subjected disproportionately to environmental hazards.

Suburbia is where the developer bulldozes out the trees, then names the streets after them.

Bill Vaughn

The rise in global consumption is tied to a capitalist system that depends upon growth for its survival. Capitalism creates a "treadmill of production" (Baer 2008; Schnaiberg 1994). Cutting back on consumption means cutting back on purchases, which leads to reduced production and the loss of profits and jobs. This treadmill necessitates creating an increasing demand for products, obtaining natural resources at minimal cost, and manufacturing products as quickly and cheaply as possible—no matter what the long-term environmental consequences.

ENVIRONMENTAL JUSTICE

In autumn 1982, nearly 500 African Americans participated in a six-week protest against a hazardous waste landfill containing cancer-causing chemicals in Warren County, North Carolina. Their protests and legal actions continued until 2002, when decontamination of the site finally began. This 20-year battle can be seen as yet another "not-in-my-backyard" (NIMBY) event in which people desire the benefits of growth but want someone else to pay for its negative effects. In any event, the Warren County struggle is viewed as a transformative moment in contemporary environmentalism: the beginning of the environmental justice movement (Bullard 2000; McGurty 2007; North Carolina Department of Environment and Natural Resources 2008).

Environmental justice is a legal strategy based on claims that racial minorities are subjected disproportionately to environmental hazards. Some observers have heralded environmental justice as the "new civil rights of the 21st century" (Kokmen 2008:42). Since the advent of the environmental justice movement, activists and scholars have identified other environmental disparities that break along racial and social class lines. In general, poor people and people of color are much more likely than others to be victimized by the everyday consequences of economic development, including air pollution from expressways and incinerators (Sandler and Pezzullo 2007).

Sociologists Paul Mohai and Robin Saha (2007) examined more than 600 hazardous waste treatment, storage, and disposal facilities in the United States. They found that non-Whites and Latinos make up 43 percent of the people who live within one mile of these dangerous sites. There are two possible explanations for this finding. One is that racial and ethnic minorities possess less power

—**SOC**THINK—

It took 20 years for the Warren County protest to succeed. Why do you think it took so long? How might access to resources shape the length of such struggles?

than others, so they cannot prevent toxic sites from being located in their backyards. The other is that they end up settling near the sites after they are constructed, because economics and the forces of discrimination push them into the least desirable living areas.

5 Movies

ENVIRONMENT on THE

Avatar
Strife erupts between humans and Na'vi over Pandora's natural resources.

An Inconvenient Truth
The truth about global warming.

Encounters at the End of the World
A documentary about the people living and working in Antarctica.

No Impact Man
A man attempts to have zero impact on the environment for a year.

WALL-E
A robot in the year 2700 discovers his destiny.

Following reports from the Environmental Protection Agency (EPA) and other organizations documenting the discriminatory location of hazardous waste sites, President Bill Clinton issued an executive order in 1994 requiring all federal agencies to ensure that low-income and minority communities have access to better information about their environment, as well as an opportunity to participate in shaping government policies that affect their health. Initial efforts to implement the policy, along with increased activity by the environmental justice movement, aroused widespread opposition because of the delays the policy imposes in establishing new industrial sites. Some observers question the wisdom of an order that slows economic development in areas that are in dire need of employment opportunities. Others counter that such businesses employ few unskilled or less skilled workers and only make the environment less livable (Stretesky 2006; D. Taylor 2000).

Meanwhile, the poor and oppressed continue to bear the brunt of environmental pollution. In the 1990s, the federal government, unable to find a disposal site for spent nuclear fuel, turned to tribal reservations. Agents eventually persuaded a tiny band of Goshute Indians in Skull Valley, Utah, to accept more than 44,000 barrels of the highly radioactive substance, which will remain dangerous for an estimated 10,000 years. The government dropped the plan only after opposition from surrounding towns and cities, whose residents objected to the movement of the material through their communities. This was not the first time the government had attempted to persuade the impoverished tribe to accept environmentally objectionable installations. The military's nerve-gas storage facility resides on or near the reservation, along with the Intermountain Power Project, which generates coal-fired electrical power for consumers in California (Eureka County 2006; Foy 2006).

In considering environmental issues, sociologists have emphasized the interconnectedness of humans and the environment, as well as the divisiveness of race and social class. Scientific findings can also play a role in our understanding of the nature and scope of environmental concerns. Of course, when such findings affect government policy and economic regulations, they become highly politicized. Such struggles are inevitable when core values and differential access to resources are at stake.

>> Environmental Problems

Unfortunately, as we have already seen, the environmental problems caused by development have effects far beyond the places where they are created. Witness Muhammad Ali,

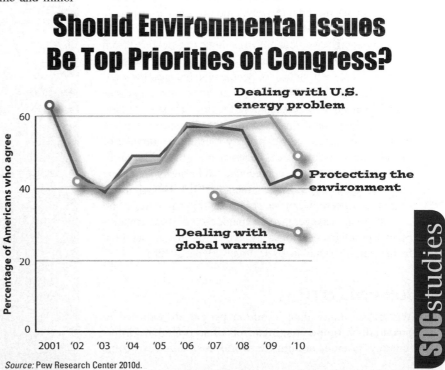

Should Environmental Issues Be Top Priorities of Congress?

Dealing with U.S. energy problem

Protecting the environment

Dealing with global warming

Percentage of Americans who agree

60

40

20

0

2001 '02 '03 '04 '05 '06 '07 '08 '09 '10

Source: Pew Research Center 2010d.

SOCstudies

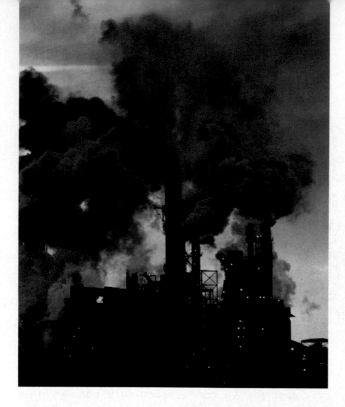

to accept smog and polluted air as normal. Urban air pollution is caused primarily by emissions from automobiles and secondarily by emissions from electric power plants and heavy industries. Smog not only limits visibility, but also can lead to health problems as uncomfortable as eye irritation and as deadly as lung cancer. Such problems are especially severe in developing countries. The WHO estimates that up to 2 million premature deaths per year could be prevented if pollutants were brought down to safer levels (World Health Organization 2008b).

People are capable of changing their behavior, but they are also often unwilling to make such changes permanent. During the 1984 Olympics in Los Angeles, authorities asked residents to carpool and stagger their work hours to relieve traffic congestion and improve the quality of the air athletes would breathe. These changes resulted in a remarkable 12 percent drop in ozone levels. After the Olympics ended, however, people reverted to their normal behavior, and the ozone levels climbed once again. Similarly, China took drastic action to ensure that Beijing's high levels of air pollution did not mar the 2008 Olympic Games. Construction work in the city ceased, polluting factories and power plants closed down, and workers

a Bangladeshi man who has had to flee floodwaters five times in the last decade. Scientists believe that global warming is to blame both for worsening monsoons and for the raging waters of the Iamuna River, swollen by abnormally high glacier melt from the Himalayas. Every time the river floods, Ali tears down his house, made of tin and bamboo, and moves to higher ground. But he is running out of land to move to. "Where we are standing, in five days it will be gone," he says. "Our future thinking is that if this problem is not taken care of, we will be swept away" (Goering 2007).

In 2010, the 40th anniversary of Earth Day in the United States, Gallup polls showed historically low levels of public concern about the environment. The percentage of people who viewed themselves as either active participants in the environmental movement or sympathetic to it declined from 71 percent in 2000 to 61 percent in 2010. During the same time period, the percentage of people who believed the environmental movement has done more harm than good rose from 21 percent to 36 percent. For the first time since Gallup started polling these questions in 2000, the percentage of people who place a higher priority on the development of oil, gas, and coal resources (even if it harms the environment) exceeded the percentage who said priority should be given to protecting the environment in 2010. Though levels of public concern about air pollution, water pollution, and global climate change have declined, each of these environmental problems continues to receive significant attention from scientists (Dunlap 2010; Jones 2010a, 2010b).

AIR POLLUTION

Worldwide, more than 1 billion people are exposed to potentially health-damaging levels of air pollution. Unfortunately, in cities around the world, residents have come

Reprinted with the permission of Mike Luckovich and Creators Syndicate.

swept roads and sprayed them with water several times a day. This temporary solution, however, has not solved China's ongoing pollution problem (*The Economist* 2008b).

WATER POLLUTION

Throughout the United States, waste materials dumped by industries and local governments have polluted streams, rivers, and lakes. Consequently, many bodies of water have become unsafe for fishing and swimming, let alone drinking. Around the world, pollution of the oceans is an issue of growing concern. The Deepwater Horizon spill in the Gulf of Mexico represents the ripple effects that such accidents can have on the environment, including the impact on birds, fish, mammals, and their habitats. According to the U.S. Fish and Wildlife Service, several endangered species face potential harm due to the spill, including the West Indian manatee, the Kemp's ridley sea turtle, the whooping crane, the Perdido Key beach mouse, and numerous others, and there are fears that the brown pelican, Louisiana's state bird, might have to return to the Endangered Species list after having been removed in November 2009.

This incident is one among many water-based accidents that have resulted in significant environmental harm. When the oil tanker *Exxon Valdez* ran aground in Prince William Sound, Alaska, in 1989, its cargo of 11 million gallons of

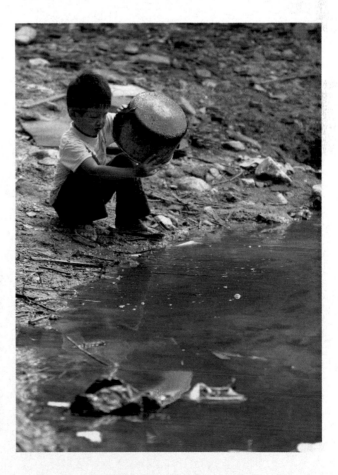

Projected Emissions of Greenhouse Gases, 2025

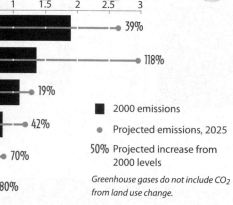

Trillions of tons of carbon equivalent

World	57%
Developed	35%
Developing	84%
U.S.	39%
China	118%
EU	19%
Former Soviet Union	42%
India	70%
Africa	80%
Brazil	68%
Japan	26%
Mexico	124%

■ 2000 emissions

● Projected emissions, 2025

50% Projected increase from 2000 levels

Greenhouse gases do not include CO_2 from land use change.

In 2000, the United States was the largest emitter of CO_2 from fossil fuels. China is expected to take the lead by 2025.

Sources: Baumert, Herzog, and Pershing 2005.

crude oil spilled into the sound and washed onto the shore, contaminating 1285 miles of shoreline. Altogether, about 11,000 people joined in a massive cleanup effort that cost more than $2 billion. Globally, oil spills occur regularly. In 2002, the oil tanker *Prestige* spilled twice as much fuel as the *Valdez*, greatly damaging coastal areas in Spain and France (ITOPF 2006).

Less dramatic than large-scale accidents or disasters, but more common in many parts of the world, are problems with the basic water supply. Worldwide, more than 884 million people lack safe and adequate drinking water, and 2.6 billion lack access to improved sanitation

facilities—a problem that further threatens the quality of water supplies. The health costs of unsafe water are enormous (World Health Organization and UNICEF 2010).

Given such water shortages, it should not come as a surprise that water is now a highly contested commodity in many parts of the world. In the United States, competition over water is intense, especially in booming Las Vegas and the Southwest. In the Middle East, the immense political challenges posed by ethnic and religious conflict are often complicated by battles over water. There, competing nations accuse each other of taking unfair advantage of existing water supplies, and water tanks are a likely target for both military forces and terrorists (Carmichael 2007).

GLOBAL CLIMATE CHANGE

The scientific evidence for global climate change is clear, consistent, and compelling, yet public opinion polls show that people remain skeptical. Global warming, the term most frequently associated with climate change, refers to the significant rise in the earth's surface temperatures that occurs when industrial gases like carbon dioxide turn the planet's atmosphere into a virtual greenhouse. Even one additional degree of warmth in the planet's average temperature increases the likelihood of wildfires, shrinking rivers and lakes, desert expansion, and torrential downpours, including typhoons and hurricanes. Despite the potential catastrophic risks, 48 percent of Americans in 2010 believed that the seriousness of global warming was generally exaggerated (Newport 2010).

Scientists now track carbon dioxide emissions around the world and can map the current and projected

Estimated Time for Each Successive Increase of 1 Billion People in World Population

Population Level	Time taken to reach new population level	Year of Attainment
First billion	Human history before 1800	1804
Second billion	123 years	1927
Third billion	32 years	1959
Fourth billion	15 years	1974
Fifth billion	13 years	1987
Sixth billion	12 years	1999
Seventh billion	13 years	2012
Eighth billion	14 years	2026
Ninth billion	17 years	2043

Source: Bureau of the Census 2008b.

contribution each country makes (see the graph on p. 368). Such analyses show the sizable and growing contribution made by the United States (Lymas 2008). For some politicians, however, the problem seems too abstract and distant. Others recognize that effective solutions demand a difficult-to-manage multinational response, and they fear that their nation may bear too much of the cost. The Kyoto Protocol, established in 1997 and enacted in 2005, was intended to provide a unified response in which the nations of the world would take collective responsibility to reduce global emissions of greenhouse gases. As of 2010, 187 countries have signed the accord, but the United States, which produces 19 percent of the world's carbon dioxide, has failed to ratify it. Opponents of the Kyoto Protocol argue that doing so would place the nation at a disadvantage in the global marketplace (Energy Information Administration 2008; United Nations Framework Convention on Climate Change 2010a).

We can again draw on world systems analysis when it comes to seeing who pays the highest price for global climate changes. Historically, core nations have been the major emitters of greenhouse gases. Today, much

manufacturing has moved to semiperiphery and periphery nations, where greenhouse gas emissions are escalating. Ironically, many of those who are now calling for a reduction in the human activity that contributes to global climate change are located in core nations, which have contributed disproportionately to the problem. We want our hamburgers, but we decry the destruction of the rain forests to create grazing land for cattle. We want inexpensive clothes and toys, but we condemn developing countries for depending on coal-fired power plants, the number of which are expected to increase 46 percent by 2030. The challenge of global climate change, then, is closely tied to global inequality (M. Jenkins 2008; Leonard 2010; Roberts, Grines, and Manale 2003).

One of the primary factors causing this global environmental crisis is the rise in global population. As of May 2010, there were 6.8 billion people on the planet, an increase of 1.7 billion since 1987. To put this in terms of the human ecology model, the more people there are on the planet, the more resources we need to use to sustain them, the more waste they produce that we must process, and the more strain we place on our capacity to house us all (Ehrlich 1968; Ehrlich and Ehrlich 1990; Ehrlich and Ellison 2002).

Technological advances also contribute to increased environmental concerns. At least since the Industrial Revolution and the invention of the steam engine, the automobile, coal-burning power plants, and more, the environmental effects of technological innovation have been extreme. Biologist and environmentalist Barry Commoner argued that additional contributors to the problem include plastics, detergents, synthetic fibers, pesticides, herbicides, and chemical fertilizers. We appreciate the lifestyles that such innovations allow us to experience, but we pay a significant price for their benefits (Commoner 1971, 1990).

THE GLOBAL RESPONSE

Globalization can be both good and bad for the environment. On the negative side, it can create a race to the bottom as polluting companies relocate to countries with less stringent environmental standards. Also of concern is that globalization allows multinationals to exploit the resources of developing countries for short-term profit. From Mexico to China, the industrialization that often accompanies globalization has increased pollution of all types.

Yet globalization can have a positive impact as well. As barriers to the international movement of goods, services, and people fall, multinational corporations have an incentive to carefully consider the cost of natural resources. As the establishment of the Kyoto Protocol demonstrated, countries around the world can come together on a global level to take action that makes a significant difference. For example, the industrialized nations that agreed to the Kyoto Protocol are on track to meet the 2010 emission reduction targets. In December 2009, nations around the world came together in

Perceptions of Global Climate Change

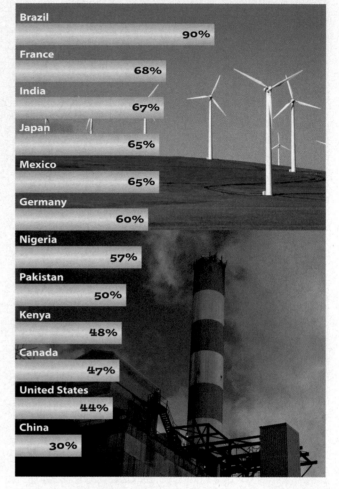

Brazil	90%
France	68%
India	67%
Japan	65%
Mexico	65%
Germany	60%
Nigeria	57%
Pakistan	50%
Kenya	48%
Canada	47%
United States	44%
China	30%

Note: Percentage of people citing global warming as a very serious problem.
Source: Pew Research Center 2009e.

Copenhagen to begin work on a new set of global environmental targets, a process that continued in Bonn, Germany, in June 2010. The goal is to establish a new global climate change treaty (United Nations Framework Convention on Climate Change 2010b). Overusing or wasting resources makes little sense, especially when they are in danger of depletion (Kwong 2005). Perhaps, as Émile Durkheim might have argued long ago, by recognizing the negative effects of our global expansion, along with our mutual interdependence, we will take the steps necessary to bring about positive social change.

There are signs that individuals, countries, and corporations are beginning to understand and appreciate our interdependence. In response, individuals are taking greater responsibility for their global impact by recycling and switching to fluorescent light bulbs (Morales 2010). Increasing numbers of corporations are "going green" and even finding profits in doing so. Sociology helps us to better see the ways we are interconnected by highlighting the significance of the system as a whole, as well as raising awareness about the inequalities that are a consequence of the global system we have constructed. Such analysis can prepare us to more effectively respond to the global challenges we face.

get Involved!

Investigate! Research the air and water quality in your community. Talk with local environmental officials about the extent to which current quality levels have improved or deteriorated in the past few years. How adequate are the indicators of quality they utilize? What evidence do leaders cite regarding the extent to which national, state, or local policies have affected water and air quality? What changes in policy may be necessary to meet desired quality goals?

For REVIEW

I. **What does sociology contribute to something as seemingly biological as health?**
    - Our understanding of what counts as health and illness is shaped by the society to which we belong. Similarly, control over resources shapes our likelihood of exposure to illness and our access to health care.

II. **What is social epidemiology?**
    - Social epidemiology involves the study of factors that shape the health status of various groups within a population. In the United States and elsewhere, social class, race and ethnicity, gender, and age all have an impact.

III. **What environmental lessons do we learn from sociology?**
    - The natural environment represents our human home, within which all social interaction occurs, and the way we organize our social relations shapes the impact we have on the environment. Countries that control a larger amount of resources have a bigger impact and therefore bear a greater responsibility for those effects.

Functionalist View

Health care is a social institution that provides for our health and welfare and thus preserves **social order.**

Society needs to take responsibility for caring for the environment because it gives us resources, serves as a waste repository, and provides a home for our species.

As we become more socially, economically, and environmentally **interdependent**, new, more global conscious, norms and values arise.

SOCIAL ORDER, INTERCONNECTEDNESS
KEY CONCEPTS

Conflict View

The medical establishment serves as an agent of **social control** by defining health and illness, reinforcing the power of professional elites.

Core nations **exploit** the natural resources of developing nations on the periphery without taking responsibility for the consequences.

Poor people and minorities suffer disproportionately from **inequlties** in health care and exposure to environmental hazards, such as toxic waste and air and water pollution.

KEY CONCEPTS
CONTROL, INEQUALITY, EXPLOITATION

Interactionist View

Patients can play an **active role** in their health both by seeking out a physician's services and by choosing whether or not to follow a doctor's orders.

Doctors tend to be trained more in clinical skills than in people skills, so their interactions with patients, as well as nurses, are somewhat **depersonalized.**

The degree to which we think significant environmental problems exist is a consequence of **socialization** by family, friends, teachers, television, and so on.

KEY CONCEPTS
ACTIVITY, INTERACTION

MAKE THE CONNECTION

After reviewing the chapter, answer the following questions:

1

How would each perspective approach the study of the Deep Horizon oil spill in the Gulf of Mexico (p. 345)?

2

What insights would we gain from each perspective regarding the current state of health care in the United States, including recent health care reform efforts (p. 353)?

3

How does the approach that the conflict perspective takes toward "environmental justice" differ from the functionalist approach (p. 362)?

4

Look at your experience with the medical world from an interactionist perspective. What were your interactions with the doctors and nurses like? Have you taken an active role or a passive role as a patient?

Pop Quiz

1. A disease that cannot be understood apart from its specific social context is an example of
   a. human ecology.
   b. culture-bound syndrome.
   c. the sick role.
   d. holistic medicine.

2. The expansion of medicine's domain of expertise and its assertion of absolute jurisdiction over many health care procedures are examples of
   a. labeling and power.
   b. social epidemiology.
   c. the medicalization of society.
   d. human ecology.

3. Which one of the following nations has the lowest infant mortality rate?
   a. the United States
   b. Sierra Leone
   c. Canada
   d. Japan

4. Compared with Whites, Blacks have higher death rates from
   a. heart disease.
   b. diabetes.
   c. cancer.
   d. all of the above.

5. The age group that is most likely to be covered by some form of health insurance is
   a. under 18.
   b. 18–34.
   c. 35–64.
   d. 65 and older.

6. Which program is essentially a compulsory health insurance plan for the elderly?
   a. Medicaid
   b. Blue Cross
   c. Medicare
   d. holistic medicine

7. Not counting prayer, what percentage of Americans reported using some form of complementary or alternative medicine in a 2007 survey?
   a. 17
   b. 38
   c. 62
   d. 84

8. The sociological perspective that emphasizes the interrelationships between people and their environment is known as
   a. human ecology.
   b. resource allocation.
   c. environmental justice.
   d. labeling theory.

9. The industrialized nations of North America and Europe account for 12 percent of the world's population. What percentage of worldwide consumption are they responsible for?
   a. 15 percent
   b. 30 percent
   c. 45 percent
   d. 60 percent

10. What is the international treaty that sought to reduce global emissions of greenhouse gases?
    a. Valdez Treaty
    b. Kyoto Protocol
    c. Port Huron Statement
    d. Gore Accord

1. (b); 2. (c); 3. (d); 4. (d); 5. (d); 6. (c); 7. (b); 8. (a); 9. (d); 10. (b)

CHANGING THE WORLD ONE CAMPUS AT A TIME

In the summer of 1964, college students traveled to Mississippi to change the world. As volunteers in Freedom Summer, their goal was to make a difference in the lives of African Americans who had been systematically denied the right to vote, quality education, and legal and political representation. The volunteers—mostly upper-middle-class White students from northern colleges—registered Black voters, established Freedom Schools, and provided legal advice and medical assistance. By the end of the summer, they had registered 17,000 voters and taught 3000 children. In 1964, 6.7 percent of voting-age African Americans in Mississippi were registered, but by 1967, 66.5 percent were (Colby 1986; McAdam 1988).

From April 18 to May 8, 2001, students at Harvard University occupied Massachusetts Hall, the location of the president's and provost's offices, as part of their Living Wage Campaign. The city of Cambridge, where Harvard is located, had passed a living-wage ordinance ensuring a minimum wage of $10 per hour, adjustable for inflation. Students argued that a school with a multibillion-dollar endowment could do better than the $6.50 many employees were receiving. After numerous attempts at negotiation, students decided to make a statement. During the sit-in, students organized daily pickets and rallies involving thousands of people. After three weeks, the administration agreed to establish a committee to implement living wage principles (Progressive Student Labor Movement 2008).

In 2007, students at Middlebury College in Vermont convinced their trustees to build a $12-million biomass power plant in keeping with their campus commitment to carbon neutrality. The plant began operation in February 2009. While a student at Cornell University in New York, Catherine McEachern was involved in a similar student movement. She says, "Global warming has been neglected by the previous generation, and we see it as an injustice that needs to be changed" (quoted in James 2008).

College students continue to fight for and bring about significant change on campuses around the world. Max Weber argued that all of us have the potential power to change our world. In fact, change will happen whether we like it or not. A key question is this: Will we be active agents seeking the change we desire or passive recipients who accept the change enacted by others?

As You READ >>

- How and why does social change happen?
- What factors shape the success of a social movement?
- What does it mean to practice sociology?

>> Global Social Change

We are at a truly dramatic era in history in terms of global social change. Within the past few decades, we have witnessed the computer revolution and the explosion of Internet connectivity; the collapse of communism; major regime changes and severe economic disruptions in Africa, the Middle East, and Eastern Europe; the spread of AIDS; the first verification of the cloning of a complex animal, Dolly the sheep; and the first major terrorist attack on U.S. soil. Today we continue to face global challenges including international terrorism, a global economic meltdown, and climate change, along with other threats.

The transformation of society has been a fundamental concern of sociologists from the very beginning. At the time of sociology's founding, social life was undergoing dramatic change. The taken-for-granted norms and values that made sense in a traditional agricultural society no longer fit with the lived experience of most people. The Industrial Revolution, the rise of capitalism, and the transformation from aristocratic to democratic rule all challenged traditional practices and beliefs. Sociological theory and research provide us with tools that allow us to make sense of where we are now and where we are headed.

The collapse of communist regimes in the former Soviet Union and the nations of Eastern Europe in the late 1980s and early 1990s, for example, took many people by surprise. Yet prior to the collapse, sociologist Randall Collins (1986, 1995) had observed a crucial sequence of events that most observers missed. Long before it happened, Collins had argued that Soviet expansionism had resulted in an overextension of resources, including disproportionate spending on the military. Such overextension strains a regime's stability. Moreover, geopolitical theory suggests that nations in the middle of a geographic region, such as the Soviet Union, tend to fragment into smaller units over time. Collins correctly predicted that the confluence of social crises on several frontiers would precipitate the collapse of the Soviet Union.

Political systems often seek to control how changes such as transfers of power happen to minimize such disruptions. In the United States, for example, political change is built into the system and arises out of the normal operation of existing practices. Barack Obama's inauguration as president occurred as a peaceful transfer of power, in spite of the fact that it represented a major shift in terms of policy and personnel. At other times, change seems more spontaneous, as was the case with the political protests in Iran that began in June 2009. Here, too, there was a presidential election, but the results were seen as illegitimate by tens of thousands of citizens. Protestors took to the streets to voice their opposition, leading to a bloody confrontation with the existing

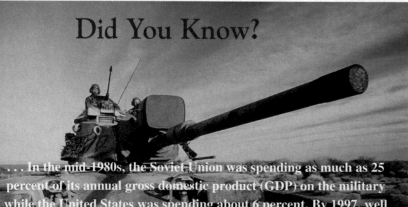

Did You Know?

...In the mid-1980s, the Soviet Union was spending as much as 25 percent of its annual gross domestic product (GDP) on the military while the United States was spending about 6 percent. By 1997, well after the collapse of the USSR, Russia's spending had fallen to about one-tenth of that amount. Currently, the United States spends more on national defense than does the rest of the world combined, which represents approximately 4 percent of its GDP.

government. However, even when seemingly impromptu challenges to the existing system of authority arise, it is possible to identify the social factors that gave rise to the protest.

Sociology helps us to understand such shifts by paying attention both to large-scale, or macro, shifts that alter the basic landscape of society and the relationships among groups, and to the small-scale, or micro, changes in social interaction within which decisions are made that can alter the course of history. We construct society through our everyday actions. As such, we have the power to change society by altering the choices we make. Of course, some people, due to their control over valued resources, have more power than do others. Sociology can better focus our attention so that we might understand which direction change might follow.

>> Sociological Perspectives on Social Change

As humans, we are creative beings. We continually innovate and experiment, developing new technologies, ideas, and ways of doing things. Each innovation represents an example of **social change,** which involves significant alteration over time in behavior patterns and culture.

> **social change** Significant alteration over time in behavior patterns and culture, including norms and values.

Social change can occur so slowly as to be almost undetectable to those it affects, but it can also happen with breathtaking rapidity. In the past century or so, for example, the U.S. population has more than doubled, the percentage

The United States: A Changing Nation

Population	1850	1940	1950	2010
Total in millions	23.3	132.1	180.7	310.2
Percentage under age 15	41%	25%	31%	20%
Education	**1850**	**1940**	**1960**	**2009**
Percentage age 25+ who have not completed high school	88%	75%	59%	14%
Percentage ages 19–24 enrolled in higher education	< 1%	8%	24%	46%
Labor Force Participation	**1850**	**1940**	**1960**	**2007**
Men working in their 20s	94%	86%	86%	85%
Women working in their 20s	22%	51%	74%	73%
Health	**1850**	**1940**	**1960**	**2010**
Physicians per 100,000 population	176	133	150	271
Life expectancy at birth, in years	38	63	70	78
Technology	**1870**	**1940**	**1960**	**2008**
Copyrights issued	5,600	176,997	243,926	232,000
Patents issued	12,137	42,238	47,170	185,000
Family	**1890**	**1940**	**1960**	**2009**
Median age at first marriage				
Men	26	24	23	28
Women	22	22	20	26
Birth rate for women, age 20–24 per 1000	168.4	135.6	258.1	106.1

Note: Data are comparable, although definitions vary somewhat across time. Education rate for 1850 is for those over age 70. Earliest birthrate is from 1905.

Source: Carter et al. 2006: vol.1: 28–29, 401–402, 440, 541, 685, 697, 709, vol. 2: 441–442, vol. 3: 422–425, 427–428; Snyder and Dillow 2010:Table 8; U.S. Census Bureau 2008a: Tables 1, 2, 7, 102, 159, 754, 756; U.S. Census Bureau 2010a:Table MS-2.

SOCstudies

of people finishing high school and attending college has skyrocketed, women have entered the paid labor force in significant numbers, life expectancy has risen, technological innovation has exploded, men and women have been marrying later, and family size has shrunk. In our global, interdependent world, there is no reason to suspect that such changes will cease, and many future changes will be difficult to predict.

Explaining social change is clearly a challenge in the diverse and complex world we inhabit. Nevertheless, sociologists have sought to analyze, interpret, and explain social change. In some instances, they have examined historical events to arrive at a better understanding of contemporary changes. We will look at change from three perspectives so that we might better identify issues we should include when considering how and why change happens.

> All change is not growth, as all movement is not forward.
>
> ———————
>
> Ellen Glasgow

THE EVOLUTION OF SOCIETIES

All societies must adapt to change. Sometimes that change is a consequence of external forces, for example, from an act of war by another nation or a natural disaster. Sometimes it results from internal innovation, such as the invention of new technologies. Change can also be gradual, something that we may not see until we take a step back and look. Other times it can come quickly, when we are called to respond to a crisis.

One approach to understanding how societies change draws upon the principle of evolution. It was inspired, in part, by Charles Darwin's (1809–1882) work on the biological evolution of species. Darwin's approach stresses a continuing progression of successive generations of life forms as they adapt to their environment. For example, human beings came at a later stage of evolution than reptiles and represent a more complex form of life. Social theorists seeking an analogy to this biological model proposed **evolutionary theory,** in which society is viewed as moving in a definite direction. Early evolutionary theorists generally agreed that society was progressing from the simple to the complex, which they assumed was superior.

Early sociologists and anthropologists believed it was possible to study what they referred to at that time as simple or "primitive" societies for clues about the

evolutionary theory A theory of social change that holds that society is moving in a definite direction.

essential building blocks that serve as the foundation for all societies. Auguste Comte (1798–1857), a founder of sociology, was an evolutionary theorist of change. He saw human societies as moving forward in their thinking, from mythology to the scientific method. Similarly, Émile Durkheim ([1893]1933) maintained that society progressed from simple to complex forms of social organization. Both Comte and Durkheim believed that by gaining a rational understanding of the principles of order and change in such societies, we would be able to more effectively shape the direction our modern, more complex societies would take.

Since that time, we have learned that the idea that all societies follow a singular path from simple to complex, from primitive to modern, is flawed. The notion that traditional societies are simple or primitive has proven to be both incorrect and ethnocentric. Such societies demonstrate significant levels of sophistication and innovation, in terms of both social relations and technological adaptation to their environments. In addition, there is no single path of social evolution that all societies must pass through. Social change can impact one area of social life, such as politics, while leaving other areas of life relatively unchanged, such as work and the economy. For example, a society might move toward a democratic form of government, but the traditional nature of work, primarily small-scale and agricultural, might stay the same.

Though there are limits to the evolutionary model of social change, it does provide a helpful metaphor when thinking about how change happens. For example, we can look to past practices to better understand where new ways of thinking and acting come from. In addition, it highlights the role that context or environment plays in shaping change. In biology, when the environment changes, mutations in species can occur, making them more fit to survive in that new context than were past generations. For Darwin, however, this did not mean that the new was superior to the old; it was simply more likely that the new would survive given changed environmental circumstances. The danger when applying this analogy to society is to assume that those who adapt to changed circumstances are superior.

EQUILIBRIUM AND SOCIAL ORDER

Another approach to understanding social change is rooted in the principle that societies naturally seek to attain stability or balance. Any social change that occurs represents necessary adjustments as society seeks to return to that state of equilibrium. For example, sociologist Talcott Parsons (1902–1979), an advocate of this approach, viewed even prolonged labor strikes or civilian riots as temporary disruptions in the status quo rather than as significant alterations in the social structure. According to his **equilibrium model,** as changes occur in one part of

SOC THINK

Why would early theorists have thought of traditional societies as "primitive"? How is this a reflection of the evolutionary theoretical paradigm they adopted?

society, adjustments must be made in other parts. If not, society's equilibrium will be threatened and strains will occur.

Parsons (1966) maintained that four processes of social change are inevitable. The first, differentiation, refers to the increasing complexity of social organization. We see this in the form of job specialization as is evident in bureaucratic systems. The transition from a healer—a single person who handles all of your health care needs—to a series of positions, including physician, anesthetist, nurse, and pharmacist, is an illustration of differentiation in the field of medicine. This process is accompanied by adaptive upgrading, in which social institutions become more

5 Movies on SOCIAL MOVEMENTS AND SOCIAL CHANGE

Gandhi
His story of change through non-violent social action.

Erin Brockovich
How one person can affect big business.

Norma Rae
Union! Union!

Milk
The story of the first openly gay elected official, Harvey Milk.

Miracle
How a game of hockey brought about the symbolic end of the Cold War.

specialized in their purposes. The division of physicians into obstetricians, internists, surgeons, and so forth is an example of adaptive upgrading.

The third process Parsons identified is the inclusion of groups that were previously excluded because of their gender, race, ethnicity, and social class. In the past two decades or so, medical schools have practiced inclusion by admitting increasing numbers of women and African Americans. Finally, Parsons contended that societies experience value generalization—the development of new values that legitimate a broader range of activities. The acceptance of preventive and alternative medicine is an example of value generalization: Society has broadened its view of health care. All four processes identified by Parsons stress consensus—societal

SOC THINK

Why might the equilibrium model have a difficult time addressing issues such as inequality and poverty as social problems to be solved?

agreement on the nature of social organization and values (Gerhardt 2002).

One of the sources of potential strain that can lead to such social adaptation involves technological innovation. As we saw in Chapter 3, sociologist William F. Ogburn (1922) distinguished between material and nonmaterial aspects of culture. Material culture includes inventions, artifacts, and technology; nonmaterial culture encompasses ideas, norms, communications, and social organization. Ogburn pointed out that technology often changes faster than do the ideas and values with which we make sense of such change. Thus, the nonmaterial culture, including values and norms, typically must respond to changes in the material culture. Ogburn introduced the term **culture lag** to refer to the period of adjustment when the nonmaterial culture is still struggling to adapt to new material conditions. One example is the Internet. Its rapid uncontrolled growth raises questions about whether to regulate it and, if so, how much.

In certain cases, the changes in the material culture can strain the relationships between social institutions. For example, the invention of the birth control pill in 1960, along with other modern forms of birth control, led to significant social changes. It helped to reduce family size at a time when large families were no longer necessary—and were even a constraint to mobility—given the shift from agricultural to industrial and service economies. It provided greater opportunity for women to pursue careers and maintain control over their fertility. In so doing, it challenged our conceptions about ideal family size and the role of women in the economy. The birth control pill also affected religious faith (among Roman Catholics, for example) because it challenged beliefs about the role of God and the value of human life in reproduction (Tentler 2004).

From Parsons's point of view, such tensions represent little more than normal adjustments needed to maintain the inevitable balance that is the natural state of all societies. Though his approach explicitly incorporates the evolutionary notion of continuing progress, the dominant theme in this model is stability. Society may change, but it remains stable through new forms of integration. For example, in place of the kinship ties that provided social cohesion in the past, people develop laws, judicial processes, and new values and belief systems. Parsons and other theorists would argue that those parts of society that persist, even

> **equilibrium model** The view that society tends toward a state of stability or balance.

COMPUTER TECHNOLOGY

In the past decade, computer access has gone global, and Internet access along with it. While the revolutions in transportation and communication have brought us together since the Industrial Revolution, the Internet provides a potential for immediate global connection that previously was virtually and physically impossible. In 2010, the Internet reached 1.8 billion users, or 27 percent of the world's population (Internet World Stats 2010a).

The Internet evolved from a computer system built in 1962 by the U.S. Defense Department to enable scholars and military researchers to continue their government work, even if part of the nation's communications system were destroyed by nuclear attack. For years, it was difficult to gain access to the Internet without holding a position at a university or a government research laboratory. Today, however, virtually anyone with sufficient resources can reach the Internet with a wireless-enabled computer, or a smartphone. People buy and sell cars, trade stocks, auction off items, research new medical remedies, vote, reconnect with long-lost friends, and coordinate social movements, to mention just a few of the thousands of possibilities (Shirky 2008).

If we look at global Internet use, the regions with the greatest number of users are Asia and Europe. Asia alone represents more than 760 million users. However, in terms of access, a larger proportion of the population in North America—about 76 percent—can connect to the Internet than in any other continent. Even though Asia has the greatest number of users, only about 20 percent of the population there has Internet access. Another sign of the global nature of this expansion has been the increase in languages used on the Internet. While English continues to lead, the number of Chinese-speaking users increased 1162 percent between 2000 and 2009, and Arabic speakers increased 2298 percent, compared to 252 percent for English (Internet World Stats 2010a, 2010b).

Unfortunately, a digital divide persists, and not everyone can get onto the information highway, especially not the less affluent. Moreover, this pattern of inequality is global. In Africa, for example, only 8.7 percent of the population has access to the Internet. The core nations that Immanuel Wallerstein described in his world systems analysis have a virtual monopoly on information technology; the peripheral nations of Asia, Africa, and Latin America depend on the core nations both for technology and for

Internet Use and Penetration by World Region

Asia   764 million users   20.1%

Europe   426 million users   53.0%

North America   260 million users   76.2%

Latin America   187 million users   31.9%

Africa   86 million users   8.7%

Middle East   58 million users   23.8%

Australia/Oceania   21 million users   60.8%

World   1.8 billion users   26.6%

10 million users

%   Penetration rate (percentage of population)

Source: Internet World Stats 2010a.

the information it provides. For example, North America, Europe, and a few industrialized nations in other regions possess almost all the world's Internet hosts—computers that are connected directly to the worldwide network.

One way to address this divide is to provide computers to people around the world who do not have them. The One Laptop per Child (OLPC) campaign, which originated at the Massachusetts Institute of Technology, is one example of a program seeking to do just that (www.laptop.org). Established in January 2005 by Nicholas Negroponte, MIT media technology professor and co-founder of MIT's Media Lab, its mission is "to create educational opportunities for the world's poorest children by providing each child with a rugged, low-cost, low-power, connected laptop with content and software designed for collaborative, joyful, self-empowered learning" (OLPC 2010). The organization designed and built durable, yet inexpensive laptop computers (called the XO) that can connect wirelessly with each other and share an Internet connection to provide access to the wider world. Negroponte's vision is to persuade individuals, foundations, and governments in industrial nations to fund the purchase and distribution of

the laptops, making them available to children for free. As of May 2010, OLPC had distributed 1.6 million computers to children around the world in places such as Peru, Haiti, Cambodia, Rwanda, Iraq, and Mongolia.

PRIVACY AND CENSORSHIP IN A GLOBAL VILLAGE

In addition to the digital divide, sociologists have also raised concerns about threats to privacy and the possibility of censorship. Recent advances have made it increasingly

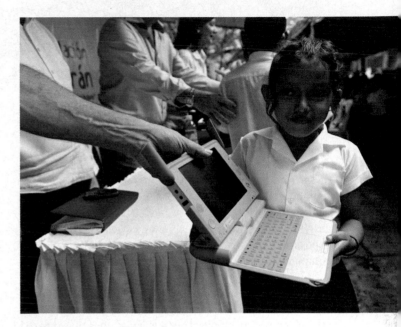

> **SOC**THINK
>
> From a purely business point of view, what would be the pros and cons of giving a free XO to every needy child in the developing world? Would the social benefits of doing so outweigh the business costs and benefits?

Internet Top 10 Languages

Millions of users

Language	Users
English	496
Chinese	408
Spanish	140
Japanese	96
Portuguese	78
French	75
German	72
Arabic	60
Russian	45
Korean	38
Rest of world languages	314

Source: Internet World Stats 2010b.

easy for business firms, government agencies, and even criminals to retrieve and store information about everything from our buying habits to our Web-surfing patterns. In public places, at work, and on the Internet, surveillance devices now track our every move, be it a keystroke or an ATM withdrawal. As technology spreads, so does the exposure to risk. In 2006, for example, the theft of a laptop computer from the home of an employee of the Veterans Administration compromised the names, Social Security numbers, and dates of birth of up to 26.5 million veterans.

At the same time that these innovations have increased others' power to monitor our behavior, they have raised fears that they might be misused for undemocratic purposes. In short, new technologies threaten not just our privacy but our freedom from surveillance and censorship (O'Harrow 2005). There is, for example, the danger that the most powerful groups in a society will use technology to violate the privacy of the less powerful. Indeed, officials in the People's Republic of China have attempted to censor online discussion groups and web postings that criticize the government. Civil liberties advocates remind us that the same abuses can occur in the United States if citizens are not vigilant in protecting their right to privacy (Liang and Lu 2010; Moyer 2010). Indeed, in April 2010, it was discovered that officials in a Pennsylvania school district had captured almost 58,000 webcam pictures of students, including images in their homes and bedrooms, using school-issued Macbook computers.

In the United States, legislation regulating the surveillance of electronic communications has not always upheld citizens' right to privacy. In 1986, the federal government passed the Electronic Communications Privacy Act, which outlawed the surveillance of telephone calls except with the permission of both the U.S. attorney general and a federal judge. Telegrams, faxes, and email did not receive the same degree of protection, however. In 2001, one month after the terrorist attacks of September 11, Congress passed the USA PATRIOT Act, which relaxed existing legal checks on surveillance by law enforcement officers. Federal agencies are now freer to gather data electronically, including credit card receipts and banking records (Etzioni 2007; Singel 2008; Zetter 2009).

In the early days of Internet expansion, many people were quite concerned about sharing any personal information online for fear that someone might use it against them. Now, with the advent of Facebook, Flickr, Twitter, and a whole host of other social networking sites, many Internet users see no such risk. People regularly share their thoughts, feelings, and actions with others, including total strangers. But Facebook's privacy setting changes in May 2010 raised red flags for many, and others have learned the hard way that schools and employers can use this information to make decisions about discipline and hiring (Finder 2006; Relerford et al. 2008; Solove 2008).

BIOTECHNOLOGY AND THE GENE POOL

Another field in which technological advances have spurred global social change is biotechnology. Sex selection of fetuses, genetically engineered organisms, the cloning of animals—these have been among the significant yet controversial scientific advances in the field of biotechnology in recent years. No phase of life now seems exempt from therapeutic or medical intervention. In fact, sociologists view many aspects of biotechnology as as an extension of the recent trend toward the medicalization of society. Through genetic manipulation, the medical profession is expanding its turf still further (Clarke et al. 2003).

Cloning Milestones

Dolly, Sheep Feb. '97

Cumulina, Mouse Oct. '97

Mira, Goat Oct. '98

Gene, Calf Aug. '97

Millie, Christa, Alexis, Carrel, & Dotcom, Piglets Mar. '00

CC, Cat Dec. '01

Taz, Mule
Dewey, Deer
Prometea, Horse May '03

Ralph, Rat Sep. '03

Snuppy, Dog Aug. '05

| 1997 | 1998 | 1999 | 2000 | 2001 | 2002 | 2003 | 2004 | 2005 |

One area of genetic modification that has raised concern involves genetically modified (GM) food. This issue arose in Europe but has since spread to other parts of the world, including the United States. The idea behind the technology is to increase food production and make agriculture more efficient and economical. But critics use the term *frankenfood* (as in Frankenstein) to refer to everything from breakfast cereals made from genetically engineered grains to "fresh" GM tomatoes. Members of the antibiotech movement object to tampering with nature and are concerned about the possible health effects of GM food. Supporters of GM food include not just biotech companies, but also those who see the technology as a way to help feed the growing populations of Africa and Asia (Bovis 2007; Schurman 2004).

Even as the genetic modification of plants continues to be a concern, the debate about the genetic manipulation of animals escalated in 1997 when scientists in Scotland announced that they had cloned a sheep, which they named Dolly. After many unsuccessful attempts, they were finally able to replace the genetic material of a sheep's egg with DNA from an adult sheep, creating a lamb that was a clone of the adult. Shortly thereafter, Japanese researchers successfully cloned cows. Since then many other species have been successfully cloned (see the timeline above), and it is now even possible to get your pet cat or dog cloned. Such accomplishments point to the possibility that in the near future, scientists may be able to clone human beings.

Manipulation that goes even further than cloning involves potentially altering species through genetic engineering. Fish and plant genes have already been mixed to create frost-resistant potato and tomato crops. More recently, human genes have been implanted in pigs to provide humanlike kidneys for organ transplants. Geneticists working with mouse fetuses have managed to disable genes that carry an undesirable trait and replace them with genes carrying a desirable trait. And in May 2010, scientists announced that they had created the first self-replicating, synthetic bacterial cell. Using a process similar to cloning, they implanted a DNA sequence created by humans into a single cell; it then successfully reproduced itself. This accomplishment was seen as a major step forward in our ability to design and create new forms of life (*Edge* 2010). Such advances raise ethical concerns related to applying such engineering to humans to eliminate disease or infirmities or to enhance physical abilities such as sight or strength (Avise 2004).

Today's biotechnology holds itself out as totally beneficial to human beings, but it is in constant need of monitoring. Biotechnological advances have raised many difficult ethical and political questions. Among them is the desirability of tinkering with the gene pool, which could alter our environment and ourselves in unexpected and unwanted ways (McKibben 2003). Even William F. Ogburn could not have anticipated the extent of such scientific developments when he first articulated the problem of culture lag in the 1920s.

—SOC THINK—

If you could modify your children's genes to protect them from genetic diseases, would you do it? How about enhancing their abilities such as eyesight, strength, or intelligence?

RESISTANCE TO TECHNOLOGY

Given such consequences, it should come as no surprise that, through the ages, there have been those who questioned whether such technological innovation equals progress. Inventions that grew out of the Industrial Revolution, for example, led to strong resistance in some countries. In England, beginning in 1811, masked craft workers took extreme measures: They mounted nighttime raids on factories and destroyed some of the new machinery. The government hunted these rebels, known as **Luddites,** and ultimately banished or hanged them. In a similar effort in France, angry workers threw their wooden shoes (sabots)

Luddites Rebellious craft workers in 19th-century England who destroyed new factory machinery as part of their resistance to the Industrial Revolution.

Five Questions to Ask When Adopting New Technology

- What is the problem to which this technology is the solution?

- Whose problem is it?

- What new problems might be created because we solve the problem?

- Which people and institutions might be most seriously harmed?

- Which people and institutions might acquire special economic and political power?

Source: Postman 1988.

Technology and Society

I confess to having mixed emotions about new technology. I love my iPhone and couldn't resist the appeal of the iPad. Yet I worry about the consequences such technologies have on my relationships with others. We are quick to adopt the latest gadgets, but what about the effects of abandoning old norms? I'm sure all of us have encountered that iPod-wearing cell-phone talker who barely seems to notice we exist. Technologies such as Facebook do enable us to maintain connections with distant friends and family. But what happens to our relationships with the people right next to us when our attention is diverted to status updates and text messages?

into factory machinery to destroy it, giving rise to the term *sabotage.* Although the resistance of the Luddites and the French workers was short-lived and unsuccessful, they have come to symbolize resistance to technology.

It would be a mistake, however, to simply dismiss the actions of the Luddites and French workers as antitechnology or irrational. Their primary concern was with the impact such technology had on their employment, their communities, and their way of life. They recognized that it would undercut taken-for-granted norms and values and fought against such threats. While it is easy to write such groups and individuals off as being against progress—or even as technophobes that fear change—their bigger concern is the impact adoption of technologies has on society. The Amish, for example, are often dismissed as backward, when, in fact, they are quite rational and deliberative about adopting technology. They carefully weigh the benefits new technologies would provide against the potential costs adoption would have on family and community life. They do not assume that, simply because something makes work easier or faster, it is necessarily better. For the Amish, working together in community is more highly valued than working more quickly in isolation (Hostetler 1993; Hurst and McConnell 2010).

Sociologist Jacques Ellul (1964, 1980, 1990) argued that the key factor to consider when analyzing our modern technological society is not simply the *technology,* by which he meant the physical tools we create as we modify our material environment, but what he referred to more generally as *technique.* By this he meant our systemic commitment to maximizing efficiency and increasing productivity in all areas of human endeavor. Success, whether in business, education, or love, is increasingly measured in quantitative terms. That which cannot be measured is suspect. For example, we see evidence of this at work in the No Child Left Behind education reforms. Performance on particular kinds of tests, in a narrow range of subjects, is becoming the primary indicator of learning. While living in a technique-focused system has the advantage of technical progress, we lose something human in the process—art, beauty, and qualitative, as opposed to quantitative, values. Ellul's concerns echo those of Max Weber about the dehumanizing consequences of bureaucracy.

Most of us today automatically adopt the latest technologies without taking time to step back and ask what consequences they might have for social order and meaning. Communications professor Neil Postman (1988, 1993, 1999) argues that, instead of passively accepting technological innovations, we should critically examine whether or not we really need them and investigate what consequences adoption might have on ourselves, our relationships, and our society (see Postman's five questions on p. 384). In a sense, Postman is calling us to recognize ways in which our choices are influenced by the technological system within which we live. Doing so enables us to resist unconscious acceptance and exercise greater freedom in the choices that we make.

>> Social Movements

We do have the power to resist change even when it seems inevitable. More than that, we also have the power to bring about positive social change. Although factors such as the physical environment, population, technology, and social inequality serve as sources of change, it is the collective effort of individuals organized in social movements that ultimately leads to change. Sociologists use the term **social movements** to refer to organized collective activities to bring about or resist fundamental change in an existing group or society. Herbert Blumer (1955:19) recognized the special importance of social movements when he defined them as "collective enterprises to establish a new order of life."

In many nations, including the United States, social movements have had a dramatic impact on the course of history and the evolution of the social structure. Consider the actions of abolitionists, suffragists, civil rights workers, and anti–Vietnam War activists. Members of each social movement stepped outside traditional channels for bringing about social change, yet they had a noticeable influence on public policy. In Eastern Europe, equally dramatic collective efforts helped to topple communist regimes in a largely peaceful manner, in nations that many observers had thought were "immune" to such social change (Marples 2004).

Social movements change how we think and act. Even if they initially fail to accomplish their explicit goals, social movements can influence cultural attitudes and expectations in ways that open people up to future change. Initially, people viewed the ideas of Margaret Sanger and other early advocates of birth control as radical, yet contraceptives are now widely available in the United States. Similarly, protests—whether against the practices of multinational corporations, same-sex marriage, the unethical treatment of animals, environmental destruction, or war—challenge us to question our taken-for-granted understandings of what is happening and why. This holds true even if we never formally participate ourselves or do not fully subscribe to all the beliefs and practices of the protestors.

> **social movement** An organized collective activity to bring about or resist fundamental change in an existing group or society.
>
> **relative deprivation** The conscious feeling of a negative discrepancy between legitimate expectations and present actualities.

At least since the work of Karl Marx, sociologists have studied how and why social movements emerge. Obviously, one factor is that people become discontented with the way things are. To explain how this develops and is transformed into action, sociologists rely on two primary explanations: relative deprivation and resource mobilization.

RELATIVE DEPRIVATION

Those members of a society who feel most frustrated with and disgruntled by social and economic conditions are not necessarily the worst off in an objective sense. Social scientists have long recognized that what is most significant is how people perceive their situation. As Marx pointed out, although the misery of the workers was important to their perception of their oppressed state, so was their position in relation to the capitalist ruling class (McLellan 2000).

The term **relative deprivation** refers to the conscious feeling of a negative discrepancy between legitimate expectations and present actualities. In other words, things aren't as good as one hoped they would be. Such a state may be characterized by scarcity rather than a complete lack of necessities. A relatively

Did You Know?

. . . In 1916, Margaret Sanger opened a family planning and birth control clinic. Nine days later, it was raided by police, and she served 30 days in jail as a result. She was undeterred and continued working to dispense birth control information.

deprived person is dissatisfied because he or she feels downtrodden relative to some appropriate reference group. Thus, blue-collar workers who live in two-family houses on small plots of land—though hardly destitute—may nevertheless feel deprived in comparison to corporate managers and professionals who live in lavish homes in exclusive suburbs (Stewart 2006).

In addition to the feeling of relative deprivation, however, two other elements must be present before discontent will be channeled into a social movement. First, people must feel that they have a right to their goals, that they deserve better than what they have. For example, the struggle against European colonialism in Africa intensified when growing numbers of Africans decided that it was legitimate for them to have political and economic independence. Second, the disadvantaged group must perceive that its goals cannot be attained through conventional means. This belief may or may not be correct. In any case, the group will not mobilize into a social movement unless there is a shared perception that members can end their relative deprivation only through collective action (Walker and Smith 2002).

resource mobilization The ways in which a social movement utilizes such resources as money, political influence, access to the media, and personnel.

Critics of this approach have noted that people don't need to feel deprived to be moved to act. In addition, this approach fails to explain why certain feelings of deprivation are transformed into social movements, whereas in other, similar situations, no collective effort is made to reshape society. Consequently, in recent years, sociologists have paid increasing attention to the forces needed to bring about the emergence of social movements (Finkel and Rule 1987; Ratner 2004).

> I cannot say whether things will get better if we change; what I can say is they must change if they are to get better.
>
> George Christoph Lichtenberg

— SOCTHINK —

Are there any issues on your campus or in your community that people persistently complain about? If so, what factors might inhibit them from organizing to bring about social change?

RESOURCE MOBILIZATION APPROACH

It takes more than desire to start a social movement. It helps to have money, political influence, access to the media, and personnel. The term **resource mobilization** refers to the ways in which a social movement utilizes such resources. The success of a movement for change will depend in good part on what resources it has and how effectively it mobilizes them (Balch 2006; J. Jenkins 2004; Ling 2006).

Sociologist Anthony Oberschall (1973:199) has argued that to sustain social protest or resistance, there must be an "organizational base and continuity of leadership." As people become part of a social movement, norms develop to guide their behavior. Members of the movement may be expected to attend regular meetings of organizations, pay dues, recruit new adherents, and boycott "enemy" products or speakers. In forming a distinct identity, an emerging social movement may give rise to special language or new words for familiar terms. In recent years, social movements have been responsible for new terms of self-reference such as *Blacks* and *African Americans* (to replace *Negroes*), *senior citizens* (to replace *old folks*), *gays* (to replace *homosexuals*), and *people with disabilities* (to replace *the handicapped*).

Leadership is a central factor in the mobilization of the discontented into social movements. Often, a movement will be led by a charismatic figure, such as occurred in the civil rights movement with Dr. Martin Luther King Jr. Charisma alone, however, may not be enough. If a group is to succeed, coordinated action is essential. As they grow, such organizations may find they need to take advantage of the efficiency that bureaucratic structures provide. This can result in their taking on some of the characteristics of the groups they were organized to protest. For example, leaders might dominate the decision-making process without directly consulting followers. The bureaucratization of social movements is not inevitable, however. More radical movements that advocate major structural change in society and embrace mass actions tend not to be hierarchical or bureaucratic (Fitzgerald and Rodgers 2000; Michels [1915] 1949).

One of the tasks such movements face is to raise consciousness among those who would be inclined to support the movement but who may lack the language or the sense of solidarity with others to mount a systematic critique of the existing system. Marx, for example, recognized the importance of recruitment when he called on workers to become aware of their oppressed status and to develop a class consciousness. Like theorists of the resource mobilization approach, Marx held that a social movement would require leaders to sharpen the awareness of the oppressed. They would need to help workers to overcome feelings of **false consciousness**—attitudes that do not reflect workers' objective position—in order to organize a revolutionary movement (see Chapter 10).

GENDER AND SOCIAL MOVEMENTS

Betty Friedan's publication of *The Feminine Mystique* in 1963 gave voice to a sense that many women had at the time that something was wrong, but they did not know that others

... Women played an active role in the civil rights movement but were often blocked from positions of leadership. Symbolizing this exclusion perhaps better than any other example was Student Nonviolent Coordinating Committee leader Stokely Carmichael's infamous line "The only position for women in SNCC is prone." Such sexism and discrimination led women to start their own organizations to fight for women's rights.

felt the same way. The book alone, however, was not enough. One of the challenges faced by women's liberation activists of the late 1960s and early 1970s was to convince women that they were being deprived of their rights and of socially valued resources. Consciousness-raising groups represented a critical tool used by women's liberation activists in the 1960s and 1970s. In these groups, women gathered to discuss topics relevant to their experience in the home, at work, in politics, and more. This helped to create a popular base that contributed to significant political and social change (Morgan 2009; Sarachild 1978).

Sociologists point out that gender continues to be an important element in understanding social movements. In our male-dominated society, women continue to find themselves cut off from leadership positions in social movement organizations. Though women often serve disproportionately as volunteers in these movements, their contributions are not always recognized, nor are their voices as easily heard as men's. Gender bias causes the real extent of their influence to be overlooked. Indeed, traditional examination of the sociopolitical system tends to focus on such male-dominated corridors of power as legislatures and corporate boardrooms, to the neglect of more female-dominated domains such as households, community-based groups, and faith-based networks. But efforts to influence family values, child rearing, relationships between parents and schools, and spiritual values are clearly significant to a culture and society (Ferree and Merrill 2000; Kuumba 2001; V. Taylor 1999, 2004).

Prior to the June 2009 presidential election in Iran, women's social movement organizations foresaw an opportunity for change and organized to take advantage of it. Almost 40 equal rights groups combined to form an organization called the "Coalition of Women's Movements to Advocate Electoral Demands." Noushin Ahmadi Khorasani (2009), a key leader of the women's rights movement in Iran, described the opportunity this way: "We could grasp this relatively short and transient moment with both hands, with hope and motivation (and looking forward to tomorrow) in order to voice our demands." During the government crackdown on the protests that followed the election, women continued to fight for change. Perhaps the most visible symbol of their fight was Neda Agha-Soltan, a protestor who was shot and bled to death in the street. The violent image was caught on video and quickly spread around the world (Gheytanchi 2009; Ravitz 2009).

NEW SOCIAL MOVEMENTS

Beginning in the late 1960s, European social scientists observed a change in both the composition and the targets of emerging social movements. Previously, traditional social movements had focused on economic issues, often led by labor unions or by people who shared the same occupation. However, many social movements that have become active in recent decades—including the second

... Martin Luther King Jr. graduated with a BA in sociology from Morehouse College in Atlanta, Georgia, in 1948.

and third waves of feminism, the peace movement, and the environmental movement—do not have the social class roots typical of the labor movements in the United States and Europe over the past century (Carty and Onyett 2006).

The term **new social movements** refers to organized collective activities that address values and social identities, as well as improvements in the quality of life. These movements may be involved in developing collective identities. Many have complex agendas that go beyond a single issue and even cross national boundaries. Educated, middle-class people are significantly represented in some of these new social movements, such as the women's movement and the movement for lesbian and gay rights (Tilly 1993, 2004).

new social movement An organized collective activity that addresses values and social identities, as well as improvements in the quality of life.

New social movements generally do not view government as their ally in the struggle for a better society. They typically do not seek to overthrow the government, but they may criticize, protest, or harass public officials. Researchers have found that members of new social movements call into question the legitimacy of arguments made by established authorities. Even scientific or technical claims, they argue, do not simply represent objective facts, but often serve specific interests. This characteristic is especially evident in the environmental and anti–nuclear power movements, whose activists present their own experts to counter those of government or big business (Clammer 2009; Jamison 2006; Rootes 2007).

The environmental movement is one of many new social movements with a worldwide focus. In their efforts to reduce air and water pollution, curtail global climate change, and protect endangered animal species, environmental activists have realized that strong regulatory measures within a single country are not sufficient. Similarly, labor union leaders and human rights advocates cannot adequately address exploitative sweatshop conditions in a developing country if a multinational corporation can simply move the factory to another country, where workers earn even less. Whereas traditional views of social movements tended to emphasize resource mobilization on a local level, new social movement theory offers a broader, global perspective on social and political activism (Obach 2004).

COMMUNICATION AND THE GLOBALIZATION OF SOCIAL MOVEMENTS

Although technological advances have contributed to some of the problems people in social movements have raised, new technologies also facilitate activism and social movement formation. Using social networking technologies, social activists can reach a large number of people around the world almost instantaneously, with relatively little effort and expense. For example, Facebook and Twitter allow organizers of social movements to enlist like-minded people without face-to-face contact or simultaneous interaction. In fact, significant social action can occur without the participants ever having met in person (Kavada 2005; Shirky 2008).

The potential power of new communication technologies was made apparent during Iran's postelection protests in June 2009. A majority of Iran's population is under 30 and technologically well connected. Before the election, young people used their online social networking skills to coordinate campaign events and raise support for candidates. After President Ahmadinejad's reelection was declared, technologies such as Twitter, Facebook, and SMS texting became critical tools for sharing information, coordinating actions, and documenting abuses by government forces. It was possible to organize rallies without revealing their location until the last minute, making it more difficult for the government to have troops in place to disperse the crowd.

Equally significant, these networking tools also were used to send stories, pictures, and video to the wider world,

SOCTHINK

Online sites such as Changemakers.net serve as information clearinghouses and networking hubs for social activists. How might the existence of such resources shape social activism both positively and negatively?

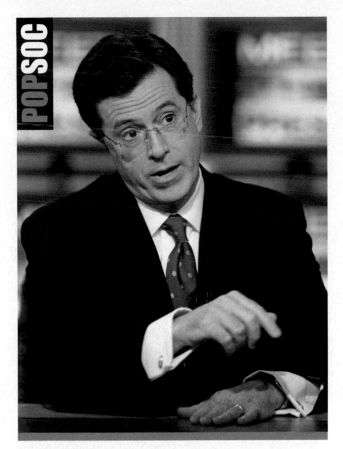

Stephen Colbert worked for several years as a sarcastic correspondent on *The Daily Show* on Comedy Central, but he became famous doing his cynical spoof of a TV talking head on his show, *The Colbert Report*. He was quite serious, however, when he gave advice in a 2006 commencement speech at Knox College. He challenged students not to give in to cynicism, telling them, "Cynicism masquerades as wisdom, but it is the farthest thing from it. Because cynics don't learn anything. Because cynicism is a self-imposed blindness, a rejection of the world because we are afraid it will hurt us or disappoint us. Cynics always say 'no.' But saying 'yes' begins things. Saying 'yes' is how things grow. Saying 'yes' leads to knowledge. 'Yes' is for young people. So for as long as you have the strength to, say 'yes.' "

revealing the brutality of the government's crackdown. The result was an outpouring of global sympathy for the protestors. Iranian authorities sought to shut down wireless phone service and restrict Internet access, including blocking sites such as YouTube and Facebook. In spite of this, people were able to use various technological hacks to get around such restrictions and spread the word (Bray 2009; Quirk 2009; Stelter and Stone 2009).

>> Sociology Is a Verb

Ultimately, social change happens because we begin to act in new ways. It involves our stepping off expected paths and, in doing so, creating new sets of norms.

Although external changes in our technological and environmental contexts do influence social change, it still takes people willing to do things differently to bring about such shifts.

Sociology is a tool that helps open up new pathways for us. By enabling us to see things we might have missed before, it helps us to view ourselves and the world around us differently. Sociology allows us to recognize how the distribution of social, cultural, and material resources gives advantage to some and disadvantage to others. It helps us to understand whether the things we do are consistent with what we claim to believe. It can inform our conversation of whether we are headed where we want to go. It does these things by getting us to pay attention to the world around us in a new way.

We need to move from thinking of sociology as only something we learn about to thinking of sociology as something we *do*. In our daily lives, sociology can help us to better understand our own individual actions and the actions of those around us. In the context of our larger society and the world, it also enables us to better appreciate the forces at work shaping outcomes—knowledge that we can then use to act in ways that make the world a better place. In both our personal and public lives, we need to practice sociology in the same way that doctors practice medicine.

PERSONAL SOCIOLOGY

Sociology can help us in our everyday lives to better understand our beliefs and actions and to make more informed choices. We learn from sociology that we are in society and society is in us. Self and society are not two separate things. Being an individual necessitates understanding the importance of place, of position, of connection, and of interaction. Though we like to believe that any choice is available to us, in reality, our options are limited.

Practicing sociology means asking uncomfortable questions and not settling for easy answers. It means taking into account the significance of both the individual and society, of both action and structure, of both freedom and constraint. It means recognizing the significance of power and the impact that access to material, social, and cultural resources has on the choices available to us. In short, as we saw in Chapter 1, doing **personal sociology** means recognizing the impact our individual position has on who we are and how we think and act, and taking responsibility for the impacts our actions have on others.

From the beginning, sociologists wanted to understand our constraints so that we might be able to change them. As sociologist Pierre Bourdieu (1998b) put it, "To those who always tax the sociologist with determinism and pessimism, I will only say that if people became fully aware of them, conscious action aimed at controlling the structural mechanisms that engender moral failure would be possible" (p. 56). In other words, we need to be honest with ourselves about the degree to which society limits our choices so that we might be empowered to make choices that are more informed and therefore more effective in helping us to attain our goals.

As individuals, we need to learn to see the degree to which we follow visible and invisible rules. We need to ask whether our current paths represent the values, norms, and goals that we really want to follow. As we have seen, the shows we watch, the things we buy, our likelihood for suicide, our chances of facing a wage gap, our perception of reality, our very selves—all are shaped by the positions we occupy. Understanding these influences empowers us to change.

PUBLIC SOCIOLOGY: TOOLS FOR CHANGE

Beyond providing a more informed understanding of why we as individuals act and think the way we do, sociology calls on us to look beyond ourselves to the world around us and ask, What might we do to make the world a better place? Sociologists since the very beginning have sought to understand and explain social processes for the purpose of shaping the future of society. **Public sociology** involves bringing the insights gained through sociological observation and analysis into the public sphere, thereby seeking to bring about positive social change. As Michael Burawoy, former president of the American Sociological Association, put it, public sociology seeks to speak to a wide audience, aiming to "enrich public debate about moral and political issues by infusing them with sociological theory and research" (Burawoy 2004:1603).

Because we construct the existing social structures through our collective and recurring actions, we bear responsibility for their consequences. Existing systems—the

> **public sociology** The process of bringing the insights gained through sociological observation and analysis into the public sphere, thereby seeking to bring about positive social change.

structure and culture we create—are not inevitable. We can choose to change them; we can act differently, as the accompanying table suggests. It can be difficult to step off the "paths of least resistance" that support the existing system (Johnson 1997), and the consequences for action and belief that run counter to the status quo can be severe. But we can do so.

What we cannot do is absolve ourselves of responsibility for the systems we end up with. In fact, to not act differently is to support the existing system of inequality. As sociologist Scott Schaffer (2004) points out, we can no longer ignore practices that violate our basic beliefs, trying to wash our hands of responsibility:

> Our hands are already dirty; the question I leave here is whether our hands will be dirtied through action intended to bring concrete, actual, enacted freedom into the world, or through our choice to preserve ourselves at the cost of all others in the here and now and in the future. (pp. 271–272)

Our cynicism and resignation only reinforce systems of oppression and violence. To not act to bring about positive change still represents a choice, and our hands are dirty either way.

By helping us to see why we think and act as we do, by helping us to clarify the relationship between belief and practice, and by helping us to better understand the consequences of difference, personal and public sociology can encourage discussion that can lead to a better future. We can use the tools of sociology to allow ourselves to enter into conversations in which we share our stories with others (both positive and negative), clarifying places where we agree and disagree, and opening ourselves up to our blind spots. We often want to avoid uncomfortable conflict, opting instead for polite discourse, but to fail to be more genuinely engaged in our cultural and structural differences virtually ensures a lack of progress toward implementing our core principles (Schaffer 2004).

> Another world is not only possible, she is on her way. On a quiet day, I can hear her breathing.
>
> **Arundhati Roy**

Citizen Activities in a Democratic Society

PRIVATE LIFE	CIVIC LIFE	
Individual activity	**Civic engagement activities**	
	Nonpolitical activities	Political participation
Family School Work	Recycling Fellowship meetings Service activities	Voting Attending political meetings Political campaigning
Cultivates personal relationships, serves individual needs—e.g., getting an education, earning a living	Provides community services and acts as a training ground for political participation	Fulfills demands of democratic citizenship

(Functions)

PRACTICING SOCIOLOGY

Change comes because people continue not only to believe that it is possible, but also to act on their hopes and dreams (see the figure on p. 391). As ethnographer Studs Terkel (2003) put it, "In all epochs, there were at first doubts and the fear of stepping forth and speaking out, but the attribute that spurred the warriors on was hope. And the *act*" (p. xviii).

We can change the world for the better. We can do so by becoming more informed about ourselves and others, and then acting on that knowledge. Here are some possibilities for action:

- *Practice personal sociology.* Become more conscious of the factors that shape your beliefs and actions.
- *Become more aware of privilege.* Identify the advantages you have, especially relative to the rest of the world; you likely have sufficient food, clothes, and shelter; you can read this; you can plan for the future; and so on.
- *Become more informed.* We have access to more information about our world now than ever. Seek it out; find out what's going on.
- *Interpret what you learn.* Analyze the information you receive. Remember that data never speak for themselves; they aren't just facts but are embedded in networks and systems that have their own interests.
- *Vote.* Elected leaders in a democracy, whether local, state, or national, are chosen by voters. It may not seem like your individual vote is significant, but the simple fact is that all those votes still add up to a winner. And even if your candidate cannot win, you can

still make a statement; for example, if you don't think any of the candidates would make a good choice, write in someone who would.
- *Participate in local politics.* Think of politics as a contact sport: Go to rallies, protests, school board meetings, city council meetings, and more. You might be surprised how much of a difference a single voice can make, especially on the local level.
- *Run for office.* Don't assume that such positions of leadership are only for others who are somehow better or more informed than you. We need more people to believe that they can lead so that we get more diversity in our leaders.
- *Volunteer.* There are local organizations in every community seeking to bring about positive social change. You might contact a local school to see if you can read to kids, work at a homeless shelter, or help build houses with Habitat for Humanity.
- *Join.* There are many organizations that provide long-term outreach opportunities, such as AmeriCorps, the Peace Corps, and the American Red Cross, in which you provide assistance to people with varieties of needs, in communities near and far.

Do You Believe You Can Effect Political Change?
External political efficacy index 1952–2008

Note: 2008 is preliminary data.

Source: American National Election Studies 2009.

in Bourdieu 1998b:55). It is only by seeing those things that limit us that we can move toward freedom.

We learn a lesson from sociology that is reminiscent of the one Ebenezer Scrooge learns in Charles Dickens' *A Christmas Carol,* written in 1843. Scrooge, a miserly businessman, thinks only of himself, caring little if anything for others, including his employee, his family, and the poor. But on Christmas Eve, he is visited by three ghosts: the Ghost of Christmas Past, the Ghost of Christmas Present, and the Ghost of Christmas Yet to Come. After each of these spirits shows him visions of their time, Scrooge repents, promising to live "an altered life" in which he will reaffirm relationships and reconnect to those around him. What is particularly interesting sociologically is the way he phrases that promise: "I will live in the Past, the Present, and the Future! The Spirits of all Three shall strive within me."

At its core, Scrooge's resolution represents what we are called to do by the sociological imagination. Just as history and biography intersect, so also do we need to understand that the past, created by the actions of ourselves and those who came before us, has shaped who we are now. As American novelist and essayist James Baldwin ([1965] 1985) wrote, "The great force of history comes from the fact that we carry it within us, are unconsciously controlled by it in many ways, and history is literally *present* in all that we do" (p. 410). Further, our present actions shape the future directions of both our lives and the lives of others in the worlds around us and of those yet to come. Like Scrooge, we can reject the myth of the isolated individual and affirm the significance of relationships and companionship (to return to one of the root word meanings of

- *Organize.* Work to bring about the world you envision; there are undoubtedly others out there who share your views. Find them and work with them, both inside and outside existing institutions, to bring about change.

- *Fight for change.* Regardless of where you are, whether in your relationships, your family, your workplace, your community, or elsewhere, work to bring about positive social change. We have the power to change the world; we can't do so in a vacuum, but if sociologists are at all correct about the social construction of reality, things could be otherwise.

As Comte wrote at sociology's very founding, "Science leads to foresight, and foresight leads to action" (quoted

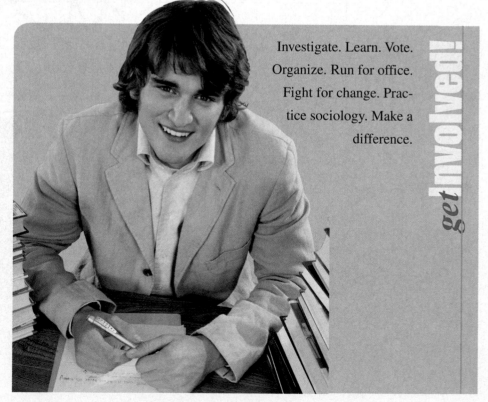

Investigate. Learn. Vote. Organize. Run for office. Fight for change. Practice sociology. Make a difference.

get involved!

sociology). By simultaneously holding the past, present, and future together in our minds, we can act to make the world a better place to live.

Sociology is more than just a noun. Sociology is a verb. It is something we do, not something we possess. Our overreliance on individualistic models, and our failure to appreciate the impact of social forces, presents a distorted picture of our freedom. An appreciation of the relationship between self and society and of the consequences of difference allows us to make more informed choices and to shape the future. It allows us to provide answers to the questions "Why do we think the way we think?" and "Why do we act the way we act?" Sociology shouldn't be something confined to college classrooms. It shouldn't be left only to professionals. We are all sociologists now, and there is work to be done.

For REVIEW

I. How and why does social change happen?
- Social change evolves out of past social practices; it represents a response by those in society to maintain social order by seeking an acceptable level of balance between stability and change; and it is influenced by the distribution of power and control over resources, which shapes what changes do or do not occur. Technological innovation has played a powerful role causing social change.

II. What factors shape the success of a social movement?
- There needs to be a sense of relative deprivation in which people have a sense that injustice exists that can and should be challenged. In addition, people must have the capacity to mobilize resources to bring about the change they seek.

III. What does it mean to practice sociology?
- Personal sociology involves better understanding the influence social factors have on our thoughts and actions and using this information to our advantage. Public sociology means taking responsibility for the collective impacts our individual actions have in shaping society and opportunity and working for positive social change.

Functionalist View

Social change is a way for society to make adjustments in order to return to a state of **stability** or balance.

The four processes of social change identified by Parsons—differentiation, adaptive upgrading, inclusion, and value generalization—stress **consensus** in society.

Social movements and protests enable us to see the dysfunctions of the existing system, and thus facilitate positive social change.

EQUILIBRIUM, CONSENSUS, STABILITY
KEY CONCEPTS

Conflict View

Groups in society that **control** valued resources can either inhibit or facilitate social change more effectively than other groups.

Though new technology can provide tools that facilitate greater freedom, those in positions of power can use it to exert greater control and surveillance.

Social change should be encouraged as a way of eliminating **inequality** and correcting social **injustice**.

CONTROL, SURVEILLANCE, VESTED INTERESTS
KEY CONCEPTS

Interactionist View

Every individual has the power to change society through the everyday **choices** he or she makes and **actions** he or she takes (i.e., words we use, relationships we build, voting, volunteering, organizing for change).

Technological innovations in communication allow us to **connect** and interact with people around the world but may also cut us off from those right next to us.

Social movements consist of the **collective activities** of individuals in search of change.

ACTION, ORGANIZATION, CONNECTION
KEY CONCEPTS

MAKE THE CONNECTION

After reviewing the chapter, answer the following questions:

1

How would each perspective explain the activism of college students described in the opening vignette (p. 373)?

2

Why does "culture lag" occur (p. 377)? Why might the interactionist perspective be particularly helpful to explain it?

3

According to each perspective, what impacts have new communication technologies (e.g. the Internet, cell phones, etc.) had on our interactions, relationships, and communities?

4

How would drawing an insight from each perspective enable you to more effectively bring about social change?

Pop Quiz

1. According to the definition, what is social change?
   a. tumultuous, revolutionary alterations that lead to changes in leadership
   b. a significant alteration over time in behavior patterns and culture
   c. regular alterations in a consistent social frame of reference
   d. subtle alterations in any social system

2. Nineteenth-century theories of social change reflect the pioneering work in biological evolution done by
   a. Albert Einstein.
   b. Harriet Martineau.
   c. James Audubon.
   d. Charles Darwin.

3. According to Talcott Parsons' equilibrium model, during which process do social institutions become more specialized in their purposes?
   a. differentiation
   b. adaptive upgrading
   c. inclusion
   d. value generalization

4. Which of the following did William F. Ogburn use to describe the period of maladjustment during which the nonmaterial culture is still struggling to adapt to new material conditions?
   a. economic shift
   b. political turmoil
   c. social change
   d. culture lag

5. The One Laptop per Child campaign was designed to overcome the problem of
   a. relative deprivation.
   b. social change.
   c. the digital divide.
   d. vested interests.

6. You are a student and do not own a car. All your close friends who are attending your college or university have vehicles of their own. You feel downtrodden and dissatisfied. You are experiencing
   a. relative deprivation.
   b. resource mobilization.
   c. false consciousness.
   d. depression.

7. It takes more than desire to start a social movement; it helps to have money, political influence, access to the media, and workers. The ways in which a social movement uses such things are referred to collectively as
   a. relative deprivation.
   b. false consciousness.
   c. resource mobilization.
   d. economic independence.

8. Karl Marx held that leaders of social movements must help workers overcome feelings of
   a. class consciousness.
   b. false consciousness.
   c. socialist consciousness.
   d. surplus value.

9. Organized collective activities that promote autonomy and self-determination, as well as improvements in the quality of life, are referred to as
   a. new social movements.
   b. social revolutions.
   c. resource mobilizations.
   d. crazes.

10. Recognizing the impact our individual position has on who we are and how we think and act, and taking responsibility for the impacts our actions have on others is known as
    a. resource mobilization.
    b. false consciousness.
    c. public sociology.
    d. personal sociology.

1. (b); 2. (d); 3. (b); 4. (d); 5. (c); 6. (a); 7. (c); 8. (b); 9. (a); 10. (d)

A

Absolute poverty   A minimum level of subsistence that no family should be expected to live below.   *250*

Achieved status   A social position that a person attains largely through his or her own efforts.   *103*

Activity theory   A theory of aging that suggests that those elderly people who remain active and socially involved will be best adjusted.   *94*

Adoption   In a legal sense, a process that allows for the transfer of the legal rights, responsibilities, and privileges of parenthood to a new legal parent or parents.   *165*

Affirmative action   Positive efforts to recruit minority group members or women for jobs, promotions, and educational opportunities.   *324*

Ageism   Prejudice and discrimination based on a person's age.   *95*

Agency   The freedom individuals have to choose and to act.   *7*

Agrarian society   The most technologically advanced form of preindustrial society. Members are engaged primarily in the production of food, but they increase their crop yields through technological innovations such as the plow.   *122*

Alienation   Loss of control over our creative human capacity to produce, separation from the products we make, and isolation from our fellow producers.   *115*

Amalgamation   The process through which a majority group and a minority group combine to form a new group.   *327*

Anomie   Durkheim's term for the loss of direction felt in a society when social control of individual behavior has become ineffective.   *13*

Anomie theory of deviance   Robert Merton's theory of deviance as an adaptation of socially prescribed goals or of the means governing their attainment, or both.   *143*

Anticipatory socialization   Processes of socialization in which a person "rehearses" for future positions, occupations, and social relationships.   *89*

Anti-Semitism   Anti-Jewish prejudice.   *337*

Apartheid   A former policy of the South African government, designed to maintain the separation of Blacks and other non-Whites from the dominant Whites.   *329*

Applied sociology   The use of the discipline of sociology with the specific intent of yielding practical applications for human behavior and organizations.   *18*

Argot   Specialized language used by members of a group or subculture.   *63*

Ascribed status   A social position assigned to a person by society without regard for the person's unique talents or characteristics.   *104*

Assimilation   The process through which a person forsakes his or her own cultural tradition to become part of a different culture.   *327*

Authority   Institutionalized power that is recognized by the people over whom it is exercised.   *211*

Avatar   A person's online representation as a character, whether in the form of a 2-D or 3-D image or simply through text.   *112*

B

Bilateral descent   A kinship system in which both sides of a person's family are regarded as equally important.   *155*

Bisexual   A category of sexual orientation that includes those who are attracted to both men and women.   *298*

Black power   A political philosophy, promoted by many younger Blacks in the 1960s, that supported the creation of Black-controlled political and economic institutions.   *331*

Borderlands   The area of common culture along the border between Mexico and the United States.   *277*

Bourgeoisie   Karl Marx's term for the capitalist class, comprising the owners of the means of production.   *241*

Brain drain   The immigration to the United States and other industrialized nations of skilled workers, professionals, and technicians who are needed in their home countries.   *349*

Bureaucracy   A component of formal organization that uses rules and hierarchical ranking to achieve efficiency.   *114*

Bureaucratization   The process by which a group, organization, or social movement increasingly relies on technical-rational decision making in the pursuit of efficiency.   *117*

C

Capitalism   An economic system based on private property, in which profit-seeking individuals, companies, and corporations compete in the marketplace.   *212*

Caste   A hereditary rank, usually religiously dictated, that tends to be fixed and immobile.   *237*

Causal logic   The relationship between a condition or variable and a particular consequence, with one event leading to the other.   *28*

Charismatic authority   Power made legitimate by a leader's exceptional personal or emotional appeal to his or her followers.   *211*

Class   A group of people who have a similar level of economic resources.   *241*

Class consciousness   In Karl Marx's view, a subjective awareness held by members of a class regarding their common vested interests and need for collective political action to bring about social change.   *241*

Class system A social ranking based primarily on economic position in which achieved characteristics can influence social mobility. *238*

Classical theory An approach to the study of formal organizations that views workers as being motivated almost entirely by economic rewards. *119*

Clinical sociology The use of the discipline of sociology with the specific intent of altering social relationships or restructuring social institutions. *20*

Closed system A social system in which there is little or no possibility of individual social mobility. *239*

Coalition A temporary or permanent alliance geared toward a common goal. *110*

Code of ethics The standards of acceptable behavior developed by and for members of a profession. *41*

Cognitive theory of development The theory that children's thought progresses through four stages of development. *79*

Cohabitation The practice of a man and a woman living together in a sexual relationship without being married. *169*

Colonialism The maintenance of political, social, economic, and cultural dominance over a people by a foreign power for an extended period. *265*

Color-blind racism The use of race-neutral principles to perpetuate a racially unequal status quo. *320*

Conflict perspective A sociological approach that assumes that social behavior is best understood in terms of tension between groups over power or the allocation of resources, including housing, money, access to services, and political representation. *17*

Conformity The act of going along with peers—individuals of our own status who have no special right to direct our behavior. *131*

Contact hypothesis The theory that in cooperative circumstances interracial contact between people of equal status will reduce prejudice. *326*

Content analysis The systematic coding and objective recording of data, guided by some rationale. *39*

Control group The subjects in an experiment who are not introduced to the independent variable by the researcher. *36*

Control theory A view of conformity and deviance that suggests that our connection to members of society leads us to systematically conform to society's norms. *134*

Control variable A factor that is held constant to test the relative impact of an independent variable. *31*

Correlation A relationship between two variables in which a change in one coincides with a change in the other. *29*

Correspondence principle The tendency of schools to promote the values expected of individuals in each social class and to prepare students for the types of jobs typically held by members of their class. *186*

Counterculture A subculture that deliberately opposes certain aspects of the larger culture. *65*

Credentialism An increase in the lowest level of education required to enter a field. *186*

Crime A violation of criminal law for which some governmental authority applies formal penalties. *137*

Cultural capital Our tastes, knowledge, attitudes, language, and ways of thinking that we exchange in interaction with others. *243*

Cultural relativism The viewing of people's behavior from the perspective of their own culture. *66*

Cultural transmission A school of criminology that argues that criminal behavior is learned through social interactions. *144*

Cultural universal A common practice or belief shared by all societies. *50*

Culture The totality of our shared language, knowledge, material objects, and behavior. *48*

Culture lag A period of adjustment when the nonmaterial culture is still struggling to adapt to new material conditions. *55*

Culture shock The feelings of disorientation, uncertainty, and even fear that people experience when they encounter unfamiliar cultural practices. *65*

Culture-bound syndrome A disease or illness that cannot be understood apart from some specific social context. *346*

Curanderismo Latino folk medicine, a form of holistic health care and healing. *354*

D

Degradation ceremony An aspect of the socialization process within some total institutions, in which people are subjected to humiliating rituals. *90*

Deindustrialization The systematic, widespread withdrawal of investment in basic aspects of productivity, such as factories and plants. *217*

Democracy In a literal sense, government by the people. *220*

Denomination A large, organized religion that is not officially linked to the state or government. *196*

Dependency theory An approach that contends that industrialized nations continue to exploit developing countries for their own gain. *266*

Dependent variable The variable in a causal relationship that is subject to the influence of another variable. *28*

Deviance Behavior that violates the standards of conduct or expectations of a group or society. *135*

Dictatorship A government in which one person has nearly total power to make and enforce laws. *220*

Differential association   A theory of deviance that holds that violation of rules results from exposure to attitudes favorable to criminal acts.   *144*

Differential justice   Differences in the way social control is exercised over different groups.   *147*

Diffusion   The process by which a cultural item spreads from group to group or society to society.   *52*

Digital divide   The relative lack of access to the latest technologies among low-income groups, racial and ethnic minorities, rural residents, and the citizens of developing countries.   *256*

Discovery   The process of making known or sharing the existence of an aspect of reality.   *52*

Discrimination   The denial of opportunities and equal rights to individuals and groups because of prejudice or other arbitrary reasons.   *320*

Disengagement theory   A theory of aging that suggests that society and the aging individual mutually sever many of their relationships.   *93*

Domestic partnership   Two unrelated adults who share a mutually caring relationship, reside together, and agree to be jointly responsible for their dependents, basic living expenses, and other common necessities.   *171*

Dominant ideology   A set of cultural beliefs and practices that helps to maintain powerful social, economic, and political interests.   *62*

Downsizing   Reductions in a company's workforce as part of deindustrialization.   *218*

Dramaturgical approach   A view of social interaction in which people are seen as theatrical performers.   *78*

E

Ecclesia   A religious organization that claims to include most or all members of a society and is recognized as the national or official religion.   *196*

Economic system   The social institution through which goods and services are produced, distributed, and consumed.   *212*

Education   A formal process of instruction in which some people consciously teach while others adopt the social role of learner.   *180*

Egalitarian family   An authority pattern in which spouses are regarded as equals.   *160*

Elite model   A view of society as being ruled by a small group of individuals who share a common set of political and economic interests.   *224*

Endogamy   The restriction of mate selection to people within the same group.   *161*

Environmental justice   A legal strategy based on claims that racial minorities are subjected disproportionately to environmental hazards.   *362*

Equilibrium model   The view that society tends toward a state of stability or balance.   *377*

Established sect   A religious group that is the outgrowth of a sect, yet remains isolated from society.   *197*

Estate system   A system of stratification under which peasants were required to work land leased to them by nobles in exchange for military protection and other services. Also known as feudalism.   *238*

Esteem   The reputation that a specific person has earned within an occupation.   *245*

Ethnic group   A group that is set apart from others primarily because of its national origin or distinctive cultural patterns.   *314*

Ethnocentrism   The tendency to assume that one's own culture and way of life represent what's normal or are superior to all others.   *65*

Ethnography   The study of an entire social setting through extended systematic observation.   *35*

Evolutionary theory   A theory of social change that holds that society is moving in a definite direction.   *376*

Exogamy   The requirement that people select a mate outside certain groups.   *161*

Experiment   An artificially created situation that allows a researcher to manipulate variables.   *36*

Experimental group   The subjects in an experiment who are exposed to an independent variable introduced by a researcher.   *36*

Exploitation theory   A belief that views racial subordination in the United States as a manifestation of the class system inherent in capitalism.   *324*

Expressive leader   The person in the family who bears responsibility for the maintenance of harmony and internal emotional affairs.   *303*

Expulsion   The systematic removal of a group of people from society.   *327*

Extended family   A family in which relatives—such as grandparents, aunts, or uncles—live in the same household as parents and their children.   *156*

F

Face-work   The efforts people make to maintain a proper image and avoid public embarrassment.   *78*

False consciousness   A term used by Karl Marx to describe an attitude held by members of a class that does not accurately reflect their objective position.   *241*

Familism   Pride in the extended family, expressed through the maintenance of close ties and strong obligations to kinfolk outside the immediate family.   *164*

Feminism   The belief in social, economic, and political equality for women.   *294*

Folkway   Norms governing everyday behavior, whose violation raises comparatively little concern.   *59*

Force   The actual or threatened use of coercion to impose one's will on others.   *211*

Formal norm   A norm that generally has been written down and that specifies strict punishments for violators.   *59*

Formal social control   Social control that is carried out by authorized agents, such as police officers, judges, school administrators, and employers.   *133*

Functionalist definition of families   A definition of families that focuses on what families do for society and for their members.   *158*

Functionalist definition of religion   The idea that religion unifies believers into a community through shared practices and a common set of beliefs relative to sacred things.   *193*

Functionalist perspective   A sociological approach that emphasizes the way in which the parts of a society are structured to maintain its stability.   *17*

Fundamentalism   Rigid adherence to core religious doctrines, often accompanied by a literal application of scripture or historical beliefs to today's world.   *194*

G

Gemeinschaft   A close-knit community, often found in rural areas, in which strong personal bonds unite members.   *120*

Gender   The social and cultural significance that we attach to the biological differences of sex.   *288*

Gender role   Expectations regarding the proper behavior, attitudes, and activities of males or females.   *81*

Generalized other   The attitudes, viewpoints, and expectations of society as a whole that a child takes into account in his or her behavior.   *77*

Genocide   The deliberate, systematic killing of an entire people or nation.   *326*

Gerontology   The study of the sociological and psychological aspects of aging and the problems of the aged.   *94*

Gesellschaft   A community, often urban, that is large and impersonal, with little commitment to the group or consensus on values.   *120*

Glass ceiling   An invisible barrier that blocks the promotion of a qualified individual in a work environment because of the individual's gender, race, or ethnicity.   *304*

Globalization   The worldwide integration of government policies, cultures, social movements, and financial markets through trade and the exchange of ideas.   *20*

Goal displacement   Overzealous conformity to official regulations of a bureaucracy.   *116*

Gross national income (GNI)   The total value of a nation's goods and services.   *273*

Group   Any number of people with shared norms, values, and goals who interact with one another on a regular basis.   *108*

H

Hate crime   A criminal offense committed because of the offender's bias against an individual based on race, religion, ethnicity, national origin, or sexual orientation.   *320*

Hawthorne effect   The unintended influence that observers of experiments can have on their subjects.   *36*

Health   As defined by the World Health Organization, a state of complete physical, mental, and social well-being, not merely the absence of disease and infirmity.   *346*

Heteronormativity   A term that sociologists use to describe the cultural presupposition that heterosexuality is the appropriate standard for sexual identity and practice and that alternative sexualities are deviant, abnormal, or wrong.   *299*

Heterosexual   A category of sexual orientation that includes those who are sexually attracted to members of the opposite sex.   *298*

Hidden curriculum   Standards of behavior that are deemed proper by society and are taught subtly in schools.   *185*

Holistic medicine   Therapies in which the health care practitioner considers the person's physical, mental, emotional, and spiritual characteristics.   *359*

Homogamy   The conscious or unconscious tendency to select a mate with personal characteristics and interests similar to one's own.   *162*

Homosexual   A category of sexual orientation that includes those who are attracted to members of the same sex.   *298*

Horizontal mobility   The movement of an individual from one social position to another of the same rank.   *240*

Horticultural society   A preindustrial society in which people plant seeds and crops rather than merely subsist on available foods.   *121*

Hospice care   Treatment of the terminally ill in their own homes, or in special hospital units or other facilities, with the goal of helping them to die comfortably, without pain.   *96*

Human ecology   The area of study concerned with the interrelationships between people and their environment.   *361*

Human relations approach   An approach to the study of formal organizations that emphasizes the role of people, communication, and participation in a bureaucracy and tends to focus on the informal structure of the organization.   *120*

Human rights   Universal moral rights possessed by all people because they are human.   *279*

Hunting-and-gathering society   A preindustrial society in which people rely on whatever foods and fibers are readily available in order to survive.   *121*

Hypothesis   A testable statement about the relationship between two or more variables.   *27*

I

I   The acting self that exists in relation to the Me.   *76*

Ideal type   An abstract model of the essential characteristics of a phenomenon.   *115*

Impression management   The altering of the presentation of the self in order to create distinctive appearances and satisfy particular audiences.   *78*

Incest taboo   The prohibition of sexual relationships between certain culturally specified relatives.   *161*

Incidence   The number of new cases of a specific disorder that occur within a given population during a stated period.   *353*

Income   Wages and salaries measured over some period of time, such as per hour or year.   *247*

Independent variable   The variable in a causal relationship that causes or influences a change in a second variable.   *28*

Index crimes   The eight types of crime reported annually by the FBI in the *Uniform Crime Reports:* murder, forcible rape, robbery, aggravated assault, burglary, larceny-theft, motor vehicle theft, and arson.   *137*

Industrial society   A society that depends on mechanization to produce its goods and services.   *122*

Infant mortality rate   The number of deaths of infants under one year old per 1000 live births in a given year.   *349*

Influence   The exercise of power through a process of persuasion.   *211*

Informal economy   Transfers of money, goods, or services that are not reported to the government.   *215*

Informal norm   A norm that is generally understood but not precisely recorded.   *59*

Informal social control   Social control that is carried out casually by ordinary people through such means as laughter, smiles, and ridicule.   *133*

In-group   Any group or category to which people feel they belong.   *108*

Innovation   The process of introducing a new idea or object to a culture through discovery or invention.   *51*

Institutional discrimination   The denial of opportunities and equal rights to individuals and groups that results from the normal operations of a society.   *303*

Instrumental leader   The person in the family who bears responsibility for the completion of tasks, focuses on distant goals, and manages the external relationship between one's family and other social institutions.   *303*

Interactionist perspective   A sociological approach that generalizes about everyday forms of social interaction in order to explain society as a whole.   *17*

Intergenerational mobility   Changes in the social position of children relative to their parents.   *240*

Interview   A face-to-face or telephone questioning of a respondent to obtain desired information.   *34*

Intragenerational mobility   Changes in social position within a person's adult life.   *240*

Invention   The combination of existing cultural items into a form that did not exist before.   *52*

Iron law of oligarchy   The principle that all organizations, even democratic ones, tend to develop into bureaucracies ruled by an elite few.   *119*

K

Kinship   The state of being related to others.   *155*

L

Labeling theory   An approach to deviance that attempts to explain why certain people are viewed as deviants while others engaged in the same behavior are not.   *146*

Laissez-faire   The principle that people should be able to compete freely, without government interference, in the capitalist marketplace.   *213*

Language   A system of shared symbols; it includes speech, written characters, numerals, symbols, and nonverbal gestures and expressions.   *55*

Law   Formal norms enforced by the state.   *59*

Liberation theology   Use of a church, primarily Roman Catholicism, in a political effort to eliminate poverty, discrimination, and other forms of injustice from a secular society.   *203*

Life chances   The opportunities people have to provide themselves with material goods, positive living conditions, and favorable life experiences.   *255*

Life course approach   A research orientation in which sociologists and other social scientists look closely at the social factors that influence people throughout their lives, from birth to death.   *88*

Looking-glass self   A theory that we become who we are based on how we think others see us.   *76*

Luddites   Rebellious craft workers in 19th-century England who destroyed new factory machinery as part of their resistance to the Industrial Revolution.   *384*

M

Machismo   A sense of virility, personal worth, and pride in one's maleness.   *164*

Macrosociology   Sociological investigation that concentrates on large-scale phenomena or entire civilizations.   *15*

Master status   A status that dominates others and thereby determines a person's general position in society.   *104*

Material culture   The physical or technological aspects of our daily lives.   *53*

Matriarchy   A society in which women dominate in family decision making.   *159*

Matrilineal descent   A kinship system in which only the mother's relatives are significant.   *156*

McDonaldization   The process by which the principles of efficiency, calculability, predictability, and control shape organization and decision making, in the United States and around the world.   *117*

Me   The socialized self that plans actions and judges performances based on the standards we have learned from others.   *76*

Mean   A number calculated by adding a series of values and then dividing by the number of values.   *34*

Mechanical solidarity   Social cohesion based on shared experiences, knowledge, and skills in which things function more or less the way they always have, with minimal change.   *120*

Median   The midpoint, or number that divides a series of values into two groups of equal numbers of values.   *34*

Microsociology   Sociological investigation that stresses the study of small groups and the analysis of our everyday experiences and interactions.   *15*

Midlife crisis   A stressful period of self-evaluation that begins at about age 40.   *90*

Minority group   A subordinate group whose members, even if they represent a numeric majority, have significantly less control or power over their own lives than the members of a dominant or majority group have over theirs.   *314*

Mixed economy   An economic system that combines elements of both capitalism and socialism.   *214*

Mode   The single most common value in a series of scores.   *35*

Model or ideal minority   A subordinate group whose members supposedly have succeeded economically, socially, and educationally despite past prejudice and discrimination.   *332*

Modernization   The far-reaching process by which nations pass from traditional forms of social organization toward those characteristic of post-Industrial Revolution societies.   *265*

Monarchy   A form of government headed by a single member of a royal family, usually a king, queen, or some other hereditary ruler.   *219*

Monogamy   A form of marriage in which one woman and one man are married only to each other.   *156*

Monopoly   Control of a market by a single business firm.   *213*

Morbidity rate   The incidence of disease in a given population.   *353*

Mores   Norms deemed highly necessary to the welfare of a society.   *59*

Mortality rate   The incidence of death in a given population.   *353*

Multinational corporation   A commercial organization that is headquartered in one country but does business throughout the world.   *267*

Multiple masculinities   The idea that men learn and play a full range of gender roles.   *292*

N

Natural science   The study of the physical features of nature and the ways in which they interact and change.   *9*

Neocolonialism   Continuing dependence of former colonies on foreign countries.   *266*

New religious movement (NRM) or cult   A small, alternative faith community that represents either a new religion or a major innovation in an existing faith.   *199*

New social movement   An organized collective activity that addresses values and social identities, as well as improvements in the quality of life.   *388*

Nonmaterial culture   Ways of using material objects, as well as customs, ideas, expressions, beliefs, knowledge, philosophies, governments, and patterns of communication.   *53*

Nonverbal communication   The use of gestures, facial expressions, and other visual images to communicate.   *57*

Norm   An established standard of behavior maintained by a society.   *59*

Nuclear family   A married couple and their unmarried children living together.   *156*

O

Obedience   Compliance with higher authorities in a hierarchical structure.   *131*

Observation   A research technique in which an investigator collects information through direct participation and/or by closely watching a group or community.   *35*

Offshoring   The transfer of work to foreign contractors.   *218*

Oligarchy   A form of government in which a few individuals rule.   *220*

Open system   A social system in which the position of each individual is influenced by his or her achieved status.   *239*

Operational definition   Transformation of an abstract concept into indicators that are observable and measurable.   *27*

Organic solidarity   A collective consciousness that rests on mutual interdependence, characteristic of societies with a complex division of labor.   *121*

Organized crime   The work of a group that regulates relations among criminal enterprises involved in illegal activities, including prostitution, gambling, and the smuggling and sale of illegal drugs.   *140*

Out-group   A group or category to which people feel they do not belong.   *108*

P

Party   The capacity to organize to accomplish some particular goal.   *242*

Patriarchy   A society in which men dominate in family decision making.   *159*

Patrilineal descent   A kinship system in which only the father's relatives are significant.   *155*

Peace The absence of war, or more broadly, a proactive effort to develop cooperative relations among nations. *229*

Personal sociology The process of recognizing the impact our individual position has on who we are and how we think and act, and of taking responsibility for the impacts our actions have on others. *118*

Pluralism Mutual respect for one another's cultures among the various groups in a society, which allows minorities to express their own cultures without experiencing prejudice. *329*

Pluralist model A view of society in which many competing groups within the community have access to government, so that no single group is dominant. *226*

Political system The social institution that is founded on a recognized set of procedures for implementing and achieving society's goals. *219*

Politics In Harold Lasswell's words, "who gets what, when, and how." *219*

Polyandry A form of polygamy in which a woman may have more than one husband at the same time. *157*

Polygamy A form of marriage in which an individual may have several husbands or wives simultaneously. *156*

Polygyny A form of polygamy in which a man may have more than one wife at the same time. *157*

Postindustrial society A society whose economic system is engaged primarily in the processing and control of information. *122*

Postmodern society A technologically sophisticated, pluralistic, interconnected, globalized society. *122*

Power The ability to exercise one's will over others even if they resist. *211*

Power elite A small group of military, industrial, and government leaders who control the fate of the United States. *224*

Prejudice A negative attitude toward an entire category of people, often an ethnic or racial minority. *319*

Prestige The respect and admiration that an occupation holds in a society. *245*

Prevalence The total number of cases of a specific disorder that exist at a given time. *353*

Primary group A small group characterized by intimate, face-to-face association and cooperation. *108*

Private troubles Obstacles that individuals face as individuals rather than as a consequence of their social position. *4*

Profane The ordinary and commonplace elements of life, as distinguished from the sacred. *103*

Proletariat Karl Marx's term for the working class in a capitalist society who lack ownership of the means of production. *241*

Protestant ethic Max Weber's term for the disciplined commitment to worldly labor driven by a desire to bring glory to God, shared by followers of Martin Luther and John Calvin. *202*

Public issues Obstacles that individuals in similar positions face; also referred to by sociologists as "social problems." *4*

Public sociology The process of bringing the insights gained through sociological observation and analysis into the public sphere, thereby seeking to bring about positive social change. *390*

Q

Qualitative research Research that relies on what is seen in field or naturalistic settings more than on statistical data. *35*

Quantitative research Research that collects and reports data primarily in numerical form. *34*

Questionnaire A printed, written, or computerized form used to obtain information from a respondent. *34*

R

Racial formation A sociohistorical process in which racial categories are created, inhibited, transformed, and destroyed. *316*

Racial group A group that is set apart from others because of physical differences that have taken on social significance. *314*

Racial profiling Any police-initiated action based on race, ethnicity, or national origin rather than on a person's behavior. *322*

Racism The belief that one race is supreme and all others are innately inferior. *319*

Random sample A sample for which every member of an entire population has the same chance of being selected. *30*

Rational-legal authority Authority based on formally agreed upon and accepted rules, principles, and procedures of conduct that are established in order to accomplish goals in the most efficient manner possible. *211*

Reference group Any group that individuals use as a standard for evaluating themselves and their own behavior. *109*

Relative deprivation The conscious feeling of a negative discrepancy between legitimate expectations and present actualities. *385*

Relative poverty A floating standard of deprivation by which people at the bottom of a society, whatever their lifestyles, are judged to be disadvantaged in comparison with the nation as a whole. *251*

Reliability The extent to which a measure produces consistent results. *31*

Religious belief A statement to which members of a particular religion adhere. *194*

Religious experience The feeling or perception of being in direct contact with the ultimate reality, such as a divine being, or of being overcome with religious emotion. *195*

Religious ritual   A practice required or expected of members of a faith.   *195*

Remittances   The monies that immigrants return to their families of origin; also called *remesas*.   *278*

Representative democracy   A form of government in which certain individuals are selected to speak for the people.   *221*

Research design   A detailed plan or method for obtaining data scientifically.   *32*

Resocialization   The process of discarding former behavior patterns and accepting new ones as part of a transition in one's life.   *89*

Resource mobilization   The ways in which a social movement utilizes such resources as money, political influence, access to the media, and personnel.   *386*

Rite of passage   A ritual marking the symbolic transition from one social position to another.   *88*

Role conflict   The situation that occurs when incompatible expectations arise from two or more social statuses held by the same person.   *105*

Role exit   The process of disengagement from a role that is central to one's self-identity in order to establish a new role and identity.   *106*

Role strain   The difficulty that arises when the same social status imposes conflicting demands and expectations.   *106*

Role taking   The process of mentally assuming the perspective of another and responding from that imagined viewpoint.   *77*

S

Sacred   Elements beyond everyday life that inspire respect, awe, and even fear.   *192*

Sample   A selection from a larger population that is statistically representative of that population.   *30*

Sanction   A penalty or reward for conduct concerning a social norm.   *61*

Sandwich generation   The generation of adults who simultaneously try to meet the competing needs of their parents and their children.   *91*

Sapir-Whorf hypothesis   The idea that the language a person uses shapes his or her perception of reality and therefore his or her thoughts and actions.   *55*

Science   The body of knowledge obtained by methods based on systematic observation.   *9*

Scientific management approach   Another name for the classical theory of formal organizations.   *119*

Scientific method   A systematic, organized series of steps that ensures maximum objectivity and consistency in researching a problem.   *26*

Second shift   The double burden—work outside the home followed by child care and housework—that many women face and few men share equitably.   *305*

Secondary analysis   A variety of research techniques that make use of previously collected and publicly accessible information and data.   *36*

Secondary group   A formal, impersonal group in which there is little social intimacy or mutual understanding.   *108*

Sect   A relatively small religious group that has broken away from some other religious organization to renew what it considers the original vision of the faith.   *197*

Secularization   Religion's diminishing influence in the public sphere, especially in politics and the economy.   *199*

Segregation   The physical separation of two groups of people in terms of residence, workplace, and social events; often imposed on a minority group by a dominant group.   *329*

Self   Our sense of who we are, distinct from others, and shaped by the unique combination of our social interactions.   *75*

Serial monogamy   A form of marriage in which a person may have several spouses in his or her lifetime, but only one spouse at a time.   *156*

Sex   The biological differences between males and females.   *288*

Sexism   The ideology that one sex is superior to the other.   *303*

Sexuality   Denotes our identities and activities as sexual beings.   *297*

Sexual orientation   The categories of people to whom we are sexually attracted.   *298*

Sick role   Societal expectations about the attitudes and behavior of a person viewed as being ill.   *348*

Significant other   An individual who is most important in the development of the self, such as a parent, friend, or teacher.   *76*

Single-parent family   A family in which only one parent is present to care for the children.   *166*

Slavery   A system of enforced servitude in which some people are owned by others as property.   *237*

Social change   Significant alteration over time in behavior patterns and culture, including norms and values.   *375*

Social control   The techniques and strategies for preventing deviant human behavior in any society.   *131*

Social disorganization theory   The theory that attributes increases in crime and deviance to the absence or breakdown of communal relationships and social institutions, such as the family, school, church, and local government.   *145*

Social epidemiology   The study of the distribution of disease, impairment, and general health status across a population.   *353*

Social inequality   A condition in which members of society have different amounts of wealth, prestige, or power.   *8*

Social institution   An organized pattern of beliefs and behavior centered on basic social needs.   *113*

Social interaction   The shared experiences through which people relate to one another.   *102*

Social mobility   Movement of individuals or groups from one position in a society's stratification system to another.   *239*

Social movement   An organized collective activity to bring about or resist fundamental change in an existing group or society.   *385*

Social network   A series of social relationships that links individuals directly to others, and through them indirectly to still more people.   *111*

Social role   A set of expectations for people who occupy a given social position or status.   *105*

Social science   The study of the social features of humans and the ways in which they interact and change.   *9*

Social structure   The way in which a society is organized into predictable relationships.   *103*

Socialism   An economic system under which the means of production and distribution are collectively owned.   *213*

Socialization   The lifelong process through which people learn the attitudes, values, and behaviors appropriate for members of a particular culture.   *72*

Societal-reaction approach   Another name for *labeling theory.*   *146*

Society   The structure of relationships within which culture is created and shared through regularized patterns of social interaction.   *49*

Sociobiology   The systematic study of how biology affects human social behavior.   *50*

Socioeconomic status (SES)   A measure of class that is based on income, education, occupation, and related variables.   *247*

Sociological imagination   An awareness of the relationship between who we are as individuals and the social forces that shape our lives.   *4*

Sociology   The systematic study of the relationship between the individual and society and of the consequences of difference.   *4*

Status   The social positions we occupy relative to others.   *103*

Status group   People who share the same preceived level of prestige.   *242*

Stereotype   An unreliable generalization about all members of a group that does not recognize individual differences within the group.   *316*

Stigma   A label used to devalue members of certain social groups.   *137*

Stratification   A structured ranking of entire groups of people that perpetuates unequal economic rewards and power in a society.   *237*

Subculture   A segment of society that shares a distinctive pattern of mores, folkways, and values that differs from the pattern of the larger society.   *63*

Substantive definition of religion   The idea that religion has a unique content or substance relating to the sacred that separates it from other forms of knowledge and belief.   *192*

Substantive definition of the family   A definition of the family based on blood, meaning shared genetic heritage, and law, meaning social recognition and affirmation of the bond including both marriage and adoption.   *155*

Survey   A study, generally in the form of an interview or questionnaire, that provides researchers with information about how people think and act.   *32*

Symbol   A gesture, object, or word that forms the basis of human communication.   *77*

Symbolic ethnicity   An ethnic identity that emphasizes concerns such as ethnic food or political issues rather than deeper ties to one's ethnic heritage.   *338*

T

Teacher-expectancy effect   The impact that a teacher's expectations about a student's performance may have on the student's actual achievements.   *185*

Technology   Cultural information about how to use the material resources of the environment to satisfy human needs and desires.   *55*

Terrorism   The use or threat of violence against random or symbolic targets in pursuit of political aims.   *229*

Theory   In sociology a set of statements that seeks to explain problems, actions, or behavior.   *10*

Total institution   An institution that regulates all aspects of a person's life under a single authority, such as a prison, the military, a mental hospital, or a convent.   *89*

Totalitarianism   Virtually complete government control and surveillance over all aspects of a society's social and political life.   *220*

Tracking   The practice of placing students in specific curriculum groups on the basis of their test scores and other criteria.   *185*

Traditional authority   Legitimate power conferred by custom and accepted practice.   *211*

Trained incapacity   The tendency of workers in a bureaucracy to become so specialized that they develop blind spots and fail to notice potential problems.   *115*

Transgender   People who appear to be biologically one sex but who identify with the gender of another.   *298*

Transnational crime   Crime that occurs across multiple national borders.   *140*

U

Underclass   The long-term poor who lack training and skills.   *252*

V

Validity   The degree to which a measure or scale truly reflects the phenomenon under study.   *31*

Value   A collective conception of what is considered good, desirable, and proper—or bad, undesirable, and improper—in a culture.   *57*

Value neutrality   Max Weber's term for objectivity of sociologists in the interpretation of data.   *42*

Variable   A measurable trait or characteristic that is subject to change under different conditions.   *27*

Vertical mobility   The movement of an individual from one social position to another of a different rank.   *240*

Vested interests   Those people or groups who will suffer in the event of social change and who have a stake in maintaining the status quo.   *378*

Victimization survey   A questionnaire or interview given to a sample of the population to determine whether people have been victims of crime.   *139*

Victimless crime   A term used by sociologists to describe the willing exchange among adults of widely desired, but illegal, goods and services.   *139*

W

War   Conflict between organizations that possess trained combat forces equipped with deadly weapons.   *226*

Wealth   The total of all a person's material assets, including savings, land, stocks, and other types of property, minus their debt at a single point in time.   *247*

White-collar crime   Illegal acts committed by affluent, "respectable" individuals in the course of business activities.   *137*

World systems analysis   A view of the global economic system as one divided between certain industrialized nations that control wealth and developing countries that are controlled and exploited.   *266*

Aaronson, Daniel, and Bhashkar Mazumder. 2007. "Intergenerational Economic Mobility in the U.S., 1940 to 2000." FRB Chicago Working Paper No. WP 2005-12, revised February 2007. Federal Reserve Bank of Chicago. Accessed June 21, 2008 (http://ssrn.com/abstract=869435).

Abercrombie, Nicholas, Stephen Hill, and Bryan S. Turner. 1980. *The Dominant Ideology Thesis.* London: George Allen and Unwin.

———. 1990. *Dominant Ideologies.* Cambridge, MA: Unwin Hyman.

———. 2006. *The Penguin Dictionary of Sociology,* 5th ed. New York: Penguin Books.

Aberle, David E., A. K. Cohen, A. K. Davis, M. J. Leng Jr., and F. N. Sutton. 1950. "The Functional Prerequisites of a Society." *Ethics* 60 (January): 100–111.

Abma, Joyce C., Gladys M. Martinez, William D. Mosher, and Brittany S. Dawson. 2004. "Teenagers in the United States: Sexual Activity, Contraceptive Use, and Childbearing, 2002." National Center for Health Statistics. *Vital and Health Statistics* 23 (24). Accessed May 12, 2010 (http://www.cdc.gov/nchs/data/series/sr_23/sr23_024.pdf).

Adair-Toteff, Christopher. 2005. "Max Weber's Charisma." *Journal of Classical Sociology* 5 (2): 189–204.

Adams, Jimi. 2007. "Stained Glass Makes the Ceiling Visible: Organizational Opposition to Women in Congregational Leadership." *Gender and Society* 21 (February): 80–115.

Adams, Samantha, and Antoinette de Bont. 2007. "Information Rx: Prescribing Good Consumerism and Responsible Citizenship." *Health Care Analysis* 15 (4): 273–290.

Addams, Jane. 1910. *Twenty Years at Hull-House.* New York: Macmillan.

———. 1930. *The Second Twenty Years at Hull-House.* New York: Macmillan.

Adler, Patricia A., and Peter Adler. 1985. "From Idealism to Pragmatic Detachment: The Academic Performance of College Athletes." *Sociology of Education* 58 (October): 241–250.

——— 1996. "Preadolescent Clique Stratification and the Hierarchy of Identity." *Sociological Inquiry* 66 (2): 111–142.

——— 2004. *Paradise Laborers: Hotel Work in the Global Economy.* Ithaca, NY: Cornell University Press.

——— 2007. "The Demedicalization of Self-Injury: From Psychopathology to Sociological Deviance." *Journal of Contemporary Ethnography* 36 (October): 537–570.

Adler, Patricia A., Peter Adler, and John M. Johnson. 1992. "Street Corner Society Revisited." *Journal of Contemporary Ethnography* 21 (April): 3–10.

Adler, Patricia A., Steve J. Kless, and Peter Adler. 1992. "Socialization to Gender Roles: Popularity Among Elementary School Boys and Girls." *Sociology of Education* 65 (July): 169–187.

Alimahomed, Sabrina. 2010. "Thinking Outside the Rainbow: Women of Color Redefining Queer Politics and Identity." *Social Identities* 16 (2): 151–168.

Allen, John L. 2008. *Student Atlas of World Politics,* 8th ed. New York: McGraw-Hill.

Allport, Gordon W. 1979. *The Nature of Prejudice,* 25th anniversary ed. Reading, MA: Addison-Wesley.

Alter, Alexandria. 2007. "Is This Man Cheating on His Wife?" *The Wall Street Journal,* August 10, p. W1. Accessed June 3, 2008 (http://online.wsj.com/article/SB118670164592393622.html).

Alvord, Lori Arviso, and Elizabeth Cohen Van Pelt. 1999. *The Scalpel and the Silver Bear.* New York: Bantam.

Amato, Paul R., and Alan Booth. 1997. *A Generation at Risk.* Cambridge, MA: Harvard University Press.

American Academy of Cosmetic Surgery. 2010. "American Academy of Cosmetic Surgery 2009 Procedural Census." Prepared by RH Research, February. Accessed April 9, 2010 (http://www.cosmeticsurgery.org/media/2009_full_report.pdf).

American Bar Association. 2009. "Death Penalty Moratorium Implementation Project." ABA Section of Individual Rights and Responsibilities. Accessed May 20, 2009 (http://www.abanet.org/moratorium/home.html).

American Federation of Teachers. 2008. "Survey and Analysis of Teacher Salary Trends 2007." Washington, DC: American Federation of Teachers, AFL-CIO. Accessed April 19, 2010 (http://archive.aft.org/salary/2007/download/AFT2007SalarySurvey.pdf).

American Jewish Committee. 2005. "2005 Annual Survey of American Jewish Opinion" Accessed June 3, 2010 (http://www.ajc.org/site/apps/nlnet/content3.aspx?c=ijIT12PHKoG&b=846741&ct=1740283).

American Sociological Association. 1997. *Code of Ethics.* Washington, DC: ASA (www.asanet.org/members/ecoderev.html).

———. 2006a. *Careers in Sociology with an Undergraduate Degree in Sociology,* 7th ed. Washington, DC: ASA.

———. 2006b. "What Can I Do with a Bachelor's Degree in Sociology?" *A National Survey of Seniors Majoring in Sociology: First Glances: What Do They Know and Where Are They Going?* Washington, DC: ASA. Accessed August 2, 2008 (http://www.asanet.org/galleries/default-file/b&b_first_report_final.pdf).

Amnesty International. 1994. *Breaking the Silence: Human Rights Violations Based on Sexual Orientation.* New York: Amnesty International.

———. 2009a. "Mexico: Two Years On: The Law to Protect Women Has Had No Impact at State Level." Accessed June 15, 2009 (www.amnesty.org/en/for-media/press-releases/mexico-two-years-law-protect-women-has-had-no-impact-state-level-2009012).

———. 2009b. "Sexual Orientation and Gender Identity." Accessed June 15, 2009 (www.amnesty.org/en/sexual-orientation-and-gender-identity).

Anagnostou, Yiorgos. 2009a. "A Critique of Symbolic Ethnicity: The Ideology of Choice?" *Ethnicities* 9 (1): 94–122.

———. 2009b. "About Facts and Fictions: Reply to Herbert Gans and Mary Waters." *Ethnicities* 9 (1).

Anderson, David, and Mykol C. Hamilton. 2005. "Gender Role Stereotyping of Parents in Children's Picture Books: The Invisible Father." *Sex Roles* 52: 145–151.

Anderson, John Ward, and Molly Moore. 1993. "Born Oppressed: Women in the Developing World Face Cradle-to-Grave Discrimination, Poverty." *Washington Post,* February 14: p. A1.

Anderson, Terry H. 2007. *The Sixties,* 3d ed. Englewood Cliffs, NJ: Prentice Hall.

Andrees, Beate, and Patrick Belser, eds. 2009. *Forced Labor: Coercion and Exploitation in the Private Economy.* Geneva: International Labour Organization.

Angelo, Megan. 2010. "Fortune 500 Women CEOs." *Fortune,* April 22. Accessed May 11, 2010 (http://money.cnn.com/galleries/2010/fortune/1004/gallery.fortune500_women_ceos.fortune/index.html).

Angier, Natalie. 2000. "Do Races Differ? Not Really, Genes Show." *New York Times,* August 22, p. F6. Accessed June 30, 2008 (http://query.nytimes.com/gst/fullpage.html?res=9E07E7DF1E3EF931A1575BC0A9669C8B63&scp=2&sq=natalie+angier&st=nyt).

Anti-Defamation League. 2009. "2008 Audit of Anti-Semitic Incidents." Accessed May 17, 2010 (http://www.adl.org/main_Anti_Semitism_Domestic/2008_Audit.htm).

Arab American Institute. 2008. "Arab Americans: Demographics." Accessed July 1, 2008 (http://www.aaiusa.org/arab-americans/22/demographics).

Arora, Neeraj K., Bradford W. Hesse, Barbara K. Rimer, K. Viswanath, Marla L. Clayman, and Robert T. Croyle. 2008. "Frustrated and Confused: The American Public Rates Its Cancer-Related Information-Seeking Experiences." *Journal of General Internal Medicine* 23 (3): 223–228.

Atchley, Robert C. 1976. *The Sociology of Retirement.* New York: Wiley.

Aud, Susan, William Hussar, Michael Planty, Thomas Snyder, Kevin Bianco, Mary Ann Fox, Lauren Frohlich, Jana Kemp, and Lauren Drake. 2010. *The Condition of Education 2010.* NCES 2010-028. National Center for Education Statistics, Institute of Education Sciences, U.S. Department of Education, Washington DC. Accessed June 2, 2010. (http://nces.ed.gov/pubs2010/2010028 .pdf).

Avise, John C. 2004. *The Hope, Hype, and Reality of Genetic Engineering: Remarkable Stories from Agriculture, Industry, Medicine, and the Environment.* New York: Oxford University Press.

B

Baby Name Wizard. 2010. "NameVoyager." Accessed April 27, 2009 (www.babynamewizard.com).

Baer, Hans. 2008. "Global Warming as a By-product of the Capitalist Treadmill of Production and Consumption—The Need for an Alternative Global System." *Australian Journal of Anthropology* 19 (1): 58–62.

Baer, Hans, and Ian Coulter. 2008. "Introduction—Taking Stock of Integrative Medicine: Broadening Biomedicine or Co-option of Complementary and Alternative Medicine?" *Health Sociology Review* 17 (4): 331–341.

Bagilhole, Barbara, and Simon Cross. 2006. "'It Never Struck Me as Female': Investigating Men's Entry into Female-Dominated Occupations." *Journal of Gender Studies* 15 (1): 35–48.

Bahr, Peter Riley. 2008. "*Cooling Out* in the Community College: What Is the Effect of Academic Advising on Students' Chances of Success?" *Research in Higher Education* 49: 704–732.

Bainbridge, William Sims. 2007. "The Scientific Research Potential of Virtual Worlds." *Science* 317 (July 27): 472–476.

Balch, Robert W. 2006. "The Rise and Fall of Aryan Nations: A Resource Mobilization Perspective." *Journal of Political & Military Sociology* 34 (1): 81–113.

Baldwin, James. [1965] 1985. "White Man's Guilt." Pp. 409–414 in *The Price of the Ticket: Collected Nonfiction, 1948–1985.* New York: St. Martin's Press.

Balfour, Gillian. 2006. "Re-imagining a Feminist Criminology." *Canadian Journal of Criminology & Criminal Justice* 48 (5): 735–752.

Banerjee, Neela. 2006. "Clergywomen Find Hard Path to Bigger Pulpit." *New York Times,* August 26, pp. A1, A11.

Barna Group. 2001. "Religious Beliefs Vary Widely by Denomination." Ventura, CA: The Barna Group. Accessed June 1, 2009 (http://www.barna.org/barna-update/article/5-barna-update/ 53-religious-beliefs-vary-widely-by-denomination).

Barnes, Patricia M., Barbara Bloom, and Richard L. Nahin. 2008. "Complementary and Alternative Medicine Use Among Adults and Children: United States, 2007." *National Health Statistics Reports* 12. Hyattsville, MD: National Center for Health Statistics. Accessed May 20, 2010 (http://nccam.nih.gov/news/2008/nhsr12 .pdf).

Barnes, Patricia M., Eve Powell-Griner, Kim McFann, and Richard L. Nahin. 2004. *Complementary and Alternative Medicine Use Among Adults, United States, 2002.* Advance Data from *Vital and Health Statistics* 343. Hyattsville, MD: National Center for Health Statistics. Accessed July 5, 2008 (http://nccam.nih.gov/news/ camsurvey_fs1.htm).

Barnett, Rosalind, and Caryl Rivers. 2004. *Same Difference: How Gender Myths Are Hurting Our Relationships, Our Children, and Our Jobs.* New York: Basic Books.

Barr, Donald A. 2008. *Health Disparities in the United States: Social Class, Race, Ethnicity, and Health.* Baltimore: Johns Hopkins University Press.

Barrett, David B., Todd M. Johnson, and Peter F. Crossing. 2006. "The 2005 Annual Megacensus of Religions." Pp. 282–283 in 2006 *Book of the Year.* Chicago: Encyclopedia Britannica.

Barrionuevo, Alexei. 2008. "Amazon's 'Forest Peoples' Seek a Role in Striking Global Climate Agreements." *New York Times,* April 6, p. 6.

Barta, Patrick, and Joel Millman. 2009. "The Great U-Turn." *The Wall Street Journal,* June 6. Accessed June 15, 2009 (http://online.wsj .com/article_email/SB124424701106590613-lMyQjAxMDI5N-DA0NzIwNDc3Wj.html).

Basso, Keith H. 1972. "Ice and Travel Among the Fort Norman Slave: Folk Taxonomies and Cultural Rules." *Language in Society* 1 (March): 31–49.

Baudrillard, Jean. [1981] 1994. *Simulacra and Simulation.* Ann Arbor: University of Michigan Press.

Baumert, Kevin, Timothy Herzog, and Jonathan Pershing. 2005. *Navigating the Numbers: Greenhouse Gas Data and International Climate Policy.* Washington, DC: World Resources Institute. Accessed August 6, 2009 (http://pdf.wri.org/navigating_numbers.pdf).

Baumgardner, Jennifer, and Amy Richards. 2000. *Manifesta: Young Women, Feminism and the Future.* New York: Farrar, Straus, and Giroux.

BBC. 2006. "Madrid Bans Waifs from Catwalks." September 13. Accessed June 7, 2008 (http://news.bbc.co.uk/2/hi/europe/ 5341202.stm).

BBC News. 2005. "Indonesian Village Report: January 12, 2005." Accessed January 19 (www.theworld.org).

Beagan, Brenda. 2003. "Teaching Social and Cultural Awareness to Medical Students: 'It's All Very Nice to Talk About It in Theory, but Ultimately It Makes No Difference.'" *Academic Medicine* 78 (6): 605–614.

Beagan, Brenda L. 2001. "'Even If I Don't Know What I'm Doing I Can Make It Look Like I Know What I'm Doing': Becoming a Doctor in the 1990s." *Canadian Review of Sociology and Anthropology* 38: 275–292.

Bearman, Peter S., James Moody, and Katherine Stovel. 2004. "Chains of Affection: The Structure of Adolescent Romantic and Sexual Networks." *American Journal of Sociology* 110 (July): 44–91.

Beauvoir, Simone de. 1952. *The Second Sex.* New York: Knopf.

Becker, Howard S. 1963. *The Outsiders: Studies in the Sociology of Deviance.* New York: Free Press.

———, ed. 1964. *The Other Side: Perspectives on Deviance.* New York: Free Press.

Beeghley, Leonard. 2007. *The Structure of Social Stratification in the United States,* 5th ed. Boston: Allyn & Bacon.

Belkin, Lisa. 2008. "When Mom and Dad Share It All." *New York Times,* June 15. Accessed June 17, 2009 (www.nytimes.com/ 2008/06/15/magazine/15parenting-t.html).

Bell, Daniel. 1953. "Crime as an American Way of Life." *Antioch Review* 13 (Summer): 131–154.

———. 1999. *The Coming of Post-industrial Society: A Venture in Social Forecasting.* With new foreword. New York: Basic Books.

———. 2001. *Liberation Theology After the End of History: The Refusal to Cease Suffering.* New York: Routledge.

Benagiano, Giuseppe, and Maurizio Mori. 2009. "The Origins of Human Sexuality: Procreation or Recreation?" *Reproductive BioMedicine Online* 18 (S1): 50–59.

Bendick Jr., Marc, Charles W. Jackson, and J. Horacio Romero. 1993. *Employment Discrimination Against Older Workers: An Experimental Study of Hiring Practices.* Washington, DC: Fair Employment Council of Greater Washington.

Benhorin, Shira, and Susan D. McMahon. 2008. "Exposure to Violence and Aggression: Protective Roles of Social Support Among Urban African American Youth." *Journal of Community Psychology* 36 (6): 723–743.

Bennett, Drake. 2010. "This Will Be on the Midterm. You Feel Me? Why So Many Colleges Are Teaching *The Wire*." *Slate,* March 24. Accessed April 9, 2010 (http://www.slate.com/id/2245788/).

Bennett, V., S. Dávila-Poblete, and M. N. Rico, eds. 2005. *Opposing Currents: The Politics of Water and Gender in Latin America.* Pittsburgh, PA: University of Pittsburgh Press.

Benschop, Yvonne. 2009. "The Micro-politics of Gendering in Networking." *Gender, Work & Organization* 16 (2): 217–237.

Berenson, Alex, and Diana B. Henriques. 2008. "Look at Wall St. Wizard Finds Magic Had Skeptics." *New York Times,* December 12. Accessed May 21, 2009 (http://www.nytimes.com/2008/12/13/ business/13fraud.html).

Bergen, Raquel Kennedy. 2006. *Marital Rape: New Research and Directions.* Harrisburg, PA: VAW Net.

Berger, Peter. 1969. *The Sacred Canopy: Elements of a Sociological Theory of Religion.* Garden City, NY: Anchor Books.

Berger, Peter, and Thomas Luckmann. 1966. *The Social Construction of Reality.* New York: Doubleday.

Berland, Gretchen K. 2001. "Health Information on the Internet: Accessibility, Quality, and Readability in English and Spanish." *Journal of the American Medical Association* 285 (March 23): 2612–2621.

Berlin, Brent, and Paul Kay. 1991. *Basic Color Terms: Their Universality and Evolution.* Berkeley: University of California Press.

Bernasek, Anna. 2006. "A Poverty Line That's Out of Date and Out of Favor." *New York Times,* August 14, p. 8.

Bernburg, Jón Gunnar, Marvin D. Krohn, and Craig Rivera. 2006. "Official Labeling, Criminal Embeddedness, and Subsequent Delinquency: A Longitudinal Test of Labeling Theory." *Journal of Research in Crime & Delinquency* 43 (1): 67–88.

Bianchi, Suzanne M., and Daphne Spain. 1996. "Women, Work, and Family in America." *Population Bulletin* 51 (December).

Bianchi, Suzanne M., John P. Robinson, and Melissa A. Milkie. 2006. *Changing Rhythms of American Family Life.* New York: Sage.

Bisi, Simonetta. 2002. "Female Criminality and Gender Difference." *International Review of Sociology* 12 (1): 23–43.

Black, Donald. 1995. "The Epistemology of Pure Sociology." *Law and Social Inquiry* 20 (Summer): 829–870.

Black, Thomas. 2009. "Mexican Factories May Cut Fewer Jobs than in 2001." *Bloomberg News,* June 1. Accessed June 15, 2009 (www.bloomberg.com/apps/news?pid=20601086&sid=aFT3Y. rFittM&refer=news).

Blaine, Tasha. 2009. *Just Like Family: Inside the Lives of Nannies, the Parents They Work for, and the Children They Love.* Boston: Houghton Mifflin Harcourt.

Blau, Peter M., and Otis Dudley Duncan. 1967. *The American Occupational Structure.* New York: Wiley.

Blauner, Robert. 1972. *Racial Oppression in America.* New York: Harper and Row.

Bligh, Michelle C., and Jeffrey C. Kohles. 2009. "The Enduring Allure of Charisma: How Barack Obama Won the Historic 2008 Presidential Election." *Leadership Quarterly* 20 (3): 483–492.

Bloemraad, Irene, Anna Korteweg, and Gökçe Yurdakul. 2008. "Citizenship and Immigration: Multiculturalism, Assimilation, and Challenges to the Nation-State." *Annual Review of Sociology* 34: 153–179.

Blossfeld, Hans-Peter. 2009. "Educational Assortative Marriage in Comparative Perspective." *Annual Review of Sociology* 35 (1): 513–530.

Blumer, Herbert. 1955. "Collective Behavior." Pp. 165–198 in *Principles of Sociology,* 2d ed., ed. Alfred McClung Lee. New York: Barnes and Noble.

Boaz, Rachel Floersheim. 1987. "Early Withdrawal from the Labor Force." *Research on Aging* 9 (December): 530–547.

Bogan, Jesse, Kerry A. Dolan, Christopher Helman, and Nathan Vardi. 2008. "Failing State." *Forbes,* December 22. Accessed June 15, 2009 (www.forbes.com/global/2008/1222/058.html).

Bohn, Roger E., and James E. Short. 2010. *How Much Information? 2009 Report on American Consumers.* San Diego: Global Information Industry Center.

Bolt, Gideon, A. Sule Ozuekren, and Deborah Phillips. 2010. "Linking Integration and Residential Segregation." *Journal of Ethnic & Migration Studies* 36 (2): 169–186.

Bonilla-Silva, Eduardo. 2004. "From Bi-racial to Tri-racial: Towards a New System of Racial Stratification in the USA." *Ethics and Racial Studies* 27 (November): 931–950.

———. 2010. *Racism Without Racists: Color-Blind Racism and the Persistence of Racial Inequality in America.* 3d ed. Lanham, MD: Rowman & Littlefield.

Booth, Alan, and Paul R. Amato. 2001. "Parental Predivorce Relations and Offspring Postdivorce Well-Being." *Journal of Marriage and the Family* 62: 197–212.

Booth, William. 2009. "In Mexico, the U.S. Downturn Hits Home." *Washington Post,* June 14. Accessed June 15, 2009 (www. washingtonpost.com/wp-dyn/content/story/2009/06/14/ST2009 061400169.html).

Bortolotti, Dan. 2006. *Hope in Hell: Inside the World of Doctors Without Borders.* Buffalo, NY: Firefly Books.

Bouis, Howarth E. 2007. "The Potential of Genetically Modified Food Crops to Improve Human Nutrition in Developing Countries." *Journal of Development Studies* 43 (1): 79–96.

Bourdieu, Pierre. 1962. *The Algerians.* Preface by Raymond Aron. Boston: Beacon Press.

———. 1984. *Distinction: A Social Critique of the Judgment of Taste.* Cambridge, MA: Harvard University Press.

———. 1986. "The Forms of Capital." Pp. 241–258 in *Handbook of Theory and Research for the Sociology of Education,* ed. J.G. Richardson. New York: Greenwood Press.

———. 1998a. *Acts of Resistance: Against the Tyranny of the Market.* New York: New Press.

———. 1998b. *On Television.* New York: New Press.

Boushey, Heather. 2009. "Gender and the Recession: Recession Hits Traditionally Male Jobs Hardest." Center for American Progress, Washington, DC. Accessed June 4, 2009 (www.americanprogress. org/issues/2009/05/gender_recession.html).

Bowles, Samuel, and Herbert Gintis. 1976. *Schooling in Capitalistic America: Educational Reforms and the Contradictions of Economic Life.* New York: Basic Books.

BP Exploration & Production Inc. 2009. *Initial Exploration Plan: Mississippi Canyon Block 252.* OCS-G 32306, February. Accessed May 19, 2010 (http://www.gomr.mms.gov/PI/PDFImages/ PLANS/29/29977.pdf).

Brand, Jennie E., and Yu Xie. 2010. "Who Benefits Most from College? Evidence for Negative Selection in Heterogeneous Economic Returns to Higher Education." *American Sociological Review* 75 (2): 273–302.

Brannigan, Augustine, and William Zwerman. 2001. "The Real 'Hawthorne Effect.'" *Society* 38 (January/February) 55–60.

Bray, Hiawatha. 2009. "Finding a Way Around Iranian Censorship." *Boston Globe,* June 19. Accessed July 1, 2009 (www.boston.com/ business/technology/articles/2009/06/19/activists_utilizing_ twitter_web_proxies_to_sidestep_iranian_censorship/).

Brewer, Cynthia A., and Trudy A. Suchan. 2001. *Mapping Census 2000: The Geography of U.S. Diversity.* Washington, DC: U.S. Government Printing Office.

Brewer, Rose M., and Nancy A. Heitzeg. 2008. "The Racialization of Criminal Punishment." *American Behavioral Scientist* 51 (January): 625–644.

Brickell, Chris. 2009. "Sexuality and the Dimensions of Power." *Sexuality & Culture* 13 (2): 57–74.

Brooks, Ann. 1997. *Postfeminisms: Feminism, Cultural Theory, and Cultural Forms.* New York: Routledge.

Brooks, Kelly D., and Kathryn Quina. 2009. "Women's Sexual Identity Patterns: Differences Among Lesbians, Bisexuals, and Unlabeled Women." *Journal of Homosexuality* 56 (8): 1030–1045.

Brown, David K. 2001. "The Social Sources of Educational Credentialism: Status Cultures, Labor Markets, and Organizations." *Sociology of Education* 74 (Extra Issue): 19–34.

Brown, George M. 2006. "Degrees of Doubt: Legitimate, Real and Fake Qualifications in a Global Market." *Journal of Higher Education Policy & Management* (1): 71–79.

Brown, Robert McAfee. 1980. *Gustavo Gutierrez.* Atlanta: John Knox.

Bruce, Steve. 2000. *Choice and Religion: A Critique of Rational Choice Theory.* New York: Oxford University Press.

Buckle, Chris, Y. M. Lisa Chuah, Calvin S. Fones, and Albert H. C. Wong. 2007. "A Conceptual History of Koro." *Transcultural Psychiatry* 44 (1): 27–43.

Bucks, Brian K., Arthur B. Kennickell, Traci L. Mach, and Kevin B. Moore. 2009. "Changes in U.S. Family Finances from 2004 to 2007: Evidence from the Survey of Consumer Finances." *Federal Reserve Bulletin* 95 (February): A1–A55.

Bullard, Robert. 2000. *Dumping in Dixie: Race, Class, and Environmental Quality*, 3d ed. Boulder, CO: Westview Press.

Bulle, Wolfgang F. 1987. *Crossing Cultures? Southeast Asian Mainland.* Atlanta: Centers for Disease Control and Prevention.

Bullough, Vern L. 1998. "Alfred Kinsey and the Kinsey Report: Historical Overview and Lasting Contributions." *Journal of Sex Research* 35 (2): 127–131.

Burawoy, Michael. 2004. "Public Sociologies: Contradictions, Dilemmas, and Possibilities." *Social Forces* 82: 1603–1618.

Bureau of Labor Statistics. 2007. "Labor Force (Demographic) Data." February 13. Accessed February 28, 2007 (www.bls.gov).

———. 2008a. "Employment Characteristics of Families in 2007." Accessed May 26, 2009 (http://www.bls.gov/news.release/famee. toc.htm).

———. 2008b. "Number of Jobs Held, Labor Market Activity, and Earnings Growth Among the Youngest Baby Boomers: Results from a Longitudinal Survey." *BLS News,* June 27. Accessed May 6, 2009 (http://www.bls.gov/news.release/pdf/nlsoy.pdf).

———. 2008c. "Highlights of Women's Earnings in 2007." U.S. Department of Labor, October, Report 1008. Accessed June 17, 2009 (www.bls.gov/cps/cpswom2007.pdf).

———. 2009a. "Mexico: Hourly Compensation Costs for Workers in Maquiladora Manufacturing Export Industries, 1975–2006." Accessed June 14, 2009 (http://stats.bls.gov/fls/flshcindmaq.htm).

———. 2009b. "International Comparisons of Hourly Compensation Costs in Manufacturing, 2007." *Bureau of Labor Statistics News,* March 26. Accessed June 14, 2009 (www.bls.gov/news.release/ pdf/ichcc.pdf).

———. 2009c. "Employment Characteristics of Families in 2008." Accessed April 11, 2010 (http://www.bls.gov/news.release/famee .toc.html).

———. 2009d. "College Enrollment and Work Activity of 2008 High School Graduates." U.S. Department of Labor, 09-0454. Accessed April 16, 2010 (http://www.bls.gov/news.release/pdf/hsgec.pdf).

———. 2009e. "Highlights of Women's Earnings in 2008." U.S. Department of Labor, July, Report 1017. Accessed May 11, 2010 (http://www.bls.gov/cps/cpswom2008.pdf).

———. 2010a. "Civilian Labor Force, 2008–2018." Employment Projections, Labor Force (Demographic) Data. Accessed April 20, 2010 (http://www/bls.gov/emp/ep_data_labor_force.htm).

———. 2010b. "Civilian Labor Force, 2019–2050." Employment Projections, Labor Force (Demographic) Data. Accessed April 20, 2010 (http://www/bls.gov/emp/ep_data_labor_force.htm).

Bureau of the Census. 2007a. *Statistical Abstract of the United States, 2008.* Washington, DC: U.S. Government Printing Office.

———. 2007b. "American Community Survey 2006" (www.census.gov).

———. 2008a. *Statistical Abstract of the United States.* Washington, DC: U.S. Government Printing Office.

———. 2008b. "Total Midyear Population for the World: 1900–2050." Data updated March 27, 2008. Accessed April 9, 2008 (www.census.gov).

Burgoon, Judee K., Laura K. Guerrero, and Kory Floyd. 2010. *Nonverbal Communication.* New York: Allyn & Bacon.

Bush, Jason. 2006. "What's Behind Russia's Crime Wave?" *Business Week,* October 19. Accessed Wednesday, May 20, 2009 (http://www.businessweek.com/globalbiz/content/oct2006/ gb20061019_110749.htm).

Butler, Daniel Allen. 1998. *Unsinkable: The Full Story.* Mechanicsburg, PA: Stackpole Books.

Butler, Robert N. 1990. "A Disease Called Ageism." *Journal of American Geriatrics Society* 38 (February): 178–180.

C

Call, V. R., and Teachman, J. D. 1991. "Military Service and Stability in the Family Life Course." *Military Psychology* 3: 233–250.

Callaway, Ewen. 2008. "Polygamy Is the Key to a Long Life." *New Scientist,* August 19. Accessed May 26, 2009 (http://www. newscientist.com/article/dn14564-polygamy-is-the-key-to-a-long-life.html).

Cañas, Jesus, and Robert W. Gilmer. 2009. "The Maquiladora's Changing Geography." Federal Reserve Bank of Dallas, *Southwest Economy:* Second Quarter. Accessed June 14, 2009 (http:// dallasfed.org/research/swe/2009/swe0902c.cfm).

Caplan, Ronald L. 1989. "The Commodification of American Health Care." *Social Science and Medicine* 28 (11): 1139–1148.

Caplow, Theodore, and Louis Hicks. 2002. *Systems of War and Peace,* 2d ed. Lanham, MD: University Press of America.

Carey, Anne R., and Elys A. McLean. 1997. "Heard It Through the Grapevine?" *USA Today,* September 15, p. B1.

Carmichael, Mary. 2007. "Troubled Waters." *Newsweek* 149 (June 4): 52–56.

Carr, Deborah. 2007. "Baby Blues." *Contexts* (Spring): 62.

Carson, Rachel. 1962. *Silent Spring.* Boston: Houghton Mifflin.

Carter, Susan B., Scott Sigmund Gartner, Michael R. Haines, Alan L. Olmstead, Richard Sutch, and Gavin Wright. 2006. *Historical Statistics of the United States: Earliest Times to the Present, Millennial Edition.* 5 vols. Cambridge: Cambridge University Press.

Carty, Victoria, and Jake Onyett. 2006. "Protest, Cyberactivism and New Social Movements: The Reemergence of the Peace Movement Post 9/11." *Social Movement Studies* 5 (3): 229–249.

Castañeda, Jorge G. 1995. "Ferocious Differences." *Atlantic Monthly* 276 (July): 68–69, 71–76.

Castells, Manuel. 1997. *The Power of Identity.* Vol. 1 of *The Information Age: Economy, Society and Culture.* London: Blackwell.

———. 1998. *End of Millennium.* Vol. 3 of *The Information Age: Economy, Society and Culture.* London: Blackwell.

———. 2000. *The Information Age: Economy, Society and Culture* (3 vols.), 2d ed. Oxford and Malden, MA: Blackwell.

Catalano, Shannan, Erica Smith, Howard Snyder, and Michael Rand. 2009. "Female Victims of Violence." Bureau of Justice Statistics, Selected Findings, September, NCJ 228356. Accessed June 2, 2010 (http://bjs.ojp.usdoj.gov/content/pub/pdf/fvv.pdf).

Catalyst. 2007. *2007 Catalyst Census of Women Board Directors, Corporate Officers, and Top Earners.* New York: Catalyst.

———. 2008. "Women and Minorities on Fortune 100 Boards." The Prout Group, the Executive Leadership Council, and the Hispanic Association on Corporate Responsibility. Accessed August 2, 2010 (http://www.catalyst.org/file/86/1-17-08%20abd%20study.pdf).

Cavalli-Sforza, L. Luca, Paolo Menozzi, and Alberto Piazza. 1994. *The History and Geography of Human Genes.* Princeton, NJ: Princeton University Press.

CBS News. 1979. Transcript of *Sixty Minutes* segment "I Was Only Following Orders." March 31, pp. 2–8.

Center for American Women and Politics. 2010. "Facts on Women Officeholders, Candidates and Voters." Eagleton Institute of Politics, Rutgers University, New Brunswick, NJ. Accessed May 11, 2010 (http://www.cawp.rutgers.edu/fast_facts/index.php).

Centers for Disease Control and Prevention. 2008 "Youth Risk Behavior Surveillance—United States, 2007." Surveillance Summaries, June 6. *Morbidity and Mortality Weekly Report* 57 (SS-4). Accessed June 1, 2010 (http://www/cdc.gov/mmwr/PDF/ss/ss5704.pdf).

Centers for Medicare and Medicaid Services. 2010a. "National Health Expenditure Web Tables." U.S. Department of Health and Human Services. Accessed May 20, 2010 (https://www.cms.gov/ NationalHealthExpendData/downloads/tables.pdf).

———. 2010b. "National Health Expenditure Projections 2009–2019." U.S. Department of Health and Human Services. Accessed May 20, 2010 (https://www.cms.gov/NationalHealthExpendData/ downloads/proj2009.pdf).

Cevallos, Diego. 2009. "Indigenous Woman Fights for Rights." *Inter Press Service,* April 1. Accessed June 15, 2009 (www.ips.org/ mdg3/mexico-indigenous-woman-on-the-offensive/#more-21).

Chambers, Samuel. 2007. " 'An Incalculable Effect': Subversions of Heteronormativity." *Political Studies* 55 (3): 656–679.

Chambliss, William. 1973. "The Saints and the Roughnecks." *Society* 11 (November/December): 24–31.

Charter, David, and Jill Sherman. 1996. "Schools Must Teach New Code of Values." *London Times,* January 15, p. 1.

Chen, Shaohua, and Martin Ravallion. 2008. "The Developing World Is Poorer Than We Thought, but No Less Successful in the Fight Against Poverty." Policy Research Working Paper 4703, World Bank Development Research Group, August 2008. Accessed June 13, 2009 (www-wds.worldbank.org/external/default/WDS Content-Server/IW3P/IB/2008/08/26/000158349_200808261132 39/Rendered/PDF/WPS4703.pdf).

———. 2009. "The Impact of the Global Financial Crisis on the World's Poorest." April 30. Accessed June 13, 2009 (www.voxeu.org/index.php?q=node/3520).

Cheng, Shu-Ju Ada. 2003. "Rethinking the Globalization of Domestic Service." *Gender and Society* 17 (2): 166–186.

Cherlin, Andrew. 2004. "The Deinstitutionalization of American Marriage." *Journal of Marriage and Family* 66: 848–861.

———. 2006. "On Single Mothers 'Doing' Family." *Journal of Marriage and Family* 68 (November): 800–803.

———. 2008a. "Can the Left Learn the Lessons of Welfare Reform?" *Contemporary Sociology* 37 (March): 101–104.

———. 2008b. *Public and Private Families: An Introduction,* 5th ed. New York: McGraw-Hill.

———. 2009. *The Marriage-Go-Round: The State of Marriage and the Family in America Today.* New York: Knopf.

Chesney-Lind, Meda. 1989. "Girls' Crime and Women's Place: Toward a Feminist Model of Female Delinquency." *Crime and Delinquency* 35: 5–29.

Chesney-Lind, Meda, and Lisa Pasko. 2004. *The Female Offender: Girls, Women, and Crime,* 2d ed. Thousand Oaks, CA: Sage.

Christian, Joseph. 2009. "Coffee Culture: A Symbol of Middle-Class Lifestyle." *China Daily,* November 3. Accessed April 1, 2010 (http://www.chinadaily.com.cn/cndy/2009-11/03/content_8903174.htm).

Cigar, Norman. 1995. *Genocide in Bosnia: The Policy of "Ethnic Cleansing."* College Station: Texas A&M University Press.

Clammer, John. 2009. "Sociology and Beyond: Towards a Deep Sociology." *Asian Journal of Social Science* 37 (3): 332–346.

Clark, Burton. 1960. "The 'Cooling-Out' Function in Higher Education." *American Journal of Sociology* 65: 569–576.

———. 1980. "The 'Cooling-Out' Function Revisited." *New Directions for Community Colleges* 32: 15–31.

Clark, Burton, and Martin Trow. 1966. "The Organizational Context." Pp. 17–70 in *The Study of College Peer Groups,* ed. Theodore M. Newcomb and Everett K. Wilson. Chicago: Aldine.

Clarke, Adele E., Janet K. Shim, Laura Maro, Jennifer Ruth Fusket, and Jennifer R. Fishman. 2003. "Bio Medicalization: Technoscientific Transformations of Health, Illness, and U.S. Biomedicine." *American Sociological Review* 68 (April): 161–194.

Clarke, Edward H. 1874. *Sex in Education; or, A Fair Chance for Girls.* Boston: James R. Osgood.

Clausen, Christopher. 2002. "To Have . . . or Not to Have." *Utne Reader,* July/August, pp. 66–70.

Clinard, Marshall B., and Robert F. Miller. 1998. *Sociology of Deviant Behavior,* 10th ed. Fort Worth, TX: Harcourt Brace.

CNN. 2006. "Skinny Models Banned from Catwalk." September 13. Accessed June 7, 2008 (http://www.cnn.com/2006/WORLD/europe/09/13/spain.models/index.html).

———. 2008. "Exit Polls." CNN Election Center 2008. Accessed May 27, 2009 (http://www.cnn.com/ELECTION/2008/results/polls/#val=USP00p3).

Cognard-Black, Andrew J. 2004. "Will They Stay, or Will They Go? Sex-Atypical Work Among Token Men Who Teach?" *Sociological Quarterly* 45: 113–139.

Colby, David C. 1986. "The Voting Rights Act and Black Registration in Mississippi." *Publius* 16 (Fall): 123–137.

Cole, Elizabeth S. 1985. "Adoption, History, Policy, and Program." Pp. 638–666 in *A Handbook of Child Welfare,* ed. John Laird and Ann Hartman. New York: Free Press.

Coleman, James William. 2006. *The Criminal Elite: Understanding White-Collar Crime,* 6th ed. New York: Worth.

Collins, Gail. 2003. *America's Women.* New York: HarperCollins.

Collins, Patricia Hill. 2000. *Black Feminist Thought,* 2d ed. New York: Routledge.

Collins, Randall. 1986. *Weberian Sociological Theory.* New York: Cambridge University Press.

———. 1995. "Prediction in Macrosociology: The Case of the Soviet Collapse." *American Journal of Sociology* 100 (May): 1552–1593.

Commission for the Status of Women. 2009. "The Fifty-Third Session of the Commission on the Status of Women." Division for the Advancement of Women, Department of Economic and Social Affairs. March 2–13, Washington, DC. Accessed June 6, 2009 (http://www.un.org/womenwatch/daw/csw/53sess.htm).

Commission on Civil Rights. 1976. *A Guide to Federal Laws and Regulations Prohibiting Sex Discrimination.* Washington, DC: U.S. Government Printing Office.

Commoner, Barry. 1971. *The Closing Circle.* New York: Knopf.

———. 1990. *Making Peace with the Planet.* New York: Pantheon Books.

Connell, R. W. 2002. *Gender.* Cambridge, UK: Polity Press.

———. 2005. *Masculinities,* 2d ed. Berkeley: University of California Press.

Connolly, Ceci. 2008. "As Latin Nations Treat Gays Better, Asylum Is Elusive." *Washington Post,* August 12. Accessed May 28, 2010 (http://www.washingtonpost.com/wp-dyn/content/article/2008/08/11/AR2008081102038.html).

Conrad, Peter. 2007. *The Medicalization of Society: On the Transformation of Human Conditions into Treatable Disorders.* Baltimore: Johns Hopkins University Press.

Cooley, Charles. H. 1902. *Human Nature and the Social Order.* New York: Scribner.

Coontz, Stephanie. 1992. *The Way We Never Were: American Families and the Nostalgia Trap.* New York: Basic Books.

———. 2005. *Marriage, a History: From Obedience to Intimacy or How Love Conquered Marriage.* New York: Viking.

———. 2006. "A Pop Quiz on Marriage." *New York Times,* February 19, p. 12.

———. 2008. "The Future of Marriage." *Cato Unbound,* January 14. Accessed August 2, 2010 (http://www.cato-unbound.org/2008/01/14/stephanie-coontz/the-future-of-marriage).

Cooper, Bruce S., and John Sureau. 2007. "The Politics of Home-schooling: New Developments, New Challenges." *Educational Policy* 21 (January and March): 110–131.

Cooper, K., S. Day, A. Green, and H. Ward. 2007. "Maids, Migrants and Occupational Health in the London Sex Industry. *Anthropology and Medicine* 14 (April): 41–53.

Corak, Miles. 2006. "Do Poor Children Become Poor Adults? Lessons from a Cross Country Comparison of Generational Earnings Mobility." Institute for the Study of Labor (IZA) Discussion Paper No. 1993, March. Accessed June 24, 2008 (http://papers.ssrn.com/sol3/papers.cfm?abstract_id=889034).

———. 2010. "Chasing the Same Dream, Climbing Different Ladders: Economic Mobility in the United States and Canada." Economic Mobility Project: An Initiative of the Pew Charitable Trusts. Accessed April 26, 2010 (http://www.economicmobility.org/assets/pdfs/PEW_EMP_US-CANADA.pdf).

Corbett, Christianne, Catherine Hill, and Andresse St. Rose. 2008. *Where the Girls Are: The Facts About Gender Equity in Education.* Washington, DC: AAUW. Accessed May 29, 2009 (http://www.aauw.org/research/upload/whereGirlsAre.pdf).

Coronado, Roberto, and Jesus Cañas. 2010. "Remittances to Mexico: Cross-Border Money Flows Slowed by U.S. Slump." Federal Reserve Bank of Dallas. *Southwest Economy* (First Quarter): 14. Accessed April 29, 2010 (http://dallasfed.org/research/swe/2010/swe1001d.pdf).

Correll, Shelley J., Stephen Benard, and In Paik. 2007. "Getting a Job: Is There a Motherhood Penalty?" *AJS* 112 (5): 1297–1338.

Corso, Regina A. 2009. "Firefighters, Scientists and Doctors Seen as Most Prestigious Occupations." *The Harris Poll* 86 (August 4). Accessed April 24, 2010 (http://www.harrisinteractive.com/vault/Harris-Interactive-Poll-Research-Pres-Occupations-2009-08.pdf).

Coser, Rose Laub. 1984. "American Medicine's Ambiguous Progress." *Contemporary Sociology* 13 (January): 9–13.

Côté, James E. 2000. *Arrested Adulthood: The Changing Nature of Identity and Maturity in the Late World.* New York: New York University.

Cox, Oliver C. 1948. *Caste, Class, and Race: A Study in Social Dynamics.* Detroit: Wayne State University Press.

Crabtree, Catherine. 2009. "Rethinking Sexual Identity." *Existential Analysis* 20 (2): 248–261.

Cross, Simon, and Barbara Bagilhole. 2002. "Girls' Jobs for the Boys? Men, Masculinity and Non-traditional Occupations." *Gender, Work, and Organization* 9 (April): 204–226.

Croucher, Sheila L. 2004. *Globalization and Belonging: The Politics of Identity in a Changing World.* Lanham, MD: Rowman & Littlefield.

Crouse, Kelly. 1999. "Sociology of the Titanic." *Teaching Sociology Listserv,* May 24.

CTIA. 2010. "Background on CTIA's Semi-annual Wireless Industry Survey." CTIA–the Wireless Association. Accessed March 30, 2010 (http://files.ctia.org/pdf/CTIA_Survey_Year_End_2009_Graphics.pdf).

Cullen, Lisa Takevchi. 2007. "Till Work Do Us Part." *Time,* October 8, pp. 63–64.

Cumming, Elaine, and William E. Henry. 1961. *Growing Old: The Process of Disengagement.* New York: Basic Books.

Currie, Elliot. 1985. *Confronting Crime: An American Challenge.* New York: Pantheon Books.

———. 1998. *Crime and Punishment in America.* New York: Metropolitan Books.

Curtiss, Susan. 1977. *Genie: A Psycholinguistic Study of a Modern Day "Wild Child."* New York: Academic Press.

D

Dahl, Robert A. 1961. *Who Governs?* New Haven, CT: Yale University Press.

Daisey, Mike. 2002. *21 Dog Years: Doing Time @ Amazon.com.* New York: Free Press.

Dalla, Rochelle L., and Wendy C. Gamble. 2001. "Teenage Mothering and the Navajo Reservation: An Examination of Intergovernmental Perceptions and Beliefs." *American Indian Culture and Research Journal* 25 (1): 1–19.

Dao, James. 1995. "New York's Highest Court Rules Unmarried Couples Can Adopt." *New York Times,* November 3, pp. A1, B2.

Darwin, Charles. 1859. *On the Origin of Species.* London: John Murray.

David, Gary. 2004. "Scholarship on Arab Americans Distorted Past 9/11." *Al Jadid* (Winter/Spring): 26–27.

———. 2008. "Arab Americans." Pp. 84–87 in *Encyclopedia of Race, Ethnicity, and Society,* vol. 1, ed. Richard T. Schaefer. Thousand Oaks, CA: Sage.

Davidov, Eldad, Peter Schmidt, and Shalom H. Schwartz. 2008. "Bringing Values Back In." *Public Opinion Quarterly* 72 (3): 420–445.

Davies, James B., Susanna Sandström, Anthony B. Shorrocks, and Edward N. Wolff. 2009 "The Level and Distribution of Global Household Wealth." National Bureau of Economic Research Working Paper 15508. Accessed May 28, 2010 (http://www.nber.org/papers/w15508).

Davis, Gerald. 2003. *America's Corporate Banks Are Separated by Just Four Handshakes.* Accessed August 2, 2010 (http://www.ns.umich.edu/index.html?Releases/2002/Dec02/chr121002).

———. 2004. "American Cronyism: How Executive Networks Inflated the Corporate Bubble." *Contexts* (Summer): 34–40.

Davis, James A., Tom W. Smith, and Peter V. Marsden. 2007. *General Social Surveys, 1972–2006: Cumulative Codebook.* Chicago: National Opinion Research Center.

Davis, Joseph E. 2006. "How Medicalization Lost Its Way." *Society* 43 (6): 51–56.

Davis, Kingsley. 1940. "Extreme Social Isolation of a Child." *American Journal of Sociology* 45 (January): 554–565.

———. 1947. "A Final Note on a Case of Extreme Isolation." *American Journal of Sociology* 52 (March): 432–437.

Davis, Kingsley, and Wilbert E. Moore. 1945. "Some Principles of Stratification." *American Sociological Review* 10 (April): 242–249.

Dawson, Lorne. 2009. "Church-Sect-Cult: Constructing Typologies of Religious Groups." Pp. 525–544 in *The Oxford Handbook of the Sociology of Religion,* ed. Peter B. Clarke. New York: Oxford University Press.

Death Penalty Information Center. 2010. "Executions in the United States: Execution Facts—Modern Era." Washington, DC, updated March 30. Accessed April 9, 2010 (http://www.deathpenaltyinfo.org/executions-united-states).

Deflem, Mathieu. 2005. "'Wild Beasts Without Nationality': The Uncertain Origins of Interpol, 1898–1910." Pp. 275–285 in *Handbook of Transnational Crime and Justice,* ed. Philip Rerchel. Thousand Oaks, CA: Sage.

DeMott, Benjamin. 1990. *The Imperial Middle: Why Americans Can't Think Straight About Class.* New York: Morrow.

DeNavas-Walt, Carmen, Bernadette D. Proctor, and Jessica C. Smith. 2009. "Income, Poverty, and Health Insurance Coverage in the United States: 2008." *Current Population Reports* P60-236(RV). Washington, DC: U.S. Government Printing Office.

———. 2009a. "Income, Poverty, and Health Insurance Coverage in the United States: 2008." *Current Population Reports* P60-236. Washington, DC: U.S. Government Printing Office. Accessed March 29, 2010 (http://www.census.gov/prod/2009pubs/p60–236.pdf).

———. 2009b. "Income, Poverty, and Health Insurance Coverage in the United States: 2008." *Current Population Reports* P60-233. Washington, DC: U.S. Government Printing Office.

Department of Health and Human Services. 2007. "HIV/AIDS Surveillance Report." Cases of HIV Infection and AIDS in the United States and Dependent Areas, Vol. 19. Centers for Disease Control and Prevention, Atlanta. Accessed June 25, 2009 (www.cdc.gov/hiv/topics/surveillance/resources/reports/2007report/pdf/2007SurveillanceReport.pdf).

Department of Homeland Security. 2006. *The Federal Response to Hurricane Katrina: Lessons Learned.* Washington, DC: U.S. Government Printing Office.

Deutscher, Eckhard. 2010. *Development Co-operation Report 2010.* An Organisation for Economic Co-operation and Development report, April 23. Paris: OECD Publishing. Accessed April 29, 2010 (http://www.oecd.org/dac/dcr).

Devitt, James. 1999. *Framing Gender on the Campaign Trail: Women's Executive Leadership and the Press.* New York: Women's Leadership Conference.

Diamond, Jared. 2008. "What's Your Consumption Factor?" *New York Times,* January 2. Accessed May 21, 2010 (http://www.nytimes.com/2008/01/02/opinion/02diamond.html).

Dickens, Charles. 1843. *A Christmas Carol.* London: Chapman and Hall. Accessed July 7, 2008 (www.gutenberg.org/dirs/4/46/46-h/46-h.htm).

Doctors Without Borders. 2010. "What Is Doctors Without Borders?" Accessed April 29, 2010 (http://www.doctorswithoutborders.org/aboutus/factsheets/What-is-MSF.pdf).

Dodgson, Mark. 2010. "Virtual Worlds the Real Deal." *The Australian,* March 31. Accessed April 8, 2010 (http://www.theaustralian.com.au/higher-education/opinion-analysis/virtual-worlds-the-real-deal/story-e6frgcko-1225847663031).

Domhoff, G. William. 1978. *Who Really Rules? New Haven and Community Power Reexamined.* New Brunswick, NJ: Transaction.

———. 2006. *Who Rules America?* 5th ed. New York: McGraw-Hill.

———. 2009. "The Power Elite and Their Challengers: The Role of Nonprofits in American Social Conflict." *American Behavioral Scientist* 52 (7): 955–973.

Doress, Irwin, and Jack Nusan Porter. 1977. *Kids in Cults: Why They Join, Why They Stay, Why They Leave.* Brookline, MA: Reconciliation Associates.

Drescher, Jack. 2010. "Queer Diagnoses: Parallels and Contrasts in the History of Homosexuality, Gender Variance, and the Diagnostic and Statistical Manual." *Archives of Sexual Behavior* 39 (2): 427–460.

Dressler, William W., Kathryn S. Oths, and Clarence C. Gravlee. 2005. "Race and Ethnicity in Public Health Research: Models to Explain Health Disparities." Pp. 231–252 in *Annual Review of Anthropology 2005*, ed. William H. Durham. Palo Alto, CA: Annual Reviews.

Duberman, Martin Bauml, Martha Vicinus, and George Chauncy Jr., eds. 1989. *Hidden from History: Reclaiming the Gay and Lesbian Past.* New York: New American Library.

Du Bois, W.E.B. [1903] 1994. *The Souls of Black Folk.* New York: Dover.

———. [1909] 1970. *The Negro American Family.* Cambridge, MA: MIT Press.

———. [1940] 1968. *Dusk of Dawn.* New York: Schocken Books.

Dubner, Stephen J. 2007. "Everything You Always Wanted to Know About Street Gangs (but Didn't Know Whom to Ask)." Freakanomics blog, *New York Times*, August 6. Accessed June 10, 2008 (http://freakonomics.blogs.nytimes.com/2007/08/06/everything-you-always-wanted-to-know-about-street-gangs-but-didnt-know-whom-to-ask/).

Dukes, Richard L., Tara M. Bisel, Karoline N. Burega, Eligio A. Lobato, and Matthew D. Owens. 2003. "Expression of Love, Sex, and Hurt in Popular Songs: A Content Analysis of All-Time Greatest Hits." *Social Science Journal*, pp. 643–650.

Duneier, Mitchell. 1994a. "On the Job, but Behind the Scenes." *Chicago Tribune,* December 26, pp. 1, 24.

———. 1994b. "Battling for Control." *Chicago Tribune,* December 28, pp. 1, 8.

———. 1999. *Sidewalk.* New York: Farrar, Straus and Giroux.

Dunlap, Riley E. 2010. "At 40, Environmental Movement Endures, with Less Consensus." Washington, DC: Gallup, Inc., April 22. Accessed May 21, 2010 (http://www.gallup.com/poll/127487/Environmental-Movement-Endures-Less-Consensus.aspx).

Durden, T. Elizabeth, and Robert A. Hummer. 2006. "Access to Health-care Among Working-Age Hispanic Adults in the United States." *Social Science Quarterly* 87 (December): 1319–1343.

Durkheim, Émile. [1887] 1972. "Religion and Ritual." Pp. 219–238 in *Émile Durkheim: Selected Writings,* ed. A. Giddens. Cambridge: Cambridge University Press.

———. [1893] 1933. *Division of Labor in Society,* trans. George Simpson. New York: Free Press.

———. [1897] 1951. *Suicide,* trans. John A. Spaulding and George Simpson. New York: Free Press.

———. [1925] 1961. *Moral Education: A Study in the Theory and Application of the Sociology of Education.* Glencoe, IL: Free Press.

———. [1895] 1964. *The Rules of Sociological Method,* trans. Sarah A. Solovay and John H. Mueller. New York: Free Press.

E

Ebaugh, Helen Rose Fuchs. 1988. *Becoming an Ex: The Process of Role Exit.* Chicago: University of Chicago Press.

Economic Mobility Project. 2007. *Economic Mobility of Immigrants in the United States.* Washington, DC: Pew Charitable Trusts.

The Economist. 2008a. "Maharishi Mahesh Yogi." (February 16): 95.

———. 2008b. "A Ravenous Dragon: A Special Report on China's Quest for Resources." (March 15): 1–22.

Edge. 2010. "On 'Creation of a Bacterial Cell Controlled by a Chemically Synthesized Genome' by Venter et al." *Edge* 318 (May 20). Accessed May 24, 2010 (http://www.edge.org/documents/archive/edge318.html#rc).

EEOC. 2008. "Age Discrimination in Employment Act (ADEA) Charges FY 1997–FY 2007." Washington, DC: U.S Equal Employment Opportunity Commission. Accessed June 27, 2008 (http://www.eeoc.gov/stats/adea.html).

Ehrlich, Paul R. 1968. *The Population Bomb.* New York: Ballantine Books.

Ehrlich, Paul R., and Anne H. Ehrlich. 1990. *The Population Explosion.* New York: Simon & Schuster.

Ehrlich, Paul R., and Katherine Ellison. 2002. "A Looming Threat We Won't Face." *Los Angeles Times,* January 20, p. M6.

Elgin, Suzette Haden. 1984. *Native Tongue.* New York: Feminist Press.

———. 1988. *A First Dictionary and Grammar of Láadan,* 2d ed. Madison, WI: Society for the Furtherance and Study of Fantasy and Science Fiction.

Elia, John P. 2003. "Queering Relationships: Toward a Paradigmatic Shift." *Journal of Homosexuality* 45 (2–4): 61–86.

Elish, Jill. 2010. "Failed College Dreams Don't Spell Depression, Study Finds." *Florida State News,* March 19. Accessed April 19, 2010 (http://www.fsu.edu/news/2010/03/19/failed.dreams/).

Elliott, Michael. 2005. "Hopelessly Devoted: Being a Fan Is Like Having Your Own Personal Time Machine." *Time,* June 20, p. 76.

Ellison, Brandy. 2008. "Tracking." Pp. 301–304 in *Encyclopedia of Race, Ethnicity, and Society,* vol. 2, ed. Richard T. Schaefer. Thousand Oaks, CA: Sage.

Ellison, Ralph. 1952. *Invisible Man.* New York: Random House.

Ellul, Jacques. 1964. *The Technological Society.* New York: Knopf.

———. 1990. *The Technological Bluff.* Grand Rapids, MI: Eerdmans.

———. 1980. *The Technological System.* New York: Continuum.

Eltman, Frank. 2007. "Wealthy Couple Charged with Slavery." Associated Press, May 24.

Ely, Robin J. 1995. "The Power of Demography: Women's Social Construction of Gender Identity at Work." *Academy of Management Journal* 38 (3): 589–634.

Emerson, Michael O., David Hartman, Karen Cook, and Douglas Massey. 2006. "The Rise of Religious Fundamentalism." *Annual Review of Sociology* 32: 127–144.

Energy Information Administration. 2008. "Emissions of Greenhouse Gases in the United States 2007." Office of Integrated Analysis and Forecasting, U.S. Department of Energy, Washington, DC. Accessed June 28, 2009 (www.eia.doe.gov/oiaf/1605/ggrpt/pdf/0573(2007).pdf).

Engels, Friedrich [1884] 1959. "The Origin of the Family, Private Property, and the State." Pp. 392–394 in *Marx and Engels: Basic Writings on Politics and Philosophy,* ed. Lewis Feuer. Garden City, NY: Anchor Books.

Escárcega, Sylvia. 2008. "Mexico." Pp. 898–902 in *Encyclopedia of Race, Ethnicity, and Society,* vol. 2, ed. Richard T. Schaefer. Thousand Oaks, CA: Sage.

Escoffier, Jeffrey. 1997. "Homosexuality and the Sociological Imagination: The 1950s and 1960s." Pp. 248–261 in *A Queer World: The Center for Lesbian and Gay Studies Reader,* ed. Martin Duberman. New York: New York University Press.

Etaugh, Claire. 2003. "Witches, Mothers and Others: Females in Children's Books." *Hilltopics* (Winter): 10–13.

Etcoff, Nancy, Susie Orbach, Jennifer Scott, and Heidi D'Agostino. 2004. "The Real Truth About Beauty: A Global Report—Findings of the Global Study on Women, Beauty and Well-Being." Commissioned by Dove, a Unilever Beauty Brand. Accessed June 28, 2008 (http://www.campaignforrealbeauty.com/uploadedfiles/DOVE_white_paper_final.pdf).

Etzioni, Amitai. 1965. *Political Unification.* New York: Holt, Rinehart and Winston.

———. 2007. "Are New Technologies the Enemy of Privacy?" *Knowledge, Technology & Policy* 20 (2): 115–119.

Eureka County. 2006. "EPA Hears Testimony on Proposed Radiation Rule." *Nuclear Waste Office Newsletter* 11 (Winter). Eureka County Yucca Mountain Information Office.

ExecuNet. 2009. "2009 Executive Job Market Intelligence Report—Executive Summary." Accessed May 12, 2009 (http://www.execunet.com/promo/pdf/EUN2009Survey_summary.pdf).

F

Fahmy, Dahlia. 2010. "Virtual Cupcakes, Teddies Generate Real Cash." *ABC News,* March 15. Accessed April 8, 2010 (http://abcnews.go.com/Business/virtual-gifts-online-cupcakes-teddies-generate-real-cash/story?id=10053231).

Faith, Nazila. 2005. "Iranian Cleric Turns Blogger in Campaign for Reform." *New York Times,* January 16, p. 4.

Farley, Melissa, and Victor Malarek. 2008. "The Myth of the Victimless Crime." *New York Times,* March 12. Accessed May 20, 2009 (http://www.nytimes.com/2008/03/12/opinion/12farley.html).

Farr, Grant M. 1999. *Modern Iran.* New York: McGraw-Hill.

Fausto-Sterling, Anne. 1993. "The Five Sexes: Why Male and Female Are Not Enough." *The Sciences* (July/August): 18–23.

———. 2000. "The Five Sexes, Revisited." *The Sciences* (July/August): 18–23.

Fearon, James D., and David D. Laitin. 2003. "Ethnicity, Insurgency, and Civil War." *American Political Science Review* 97 (March): 75–90.

Featherman, David L., and Robert M. Hauser. 1978. *Opportunity and Change.* New York: Aeodus.

Federal Bureau of Investigation. 2009. "Organized Crime." Accessed May 20, 2009 (http://www.fbi.gov/hq/cid/orgcrime/ocshome.htm).

Felson, David, and Akis Kalaitzidis. 2005. "A Historical Overview of Transnational Crime." Pp. 3–19 in *Handbook of Transnational Crime and Justice,* ed. Philip Reichel. Thousand Oaks, CA: Sage.

Ferree, Myra Marx, and David A. Merrill. 2000. "Hot Movements, Cold Cognition: Thinking About Social Movements in Gendered Frames." *Contemporary Society* 29 (May): 454–462.

Fields, Jason. 2004. "America's Families and Living Arrangements: 2003." *Current Population Reports* P20-553. Washington, DC: U.S. Government Printing Office.

Finder, Alan. 2006. "For Some, Online Persona Undermines a Résumé." *New York Times,* June 11. Accessed June 30, 2009 (www.nytimes.com/2006/06/11/us/11recruit.html).

Findlen, Barbara, ed. 1995. *Listen Up: Voices From the Next Feminist Generation.* Seattle, WA: Seal Press.

Fine, Gary C. 2008. " Robbers Cave." Pp. 1163–1164 in *Encyclopedia of Race, Ethnicity, and Society,* vol. 3, ed. Richard T. Schaefer. Thousand Oaks, CA: Sage.

Finkel, Steven E., and James B. Rule. 1987. "Relative Deprivation and Related Psychological Theories of Civil Violence: A Critical Review." *Research in Social Movements* 9: 47–69.

Fiscella Kevin, and Kathleen Holt. 2008. "Racial Disparity in Hypertension Control: Tallying the Death Toll." *Annals of Family Medicine* 6: 497–502.

Fisher, Gordon M. 1992. "The Development and History of the Poverty Thresholds." *Social Security Bulletin* 55 (4): 3–14. Accessed April 25, 2010 (http://www.ssa.gov/history/fisheronpoverty.html).

———. 2008. "Remembering Mollie Orshansky—the Developer of the Poverty Thresholds." *Social Security Bulletin* 68 (3): 79–83. Accessed April 25, 2010 (http://www.ssa.gov/policy/docs/ssb/v68n3/v68n3p79.pdf).

Fishman, Charles. 2006. *The Wal-Mart Effect: How the World's Most Powerful Company Really Works—and How It's Transforming the American Economy.* New York: Penguin Books.

Fitzgerald, Kathleen J., and Diane M. Rodgers. 2000. "Radical Social Movement Organization: A Theoretical Model." *Sociological Quarterly* 41 (4): 573–592.

Forsythe, David P. 1990. "Human Rights in U.S. Foreign Policy: Retrospect and Prospect." *Political Science Quarterly* 105 (3): 435–454.

Fortune. 2009. "Global 500: World's Largest Corporations." *Fortune* 160 (July 20). Accessed April 28, 2010 (http://money.cnn.com/magazines/fortune/global500/2009/full_list/).

Foy, Paul. 2006. "Interior Rejects Goshute Nuclear Waste Stockpile." *Indian Country Today* 20 (September 18): 1.

Franklin, John Hope, and Alfred A. Moss. 2000. *From Slavery to Freedom: A History of African Americans,* 8th ed. Upper Saddle River, NJ: Prentice Hall.

Freidson, Eliot. 1970. *Profession of Medicine.* New York: Dodd, Mead.

French, Howard W. 2000. "The Pretenders." *New York Times Magazine,* December 3, pp. 86–88.

Freudenburg, William R. 2005. "Seeing Science, Courting Conclusions: Reexamining the Intersection of Science, Corporate Cash, and the Law." *Sociological Forum* 20 (March): 3–33.

Friedan, Betty. 1963. *The Feminine Mystique.* New York: Dell.

Friman, H. Richard. 2004. "The Great Escape? Globalization, Immigrant Entrepreneurship and the Criminal Economy." *Review of International Political Economy* 11 (1): 98–131.

Furedi, Frank. 2006. "The End of Professional Dominance." *Society* 43 (6): 14–18.

Furman, Nelly, David Goldberg, and Natalia Lusin. 2007. "Enrollments in Languages Other Than English in United States Institutions of Higher Education, Fall 2006." Modern Language Association, November 13. Accessed May 3, 2009 (http://www.mla.org/pdf/06enrollmentsurvey_final.pdf).

Furstenberg, Frank F. 2007. "The Making of the Black Family: Race and Class in Qualitative Studies in the Twentieth Century." *Annual Review of Sociology* 33: 429–348.

Furstenberg, Sheela Kennedy Jr., Vonnie C. McCloyd, Rubén G. Rumbaut, and Richard A. Setterstein Jr. 2004. "Growing Up Is Harder to Do." *Contexts* 3: 33–41.

Fuson, Ken. 2008. "Raid Mars Future for 3 Graduating Today from Postville." *Des Moines Register,* May 25. Accessed June 29, 2008 (http://www.desmoinesregister.com/apps/pbcs.dll/article?AID=/20080525/NEWS/805250327/1001&theme=POSTVILLE_ICE_RAID).

Fussell, Elizabeth. 2006. "Leaving New Orleans: Social Stratification, Networks, and Hurricane Evacuation." Understanding Katrina: Perspectives from the Social Sciences, Social Science Research Council, Brooklyn, NY. Accessed June 10, 2009 (http://understandingkatrina.ssrc.org/Fussell).

Fussell, Paul. 1992. *Class: A Guide Through the American Status System.* New York: Touchstone.

Fuwa, Makiko. 2004. "Macro-level Gender Inequality and the Division of Household Labor in 22 Countries." *American Sociological Review* 69 (December): 751–767.

G

Neal Gabler. 2006. *Walt Disney: The Triumph of the American Imagination.* New York: Knopf.

Gallup. 2008a. "Abortion." Accessed March 6, 2008 (www.gallup.com).

———. 2008b. "Homosexual Relations." Accessed March 6, 2008 (www.gallup.com).

———. 2008c. "Religion." Accessed March 14, 2008 (www.gallup.com).

———. 2008d. "Environment." Accessed March 18, 2008 (www.gallup.com).

———. 2009. "Military and National Defense." Washington, DC: Gallup, Inc. Accessed June 3, 2009 (www.gallup.com/poll/1666/military-national-defense.aspx).

———. 2010. "Abortion." Washington, DC: Gallup, Inc. Accessed May 5, 2010 (http://www.gallup.com/poll/1576/abortion.aspx).

Gans, Herbert. 1971. "The Uses of Poverty: The Poor Pay All." *Social Policy,* July/August, Pp. 20–24.

———. 2009. "Reflections on Symbolic Ethnicity: A Response to Y. Anagnostou." *Ethnicities* 9 (1): 123–130.

García-Moreno, Claudia, Henrica A.F.M. Jansen, Mary Ellsberg, Lori Heise, and Charlotte Watts. 2005. *WHO Milti-country Study on Women's Health and Domestic Violence Against Women: Initial Results on Prevalence, Health Outcomes and Women's Responses.* Geneva: World Health Organization. Accessed June 2, 2010 (http://www.who.int/gender/violence/who_multicountry_study/en/index.html).

Gardner, Gary. 2008. "Microfinance Surging." *World Watch* 21 (November/December): 30.

Gardner, Gary, Erik Assadourian, and Radhika Sarin. 2004. "The State of Consumption Today." Pp. 3–21 in *State of the World 2004,* ed. Brian Halweil and Lisa Mastny. New York: Norton.

Garfinkel, Harold. 1956. "Conditions of Successful Degradation Ceremonies." *American Journal of Sociology* 61 (March): 420–424.

Gaviria, Marcela, and Martin Smith. 2009. "The Madoff Affair." *PBS Frontline,* May 12. Accessed May 21, 2009 (http://www.pbs.org/wgbh/pages/frontline/madoff).

Geist, Claudia. 2005. "The Welfare State and the Home: Regime Differences in the Domestic Division of Labour." *European Sociological Review 2005* 21 (1): 23–24.

Gendell, Murray. 2008. "Older Workers: Increasing Their Labor Force Participation and Hours of Work." *Monthly Labor Review,* January, pp. 41–54.

Gentleman, Amelia. 2007. "Police Ignore Serial Killings in Delhi Slum, Exposing Unequal Justice for India's Poor." *New York Times,* January 7, p. 8.

Gerhardt, Uta. 2002. *Talcott Parsons: An Intellectual Biography.* New York: Cambridge University Press.

Gerth, H. H., and C. Wright Mills. 1958. *From Max Weber: Essays in Sociology.* New York: Galaxy.

Gheytanchi, Elham. 2009. "Iranian Women Lead the Protests." *San Francisco Chronicle,* June 29. Accessed June 30, 2009 (www.sfgate.com/cgi-bin/article.cgi?f=/c/a/2009/06/29/ED8618EMUC.DTL).

Gibson, Campbell, and Kay Jung. 2002. "Historical Census Statistics on Population Totals by Race, 1790 to 1990, and by Hispanic Origin, 1970 to 1990, for the United States, Regions, Divisions, and States." Population Division, U.S. Census Bureau, Washington, DC, September, Working Paper Series No. 56. Accessed May 17, 2010 (http://www.census.gov/population/www/documentation/twps0056/twps0056.html).

Giordano, Peggy C. 2003. "Relationships in Adolescence." Pp. 257–281 in *Annual Review of Sociology, 2003,* ed. Karen S. Cook and John Hagan. Palo Alto, CA: Annual Reviews.

Giroux, Henry A. 1988. *Schooling and the Struggle for Public Life: Critical Pedagogy in the Modern Age.* Minneapolis: University of Minnesota Press.

Gitlin, Todd. 1993. *The Sixties: Years of Hope, Days of Rage.* New York: Bantam Books.

Glassner, Barry. 2010. "Still Fearful." *Chronicle of Higher Education* 56 (January 22): B11–B12.

Glaze, Lauren E., and Thomas P. Bonczar. 2009. "Probation and Parole in the United States, 2008." *Bureau of Justice Statistics Bulletin,* December, NCJ 228230. Accessed April 9, 2010 (http://bjs.ojp.usdoj.gov/content/pub/pdf/ppus08.pdf).

Glenn, David. 2007. "Anthropologists in a War Zone: Scholars Debate Their Role." *Chronicle of Higher Education* 54 (September 30): A1, A10–A12.

Goering, Laurie. 2007. "The First Refugees of Global Warming." *Chicago Tribune,* May 2, pp. 1, 25.

Goffman, Erving. 1959. *The Presentation of Self in Everyday Life.* New York: Doubleday.

———. 1961. *Asylums: Essays on the Social Situation of Mental Patients and Other Inmates.* Garden City, NY: Doubleday.

———. 1963. *Stigma: Notes on Management of Spoiled Identity.* Englewood Cliffs, NJ: Prentice Hall.

———. 1979. *Gender Advertisements.* Cambridge, MA: Harvard University Press.

Goldscheider, Frances, Gayle Kaufman, and Sharon Sassler. 2010. "Navigating the 'New' Marriage Market: How Attitudes Toward Partner Characteristics Shape Union Formation." *Journal of Family Issues* 30 (6): 719–737.

Goldstein, Melvyn C., and Cynthia M. Beall. 1981. "Modernization and Aging in the Third and Fourth World: Views from the Rural Hinterland in Nepal." *Human Organization* 40 (Spring): 48–55.

Gomez, Jewelle L. 1997. "The Event of Becoming." Pp. 17–23 in *A Queer World: The Center for Lesbian and Gay Studies Reader,* ed. Martin Duberman. New York: New York University Press.

Goodwin Paula Y., William D. Mosher, and Anjani Chandra. 2010. "Marriage and Cohabitation in the United States: A Statistical Portrait Based on Cycle 6 (2002) of the National Survey of Family Growth." *Vital and Health Statistics,* 23 (28). National Center for Health Statistics, Washington, DC.

Gottfredson, Michael, and Travis Hirschi. 1990. *A General Theory of Crime.* Palo Alto, CA: Stanford University Press.

Gottlieb, Lori. 2006. "How Do I Love Thee?" *Atlantic Monthly,* March, pp. 58, 60, 62–68, 70.

Gould, Elise. 2008. "The Erosion of Employer-Sponsored Health Insurance: Declines Continue for the Seventh Year Running." EPI Briefing Paper No. 223, October 9. Washington, DC: Economic Policy Institute. Accessed June 26, 2009 (http://epi.3cdn.net/d1b4356d96c21c91d1_ilm6b5dua.pdf).

Gould, Larry A. 2002. "Indigenous People Policing Indigenous People: The Potential Psychological and Cultural Costs." *Social Science Journal* 39: 171–188.

Gouldner, Alvin. 1960. "The Norm of Reciprocity." *American Sociological Review* 25 (April): 161–177.

———. 1970. *The Coming Crisis of Western Sociology.* New York: Basic Books.

Government Accountability Office. 2003. *Women's Earnings: Work Patterns Partially Explain Difference Between Men's and Women's Earnings.* Washington, DC: U.S. Government Printing Office.

Gramsci, Antonio. 1929. *Selections from the Prison Notebooks,* ed. and trans. Quintin Hoare and Geoffrey Nowell Smith. London: Lawrence and Wishort.

Gray, John. 1992. *Men Are from Mars, Women Are from Venus: A Practical Guide for Improving Communication and Getting What You Want in Your Relationships.* New York: Harper Collins.

Green, Alexander R., Dana R. Carney, Daniel J. Pallin, Long H. Ngo, Kristal L. Raymond, Lisa I. Iezzoni, and Mahzarin R. Banaji. 2007. "Implicit Bias Among Physicians and Its Prediction of Thrombolysis Decisions for Black and White Patients." *Journal of General Internal Medicine* 9 (September): 1231–1238.

Greenhouse, Steven. 2007. "Low Pay and Broken Promises Greet Guest Workers in U.S." *New York Times,* February 28, p. A14.

———. 2008. "Queens Factory Is Found to Owe Workers $5.3 Million." *New York Times,* July 23. Accessed June 20, 2009 (http://cityroom.blogs.nytimes.com/2008/07/23/a-queens-sweatshop-found-to-owe-workers-53-million/).

Greenspan, Alan. 2005. "Testimony." Hearing Before the Committee on Banking, Housing, and Urban Affairs, United States Senate One Hundred Ninth Congress, S. Hrg. 109–204. Accessed June 6, 2009 (http://frwebgate.access.gpo.gov/cgi-bin/getdoc.cgi?dbname=109_senate_hearings&docid=f:24852.pdf).

Grieco, Elizabeth M., and Rachel C. Cassidy. 2001. "Overview of Race and Hispanic Origin." *Current Population Reports,* Ser. CENBR/01–1. Washington, DC: U.S. Government Printing Office.

Groeneveld, Elizabeth. 2009. "'Be a Feminist or Just Dress Like One': BUST, Fashion and Feminism as Lifestyle." *Journal of Gender Studies* 18 (2): 179–190.

Gross, Jane. 2005. "Forget the Career. My Parents Need Me at Home." *New York Times,* November 24, pp. A1, A20.

———. 2007. "U.S. Joins Overseas Adoption Overhaul Plan." *New York Times,* December 11, p. A25.

Groza, Victor, Scott Ryan, and Sara Thomas. 2008. "Institutionalization, Romanian Adoptions and Executive Functioning." *Child & Adolescent Social Work Journal* 25 (3): 185–204.

Guatemala Times. 2009. "Increase of Guatemala Remittances in 2008." *Guatemala Times,* January 9. Accessed May 17, 2010 (http://www.guatemala-times.com/news/guatemala/629-increase-of-guatemala-remittances-in-2008.html).

Guerrera, Francesco, and Andrew Ward. 2007. "Women on March to Top of U.S. Companies." *Financial Times,* March 28, p.17.

Guglielmo, Jennifer. 2003. "White Lies, Dark Truths." Pp. 1–14 in *Are Italians White? How Race Is Made in America,* ed. Jennifer Guglielmo and Salvatore Salerno. New York: Routledge.

Gurari, Inbal, John Hetts, and Michael Strube. 2006. "Beauty in the 'I' of the Beholder: Effects of Idealized Media Portrayals on Implicit Self-Image." *Basic & Applied Social Psychology* 28 (3): 273–282.

Gutiérrez, Gustavo. 1990. "Theology and the Social Sciences." Pp. 214–225 in *Liberation Theology at the Crossroads: Democracy or Revolution?* ed. Paul E. Sigmund. New York: Oxford University Press.

H

Halle, David. 1993. *Inside Culture: Art and Class in the American Home*. Chicago: University of Chicago Press.

Halperin, David M. 2009. "Thirteen Ways of Looking at a Bisexual." *Journal of Bisexuality* 9 (3/4): 451–455.

Hamilton, Mykol C., David Anderson, Michelle Broaddus, and Kate Young. 2006. "Gender Stereotyping and Underrepresentation of Female Characters in 200 Popular Children's Books: A Twenty-first Century Update." *Sex Roles* 55 (11/12): 757–765.

Harding, Sandra. 2004. "Introduction: Standpoint Theory as a Site of Political, Philosophic, and Scientific Debate." Pp. 1–16 in *The Feminist Standpoint Theory Reader: Intellectual and Political Controversies*, ed. Sandra Harding. New York: Routledge.

Harding, Sandra, ed. 2003. *The Feminist Standpoint Theory Reader: Intellectual and Political Controversies*. New York: Routledge.

Hardt, Michael, and Antonio Negri. 2009. *Commonwealth*. Cambridge, MA: Belknap Press.

Harlow, Harry F. 1971. *Learning to Love*. New York: Ballantine Books.

Harrington, Michael. 1962. *The Other America: Poverty in the United States*. Baltimore: Penguin Books.

———. 1980. "The New Class and the Left." Pp. 123–138 in *The New Class*, ed. B. Bruce Briggs. Brunswick, NJ: Transaction.

Hart, Betty, and Todd R. Risley. 1995. *Meaningful Differences in the Everyday Experience of Young American Children*. Baltimore: Paul H. Brookes.

Hart, Zachary P., Vernon D. Miller, and John R. Johnson. 2003. "Socialization, Resocialization and Communication Relationships in the Context of an Organizational Change." *Communication Studies* 54 (4): 483–495.

Hartsock, Nancy C. M. 1983. "The Feminist Standpoint: Developing the Ground for a Specifically Feminist Historical Materialism." Pp. 283–310 in *Discovering Reality: Feminist Perspectives in Epistemology, Methodology, and Philosophy of Science*, ed. Sandra Harding and Merrill B. Hintikka. Dordrect: Reidel.

Haskins, Ron. 2008. "Wealth and Economic Mobility." Chap. 4 in *Getting Ahead or Losing Ground: Economic Mobility in America*. Washington, DC: Pew Charitable Trusts. Accessed August 2, 2010 (http://economicmobility.org/assets/pdfs/EMP_Wealthand EconomicMobility_ChapterIV.pdf).

Hausmann, Ricardo, Laura D. Tyson, and Saadia Zahidi. 2009. *The Global Gender Gap Report 2009*. Geneva: World Economic Forum. Accessed May 11, 2010 (http://www.weforum.org/pdf/ gendergap/report2009.pdf).

Haviland, William A., Harald E. L. Prins, Dana Walrath, and Bunny McBride. 2005. *Cultural Anthropology: The Human Challenge*, 11th ed. Belmont, CA: Wadsworth.

He, Wan, Manisha Sengupta, Victoria A. Velkoff, and Kimberly A. DeBarros. 2005 "65+ in the United States: 2005." *Current Population Reports* P23-209. Washington, DC: U.S. Government Printing Office.

Heatherton, Todd F., and James Sargent. 2009. "Does Watching Smoking in Movies Promote Teenage Smoking?" *Current Directions in Psychological Science* 18 (2): 63–67.

Heilman, Madeline E. 2001. "Description and Prescription: How Gender Stereotypes Prevent Women's Ascent up the Organizational Ladder." *Journal of Social Issues* 57 (4): 657–674.

Henriques, Diana B., and Jack Healy. 2009. "Madoff Goes to Jail After Guilty Pleas." *New York Times,* March 12. Accessed May 21, 2009 (http://www.nytimes.com/2009/03/13/business/13madoff .html).

Herek, Gregory M. 2004. "Beyond 'Homophobia.' Thinking About Sexual Prejudice and Stigma in the Twenty-first Century." *Sexuality Research & Social Policy* 1 (2): 6–24.

———. 2007. "Confronting Sexual Stigma and Prejudice: Theory and Practice." *Journal of Social Issues* 63 (4): 905–925.

Heron, Melonie, Donna L. Hoyert, Sherry L. Murphy, Jiaquan Xu, Kenneth D. Kochanek, and Betzaida Tejada-Vera. 2009. "Deaths: Final Data for 2006." *National Vital Statistics Reports* 57 (14). Hyattsville, MD: National Center for Health Statistics.

Hertz, Rosanna. 2006. *Single by Chance. Mothers by Choice*. New York: Oxford University Press.

Hetherington, E. Mavis, and John Kelly. 2002. *For Better or for Worse: Divorce Reconsidered*. New York: Norton.

Higgins, George E., Richard Tewksbury, and Elizabeth Mustaine. 2007. "Sports Fan Binge Drinking: An Examination Using Low Self-Control and Peer Association." *Sociological Spectrum* 27 (4): 389–404.

Higgins, Michelle. 2008. "No Shoes, No Shirt, No Worries." *New York Times,* April 27. Accessed August 5, 2009 (http://travel.nytimes .com/2008/04/27/travel/27nude.html).

Hirschi, Travis. 1969. *Causes of Delinquency*. Berkeley: University of California Press.

Hirschman, Charles, and Irina Voloshin. 2007. "The Structure of Teenage Employment: Social Background and the Jobs Held by High School Seniors." *Research in Social Stratification and Mobility* 25: 189–203.

Hitlin, Steven, and Jane Allyn Piliavin. 2004. "Values: Reviving a Dormant Concept." Pp. 359–393 in *Annual Review of Sociology 2004*, ed. Karen S. Cook and John Hagan. Palo Alto, CA: Annual Review of Sociology.

Hochschild, Arlie Russell. 1989. *The Second Shift: Working Parents and the Revolution at Home*. New York: Viking Press.

———. 1990. "The Second Shift: Employed Women Are Putting in Another Day of Work at Home." *Utne Reader* 38 (March/April): 66–73.

———. 2005. *The Commercialization of Intimate Life: Notes from Home and Work*. Berkeley: University of California Press.

Holden, Constance. 1980. "Identical Twins Reared Apart." *Science* 207 (March 21): 1323–1328.

———. 1987. "The Genetics of Personality." *Science* 257 (August 7): 598–601.

Holder, Kelly. 2006. "Voting and Registration in the Election of November 2004." *Current Population Reports* P20–556. Washington, DC: U.S. Government Printing Office.

Hollingshead, August B. 1975. *Elmtown's Youth and Elmtown Revisited*. New York: Wiley.

Holmes, Mary. 2006. "Love Lives at a Distance: Distance Relationships over the Lifecourse." *Sociological Research Online* 11 (3).

Homans, George C. 1979. "Nature Versus Nurture: A False Dichotomy." *Contemporary Sociology* 8 (May): 345–348.

Home School Legal Defense Association. 2005. "State Laws" and "Academic Statistics on Homeschooling." Accessed August 2, 2010 (www.hslda.org)

Hondagneu-Sotelo, Pierrette, ed. 2003. *Gender and U.S. Immigration. Contemporary Trends*. Berkeley: University of California Press.

Hootman, J., J. Bolen, C. Helmick, and G. Langmaid. 2006. "Prevalence of Doctor-Diagnosed Arthritis and Arthritis-Attributable Activity Limitation—United States, 2003–2005." *Morbidity and Mortality Weekly Report* 55 (40): 1089–1092.

Horowitz, Helen Lefkowitz. 1987. *Campus Life*. Chicago: University of Chicago Press.

Horrigan, John B. 2007. *A Typology of Information and Communication Technology Users*. Washington, DC: Pew Internet and American Life Project.

———. 2009. "Home Broadband Adoption 2009." Pew Internet and American Life Project, Pew Research Center, Washington, DC. Accessed April 26, 2010 (http://www.pewinternet.org/~ /media// Files/Reports/2009/Home-Broadband-Adoption-2009.pdf).

Hostetler, John A. 1993. *Amish Society,* 4th ed. Baltimore: Johns Hopkins University Press.

Hout, Michael, and Claude S. Fischer. 2002. "Why More Americans Have No Religious Preference: Politics and Generations." *American Sociological Review* 67 (April): 165–190.

Howard, Russell D., and Reid L. Sawyer. 2003. *Terrorism and Counterterrorism: Understanding the New Security Environment.* Guilford, CT: McGraw-Hill/Dushkin.

Huang, Gary. 1988. "Daily Addressing Ritual: A Cross-Cultural Study." Paper presented at the annual meeting of the American Sociological Association, Atlanta.

References

Hughes, Everett. 1945. "Dilemmas and Contradictions of Status." *American Journal of Sociology* 50 (March): 353–359.

Human Rights Campaign. 2009. "Maps of State Laws & Policies." Accessed May 27, 2009 (http://www.hrc.org/about_us/state_laws .asp).

———. 2010. "Marriage Equality & Other Relationship Recognition Laws." Human Rights Campaign, Washington, DC, April 2. Accessed April 14, 2010 (http://www.hrc.org/documents/ Relationship_Recognition_Laws_Map.pdf).

Hunter, Herbert M., ed. 2000. *The Sociology of Oliver C. Cox: New Perspectives: Research in Race and Ethnic Relations,* vol. 2. Stamford, CT: JAI Press.

Hurst, Charles E., and David L. McConnell. 2010. *An Amish Paradox: Diversity and Change in the World's Largest Amish Community.* Baltimore: Johns Hopkins University Press.

I

Ignatiev, Noel. 1995. *How the Irish Became White.* New York: Routledge.

Igo, Sarah E. 2007. *The Average American: Surveys, Citizens, and the Making of a Mass Public.* Cambridge, MA: Harvard University Press.

INEGI. 2009. "Mujeres y Hombres en México 2005. Anexo estadístico." Instituto Nacional de Estadística y Geografía. Accessed June 14, 2009 (www.inegi.org.mx/inegi/contenidos/espanol/bvinegi/ productos/integracion/sociodemografico/mujeresyhombres/2005/ anexo_2005.xls).

Inglehart, Ronald, Pippa Norris, and Christian Welzel. 2002. "Gender Equality and Democracy." *Comparative Sociology* 1 (3/4): 321–346.

Innocence Project. 2009. "Innocence Project Case Profiles." Accessed May 20, 2009 (http://www.innocenceproject.org/know/).

———. 2010. "Innocence Project Case Profiles." Accessed May 5, 2010 (www.innocenceproject.org/know/).

INPE. 2010. "Specific Data of PRODES/INPE Confirms the Range of the Amazon Deforestation." Instituto Nacional de Pesquisas Espaciais, April 29. Accessed May 21, 2010 (http://www.inpe.br/ingles/ news/news_dest117.php).

International Centre for Prison Studies. 2010. "Prison Brief—Highest to Lowest Rates: Entire World—Prison Population Rates per 100,000 of the National Population." School of Law, King's College, University of London, United Kingdom. Accessed April 9, 2010 (http://www.kcl.ac.uk/depsta/law/research/icps/worldbrief/ wpb_stats.php?area=all&category=wb_poprate).

International Institute for Democracy and Electoral Assistance. 2010. "Voter Turnout Database." Accessed April 23, 2010 (http://www. idea.int/vt/view_data.cfm).

International Telecommunications Union. 2010. "ICT Statistics Database: Country Data by Region—2008." Accessed April 1, 2010 (http://www.itu.int/ITU-D/icteye/indicators/indicators.aspx).

Inter-Parliamentary Union. 2010. "Women in National Parliaments: Situation as of 28 February 2010." Accessed April 23, 2010 (http:// www.ipu.org/wmn-e/classif.htm).

Internal Revenue Service. 2008. "Fiscal Year 2008 Enforcement Results." Accessed June 6, 2009 (www.irs.gov/pub/irs-news/2008_ enforcement.pdf).

———. 2009. "The 400 Individual Income Tax Returns Reporting the Highest Adjusted Gross Incomes Each Year, 1992–2006." Accessed June 6, 2009 (www.irs.gov/pub/irs-soi/06intop400.pdf).

International Institute for Democracy and Electoral Assistance. 2009. "Voter Turnout Database." Accessed June 2, 2009 (www.idea.int/ vt/view_data.cfm).

International Labour Organization. 2008. *World of Work Report 2008: Income Inequalities in the Age of Financial Globalization.* Geneva International Institute for Labour Studies. Accessed June 12, 2009 (www.ilo.org/public/english/bureau/inst/download/world08.pdf).

International Monetary Fund. 2000. *World Economic Outlook: Asset Prices and the Business Cycle.* Washington, DC: IMF.

———. 2008. "IMF Helping Countries Respond to Food Price Crisis." *IMF Survey Magazine: In the News,* June 3. Washington, DC: IMF. Accessed August 2, 2010 (http://www.imf.org/external/pubs/ft/ survey/so/2008/NEW060308A.htm).

International Telecommunications Union. 2009. "ICT Statistics Database." Accessed May 6, 2009 (http://www.itu.int/ITU-D/ icteye/Indicators/Indicators.aspx).

Internet World Stats. 2010a. "Internet Usage Statistics: The Internet Big Picture." Accessed May 23, 2010 (http://www.internetworldstats .com/stats.htm).

———. 2010b. "Internet World Users by Language: Top 10 Languages." Accessed May 23, 2010 (http://www.internetworldstats.com/stats7 .htm).

Ionescu, Carmiola. 2005. "Romania's Abandoned Children Are Still Suffering." *Lancet* 366 (9497): 1595–1596.

Isaacs, Julia B. 2007a. *Economic Mobility of Families Across Generations.* Washington, DC: Economic Mobility Project, Pew Charitable Trusts.

———. Julia B. 2007b. *Economic Mobility of Men and Women.* Washington, DC: Economic Mobility Project.

———. 2007c. *Economic Mobility of Black and White Families.* Washington, DC: Economic Mobility Project.

———. 2008. "Economic Mobility of Black and White Families." *Economic Mobility Project,* Pew Charitable Trusts, November. Accessed June 21, 2009 (www.brookings.edu/reports/2008/~/ media/Files/rc/reports/2008/02_economic_mobility_sawhill/02_ economic_mobility_sawhill_ch6.pdf).

Isaacs, Julia B., Isabel V. Sawhill, and Ron Haskins. 2008. *Getting Ahead or Losing Ground: Economic Mobility in America.* Washington, DC: Pew Charitable Trust.

ITOPF. 2006. "Statistics: International Tanker Owners Pollution Federation Limited." Accessed May 2, 2007 (www.itopf.com/stats.html).

J

Jackson, Jerlando, and Elizabeth O'Callaghan. 2009. "What Do We Know About Glass Ceiling Effects? A Taxonomy and Critical Review to Inform Higher Education Research." *Research in Higher Education* 50 (5): 460–482.

Jacobs, David, Zhenchao Qian, Jason T. Carmichael, and Stephanie L. Kent. 2007. "Who Survives on Death Row? An Individual and Contextual Analysis." *American Sociological Review* 72 (August): 610–632.

James, Susan Donaldson. 2008. "Students Use Civil Rights Tactics to Combat Global Warming." *ABC News,* January 19. Accessed August 2, 2010 (http://abcnews.go.com/Technology/ GlobalWarming/story?id=2805553&page=1).

———. 2008. "Wild Child Speechless After Tortured Life: Abandoned by Doctors and Mother, Abused in Foster Care, 'Genie' Regressed." *ABC News Online,* May 19. Accessed May 5, 2009 (http://abcnews.go.com/Health/Story?id=4873347&page=1).

Jamison, Andrew. 2006. "Social Movements and Science: Cultural Appropriations of Cognitive Praxis." *Science as Culture* 15 (1): 45–59.

Jargowsky, Paul A., and Rebecca Yang. 2006. "The 'Underclass' Revisited: A Social Problem in Decline." *Journal of Urban Affairs* 28 (1): 55–70.

Jaye, Chrystal, Tony Egan, and Sarah Parker. 2006. "'Do as I Say, Not as I Do': Medical Education and Foucault's Normalizing Technologies of Self." *Anthropology & Medicine* 13 (2): 141–155.

Jenkins, J. Craig. 2004. "Social Movements: Resource Mobilization Theory." Pp. 14368–14371 in *International Encyclopedia of the Social and Behavioral Sciences,* ed. Neil J. Smelser and Paul B. Baltes. New York: Elsevier.

Jenkins, Matt. 2008. "A Really Inconvenient Truth." *Miller-McCure* 1 (March/April): 38–41.

Jenness, Valerie, David A. Smith, and Judith Stepan-Norris. 2006. "Pioneer Public Sociologist C. Wright Mills, 50 Years Later." *Contemporary Sociology* 35 (6): 7–8.

Johnson, Allan G. 1997. *The Forest and the Trees: Sociology as Life, Practice, and Promise.* Philadelphia: Temple University Press.

Johnson, Tallese D. 2008. "Maternity Leave and Employment Patterns: 2001–2003." *Current Population Reports,* P70-113. Washington, DC: U.S. Census Bureau.

Johnston, David Cay. 1994. "Ruling Backs Homosexuals on Asylum." *New York Times,* June 12, pp. D1, D6.

Jones, Jeffrey M. 2010a. "Americans Prioritize Energy over Environment for First Time." Washington, DC: Gallup, Inc. April 6. Accessed May 21, 2010 (http://www.gallup.com/poll/127220/Americans-Prioritize-Energy-Environment-First-Time.aspx).

———— 2010b. "In U.S., Many Environmental Issues at 20-Year-Low Concern." Washington, DC: Gallup, Inc. March 16. Accessed May 21, 2010 (http://www.gallup.com/poll/126716/Environmental-Issues-Year-Low-Concern.aspx).

Jones, Nicholas A. 2005. *We the People of More than One Race in the United States.* Census 2000 Special Reports, CENSR-22. Washington, DC: U.S. Government Printing Office.

Joseph, Jay. 2004. *The Gene Illusion: Genetic Research in Psychiatry and Psychology Under the Microscope.* New York: Algora Books.

Josephson Institute of Ethics. 2008. "The Ethics of American Youth—2008 Summary." Josephson Institute's 2008 Report Card on the Ethics of American Youth. Accessed May 2, 2009 (http://charactercounts.org/programs/reportcard/).

Jost, Kenneth. 2008. "Women in Politics."*CQ Researcher* 18 (March 21).

Juergensmeyer, Mark. 2003. *Terror in the Mind of God: The Global Rise of Religious Violence,* 3d ed. Berkeley: University of California Press.

K

Kaiser Family Foundation. 2005. *Sex on TV: 2005.* Santa Barbara, CA: Kaiser Family Foundation.

————. 2009. "Trends in Health Care Costs and Spending." Kaiser Family Foundation Publication #7692–02, March, Menlo Park, CA. Accessed June 26, 2009 (www.kff.org/insurance/upload/7692_02.pdf).

Kalev, Alexandria, Frank Dobbin, and Erin Kelly. 2006. "Best Practices or Best Guesses? Assessing the Efficacy of Corporate Affirmative Action and Diversity Policies." *American Sociological Review* 71: 589–617.

Kalish, Richard A. 1985. *Death, Grief, and Caring Relationships,* 2d ed. Monterey, CA: Brooks/Cole.

Kalita, S. Mitra. 2006. "On the Other End of the Line." *Washington Post National Weekly Edition,* January 9, pp. 20–21.

Kalmijn, Matthijs. 1991. "Status Homogamy in the United States." *American Journal of Sociology* 97 (2): 496–523.

———— 1998. "Intermarriage and Homogamy: Causes, Patterns, Trends." *Annual Review of Sociology* 24: 395–412.

Kamp, Marianne. 2008. *The New Woman in Uzbekistan.* Seattle: University of Washington Press.

Kanter, Rosabeth Moss. 1993. *Men and Women of the Corporation.* New York: Basic Books.

Kapstein, Ethan B. 2006. "The New Global Slave Trade." *Foreign Affairs* 85 (November/December): 103–115.

Karney, Benjamin R., and John S. Crown. 2007. "Families Under Stress: An Assessment of Data, Theory, and Research on Marriage and Divorce in the Military." Santa Monica, CA: RAND Corporation.

Kasavin, Greg. 2003. "Real Life: The Full Review." GameSpot, July 11. Accessed June 3, 2008 (http://www.gamespot.com/gamespot/features/all/gamespotting/071103minusworld/1.html).

Katz, Jason. 1999. *Tough Guise: Violence, Media, and the Crisis in Masculinity.* Video. Directed by Sut Jhally. Northampton, MA: Media Education Foundation.

Kavada, Anastasia 2005. "Exploring the Role of the Interest in the 'Movement for Alternative Globalization': The Case of the Paris 2003 European Social Forum." *Westminster Papers in Communication and Culture* 2 (1): 72–95.

Kempadoo, Kamala, and Jo Doezema, eds. 1998. *Global Sex Workers: Rights, Resistance, and Redefinition.* New York: Routledge.

Kennickell, Arthur B. 2009. "Ponds and Streams: Wealth and Income in the U.S., 1989 to 2007." Finance and Economics Discussion Series, Divisions of Research & Statistics and Monetary Affairs, Federal Reserve Board, Washington, DC. Accessed June 7, 2009 (www.federalreserve.gov/pubs/feds/2009/200913/200913pap.pdf).

Kentor, Jeffrey, and Yong Suk Jang. 2004. "Yes, There Is a (Growing) Transnational Business Community." *International Sociology* 19 (September): 355–368.

Kerbo, Harold R. 2009. *Social Stratification and Inequality: Class Conflict in Historical, Comparative, and Global Perspective,* 7th ed. New York: McGraw-Hill.

Khorasani, Noushin Ahmadi. 2009. "How Social Movements Can Change Iran." *The Mark,* June 11. Accessed June 30, 2009 (www.themarknews.com/articles/290-how-social-movements-can-change-iran).

Kilbourne, Jean. 2010. *Killing Us Softly 4: Advertising's Image of Women.* Video. Produced and directed by Sut Jhally. Northampton, MA: Media Education Foundation.

Kilpatrick, Dean G., Heidi S. Resnick, Kenneth J. Ruggiero, Lauren M. Conoscenti, and Jenna McCauley. 2007. "Drug-Facilitated, Incapacitated, and Forcible Rape: A National Study." National Institute of Justice Grant No. 2005-Wg-BX-0006. Accessed June 1, 2010 (http://www.ncjrs.gov/pdffiles1/nij/grants/219181.pdf).

Kim, Kwang Chung. 1999. *Koreans in the Hood: Conflict with African Americans.* Baltimore: Johns Hopkins University Press.

Kimmel, Michael. 2004. *The Gendered Society,* 2d ed. New York: Oxford University Press.

Kinsella, Kevin, and David R. Phillips. 2005. "Global Aging: The Challenge of Success." *Population Bulletin* 60 (March).

Kinsey, Alfred C., Wardell B. Pomeroy, and Paul H. Gebhard. 1953. *Sexual Behavior in the Human Female.* Philadelphia: Saunders.

Kinsey, Alfred C., Wardell B. Pomeroy, and Clyde E. Martin. 1948. *Sexual Behavior in the Human Male.* Philadelphia: Saunders.

Kirby, Emily Hoban, and Kei Kawashima-Ginsberg. 2009. "The Youth Vote in 2008." Fact Sheet, Center for Information & Research on Civic Learning & Engagement, April. Accessed June 18, 2009 (www.civicyouth.org/PopUps/FactSheets/FS_youth_Voting_2008.pdf).

Kitchener, Richard F. 1991. "Jean Piaget: The Unknown Sociologist." *British Journal of Sociology* 42 (September): 421–442.

Klein, Stefan. 2006. *The Science of Happiness: How Our Brains Make Us Happy—And What We Can Do to Get Happier.* New York: Marlowe.

Kleinknecht, William. 1996. *The New Ethnic Mobs: The Changing Face of Organized Crime in America.* New York: Free Press.

Kliewer, Wendy, and Terri N. Sullivan. 2009. "Community Violence Exposure, Threat Appraisal, and Adjustment in Adolescents." *Journal of Clinical Child & Adolescent Psychology* 37 (4): 860–873.

Klinenberg, Eric. 2002. *Heat Wave: A Social Autopsy of Disaster in Chicago.* Chicago: University of Chicago Press.

Knudson, Tom. 2006. "Promises and Poverty: Starbucks Calls Its Coffee Worker-Friendly—but in Ethiopia, a Day's Pay Is a Dollar." *Sacramento Bee,* September 23. Accessed June 12, 2009 (www.sacbee.com/502/story/393917.html).

————. 2007. "Investigative Report: Promises and Poverty." *Sacramento Bee,* September 23. Accessed August 6, 2009 (www.sacbee.com/502/story/393917.html).

Kochhar, Rakesh. 2004. *The Wealth of Hispanic Households: 1996 to 2002.* Washington, DC: Pew Hispanic Center.

Kochhar, Rakesh, Ana Gonzalez-Barrera, and Daniel Dockterman. 2009. "Through Boom and Bust: Minorities, Immigrants and Homeownership." Pew Hispanic Center, May 12. Accessed June 22, 2009 (http://pewhispanic.org/files/reports/109.pdf).

Koerner, Brendan I. 2003. "What Does a 'Thumbs Up' Mean in Iraq?" *Slate,* March 28. Accessed May 3, 2009 (http://www.slate.com/id/2080812).

Kokmen, Leyla. 2008. "Environmental Justice for All." *Utne Reader,* March/April, pp. 42–46.

Korczyk, Sophie M. 2002. *Back to Which Future? The U.S. Aging Crisis Revisited.* Washington, DC: AARP.

Kosmin, Barry A., and Ariela Keysar. 2009. *American Religious Identification Survey: ARIS 2008 Summary Report.* Hartford, CT: Trinity College. Accessed June 1, 2009 (http://b27.cc.trincoll.edu/weblogs/AmericanReligionSurvey-ARIS/reports/ARIS_Report_2008.pdf).

Kottak, Conrad. 2004. *Anthropology: The Explanation of Human Diversity.* New York: McGraw-Hill.

Kozol, Jonathan. 2005. *The Shame of the Nation: The Restoration of Apartheid Schooling in America.* New York: Crown.

Kraybill, Donald. 2001. *The Riddle of Amish Culture,* rev. ed. Baltimore: Johns Hopkins University Press.

Krebs, Christopher P., Christine H. Lindquist, Tara D. Warner, Bonnie S. Fisher, and Sandra L. Martin. 2007. "The Campus Sexual Assault (CSA) Study, Final Report." National Institute of Justice Grant No. 2004-WG-BX-0010. Accessed June 1, 2010 (http://www.ncjrs.gov.pdffiles1/nij/grants/221153.pdf).

Kreider, Rose M. 2008. "Living Arrangements of Children: 2004." *Current Population Reports,* No. 114. Washington, DC: U.S. Government. Printing Office.

Kristof, Nicholas D., and Sheryl WuDunn. 2009. *Half the Sky: Turning Oppression into Opportunity for Women Worldwide.* New York: Knopf.

Kroll, Luisa, and Allison Fass. 2006. "The World's Billionaires." *Forbes,* March 9.

Kroll, Luisa, and Matthew Miller. 2010. "The World's Billionaires." *Forbes,* March 10. Accessed April 29, 2010 (http://www.forbes.com/2010/03/10/worlds-richest-people-slim-gates-buffett-billionaires-2010_land.html).

Kronstadt, Jessica, and Melissa Favreault. 2008. "Families and Economic Mobility." Washington, DC: Economic Mobility Project. Accessed August 13, 2008 (www.economicmobility.org/reports_and_research/literature_reviews?id=0004).

Kruttschnitt, Candace, and Kristin Carbone-Lopez. 2006. "Moving Beyond the Stereotypes: Women's Subjective Accounts of Their Violent Crime." *Criminology* 44 (2): 321–352.

Kübler-Ross, Elisabeth. 1969. *On Death and Dying.* New York: Macmillan.

Kuumba, M. Bahati. 2001. *Gender and Social Movements.* Lanham, MD: AltaMira Press.

Kwong, Jo. 2005. "Globalization's Effects on the Environment." *Society* 42 (January/February): 21–28.

Kyckelhahn, Tracey, Allen J. Beck, and Thomas H Cohen. 2009. "Characteristics of Suspected Human Trafficking Incidents, 2007–08." Bureau of Justice Statistics, Special Reports, January, NCJ 224526. Accessed June 2, 2010 (http://bjs.ojp.usdoj.gov/content/pub/pdf/cshti08.pdf).

L

Lacey, Marc. 2008. "Hunger in Haiti Increasing Rapidly." *International Herald Tribune,* April 17. Accessed August 12, 2008 (http://www.iht.com/articles/2008/04/17/news/Haiti.php).

Ladner, Joyce. 1973. *The Death of White Sociology.* New York: Random Books.

Lambert, Emily. 2009. "Nimby Wars." *Forbes* 183 (February 16): 98–101. Accessed June 29, 2009 (www.forbes.com/forbes/2009/0216/098.html).

Landale, Nancy S., and R. S. Oropesa. 2007. "Hispanic Families: Stability and Change." *Annual Review of Sociology* 33: 381–405.

Langhout, Regina D., and Cecily A. Mitchell. 2008. "Engaging Contexts: Drawing the Link Between Student and Teacher Experiences of the Hidden Curriculum." *Journal of Community & Applied Social Psychology* 18 (6): 593–614.

Lareau, Annette. 2003. *Unequal Childhoods: Class, Race, and Family Life.* Berkeley: University of California Press.

Larson, Edward J. 2006. *Summer for the Gods: The Scopes Trial and America's Continuing Debate over Science and Religion.* New York: Basic Books.

Lasker, John. 2008. "Inside Africa's PlayStation War." *Toward Freedom,* July 8. Accessed June 3, 2009 (http://towardfreedom.com/home/content/view/1352/1).

Lasswell, Harold D. 1936. *Politics: Who Gets What, When, How.* New York: McGraw-Hill.

Laumann, Edward O., John H. Gagnon, Robert T. Michael, and Stuart Michaels. 1994. *The Social Organization of Sexuality: Sexual Practices in the United States.* Chicago: University of Chicago Press.

Leadley, Jennifer. 2009. "Women in U.S. Academic Medicine: Statistics and Benchmarking Report, 2008–2009." Association of American Medical Colleges. Accessed May 20, 2010 (https://services.aamc.org/publications/showfile.cfm?file=version158.pdf&prd_id=295&prv_id=366&pdf_id=158).

Le Bon, Gustav. 1895. *The Crowd: A Study of the Popular Mind.* New York: Macmillan.

Leavell, Hugh R., and E. Gurney Clark. 1965. *Preventive Medicine for the Doctor in His Community: An Epidemiologic Approach,* 3d ed. New York: McGraw-Hill.

LeClaire, Jennifer. 2009. "Sixty Percent of the World Uses Cell Phones." *Mobile Tech Today.* Accessed May 6, 2009 (http://www.mobile-tech-today.com/story.xhtml?story_id=65006).

Lengermann, Patricia Madoo, and Jill Niebrugge-Brantley. 1998. *The Women Founders: Sociology and Social Theory, 1830–1930.* Boston: McGraw-Hill.

Leonard, Annie. 2010. *The Story of Stuff: How Our Obsession with Stuff Is Trashing the Planet, Our Communities, and Our Health—and a Vision for Change.* New York: Free Press.

Leonhardt, David. 2007. "Middle-Class Squeeze Comes with Nuances." *New York Times,* April 25, pp. C1, C12.

Levine, Kenneth J., and Cynthia A. Hoffner. 2006. "Adolescents' Conceptions of Work: What Is Learned from Different Sources During Anticipatory Socialization?" *Journal of Adolescent Research* 21 (6): 647–669.

Levitt, Steven D., and Stephen J. Dubner. 2005. *Freakonomics: A Rogue Economist Explores the Hidden Side of Everything.* New York: Morrow.

Lewin, Tamar. 2008. "College May Become Unaffordable for Most in U.S." *New York Times,* Decemeber 3. Accessed May 19, 2010 (http://www.nytimes.com/2008/12/03/education/03college.html).

Leys, Tony. 2008. "New Faces Endure Same Struggle." *Des Moines Register,* May 18, pp. 1, 11.

Liang, Bin, and Hong Lu. 2010. "Internet Development, Censorship, and Cyber Crimes in China." *Journal of Contemporary Criminal Justice* 26 (1): 103–120.

Ling, Peter. 2006. "Social Capital, Resource Mobilization and Origins of the Civil Rights Movement." *Journal of Historical Sociology* 19 (2): 202–214.

Lino, Mark, and Andrea Carlson. 2009. *Expenditures on Children by Families, 2008.* Center for Nutrition Policy and Promotion, Miscellaneous Publication No. 1528-2008. U.S. Department of Agriculture, Washington, DC. Accessed April 13, 2010 (http://www.cnpp.usda.gov/Publications/CRC/crc2008.pdf).

Liptak, Adam. 2006. "The Ads Discriminate, but Does the Web?" *New York Times,* March 5, p. 16.

———. 2008a. "Damages Cut Against Exxon in *Valdez* Case." *New York Times,* June 26. Accessed April 27, 2009 (http://www.nytimes.com/2008/06/26/washington/26punitive.html).

———. 2008b. "From One Footnote, a Debate over the Tangles of Law, Science and Money." *New York Times,* June 26. Accessed April 27, 2009 (http://www.nytimes.com/2008/11/25/washington/25bar.html).

List, Justin M. 2009. "Justice and the Reversal of the Healthcare Worker 'Brain-Drain.'" *American Journal of Bioethics* 9 (3): 10–12.

Logue, Susan. 2009. "Poll: More Newlyweds Met Online." *Voice of America News,* March 27. Accessed May 26, 2009 (http://www.voanews.com/english/archive/2009–03/2009–03–27-voa17.cfm).

Lopata, Helena Znaniecki. 1971. *Occupation: Housewife.* New York: Oxford University Press.

Lopez, Mark Hugo, and Paul Taylor. 2009. "Dissecting the 2008 Electorate: Most Diverse in U.S. History." Pew Research Center, Washington, DC, April 30. Accessed June 18, 2009 (http://pewresearch.org/assets/pdf/dissecting-2008-electorate.pdf).

Lorber, Judith. 1994. *Paradoxes of Gender.* New Haven, CT: Yale University Press.

Lotz, Amanda D. 2007. "Theorising the Intermezzo: The Contributions of Postfeminism and Third Wave Feminism." Pp. 71–85 in *Third Wave Feminism: A Critical Exploration,* expanded 2d ed., ed. Stacy Gillis, Gillian Howie, and Rebecca Munford. New York: Palgrave Macmillan.

Louie, Miriam Ching Yoon. 2001. *Sweatshop Warriors: Immigrant Women Workers Take on the Global Factory.* Cambridge, MA: South End Press.

Lovgren, Stefan. 2006. "Can Cell-Phone Recycling Help African Gorillas?" *National Geographic News,* January 20. Accessed June 3, 2009 (http://news.nationalgeographic.com/news/2006/01/0120_060120_cellphones.html).

Lucal, Betsy. 2010. "Better Informed, Still Skeptical: Response to Machalek and Martin." *Teaching Sociology* 38 (1): 46–49.

Lu, Haoting. 2009. "Starbucks Pushes China Sales with Local Brew." *China Daily,* February 5. Accessed May 2, 2009 (http://www.chinadaily.com.cn/bizchina/2009–02/05/content_7447136.htm).

Lukács, Georg. 1923. *History and Class Consciousness.* London: Merlin.

Lumpe, Lora. 2003. "Taking Aim at the Global Gun Trade." *Amnesty Now* (Winter): 10–13.

Lundquist, Jennifer Hickes. 2006. "Choosing Single Motherhood." *Contexts* 5 (Fall): 64–67.

Lyall, Sarah. 2002. "For Europeans, Love, Yes; Marriage, Maybe." *New York Times,* March 24, pp. 1–8.

Lymas, Mark. 2008. *Six Degrees: Our Future on a Hotter Planet.* Washington, DC: National Geographic.

Lynn, Barry C. 2003. "Trading with a Low-Wage Tiger." *The American Prospect* 14 (February): 10–12.

Lytton, Hugh, and David M. Romney. 1991. "Parents' Differential Socialization of Boys and Girls: A Meta-analysis." *Psychological Bulletin* 109 (2): 267–296.

M

MacEachern, Scott. 2003. "The Concept of Race in Anthropology." Pp. 10–35 in *Race and Ethnicity: An Anthropological Focus on the United States and the World,* ed. R. Scupin. Upper Saddle River, NJ: Prentice Hall.

MacFarquhar, Neil. 2008. "Resolute or Fearful, Many Muslims Turn to Home Schooling." *New York Times,* March 26, p. A1.

Machalek, Richard, and Michael W. Martin. 2010. "Evolution, Biology, and Society: A Conversation for the 21st-Century Classroom." *Teaching Sociology* 38 (1): 35–45.

Machan, Dyan. 2010. "Entrepreneurs Doing Business by Avatar." *SmartMoney,* April 7. Accessed April 8, 2010 (http://www.smartmoney.com/personal-finance/employment/Entrepreneurs-Doing-Business-by-Avatar/).

Maher, Timothy M. 2008. "Police Chiefs' Views on Police Sexual Misconduct." *Police Practice & Research* 9 (3): 239–250.

Mahy, Mary, Jean-Michel Tassie, Peter D. Ghys, John Stover, Michel Beusenberg, Priscilla Akwara, and Yves Souteyrand. 2010. "Estimation of Antiretroviral Therapy Coverage: Methodology and Trends." *Current Opinion in HIV and AIDS* 5 (1): 97–102.

Malacrida, Claudia. 2005. "Discipline and Dehumanization in a Total Institution: Institutional Survivors' Descriptions of Time-Out Rooms." *Disability & Society* 20 (5): 523–537.

Malcolm X, with Alex Haley. 1964. *The Autobiography of Malcolm X.* New York: Grove.

Mandel, Stephen. 2008. *Debt Relief as if Justice Mattered.* London: New Economics Foundation.

Mangan, Katherine. 2006. "Survey Finds Widespread Cheating in M.B.A. Programs." *Chronicle of Higher Education,* September 19. Accessed June 6 (http://chronicle.com/daily/2006/09/2006091902n.htm).

Mangum, Garth L., Stephen L. Mangum, and Andrew M. Sum. 2003. *The Persistence of Poverty in the United States.* Baltimore: Johns Hopkins University Press.

Mann, Horace. [1848] 1957. "Report No. 12 of the Massachusetts School Board." Pp. 79–97 in *The Republic and the School: Horace Mann on the Education of Free Men,* ed. L. A. Cremin. New York: Teachers College.

Manning, Jennifer E. 2010. "Membership of the 111th Congress: A Profile." A Congressional Research Service Report for Congress, Washington, DC, February 4. Accessed April 23, 2010 (http://assets.opencrs.com/rpts/R40086_20100204.pdf).

Mapel, Tim. 2007. "The Adjustment Process of Ex-Buddhist Monks to Life After the Monastery." *Journal of Religion & Health* 46 (1): 19–34.

Marijuana Policy Project. 2008. "State-by-State Medical Marijuana Laws: 2008." Washington, DC: Marijuana Policy Project. Accessed May 19, 2009 (http://www.mpp.org/assets/pdfs/download-materials/SBSR_NOV2008.pdf).

Marples, David R. 2004. *The Collapse of the Soviet Union, 1985–1991.* New York: Pearson Longman.

Martineau, Harriet. [1837] 1962. *Society in America.* Edited, abridged, with an introductory essay by Seymour Martin Lipset. Garden City, NY: Doubleday.

———. [1838] 1989. *How to Observe Morals and Manners.* Philadelphia: Leal and Blanchard. Sesquentennial edition, ed. M. R. Hill. New York: Transaction.

Marx, Karl. [1845] 2000. "German Ideology." Pp. 175–208 in *Karl Marx: Selected Writings,* 2d ed., ed. David McLellan. New York: Oxford University Press.

———. [1867] 2000. "Capital." Pp. 452–546 in *Karl Marx: Selected Writings,* 2d ed., ed. David McLellan. New York: Oxford University Press.

Marx, Karl, and Friedrich Engels. [1847] 1955. *Selected Work in Two Volumes.* Moscow: Foreign Languages Publishing House.

———. (1848) 1998. *The Communist Manifesto: A Modern Edition.* New York: Verso.

Massey, Douglas S. 1998. "March of Folly: U.S. Immigration Policy After NAFTA." *The American Prospect,* March/April, pp. 22–23.

———. 2007. *Categorically Unequal: The American Stratification System.* New York: Sage.

———. 2008. *New Faces in New Places: The Changing Geography of American Immigration.* New York: Sage.

Mathews, T. J., and Marian F. MacDorman. 2010. "Infant Mortality Statistics from the 2006 Period Linked Birth/Infant Death Data Set." *National Vital Statistics Reports* 58 (17). Hyattsville, MD: National Center for Health Statistics. Accessed May 20, 2010 (http://www.cdc.gov/nchs/data/nvsr/nvsr58/nvsr58_17.pdf).

Mayeux, Lara, Marlene J. Sandstrom, and Antonius H. N. Cillessen. 2008. "Is Being Popular a Risky Proposition?" *Journal of Research on Adolescence* 18 (1): 49–74.

Mayo, Elton. 1933. *The Human Problems of an Industrial Civilization.* London: Macmillan.

McCabe, Donald L., Kenneth D. Butterfield, and Linda Klebe Treviño. 2006. "Academic Dishonesty in Graduate Business Programs: Prevalence, Causes, and Proposed Action." *Academy of Management Learning & Education* 5 (3): 294–305.

McAdam, Doug. 1988. *Freedom Summer.* New York: Oxford University Press.

McCabe, Janice. 2005. "What's in a Label? The Relationship Between Feminist Self-Identification and 'Feminist' Attitudes Among U.S. Women and Men." *Gender & Society* 19 (4): 480–505.

McCombs, Brady. 2009. "Death Count Rises with Border Restrictions." *Arizona Daily Star,* May 17. Accessed June 13, 2009 (www.azstarnet.com/sn/border/293256).

McDonald, Michael. 2009. "Election of a Century?" United States Elections Project. Accessed June 2, 2009 (http://elections.gmu.edu/Election_of_a_Century.html).

McDowell, David J., and Ross D. Parke. 2009. "Parental Correlates of Children's Peer Relations: An Empirical Test of a Tripartite Model." *Developmental Psychology* 45 (1): 224–235.

McGue, Matt, and Thomas J. Bouchard Jr. 1998. "Genetic and Environmental Influence on Human Behavioral Differences." Pp. 1–24 in *Annual Review of Neurosciences.* Palo Alto, CA: Annual Reviews.

McGurty, Eileen. 2007. *Transforming Environmentalism: Warren County, PCBs, and the Origins of Environmental Justice.* Piscataway, NJ: Rutgers University Press.

McIntosh, Peggy. 1988. "White Privilege and Male Privilege: A Personal Account of Coming to See Correspondence Through Work and Women's Studies." Working Paper No. 189, Wellesley College Center for Research on Women, Wellesley, MA.

McKibben, Bill. 2003. *Enough: Staying Human in an Engineered Age.* New York: Henry Holt.

McKown, Clark and Rhona S. Weinstein. 2008. "Teacher Expectations, Classroom Context, and the Achievement Gap." *Journal of School Psychology* 46 (3): 235–261.

McLaughlin, Emma, and Nicola Kraus. 2002. *The Nanny Diaries: A Novel.* New York: St. Martin's Press.

McLellan, David, ed. 2000. *Karl Marx, Selected Writings,* rev. ed. New York: Oxford University Press.

Mead, George H. 1934. *Mind, Self and Society,* ed. Charles W. Morris. Chicago: University of Chicago Press.

———. 1964a. *On Social Psychology,* ed. Anselm Strauss. Chicago: University of Chicago Press.

———. 1964b. "The Genesis of the Self and Social Control." Pp. 267–293 in *Selected Writings: George Herbert Mead,* ed. Andrew J. Reck. Indianapolis: Bobbs-Merrill.

Mead, Margaret. [1935] 2001. *Sex and Temperament in Three Primitive Societies.* New York: Perennial, HarperCollins.

Meara Ellen R., Seth Richards, and David M. Cutler. 2008. "The Gap Gets Bigger: Changes in Mortality and Life Expectancy, by Education, 1981–2000." *Health Affairs* 27 (2): 350–360.

Mehl, Matthias R., Simine Vazire, Nairán Ramírez-Esparza, Richard B. Slatcher, and James W. Pennebacker. 2007. "Are Women Really More Talkative than Men?" *Science* 317 (July 6): 82.

Meier, Robert F., and Gilbert Geis. 1997. *Victimless Crime? Prostitution, Drugs, Homosexuality, Abortion.* Los Angeles: Roxbury Books.

Melby, Todd. 2007. "Exploring Why We Have Sex." *Contemporary Sexuality* 41 (October): 1, 4–6.

———. 2009. "Creating the DSM-V." *Contemporary Sexuality* 43 (3): 1, 4–6.

Mendez, Jennifer Bickman. 1998. "Of Mops and Maids: Contradictions and Continuities in Bureaucratized Domestic Work." *Social Problems* 45 (February): 114–135.

Merton, Robert. 1948. "The Bearing of Empirical Research upon the Development of Social Theory." *American Sociological Review* 13 (October): 505–515.

———. 1968. *Social Theory and Social Structure.* New York: Free Press.

Merton, Robert K., and Alice S. Kitt. 1950. "Contributions to the Theory of Reference Group Behavior." Pp. 40–105 in *Continuities in Social Research: Studies in the Scope and Methods of the American Soldier,* ed. Robert K. Merton and Paul L. Lazarsfeld. New York: Free Press.

Meston, Cindy M., and David M. Buss. 2007. "Why Humans Have Sex." *Archives of Sexual Behavior* 36: 477–507.

———. 2009. *Why Women Have Sex: Understanding Sexual Motivations—From Adventure to Revenge (and Everything in Between).* New York: Henry Holt.

Michels, Robert. [1915] 1949. *Political Parties.* Glencoe, IL: Free Press.

Milgram, Stanley. 1963. "Behavioral Study of Obedience." *Journal of Abnormal and Social Psychology* 67 (October): 371–378.

———. 1975. *Obedience to Authority: An Experimental View.* New York: Harper & Row.

Milillo, Diana. 2008. "Sexuality Sells: A Content Analysis of Lesbian and Heterosexual Women's Bodies in Magazine Advertisements." *Journal of Lesbian Studies* 12 (4): 381–392.

Miller, David L., and JoAnne DeRoven Darlington. 2002. "Fearing for the Safety of Others: Disasters and the Small World Problem." Paper presented at the annual meeting of the Midwest Sociological Society, Milwaukee, WI.

Millett, Kate. 1970. *Sexual Politics.* Garden City, NY: Doubleday.

Mills, C. Wright. [1956] 2000. *The Power Elite.* New edition with afterword by Alan Wolfe. New York: Oxford University Press.

———. [1959] 2009. *The Sociological Imagination.* New York: Oxford University Press.

Milner Jr., Murray. 2006. *Freaks, Geeks, and Cool Kids: American Teenagers, Schools, and the Culture of Consumption.* New York: Routledge.

Minnesota Center for Twin and Family Research. 2008. "Minnesota Center for Twin and Family Research." Accessed January 7 (http://mctfr.psych.umn.edu/research).

Minority Rights Group International. 2007. "World Directory of Minorities and Indigenous Peoples–Mexico: Overview." Geneva: United Nations High Commissioner for Refugees. Accessed June 14, 2009 (www.unhcr.org/refworld/docid/4954ce409a.html).

Mirapaul, Matthew. 2001. "How the Net Is Documenting a Watershed Moment." *New York Times,* October 15, p. E2.

Mishel, Lawrence, Jared Bernstein, and Heide Shierholz. 2009. *The State of Working America 2008/2009.* Ithaca, NY: ILR Press.

Mizruchi, Mark S. 1996. "What Do Interlocks Do? An Analysis, Critique, and Assessment of Research on Interlocking Directorates." Pp. 271–298 in *Annual Review of Sociology,* ed. John Hagan and Karen Cook. Palo Alto, CA: Annual Reviews.

Moen, Phyllis, and Patricia Roehling. 2005. *The Career Mystique: Cracks in the American Dream.* Lanham, MD: Rowman & Littlefield.

Mohai, Paul, and Robin Saha. 2007. "Racial Inequality in the Distribution of Hazardous Waste: A National-Level Reassessment." *Social Problems* 54 (3): 343–370.

Monaghan, Peter. 1993. "Sociologist Jailed Because He 'Wouldn't Snitch' Ponders the Way Research Ought to Be Done." *Chronicle of Higher Education* 40 (September 1): A8, A9.

Montagu, Ashley, 1997. *Man's Most Dangerous Myth: The Fallacy of Race,* 6th ed., abridged student ed. Walnut Creek, CA: AltaMira Press.

Moore, David W. 2002. "Americans' View of Influence of Religion Settling Back to Pre–September 11 Levels." *Gallup Poll Tuesday Briefing,* December 31.

Moore, Molly. 2006. "Romance, but Not Marriage." *Washington Post National Weekly Edition,* November 27, p. 18.

Moore, Wilbert E. 1968. "Occupational Socialization." Pp. 861–883 in *Handbook of Socialization Theory and Research,* ed. David A. Goslin. Chicago: Rand McNally.

Morales, Lymari. 2010. "Green Behaviors Common in U.S., but Not Increasing." Washington; DC: Gallup, Inc., April 9. Accessed May 21, 2010 (http://www.gallup.com/poll/127292/Green-Behaviors-Common-Not-Increasing.aspx).

Morgan, Sue. 2009. "Theorising Feminist History: A Thirty-Year Retrospective." *Women's History Review* 18 (3): 381–407.

Morin, Rich, and Paul Taylor. 2009. "Oldest Are Most Sheltered: Different Age Groups, Different Recessions." Pew Research Center, May 14. Accessed August 6, 2009 (http://pewsocialtrends.org/assets/pdf/recession-and-older-americans.pdf).

Morse, Arthur D. 1967. *While Six Million Died: A Chronicle of American Apathy.* New York: Ace.

Morselli, Carlo, Pierre Tremblay, and Bill McCarthy. 2006. "Mentors and Criminal Achievement." *Criminology* 44 (1): 17–43.

Mortimer, Jeylan T., and Michael J. Shanahan, eds. 2006. *Handbook of the Life Course.* New York: Springer Science and Business Media.

Mosher William D., Anjani Chandra, and Jo Jones. 2005. "Sexual Behavior and Selected Health Measures: Men and Women 15–44 Years of Age, United States, 2002." *Advance Data from Vital and Health Statistics* 362. Hyattsville, MD: National Center for Health Statistics.

Moss, Michael, and Ford Fessenden. 2002. "New Tools for Domestic Spying, and Qualms." *New York Times,* December 10, pp. A1, A18.

Moyer, Michael. 2010. "Internet Ideology War." *Scientific American* 302 (4): 14–16.

Ms. 2006. "The *Ms.* Poll: Support High for Being a Feminist." *Ms.* 16 (3): 44.

Munford, Rebecca. 2007. "'Wake Up and Smell the Lipgloss': Gender, Generation, and the (A)Politics of Girl Power." Pp. 266–279 in *Third Wave Feminism: A Critical Exploration,* expanded 2d ed., Stacy Gillis, Gillian Howie, and Rebecca Munford. New York: Palgrave Macmillan.

Murdock, George P. 1945. "The Common Denominator of Cultures." Pp. 123–142 in *The Science of Man in the World Crisis,* ed. Ralph Linton. New York: Columbia University Press.

———. 1949. *Social Structure.* New York: Macmillan.

———. 1957. "World Ethnographic Sample." *American Anthropologist* 59 (August): 664–687.

N

Nanda, Serena. 1997. "The Hijras of India." Pp. 82–86 in *A Queer World: The Center for Lesbian and Gay Studies Reader,* ed. Martin Duberman. New York: New York University Press.

Naples, Nancy. 2003. *Feminism and Method: Ethnography, Discourse Analysis, and Activist Research.* New York: Routledge.

National Cancer Institute. 2008. *The Role of the Media in Promoting and Reducing Tobacco Use.* Tobacco Control Monograph No. 19. National Institutes of Health, National Cancer Institute, NIH Pub. No. 07-6242. Bethesda, MD: U.S. Department of Health and Human Services.

National Center for Health Statistics. 2009. *Health, United States, 2009: With Special Feature on Medical Technology.* Hyattsville, MD. Accessed May 17, 2010 (http://www.cdc.gov/nchs/data/hus/hus09.pdf).

———. 2009. "National Marriage and Divorce Rate Trends." National Vital Statistics System, Centers for Disease Control and Prevention, Atlanta. Accessed April 13, 2010 (http://www.cdc.gov/nchs/nvss/marriage_divorce_tables.htm).

———. 2010. *Health, United States, 2009: With Special Feature on Medical Technology.* Hyattsville, MD. Accessed May 20, 2010 (http://www.cdc.gov/nchs/data/hus/hus09.pdf).

National Counterterrorism Center. 2010. "Worldwide Incidents Tracking System." Report generated for incidents between January 1, 2009 and December 31, 2009. Accessed April 23, 2010 (https://wits.nctc.gov/FederalDiscoverWITS/index.do?Rcv=Incident&t=Reports&Nf=p_IncidentDate|GTEQ+2009 0101||p_IncidentDate|LTEQ+20091231&N=0).

National Institute of Justice. 2007. "Transnational Organized Crime." U.S. Department of Justice. Accessed May 20, 2009 (http://www.ojp.usdoj.gov/nij/topics/crime/transnational-organized-crime/welcome.htm).

Neiwert, David A. 2005. *Strawberry Days: How Internment Destroyed the Japanese Community.* New York: Palgrave Macmillan.

Neuman, W. Lawrence. 2006. *Social Research Methods: Qualitative and Quantitative Approaches,* 6th ed. Boston: Allyn & Bacon.

Neumark, David. 2008. "Reassessing the Age Discrimination in Employment Act." Washington, DC: AARP Public Policy Institute. Accessed June 27, 2009 (http://www.aarp.org/research/work/agediscrim/2008_09_adea.html).

Newman, Katherine, and Cybelle Fox. 2009. "Repeat Tragedy: Rampage Shootings in American High School and College Settings, 2002–2008." *American Behavioral Scientist* 52 (9): 1286–1308.

Newport, Frank. 2010. "Americans' Global Warming Concerns Continue to Drop." Washington, DC: Gallup, Inc. March 11. Accessed May 21, 2010 (http://www.gallup.com/poll/126560/Americans-Global-Warming-Concerns-Continue-Drop.aspx).

New York Times. 2006. "Questions Couples Should Ask (or Wish They Had) Before Marrying." *New York Times,* December 17. Accessed August 6, 2009 (www.nytimes.com/2006/12/17/fashion/weddings/17FIELDBOX.html).

Newman, William M. 1973. *American Pluralism: A Study of Minority Groups and Social Theory.* New York: Harper & Row.

NFHS. 2009. "2008–09 High School Athletics Participation Survey." National Federation of State High School Associations, Indianapolis. Accessed April 16, 2010 (http://www.nfhs.org/WorkArea/linkit.aspx?LinkIdentifier=id&ItemID=3506).

Nicolas, Guerda, Angela M. DeSilva, Kathleen S. Grey, and Diana Gonzalez-Eastep. 2006. "Using a Multicultural Lens to Understand Illnesses Among Haitians Living in America." *Professional Psychology: Research & Practice* 37 (6): 702–707.

Nielsen, Joyce McCarl, Glenda Walden, and Charlotte A. Kunkel. 2000. "Gendered Heteronormativity: Empirical Illustrations in Everyday Life." *Sociological Quarterly* 41 (2): 283–296.

Nobles, Melissa. 2000. "History Counts: A Comparative Analysis of Racial/Color Categorization in U.S. and Brazilian Censuses." *American Journal of Public Health* 90: 1738–1745.

Nofziger, Stacey, and Hye-Ryeon Lee. 2006. "Differential Associations and Daily Smoking of Adolescents: The Importance of Same-Sex Models." *Youth & Society* 37 (4): 453–478.

Nolan, Patrick, and Gerhard Lenski. 2006. *Human Societies: An Introduction to Macrosociology,* 10th ed. Boulder, CO: Paradigm.

Norris, Pippa, and Ronald Inglehart. 2004. *Sacred and Secular: Religion and Politics Worldwide.* Cambridge: Cambridge University Press.

North Carolina Department of Environment and Natural Resources. 2008. "Warren County PCB Landfill Fact Sheet." Accessed April 9, 2008 (www.wastenotnc.org/WarrenCo_Fact_Sheet.htm).

Norwegian Ministry of Children and Equality. 2009. "Women in Norwegian Politics." Norway, the Official Site in the United States. Accessed June 18, 2009 (www.norway.org/policy/gender/politics/politics.htm).

O

Oakes, Jeannie. 2008. "Keeping Track: Structuring Equality and Inequality in an Era of Accountability." *Teachers College Record* 110 (3): 700–712.

Obach, Brian K. 2004. *Labor and the Environmental Movement: The Quest for Common Ground.* Cambridge, MA: MIT Press.

Oberschall, Anthony. 1973. *Social Conflict and Social Movements.* Englewood Cliffs, NJ: Prentice Hall.

O'Connell, Martin, and Daphne Lofquist. 2009. "Counting Same Sex Couples: Official Estimates and Unofficial Guesses." Annual meeting of the Population Association of America, Detroit, April 30–May 2, 2009. Accessed May 27, 2009 (http://www.census.gov/population/www/socdemo/files/counting-paper.pdf).

O'Connor, Anne-Marie. 2004. "Time of Blogs and Bombs." *Los Angeles Times,* December 27, pp. E1, E14–E15.

O'Harrow Jr., Robert. 2005. "Mining Personal Data." *Washington Post National Weekly Edition* (February 6), pp. 8–10.

OECD. 2009. "Education at a Glance: 2009." Paris: Organisation for Economic Co-operation and Development. Accessed April 14, 2010 (http://www.oecd.org/dataoecd/41/25/43636332.pdf).

———. 2009. "Society at a Glance 2009: OECD Social Indicators." Paris: Organisation for Economic Co-operation and Development. Accessed June 7, 2009 (http://dx.doi.org/10.1787/550407525853).

———. 2010. "Development Aid Rose in 2009 and Most Donors Will Meet 2010 Aid Targets." Organization for Economic Co-operation and Development, April 14. Accessed April 28, 2010. (http://www.oecd.org/document/11/0,3343,en_2649_34487_44981579_1_1_1,00.html).

Office of Immigration Statistics. 2007. "2006 Yearbook of Immigration Statistics." Washington, DC: U.S. Department of Homeland Security.

Office of Justice Programs. 1999. "Transnational Organized Crime." *NCJRS Catalog* 49 (November/December): 21.

Ogburn, William F. 1922. *Social Change with Respect to Culture and Original Nature.* New York: Huebsch (reprinted 1966, New York: Dell).

References

Ogburn, William F., and Clark Tibbits. 1934. "The Family and Its Functions." Pp. 661–708 in *Recent Social Trends in the United States,* ed. Research Committee on Social Trends. New York: McGraw-Hill.

Okrent, Arika. 2010. "The New Klingon Without So Much as a Dictionary, Avatar Fans Are Learning How to Speak Na'vi." *Slate,* March 24. Accessed March 31, 2010 (http://www.slate.com/id/2248683/).

———. 2009. *In the Land of Invented Languages: Esperanto Rock Stars, Klingon Poets, Loglan Lovers, and the Mad Dreamers Who Tried to Build a Perfect Language.* New York: Spiegel and Grau.

Oliver, Melvin L., and Thomas M. Shapiro. 1995. *Black Wealth/ White Wealth: New Perspectives on Racial Inequality.* New York: Routledge.

OLPC. 2010. "One Laptop per Child: Vision." One Laptop per Child, Cambridge, MA. Accessed May 23, 2010 (http://laptop.org/en/vision/index.shtml).

Omi, Michael, and Howard Winant. 1994. *Racial Formation in the United States: From the 1960s to the 1990s,* 2d ed. New York: Routledge.

Onishi, Norimitso. 2003. "Divorce in South Korea: Striking a New Attitude." *New York Times,* September 21, p. 19.

Orshansky, Mollie. 1965. "Counting the Poor: Another Look at the Poverty Profile." *Social Security Bulletin* 28 (1): 3–29

Ortman, Jennifer M., and Christine E. Guarneri. 2008. "United States Population Projections: 2000 to 2050." 2009 National Population Projections, U.S. Census Bureau. Accessed May 17, 2010 (http://www.census.gov/population/www/projections/analytical-document09.pdf).

Osberg, Lars, and Timothy Smeeding. 2006. "'Fair' Inequality? Attitudes Toward Pay Differentials: The United States in Comparative Perspective." *American Sociological Review* 71 (June): 450–473.

P

Padian, Kevin. 2007. "The Case of Creation." *Nature* 448 (July 19): 253–254.

Pager, Devah. 2003. "The Mark of a Criminal Record." *American Journal of Sociology* 108 (March): 937–975.

Pager, Devah, and Hana Shepherd. 2008. "The Sociology of Discrimination: Racial Discrimination in Employment, Housing, Credit, and Consumer Markets." *Annual Review of Sociology* 34: 181–209.

Painter, Nell Irvin. 2010. *The History of White People.* New York: Norton.

Palm, Cheryl, Stephen A. Vosti, Pedro A. Sanchez, and Polly J. Ericksen, eds. 2005. *Slash-and-Burn Agriculture: The Search for Alternatives.* New York: Columbia University Press.

Park, Kristin. 2005. "Choosing Childlessness: Weber's Typology of Action and Motives of the Voluntarily Childless." *Sociological Inquiry,* August, pp. 372–402.

Park, Robert E. 1922. *The Immigrant Press and Its Control.* New York: Harper.

Parker, Alison. 2004. "Inalienable Rights: Can Human-Rights Law Help to End U.S. Mistreatment of Noncitizens?" *American Prospect,* October, pp. A11–A13.

Parker, Richard. 2009. "Sexuality, Culture and Society: Shifting Paradigms in Sexuality Research." *Culture, Health & Sexuality* 11 (3): 251–266.

Parsons, Talcott. 1951. *The Social System.* New York: Free Press.

———. 1966. *Societies: Evolutionary and Comparative Perspectives.* Englewood Cliffs, NJ: Prentice Hall.

———. 1975. "The Sick Role and the Role of the Physician Reconsidered." *Milbank Medical Fund Quarterly Health and Society* 53 (Summer): 257–278.

Parsons, Talcott, and Robert Bales. 1955. *Family: Socialization, and Interaction Process.* Glencoe, IL: Free Press.

Pascoe, C. J. 2007. *Dude You're a Fag: Masculinity and Sexuality in High School.* Berkeley: University of California Press.

Passel, Jeffrey S., and D'Vera Cohn. 2009. "A Portrait of Unauthorized Immigrants in the United States." Pew Hispanic Center Report, April 14. Pew Research Center, Washington, DC. Accessed June 21, 2009 (http://pewhispanic.org/files/reports/107.pdf).

———. 2009. "Mexican Immigrants: How Many Come? How Many Leave?" Pew Hispanic Center Report, July 22. Pew Hispanic Center, Washington, DC. Accessed April 29, 2010 (http://pewhispanic.org/files/reports/112.pdf).

Passero, Kathy. 2002. "Global Travel Expert Roger Axtell Explains Why." *Biography,* July, pp. 70–73, 97–98.

Patterson, Thomas E. 2003. *We the People,* 5th ed. New York: McGraw-Hill.

Pattillo, Mary. 2005. "Black Middle-Class Neighborhoods." *Annual Review of Sociology* 31: 305–329.

Paxton, Pamela, Sheri Kunovich, and Melanie M. Hughes. 2007. "Gender in Politics." Pp. 263–285 in *Annual Review of Sociology* 2007. Palo Alto, CA: Annual Reviews.

Pear, Robert. 2008. "Gap in Life Expectancy Widens for the Nation." *New York Times,* March 23. Accessed June 26, 2009 (www.nytimes.com/2008/03/23/us/23health.html).

Peattie, Lisa, and Martin Rein. 1983. *Women's Claims: A Study in the Political Economy.* New York: Oxford University Press.

Peel, Lilly. 2008. "Matchmaker, Matchmaker Make Me a Match…If the Algorithms Agree." *Times Online,* October 6. Accessed May 26, 2009 (http://business.timesonline.co.uk/tol/business/industry_sectors/technology/article4887501.ece).

Perrow, Charles. 1986. *Complex Organizations,* 3d ed. New York: Random House.

Pershing, Jana L. 2003. "Why Women Don't Report Sexual Harassment: A Case Study of an Elite Military Institution." *Gender Issues* 21 (4): 3–30.

Peterson, Karen. S. 2003. "Unmarried with Children: For Better or Worse." *USA Today,* August 18, pp. 1A, 8A.

Petrovic, Drazen. 1994. "Ethnic Cleansing—an Attempt at Methodology." *EJIL* 5: 1–19.

Pew Hispanic Center. 2009. "Mexican Immigrants in the United States, 2008." Pew Research Center Fact Sheet, April 15. Accessed June 21, 2009 (http://pewhispanic.org/files/factsheets/47.pdf).

Pew Research Center. 2006. "More Americans Discussing—and Planning—End-of-Life Treatment." Pew Research Center for the People & the Press, Washington, DC, January 5. Accessed June 18, 2009 (http://people-press.org/reports/pdf/266.pdf).

———. 2007. "Optimism About Black Progress Declines: Blacks See Growing Values Gap Between Poor and Middle Class." Washington, DC: Pew Research Center. Accessed July 1, 2008 (http://pewsocialtrends.org/assets/pdf/Race.pdf).

———. 2008a. "U.S. Religious Landscape Survey." Pew Forum on Religion in Public Life. Washington, DC: Pew Research Center. Accessed June 14, 2008 (http://religions.pewforum.org/pdf/report-religious-landscape-study-full.pdf).

———. 2008b. "Election-Year Economic Ratings Lowest Since '92: An Even More Partisan Agenda for 2008." Pew Research Center for the People & the Press. Washington, DC: Pew Research Center. Accessed July 4, 2008 (http://people-press.org/reports/display.php3?ReportID=388).

———. 2009a. "Independents Take Center Stage in Obama Era." Pew Research Center for the People & the Press, May 21. Accessed June 2, 2009 (http://people-press.org/report/?pageid=1516).

———. 2009b. "Confidence in Obama Lifts U.S. Image Around the World." Pew Global Attitudes Project, July 23. Accessed April 8, 2010 (http://pewglobal.org/reports/pdf/264.pdf).

———. 2009c. "Majority Continues to Support Civil Unions: Most Still Oppose Same-Sex Marriage." Pew Research Center for the People & the Press, Washington, DC, October 9. Accessed April 14, 2010 (http://people-press.org/reports/pdf/553.pdf).

———. 2009d. "The Stronger Sex—Spiritually Speaking." Pew Forum on Religion & Public Life, February 26. Accessed April 19, 2010 (http://pewforum.org/docs/?DocID=403).

———. 2009e. "End of Communism Cheered but Now with More Reservations: Two Decades After the Wall's Fall." Pew Global

Attitudes Project, November 2. Accessed April 23, 2010 (http://pewglobal.org/reports/pdf/267.pdf).

———. 2010. "Public's Priorities for 2010: Economy, Jobs, Terrorism." Pew Research Center for the People & the Press, January 25. Accessed May 21, 2010 (http://people-press.org/reports/pdf/584.pdf).

———. 2010a. "Millennials: A Portrait of Generation Next." Pew Research Publications, February. Accessed April 8, 2010 (http://pewsocialtrends.org/assets/pdf/millennials-confident-connected-open-to-change.pdf).

———. 2010b. "Broad Public Support for Legalizing Medical Marijuana." Pew Research Center for the People & the Press, Washington, DC, April 1. Accessed April 9, 2010 (http://pewresearch.org/pubs/1548/broad-public-support-for-legalizing-medical-marijuana).

———. 2010c. "Trust in Government Database: 1958–2010." Accessed April 23, 2010 (http://people-press.org/trust/trust-database.xls).

Pfeifer, Mark. 2008. "Vietnamese Americans." Pp. 1365–1368 in *Encyclopedia of Race, Ethnicity, and Society,* vol. 3, ed. Richard T. Schaefer. Thousand Oaks, CA: Sage.

Phillips, Katherine A., Katie A. Liljenquist, and Margaret A. Neale. 2009. "Is the Pain Worth the Gain? The Advantages and Liabilities of Agreeing with Socially Distinct Newcomers." *Personality and Social Psychology Bulletin* 35 (3): 336–350.

Piaget, Jean. 1954. *The Construction of Reality in the Child,* trans. Margaret Cook. New York: Basic Books.

Piketty, Thomas, and Emmanuel Saez. 2009. "Tables and Figures Updated to 2006 for Income Inequality in the United States, 1913–1998," *Quarterly Journal of Economics,* February 2003." Accessed April 25, 2010 (http://www.econ.berkeley.edu/~sacz/TabFig2007.xls).

Pinderhughes, Dianne. 1987. *Race and Ethnicity in Chicago Politics: A Reexamination of Pluralist Theory.* Urbana: University of Illinois Press.

Pinkerton, James P. 2003. "Education: A Grand Compromise." *Atlantic Monthly* 291 (January/February): 115–116.

Pinnow, Ellen, Pellavi Sharma, Ameeta Parekh, Natalie Gevorkian, and Kathleen Uhl. 2009. "Increasing Participation of Women in Early Phase Clinical Trials Approved by the FDA." *Women's Health Issues* 19 (2): 89–92.

Planty, M., W. Hussar, T. Snyder, G. Kena, A. Kewal-Ramani, J. Kemp, K. Bianco, and R. Dinkes. 2009. *The Condition of Education 2009.* NCES 2009-081. Washington, DC: National Center for Education Statistics, Institute of Education Sciences, U.S. Department of Education. Accessed May 29, 2009 (http://nccs.ed.gov/pubs2009/2009081.pdf).

Planty, M., W. Hussar, T. Snyder, S. Provasnik, G. Kena, R. Dinkes, A. Kewal-Ramani, and J. Kemp. 2008. *The Condition of Education 2008.* NCES 2008-031. Washington, DC: National Center for Education Statistics, Institute of Education Sciences, U.S. Department of Education. Accessed June 14, 2008 (http://nces.ed.gov/pubs2008/2008031.pdf).

Pollini, Jacques. 2009. "Agroforestry and the Search for Alternatives to Slash-and-Burn Cultivation: From Technological Optimism to a Political Economy of Deforestation." *Agriculture, Ecosystems & Environment* 133 (1/2): 48–60.

Pollster.com. 2010. "National Party Identification (All Adults)." Accessed April 23, 2010 (http://www.pollster.com/polls/us/party-id.php).

Popenoe, David, and Barbara Dafoe Whitehead. 1999. *Should We Live Together? What Young Adults Need to Know About Cohabitation Before Marriage.* Rutgers, NJ: National Marriage Project.

Population Reference Bureau. 2009. *2009 World Population Data Sheet.* Washington, DC. Accessed May 20, 2010 (http://www.prb.org/Publications/Datasheets.aspx).

Porter, Roy. 1998. *The Greatest Benefit to Mankind: A Medical History of Humanity.* New York: HarperCollins.

———. 2004. *Blood and Guts: A Short History of Medicine.* New York: Norton.

Postman, Neil. 1988. "Questioning the Media." Video. The January Series, January 12. Grand Rapids, MI: Calvin College.

———. 1993. *Technopoly: The Surrender of Culture to Technology.* New York: Vintage Books.

———. 1999. *Building a Bridge to the 18th Century: How the Past Can Improve Our Future.* New York: Knopf.

Potts, John. 2009. *A History of Charisma.* New York: Palgrave Macmillan.

Preves, Sharon S. 2000. "Negotiating the Constraints of Gender Binarism: Intersexuals' Challenge to Gender Categorization." *Current Sociology* 48 (3): 27–50.

Pridemore, William Alex. 2003. "Measuring Homicide in Russia: A Comparison of Estimates from the Crime and Vital Statistics Reporting Systems." *Social Science & Medicine* 57 (8): 1343–1354.

ProCon.org. 2009. "Medical Marijuana: Votes and Polls, National." Accessed May 19, 2009 (http://medicalmarijuana.procon.org/viewadditionalresource.asp?resourceID=000151).

Progressive Student Labor Movement. 2008. "A Brief History of the Living Wage Debate at Harvard." Accessed July 7 (http://www.hcs.harvard.edu/~pslm/livingwage/timeline.html).

Prohaska, Ariane, and Jeannine Gailey. 2010. "Achieving Masculinity Through Sexual Predation: The Case of Hogging." *Journal of Gender Studies* 19 (1): 13–25.

Provasnik, S., and Planty, M. 2008. *Community Colleges: Special Supplement to the Condition of Education 2008.* NCES 2008-033. Washington, DC: National Center for Education Statistics, Institute of Education Sciences, U.S. Department of Education. Accessed May 31, 2009 (http://nces.ed.gov/pubs2008/2008033.pdf).

Prus, Steven G. 2007. "Age, SES, and Health: A Population-Level Analysis of Health Irregularities over the Lifecourse." *Sociology of Health and Illness* 29 (March): 275–296.

Pryor, John H., Sylvia Hurtado, Linda DeAngelo, Laura Palucki Blake, and Serge Tran. 2009. *The American Freshman: National Norms for Fall 2009.* Los Angeles: Higher Education Research Institute, UCLA.

Pryor, J. H., S. Hurtado, L. DeAngelo, J. Sharkness, L. C. Romero, W. S. Korn, and S. Tran. 2008. *The American Freshman: National Norms for Fall 2008.* Los Angeles: Higher Education Research Institute, UCLA.

Pryor, John H., Sylvia Hurtado, Jessica Sharkness, and William S. Korn. 2007a. *The American Freshman: National Norms for Fall 2007.* Los Angeles: Higher Education Research Institute, UCLA.

Pryor, John H., Sylvia Hurtado, Victor B. Saenz, José Luis Santos, and William S. Korn. 2007. *The American Freshman: Forty-Year Trends.* Los Angeles: Higher Education Research Institute, UCLA.

Q

Quinney, Richard. 1970. *The Social Reality of Crime.* Boston: Little, Brown.

———. 1974. *Criminal Justice in America.* Boston: Little, Brown.

———. 1979. *Criminology,* 2d ed. Boston: Little, Brown.

———. 1980. *Class, State and Crime,* 2d ed. New York: Longman.

Quirk, Patrick W. 2009. "Iran's Twitter Revolution." *The Epoch Times,* June 24. Accessed July 1, 2009 (www.theepochtimes.com/n2/content/view/18593).

Quisumbing, Agnes, Ruth Meinzen-Dick, and Lucy Bassett. 2008. "Helping Women Respond to the Global Food Price Crisis." IFPRI Policy Brief 7, October. Accessed June 18, 2009 (www.ifpri.org/pubs/bp/bp007.pdf).

R

Radovich, Sasha. 2006. *The Global Alliance for Workers and Communities: Lessons Learned About Partnership Goverance and Accountability from a Milti-stakeholder Initiative.* London: AccountAbility. Accessed May 28, 2010 (http://info.worldbank.org/etools/docs/library/238370/The%2520Global%2520Alliance%2520for%2520Workers%2520and%2520Communities.pdf).

Rainie, Lee. 2001. *The Commons of the Tragedy.* Washington, DC: Pew Internet and American Life Project.

Rand, Michael R. 2008. "Criminal Victimization, 2007: National Crime Victimization Survey." *Bureau of Justice Statistics Bulletin,* December, NCJ 224390. Accessed May 20, 2009 (http://www.ojp.usdoj.gov/bjs/pub/pdf/cv07.pdf).

Rand, Michael R. 2009. "Criminal Victimization, 2008: National Crime Victimization Survey." *Bureau of Justice Statistics Bulletin,* September, NCJ 227777. Accessed April 9, 2010 (http://bjs.ojp.usdoj.gov/content/pub/pdf/cv08.pdf).

Rand, Robert. 2006. *Tamerlane's Children: Dispatches from Contemporary Uzbekistan.* Oxford: Oneworld Publications.

Ratner, Carl. 2004. "A Cultural Critique of Psychological Explanations of Terrorism." *Cross-Cultural Psychology Bulletin* 38 (1/2): 18–24.

Ravitz, Jessica. 2009. "Neda: Latest Iconic Image to Inspire." *CNN,* June 24. Accessed June 30, 2009 (www.cnn.com/2009/WORLD/meast/06/24/neda.iconic.images/).

Ray, Julie, and Rajesh Srinivasan. 2010a. "Afghans More Skeptical of U.S. Leadership, Troops in 2009." Washington, DC: Gallup, Inc. Accessed March 28, 2010 (http://www.gallup.com/poll/125537/Afghans-Skeptical-Leadership-Troops-2009.aspx).

———. 2010b. "Taliban Increasingly Unpopular in Pakistan." Washington, DC: Gallup, Inc. Accessed March 28, 2010 (http://www.gallup.com/poll/126602/Taliban-Increasingly-Unpopular-Pakistan.aspx).

Reddy, Gayatri. 2005. *With Respect to Sex: Negotiating Hijra Identity in South India.* Chicago: University of Chicago Press.

Reel, Justine J., Sonya SooHoo, Julia Franklin Summerhays, and Diane Gill. 2008. "Age Before Beauty: An Exploration of Body Image in African-American and Caucasian Adult Women." *Journal of Gender Studies* 17 (4): 321–330.

Reeves, Scott, Sioban Nelson, and Merrick Zwarenstein. 2008. "The Doctor–Nurse Game in the Age of Interprofessional Care: A View from Canada." *Nursing Inquiry* 15 (1): 1–2.

Reid, Luc. 2006. *Talk the Talk: The Slang of 65 American Subcultures.* Cincinnati: Writer's Digest Books.

Reinharz, Shulamit. 1992. *Feminist Methods in Social Research.* New York: Oxford University Press.

Reitzes, Donald C., and Elizabeth J. Mutran. 2004. "The Transition to Retirement: Stages and Factors that Influence Retirement Adjustment." *International Journal of Aging & Human Development* 59 (1): 63–84.

Relerford, Patrice, Chao Xiong, Michael Rand, and Curt Brown. 2008. "42 Students Questioned, 13 Disciplined." *Minneapolis Star-Tribune,* January 10. Accessed June 30, 2009 (www.startribune.com/local/west/13663951.html).

Religious Tolerance. 2008. "Female Genital Mutilation (FGM): Informational Materials." Accessed March 1, 2008 (www.religioustolerance.org).

Renegar, Valerie R., and Stacey K. Sowards. 2009. "Contradiction as Agency: Self-Determination, Transcendence, and Counter-imagination in Third Wave Feminism." *Hypatia* 24 (2): 1–20.

Reynolds, John R., and Chardie L. Baird. 2010. "Is There a Downside to Shooting for the Stars? Unrealized Educational Expectations and Symptoms of Depression." *American Sociological Review* 75 (1): 151–172.

Ribando, Clare M. 2008. *CRS Report for Congress: Trafficking in Persons.* Washington, DC: Congressional Research Service.

Richtel, Matt. 2006. "The Long-Distance Journey of a Fast-Food Order." *New York Times,* April 11. Accessed May 13, 2009 (http://www.nytimes.com/2006/04/11/technology/11fast.html).

Rideout, Victoria, Donald F. Roberts, and Ulla G. Foehr. 2005. *Generation M: Media in the Lives of 8–18-Year-Olds.* Menlo Park, CA: Kaiser Family Foundation.

Rideout, Victoria J., Ulla G. Foehr, and Donald F. Roberts. 2010. *Generation M2: Media in the Lives of 8–18-Year-Olds.* Kaiser Family Foundation Study, Menlo Park, CA, January. Accessed April 30, 2010 (http://www.kff.org/entmedia/8010.cfm)

Ridgeway, Greg. 2007. "Analysis of Racial Disparities in the New York Police Department's Stop, Question, and Frisk Practices." Santa Monica, CA: RAND Corporation.

Rieker, Patricia R., and Chloe E. Bird. 2000. "Sociological Explanations of Gender Differences in Mental and Physical Health." Pp. 98–113 in *Handbook of Medical Sociology,* ed. Chloe Bird, Peter Conrad, and Allan Fremont. New York: Prentice Hall.

Risman, Barbara J. 1986. "Can Men 'Mother'? Life as a Single Father." *Family Relations* 35: (1): 95–102.

Risman, Barbara J., and Danette Johnson-Sumerford. 1998. "'Doing It Fairly: A Study of Postgender Marriages." *Journal of Marriage and Family* 60 (1): 23–40.

Ritzer, George. 2008. *The McDonaldization of Society 5.* Thousand Oaks, CA: Sage.

Roberson, Debi, Ian Davies, and Jules Davidoff. 2000. "Color Categories Are Not Universal: Replications and New Evidence from Stone Age Culture." *Journal of Experimental Psychology* 129 (3): 369–398.

Roberts, J. Timmons, Peter E. Grines, and Jodie L. Manale. 2003. "Social Roots of Global Environmental Change: A World-Systems Analysis of Carbon Dioxide Emissions." *Journal of World-Systems Research* 9 (Summer): 277–315.

Robison, Jennifer. 2002. "Should Mothers Work?" Gallup, Inc., August 27. Accessed June 17, 2009 (www.gallup.com/poll/6676/Should-Mothers-Work.aspx).

Rodriguez, Richard. 2002. *Brown: The Last Discovery of America.* New York: Penguin Books.

Rodwan Jr., John 2010. "Bottled Water Statistics 2009: Challenging Circumstances Persist, Future Growth Anticipated." *Bottled Water Reporter* 50 (April/May): 10–16. Accessed May 21, 2010 (http://www.bottledwater.org/content/455/bottled-water-reporter).

Roediger, David R. 2005. *Working Toward Whiteness: How America's Immigrants Became White.* New York: Basic Books.

Rootes, Christopher. 2007. "Acting Locally: The Character, Contexts and Significance of Local Environmental Mobilisations." *Environmental Politics* 16 (5): 722–741.

Roscigno, Vincent J. 2010. "Ageism in the American Workplace." *Contexts* 9 (1):16–21.

Roscoe, Will. 1997. "Gender Diversity in Native North America: Notes Toward a Unified Analysis." Pp. 65–81 in *A Queer World: The Center for Lesbian and Gay Studies Reader,* ed. Martin Duberman. New York: New York University Press.

Rose, Arnold. 1951. *The Roots of Prejudice.* Paris: UNESCO.

Rosenfeld, Michael J. 2008. "Racial, Educational and Religious Endogamy in the United States: A Comparative Historical Perspective." *Social Forces* 87 (1): 1–33.

Rosenthal, Robert, and Lenore Jacobson. 1968. *Pygmalion in the Classroom.* New York: Holt.

Rosenwald, Michael S. 2010. "Second Life's Virtual Money Can Become Real-Life Cash." *Washington Post,* March 8. Accessed April 8, 2010 (http://www.washingtonpost.com/wp-dyn/content/article/2010/03/07/AR2010030703524.html).

Rosin, Hanna. 2007. *God's Harvard: A Christian College on a Mission to Save America.* New York: Harcourt.

Rossi, Alice S. 1968. "Transition to Parenthood." *Journal of Marriage and the Family* 30 (February): 26–39.

———. 1984. "Gender and Parenthood." *American Sociological Review* 49 (February): 1–19.

Rossides, Daniel W. 1997. *Social Stratification: The Interplay of Class, Race, and Gender,* 2d ed. Upper Saddle River, NJ: Prentice Hall.

Rothstein, Richard. 2009. "Equalizing Opportunity: Dramatic Differences in Children's Home Life and Health Mean that Schools Can't Do It Alone." *American Educator* 33 (2): 4–7, 45–46. Accessed April 26, 2010 (http://archive.aft.org/pubs-reports/american_educator/issues/summer2009/equalizingopportunity.pdf).

Rotolo, Thomas, and John Wilson. 2007. "Sex Segregation in Volunteer Work." *Sociological Quarterly* 48: 559–585.

Rowland, Christopher, ed. 2007. *The Cambridge Companion to Liberation Theology,* 2d ed. New York: Cambridge University Press.

Rubie-Davies, Christine M. 2010. "Teacher Expectations and Perceptions of Student Attributes: Is There a Relationship?" *British Journal of Educational Psychology* 80 (1): 121–135.

Rubin, Alissa J. 2003. "Pat-Down on the Way to Prayer." *Los Angeles Times,* November 25, pp. A1, A5.

Rutter, Michael. 2010. "Gene Environment Interplay." *Depression and Anxiety* 27: 1–4.

Rutter, Michael, Terrie E. Moffitt, and Avshalom Caspi. 2006. "Gene-Environment Interplay and Psychopathology: Multiple Varieties but Real Effects." *Journal of Child Psychology and Psychiatry* 47 (3/4): 226–261.

Rymer, Russ. 1993. *Genie: An Abused Child's Flight from Science.* New York: HarperCollins.

S

Saad, Lydia. 2004. "Divorce Doesn't Last." *Gallup Poll Tuesday Briefing,* March 30 (www.gallup.com).

Sachs, Jeffrey D. 2005a. *The End of Poverty: Economic Possibilities for Our Time.* New York: Penguin Books.

———. 2005b. "Can Extreme Poverty Be Eliminated?" *Scientific American* 293 (September): 56–65.

Sacks, Peter. 2007. *Tearing Down the Gates: Confronting the Class Divide in American Education.* Berkeley: University of California Press.

Samuelson, Paul A., and William D. Nordhaus. 2005. *Economics,* 18th ed. New York: McGraw-Hill.

Sanday, Peggy Reeves. 2002. *Women at the Center: Life in a Modern Matriarchy.* Ithaca, NY: Cornell University Press.

———. 2008. Homepage. Accessed March 15 (www.sas.upenn. edu/~psanday).

Sandler, Ronald, and Phaedra C. Pezzullo, eds. 2007. *Environmental Justice and Environmentalism: The Social Justice Challenge to the Environmental Movement.* Cambridge: MIT Press.

Sanyal, Paromita. 2009. "From Credit to Collective Action: The Role of Microfinance in Promoting Women's Social Capital and Normative Influence." *American Sociological Review* 74 (4): 529–550.

Sarachild, Kathie. 1978. "Consciousness-Raising: A Radical Weapon." Pp. 144–150 in *Feminist Revolution.* New York: Random House. Accessed June 30, 2009 (http://scriptorium.lib.duke.edu/wlm/fem/sarachild.html).

Sargent, John, and Linda Matthews. 2009. "China Versus Mexico in the Global EPZ Industry: Maquiladoras, FDI Quality, and Plant Mortality." *World Development* 37 (6): 1069–1082.

Sassen, Saskia. 2005. "New Global Classes: Implications for Politics." Pp. 143–170 in *The New Egalitarianism,* ed. Anthony Giddens and Patrick Diamond. Cambridge, UK: Polity Press.

Sawhill, Isabel V. 2006. "Teenage Sex, Pregnancy, and Nonmarital Births." *Gender Issues* 23 (4): 48–59.

Scarce, Rik. 1994. "(No) Trial (but) Tribulations: When Courts and Ethnography Conflict." *Journal of Contemporary Ethnography* 23 (July): 123–149.

———. 1995. "Scholarly Ethics and Courtroom Antics: Where Researchers Stand in the Eyes of the Law." *American Sociologist* 26 (Spring): 87–112.

———. 2005. "A Law to Protect Scholars." *Chronicle of Higher Education,* August 12, p. 324.

Scelfo, Julie. 2008. "Baby You're Home." *New York Times,* November 12. Accessed June 29, 2009 (www.nytimes.com/2008/11/13/garden/13birth.html).

Schachtman, Tom. 2006. *Rumspringa: To Be or Not to Be Amish.* New York: North Point Press.

Schaefer, Richard T. 1998a. "Differential Racial Mortality and the 1995 Chicago Heat Wave." Paper presented at the annual meeting of the American Sociological Association, August, San Francisco.

———. 1998b. *Alumni Survey.* Chicago: Department of Sociology, De Paul University.

———. 2006. *Racial and Ethnic Relations,* 10th ed. Upper Saddle River, NJ: Prentice Hall.

———. 2009. *Sociology: A Brief Introduction,* 8th ed. New York: McGraw-Hill.

Schaefer, Richard T., and William W. Zellner. 2007. *Extraordinary Groups,* 8th ed. New York: Worth.

Schaffer, Scott. 2004. *Resisting Ethics.* New York: Palgrave Macmillan.

Scharnberg, Kirsten. 2007. "Black Market for Midwives Defies Bans." *Chicago Tribune,* November 25, pp. 1, 10.

Schelly, David, and Paul B. Stretesky. 2009. "An Analysis of the 'Path of Least Resistance' Argument in Three Environmental Justice Success Cases." *Society & Natural Resources* 22 (4): 369–380.

Schmeeckle, Maria. 2007. "Gender Dynamics in Stepfamilies: Adult Stepchildren's Views." *Journal of Marriage and Family* 69 (February): 174–189.

Schmeeckle, Maria, Roseann Giarrusso, Du Feng, and Vern L. Bengtson. 2006. "What Makes Someone Family? Adult Children's Perceptions of Current and Former Stepparents." *Journal of Marriage and Family* 68 (August): 595–610.

Schmidt, Peter. 2008. "A University Examines Underlying Problems After Racist Incidents." *Chronicle of Higher Education* 54 (March 14): A18–A21.

Schnaiberg, Allan. 1994. *Environment and Society: The Enduring Conflict.* New York: St. Martin's Press.

Schur, Edwin M. 1965. *Crimes Without Victims: Deviant Behavior and Public Policy.* Englewood Cliffs, NJ: Prentice Hall.

———. 1968. *Law and Society: A Sociological View.* New York: Random House.

———. 1985. "'Crimes Without Victims: A 20-Year Reassessment." Paper presented at the annual meeting of the Society for the Study of Social Problems.

Schurman, Rachel. 2004. "Fighting 'Frankenfoods': Industry Opportunity Structures and the Efficacy of the Anti-biotech Movement in Western Europe." *Social Problems* 51 (2): 243–268.

Schwartz, Shalom H., and Anat Bardi. 2001. "Value Hierarchies Across Cultures: Taking a Similarities Perspective." *Journal of Cross-Cultural Perspective* 32 (May): 268–290.

Scott, Greg. 2005. "Public Symposium: HIV/AIDS, Injection Drug Use and Men Who Have Sex with Men." Pp. 38–39 in *Scholarship with a Mission,* ed. Susanna Pagliaro. Chicago: De Paul University.

Second Life. 2010a. "Economic Statistics." San Francisco: Linden Research. Accessed April 8, 2010 (http://secondlife.com/statistics/economy-data.php).

———. "2009 End of Year Second Life Economy Wrap-Up (Including Q4 Economy in Detail)." Blogpost, January 19. San Francisco: Linden Research. Accessed April 8, 2010 (https://blogs.secondlife.com/community/features/blog/2010/01/19/2009-end-of-year-second-life-economy-wrap-up-including-q4-economy-in-detail).

Shah, Anup. 2010. "Poverty Facts and Stats." *Global Issues,* March 22. April 28, 2010 (http://www.globalissues.org/article/26/poverty-facts-and-stats).

Shaheen, Jack. 2006. *Reel Bad Arabs: How Hollywood Vilifies a People* Video. Directed by Sut Jhally. 50 minutes. Northampton, MA: Media Education Foundation.

———. 2009. *Reel Bad Arabs: How Hollywood Vilifies a People,* 2d ed. New York: Olive Branch Press.

Shapiro, Samantha M. 2009. "Can the Muppets Make Friends in Ramallah?" *New York Times,* October 4. Accessed April 6, 2010 (http://www.nytimes.com/2009/10/04/magazine/04sesame-t.html).

Shaw, Clifford R., and Henry D. McKay. 1969. *Juvenile Delinquency and Urban Areas.* Chicago: University of Chicago Press.

Shenk, David. 2010. *The Genius in All of Us: Why Everything You've Been Told About Genetics, Talent, and IQ Is Wrong.* New York: Doubleday.

Sherkat, Darren E. 2004. "Religious Intermarriage in the United States: Trends, Patterns, and Predictors." *Social Science Research* 33 (4): 606–625.

Sheskin, Ira M., and Arnold Dashefsky. 2007. "Jewish Population of the United States, 2006." In *American Jewish Year Book 2006,* ed. David Singer and Lawrence Grossman. New York: American Jewish Committee.

Shi, Yu. 2008. "Chinese Immigrant Women Workers: Everyday Forms of Resistance and 'Coagulate Politics.'" *Communication and Critical/Cultural Studies* 5 (4): 363–382.

Shields, Stephanie A. 2008. "Gender: An Intersectionality Perspective." *Sex Roles* 59 (5/6): 301–311.

Shipler, David K. 2004. *The Working Poor: Invisible in America.* New York: Knopf.

Shirky, Clay. 2008. *Here Comes Everybody: The Power of Organizing Without Organizations.* New York: Penguin Books.

Shostak, Arthur B. 2002. "Clinical Sociology and the Art of Peace Promotion: Earning a World Without War." Pp. 325–345 in *Using Sociology: An Introduction from the Applied and Clinical Perspectives,* ed. Roger A. Straus. Lanham, MD: Rowman & Littlefield.

Showden, Carisa R. 2009. "What's Political About the New Feminisms?" *Frontiers: A Journal of Women Studies* 30 (2): 166–198.

Shupe, Anson D., and David G. Bromley. 1980. "Walking a Tightrope." *Qualitative Sociology* 2: 8–21.

Silicon Valley Cultures Project. 2004. The Silicon Valley Cultures Project website. Accessed February 3, 2005 (www2.sjsu.edu/depts/anthropology/svcp).

Silver, Ira. 1996. "Role Transitions, Objects, and Identity." *Symbolic Interaction* 10 (1): 1–20.

Simmons, Robin. 2009. "Entry to Employment: Discourses of Inclusion and Employability in Work-Based Learning for Young People." *Journal of Education & Work* 22 (2): 137–151.

Simmons, Tavia, and Martin O'Connell. 2003. "Married-Couple and Unmarried-Partner Households: 2000." *Census 2000 Special Reports,* CENBR-5. Washington, DC: U.S. Government Printing Office.

Singel, Ryan. 2008. "FBI Tried to Cover Patriot Act Abuses with Flawed, Retroactive Subpoenas, Audit Finds." *Wired,* March 13. Accessed June 30, 2009 (www.wired.com/threatlevel/2008/03/fbi-tried-to-co).

Sisson, Carmen K. 2007. "The Virtual War Family." *Christian Science Monitor,* May 29.

Smith, Adam. [1776] 2003. *The Wealth of Nations.* New York: Bantam Classics.

Smith, Craig. 2006a. "Romania's Orphans Face Widespread Abuse, Group Says." *New York Times,* May 10, p. A3.

Smith, Craig S. 2006b. "Warm and Fuzzy TV, Brought to You by Hamas." *New York Times,* January 18. Accessed April 5, 2010 (http://www.nytimes.com/2006/01/18/international/middleeast/18hamas.html).

Smith, Denise. 2003. "The Older Population in the United States: March 2002." U.S. Census Bureau *Current Population Reports,* P20–546. Washington, DC. Accessed June 18, 2009 (www.census.gov/prod/2003pubs/p20–546.pdf).

Smith, Dorothy E. 1987. *The Everyday World as Problematic: A Feminist Sociology.* Boston: Northeastern University Press.

Smith, Tom W. 2003. *Coming of Age in 21st Century America: Public Attitudes Toward the Importance and Timing of Transition to Adulthood.* Chicago: National Opinion Research Center.

———. 2004. "Coming of Age in Twenty-first Century America: Public Attitudes Towards the Importance and Timing of Transitions to Adulthood." *Ageing International* 29 (2): 136–148.

———. 2006. "American Sexual Behavior: Trends, Socio-Demographic Differences, and Risk Behavior." National Opinion Research Center, University of Chicago, GSS Topical Report No. 25. Updated March, 2006. Accessed May 12, 2010 (http://www.norc.org/NR/rdonlyres/2663F09F-2E74-436E-AC81-6FFBF288E183/0/AmericanSexualBehavior2006.pdf).

Snyder, T. D., and S. A. Dillow. 2010. *Digest of Education Statistics 2009.* NCES 2010–013. Washington, DC: National Center for Education Statistics, Institute of Education Sciences, U.S. Department of Education. Accessed April 16, 2010 (http://nces.ed.gov/pubs2010/2010013.pdf).

Social Security Administration. 2008. "Fast Facts & Figures About Social Security, 2008." SSA Publication No. 13–11785. Social Security Administration, Office of Research, Evaluation, and Statistics, Washington, DC. Accessed June 18, 2009 (www.ssa.gov/policy/docs/chartbooks/fast_facts/2008/fast_facts08.pdf).

Solidarity Center. 2009. *2009 Annual Report.* Solidarity Center, AFL-CIO, Washington, DC. Accessed May 28, 2010 (http://www.solidaritycenter.org/files/pubs_annual_report_2009.pdf).

Solove, Daniel J. 2008. "Do Social Networks Bring the End of Privacy?" *Scientific American* 299 (September): 100–106.

Accessed June 30, 2009 (www.scientificamerican.com/article.cfm?id=do-social-networks-bring).

Sorokin, Pitirim A. [1927] 1959. *Social and Cultural Mobility.* New York: Free Press.

Spalter-Roth, Roberta, and Nicole Van Vooren. 2008a. "What Are They Doing with a Bachelor's Degree in Sociology?" American Sociological Association Department of Research and Development. Washington, DC: Association. Accessed March 25, 2010 (http://www.asanet.org/images/research/docs/pdf/What%20Are%20They%20Doing%20with%20BA%20in%20Soc.pdf).

———. 2008b. "Pathways to Job Satisfaction." American Sociological Association Department of Research and Development. Washington, DC: Association. Accessed March 25, 2010 (http://www.asanet.org/images/research/docs/pdf/Pathways%20to%20Job%20Satisfaction.pdf).

———. 2009. "Idealists vs. Careerists: Graduate School Choices of Sociology Majors." American Sociological Association Department of Research and Development. Washington DC: ASA. Accessed March 25, 2010 (http://www.asanet.org/images/research/docs/pdf/Idealist%20vs%20Careerisst.pdf).

Sprague, Joey. 2005. *Feminist Methodologies for Critical Research: Bridging Differences.* Lanham, MD: AltaMira Press.

Stack, Carol. 1974. *All Our Kin: Strategies for Survival in a Black Community.* New York: Harper & Row.

Standish, Peter, and Steven Bell. 2008. *Culture and Customs of Mexico.* Santa Barbara, CA: Greenwood Press.

Stark, Rodney, and William Sims Bainbridge. 1979. "Of Churches, Sects, and Cults: Preliminary Concepts for a Theory of Religious Movements." *Journal for the Scientific Study of Religion* 18 (June): 117–131.

———. 1985. *The Future of Religion.* Berkeley: University of California Press.

Starr, Paul. 1982. *The Social Transformation of American Medicine.* New York: Basic Books.

State of Arizona. 2010. "Senate Bill 1070: Support Our Law Enforcement and Safe Neighborhoods Act." Forty-ninth Legislature, Second Regular Session. Accessed May 16, 2010 (http://www.azleg.gov/legtext/49leg/2r/bills/sb1070s.pdf).

Stavenhagen, Rodolfo. 1994. "The Indian Resurgence in Mexico." *Cultural Survival Quarterly* (Summer/Fall): 77–80.

Steele, Jonathan. 2005. "Annan Attacks Britain and U.S. over Erosion of Human Rights." *Guardian Weekly,* March 16, p. 1.

Steidle, Brian. 2007. *The Devil Came on Horseback: Bearing Witness to the Genocide in Darfur.* New York: PublicAffairs.

Stein, Arlene. 2010. "The Incredible Shrinking Lesbian World and Other Queer Conundra." *Sexualities* 13 (1): 21–32.

Stein, Leonard I. 1967. "The Doctor–Nurse Game." *Archives of General Psychology* 16: 699–703.

Stein, Leonard, David T. Watts, and Timothy Howell. 1990. "The Doctor–Nurse Game Revisited." *New England Journal of Medicine* 322 (8): 546–549.

Stelter, Brian, and Brad Stone. 2009. "Web Pries Lid of Iranian Censorship." *New York Times,* June 22. Accessed July 1, 2009 (www.nytimes.com/2009/06/23/world/middleeast/23censor.html).

Stenning, Derrick J. 1958. "Household Viability Among the Pastoral Fulani." Pp. 92–119 in *The Developmental Cycle in Domestic Groups,* ed. John R. Goody. Cambridge: Cambridge University Press.

Steward, Samuel M. 1990. *Bad Boys and Tough Tattoos: A Social History of the Tattoo with Gangs, Sailors, and Street-Corner Punks.* Binghamton, NY: Harrington Park Press.

Stewart, Quincy Thomas. 2006. "Reinvigorating Relative Deprivation: A New Measure for a Classic Concept." *Social Science Research* 35 (3): 779–802.

Stewart, Susan D. 2007. *Brave New Stepfamilies: Diverse Paths Toward Stepfamily Living.* Thousand Oaks, CA: Sage.

Stitt, Carmen, and Dale Kunkel. 2008. "Food Advertising During Children's Television Programming on Broadcast and Cable Channels." *Health Communication* 23: 573–584.

Stratton, Terry D., and Jennifer L. McGivern-Snofsky. 2008. "Toward a Sociological Understanding of Complementary and Alternative

Medicine Use." *Journal of Alternative and Complementary Medicine* 14 (6): 777–783.

Strauss, Gary. 2002. "'Good Old Boys' Network Still Rules Corporate Boards." *USA Today,* November 1, pp. B1, B2.

Stretesky, Paul B. 2006. "Corporate Self-Policing and the Environment." *Criminology* 44 (3): 671.

Strier, Roni. 2010. "Women, Poverty, and the Microenterprise: Context and Discourse." *Gender, Work & Organization* 17 (2): 195–218.

Stryker, Susan. 2007. "Transgender Feminism: Queering the Woman Question." Pp. 59–70 in *Third Wave Feminism: A Critical Exploration,* expanded 2nd ed., Stacy Gillis, Gillian Howie, and Rebecca Munford. New York: Palgrave Macmillan.

Sudan Tribune. 2008. "Darfur's Poorest Squeezed by Ration Cuts." June 22. Accessed August 12, 2008 (http://www.sudantribune.com/spip.php?article27608).

Suitor, J. Jill, Staci A. Minyard, and Rebecca S. Carter. 2001. "'Did You See What I Saw?' Gender Differences in Perceptions of Avenues to Prestige Among Adolescents." *Sociological Inquiry* 71 (Fall): 437–454.

Sullivan, Harry Stack. [1953] 1968. *The Interpersonal Theory of Psychiatry,* ed. Helen Swick Perry and Mary Ladd Gawel. New York: Norton.

Sullivan, Kevin. 2006. "In War-Torn Congo, Going Wireless to Reach Home." *Washington Post,* July 9. Accessed May 6, 2009 (http://www.washingtonpost.com/wp-dyn/content/article/2006/07/08/AR2006070801063.html).

Sumner, William G. 1906. *Folkways.* New York: Ginn.

Sun, Yongmin, and Yuanzhang Li. 2008. "Stable Postdivorce Family Structures During Late Adolescence and Socioeconomic Consequences in Adulthood." *Journal of Marriage & Family* 70 (1): 129–143.

Sutcliffe, Bob. 2002. *100 Ways of Seeing an Unequal World.* London: Zed Books.

Sutherland, Edwin H. 1940. "White-Collar Criminality." *American Sociological Review* 5 (February): 1–11.

———. 1949. *White Collar Crime.* New York: Dryden.

———. 1983. *White Collar Crime: The Uncut Version.* New Haven, CT: Yale University Press.

Sutherland, Edwin H., Donald R. Cressey, and David F. Luckenbill. 1992. *Principles of Criminology,* 11th ed. New York: Rowman & Littlefield.

Sutton, Philip W. 2007. *The Environment: A Sociological Introduction.* Malden, MA: Polity Press.

Swatos Jr., William H., ed. 1998. *Encyclopedia of Religion and Society.* Lanham, MD: AltaMira Press.

Swidler, Ann. 1986. "Culture in Action: Symbols and Strategies." *American Sociological Review* 51 (April): 273–286.

Szasz, Thomas S. 1971. "The Same Slave: An Historical Note on the Use of Medical Diagnosis as Justificatory Rhetoric." *American Journal of Psychotherapy* 25 (April): 228–239.

T

Tafur, Maritza Montiel, Terry K. Crowe, and Eliseo Torres. 2009. "A Review of Curanderismo and Healing Practices Among Mexicans and Mexican Americans." *Occupational Therapy International* 16 (1): 82–88.

Taha, T. A. 2007. "Arabic as 'A Critical-Need' Foreign Language in Post–9/11 Era: A Study of Students' Attitudes and Motivation." *Journal of Instructional Psychology* 34 (3): 150–160.

Tate, Shirley Anne. 2009. *Black Beauty: Aesthetics, Stylization, Politics.* Burlington, VT: Ashgate.

Taylor, Dorceta E. 2000. "The Rise of the Environmental Justice Paradigm." *American Behavioral Scientist* 43 (January): 508–580.

Taylor, Jonathan B., and Joseph P. Kalt. 2005. *American Indians on Reservations: A Data Book of Socioeconomic Change Between the 1990 and 2000 Censuses.* Cambridge, MA: Harvard Project on American Indian Development.

Taylor, Paul, and Richard Morin. 2008. "Americans Say They Like Diverse Communities; Election, Census Trends Suggest Otherwise." Pew Research Center Report, December 2. Accessed May 17, 2010 (http://pewsocialtrends.org/assets/pdf/diverse-political-communities.pdf).

Taylor, Paul, Rich Morin, Kim Parker, D'Vera Cohn, and Wendy Wang. 2009. *Growing Old in America: Expectations vs. Reality.* Pew Research Center Social & Demographic Trends Project, January. Accessed April 5, 2010 (http://pewsocialtrends.org/assets/pdf/Getting-Old-in-America.pdf).

Taylor, Verta. 1999. "Gender and Social Movements: Gender Processes in Women's Self-Help Movements." *Gender and Society* 13: 8–33.

———. 2004. "Social Movements and Gender." Pp. 14348–14352 in *International Encyclopedia of the Social and Behavioral Sciences,* ed. Neil J. Smelser and Paul B. Baltes. New York: Elsevier.

Tejada-Vera, Betzaida, and Paul D. Sutton. 2009. "Births, Marriages, Divorces, and Deaths: Provisional Data for 2008." *National Vital Statistics Reports* 57 (19). Hyattsville, MD: National Center for Health Statistics. Accessed April 11, 2010 (http://www.cdc.gov/nchs/data/nvsr/nvsr57/nvsr57_19.pdf).

Tejada-Vera, Betzaida, and Paul D. Sutton. 2010. "Births, Marriages, Divorces, and Deaths: Provisional Data for July 2009." *National Vital Statistics Reports* 58 (15). Hyattsville, MD: National Center for Health Statistics. Accessed April 14, 2010 (http://www.cdc.gov/nchs/data/nvsr/nvsr58/nvsr58_15.pdf).

Tentler, Leslie Woodcock. 2004. *Catholics and Contraception: An American History.* Ithaca, NY: Cornell University.

Terkel, Studs. 2003. *Hope Dies Last: Keeping the Faith in Difficult Times.* New York: New Press.

Terry, Sara. 2000. "Whose Family? The Revolt of the Child-Free." *Christian Science Monitor,* August 29, pp. 1, 4.

Tertilt, Michèle. 2005. "Polygyny, Fertility, and Savings." *Journal of Political Economy* 113 (6): 1341–1370.

Thernsrom, Melanie. 2005. "The New Arranged Marriage." *New York Times,* February 13. Accessed April 14, 2010 (http://www.nytimes.com/2005/02/13/magazine/13MATCHMAKING.html).

Thomas, Adam, and Isabel Sawhill. 2002. "For Richer and Poorer: Marriages as an Antipoverty Strategy." *Journal of Policy Analysis and Management* 21 (4): 587–599.

Thomas, Gordon, and Max Morgan Witts. 1974. *Voyage of the Damned.* Greenwich, CT: Fawcett Crest.

Thomas, William I., and Dorothy Swain Thomas. 1928. *The Child in America: Behavior Problems and Programs.* New York: Knopf.

Thomson, Elizabeth, and Eva Bernhardt. 2010. "Education, Values, and Cohabitation in Sweden." *Marriage & Family Review* 46 (1/2): 1–21.

Thornberg, Robert. 2008. "'It's Not Fair!'—Voicing Pupils' Criticisms of School Rules." *Children & Society* 22 (6): 418–428.

Tierney, John. 2003. "Iraqi Family Ties Complicate American Efforts for Change." *New York Times,* September 28, pp. A1, A22.

Tilly, Charles. 1993. *Popular Contention in Great Britain 1758–1834.* Cambridge, MA: Harvard University Press.

———. 2004. *Social Movements, 1768–2004.* Boulder, CO: Paradigm.

Tolbert, Kathryn. 2000. "In Japan, Traveling Alone Begins at Age 6." *Washington Post National Weekly Edition* 17, May 15, p. 17.

Tonkinson, Robert. 1978. *The Mardudjara Aborigines.* New York: Holt.

Tönnies, Ferdinand. [1887] 1988. *Community and Society.* Rutgers, NJ: Transaction.

Toossi, Mitra. 2007. "Labor Force Projections to 2016: More Workers in Their Golden Years." *Monthly Labor Review,* November, pp. 33–52.

Torres, Lourdes. 2008. "Puerto Rican Americans" and "Puerto Rico." Pp. 1082–1089, vol. 3, in *Encyclopedia of Race, Ethnicity, and Society,* ed. Richard T. Schaefer. Thousand Oaks, CA: Sage.

Traugott, Michael W. 2005. "The Accuracy of the National Preelection Polls in the 2004 Presidential Election." *Public Opinion Quarterly* 69 (5): 642–654.

Ture, Kwame, and Charles Hamilton. 1992. *Black Power: The Politics of Liberation,* rev. ed. New York: Vintage Books.

Twitchell, James B. 2000. "The Stone Age." Pp. 44–48 in *Do Americans Shop Too Much?* ed. Juliet Schor. Boston: Beacon Press.

UNAIDS. 2009. *AIDS Epidemic Update: November 2009.* Geneva: UNAIDS. Accessed May 20, 2010 (http://data.unaids.org/pub/Report/2009/JC1700_Epi_Update_2009_en.pdf).

UNCTAD. 2009. "Mainstreaming Gender in Trade Policy." United Nations Conference on Trade and Development, March 10–11, Geneva. Accessed June 18, 2009 (www.unctad.org/Templates/WebFlyer.asp?intItemID=4760&lang=1)

United Nations. 2008. *The Millennium Development Goals Report 2008.* New York: United Nations. Accessed June 13, 2009 (www.un.org/millenniumgoals/2008highlevel/pdf/newsroom/mdg%20reports/MDG_Report_2008_ENGLISH.pdf).

———. 2009a. *International Migration Report 2006: A Global Assessment.* Department of Economic and Social Affairs, Population Division. Accessed June 21, 2009 (www.un.org/esa/population/publications/2006_MigrationRep/report.htm).

———. 2009b. *World Marriage Data 2008.* UN Department of Economic and Social Affairs, Population Division, POP/DB/Marr/Rev2008. Accessed April 11, 2010 (http://www.un.org/esa/population/publications/WMD2008/Main.html).

———. 2009c. *World Contraceptive Use 2009.* UN Department of Economic and Social Affairs, Population Division, POP/DB/CP/Rev2009. Accessed May 12, 2010 (http://www.un.org/esa/population/publications/WCU2009/WCP_2009/Data.html).

———. 2010. *Special Rapporteur on Contemporary Forms of Slavery.* Office of the High Commissioner for Human Rights, Geneva. Accessed April 24, 2010 (http://www2.ohchr.org/english/issues/slavery/rapporteur/index.htm).

United Nations Development Programme. 2000. *Poverty Report 2000: Overcoming Human Poverty.* Washington, DC: UNDP.

———. 2008. *Human Development Indices: A Statistical Update 2008.* New York: UNDP. Accessed June 7, 2009 (http://hdr.undp.org/en/media/HDI_2008_EN_Complete.pdf).

———. 2009. *Human Development Report 2009—Overcoming Barriers: Human Mobility and Development.* Accessed May 28, 2010 (http://hdr.undp.org/en/media/HDR_2009_EN_Complete.pdf).

United Nations Framework Convention on Climate Change. 2010a. "Status of Ratification of the Kyoto Protocol." Accessed June 8, 2010 (http://unfccc.int/playground/items/5524.php).

———. 2010b. "Bonn Climate Change Talks—June 2010." Accessed June 8, 2010 (http://unfccc.int/2860.php).

United Nations Population Division. 2005. *World Fertility Report 2003.* New York: UNPD.

UN News Service. 2010. "Darfur: Security Council Warned of 'Significant Challenges' to Peace Process." UN News Centre, May 20. Accessed May 28, 2010. (http://www.un.org/apps/news/story.asp?NewsID=34761&Cr=&Crl=).

Urbina, Ian. 2004. "Disco Rice, and Other Trash Talk." *New York Times,* July 31, p. A11.

U.S. Census Bureau. 1975. *Historical Statistics of the United States, Colonial Times to 1970.* Washington, DC: U.S. Government Printing Office.

———. 1994. *Statistical Abstract of the United States: 1994* (114th ed.). Washington, DC: U.S. Government Printing Office. Accessed April 13, 2010 (http://www2.census.gov/prod2/statcomp/documents/1994-01.pdf).

———. 1998. "Interracial Tables." Washington, DC: U.S. Census Bureau. Accessed April 12, 2010 (http://www.census.gov/population/www/socdemo/interrace.html).

———. 2004. "Current Population Survey (CPS)—Definitions and Explanations." Washington, DC: U.S. Census Bureau. Accessed June 8, 2008 (http://www.census.gov/population/www/cps/cpsdef.html).

———. 2007. "Marriage and Divorce: 2004 SIPP Report." Washington, DC: U.S. Census Bureau. Accessed April 13, 2010 (http://www.census.gov/population/www/socdemo/marr-div.html).

———. 2008a. "Current Population Survey (CPS)—Definitions and Explanations." Washington, DC: U.S. Census Bureau. Accessed May 22, 2009 (http://www.census.gov/population/www/cps/cpsdef.html).

———. 2008b. "PPL Table 1B: Child Care Arrangements of Preschoolers Under 5 Years Old Living with Mother, by Employment Status of Mother and Selected Characteristics: Spring 2005 (Percentages)." *Who's Minding the Kids? Child Care Arrangements: Spring 2005.* Accessed May 6, 2009 (http://www.census.gov/population/www/socdemo/child/ppl-2005.html).

———. 2008c. *Statistical Abstract of the United States: 2009* (128th ed.). Washington, DC: Author.

———. 2008d. "Table PINC-03. Educational Attainment—People 25 Years Old and Over, by Total Money Earnings in 2007, Work Experience in 2007, Age, Race, Hispanic Origin, and Sex." Annual Social and Economic Supplement. Washington, DC: U.S. Census Bureau. Accessed May 29, 2009 (http://www.census.gov/hhes/www/macro/032008/perinc/new03_000.htm).

———. 2008e. "Historical Income Tables—Households." Accessed June 6, 2009 (www.census.gov/hhes/www/income/histinc/inchhtoc.html).

———. 2008f. "2007 Poverty Table of Contents." Current Population Survey 2008 Annual Social and Economic Supplement. Accessed June 8, 2009 (http://www.census.gov/hhes/www/macro/032008/pov/new46_100125_01.htm).

———. 2008g. "2008 National Population Projections: Tables and Charts." Accessed June 18, 2009 (www.census.gov/population/www/projections/tablesandcharts.html).

———. 2008h. "2007 American Community Survey 1-Year Estimates." American FactFinder. Accessed June 19, 2009 (http://factfinder.census.gov/home/saff/main.html).

———. 2009a. "Families and Living Arrangements." Washington, DC: U.S. Census Bureau. May 23, 2009 (http://www.census.gov/population/www/socdemo/hh-fam.html).

———. 2009b. "Educational Attainment." Washington, DC: U.S. Census Bureau. Accessed May 28, 2009 (http://www.census.gov/population/www/socdemo/educ-attn.html).

———. 2009c. "Tables of Alternative Poverty Estimates: 2007." Accessed June 8, 2009 (http://www.census.gov/hhes/www/povmeas/tables.html).

———. 2009d. "Person Income Table of Contents." Annual Social and Economic Supplement. Current Population Survey. Washington, DC: U.S. Census Bureau. Accessed March 28, 2010 (http://www.census.gov/hhes/www/cpstables/032009/perinc/toc.htm).

———. 2009e. "Who's Minding the Kids? Child Care Arrangements." Survey of Income and Program Participation Panel, Summer 2006. Accessed April 3, 2010 (http://www.census.gov/population/www/socdemo/child/tables-2006.html).

———. 2009f. *Statistical Abstract of the United States: 2010* (129th ed.). Washington, DC: U.S. Government Printing Office. Accessed April 5, 2010 (http://www.census.gov/compendia/statab/).

———. 2009g. "Table PINC-03. Educational Attainment—People 25 Years Old and Over, by Total Money Earnings in 2007, Work Experience in 2007, Age, Race, Hispanic Origin, and Sex." Annual Social and Economic Supplement. Washington, DC: U.S. Census Bureau. Accessed April 15, 2010 (http://www.census.gov/hhes/www/cpstables/032009/perinc/new03_000.htm).

———. 2009h. "Voting and Registration in the Election of November 2008—Detailed Tables." Accessed April 23, 2010 (http://www.census.gov/hhes/www/socdemo/voting/publications/p20/2008/tables.html).

———. 2009i. "Historical Income Tables—Households." Accessed April 25, 2010 (http://www.census.gov/hhes/www/income/histinc/inchhtoc.html).

———. 2009j. "2008 American Community Survey 1-Year Estimates." American Community Survey, American FactFinder. Accessed May 13, 2010 (http://factfinder.census.gov/home/saff/main.html).

———. 2010a. "Families and Living Arrangements." Washington, DC: U.S. Census Bureau. Accessed April 11, 2010 (http://www.census.gov/population/www/socdemo/hh-fam.html).

————. 2010b. "Observations from the Interagency Technical Working Group on Developing a Supplemental Poverty Measure." Accessed April 25, 2010 (http://www.census.gov/hhes/www/poverty/SPM_TWGObservations.pdf).

————. 2010c. "The Questions on the Form." Accessed May 16, 2010 (http://2010.census.gov/2010census/pdf/2010_Questionnaire_Info.pdf).

U.S. Commission on Civil Rights. 2009. "Racial Categorization in the 2010 Census: A Briefing Before the United States Commission on Civil Rights Held in Washington, DC, April 7, 2006." Briefing Report. Accessed May 16, 2010 (http://www.usccr.gov/pubs/RC2010Web_Version.pdf).

U.S. Department of Agriculture. 2007. "International Macroeconomic Data Set." Economic Research Service. Accessed August 6, 2009 (www.ers.usda.gov/data/macroeconomics).

U.S. Department of Homeland Security. 2009. *Yearbook of Immigration Statistics: 2008*. Washington, DC: U.S. Department of Homeland Security, Office of Immigration Statistics. Accessed April 29, 2010 (http://www.dhs.gov/files/statistics/publications/yearbook.shtm).

U.S. Department of Justice. 1999. "Ten-Year Program to Compensate Japanese Americans Interned During World War II Closes Its Doors." Press release No. 059, February 19. Accessed June 3, 2010 (http://www.justice.gov/opa/pr/1999/February/059cr.htm).

————. 2008a. *Crime in the United States, 2007*. Washington, DC: U.S. Department of Justice, Federal Bureau of Investigation. Accessed May 20, 2009 (http://www.fbi.gov/ucr/cius2007/index.html).

————. 2008b. "Crime Clock: 2007." *Crime in the United States, 2007*. Washington, DC: U.S. Department of Justice, Federal Bureau of Investigation. Accessed May 20, 2010 (http://www.fbi.gov/ucr/cius2007/about/crime_clock.html).

————. 2009a *Crime in the United States, 2008*. Washington, DC: U.S. Department of Justice, Federal Bureau of investigation. Accessed April 9, 2010 (http://www.fbi.gov/ucr/cius2008/index.html).

————. 2009b. "Crime Clock: 2008." *Crime in the United States, 2008*. Washington, DC: U.S. Department of Justice, Federal Bureau of Investigation. Accessed April 9, 2010 (http://www.fbi.gov/ucr/cius2008/about/crime_clock.html).

U.S. Department of State. 2009. *FY 2009 Annual Report on Intercountry Adoptions*. U.S. Department of State, Washington, DC, November. Accessed April 13, 2010 (http://www.adoption.state.gov/pdf/fy2009_annual_report.pdf).

————. 2010. *Trafficking in Persons Report*. Office of the Under Secretary for Democracy and Global Affairs and Bureau of Public Affairs, Washington, DC, Publication 11407, June 2009. Accessed April 29, 2010 (www.state.gov/g/tip).

U.S. Surgeon General. 1999. "Overview of Cultural Diversity and Mental Health Services." In Chap. 2, *Surgeon General's Report on Mental Health*. Washington, DC: U.S. Government Printing Office.

U.S. Trade Representative. 2003. *2002 Annual Report*. Washington, DC: U.S. Government Printing Office.

Utne, Leif. 2003. "We Are All Zapatistas." *Utne Reader*, November/December, pp. 36–37.

V

van den Bergh, Linda, Eddie Denessen, Lisette Hornstra, Marinus Voeten, and Rob W. Holland. 2010. "The Implicit Prejudiced Attitudes of Teachers: Relations to Teacher Expectations and the Ethnic Achievement Gap." *American Educational Research Journal*, January. doi: 10.3102/0002831209353594.

Van Dijk, Jan., John van Kesteren, and Paul Smit. 2007. *Criminal Victimisation in International Perspective, Key Findings from the 2004–2005 ICVS and EU ICS*. The Hague: Boom Legal Publishers. Accessed May 20, 2009 (http://rechten.uvt.nl/icvs/pdffiles/ICVS2004_05.pdf).

Vanderstraeten, Raf. 2007. "Professions in Organizations, Professional Work in Education." *British Journal of Sociology of Education* 28 (5): 621–635.

Vasagar, Jeeran. 2005. " 'At Last Rwanda Is Known for Something Positive.' " *Guardian Weekly,* July 22, p. 18.

Veblen, Thorstein. [1899] 1964. *Theory of the Leisure Class*. New York: Macmillan.

————. 1919. *The Vested Interests and the State of the Industrial Arts*. New York: Huebsch.

Veenhoven, Ruut. 2009. "Average Happiness in 148 Nations 2000–2009." World Database of Happiness, Rankreport Average Happiness, version 10/09. Accessed March 23, 2010 (http://worlddatabaseofhappiness.eur.nl/hap_nat/findingreports/RankReport_AverageHappiness.htm).

Venkatesh, Sudhir. 2006. *Off the Books: The Underground Economy of the Urban Poor*. Cambridge, MA: Harvard University Press.

————. 2008. *Gang Leader for a Day: A Rogue Sociologist Takes to the Street*. New York: Penguin Books.

Venter, Craig. 2000. "Remarks at the Human Genome Announcement, at the Whitehouse." Accessed June 30, 2008 (http://www.celera.com/celera/pr_1056647999).

Villarreal, Andrés. 2004. "The Social Ecology of Rural Violence: Land Scarcity, the Organization of Agricultural Production, and the Presence of the State." *American Journal of Sociology* 110 (September): 313–348.

Virtcom. 2009. "Board Diversification Strategy: Realizing Competitive Advantage and Shareholder Value." A Whitepaper by Virtcom Consulting, prepared for CalPERS. Accessed June 22, 2009 (www.calpers-governance.org/docs-sof/marketinitiatives/initiatives/board-diversity-white-paper.pdf).

Vowell, Paul R., and Jieming Chen. 2004. "Predicting Academic Misconduct: A Comparative Test of Four Sociological Explanations." *Sociological Inquiry* 74 (2): 226–249.

W

Wais, Erin. 2005. "Trained Incapacity: Thorstein Veblen and Kenneth Burke." *KB Journal* 2 (1). Accessed May 13, 2009 (http://www.kbjournal.org/node/103).

Waites, Matthew. 2009. "Critique of 'Sexual Orientation' and 'Gender Identity' in Human Rights Discourse: Global Queer Politics Beyond the Yogyakarta Principles." *Contemporary Politics* 15 (1): 137–156.

Waldman, Amy. 2004a. "India Takes Economic Spotlight, and Critics Are Unkind." *New York Times,* March 7, p. 3.

———— 2004b. "Low-Tech or High, Jobs Are Scarce in India's Boon." *New York Times,* May 6, p. A3.

————. 2004c. "What India's Upset Vote Reveals: The High Tech Is Skin Deep." *New York Times,* May 15, p. A5.

Walker, Iain, and Heather J. Smith, eds. 2002. *Relative Deprivation: Specification, Development, and Integration*. New York: Cambridge University Press.

Walker, Rebecca. 1992. "Becoming the Third Wave." *Ms.,* January, pp. 39–41.

————. 1995. *To Be Real: Telling the Truth and Changing the Face of Feminism*. Berkeley: University of California Press.

Wallerstein, Immanuel. 1974. *The Modern World System*. New York: Academic Press.

————. 1979a. *Capitalist World Economy*. Cambridge, UK: Cambridge University Press.

————. 1979b. *The End of the World as We Know It: Social Science for the Twenty-first Century*. Minneapolis: University of Minnesota Press.

————. 2000. *The Essential Wallerstein*. New York: New Press.

————. 2004. *World-Systems Analysis: An Introduction*. Durham, NC: Duke University Press.

Wallerstein, Immanuel. 2010. "Structural Crises." *New Left Review* 62 (March/April): 133–142.

Wallerstein, Judith S., Julia M. Lewis, and Sandra Blakeslee. 2000. *The Unexpected Legacy of Divorce: A 25-Year Landmark Study*. New York: Basic Books.

Wallis, Claudia. 2008. "How to Make Great Teachers." *Time,* February 25, pp. 28–34.

Walpole, Marybeth. 2007. "Economically and Educationally Challenged Students in Higher Education: Access to Outcomes." *ASHE Higher Education Report* 33 (3).

Warner, R. Stephen. 2005. *A Church of Our Own: Disestablishment and Diversity in American Religion.* New Brunswick, NJ: Rutgers University Press.

———. 2007. "The Role of Religion in the Process of Segmented Assimilation." *Annals of the American Academy of Political and Social Science* 612 (1): 100–115.

Warren, Patricia, Donald Tomaskovic-Devey, William Smith, Matthew Zingraff, and Marcinda Mason. 2006. "Driving While Black: Bias Processes and Racial Disparity in Police Stops." *Criminology* 44 (3): 709–738.

Wartella, Ellen, Aletha C. Huston, Victoria Rideout, and Michael Robb. 2009. "Studying Media Effects on Children: Improving Methods and Measures." *American Behavioral Scientist* 52 (8): 1111–1114.

Washington, Harriet A. 2006. *Medical Apartheid: The Dark History of Medical Experimentation on Black Americans from Colonial Times to the Present.* New York: Doubleday.

Waters, Mary C. 2009. "Social Science and Ethnic Options." *Ethnicities* 9 (1): 130–135.

Watts, Duncan J. 2004. "The 'New' Science of Networks." Pp. 243–270 in *Annual Review of Sociology 2004,* ed. Karen S. Cook and John Hagan. Palo Alto, CA: Annual Reviews.

Weber, Max. [1913–1922] 1947. *The Theory of Social and Economic Organization,* trans. A. Henderson and T. Parsons. New York: Free Press.

———. [1904] 1949. *Methodology of the Social Sciences,* trans. Edward A. Shils and Henry A. Finch. Glencoe, IL: Free Press.

———. [1904] 2009. *The Protestant Ethic and the Spirit of Capitalism,* trans. Talcott Parsons. New York: Scribner.

———. [1916] 1958a. "Class, Status, Party," Pp. 180–195 in *From Max Weber: Essays in Sociology,* ed. H. H. Gerth and C. Wright Mills. New York: Oxford University Press.

———. [1916] 1958b. *The Religion of India: The Sociology of Hinduism and Buddhism.* New York: Free Press.

———. [1921] 1958c. "Bureaucracy." Pp. 196–244 in *From Max Weber: Essays in Sociology,* ed. H. H. Gerth and C. Wright Mills. New York: Oxford University Press.

Wechsler Henry, and Toben F. Nelson. 2008. "What We Have Learned from the Harvard School of Public Health College Alcohol Study: Focusing Attention on College Student Alcohol Consumption and the Environmental Conditions that Promote It." *Journal of Studies on Alcohol and Drugs* 69 (4): 481–490.

Wechsler, Henry, J. E. Lee, M. Kuo, M. Seibring, T. F. Nelson, and H. Lee. 2002. "Trends in College Binge Drinking During a Period of Increased Prevention Efforts: Findings from Four Harvard School of Public Health College Alcohol Surveys: 1993–2001." *Journal of American College Health* 50 (5): 203–217.

Weinberg, Daniel H. 2004. "Evidence from Census 2000 About Earnings by Detailed Occupation for Men and Women." Census 2000 Special Reports, CENSR-15. Washington, DC: U.S. Census Bureau. Accessed June 26, 2008 (http://www.census.gov/prod/2004pubs/censr-15.pdf).

———. 2007. "Earnings by Gender: Evidence from Census 2000." *Monthly Labor Review,* July/August, pp. 26–34.

Weinstein, Henry. 2002. "Airport Screener Curb Is Regretful." *Los Angeles Times,* November 16, pp. B1, B14.

Weiss, Michael J. 2000. *The Clustered World: How We Live, What We Buy, and What It All Means About Who We Are.* Boston: Little, Brown.

Wells-Barnett, Ida B. [1928] 1970. *Crusade for Justice: The Autobiography of Ida B. Wells,* ed. Alfreda M. Duster. Chicago: University of Chicago Press.

West, Candace, and Don H. Zimmerman 1987. "Doing Gender." *Gender and Society* 1 (June): 125–151.

Wethington, Elaine. 2000. "Expecting Stress: Americans and the 'Midlife Crisis.' " *Motivation & Emotion* 24 (2): 85–103.

Whorton, James C. 2002. *Nature Cures: The History of Alternative Medicine in America.* New York: Oxford University Press.

Whyte, William Foote. [1943] 1981. *Street Corner Society: Social Structure of an Italian Slum,* 3d ed. Chicago: University of Chicago Press.

WICHE. 2008. "Knocking at the College Door: Projections of High School Graduates by State and Race/Ethnicity 1992–2022." Boulder, CO: Western Interstate Commission for Higher Education. Accessed April 19, 2010 (http://wiche.edu/info/publications/knocking_complete_book.pdf).

Wickman, Peter M. 1991. "Deviance." Pp. 85–87 in *Encyclopedic Dictionary of Sociology,* 4th ed., ed. Dushkin Publishing Group. Guilford, CT: Dushkin.

Wierzbicka, Anna. 2008. "Why There Are No 'Colour Universals' in Language and Thought." *Journal of the Royal Anthropological Institute* 14 (2): 407–425.

Wilford, John Noble. 1997. "New Clues Show Where People Made the Great Leap to Agriculture." *New York Times,* November 18, pp. B9, B12.

Williams, Alicia, John Fries, Jean Koppen, and Robert Prisuta. 2010. *Connecting and Giving: A Report on How Midlife and Older Americans Spend Their Time, Make Connections and Build Communities.* Washington, DC: AARP.

Williams, David R., and Chiquita Collins. 2004. "Reparations." *American Behavioral Scientist* 47 (March): 977–1000.

Williams, Kristine N., and Carol A. B. Warren. 2009. "Communication in Assisted Living." *Journal of Aging Studies* 23 (1): 24–36.

Williams, Mike. 2008. "Rising Cost of Food Devastates Haiti." *Atlanta Journal Constitution,* June 17. Accessed August 12 (http://www.ajc.com/news/content/news/stories/2008/06/16/haiti_food_crisis.html).

Williams, Richard Allen. 2007. "Cultural Diversity, Health Care Disparities, and Cultural Competency in American Medicine." *Journal of the American Academy of Orthopaedic Surgeons* 15: S52–S58.

Williams Jr., Robin M. 1970. *American Society,* 3d ed. New York: Knopf.

Wills, Jeremiah B., and Barbara J. Risman. 2006. "The Visibility of Feminist Thought in Family Studies." *Journal of Marriage and Family* 68 (August): 690–700.

Wilson, Carl. 2007. *Let's Talk About Love: A Journey to the End of Taste.* New York: Continuum.

Wilson, Robin. 2007. "The New Gender Divide." *Chronicle of Higher Education* 53 (January 26): A36–A39.

Wilson, William Julius. 1980. *The Declining Significance of Race: Blacks and Changing American Institutions,* 2d ed. Chicago: University of Chicago Press.

———. 1987. *The Truly Disadvantaged: The Inner City, the Underclass and Public Policy.* Chicago: University of Chicago Press.

———. 1996. *When Work Disappears: The World of the New Urban Poor.* New York: Knopf.

———. 1999. *The Bridge over the Racial Divide: Rising Inequality and Coalition Politics.* Berkeley: University of California Press.

———. 2008. "The Political and Economic Forces Shaping Concentrated Poverty." *Political Science Quarterly* 123 (4): 555–571.

———. 2009. *More than Just Race: Being Black and Poor in the Inner City.* New York: Norton.

Wilper, Andrew P., Steffie Woolhandler, Karen E. Lasser, Danny McCormick, David H. Bor, and David U. Himmelstein. 2009. "Health Insurance and Mortality in US Adults." *American Journal of Public Health* 99 (12): 2289–2295.

Winseman, Albert L. 2005. "Religion in America: Who Has None?" December 6. Accessed March 4, 2007 (www.gallup.com).

Wirth, Louis. 1931. "Clinical Sociology." *American Journal of Sociology* 37 (July): 49–60.

Withrow, Brian L. 2006. *Racial Profiling: From Rhetoric to Reason.* Upper Saddle River, NJ: Prentice Hall.

Witte, Griff. 2005. "The Vanishing Middle Class." *Washington Post National Weekly Edition,* September 27, pp. 6–9.

Wolf, Naomi. 1992. *The Beauty Myth: How Images of Beauty Are Used Against Women.* New York: Anchor.

Women and Work Commission. 2006. "Shaping a Fairer Future." Presented to the Prime Minister by Baroness Prosser of Battersea,

February 2006. Accessed June 18, 2009 (http://www.equalities. gov.uk/pdf/Shaping%20a%20Fairer%20Future%20report.pdf).

Word, David L., Charles D. Coleman, Robert Nunziator, and Robert Kominski. 2007. "Demographic Aspects of Surnames from Census 2000." Accessed January 2, 2008 (www.census.gov/genealogy/www/surnames.pdf).

World Bank. 2003. *World Development Report 2003: Sustainable Development in a Dynamic World.* Washington, DC: World Bank.

————. 2006. "India, Inclusive Growth and Service Delivery: Building on India's Success." Development Policy Review, Report No. 34580-IN. Accessed June 13, 2009 (http://siteresources.worldbank.org/SOUTHASIAEXT/Resources/DPR_FullReport.pdf).

————. 2009a. "Gross National Income per Capita 2007," Atlas Method and PPP." *World Development Indicators 2009.* Accessed June 11, 2009 (http://siteresources.worldbank.org/DATASTATISTICS/Resources/GNIPC.pdf).

————. 2009b. "Gross Domestic Product 2007." *World Development Indicators 2009.* Accessed June 12, 2009 (http://siteresources.worldbank.org/DATASTATISTICS/Resources/GDP.pdf).

————. 2009c. *World Development Indicators 2009.* New York: World Bank.

————. 2010. *World Development Indicators.* Accessed April 29, 2010 (http://data.worldbank.org/indicator).

————. 2010a. "Health Expenditure, Public (% of Total Health Expenditure): 2007." *World Development Indicators.* Accessed April 25, 2010 (http://data.worldbank.org/indicator/SH.XPD.PUBL).

————. 2010b. "GNI per Capita, Atlas Method (Current US$): 2008." *World Development Indicators.* Accessed April 27, 2010 (http://data.worldbank.org/indicator/NY.GNP.PCAP.CD).

————. 2010c. "GDP (Current US$): 2008." *World Development Indicators.* Accessed April 28, 2010 (http://data.worldbank.org/indicator/NY.GDP.MKTP.CD).

————. 2010d. "Income Share Held by Highest 20%." *World Development Indicators.* Accessed April 28, 2010 (http://data.worldbank.org/indicator/SI.DST.05TH.20).

————. 2010e. "Income Share Held by Lowest 20%." *World Development Indicators.* Accessed April 28, 2010 (http://data.worldbank.org/indicator/SI.DST.FRST.20).

————. 2010f. "Share of Women Employed in the Nonagricultural Sector (% of Total Nonagricultural Employment)." *World Development Indicators.* Accessed April 28, 2010 (http://data.worldbank.org/indicator/SI.EMP.INSV.FE.ZS).

————. 2010g. *The MDGs After the Crisis: Global Monitoring Report 2010.* Washington, DC: World Bank.

————. 2010h. "Mortality Rate, Infant (per 1,000 Live Births)." *World Development Indicators.* Accessed April 28, 2010 (http://data.worldbank.org/indicator/SP.DYN.IMRT.IN).

World Health Organization. 2005. *WHO Global Atlas of Traditional, Complementary, and Alternative Medicine.* Geneva: WHO Press.

————. 2008a. "Traditional Medicine." Fact Sheet No. 134, December. Accessed May 21, 2010 (http://www.who.int/mediacentre/factsheets/fs134/en/print.html).

————. 2008b. "Air Quality and Health." Fact Sheet No. 313, August. Accessed May 21, 2010 (http://www.who.int/mediacentre/factsheets/fs313/en/print.html).

————. 2010. *World Health Statistics 2010.* Geneva: WHO Press. Accessed May 20, 2010 (http://www.who.int/whosis/whostat/en/).

World Health Organization and UNICEF. 2010. *Progress on Sanitation and Drinking-Water: 2010 Update.* WHO, Geneva and UNICEF, New York. Accessed May 21, 2010 (http://whqlibdoc.who.int/publications/2010/9789241563956_eng_full_text.pdf).

World Values Survey. 2009. "Online Data Analysis." Accessed May 17, 2010 (http://www/wvsevsdb.com/wvs/WVSAnalize.jsp).

X

Xu, Jiaquan, Kenneth D. Kochanek, Sherry L. Murphy, and Betzaida Tejada-Vera. 2010. "Deaths: Final Data for 2007." *National Vital Statistics Reports* web release 58 (19). Hyattsville, MD: National Center for Health Statistics. Accessed May 20, 2010 (http://www.cdc.gov/nchs/data/nvsr/nvsr58/nvsr58_19.pdf).

Y

Yinger, J. Milton. 1970. *The Scientific Study of Religion.* New York: Macmillan.

Yogyakartaprinciples.org. 2007. *The Yogyakarta Principles: Principles on the Application of International Human Rights Law in Relation to Sexual Orientation and Gender Identity.* Accessed May 11, 2010 (http://www.yogyakartaprinciples.org/principles_en.pdf).

Yoong, Nicholas, and Eric Young. 2007. "2007 Corporate Board Report Card: A Report on Directors of Asian Ethnicity on Fortune 500 Boards." A Project of the Corporate Board Initiative of the Committee of 100, Inc., New York. Accessed June 20, 2009 (www.committee100.org/initiatives/corporate_board/2007%20May%20C-100%20Report%20Card.PDF).

Z

Zarembo, Alan. 2004. "A Theater of Inquiry and Evil." *Los Angeles Times,* July 15, pp. A1, A24, A25.

Zauzmer, Julie M. 2010. "Acceptance Rate Falls to New Low." *Harvard Crimson,.* March 31. Accessed April 15, 2010 (http://www.thecrimson.com/article/2010/3/31/financial-aid-percent-students/).

Zellner, William M., and Richard T. Schaefer. 2006. *Extraordinary Groups,* 8th ed. New York: Worth.

Zetter, Kim. 2009. "FBI Use of Patriot Act Authority Increased Dramatically in 2008." *Wired,* May 19. Accessed June 30, 2009 (www.wired.com/threatlevel/2009/05/fbi-use-of-patriot-act-authority-increased-dramatically-in-2008).

Zimbardo, Philip G. 2007. *The Lucifer Effect: Understanding How Good People Turn Evil.* New York: Random House.

Zimmerman, Amber Lynn, M. Joan McDermott, and Christina M. Gould. 2009. "The Local Is Global: Third Wave Feminism, Peace, and Social Justice." *Contemporary Justice Review* 12 (1): 77–90.

Zola, Irving K. 1972. "Medicine as an Institution of Social Control." *Sociological Review* 20 (November): 487–504.

————. 1983. *Socio-Medical Inquiries.* Philadelphia: Temple University Press.

Zweigenhaft, Richard L., and G. William Domhoff. 2006. *Diversity in the Power Elite: How It Happened, Why It Matters,* 2d ed. New York: Rowman & Littlefield.

Front Matter

p. iT, © DynamicGraphics/JupiterImages; p. iB, © istockphoto.com/ DNY59; p. ivT, © William B. Plowman/NBC NewsWire via AP Images; p. ivB, © Win McNamee/Getty Images; p. viT, © iStockphoto .com/Jacob Wackerhause; p. viB, © iStockphoto.com/Pamela Moore; p. viiT, © Elizabeth Dalziel/AP/WIde World; p. viiB, © iStockphoto .com/David H. Lewis; p. viiiT, © Peter Menzel/From the book "Hungry Planet, What the World Eats" by Peter Menzel and Faith D'Aluisio/ www.menzelphoto.com; p. viiiB, © iStockphoto.com/Ekaterina Monakhov; p. ix, © iStockphoto.com/Carrie Bottomley; p. xT, © iStockphoto.com/Grigory Bibikov; p. xB, © iStockphoto.com/Rich Legg; p. xi, © Pavel Filatov/Alamy; p. xiiL, © iStockphoto.com/Victor Maffe; p. xiiR, © image100/Corbis; p. xiiiT, © iStockphoto.com/Yanik Chauvin; p. xiiiB, © Frans Lanting/Corbis; p. xiv, © istockphoto.com/ Jan Bryson; p. xv, © iStockphoto.com/Faut Kose.

Chapter 1

p. 2, © Justin Sullivan/Getty Images; p. 4L, © Orlando Sierra/AFP/ Getty Images; p. 4M, © Rebecca Cook/Reuters/Corbis; p. 4R, © Tim Mosenfelder/Getty Images; p. 5B, © PhotoDisc/Getty Images; p. 7, © Orlando Sierra/AFP/Getty Images; p. 9, Ryan McVay/Getty Images. Background: © iStockphoto.com/morganl, Polaroid emulsion transfer: © iStockphoto.com/morganl; p. 10, © Mark Downey/Master-file; p. 12T, © Robert Walker/Hulton Archive/Getty Images; p. 12B, © Rebecca Cook/Reuters/Corbis; p. 13, © Tim Mosenfelder/Getty Images; p. 14T, © Bettmann/Corbis, Frame: © iStockphoto.com/ Pomortzeff; p. 14BL, Library of Congress Prints and Photographs Division. LC-USZ62-16530.jpg, Frame: © iStockphoto.com/Peter Zele; p. 14BR, © Hulton Archive/Getty Images, Frame: © iStock-photo.com/Lou Oates; p. 15T, Ryan McVay/Riser/Getty Images; p. 15B, © Mike Segar/Reuters/Corbis; p. 17, © Hulton Archive/Getty Images, Frame: © iStockphoto.com/Andrea Gingerich; p. 18, © iStockphoto.com/vofpalabra; p. 19, © Stockbyte/PunchStock; p. 20L, Medioimages/PictureQuest; p. 20R, Comstock Images/Alamy; p. 21, © Doug Menuez/Getty Images.

Chapter 2

p. 24, © Spencer Platt/Getty Images; p. 26L, © iStockphoto.com/Geor-gina Palmer; p. 26M, © Sally and Richard Greenhill/Alamy; p. 26R, © Frank Trapper/Corbis; p. 27, Mike Kemp/Getty Images; p. 28, © Peter Dazeley/The Image Bank/Getty Images; p. 29, © iStockphoto.com/Ste-fano Maccari; p. 30T, © Veer; p. 30B, © iStockphoto.com/Tatiana Pop-ova; p. 31, © iStockphoto.com/Jerry Koch; p. 32, © Hill Street Studios/ Blend Images/Getty Images; p. 33, © Bettmann/Corbis; p. 34, © iStockphoto.com/Georgina Palmer; p. 35, © Sally and Richard Green-hill/Alamy; p. 37T, © The McGraw-Hill Companies, Inc./Jill Braaten, pho-tographer; p. 37B, © Masterfile (Royalty-Free Division); p. 38, © Penny Gentieu/Jupiter Images/Getty Images; p. 39T, © Scott Barbour/Getty Images; p. 39B, © Weinstein Company/courtesy Everett Collection; p. 40T, © iStockphoto.com/Grafisimo; p. 40BL, © Fox/Photofest; p. 40BR, © Frank Trapper/Corbis; p. 41, © Siqui Sanchez/The Image Bank/Getty Images; p. 43, © Digital Vision Ltd./SuperStock.

Chapter 3

p. 46, © Roger Bamber/Alamy; p. 48TL, © AP/Wide World Photos; p. 48TM, © Peter Menzel/From the book "Hungry Planet, What the World Eats" by Peter Menzel and Faith D'Aluisio/ www.menzelphoto.com; p. 48TR, © Under-wood & Underwood/Corbis; p. 48B, © The Granger Collection, New York; p. 49T, © AP/Wide World Photos; p. 49B, Wicked Artwork and logo © ® 2011 Wicked LLC. All Rights Reserved; p. 50, © Peter Menzel/

From the book "Hungry Planet, What the World Eats" by Peter Menzel and Faith D'Aluisio/www.menzelphoto.com; p. 52, © AP/Wide World Photos; p. 53, Courtesy Apple; p. 54T, © Paramount/Courtesy Everett Collection; p. 54B, © Royalty-Free/Corbis; p. 56T, TM & Copyright © 20th Century Fox. All rights reserved/Courtesy Everett Collection; p. 56B, Jean-Christophe Verhaegen/AFP/Getty Images; p. 57, © Jupi-terImages/BananaStock/Alamy; p. 58TL, © dbimages/Alamy; p. 58TR, © iStockphoto.com/Mustafa Deliormanli; p. 58B, © ballyscanion/ PhotoDisc/Getty Images; p. 60, Dress: © iStockphoto.com/Igor Ter-ekhov, Jeans: © iStockphoto.com/Andrey Armyagov; p. 61, © Karim Sahib/AFP/Getty Images; p. 62, © Rob Crandall/The Image Works; p. 63, © Underwood & Underwood/Corbis; p. 64, RubberBall Produc-tions; p. 65T, © Marvy!/Corbis; p. 65B, © Frans Lemmens/Iconica/ Getty Images; p. 66, © moodboard/Corbis.

Chapter 4

p. 70, © Frank Siteman/Stone/Getty Images; p. 72TL, © Nevada Wier/ Getty Images; p. 72TM, © Thomas S. England/Photo Researchers, Inc.; p. 72TR, © Royalty-Free/Corbis; p. 72B, Creatas Images; p. 73T, © Inti St. Clair/Digital Vision/Getty Images; p. 73B, © Mary Evans Picture Library/The Image Works; p. 73B, Album: © iStockphoto .com/Mike Bentley; p. 74T, © Nina Leen/Time & Life Pictures/Getty Images; p. 74B, Barbara Penoyar/Getty Images; p. 75, © Digital Vision/Alamy; p. 76, © Somos/Veer/Getty Images; p. 77, © AP/Wide World Photos; p. 78, © Stockbyte/Getty Images; p. 79, Ryan McVay/ Getty Images; p. 80, © Mark Wilson/Getty Images; p. 81T, © Bill Pug-liano/Getty Images; p. 81B, © blue jean images/Getty Images; p. 82, © The McGraw-Hill Companies, Inc./Jill Braaten, photographer; p. 83, Photo: Michael Yarish/© Fox Television/Courtesy: Everett Collection; p. 84T, © iStockphoto.com/Andrea Gingerich; p. 84B, © iStockphoto. com/Dan Wilton; p. 85, © Chris Jackson/Getty Images; p. 86T, © iStockphoto.com/Tatiana Popova; p. 86B, Laptop: © iStockphoto.com/ Andres Peiro Palme, Woman: © iStockphoto.com/Anna Bryukhanova; p. 87T, © IT Stock Free; p. 87B, © Nevada Wier/Getty Images; p. 88T, © William Thomas Cain/Getty Images; p. 88B, © Thomas S. England/ Photo Researchers, Inc.; p. 90, © Justin Sullivan/Getty Images; p. 91T, © Paula Bronstein/Getty Images; p. 92L, © iStockphoto.com/Justin Sneddon; p. 92R, Ryan McVay/Getty Images; p. 93, © Luedke and Sparrow/Digital Vision/Getty Images; p. 94, © Harold Eisenberger/ LOOK/Getty Images; p. 95TL, © Royalty-Free/Corbis; p. 95TR, © iStockphoto.com/Lisa F. Young; p. 95B, © Royalty-Free/Corbis; p. 97, PhotoDisc/Getty Images.

Chapter 5

p. 100, © R1/Alamy; p. 102L, Brand X Pictures; p. 102M, © The McGraw-Hill Companies, Inc./John Flournoy, photographer; p. 102R, © Reza Estakhrian/Reportage/Getty Images; p. 103, © AP/Wide World Photos; p. 104T, Amos Morgan/Getty Images; p. 103BL, Brand X Pic-tures; p. 104BR, © Jim West/The Image Works; p. 106, © ImageDJ/ Alamy; p. 107, © China Photos/Getty Images; p. 107T, Courtesy of Central College. Photo by Dan Vander Beek; p. 108B, © Keith Sra-kocic/AP Photo; p. 109, © The McGraw-Hill Companies, Inc./John Flournoy, photographer; p. 110, © Reza Estakhrian/Reportage/Getty Images; p. 111, © Stockbyte/Getty Images; p. 112, Ryan McVay/Getty Images; p. 113T, © iStockphoto.com/Dean Turner; p. 113B, © Daniel Barry/Getty Images; p. 114, © Bob Pearson/epa/Corbis; p. 115T, © Gary S. Chapman/Getty Images; p. 115B, © iStockphoto.com/Mark Evans; p. 116T, © David S. Holloway/Getty Images; p. 116B, Pola-roids on clothes line: © iStockphoto.com/David Franklin; p. 116BL, © Custom Medical Stock Photo/Alamy; p. 116BM, Adam Crowley/ Getty Images; p. 116BR, © Muntz/Taxi/Getty Images; p. 117, © Kazuhiro Tanda/Taxi Japan/Getty Images; p. 118, Manchan/Getty Images; p. 121, PhotoDisc/Getty Images; p. 122, © Frederick M. Brown/Getty Images; p. 124, © Digital Vision Ltd./SuperStock; p. 125, © Veer.

Chapter 6

p. 128, © Comstock/JupiterImages; p. 130TL, © Leonard McLane/ Digital Vision/Getty Images; p. 130TM, Brand X Pictures; p. 130TR, © Masterfile (Royalty-Free Division); p. 130B, © Comedy Central/ Courtesy: Everett Collection; p. 131T, © Dave Robertson/Masterfile; p. 131B, © AP/Wide World Photos; p. 132, From the film OBEDI- ANCE ©1968 by Stanley Milgram, © renewed 1993 by Alexandra Milgram, distributed by Penn State Media Sales; p. 133, Bottle cap: © iStockphoto.com/Luis Carlos, bottle: iStockphoto.com/Dmitry Bomshtein; p. 134T, © istockphoto.com/MirkaMoksha; p. 134B, Burke/Triolo/Brand X Pictures/Jupiterimages; p. 135T, © Leonard McLane/Digital Vision/Getty Images; p. 135B, © Jose Luis Roca/AFP/ Getty Images; p. 136T, © AP/Wide World Photos; p. 136M, Comstock Images/Alamy; p. 136B, © Masterfile (Royalty-Free Division); p. 137, © iStockphoto.com/Floortje; p. 138T, © iStockphoto.com/ Tamás Dernovics; p. 138B, Brand X Pictures; p. 140, © HBO/Cour- tesy Everett Collection; p. 141, © Trista Weibell/iStockphoto.com; p. 143, Photo Justin Lubin/© NBC/Courtesy Everett Collection; p. 144, Getty Images/Digital Vision; p. 145, © rubberball/Getty Images; p. 146, © SCPhotos/Alamy; p. 148, Amos Morgan/Getty Images; p. 149, BananaStock/JupiterImages.

Chapter 7

p. 152, Dex Image/Getty Images; p. 154TL, Brand X Pictures/Jupi- terimages; p. 154TM, TM & © Fox Searchlight. All rights reserved/ Courtesy Everett Collection; p. 154TR, © Justin Sullivan/Getty Images; p. 154M, © David Noble Photography/Alamy; p. 154B, © iStockphoto.com/Jeremy Edwards; p. 155, ABC-TV/The Kobal Collection/Eric McCandless; p. 156, © Royalty-Free/Corbis; p. 158T, © HBO/courtesy Everett Collection; p. 158B, Brand X Pictures/Jupi- terimages; p. 159, © Comstock/PunchStock; p. 160, © iStockphoto/ MistikasS; p. 161L, © Erica Simone Leeds; p. 161R, Don Tremain/ Getty Images; p. 162, Burke/Triolo Productions/Getty Images; p. 164, TM & © Fox Searchlight. All rights reserved/Courtesy Everett Collec- tion; p. 165, © James Devaney/WireImage/Getty Images; p. 166, © Brand X Pictures/Jupiterimages; p. 167, © Universal/Courtesy Everett Collection; p. 168, © Royalty-Free/Corbis; p. 170, © Justin Sullivan/Getty Images; p. 171, © Angela Wyant/Stone/Getty Images; p. 172T, Wedding picture: © iStockphoto.com/bitter, Frame: © iStockphoto.com/sxasher; p. 172BL, TLC-TV/The Kobal Collec- tion; p. 172BR, © Erin Patrice O'Brien/Digital Vision/Getty Images; p. 173T, © iStockphoto.com/Jennifer Trenchard; p. 173B, CMCD/ Getty Images; p. 174, Getty Images/Digital Vision.

Chapter 8

p. 178, © Gavriel Jecan/Getty Images; p. 180TL, © CinemaPhoto/Corbis; p. 180TM, © GOODSHOOT/Alamy; p. 180TR, © Brand X Pictures/ PunchStock; p. 180B, © iStockphoto.com/Borut Trdina; pp. 181, © iStockphoto.com/Forest Woodward; p. 183, © AP Photo/Gerald Herbert; p. 185, Photodisc/Getty Images; p. 186T, © PhotoAlto/PunchStock; p. 186B, Photodisc/Getty Images; p. 187, Mike Kemp/Getty Images; p. 189, © iStockphoto.com/Robert Hunt; p. 190, © CinemaPhoto/Corbis; p. 191, © iStockphoto.com/Michael Ciranni; p. 192, © Javier Pierini/Getty Images; p. 193T, PhotoDisc/Getty Images; p. 193B, © GOODSHOOT/ Alamy; p. 195, DAJ/Getty Images; p. 196, © Jeff Greenberg/The Image Works; p. 198T, © Robert Davis; p. 198B, © Brand X Pictures/Punch- Stock; p. 200, © Stockdisc/PunchStock; p. 201, © Pavel Filatov/Alamy; p. 204T, M. Freeman/PhotoLink/Getty Images; p. 204B, © Syracuse News- papers/The Image Works; p. 205, © Brand X/SuperStock.

Chapter 9

p. 208, © Saul Loeb/AFP/Getty Images; p. 210TL, © Jorge Rey/Getty Images; p. 210TM, © Peter Macdiarmid/Getty Images; p. 210TR,

© AFP/Getty Images; p. 210M, © Jeff J. Mitchell/Getty Images; p. 210B, © Steve Granitz/WireImage/Getty Images; p. 211, © Elliott & Fry/Hulton Archive/Getty Images; p. 212, © Comstock Images/Alamy; p. 213T, © The McGraw-Hill Companies, Inc./John Flournoy, photog- rapher; p. 213B, © Rob Wilkinson/Alamy; p. 214, © Jorge Rey/Getty Images; p. 215, © iStockphoto.com/Amanda Rohde; p. 216, © iStockphoto.com/René Mansi; p. 217, © Tony Savino/Corbis; p. 219L, PhotoLink/Getty Images; p. 219R, © Peter Macdiarmid/Getty Images; p. 220L, © AFP/Getty Images; p. 220R, National Archives and Records Administration; p. 221T, © iStockphoto.com/Ugur Evirgen; p. 221B, © Frank Micelotta/Getty Images; p. 222T, Brand X Pictures/PunchStock; p. 222B, Ryan McVay/Getty Images; p. 223, Library of Congress, Prints and Photographs Division [LC-USZ62-53202]; p. 225, © istockphoto .com/Ben and Kristen Bryant; p. 226, © Last Resort/PhotoDisc/Getty Images; p. 227, © iStockphoto.com/Valerie Loiseleux; p. 228T, Courtesy Everett Collection; p. 228B, © Tariq Mahmood/AFP/Getty Images; p. 230, Amos Morgan/Getty Images; p. 233, © Fancy Photography/Veer.

Chapter 10

p. 234, © Sean Gallup/Getty Images; p. 236TL, © Dr. Parvinder Sethi; p. 236TM, © Peter Turnley/Corbis; p. 236TR, © Robyn Beck/AFP/Getty Images; p. 236B, © Bettmann/Corbis; p. 237T, © Per-Anders Pettersson/ Getty Images; p. 237B, © Dr. Parvinder Sethi; p. 238T, © Arnaldo Mag- nani/Getty Images; p. 238B, © Jacobs Stock Photography/Photographer's Choice/Getty Images; p. 239, © Gabe Palmer/Corbis; p. 241, © iStock- photo.com/James Reilly Wilson; p. 242, © Peter Turnley/Corbis; p. 243, Photo: ABC/Alex Mehl, © ABC/Courtesy Everett Collection; p. 244, Courtesy Romain Jerome; p. 245, © Brand X Pictures/PunchStock; p. 246, Surgeon: © iStockphoto.com/Michael Krinke, Garbage man: © iStockphoto.com/Mike Clarke; p. 247L, © Bananastock/Alamy; p. 247R, © iStockphoto.com/Ivan Bajic; p. 248, © Tana Lee Alves/WireI- mage/Getty Images; p. 249, © Brand X Pictures/PunchStock; p. 250T, © iStockphoto.com/Jason R Warren; p. 250B, © Robyn Beck/AFP/Getty Images; p. 251, © Royalty-Free/Corbis; p. 252, African-American woman (TL): © iStockphoto.com/James Pauls, Asian woman with head in hand (TR): © iStockphoto.com/Eduardo Jose Bernardino, White girl sitting on stairs (BL): © iStockphoto.com/Stockphoto4u, Man with beard standing in street (BM): © iStockphoto.com/Ivar Teunissen, Children eating lunch (BR): David Buffington/Getty Images; p. 254T, TRBfoto/Getty Images; p. 254B, © Gary S. Chapman/Photographer's Choice/Getty Images; p. 256T, © iStockphoto.com/Alex Potemkin; p. 256B, © Michele West- morland/PhotoDisc/Getty Images; p. 257L, Digital Vision; p. 257R, © SuperStock.

Chapter 11

p. 260, © Mario Tama/Getty Images; p. 262TL, © Chien-min Chung/ Getty Images; p. 262TM, © AP/Wide World Photos; p. 262TR, © Marco Di Lauro/Getty Images; p. 262B, © Getty Images; p. 263L, © Photofusion Picture Library/Alamy; p. 263R, © Henning Kaiser/ DDP/Getty Images; p. 264T, © iStockphoto.com/Rafael Laguillo; p. 264B, © Chien-min Chung/Getty Images; p. 265, Library of Con- gress; p. 266, © Warner Brothers/Courtesy Everett Collection; p. 267, © Picturenet/Blend Images/Getty Images; p. 269T, © Siqui Sanchez/ The Image Bank/Getty Images; pp. 269B, 271, © AP/Wide World Pho- tos; p. 272, © iStockphoto.com/Leon Bonaventura; p. 273T, © Image Club; p. 274, © iStockphoto.com/Frank van den Bergh; p. 275B, © iStockphoto.com/Randolf Jay Braun; p. 275T, © Photos.com Select/ Index Stock; p. 275B, Pixtal/age footstock; p. 278, © Marco Di Lauro/ Getty Images; p. 279, © Paula Bronstein/Getty Images; p. 282, Amos Morgan/PhotoDisc/Getty Images; p. 285, © Royalty-Free/Corbis.

Chapter 12

p. 286, © Nicholas D. Kristof/The New York Times/Redux; p. 288TL, © Art Montes De Oca/Taxi/Getty Images; p. 288TM, © Thomas Northcut/

Digital Vision/Getty Images; p. 288TR, Photo: Carin Baer/© Fox Television/Courtesy: Everett Collection; p. 288B, © 1998 Image Ideas, Inc.; p. 289T, © Getty Images; p. 289B, © iStockphoto.com/Olivier Blondeau; p. 290, © Art Montes De Oca/Taxi/Getty Images; p. 291T, © Dove/PA Wire URN:8069588 (Press Association via AP Images); p. 291B, © iStockphoto.com/Christine Balderas; p. 295B, © Brand X Pictures/PunchStock; p. 296T, © AP/Wide World Photos; p. 296B, © Scott J. Ferrell/Getty Images; p. 297, Index Stock/Getty Images; p. 298, Scale: Comstock Images/Alamy, Bride and groom: © Image Club, Groom and groom: Photodisc/Getty Images; p. 299T, © AP Photo/Hermann J. Knippertz; p. 299B, Photo: Carin Baer/© Fox Television/Courtesy: Everett Collection; p. 300, © AP Photo; p. 302, © Steven Lawton/FilmMagic/Getty Images; p. 303, © AP Photo/NYC Department of Health and Mental Hygiene; p. 304T, © Thomas Northcut/Digital Vision/Getty Images; p. 304B, © iStockphoto.com/Jason Lugo; p. 305, © Royalty-Free/Corbis; p. 306T, C Squared Studios/Getty Images; p. 306B, © iStockphoto.com/Anton Seleznev; p. 307B, © Tetra Images/Getty Images; p. 308T, © Elisabetta Villa/Getty Images; p. 308B, Bucket: © iStockphoto.com/Jack Jelly, Briefcase: © iStockphoto.com/Anna Bryukhanova; p. 309, © Superstock.

Chapter 13

p. 312, © Shaun Botterill/Getty Images; p. 314TL, © AP/Wide World Photos; p. 314TM, © William Campbell/Sygma/Corbis; p. 314TR, © David McNew/Getty Images; p. 314B, © Andersen Ross/Blend Images/Getty Images; p. 315, © Jeff Greenberg/Alamy; p. 317T, © Richard Heathcote/Getty Images; p. 317B, © Stephen Chernin/Getty Images; p. 318T, Ryan McVay/Getty Images; p. 318B, © AP/Wide World Photos; p. 319, © Bruce Roberts/Photo Researchers, Inc.; p. 320T, © iStockphoto.com/Duncan Walker; p. 320B, © William Campbell/Sygma/Corbis; p. 321T, © iStockphoto.com/Skip ODonnell.; p. 321B, © Bettmann/Corbis; p. 322T, Don Farrall/Getty Images; p. 322B, © Kathleen Finlay/Masterfile; p. 324T, © Francis Miller/Time Life Pictures/Getty Images; p. 324B, © Jim West/The Image Works; p. 326, © AP/Wide World Photos; p. 327B, Nicole Rivelli/© NBC/Courtesy Everett Collection; p. 328T, © Digital Vision/Getty Images; p. 328B, © Daniel Berehulak/Getty Images; p. 329, © David McNew/Getty Images; pp. 330TL, 330TR, © Copyright 1997 IMS Communications Ltd/Capstone Design. All Rights Reserved; p. 330M, © liquidlibrary/PictureQuest; p. 330B, Ryab McVay/Getty Images; p. 331T, © iStockphoto.com/Jaroslaw Wojcik; p. 331B, © Walt Disney Co./courtesy Everett Collection; p. 336, PhotoDisc/Getty Images; p. 337, © Royalty-Free/CORBIS; p. 340, © iStockphoto.com/Steve Dibblee; p. 341, © Comstock/PictureQuest.

Chapter 14

p. 344, © Hans Deryk/Reuters/Landov; p. 346TL, Anthony Saint James/Getty Images; p. 346TM, © China Photos/Getty Images; p. 346TR, © Brand X Pictures/Jupiterimages; p. 346B, Photo by Rex Features/Courtesy Everett Collection; p. 347, Ryan McVay/Getty Images; p. 349T, Blend Images/Getty Images; p. 350, © The McGraw-Hill Companies, Inc./Christopher Kerrigan, photographer; p. 352T, © Jean-Marc Giboux/Getty Images; p. 352B, RubberBall Productions; p. 355T, © Fancy Photography/Veer; p. 355B, © iStockphoto.com/Don Bayley; p. 356, Comstock Images/Alamy; p. 357T, Jules Frazier/Getty Images; p. 357B, Photo: Chris Haston/© FOX /Courtesy Everett Collection; p. 358T, © iStockphoto.com/Grigory Bibikov; p. 358B, © Chip Somodevilla/Getty Images; p. 359T, Anthony Saint James/Getty Images; p. 359B, © iStockphoto.com/Duncan Walker; p. 360T, © Paul Miles/Axiom Photographic Agency/Getty Images; p. 360B, © Royalty-Free/Corbis; p. 361T, © Digital Vision Ltd.; p. 361B, © Digital Vision/PunchStock; p. 364T, Steve Cole/Getty Images; p. 364B, © Bruce Dale/National Geographic/Getty Images; p. 365, © China Photos/Getty Images; p. 366, Ryan McVay/Getty Images; p. 367, © Brand X Pictures/Jupiterimages; p. 368T, Wind farm: © iStockphoto.com/Mark Trost, Smokestacks: Stockbyte/PunchStock; p. 368B, © Royalty-Free/Corbis; p. 369, © Stockbyte/PunchStock.

Chapter 15

p. 372, © Mandel Ngan/AFP/Getty Images; p. 374TM, © Alex Wong/Getty Images; p. 374TR, © 20th Century Fox Film Corp. All rights reserved./Courtesy Everett Collection; p. 374B, © Digital Vision/Getty Images; p. 375, © iStockphoto.com/Lara Seregni; p. 378, © AP/Wide World Photos; p. 379L, © The McGraw-Hill Companies/Lars Niki, photographer; p. 379R, Ryan McVay/Getty Images; p. 381, © Elmer Martinez/AFP/Getty Images; p. 382B, © Photodisc/PunchStock; p. 383T, Calf: © iStockphoto.com/Eric Isselée, goat: © iStockphoto.com/Eric Isselée, pig: Ryan McVay/Getty Images, cat: © iStockphoto.com/Blackbeck, rat: © iStockphoto.com/Butinova Elena; p. 383B, © Getty Images; p. 384, © iStockphoto.com/Clint Hild; p. 385, Library of Congress; p. 387T, © Bettmann/Corbis; p. 387B, © Popperfoto/Getty Images; p. 388T, © Mario Tama/Getty Images; p. 388B, Digital Vision/PunchStock; p. 389, © Alex Wong/Getty Images; p. 391, © Kerry-Edwards 2004, Inc./Sharon Farmer, photographer; p. 392T, © 20th Century Fox Film Corp. All rights reserved./Courtesy Everett Collection; p. 392B, © Royalty-Free/Corbis; p. 393, © Digital Vision/Getty Images.

Figures/Text

p. 7, © The New Yorker Collection 1992 Warren Miller from cartoonbank.com. All rights reserved; p. 8, From Kaiser State Health Facts, www.statehealthfacts.org. Reprinted with permission from the Henry J. Kaiser Family Foundation. The Kaiser Family Foundation is a non-profit private operating foundation, based in Menlo Park, California, dedicated to producing and communicating the best possible analysis and information on health issues; p. 19, Adapted from American Sociological Association Research and Development, "What Can I Do with A Bachelor's Degree in Sociology? A National Survey of Seniors Majoring in Sociology: First Glances: What Do They Know and Where Are They Going?" (January 2006): 29, Table 5. Reprinted by permission of the American Sociological Association; p. 29, Courtesy Randall Munroe, www.xkcd.com; p. 33, Copyright © 2001–2008 by Stuart Eugene Thiel. All rights reserved; p. 37, Adapted from Devah Pager, "The Mark of a Criminal Record" from *American Journal of Sociology* 108.5 (March 2003): 958, Figure 6. Copyright © 2003 by The University of Chicago. Reprinted with the permission of The University of Chicago Press; p. 53, © 2010 CTIA—The Wireless Association; p. 84, Copyright © 2010 Henry J. Kaiser Family Foundation. Reprinted with permission from the Henry J. Kaiser Family Foundation. The Kaiser Family Foundation is a non-profit private operating foundation, based in Menlo Park, California, dedicated to producing and communicating the best possible analysis and information on health issues; p. 89, From Tom Smith, "Coming of Age in 21st Century America: Public Attitudes Toward the Importance and Timing of Transition to Adulthood" (Chicago: NORC, 2003). Reprinted with the permission of National Opinion Research Center; p. 93, © The New Yorker Collection 2000 Victoria Roberts from cartoonbank.com; p. 111, Adapted from Peter Bearman, James Moody, and Katherine Stovel, "Chains of Affection: The Structure of Adolescent Romantic and Sexual Networks" from *Journal of Sociology* 110.1 (July 2004): 58, Copyright © 2004 by University of Chicago Press. Reprinted with permission; p. 112, Toles © 2000 The Washington Post. Watterson. Reprinted by permission of Universal Uclick. All rights reserved; p. 114, Cartoon by Chris Wildt, www.CartoonStock.com; p. 134, Marijuana Policy Project (2008). Reprinted by permission; p. 138, © The New Yorker Collection 2002 Alex Gregory from cartoonbank.com. All rights reserved; p. 141, © International Centre for Prison Studies, Kings College, London. Author: Ray Walmslay; p. 160, From *The New York Times* (December 17, 2006). Copyright © 2006 by The New York Times Company. All rights reserved. Used by permission and protected by the Copyright Laws of the United States. The printing, copying, redistribution, or retransmission of the Material without express written permission is prohibited; p. 170, © 2010 Human Rights Campaign. Reprinted with permission; p. 171, © 2006 Human Rights Campaign. Reprinted with permission; p. 183, © 1993 Kirk Anderson. Reprinted with the permission of Kirk Anderson,